Philadelphia

Philadelphia

A Narrative History

Paul Kahan

PENN

UNIVERSITY OF PENNSYLVANIA PRESS

PHILADELPHIA

Published by
University of Pennsylvania Press
Philadelphia, Pennsylvania 19104-4112
www.pennpress.org

Printed in the United States of America on acid-free paper
10 9 8 7 6 5 4 3 2 1

Hardcover ISBN: 978-1-5128-2629-6
eBook ISBN: 978-1-5128-2630-2

A catalogue record for this book is available
from the Library of Congress.

To J. R. King, my favorite Philadelphia lawyer

If you're off to Philadelphia in the morning,
You mustn't take my stories for a guide.
There's little left, indeed, of the city you will read of,
And all the folk I write about have died.
—Rudyard Kipling, "Philadelphia," 1910

CONTENTS

Introduction

As it entered the third decade of the twenty-first century, Philadelphia boasted a racially, ethnically, and religiously diverse population. Indeed, modern American cities are the most diverse places in the United States, but in Philadelphia's case, diversity has always been a core characteristic. Even before Pennsylvania's founder, William Penn, arrived in the region in 1682, the Delaware Valley was home to a heterogeneous mix of Native Americans, Africans, Dutch, English, Finns, and Swedes. Penn's famed religious tolerance encouraged emigration to Pennsylvania and swelled the colony's population, which by the end of the eighteenth century included French, German, Irish, Scottish, and Welsh. During the nineteenth century, Russians, Italians, Poles, and Chinese settled in the region, followed by Dominicans, Haitians, Indians, Jamaicans, Koreans, Puerto Ricans, and Vietnamese (to name just a few) in the twentieth. In short, diversity is a cornerstone of Philadelphia's story and is therefore one of this book's major themes.

One by-product of that diversity was political and social conflict between the city's various ethnic and racial groups, which is the book's second theme: individual and institutionalized racism, xenophobia, homophobia, and religious intolerance have left an indelible mark on the city politically, geographically, and economically. Throughout its history, the City of Brotherly Love has frequently failed to live up to its nickname.[1] Moreover, while conflict was pervasive, it was not inevitable. One persistent element has been racism and anti-Black and anti-brown terrorism, both individual and state sponsored (the so-called Cradle of Liberty has a long and troubling history of police brutality that continues to this day). Racism and bigotry also help explain why cities like Philadelphia are nearly constant targets of "reform."

A related theme is the role that persistent antiurbanism has played in the city's history.[2] Antiurbanism has deep and pernicious roots in US culture. George Washington once asserted, "The tumultuous populace of large cities are ever to be dreaded," while Thomas Jefferson, writing to Philadelphian Benjamin Rush in 1800, called cities "pestilential to the morals, the health and the liberties of man."[3] Jefferson was not the last US thought leader to disparage cities: three-time presidential nominee and secretary of state William Jennings Bryan delivered a fiery speech at the 1896 Democratic National Convention in which he thundered, "Burn down your cities and leave our farms, and your cities will spring up again as if by magic," while his contemporary, President Theodore Roosevelt, deplored "the evils of city life" and vowed to reform them.[4] President Franklin D. Roosevelt, whose New Deal in the 1930s helped forge a powerful political coalition that included large swaths of urban workers, nevertheless, in the words of one aide, "always did, and always would think people better off in the country and would regard cities as rather hopeless."[5] Even Penn's plan for Philadelphia—a city he described as a "greene country towne"—reflected some antiurban beliefs about the deleterious effects of city living for the morals and health of urbanites.

A fourth theme thus concerns the uses of space and the evolution of Philadelphia's physical form. While we tend to take Philadelphia's location, and even its existence, for granted, the city did not simply appear: it was planned, planted, and cultivated. Philadelphia has always been a place where carefully curated spaces and structures (buildings, public art, etc.) were intended to foster specific values and encourage citizens to behave in "virtuous" ways.[6] The faith in the power of buildings, space, and public art to influence citizens' behavior spans Philadelphia's history and is visible in William Penn's plan for the city, John Haviland's design for Eastern State Penitentiary, Jacques Gréber's outline of what is now called the Benjamin Franklin Parkway, and Edmund Bacon's ambitious urban renewal program in Society Hill.[7] This is not to say that the elites' goals remained consistent over time, or that they were a monolithic or homogeneous group. In fact, the beliefs of architects, city planners, and political leaders about how and where Philadelphians ought to live consistently ran headlong into ordinary citizens' use of public and private spaces, which they adapted to fit their own needs and desires, putting them to use for a broad range of often contradictory political, social, and cultural movements. This created a persistent conflict between organic and controlled development of Philadelphia's space, which often pitted elites against ordinary citizens, a key element of Philadelphia's story and one that has indelibly shaped the city's development and culture. It also helps explain the heated conflicts over statues of such divisive figures as Christopher Columbus and former mayor Frank Rizzo. This fact reminds us that the city's history does not speak for itself and that history's "meaning" remains contested.

These themes are not unique to Philadelphia, so it is worth asking: do we need a new narrative history of Philadelphia? Obviously, my answer is yes. Philadelphia is not just any city, and its story, while similar in some respects to the stories of other American cities, does not exactly mirror the histories of New York, Boston, or Los Angeles. Home to the so-called Birthplace of America (Independence Hall), Philadelphia, for the eighteenth and much of the nineteenth centuries, was arguably the most important city in North America and has played a crucial role in regional, state, and national history since its founding in 1682. Moreover, Philadelphia plays an incredibly important symbolic role in the story of the American Revolution and the early political history of the United States.

Ironically, given the central role the city occupies in national history, Philadelphia does a terrible job remembering most of its own history. At first glance, this statement might seem absurd, given the large number of nationally significant museums and historic sites in the city and the role that history tourism plays in the region's economy. Yet the truth of this assertion is demonstrated by two events that took place nearly simultaneously as I was finishing the manuscript for this book. The first was the transfer of the defunct Philadelphia History Museum's collection of approximately 130,000 artifacts and documents to Drexel University. The Philadelphia History Museum at the Atwater Kent (formerly known as the Atwater Kent Museum) operated from 1938 to 2018, when it closed its doors due to financial troubles. It was only the second museum in the United States dedicated to the history of a city (the first being the Museum of the City of New York, which opened in 1924). Philadelphia's charter obligated the city to financially support the museum, but in 2018 the city eliminated the modest funding it provided, and the Philadelphia History Museum closed. As of this writing, it is not clear how, when, or if Drexel University will make the Philadelphia History Museum's collection available to the public.

Meanwhile, just over a year before the Philadelphia History Museum closed, the Museum of the American Revolution, after more than a decade in development, opened just a few blocks from the Philadelphia History Museum. The Museum of the American Revolution's board of directors had managed to raise $173 million to construct a 118,000-square-foot building filled with unique and priceless artifacts, including George Washington's campaign tent. Even during the height of the COVID-19 pandemic, the museum attracted 20,000 visitors between October 2020 and September 2021, and in 2022 the Museum of the American Revolution received a $50 million gift from the estate of H. F. "Gerry" Lenfest, a lawyer and media executive. Lenfest had served on the museum's board of directors, was its largest single donor, and played a key role in raising an additional $20 million on the museum's behalf before his death in 2018. Given those facts, it is not surprising that Lenfest's estate donated a substantial sum to the Museum of the American Revolution, but the juxtaposition of a massive donation going to that institution at nearly the same time as the

Philadelphia History Museum's collection was transferred to a private organization with little oversight about how it would be made available to the public is nonetheless illuminating. The juxtaposition of these two events demonstrates that while the Revolution and the framers' legacies are being preserved and made accessible to the public, the stories of Philadelphia's ordinary citizens are passing out of view.

However, this is consistent with the fact that Philadelphia has long privileged its colonial and revolutionary past above other periods in the city's history, for a variety of economic, cultural, and political reasons. Since at least the beginning of the nineteenth century, tourists have visited the city to see Philadelphia's rich collection of revolutionary-era buildings and sites. As these buildings aged or the sites were threatened with demolition, various private organizations (and later government agencies) tried to preserve them. However, identifying which sites and buildings would be preserved and how they would be interpreted was a contentious endeavor, reflecting the contradictory stories about the city's past and the fact that the stories we tell about a place and the objects we preserve reveal as much about what we value in the present as they do about the lived experience of people in the past. Moreover, that carefully cultivated popular connection between Philadelphia and the American Revolution indelibly linked the city (and certain iconic buildings such as Independence Hall or artifacts like the Liberty Bell) to values (e.g., liberty). As a result, Philadelphia has been a potent backdrop for a variety of sometimes contradictory political and social causes, transforming the city from simply a place into a symbol. However, the meaning of these events and objects remains contested, and the heavy focus on the colonial and revolutionary eras has frequently come at the expense of other periods of the city's history.

My goal in writing this book is to construct a broader narrative history and, in so doing, create what literary critic Van Wyck Brooks more than a century ago called a "usable past." Writing in 1918, Brooks asserted (correctly, in my view) that "every people selects from the other experience of every other people whatever contributes most vitally to its own development."[8] Yet before you condemn me for my lack of objectivity, let me point out that I am simply following the example of generations of Philadelphians (and Americans) who have drawn upon the city's history and historical treasures to answer the questions that confront them in their presents. In fact, many of the events I describe in the following chapters will seem eerily contemporary even though they happened decades or even centuries ago. The same, however, can be said of the United States, and the search for a usable past requires us to put aside the comforting blanket of misty-eyed nostalgia for a history that never was.

That being said, this book is not intended to be the final word on Philadelphia's history. No single volume could do justice to Philadelphia's richly complex history to tell every possible tale. Plenty of individuals and events described only briefly (or not at all) in this book have been the focus of volumes in their own right, and many others should be. My goal in writing *Philadelphia: A Narrative History* is to provide readers with an accessible interpretive history of the city from its founding to the present. My hope is that the book will demonstrate to readers that history doesn't just happen. Instead, it is driven by individual choices made at a variety of levels. In more concrete terms, Philadelphia's current reality did not just happen; it is the result of choices. A better future requires understanding the decisions that created the present for, as Jack Burden, the narrator of Robert Penn Warren's 1946 masterpiece, *All the King's Men*, notes, "only out of the past can you make the future."[9]

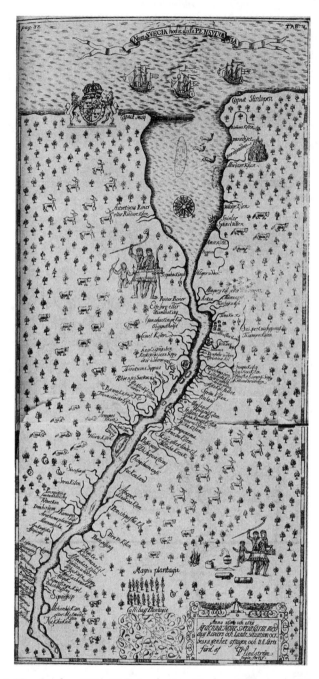

Figure 1. New Sweden, 1664–65. Beinecke Rare Book and Manuscript Library, Yale University. This map depicts the presence of Native Americans, the abundance of trees, and the importance of riverways to the area that would later become Philadelphia.

CHAPTER 1

Philadelphia Before 1681

Philadelphia's history does not start with Pennsylvania's founding in 1681. Millennia before the first Europeans arrived, Native Americans inhabited the land on which the city later arose. Moreover, for nearly a half century before the English Crown granted William Penn a charter to establish the colony, a small but diverse population of several hundred Native Americans, Africans, English, Swedes, Dutch, and Finns lived in and around where the Delaware and Schuylkill Rivers meet. Decentralized control, distance from their homelands, and the profit motive thus worked to weaken colonists' attachment to their home countries. In turn, the various regimes that controlled the Delaware Valley during this period were willing to accept these polyglot populations provided they did not threaten the fragile colonial order.[1] This situation laid the groundwork for what Penn later called his "Holy Experiment."

The first inhabitants of the region arrived during the last Ice Age (between 30,000 and 10,000 years ago). They crossed over a land bridge spanning the Bering Strait and connecting modern-day Alaska and Siberia. Successive generations migrated east across the continent, arriving in the Delaware Valley about 18,000 years ago. There were three subsequent periods of Native American development in what is now Pennsylvania. The first, from 18,000 to 8,000 years ago, is known as the Paleo-Indian period. During that period, a mix of lush forests and open grasslands provided a rich mix of fruit, nuts, and roots, as well as several mammals to hunt. Estimates are that approximately 150 people lived in the region, divided into several small and highly mobile bands of hunter-gatherers.[2] Later, as the climate became drier, several waterways shrank or dried up entirely, severely diminishing the amount of food resources.[3] In this period, small groups migrated in a seasonal cycle to maximize their access to food resources.

Finally, from 3,000 to 400 years ago the Woodland period occurred. The shift from the Archaic to the Woodland was not abrupt; some scholars point to a transition period of approximately 1,600 years. The Woodland period is itself divided into three periods: early (2,700 to 2,100 years ago), mid (2,100 to 1,100 years ago), and late (900 to 1600 CE). By the late Woodland period, Native groups had developed more-effective foraging strategies and begun supplementing their hunting and gathering with small-scale cultivation of crops. They had also adopted the bow and arrow to hunt but were more dependent on crops than people in previous eras. The best estimates for this period put the entire Native population in the region of modern-day Pennsylvania at approximately 9,000 to 10,000 people, divided into several groups: the Monongahela (southwest), the Owasco (northern central), and the Shenks Ferry (south central).[4] At the site of modern-day Philadelphia lived several bands of Native Americans collectively known as the Lenni Lenape, or "original man."

The Lenape were seminomadic foragers and fishers who lived near what we now call the Delaware River in a roughly triangle-shaped territory that stretched from present-day Delaware's Cape Henlopen north to what is now Trenton, New Jersey, and west to the Schuylkill River's edge.[5] The Lenape spoke an Algonquin dialect known as Unami; they were among several Native groups in the region that spoke Algonquin dialects, including the Munsee-speaking people to the north (whose territory stretched into the Hudson River Valley).[6] The Lenape's connection to the Delaware River led Europeans to indiscriminately call them and the Munsee "River Indians" and later the Delaware.[7] While this clearly ignored crucial differences between groups, identifying them as "river Indians" did capture just how central particular rivers (which provided food, created floodplains of rich soil ideal for agriculture, and functioned as travel routes) were to their lives.[8] Like many other Native groups, the Lenape occupied a core area surrounded by the buffer zones that separated them from other nearby Native groups; frequently, buffer zones overlapped (as in the case of the Munsee to the north and the Susquehannock to the west).[9]

The Lenape lived in kin-based bands or villages that scholars estimate ranged in size from fifty to perhaps as many as two hundred people.[10] Bands interacted with one another, though cultural differences existed between villages (such as in the diversity of building styles they employed), creating some identifiable subgroups within the Lenape (such as the Armewamese, Cohansey, Mante, Minisink, and Sickoneysink, to name just a few).[11] Lenape bands typically summered along the Delaware River's banks, where they fished, foraged, and raised small amounts of maize, beans, and squash.[12] Approximately every five to ten years, once resources in the local area were exhausted, bands migrated to new "stations" along the Delaware River.[13] Lenape bands lacked chiefs, having instead sachems, who were more "first among equals" than rulers. Being sachem conferred no benefits, so, like all Lenape, they foraged, fished, and hunted.[14] Lenape women tended the crops and children, while male Lenape hunted and fished, usually at some distance from the village.[15] Because the Lenape culture was matrilineal (meaning that political power and social position flowed through the mother rather than the father), women played a key role in selecting the band's sachem, even functioning as a "chief-maker."[16] There was no central government overseeing the loosely affiliated villages, and Lenape bands operated with a great deal of autonomy, making large-scale military mobilization all but impossible.[17]

By the early 1600s, Europeans reached the Delaware Valley. Like the Lenape, the Europeans were attracted to the Delaware River because it provided resources and inland access. In 1645, an Englishman described the Delaware as "a very great river, very fruitfull, [which] will contayne more people than all New England beside."[18] Writing in 1649, one Dutch visitor to the region described the Delaware as "one of the best, finest, and pleasantist rivers in the world, on account of its own and other attendant conveniences. Fourteen streams flow into this river, the smallest of them navigable for two or three leagues, and every where, on both sides, are pretty good flats in great abundance."[19] The Delaware River was deep enough to allow large sailing ships to travel as far as present-day Trenton, and many of its tributaries could carry large ships into the interior. Furthermore, the Delaware Valley was home to an abundance of animals, including bears, rabbits, foxes, and beavers, which appealed to Europeans because fur was in high demand in the cold climate of northeastern Europe. Three European nations—the Netherlands, England, and Sweden—vied for control over the Delaware Valley during the first half of the seventeenth century.

Though likely not the first European visitors to the region, the earliest white settlers in the Delaware Valley were the Dutch.[20] In 1609, Henry Hudson, commanding the Dutch ship *Halve Maen*, sailed into the Delaware Bay while searching for the Northwest Passage. Employed by the Dutch East India Company, which was chartered in 1602 and granted a monopoly on the Dutch spice trade, Hudson and his crew (a mixed band of approximately twenty Dutch and English sailors) found "a white sandy beach . . . beyond which the land was full of trees."[21] When sandy shoals stymied the *Halve Maen*'s progress up the Delaware, Hudson sailed back down the river and then north along the Eastern Seaboard, eventually sailing into New York Bay.

In late 1615, Dutch explorer Cornelius Hendrickson sailed into the Delaware Bay, going as far north as the Schuylkill River looking for a place to build a trading post. Soon after, the Dutch established seasonal trading posts along the Delaware River, and by the mid-1620s, the Dutch West India Company (established in 1601 and granted a monopoly on trade in the Dutch West Indies) had established regular trading links with the Lenape's western neighbors, the Susquehannock, who quickly came to dominate the pelt trade. One trade good was wampum, or cylindrical white or blue-black beads that were cut, polished, and strung together. The strings of woven beads were worn decoratively, but they also functioned as a form of pictographic history text. Traders exchanged European goods for beads and then in turn traded the beads for pelts. The introduction of European tools into North America increased the production of wampum in New England and New Amsterdam (as the Dutch settlement on the southern tip of Manhattan island was known), while the pelt trade encouraged the Natives to overharvest, devastating the local animal population.[22] Worse, it spurred a decade-long war between the Lenape and the Susquehannock, Iroquoian-speaking Native Americans who lived along the Susquehanna River.[23]

Initially, the Dutch behaved as traders, not colonizers, so they left a light footprint in North America.[24] In 1624, the Dutch West India Company established a small settlement on Burlington (or Matinicunk) Island (near present-day Bristol, Pennsylvania) and two years later a trading post called Fort Nassau (located at present-day Gloucester, New Jersey). Both sites were hardly colonies: they were occupied seasonally, and only intermittently at that, so the Natives perceived little threat from the Dutch. However, things changed in 1631, when the Dutch established a plantation station called Swanendael (near present-day Lewes, Delaware) at the mouth of the Delaware Bay. Almost immediately, this led to a misunderstanding that turned deadly. To mark their new possession, the Dutch hammered a tin sign on a tree. However, a local Native took the sign down and converted it into pipes. The Dutch complained to their Sickoneysink contacts, who murdered the offender and brought his severed head to the Dutch. In retaliation, the murdered man's friends attacked Swanendael and killed its inhabitants, which discouraged Dutch settlement in the area for a generation.[25]

Encounters between Europeans and Native Americans led to cultural dislocations on both sides. For instance, illness seriously reduced the Lenape population (though not nearly as badly as some other Native groups) in the two decades after 1630.[26] European goods gradually filtered into the Delaware Valley, and the Natives enthusiastically adopted European technology; within a century, most of their "tools and ornaments [were] replaced by European goods."[27] Nor were goods the only things exchanged. The shortage of European women encouraged sexual contact between Natives and Europeans. The Lenape had given the Europeans "their daughters to sleep with, by whom they had begotten children, and there roved many an Indian who was begotten by a [European]."[28] Though the Lenape had traditionally grown small plots of maize near their summer stations along the Delaware River, they temporarily increased the amount they grew to trade with the Swedes. This shift also led to an important development: the massing of Lenape at Passyunk (on the Schuylkill River's eastern shore near where the rivers converge with the Delaware) rather than at several stations along the Delaware River.[29] Lenape also began selling Europeans small parcels of land, but they understood land sales differently from Europeans, with the former believing they were selling only temporary usage rights, whereas the latter insisted they were purchasing the land "free and clear."[30] This basic misunderstanding plagued Native-European relations for decades and spurred much of the conflict between these groups. For now, however, the relatively small European population and the wide distances between settlements militated against conflict, and the Lenape effectively retained control of the region.[31]

The Dutch were not the only Europeans eyeing the Delaware Valley. The English also wanted a piece of the region's fur trade. English pretensions to the continent harkened back to John Cabot's 1497 "discovery" of North America's eastern coast. Cabot was an Italian (Giovanni Caboto) sailing under letters patent from England's King Henry VII that entitled him to all the land between present-day Columbia, South Carolina, and Port Chester, New York, a massive swath of territory that included land the Dutch also claimed. More than one hundred years later, in 1610, English adventurer Captain Samuel Argall, an employee of the Virginia Company of London, explored what he later described as "a very great bay."[32] Unaware of Hudson's visit the year before, Argall named the bay he "discovered" for Virginia's governor for life and captain general, Thomas West, the twelfth Baron De La Warr, which eventually evolved into "Delaware." In the fall of 1633, King Charles I granted Captain Thomas Yong a commission to explore uninhabited parts of Virginia, establish a settlement or settlements, and retain a portion of whatever wealth he discovered. In the summer of 1634, Yong sailed into the Delaware Bay and renamed its river the Charles River, after the king. Yong was distressed to discover a Dutch trading vessel in the bay. Meeting with the ship's captain, who asserted his right to trade in the area under a commission granted by the governor of New Netherland, Yong said he "knew of no such Governor, nor no such place as new Netherlands" and told them "this Country did belong to the crowne of England."[33]

In 1641, a small group of Englishmen led by George Lamberton and Nathaniel Turner and representing the Delaware Company of New Haven sailed into Delaware Bay to purchase land for a colony. They did so along the Schuylkill River in current-day Philadelphia and at Varkens Kill (in what is now Salem Creek, New Jersey). Within a year, several dozen Englishmen settled and began undercutting the Swedish and Dutch in the pelt trade. As a result, the Dutch forcibly expelled the English from their site on the Schuylkill River and burned their settlement, while the English colonists at Varkens Kill eventually came under Swedish control. Though a setback, it was only temporary and in no way diminished English interest in settling the Delaware Valley.[34]

The following year, Sir Edmund Plowden, a wealthy Englishman from a distinguished family, attempted to colonize the Delaware Valley under the terms of a charter granted by Charles I in 1634. Plowden's grant entitled him to substantial land in present-day Virginia, Maryland, Pennsylvania, and New Jersey, which overlapped the grant of Cecil Calvert, 2nd Baron Baltimore, of present-day Maryland. Lord Baltimore, as he was known, was "First Lord Proprietary, Earl Palatine of the Provinces of Maryland and Avalon in America" because Charles I granted him a charter in 1632 for a colony in the Chesapeake Bay. The overlap between Baltimore's and Plowden's charters was no accident: it incentivized both men to settle the land to establish their individual claims, thereby securing the area against the Dutch.[35] English monarchs' habit of dispensing overlapping charters and land grants was to profoundly shape Pennsylvania's development. Plowden's mission to establish a colony to be called New Albion coincided with the outbreak of the English Civil War (1642–1651), which led to the trial and execution of King Charles I in 1649, limiting support for the venture in England. A small cadre of indentured servants mutinied against Plowden while traveling to the Delaware Valley. The mutineers left Plowden and his two pages on an island off Virginia's Cape Charles, then sailed to Fort Elfsborg in New Sweden (a Swedish colony founded in 1638 that by 1642 centered on the Delaware River and stretched from present-day Trenton, New Jersey, to Lewes, Delaware), apparently with the idea that they take refuge with the Swedes.[36] Much to the mutineers' surprise, the Swedes arrested them and turned them over to Plowden (who had been rescued from his island imprisonment by the English in Virginia). Plowden's dream did not die easily: he made it back to England in 1649, intending to return with another crew and settle New Albion. Ultimately, this never came to pass, and Plowden made no more attempts to settle his land grant; he died in 1659, but the English dream of controlling the Delaware Valley lived on.

English colonization attempts of the Delaware Valley played out in the context of more than a century of political, cultural, and social upheaval in England. Beginning in 1532, England's King Henry VIII broke with the Roman Catholic Church and established the Church of England (whose members were called Anglicans), touching off the English wave of the Protestant Reformation. The Protestant Reformation (of which the emergence of the Church of England was one manifestation) opened the floodgates of religious conflict in England. For some individuals, Queen Elizabeth I's policies in the late 1500s did not go far enough, and they sought to "purify" the Church of England of all Catholic influences. They became known as Puritans, and they played an outsized role in English politics and the colonization of North America. A century later another sect emerged that had a profound impact: the Religious Society of Friends, or

Quakers. Founded in 1647 by George Fox, the son of a wealthy weaver, Quakers abjured violence and believed in the equality of all before God. This was a radical notion that threatened the government of England because the English monarch stood atop the Church of England's hierarchy. Though Quakers were a tiny minority (accounting for less than 1 percent of the population of England, Wales, Scotland, and Ireland), their unwillingness to acknowledge the state's authority in several key respects made them a threat.[37] In 1653, Oliver Cromwell became lord protector of England, Scotland, and Ireland, and he used his position to enforce widespread discrimination against Catholics and Quakers.

The last European power to seriously consider colonizing the Delaware Valley during this period proved to be the most successful, at least initially. Under the reign of King Gustavus Adolphus, Sweden achieved military supremacy in the early stages of the Thirty Years' War (1618–1648) and had pretensions to world-power status. One element of those pretensions was the establishment of North American colonies. Adolphus's daughter and successor, Queen Christina, continued her father's efforts, albeit less enthusiastically, which contributed to their eventual failure. In March 1638, Peter Minuit—the man who in 1626 purchased Manhattan Island on behalf of the Dutch West India Company and served as its governor for six years—established the New World's first Swedish colony, New Sweden, on the Delaware Peninsula for his new employer, the Swedish South Company.

Minuit himself was the sort of multicultural character who crops up frequently in the story of early settlements in the Delaware Valley. Born in what is now Germany, Minuit migrated in 1625 to the Netherlands, where he worked for the Dutch West India Company until he was dismissed over an internal power struggle. He was then hired by the New Sweden Company and commanded a largely Dutch crew. Landing at Swedes' Landing (now Wilmington, Delaware), Minuit and his crew purchased land from the local Natives and established Fort Christina, a trading post at the mouth of the Christina River (a place known to the Swedes as Minquas Kill). Manned by only about thirty people—all men—it was hardly an auspicious beginning to the Delaware Valley's first permanent European settlement.

Minuit was aware of English interest in the Delaware Valley because in 1632, the English arrested him for trading in the king's territory while governor of New Netherland. The Swedes' goal seems to have been to legitimize their claim to the territory by creating facts on the ground that would cement their claims. In 1640, the Swedes purchased additional land from the Lenape, this time in the Delaware Valley between the Schuylkill River and the Falls of the Delaware (located in present-day Bucks County, Pennsylvania, not far from Trenton, New Jersey). That same year a Dutchman named Peter Hollander Ridder arrived at Fort Christina to assume the role of governor, bringing with him a cargo of "involuntary emigrants" composed of convicts, debtors, and deserters from the army forced to emigrate by Swedish authorities.[38] The following year thirty-five additional Europeans arrived in the colony. Among them were a handful of Finns (Finland was ruled by the Swedes during this period). Collectively, the colony's European inhabitants professed a broad range of Christian sects, including Catholicism, Lutheranism, Anabaptism, and Puritanism, and the need for colonists forced the government to exercise de facto religious toleration.[39]

New Sweden expanded rapidly, at least in terms of physical size. By 1642, at least one Swedish settler, Olof Persson Stille, had settled in what later became Pennsylvania at a site known as Techoherassi (now Eddystone, south and west of Philadelphia on the banks of the Delaware), and over the next three years Swedes settled on the western bank of the Schuylkill River (Kingsessing) and on Tinicum Island. At that point, New Sweden consisted of several small homesteads stretching from the Delaware Bay to north of present-day Philadelphia. The homesteads were simple affairs, reflecting both the abundance of wood available in the area and the shortage of finished products (such as nails) coming from Europe. Jasper Danckaerts, who visited the region in 1679, described the Swedes as living in "block-houses, being nothing else than entire trees, split through the idle, or squared out of the rough, and placed in the form of a square, upon each other, as high as they wish to have the house . . . the whole structure is thus made, without a nail or spike."[40]

In terms of European population growth, the colony languished: as late as 1648, seventy-nine men called New Sweden home, and only twenty-eight of those were freemen. The rest were servants, soldiers, or (in at least one instance) enslaved.[41] One reason New Sweden's population failed to grow was that there were few women, a problem that the Swedish South Company failed to rectify.[42] In fact, the Swedish government was indifferent to New Sweden's success: during the colony's seventeen years of existence, only eleven ships arrived to provide the colony with supplies and people (and this in an era when most other colonies received at least annual shipments from their home countries).[43] In part this was because Sweden was embroiled in the Thirty Years' War, which distracted Queen Christina's government and choked off supplies.

Peter Hollander Ridder's term as governor of New Sweden ended in 1643, and he was replaced by Johan Björnsson Printz. Few men loomed as large in the Delaware Valley's early history as Printz, both figuratively and literally: over six feet tall and weighing between three hundred and four hundred pounds, Printz was a dominating presence (the Lenape called him "Big Belly"). Printz understood impression management, commissioning a suit of clothes made entirely of wampum. This commodity, rare and highly prized in the Delaware Valley, projected an image of wealth to the local Lenape.[44] Massachusetts Bay Governor John Winthrop, who corresponded with the Swede, described Printz as "a man very furious and passionate, cursing and swearing."[45]

Daunting challenges faced Printz when he arrived in February 1643: the fur trade had not met investors' expectations. As a result, there was little inclination in the Swedish court to support the colony economically or militarily, and the lack of wampum put it at a relative disadvantage when it came to trading with the Lenape, who were far less accommodating than they had been a decade earlier.[46] The mania for pelts encouraged other Native groups, including the Iroquois in western New York, to compete for increasingly scarce resources. Consequently, in 1636, the Susquehannock and the Lenape formed a tacit alliance against the other Native groups. As a result, the Lenape became far more assertive in their dealings with European traders than they had been.[47] Labor was in short supply, particularly after 20 percent of the population died of illness during the fall of 1644.[48] Worse, that winter Printz's manor house and nearby Fort New Gothenburg burned to the ground, consuming the Swedes' gunpowder and supplies.[49] The prevalence of mosquitoes was both an annoyance (the settlers took to calling the area "Fort Mosquitoburg") and a health concern.[50] Finally, New Sweden's main economic activity was trading, and what agriculture existed failed to sustain the colony. The Delaware Valley's waterways, which made the area so attractive to Europeans, allowed the Swedes to become the leading intermediaries, purchasing English and Dutch goods to trade with the Susquehannock (and later the Lenape) for pelts and other exports, but this did little to make New Sweden self-sufficient.

Consequently, the Swedes relied on trade with the Dutch, English, and Natives.[51] For instance, merchants from New England and New Netherland came to New Sweden to trade wampum and grain for pelts; the Swedes consumed the grain and traded the wampum to the local Natives for pelts.[52] This made New Sweden particularly vulnerable to economic warfare and heavily dependent on local Native Americans.[53] Printz pushed the colonists under his command to stop cultivating maize, which the Lenape and other Native groups would sell cheaply, and focus instead on tobacco, which could be traded at a profit in New Amsterdam or New England in exchange for tools and other goods. Eventually, tobacco became one of the region's key exports, but, despite Printz's efforts, it was not grown there, only shipped.[54] While this improved the colony's profitability, it did nothing to make the colony self-sufficient, and conditions remained miserable.

Necessity thus forced Printz to be diplomatic in dealing with what he called his "evil neighbors" because his forces were tiny (Fort New Gothenburg, the seat of Swedish government in the region, was manned by eight soldiers and two gunners).[55] He relied on guile and deception to play the Natives, English, and Dutch off one another whenever possible. For instance, in 1644, Printz successfully defended Swedish prerogatives in the Delaware Valley from English and Dutch encroachment by pitting his rivals against each other. That year a group of English explorers from Boston appeared at Fort Elfsborg (on the Delaware's eastern bank in present-day New Jersey). Thinking quickly, Printz dispatched a letter to the Dutch commander of Fort Nassau informing him of the English expedition and warning that their intention was to cut off Dutch trade with the Native Americans. Printz was friendly to the English, assuring them of free passage through Swedish territories, expecting (correctly, as it turned out) that the Dutch would prevent the expedition from sailing north along the Delaware. In this way Printz got what he wanted: the English were prevented from staking a claim to the Delaware Valley (at least temporarily), and Winthrop blamed the Dutch, not the Swedes. Printz then negotiated the release of English prisoners held by local Natives and hosted the Englishmen until they could be returned to Boston, further ingratiating himself to the English.[56]

By the early 1640s, the Delaware Valley was becoming a crowded neighborhood. Yet despite their keen interest in controlling it, the Dutch, English, and Swedes also sought to avoid any direct conflict that could lead to a war with each other or with the Natives.[57] Direct conflict was out of the question because of the weakness of the colonies and the concern it would lead to a wider war (in fact, Peter Minuit had correctly bet on Dutch reticence to forcibly confront him when he established New Sweden in 1638). The various colonists' attachment to their home countries was weak; at several junctures during this period, colonists swore oaths of allegiance to foreign powers that claimed to control the territory in which they were settled (in reality the Lenape's numerical advantage ensured they remained in control of the Delaware Valley).[58] Moreover, trade between the colonies was brisk, which brought them into contact with one another and made leaders loath to pursue open hostilities. Circumstances, not principle, dictated keeping the peace between the Delaware Valley's many inhabitants, which fostered a legacy of de facto toleration that William Penn continued and expanded. Nevertheless, the colonial powers were "passively hostile" toward one another, probing for ways to extend their control over the Delaware Valley without provoking the other powers.[59]

Things began changing in the late 1640s. In 1647, the Dutch West India Company replaced New Amsterdam's director general, William Kieft, with Peter Stuyvesant. Like Printz, Stuyvesant was a colorful character: expelled from the University of Franeker for seducing his landlord's daughter, he had served as the Dutch West India Company's director general of several of its Caribbean colonies and lost his right leg in combat with the Spanish. Kieft's administration of New Amsterdam had been disastrous, and the colony was at low ebb when Stuyvesant arrived in August 1647. Unlike his predecessor, Stuyvesant was an autocrat who aggressively pursued Dutch prerogatives in the Delaware Valley, correctly understanding that he was militarily superior to the Swedes in that region. Stuyvesant's arrival put in motion the deterioration of Swedish-Dutch relations that led, ultimately, to English domination of the Delaware Valley.[60]

In 1648, the Dutch purchased land from the Lenape and built Fort Beversreede on the Schuylkill's eastern banks (about a mile south of the present-day Passyunk Avenue Bridge). However, the Swedes frustrated the Dutch attempt to settle the area: in one instance, Printz's son, Gustaf, pulled down a Dutch settler's house. The apple did not fall far from the tree, because Printz himself bragged in 1650 about how "a few times and in several places [the Dutch had] begun to build within our poles and limits, but I have immediately let it be torn down again . . . [in the hope that] the Hollanders will quickly get tired and give up this in no less manner than the Puritans have done, who in the beginning were the most violent, but now they leave us entirely."[61] Sometimes Printz's actions bordered on the comical: at one point, he had a massive blockhouse constructed near Fort Beversreede that obstructed the fort's view of the river, rendering it useless for surveillance. Adriaen van der Donck, writing in 1650, complained that the Swedes had the Schuylkill "almost entirely under their dominion," while Cornelius Van Tienhoven, New Amsterdam's secretary, sputtered, "The Swedes do here as they please. The house which they have built at Beversreede, is the greatest insult that could be offered. They have also occupied all the land around the fort upon which they have planted Indian corn this year, so that we have not near the fort as much land that we can make a little garden in the spring. It is a shame that they act thus."[62]

The Dutch decided to force the issue in May 1651. That month a Dutch ship from New Amsterdam appeared and menaced Fort Christina. Printz bared his teeth by dispatching a small yacht with cannon and thirty men, and the Dutch ship sailed away, leading the Swede to brag, "And thus we secured the river open."[63] His triumph was short lived: the following month eleven Dutch ships appeared on the Delaware and announced their arrival with an ostentatious show of "drumming and cannonading."[64] Meanwhile, Governor Stuyvesant marched overland to Fort Nassau at the head of a force of 125 men. Rendezvousing with his fleet, Stuyvesant sent Printz a letter asserting Dutch ownership of the Delaware Valley by right of discovery.[65] Moreover, Stuyvesant had lined up the support of some Lenape sachems, who agreed to let him build a fort in territory they claimed to control. Though their claims were suspect, it was in Stuyvesant's interests to ignore that inconvenient fact.[66]

Clearly, Stuyvesant meant business, but he could not simply force the Swedes out of the Delaware Valley because, like Printz, his employers, the Dutch West India Company, warned him "to be very cautious in the intercourse with the Swedes [and to avoid] . . . as much as possible to give them cause for complaints and dissatisfaction, as it is not desirable to add to the Company's enemies at this time."[67] In an attempt to undermine Swedish control of the Delaware River, Stuyvesant built Fort Casimir (near present-day New Castle, Delaware) and abandoned Forts Beversreede and Nassau. Fort Casimir was an imposing structure, two hundred feet long by one hundred feet wide, and boasted twelve gun emplacements supplemented by two Dutch warships. Stuyvesant abandoned Fort Nassau, concentrating his forces at Fort Casimir. Outmanned and outgunned, Printz consolidated his meager forces at Forts Gothenburg and Christina, but the Dutch clearly controlled access to the Delaware River from the Atlantic. The Dutch allowed English goods to flow to the Swedish settlements, though they taxed them heavily. Given that trade with the colony was still not self-sufficient and that the Swedes could not rely on being supplied from home (there had been no ships from Sweden in three years), increasing the cost of goods was sure to drive away colonists. Stuyvesant was thus playing the long game in the hope that time would weaken the Swedes and create an opportunity for the Dutch.[68]

Time was on Stuyvesant's side: due to the awful conditions in New Sweden, the number of Swedes in the colony ebbed, and those who remained became ornery. In the summer of 1653, twenty-two (representing approximately a third of the colony's population) signed a petition demanding Printz redress their grievances, which included allegations that they were not safe in their property and complaints that he was brutal and greedy. Printz took strong action against the man he believed to be the ringleader, having him shot by firing squad, and this seemed to intimidate the rest of the colony. Disgusted and frustrated by life in the colony, Printz departed for home, leaving the colony under the command of his son-in-law, Johan Papegoja. Papegoja turned out to be as brutal as his predecessor. When fifteen freemen abandoned New Sweden to live under Dutch rule, Papegoja paid several local Natives to hunt down and return the escaped men, dead or alive.[69]

By the following year, the seventy-odd colonists remaining in New Sweden (many of whom were living among the Lenape in an area of present-day Philadelphia called Kingsessing) seriously debated moving to New Netherland. These deliberations ended when an unexpected development occurred: a Swedish ship, the *Eagle*, arrived carrying 250 colonists and the new governor, Johan Risingh. Like his predecessor, Risingh faced several challenges: shortly after his arrival, he complained that Fort Elfsbourg was "dilapidated and abandoned," while the colonists "were completely destitute."[70] Risingh immediately laid plans to reverse Dutch encroachments in Delaware Valley, and within weeks he had captured the badly undermanned Fort Casimir (which he renamed Fort Trefaldighet) without firing a shot. All Europeans living in the area became Swedish subjects, a further indication of the fluidity of national identity in the New World. Shortly after arriving in New Sweden, Risingh reported that the colony had more than 350 inhabitants, which taxed the colony's ability to produce enough food to feed everyone. Risingh introduced reforms designed to improve conditions, make the colony self-sufficient, and thereby encourage more immigration to New Sweden, but many of the Dutch then living in the area decamped for New Amsterdam, further diminishing his military strength.

Within a month of Risingh's arrival, the English visited the new governor and asserted their ownership of the Delaware River on the basis of having discovered it and it having been granted by the English Crown. Risingh was caught in a bind: as he noted in his journal, "Our orders issued in Sweden stated that we should not only procure the mouth of the river and occupy the fort . . . but we should also force other nations from the territory, *all, however, without hostilities*" (my emphasis).[71] The Swedish government considered the English a greater threat to the colony than the Dutch. Risingh had been instructed to tolerate the Dutch in territory that the Swedish claimed lest, by expelling the Dutch, "the same fort should fall into the hands of the English as the strongest, and consequently the most dangerous" rival in the region.[72] It is worth noting that even as the English demanded that the Swedes leave the Delaware Valley, they remained willing to trade with the Swedes, an indication that colonists often placed personal gain over national identity.

While Risingh deliberated his next move (like Printz, he depended on the English for supplies but was loath to surrender Swedish claims to the area), a handful of Englishmen in New Haven laid plans to colonize the Delaware Valley. On July 10, 1654, Swedish guards captured nine Englishmen who had come to colonize the area because of rumors that the Swedes had either left or died. Risingh decided the men were spies and sent them back to New England, but it was clear that Englishmen to Risingh's north and south coveted New Sweden.[73] As a precaution, Risingh met with local Native bands to state the Swedes' friendship and confirm the validity of the land sales on which New Sweden based its claims to the area. Risingh and the Natives signed a treaty of friendship whose provisions—a commitment to share intelligence about common enemies, regular consultations, and joint access to shared lands—William Penn later adopted for his treaties with the Lenape.[74]

English plans to settle New Sweden also threatened Stuyvesant's claims to the Delaware Valley because New Amsterdam could potentially be sandwiched between two hostile English colonies. Fearful of events moving faster than he could control, in late summer of 1655, Stuyvesant made his move: he dispatched several ships to the Delaware River, retaking Fort Casimir on September 1. Two weeks later Fort Christina capitulated, thereby officially bringing New Sweden to an end. Risingh and about three dozen Swedes were returned to Sweden on a Dutch ship, while the remaining mix of Swedes, Finns, English, and Dutch were forced to swear allegiance to the Netherlands. The overwhelming majority of New Sweden's inhabitants elected to remain in the Delaware Valley (perhaps believing that Dutch control would be temporary), and the Dutch treated them relatively well, granting them some measure of autonomy in their local affairs. Again, this was more about pragmatism than altruism, because Dutch officials lacked the power to coerce New Sweden's population and feared that Sweden would try to reconquer the area.[75]

The Dutch takeover of New Sweden did nothing to obviate English interest in the region. Following the ascension of Charles II to the English throne in 1660, England adopted several mercantilist policies aimed at undermining Dutch dominance of world trade and thereby weakening Dutch control of the Delaware Valley. Initially, the Dutch adopted a conciliatory posture toward the English by giving Charles paintings, sculptures, furniture, and even a yacht. However, English advocates of aggressive action toward the Netherlands, including the king's brother, James, Duke of York, gained influence with Charles, and enthusiasm for war was widespread in England. English privateers attacked and seized Dutch ships, and in late 1663, Admiral Robert Holmes began capturing the Netherlands' trading posts in West Africa. Charles gave James all the land between the Delaware's eastern shore and the west bank of the Connecticut River, a huge swath of territory that the English Crown did not actually control. In August 1664, a squadron of English frigates commanded by Richard Nicolls (a friend and political ally of James's) appeared in New Amsterdam's harbor and disgorged three hundred troops. Nicolls demanded the surrender of New Netherland. He met no resistance, and Stuyvesant, recognizing the military superiority of the English, negotiated the best terms he could. Under the articles Nicolls signed on September 29, 1664, the English committed themselves to protect the property of Dutch citizens who chose to remain in New Netherland (now renamed New York in honor of Nicolls's patron, James, Duke of York). Nicolls became New York's first English governor. As part of the transfer, the English now controlled the Delaware Valley. Nicolls dispatched Sir Robert Carr to oversee the Delaware Valley's surrender to English control. Carr easily took possession of Forts Casimir and Christina and required the region's inhabitants to swear allegiance to the English Crown. Carr was not subtle: he demolished a Mennonite settlement at Horekill (near present-day Lewes, Delaware) and carried away everything he could.[76] This was the exception rather than the rule because the English, like the Dutch and the Swedes before them, lacked the military power to effectively subdue the region; as always, circumstances dictated peaceful coexistence, not military conflict. In 1671, New York's governor, Francis Lovelace, ordered a census of people living in the Delaware Valley to tax the region's inhabitants more effectively. Not surprisingly, the area was sparsely populated (fewer than two hundred households), and while there were a few Englishmen, most European residents were Swedes, Finns, and Dutch (the census did not count Native Americans).[77]

Consequently, the English more or less tolerated the region's polyethnic population, allowing the Swedes to renovate a blockhouse in Wicaco to use as a church. This was far from altruism, because the English needed the Delaware Valley's inhabitants. Just as when the Dutch took over New Sweden, Swedes and Finns worked as translators connecting the English to the Lenape. The inhabitants of the Delaware Valley in 1664 had little reason to believe that English dominion of the region would be permanent; after all, over the preceding quarter century, control over the region had shifted several times, and in 1673, the Dutch briefly recaptured New York.[78] Yet England's takeover of the region marked a decisive turning point in the Delaware Valley's history. While the region would remain ethnically diverse, in the coming decades one power—England—would exercise uncontested political and economic domination in the Delaware Valley.[79] That dominance made it possible for William Penn to establish his utopian colony, a place he hoped would protect religious freedom while also turning a profit. As the succeeding chapters illustrate, Pennsylvania built on traditions established during the seventeenth century (most notably being home to an ethnically diverse population), but political, economic, racial, and cultural conflict ensured it would never be the "peaceable kingdom" Penn envisioned.

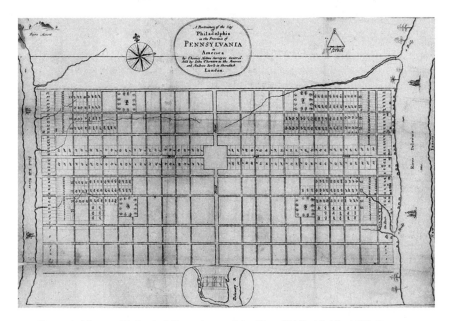

Figure 2. Thomas Holme's *A Portraiture of the City of Philadelphia*, 1683. Barry
Lawrence Ruderman Map Collection, Stanford University. The map depicts
the city's famed grid layout and a number of public squares, but it was largely
aspirational: it would be more than a century before the city stretched between
the rivers.

CHAPTER 2

The Founding of Philadelphia, 1681–1718

The Delaware Valley was hardly an uninhabited wilderness when William Penn arrived: instead, it was home to a small but ethnically and religiously diverse population of English, Scottish, Swedish, Dutch, and Indigenous peoples. In fact, Penn's famed "Holy Experiment" in religious toleration owed much to the groundwork laid by the half century of Lenape and European interaction in the Delaware Valley.[1] King Charles II's grant to William Penn of the land that became Pennsylvania inaugurated a period of massive migration that reshaped the region. Between 1681 and 1682, at least twenty-three ships disgorged would-be settlers in the Delaware Valley, dwarfing the number of Swedes who had immigrated to the region during New Sweden's entire existence.[2] There they continued the de facto tolerance that had prevailed over the preceding half century.[3] Yet tolerance had its limits, and far from the peaceable (and profitable) kingdom Penn hoped to establish, Pennsylvania was riven by cultural and political conflict.[4] Moreover, though Philadelphia was well on its way to becoming North America's largest and most economically important city by the time Penn died in 1718, his attempt to shape Philadelphians' behavior through the manipulation of space—most evident in his design for the city—utterly failed. While Penn's heterogeneous settlers failed to fully embrace his utopian vision, they too shaped Philadelphia's footprint, culture, and economy in enduring ways.[5]

Though Pennsylvania (the so-called Quaker State) is often imagined to be the first Quaker settlement in North America, members of the Religious Society of Friends had been on the continent since at least 1655, when Mary Fisher and Ann Austin arrived in Boston from Barbados.[6] That city's Puritan authorities arrested the would-be Quaker missionaries almost immediately, imprisoning them in near total isolation, destroying their tracts, and examining them for signs of witchcraft.[7] After five weeks the authorities shipped Austin and Fisher back to Barbados, but their mission was not a total failure: they had managed to convert an innkeeper, Nicholas Upsall, who took pity on the prisoners and

bribed local officials to meet with the Quaker women. Following Upsall's con-
version to Quakerism, Puritan authorities expelled him from Boston. He settled
in Sandwich, a town on Cape Cod, and in 1657 helped found the first Monthly
Meeting of the Religious Society of Friends in North America.[8] From this small
seed, Quakerism spread in North America. In 1674, John Fenwick and Edward
Byllynge purchased from Lord John Berkeley, the first Baron Berkeley of Strat-
ton, the latter's interest in New Jersey, creating a separate colony: West Jersey.[9]
By 1681, a significant English settlement existed near the Falls of the Delaware
in present-day Bucks County, and there was even a small group of Friends living in present-day Philadelphia, near what is today Kensington.[10] When Fenwick and Byllynge argued about their ownership of the land, English Quakers
turned to William Penn and two other Quaker trustees to resolve the conflict.
Penn and his fellow trustees awarded Byllynge 90 percent of the land, and when
he was unable to service his debts, they took on the active management of the
colony's affairs.

Penn promoted religious freedom in West Jersey, billing the colony as a
haven for Quakers.[11] Intensifying political conflict in England, coupled with
increased religious persecution, was one reason so many Quakers migrated to
the Jerseys. In 1660, Parliament proclaimed Charles II (the son of Charles I)
king. In the first few years of Charles II's reign, Parliament passed several laws
designed to discourage dissent from Anglicanism. However, despite his many
faults, Charles II was far more tolerant of dissent than Parliament, and in 1672
he issued the Royal Declaration of Indulgence, which granted religious freedom to Roman Catholics and dissenters. Hardliners in Parliament forced the
king to rescind the declaration and enforce the Test Acts, which mandated that
public officials deny Catholic doctrine and take communion in the Church
of England. The attacks on Catholicism spilled over into intolerance toward
Quakers, 20,000 of whom (representing almost half the sect's membership in
England) faced fines or imprisonment between 1660 and 1688.[12] It was under
these circumstances that William Penn approached Charles II in June 1680
with a bold strategy: creating a colony in North America where Quakers and
other religious minorities could migrate.

William Penn was born in October 1644 to Sir William Penn and his wife,
Margaret Jasper Penn. At the time of William's birth, his father served as an
admiral, fighting for Parliament during the First English Civil War, though his
allegiances shifted with the political winds: by the late 1640s, he was (at least
tacitly) a royalist. Sir William's political savvy paid dividends: he was elected to
Parliament in 1660 and became close to King Charles II's brother (and future
king) James, Duke of York. Sir William Penn's wealth and political influence
allowed him to send his son to Oxford, where William refused to attend daily

worship and was expelled. In response, Sir William beat his son with a cane and sent the young man to live in France, where he stayed two years. Upon his return to England, William studied law briefly and even shadowed his father on the admiral's ship. When the admiral was laid low by gout in 1666, he sent William to Ireland to look after the family's landholdings.[13]

During his time in Ireland, Penn began attending Quaker meetings, eventually joining the Society of Friends. Penn's father responded by disinheriting him and forcing the younger man from the family house. Penn went to live with various Quaker families and became close with George Fox, eventually contributing the introduction to the *Journal of George Fox* and playing a key role in the development of Quaker theology. Shortly before Admiral Penn's death, father and son reconciled. When Sir William Penn died in 1670, he left William an estate large enough to provide him an annual income of £1,500. More importantly, Charles II owed Sir William £16,500 upon the latter's death. A decade later, the king was unable to pay the debt because of his tense relations with Parliament (which had the right to levy taxes), so William's request of land in lieu of cash seemed like an ideal way to discharge Charles's debt to the Penn family, and the king's brother, James, recommended granting the request.[14] In the royal charter, Charles granted Penn all land west of the Delaware River "from twelve miles distance Northwards of New Castle" between the fortieth and forty-third parallels, a total of forty-five thousand square miles.[15] Charles insisted that William name the colony after the latter's father, so Penn dubbed it Pennsylvania, or "Penn's woods." Unlike other English charters, such as those for Virginia and Massachusetts Bay, which the Crown conferred upon corporations, Charles II granted the land directly to Penn and gave him full governing rights, making Pennsylvania a proprietary colony and Penn its proprietor.

Creating a religious safe haven for Quakers was only one aspect of Penn's goal for Pennsylvania.[16] Penn also saw the colony as a profit-making venture: his plan was to sell five-thousand-acre tracts of land for £100 and a quitrent (a fixed rent paid to a feudal lord in lieu of military services or work) of one shilling per one hundred acres, which would provide ongoing, passive income (though he was willing to forgo the quitrent in exchange for an upfront payment of eighteen shillings per one hundred acres), which was lower than the cost of land in England.[17] Penn initiated an extensive marketing campaign across western Europe with the intention of enticing immigration to Pennsylvania, tapping a network of Quaker communities in Wales, Rotterdam, and Ireland. To further encourage emigration to the colony, Penn initially offered those importing indentured servants (individuals who agreed to a fixed term of service in exchange for passage to North America) fifty acres per servant. Once their indentures expired, the servants themselves would receive fifty acres.[18]

Penn also offered purchasers ten acres in Philadelphia for every five hundred acres of land in Pennsylvania they purchased, but this was later reduced when it became clear that such terms were unsustainable.[19]

Initially, land sold briskly: before the year was out, Penn had sold approximately three hundred thousand acres, and by 1685, that number had jumped to seven hundred thousand acres.[20] Welsh Quakers were some of the earliest purchasers of land in Pennsylvania, buying forty thousand acres covering sixty-two square miles north of Philadelphia on the Schuylkill's west bank.[21] A German named Francis Daniel Pastorius, acting on behalf of the Frankfurt Land Company (representing German Quakers, Mennonites, and Pietists), purchased fifteen thousand acres in 1683, eventually founding a settlement called Germantown, about a two-hour walk from Philadelphia. The Frankfurt Land Company's directors were speculators, not colonists, and none except Pastorius ever immigrated to Pennsylvania. That being said, German immigration—which included Mennonites, Dunkers, Calvinists of various types, and Lutherans (the most numerous)—to Pennsylvania was so substantial that the first Bible printed in Pennsylvania was in German and predated an English version by nearly four decades.[22] In the century after Pennsylvania's founding, the colony received approximately seventy-five thousand German immigrants, nearly three out of four who migrated to North America during this period.[23] Germantown's growth was so great that the village was granted a charter of incorporation in 1691 (which it forfeited in 1701), the same year as Philadelphia's. Germans pushed farther into the colony's interior in search of land, and in 1702, a second German community, Skippack, was founded in what is now Montgomery County.

Of course, in addition to a small number of Europeans, Pennsylvania was populated by Native Americans, who also needed to be considered when it came to implementing Penn's vision for the new colony. In August 1681, Deputy Governor William Markham (Penn's first cousin) arrived in the colony, and the following July he and sixteen Lenape sachems signed the colony's first treaty. In exchange for guns, ammunition, tools, rum, and wampum, as well as Dutch guilders, the Natives ceded land between the Neshaminy Creek and the Delaware River. The terms of these land cessions, with their attendant promises—regular consultations, pledges to warn of imminent enemy attacks—built on precedents established by the Swedes in their relations with the Natives.[24] According to tradition, the Lenape gave Penn a wampum belt depicting a Native and a European holding hands.[25] The following summer Penn himself signed two additional treaties with local Lenape leaders, purchasing additional land.[26] Supposedly, Penn and the Lenape negotiated this purchase under an elm tree along the Delaware River (now known as Penn Treaty Park), an event artist

Benjamin West depicted almost a century later in his well-known painting *Penn's Treaty with the Indians.*[27]

This was far from the end of the Penn-Lenape relationship: between 1682 and 1684, Penn (who arrived in Pennsylvania in October 1682) signed a dozen treaties with various Native groups living in the Delaware Valley.[28] Penn carried on a "friendly correspondence" with Native leaders and hosted various Native delegations at his country home, Pennsbury.[29] It was not unusual to encounter Native Americans in Philadelphia and in the surrounding region well into the eighteenth century, and in February 1688, the governor's council ordered that local Natives be offered extra provisions as an incentive to kill wolves.[30] One result of Penn's approach was significantly less conflict with the local Native Americans than in other colonies, which made Pennsylvania attractive to settlers and investors and aided its growth.

That is not to say that European-Native relations were totally harmonious in Pennsylvania during this period. As noted in Chapter 1, the Lenape had a different conception of land ownership than Europeans. To some extent, when the European population was small, these differing understandings of land ownership were not a problem; after all, Europeans were so few and so widely dispersed that they did not impinge on the Lenape's land use. That changed once the Delaware Valley's European population exploded in the 1680s. As early as 1684, the difference between Native and European understandings of land ownership, coupled with the rapid migration of Europeans to the region, caused conflict.[31] In 1685, Tammany (or Tamanend), a Lenape sachem whom Penn had interacted with in the past, threatened settlers in Bucks County with violence if they did not leave the area. The settlers took the threats seriously enough that several fled to West Jersey. In response, Penn instructed his surveyor, Thomas Holme, to "make [the Lenape] keep their word," recommending a carrot-and-stick approach. According to Penn, "If they see you use them severely when rogueish, and kindly, when just, they will demean themselves accordingly." Lest Holme misunderstand his meaning, Penn went on to say, "If the Indians will not punish [Tammany], we will and must, for they must never see you afraid of executing the justice they ought to do."[32] Writing in 1701, one Pennsylvanian noted, "The Aborigines or Indians . . . are angered at the bad living of the Christians, especially at the system of trading which is driven with them, and they only learn vices which they did not have formerly, such as drunkenness, stealing, &c."[33] Samuel Guldin, who came to Pennsylvania in 1710, noted that the colony's Natives complained to him that the quantity of game animals had "much decreased in number" since Penn's arrival. According to the Natives, the European settlers "have shot deer simply for the skins but allowed the meat to spoil. Thus, the unrighteous mammon and avarice have already spoiled this hitherto guiltless land."[34]

In addition, it was not entirely clear how far Penn's writ ran. In a letter to his wife penned in December 1681, Deputy Governor Markham called Pennsylvania "a very fine Country . . . very Healthy," though he lamented the fact that it was "overgrown with Woods." He noted that "Provisions of all sorts are . . . plentiful: *Venison* especially." To a friend in London, Markham reported that Pennsylvania had "*good Air*" and contained an "abundance of good *Fruits*: all sorts of *Apples, Cherries, Pears, good Plumbs*."[35] When William Penn arrived in New Castle on October 27, 1682, he received a warm welcome from the region's European inhabitants.[36] The warmth of his reception belied the fact that he faced several thorny problems, the most pressing of which was defining the colony's actual boundary with Maryland. Though the charter seemed clear on this issue—establishing the colony's southern border at the fortieth parallel—there were problems. Penn's charter defined Pennsylvania's southern boundary on the location of New Castle, which was below the fortieth parallel, making the charter self-contradictory. This was no small issue: at stake were the rich farmlands of Upland (now Chester County) and the favorable location of Philadelphia.[37]

On the surface, Penn and Charles Calvert, third Lord Baltimore (henceforth Baltimore), had some similarities: both were religious minorities (Penn a Quaker, Calvert a Catholic) who hoped their colonies would serve as refuges for their persecuted coreligionists. In 1632, Charles I granted to Baltimore's father, Cecil Calvert, second Lord Baltimore, a charter for land in North America "which lieth under the Fortieth Degree of North Latitude from the Equinoctial, where New England is terminated; And all that Tract of Land within the Metes underwritten (that is to say) passing from the said Bay, called Delaware Bay, in a right Line, by the Degree aforesaid."[38] Crucially, Baltimore's charter included the phrase *hactenus inculta* ("now uncultivated"), which could be interpreted as limiting Baltimore to land under the fortieth parallel that was uninhabited by Europeans. *Hactenus inculta* and similar phrases were in English charters during this period, and the reason was straightforward: as Chapter 1 made clear, European powers settling in North America tried to avoid conflict with one another.[39] When Charles II ascended to the throne in 1660, he confirmed the charter, and the king's charter to Penn—which set Pennsylvania's lower boundary at the fortieth parallel—seemingly reinforced Baltimore's claim.[40]

Markham tried to negotiate with Baltimore over the boundary issue but fell ill shortly after arriving in Pennsylvania, so discussions got nowhere. Meanwhile, Penn worked to undermine the allegiances of people living in the disputed area by discouraging them from paying taxes in Maryland.[41] Baltimore responded to Penn's provocation by dispatching military forces to collect taxes from people living in the disputed area.[42] In 1682, Penn convinced James, Duke of York, to sell him the "three lower counties" (today's state of Delaware), which further threatened Baltimore's claim to the disputed land.[43] Baltimore responded by intimating to the inhabitants of Delaware he would confiscate their lands if they did not submit to his authority.[44] Clearly, Penn and Baltimore were unwilling or unable to settle the dispute between themselves, necessitating the Crown's involvement.

Crucially, Baltimore's 1632 charter included clause 22, which in part read, "If, peradventure, hereafter it may happen, that any Doubts or Questions should arise concerning the true Sense and Meaning of any Word, Clause, or Sentence, contained in this our present Charter . . . [t]hat Interpretation to be applied always, and in all Things, and in all Courts and Judicatories whatsoever, to obtain which shall be judged to be the more beneficial, profitable, and favorable to the aforesaid now Baron of Baltimore, his Heirs and Assigns: *Provided always, that no Interpretation thereof be made, whereby God's holy and true Christian Religion, or the Allegiance due to Us, our Heirs and Successors, may in any wise suffer by Change, Prejudice, or Diminution*" (my emphasis).[45] In 1684, Baltimore sailed for England to have the king settle the matter. Penn quickly followed, and both men hoped the issue would be decided in their favor. On paper, Baltimore had the stronger claim: after all, both charters agreed on the fortieth parallel as the boundary between the two colonies.

King Charles delegated to his Board of Trade the responsibility for adjudicating the dispute, and in 1685 it ruled in Penn's favor. The Board of Trade concluded that because Baltimore's charter included the phrase *hactenus inculta*, it specifically excluded from his lands those that were settled by Europeans at the time his charter was issued. Because Penn offered depositions attesting to the presence of Swedes in the disputed territory prior to Baltimore's charter (and because Penn's charter had no similar limitation), Baltimore had no title to the disputed land. It certainly did not hurt Penn's case that seven months before the Board of Trade rendered its verdict, James had succeeded his brother, becoming King James II. Given that James preferred Penn to Baltimore, it would have been politically unwise for the Board of Trade to rule in Baltimore's favor.[46] However, the Board of Trade's decision was far from the last word on the matter, and the issue lingered until the establishment of the Mason–Dixon Line in 1767.

Moreover, changing political winds in England threatened Penn's charter. The Glorious Revolution of 1688 swept King James II from power, depriving Penn of his most powerful champion. As a result, in 1692, Penn lost control of the colony, ostensibly because of Pennsylvania's unwillingness to provide money and men to support England's military effort during King William's War (1688–1697) but more likely because of Penn's closeness to the deposed James. King William III, who replaced James II on the English throne in 1689 following the latter's deposition, appointed Benjamin Fletcher colonial governor of Pennsylvania.

Fletcher found Pennsylvania highly factionalized and "nearly impossible to govern."[47] Fletcher did himself no favors by initially trying to coerce the region's Quaker officeholders into taking an oath mandated in England (which was explicitly designed to discriminate against dissenters generally and the Quakers in particular, whose faith precluded oath taking). Popular opposition forced Fletcher to back down and accept an affirmation.[48] Penn eventually managed to persuade the Crown to return the colony to his control in 1694, and the Crown worked out a tacit arrangement with the Pennsylvania Assembly whereby any money granted by it for the monarchs would be used for strictly nonviolent purposes, a compromise that held for more than a half century.[49]

Nor were all Penn's problems external: from the beginning, the colony was riven by political conflict.[50] Penn's charter obligated him to solicit the "advice, assent and approbation" of the colony's freemen when it came to enacting laws, though the document said little about what this would look like in practice.[51] Penn's 1682 Frame of Government called for a governor, a governor's council, and an elective Assembly of up to two hundred members.[52] Under Penn's plan, the governor and his council originated bills, which the Assembly voted to accept or reject, making it the clearly subordinate body.[53] Penn intended the Assembly to sit only nine days per year, and it met wherever space was available (such as at meetinghouses, schoolhouses, or even private homes rented for the purpose).[54] In 1683, Penn modified the colony's government structure by shrinking the Assembly (to seventy-two) and the governor's council, beginning a process that led to Pennsylvania having the highest representative-to-constituent ratio of all the colonies in British North America by the time of the Revolution.[55]

In 1684, Penn returned to England, giving the Assembly the upper hand in its conflict with him as proprietor. In 1696, it successfully pressured Deputy Governor Markham into promulgating a new Frame of Government, giving the Assembly the power to propose legislation and eliminating the nine-day limit on its sessions. When Penn returned to the colony in 1699, he asserted that the 1683 Frame of Government remained in force. Unfortunately, circumstances again conspired against him: in the summer of 1701, Penn learned that Parliament was debating a Reunification Bill that would have voided proprietary colonies' charters, bringing them back under direct royal control. Fearing for his investment and the future of his coreligionists in Pennsylvania, Penn decided he had to return to England, believing "no man living can defend us or bargain better for us than myself."[56] That may have been true, but the Assembly took advantage of Penn's imminent departure to press for greater power. Thus, shortly before departing the colony in 1701 (for what would be the last time), Penn assented to a new Charter of Privileges, which made the governor's council strictly advisory and allowed the Assembly to define the length of its session.

This was a net gain for the Assembly, which became more powerful than the colony's governors (due to controlling the purse) and remained the nexus of Quaker political strength in Pennsylvania for decades.[57]

The 1701 charter did not end the conflict between Penn and the Assembly. By now Penn's supporters and opponents had coalesced into two loose factions. The latter group came to be called the Anti-Proprietary Party (for their opposition to the colony's proprietor) and were led by David Lloyd, a Welsh Quaker who emigrated to Pennsylvania in 1686. Penn had appointed Lloyd attorney general but removed him in 1699, at which point Lloyd turned against his former benefactor. For most of the first decade of the eighteenth century, Lloyd's Anti-Proprietary faction controlled the Assembly, and he served as speaker for much of that time, ensuring conflict between Penn and the Assembly. Penn's supporters, the Proprietary Party, were led by James Logan, the colonial secretary. Shortly before leaving Pennsylvania in 1701, Penn delivered a message to the Assembly that expressed his frustration. Calling the members "Friends," he nonetheless declared, "Your union is what I desire; but your peace and accommodating of one another, is what I expect from you. . . . Make me not sad."[58]

When velvet words failed to achieve Penn's goals, he employed the iron fist. In 1704, he appointed John Evans deputy governor. Evans was not a Quaker, and his tenure was tumultuous, in part because he publicly called for troops to assist other colonies in Queen Anne's War (1702–1713), a decade-long struggle between Great Britain, France, Spain, and their respective Native allies in North America. When his initial call for volunteers went unheeded, Evans dispatched a messenger to ride into Philadelphia during the annual fair and spread rumors that French troops had invaded Delaware and were marching north. Then Evans himself rode into the city, sword drawn, and called for volunteers to join him in defending the colony. None of the rumors were true, but Evans's actions caused a widespread panic, and some Philadelphians dumped valuables down privies or wells and fled the city. No one rallied to Evans's cause, and it soon became apparent that the deputy governor had concocted the whole thing, further eroding his standing with Pennsylvanians.[59]

In 1709, Penn recalled Evans and appointed Charles Gookin, a former soldier, to be Pennsylvania's deputy governor. During the first five years of Gookin's term, he worked reasonably well with the Assembly, but beginning in 1714, relations started to deteriorate, largely because of the deputy governor's increasingly bizarre behavior. In February 1714, he berated a committee from the Assembly over an apparently minor inconvenience. Two years later, Gookin accused Richard Hill, speaker of the Assembly, and James Logan, William Penn's secretary, of being "inimical to the government of Great Britain." Gookin further enraged the Assembly that September by refusing to prosecute

Hugh Lowdon, a Philadelphian who threatened Speaker Hill at gunpoint.[60] At another point, Gookin kicked one of the judges of the Supreme Court over some minor affront.[61] Shortly thereafter the council petitioned Penn to remove Gookin, and the proprietor complied, appointing Sir William Keith, whose tenure lasted until 1726.

Despite all these setbacks and disappointments, Penn realized his dream of creating a mercantile capital—Philadelphia—though, like everything about his colony, it was not an unalloyed success.[62] From the very beginning, one of Penn's highest priorities was establishing a city to serve as a center of mercantile activity and the colony's capital. The city's very name—Greek for "brotherly love"—spoke to Penn's aspirations: Philadelphia had been a wealthy trading city in Asia Minor beginning around 189 BCE. While Philadelphia is famed for being a "planned" city, that reputation has obscured the reality that from the beginning, its development was far more organic than is generally supposed, driven by economic, political, and cultural pressures.[63] Initially, Penn selected for Philadelphia a site at the confluence of the Delaware and Schuylkill Rivers, which offered several advantages. One was that it ensured many lots would be on the river, an attractive feature for a city explicitly designed to be a shipping center.[64] In 1682, Penn's advance agents purchased the territory from three Swedish brothers, the Svensons (they were given land on the Schuylkill north of Lemon Hill).[65] Shortly thereafter, Penn purchased another mile of land fronting the Schuylkill's eastern shore. At this point, the site for Philadelphia was a one-by-two-mile rectangle stretching between the two rivers, bounded by what would become Vine Street to the north and Cedar Street to the south, comprising about 1,200 acres. The planned city would be built on a grid pattern, with streets meeting at ninety-degree angles. Thomas Holme, the colony's first surveyor general, drafted a plan that called for the city to be divided into quadrants, each with a public square just north of its center. At the intersection of High and Broad Streets would be a fifth square for buildings related to public affairs.[66] In 1683, Penn issued a letter to the Free Society of Traders that included the following description of Philadelphia:

> The *City* . . . consists of a large *Front-street* to each River, and a *High-street* (near the middle) from Front (or River) to Front, of one hundred Foot broad, and a *Broad-street* in the middle of the City, from fide to fide, of the like breadth. In the Center of the City is a *Square* of ten Acres; at each Angle are to be Houses for *publick Affairs*. . . . There are also in each Quarter of the City a *Square* of eight Acres, to be for the like Uses, as the *Moore-fields* in *London*; and *eight Streets*, (besides the *High-street*), that run from Front to Front, and twenty Streets, (besides the

Broad-street) that run cross the City, from fide to fide; all these Streets are of *fifty Foot breadth*.[67]

Philadelphia's distinctive grid plan was not unique to the City of Brotherly Love, but it came to be a feature closely associated with the city and reflected Penn's desire to use physical space to foster an orderly and harmonious society by controlling where his purchasers lived.[68]

Penn's vision did not stop at the city's outline: he sought to dictate the types of houses his colonists would build. In his instructions for settling the colony, delivered in September 1681, Penn suggested, "Let every House be placed, if the Person pleases, in [the] middle of its [plot], as to the breadth way of it, that so there may be ground on each side for Gardens or Orchards, or [fields], [that] it may be a greene County Towne, [which] will never be burnt, and allwayes be wholesome."[69] Initially, many new arrivals adopted what was called the "Swedish mode" for building their houses: basically, rough-hewn wooden cabins approximately thirty by eighteen feet. The shortage of nails and of blacksmiths meant that as much as possible, the cabins had to be built without nails. These were clearly designed to be temporary structures until more-suitable building materials became available.[70]

Fortunately for this scheme, Philadelphia lies atop high-grade red clay, the ideal material for making bricks.[71] In 1684, Penn directed that a stone quarry be opened on the Schuylkill's east bank, an area that the proprietor renamed Fairmount.[72] Consequently, Philadelphians soon began building houses from brick; as one Philadelphian noted in August 1685, "Some that built Wooden Houses, are sorry for it: Brick building is said to be as cheap: Bricks are exceeding good . . . now many Brick Houses are going up, with good cellars."

In 1684, Penn estimated that Philadelphia contained just over 350 homes; two years later that number had jumped to approximately 600.[73] The easy availability of brick and stone led to the creation of large and ornate mansions, such as Samuel Carpenter's Slate Roof House (on Second Street between Chestnut and Walnut), which served as Penn's city residence when he returned to Pennsylvania in 1699.[74] At the other end of the spectrum, some immigrants settled along the banks of the Wissahickon Creek (a tributary of the Schuylkill that runs through Germantown). Under the leadership of Johann Kelpius, a German Pietist and mystic, members of the self-styled Society of the Woman in the Wilderness (named for a woman in the Book of Revelation who took refuge in the wilderness to avoid the apocalypse) lived in caves as hermetic ascetics.[75] In short, from the very beginning, individuals resisted Penn's utopian vision, setting in motion a conflict between top-down urban planners and ordinary Philadelphians that continues to the present.

However, it was not just recalcitrant colonists; nature itself refused to bend to Penn's vision. As an inducement to potential buyers, Penn offered a "bonus" of land in Philadelphia. The problem was that the site was not large enough to accommodate all the "bonus" land Penn had promised his purchasers, and making good on those promises would have required more than an eightfold expansion in the city's size. Penn elected to give his purchasers their bonus land in the "liberties," a sixteen-thousand-acre spread of land to the city's north and west bounded in the south by Cohoquinoque Creek (later called Pegg's Run) and in the north by Cohocksink Creek.[76] Penn awarded the best lots (such as those fronting the Delaware River) in the city to his largest purchasers. Those purchasing ten thousand acres of land would receive just over two hundred feet of riverfront land (half on the Delaware and half on the Schuylkill), while those who bought five hundred acres could count on just over one hundred feet of riverfront land and a 132-by-306-foot-deep lot on High Street (today's Market Street). Those who purchased fewer than five hundred acres received only interior lots.[77] Penn also allowed for renters, who (he expected) would lease city lots directly from him at a cost of about one shilling per ten feet of frontage.[78]

Being a "first purchaser" conveyed status and privilege, but even among this elite group there was a pecking order.[79] Penn favored the Free Society of Traders by offering its members the best lots in Philadelphia because he believed this would most likely encourage Philadelphia's growth.[80] This may have been true, but it antagonized Penn's other investors. One consequence was that the Assembly refused to ratify the society's charter, thereby preventing it from taking possession of its bonus lands in the city.[81] Penn responded by giving the society a square of land of one hundred acres just south of the city, stretching from a prominent hill to the Schuylkill's east bank. The Free Society of Traders erected a warehouse on the hill, which gave the area its name: Society Hill. In addition, the society's allotment of liberty lands included a sawmill in the northern section of the liberties that came to be known as the Manor of Frank and later Frankford. One reason Penn allotted the society this land was that he believed its members were best able to operate the mill and thereby foster the city's development.[82] Penn also showed a marked preference for people who actually emigrated to Pennsylvania over absentee investors, giving the former lots on or near the Delaware and allotting the latter parcels fronting the Schuylkill.[83]

Almost immediately, European immigrants began arriving in the new colony. Attracted by religious toleration, members of a variety of sects migrated to Pennsylvania, and during the Pennsylvania Assembly's first session in 1682, it adopted a liberal naturalization act, guaranteeing to everyone who availed themselves of it the same rights and privileges as those enjoyed by English Quakers. Writing several decades after the event, one 1682 arrival recalled landing in Philadelphia and finding "neither house nor shelter . . . but the wild woods, nor anyone to welcome them to the land. A poor look out this, for persons who had been so long at sea."[84] This was perhaps an overstatement; in reality, the current site of Philadelphia had several European households when this letter writer arrived in the summer of 1682, and there was at least one tavern, the Blue Anchor, located in the middle of what is now Front Street just north of Dock Street.[85] Nevertheless, the writer's larger point—that the area was sparsely populated and lacked sufficient housing to accommodate the flood of new arrivals—is valid: with winter fast approaching, they were forced to throw up makeshift dwellings they called "caves." These caves were little more than shallow holes dug in the soft ground alongside the Delaware and then covered by a patchwork of tree limbs, rushes, and other debris.[86] One Welsh immigrant described Philadelphia in the fall of 1682:

> By this time there was a kind of neighbourhood here, although as neighbours they could little benefit each other. They were sometimes employed in making huts beneath some cliff, or under the hollow banks of rivulets, thus sheltering themselves where their fancy dictated. There was neither cows nor horses to be had at any price . . . yet no one was in want, and all were much attached to each other; indeed, much more so, perhaps than many who have every outward comfort this world can afford.[87]

Fortunately, the new settlers were blessed with a mild winter. Writing the following year, Penn described the weather in Pennsylvania from his arrival in late October through the beginning of December as "rather like an English mild Spring." The weather became frosty thereafter but not as bad as in England, with "Skie as clear as in Summer . . . I remember not, that I wore more Clothes than in England."[88]

Immigration rapidly transformed the region: by 1686, one visitor claimed that the new colony had one hundred villages.[89] Between 1690 and 1700, southeastern Pennsylvania's population grew by nearly 250 percent, from 8,800 to 21,000. In the decade that followed, the population grew by 25 percent, to 28,000, and by 1720 it stood at 37,000. Philadelphia's population growth was more modest; the city swelled from 2,031 inhabitants to 4,883 over the same period, almost entirely because of immigration (in fact, the city experienced a negative birth rate during this period, meaning deaths outpaced births).[90] As in earlier periods, women were scarce, which pushed down the birth rate. Writing in 1698, nearly twenty years after Pennsylvania's founding, one colonist noted that "women are not yet very numerous."[91] Of those who did arrive, many were indentured servants who were barred from marriage until completing their term of service, which retarded natural growth.[92] Nevertheless, just over a year after landing in Pennsylvania, Penn could legitimately boast, "Whatever men may say, our Wildernesse flourishes as a Garden, and our dessert [sic] springs like a Green field."[93]

Penn hoped Philadelphia would grow into a commercial powerhouse, a node for exporting the colony's agricultural produce.[94] The city attracted a broad array of merchants and artisans: 62 percent of Penn's first purchasers identified as merchants, shopkeepers, or artisans (compared with 23 percent who identified as farmers), a fact that laid the groundwork for Philadelphia's swift emergence as one of North America's leading mercantile centers.[95] In the first three decades of the city's existence, shipbuilding became one of Philadelphia's leading industries. This was not accidental, as Penn encouraged individuals connected with the shipbuilding trade to immigrate to Philadelphia.[96] The city's first seal prominently featured a ship, a reminder of how important shipping and shipbuilding would be to Philadelphia's early growth.[97] Penn specifically instructed his advance agents to locate the city along the Delaware River at a place convenient for large ships to dock, and within Penn's lifetime, several wharves, along with large, modern equipment for loading and unloading cargo, appeared along the river.[98] Surveyor Thomas Holme described Philadelphia as "placed and modelled between two Navigable Rivers upon a Neck of Land, [so] that Ships may rife in good Anchorage, in six or eight Fathom Water in both Rivers, close to the City."[99] A visitor to the city in the late 1690s noted, "They have Curious Wharfs and also several large and fine Timber Yards . . . where are built Ships of considerable Burthen; they Car their Goods from that Wharf into the City of Philadelphia, under an Arch, over which part of the Street is built, which is called [Arch Street], besides other Wharfs, as High-Street Wharf . . . and Vine Street Wharf, and all those are Common Wharfs."[100] By Penn's death, Philadelphia had grown into the region's preeminent port, allowing Benjamin Franklin to crow in 1729 that in Philadelphia "*Ship-Building* [is] as much as possible advanced."[101]

Consequently, Philadelphia's merchants became some of the city's most politically powerful individuals.[102] Moreover, the city's strong shipbuilding infrastructure encouraged the colony's economic development: Pennsylvania's farmers grew grain and raised livestock, which they then transported to Philadelphia for distribution throughout North America and for shipment to Europe. Philadelphia became a leading exporter of tobacco, continuing a pattern established by the Swedes.[103] Foreshadowing Philadelphia's emergence as a key publishing hub in the nineteenth century, a German immigrant named William Rittenhouse constructed the colonies' first papermill in 1690 along the Monoshone Creek, a tributary of the Wissahickon, near Germantown.

Almost immediately, Philadelphians pressured Penn to grant them the right to build on the east side of Front Street, which would limit access to the Delaware River. The proprietor reluctantly agreed because, while he strongly believed that everyone should be able to access the Delaware River, he simply could not afford to turn down quitrents that could be from this land.[104] Following Penn's departure for England in August 1684, growth along the Delaware River's bank continued to such a degree that in 1690, his representatives promulgated the "Regulation of the Bank of the River Delaware" in order to tame the haphazard development.[105] The development along the Delaware's bank displeased Penn, and in 1694, he commissioned the construction of ten public staircases along the river's bank to ensure that all Philadelphians had access to the river (the Wood Street Riverbank Steps are the only set still in existence). In 1703, Penn went further, instructing his secretary, James Logan, that no further bank lots should be granted without his permission.[106] By then it was too late: the genie could not be forced back into the lamp.[107]

In response to Philadelphians' requests, on March 20, 1691, Penn issued a charter officially designating the settlement a city and declaring that Philadelphia "shall extend the Limits and Bounds as it is layd out between Delaware and Skoolkill." Philadelphia's charter embodied two contradictory impulses: it proclaimed very broad suffrage rights while at the same time giving most of the governing power to aldermen and councilmen with lifetime tenure.[108] Under the charter's terms, Penn appointed the city's first mayor, Humphrey Morrey.[109] A wealthy merchant who had immigrated to Pennsylvania in 1683, Morrey served as both a justice of the peace and in the colonial Assembly before becoming mayor, a position he held for ten years. In 1701, shortly before leaving Pennsylvania for the last time, Penn chartered a municipal corporation for Philadelphia. Municipal corporations were medieval legal devices granted by a king or feudal lord designed to "contract out" certain governing functions to local leaders.[110] English proprietors in North America were particularly enthusiastic about municipal corporations because these devices allowed them to control trade and thereby maximize revenue from their colonial possessions.[111] The corporation's purpose was to encourage immigration to Pennsylvania generally and Philadelphia specifically, to provide more effective city government, and to regulate commerce within the city. The municipal charter created a city government composed of twelve common councilmen (initially appointed and then elected by "free Denizens of this Province, and are the Age of Twenty-One Years or upwards, and Inhabitants of the said City, and have an Estate or Freehold therein, or are worth Fifty Pounds in Money or other Stock, and have been Resident in the City for a Space of Two Years") and eight aldermen (who held their positions for life and annually chose one of their number to serve as mayor).[112]

Philadelphia's first mayor under the new charter was Edward Shippen. Appointed by Penn in 1701, Shippen was elected to the mayoralty by the city's aldermen in 1702, making him the city's first elected mayor. This was hardly the honor it would later become because the city's mayor had little executive power and was required to perform several time-consuming chores (such as enforcing commercial regulations in Philadelphia's shops). Given that the city hosted a market on Wednesday and Saturday each week, as well as two annual fairs, and was home to more than one hundred shopkeepers and craftspeople, the mayor's duties were onerous and costly.[113] For instance, the mayor was expected to fete the other members of the municipal corporation at his own expense.[114] Until 1760, the job was unpaid, meaning that in practice only wealthy men could hold the office.[115] Perhaps it is no surprise that the mayoralty was more often considered a burden than an honor, and why in 1706, Alderman Joseph Story paid a hefty fine—£20—rather than serve as mayor.[116]

Reflecting Philadelphia's growing prominence, in 1709, the provincial council began construction on a proper courthouse (up to this point, Philadelphia's magistrates conducted business in an alehouse). Reflecting the close relationship between commerce and government, the provincial council chose to build the new courthouse on Market Street near Second Street, directly across from the Quakers' Great Meetinghouse, which housed that sect's quarterly and yearly gatherings. Completed in 1718, Philadelphia's new courthouse became the center of the city's political life: voters cast ballots there, and governors were presented to the city on the building's steps.[117] In practice, the municipal corporation had exercised little power, and the colonial Assembly did most of the governing. Most of the members of Pennsylvania's provincial council and a few members of the colonial Assembly also served as members of Philadelphia's municipal corporation.[118]

Despite the city's failure to totally live up to his vision, Penn took considerable pride in the city's growth, boasting in 1701, "This year the customs [revenue] from Pennsylvania [amounts to] £8,000. The year I arrived there [the second time], in 1699, it was but £1,500—a good encouragement for me and the country. New York has not half of it!"[119] Naturally, Pennsylvania's growth did not go unnoticed. In 1696, New York's governor, Benjamin Fletcher, complained that Philadelphia had overtaken Manhattan in volume of trade, which he attributed to Pennsylvania's taxes being lower than New York's because of the latter's need to defend against the Iroquois, a backhanded vindication of Penn's relatively enlightened policy toward the Lenni Lenape.[120] Boston, established in 1630, dwarfed its southern rival in trade and in the number of ships, and the Puritan city remained a key port for importing European goods into the North American colonies, but the writing was on the wall: by 1717, Philadelphia was home to ten thousand people and was well on its way to becoming North America's leading port.[121]

Despite this, the city faced some serious challenges. One was that the corporation, which lacked the power to impose taxes, was cash poor; it relied on fees and rental payments for income. As a result, large-scale construction projects, such as building the market at Second and Market Streets, more often relied on charitable donations and voluntary associations than on public funds and public officials. Recognizing the problem, in June 1712, the Assembly (which had its own money problems) passed "An Act for raising Money on the Inhabitants of the City of Philadelphia, for the publick Use and Benefit thereof," which mandated the election of six assessors responsible for collecting taxes sufficient to meet the city's debt and public works needs, but even this failed to solve the city's fiscal problems.[122]

There were other problems as well. One was the prevalence of drunkenness. The city took steps to combat drinking and the wanton behavior that often followed: in 1685, the governor's council ordered the "caves" along the Delaware—which often served as unlicensed taverns—demolished, but this did not end the problem of drunken misbehavior. In 1708, Deputy Governor John Evans was involved in a "riotous assembly" in one of the city's taverns. When the constable arrived to break it up, Evans responded by flogging and then imprisoning the man.[123] Part of the problem was that taverns served as places to conduct business or keep up on the latest news, which certainly encouraged Philadelphians to drink alcohol. Many taverns also cultivated an image of roguishness, as their names (such as the Man Full of Troubles, built in 1759 on Spruce Street just east of Second and the only prerevolutionary-era tavern still standing in Philadelphia) demonstrate.

Closely related to alcohol abuse was crime, which concerned Philadelphians almost from the moment they arrived. In late 1682, the governor's council ordered the construction of a cage to detain lawbreakers; within three years the county rented a private house to serve as a jail.[124] By 1717, crime was enough of a concern that "sundry persons" were willing to donate money to build a jail, which opened in 1723.[125] However, the colony lacked a consistent and effective law-enforcement system and was therefore unable to deal with breaches of the peace. In 1704, Penn's son William Penn Jr. was involved in what amounted to a bar brawl at Enoch Story's Tavern (near Christ Church). Apparently, Penn and his friends were carousing, and when the night watchmen arrived at the tavern to quiet them down, they responded by beating the watchmen. Governor Evans later intervened to prevent the matter from making it to court, and shortly thereafter Penn left Pennsylvania.[126] In 1714, two Philadelphians, John Smith and William Jones, had the Reverend Francis Phillips, then serving as Christ Church's minister, dragged out of his house and arrested. Apparently, Phillips had claimed to have slept with the wives of several prominent men in the city. Between two hundred and three hundred members of Christ Church descended on the jail and successfully demanded Phillips's release. Over the next few days, Phillips's accusers had their property vandalized.[127] Clearly, even in the Quaker colony, violence and impiety were not unheard of.

Moreover, Philadelphia's economic growth created winners and losers, and the city was ill-equipped to deal with poverty. The Pennsylvania Assembly made things worse by allowing imprisonment for debt, which, in a city short on cash, strained Philadelphia's limited law-enforcement apparatus. In his *Annals*, antiquarian and historian John F. Watson described the plight of one shopkeeper placed in the stocks outside the jail. The man's crime was debt, and he "made his amends, by having his face pelted with innumerable eggs, and his ears clipt adroitly by the 'delicate pocket scissors' of the sheriff—he holding up his clippings to the gaze and shouts of the populace."[128] One consequence is that as early as 1705, the city was forced to appoint overseers to deal with the city's impoverished, though the problem only got worse and more obvious over the course of the eighteenth century.[129] Reflecting the mindset that economic failure was rooted in moral shortcomings, in 1718, the Assembly passed a law requiring recipients of public charity to identify themselves by wearing a *P* (for pauper) on their clothing. Yet these efforts to shame charity recipients into economic success largely failed, and poverty bedeviled Philadelphia over the coming centuries.

One downside of Philadelphia's large shipping business was that the vessels arriving in the city often carried Caribbean diseases. These were devastating, given that the city was an ideal breeding ground for illness.[130] The area around Philadelphia was incredibly moist: there was a swampy area just south of the Blue Anchor Tavern during this period and a sizable duck pond a few blocks west, and at various times water pooled into a pond on Third Street just north of Pine Street.[131] The abundance of slow-moving or standing water bred insects, which in turn spread diseases that help explain the city's high mortality rate. Writing to his family in North Wales from a settlement near present-day Bryn Mawr in mid-1698, one correspondent noted, "It has been a very sickly season here ye last fall & winter; several died of our Countrymen."[132] The following summer, yellow fever racked the city, so in 1700, the Assembly passed a law preventing any ship with sick passengers or crew from docking until the illness had run its course; Pennsylvania was the first colony to pass such a law.[133] One man who emigrated to the city during this period recalled that his stepmother was constantly sick with "tertian ague" (malaria), which she had developed while living in Pennsylvania.[134] Even ten years later, Andreas Sandel, pastor of Gloria Dei (Philadelphia's Swedish Lutheran Church and the oldest church in Pennsylvania), noted, "It has been very sickly in Philadelphia this Winter and many have died."[135]

Despite its growth, Philadelphia was still tiny by modern standards and remained surrounded by several small European and Native settlements. Swedish communities remained at Wicaco and Moyamensing, and a growing community of Swedes and English settled beyond the liberties in Byberry. Land travel between these sections was difficult because of the generally poor roads. One contemporary described the road connecting Philadelphia and Germantown as "clayey and mirey" and pockmarked by a "fearful quicksand."[136] Moreover, it was not unusual to see wild animals—turkeys, wolves, and even bears—in the nearby countryside or, on more than one occasion, even in the city.[137] Some Philadelphians allowed their pigs and goats to forage in the streets (despite a 1693 statute prohibiting "hoggs going at large in Philadelphia"), a fact that surely did nothing to improve the healthiness of life in the city; this practice continued into the nineteenth century.[138]

While Pennsylvania was justly celebrated for its expansive religious tolerance, ministers faced daunting challenges: their congregants were widely dispersed, which made ministering to them difficult. Frequently, non-Quaker ministers cooperated, or at least socialized. For instance, Gloria Dei's pastor, Andreas Sandel, noted that "English clergymen" invited him to visit Philadelphia's most prominent Englishmen "in order to become acquainted with them." These "English clergymen" frequently called on Sandel, and he often reciprocated, even visiting their churches. When Sandel married, Deputy Governor John Evans attended the wedding despite not being a Lutheran, and his journal makes clear that intermarriage between the sects was not unheard of.[139] When Francis Phillips, the Anglican minister of Christ Church, was jailed as a result of a sex scandal, prominent members of the congregation turned to Sandel to preach in Phillips's absence.[140] Early on, the city's Baptists and Presbyterians shared a single church building on the corner of Second and Chestnut Streets.[141]

Religious tolerance did not, however, mean "anything went" in Pennsylvania: despite Penn's tolerance of religious diversity, he nonetheless was strongly committed to building an orderly community that enforced what he considered to be moral behavior.[142] Penn's charter conveyed upon the proprietor sweeping authority (his power was subordinate only to the Crown), making Pennsylvania essentially a feudal fiefdom.[143] Penn himself declared in the preface to his Frame of Government that "liberty without obedience is confusion, and obedience without liberty is slavery."[144] There were thus limits to religious toleration in Pennsylvania, and while Pennsylvanians did not have to be Quakers, they had to behave according to Penn's moral code. Failure to do so, or to show him proper deference, could have brutal consequences. For instance, in 1684, Penn ordered Anthony Weston whipped on three consecutive days in Philadelphia's marketplace as punishment for presenting a "disrespectful" paper to the governor's council.[145] At various points, the proprietor or his representatives suppressed articles or pamphlets critical of Pennsylvania's government, even going so far as briefly confiscating William Bradford's printing press after he published controversial pamphlets.[146]

Moreover, tolerance was not the same thing as political equality. As a persecuted minority, Quakers believed they needed to control the community lest they be persecuted in their own colony. Nor were these fears unfounded; at least some of the colony's Anglicans wanted Pennsylvania to adopt legislation similar to England's 1689 Toleration Act, which allowed dissenters freedom of worship but barred them from universities and government service.[147] Thus, Pennsylvania's Quakers made clear the colony was a Quaker enterprise and, though some non-Quakers served in the colonial government, was dominated by members of the Religious Society of Friends.[148] Justus Falckner, a Lutheran minister living in Germantown, complained in 1701 that although the colony was populated by "almost innumerable sects," Penn "favors [Quakers]."[149] As far as Penn was concerned, "King Charles, King James, and King William knew [Pennsylvania to be] a Quaker colony; it was so intended."[150] Frustration with the Quaker elite pushed many of the Delaware Valley's inhabitants to move to West Jersey or into Pennsylvania's interior.[151]

One group faced significant discrimination: Catholics. Anti-Catholicism was a defining impulse of English politics in the sixteenth and seventeenth centuries, and toleration of Catholicism threatened Penn's standing with the English Crown.[152] Writing to James Logan from England in the summer of 1708, Penn noted, "Here is a complaint against your Government, that you suffer publick Mass in a scandalous manner." Though he does not instruct Logan to do anything about the situation, the implication that *something* should be done is quite clear.[153] In addition, while religious minorities enjoyed the right of religious toleration themselves, that did not stop them from trying to evangelize their fellow colonists. Writing in 1701, Justus Falckner bragged that he had been "the means of influencing divers Germans by our example, so they now and then come to the assemblies even though they do not know the language. Still, they are gradually being redeemed from barbarism and becoming accustomed to an orderly outward service."[154] Francis Daniel Pastorius, writing to friends in 1683, described his purpose in establishing Germantown as "maintain[ing] a separate little province, and thus feel more secure from all oppression."[155]

However, Pennsylvania's Quakers were far from united, a fact that contributed to the Keithian schism, a conflict named for a Quaker convert named George Keith. Born in Scotland, Keith converted to Quakerism in the 1660s and accompanied Penn and George Fox on a missionary trip to Germany in 1677. He was thus an early, and important, member of the Religious Society of Friends in England and even served as surveyor general of East Jersey, where he plotted the border (known as the Keith line) between the two Jersey colonies. In 1689, Keith became headmaster of Philadelphia's Friends School. What he found in Philadelphia troubled him: the city's Friends had (in Keith's view) strayed too far from its founding principles by pursuing worldly goods and ignoring spiritual matters. Keith began arguing that Quakers should adopt more orthodox positions regarding the divinity of Christ, but the Philadelphia Yearly Meeting (the central organizing body for regional Quaker meetings) rejected his arguments.[156] By this point, Keith and his followers were holding separate meetings, and in 1692, he published a pamphlet, *Some Reasons and Causes of the Late Separation*, which laid out his position in the most public forum yet. In response, the Philadelphia Yearly Meeting disowned Keith and his followers. Worse, civil authorities (all Quakers) tried and convicted Keith and some of his followers of sedition and slander. This points to a central element of the Keithian schism: it transcended doctrinal conflict and bled into politics. Even in religiously tolerant Pennsylvania, Quakers controlled the mechanisms of government, and Keith's assertion that Quakers should not hold public office directly threatened the status of Pennsylvania's (Quaker) political elite.[157] In 1694, George Keith decamped for London, and his followers began fighting among themselves, with most eventually leaving the Religious Society of Friends for other Christian denominations. In that sense, the Keithians lost the conflict, but the Keithian schism demonstrated the roiling tensions at work in Pennsylvania.

One tension that directly threatened Quaker unity was enslavement. Enslaved Africans were present in the mid-Atlantic when Charles II granted Penn his charter in 1681, but slavery metastasized under Quaker government: in 1684, 150 enslaved people (the equivalent of 3 percent of Pennsylvania's population and 13 percent of Philadelphia's) were "imported" into Pennsylvania aboard the slave ship *Isabella*. Enslaved Africans were quickly integrated into the colony's economy, and many prominent Pennsylvanians were enslavers.[158] These included William Penn; Philadelphia's first mayor, Humphrey Morrey; and Chief Justice of the Provincial Supreme Court Nicholas More.[159] In fact, many of the city's most prominent merchants enslaved Africans, and enslaved people accounted for more than 10 percent of Philadelphia's population in the 1690s and nearly 20 percent between 1700 and 1710, while nearly one in seven white Philadelphia families enslaved Africans during roughly the same period.[160]

Slavery's ubiquity did not make it uncontroversial.[161] In April 1688, four Quaker residents of Germantown—Francis Daniel Pastorius, Gerrit Hendricks, Derick op den Graeff, and Abraham op den Graeff—addressed a protest to the local Quaker Meeting denouncing slavery and drawing explicit parallels between religious persecution and enslavement.[162] "In Europe there are many oppressed for Conscience sacke; and here there are those oppressed wch are of a black Colour. And we, who know that men must not comitt adultery, some doe comitt adultery in others, separating wifes from their housbands, and giving them to others and some sell children of those poor Creatures to other men. Oh! Doe consider well this things, you who doe it, if you would be done at this manner? And if it is it done according Christianity?"[163] They were not the only ones: in 1693, George Keith took the provocative step of publishing *An Exhortation & Caution to Friends Concerning Buying or Keeping of Negroes*, one of the earliest English-language antislavery tracts in in North America.[164] Quaker magistrates, outraged by the pamphlet, forced its printer, William Bradford, out of Pennsylvania, though his son Andrew (also a printer) returned to the city in 1718.[165] One resident of Germantown celebrated the Keithian schism, writing:

> Hence the eyes of many have been opened to see that they have erred against God's Writ and they have publicly seceded. This has produced such a shattering among them that one piece of their meeting-customs lies splintered here, another there; there is some sighing on account of the vanity and folly of their teachers, some of whom have gone so far, as to consider the inward light, such as heathens have, sufficient for salvation, thus degrading Christ, His justification, blood and death. These and other absurdities have gained ground among them because of their ignorance of Scripture, which many of them . . . have ceased to hold in honor.[166]

Nor was it just the Keithians who raised the issue: some orthodox Quakers expressed concern about enslavement. For instance, William Southeby, in 1696, wrote an impassioned address, "To Friends and All whom it may Concern," that attacked enslavement.[167] That same year Cadwalader Morgan, a Quaker living in Merion, wrote to the Philadelphia Yearly Meeting claiming that God had "made known to me whether it was his will if I should buy of [enslaved Africans] or no. . . . it was not Long before he made it known unto me That I should not be Concerned with them. And afterwards I had no freedom to buy or take any of them upon any account."[168] Beginning in 1696, the Philadelphia Yearly Meeting discouraged the importation of enslaved people, though this fell short of an outright ban on the practice. Two years later "it was Agreed that Endevors should bee used to put A stop to the Importing of [enslaved people]," though no specific actions were suggested.[169] In 1700, the Assembly did levy a tariff of twenty shillings for every enslaved adult entering the colony (raised to forty shillings in 1706), though this was an attempt to raise revenue rather than discourage the importation of enslaved people, a reflection of the fact that slavery was a vital part of Pennsylvania's economy in the late seventeenth and early eighteenth centuries.[170]

Yet by 1710, there was growing pressure to abolish the slave trade, and enslavement among Philadelphians declined for several decades thereafter.[171] In 1711, the Philadelphia Yearly Meeting again encouraged the colony's merchants to avoid the slave trade, and when in 1715 the Chester Meeting asked for guidance in dealing with Quakers who purchased or sold enslaved people, the Philadelphia Yearly Meeting's advice was to gently press such Friends to "avoid the practice."[172] Even this was a step too far for Isaac Norris, a prominent Philadelphian and slaver who complained in 1715 of the "warm pushing by some Friends, of Chester chiefly, in the business of negroes. Their aim was to obtain a [rule] that none should buy them for the future."[173] But Norris was fighting a losing battle. In 1712, the had Assembly passed a tariff of £20 per enslaved person, which was clearly designed to discourage slave imports out of concern over rebellions of the enslaved like the one in New York earlier in the year.[174] Though the Assembly reduced the tariff in 1715 to £5 per head, it had the intended result: the total number of enslaved people imported into Pennsylvania dropped sharply around 1720 (though it briefly spiked in the mid-1730s and again in the mid-1760s).[175] Moreover, opposition to slavery was hardly the same as believing in racial equality, and racism continued to plague the city throughout the coming centuries.

Thus, when William Penn died in 1718, Pennsylvania was far from the harmonious utopia he had envisioned: while it had grown spectacularly, that growth had created several unintended consequences. An ethnically and racially heterogeneous group, Philadelphians were tolerant, but only up to a point. Meanwhile, the colony and city were riven by political conflict, and Philadelphia's growth thoroughly undermined Penn's vision for the city as a "greene country towne," with purchasers subdividing lots and trying to restrict access to desirable plots. Yet despite all the hardships, life in the City of Brotherly Love offered many new arrivals opportunities they might not have ever had. As one Philadelphian put it in 1698, "Some came here might have better staid in their own country, & it is my thought yt great many more whould have done better here yt ever they are like to do in their own country."[176]

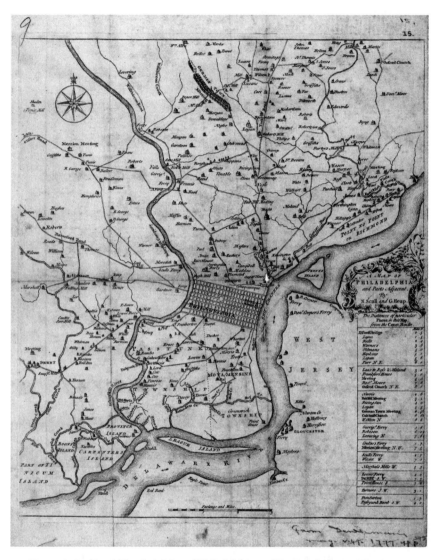

Figure 3. Scull and Heap's *A Map of Philadelphia and Parts Adjacent*, 1755.
Library of Congress, Geography and Map Division. Though the second largest
city in the British Empire and the largest in North America, Philadelphia in the
mid-eighteenth century was still an overgrown town surrounded by family farms
and small villages.

CHAPTER 3

Franklin's Philadelphia, 1718–1765

When William Penn died in 1718, Philadelphia was a thriving, multiethnic, and religiously diverse mercantile center, as he had hoped. However, in many ways, the city had fallen short of Penn's vision for a "greene country towne." Municipal government often failed to meet Philadelphians' needs, so citizens turned to private organizations to help achieve public ends (a practice called volunteerism), with limited success. One reason that municipal government and volunteerism failed was the proliferation of challenges that the city faced. Philadelphia's growth into a regional and empire-wide shipping center made it vulnerable to booms and busts of the business cycle, exacerbating economic inequality. Immigration swelled the colony's population but also contributed to ethnic and religious conflict. In addition, Philadelphia's economy relied on various forms of unfree labor, including the enslavement of Africans, which became increasingly controversial over the course of the eighteenth century. Moreover, Philadelphia's role as British North America's leading port embroiled the city in the Crown's colonial wars. This forced the colony's Quaker elite to choose between their pacifist principles and the growing political pressure to defend Pennsylvania against incursions from Britain's enemies. Finally, the rejection by Penn's sons of his comparatively benevolent attitude toward Native Americans led to increased conflict between colonists and Natives, which fostered antiurbanism among individuals in the backcountry who felt the Philadelphia-based Assembly was ignoring their concerns. All these issues came to a head during the French and Indian War, a conflict that paved the way for revolution just a decade later.

After Penn's death, ownership of Pennsylvania passed to Penn's widow, Hannah. Following Hannah's death in 1726, the proprietorship of Pennsylvania passed to her sons, Thomas, John, and Richard. During this tumultuous period of changing leadership, Pennsylvania was racked by a depression set off by the collapse of the South Sea Company, a British firm granted a monopoly of Great Britain's trade with South America. This depression drained specie (gold and silver coin) from the colonies, strangling business. It was not a new problem:

England during the seventeenth and eighteenth centuries operated under an economic system called mercantilism, whose adherents asserted that countries should adopt policies designed to maximize exports and minimize imports. One result of these policies was that British merchants accumulated large stores of coins, leaving colonists perennially starved for cash.[1] In 1723 the Assembly established a land bank, which lent paper currency to the colony's subjects, who in turn offered property as collateral. The land bank had two purposes: injecting liquidity into the economy and providing revenue for the colony (the colony received interest on the loans).[2] Deputy Governor William Keith championed these proposals, which made him popular with the city's artisans and workers but put him at odds with Philadelphia's merchants, many of whom were allied with the proprietor. They worried that a colonial emission of paper currency would complicate trade with England, while the colonial secretary, James Logan, was concerned that emissions of paper money would erode the values of the rents due to the Penn family.[3] In 1726, the Penns replaced Keith with Patrick Gordon. In response, Keith successfully sought election to the Assembly, mostly by organizing two political clubs, the Gentlemen's Club and the Leather Apron Club, which mobilized his supporters and ensured he remained a formidable political force in Pennsylvania.

In 1732, Thomas Penn came to Pennsylvania committed to doing what his father never could: make the colony profitable.[4] He was followed by his brother John ("the American," so called because he was the only one of Penn's children born in the colonies) in 1734, but John stayed for only a year, and he died in 1746. Thomas believed the first step to making Pennsylvania profitable was to recover power ceded to or grabbed by the Assembly over the preceding decades. Following Gordon's departure in 1736, the deputy governor's office remained vacant for two years, during which James Logan—then serving as the governor's council president and a strong supporter of the proprietors—was the colony's de facto deputy governor. But he lost the war on paper money: by the mid-1740s, Pennsylvania had issued approximately £80,000, mostly to small farmers and mechanics. Paper currency was so ubiquitous that one visitor in 1750 claimed that "everything is paid for with stamped paper money."[5]

Conflict over paper money was only one in a series of political battles during this period, leading to the emergence of what historians have identified as two parties. The Proprietary Party, so-called because it supported the Penn family's interests, dominated Philadelphia's municipal corporation.[6] The Proprietary Party is a misnomer because it was not so much a cohesive organization with an effective leadership system as an aggregation of people who, for a variety of reasons, were invested in the continuance of proprietary government in Pennsylvania.[7] This fact, as well as the antidemocratic features of proprietary government, put them at a disadvantage when it came to colonial politics.[8] They were opposed in the colonial Assembly by the Anti-Proprietary Party (usually called the Quaker Party), made up largely of Quakers and Germans (of both the Reformed Churches and the Pietistic sects), ensuring a tense relationship between the Assembly and the city's government.[9] In 1740, Thomas Penn tried to bar Quakers from serving in the Assembly by requiring them to take oaths, a clear attempt to regain power lost to the body over the preceding decades.[10] This move failed in large part because the Quaker Party was substantially better organized than its opponents.[11]

In general, politics during this period was raucous, and elections were alcohol-drenched affairs characterized by violence and voter intimidation.[12] According to one chronicle, in 1729, a mob of two hundred club-wielding men from the surrounding counties entered the city "to overawe the Assembly, and to storm the government and council."[13] Tensions between Deputy Governor George Thomas (who had assumed the position in 1738 due to Patrick Gordon's death in 1736) over Pennsylvania's lack of support for English efforts during the War of Jenkins' Ear (a nine-year conflict between Great Britain and Spain that began in 1739) intensified. In the elections of 1740, the Quaker Party successfully turned out several hundred Germans, who tipped the balance in the Quakers' favor, leading to gripes about illegal voting by unnaturalized German immigrants.[14] Moreover, casting ballots had a running-the-gauntlet flavor: voters had to ascend a flight of stairs to deposit their vote with election officials on the courthouse's second-floor balcony, and Quaker Party members packed the stairway to prevent Proprietary Party members from voting.[15] This combustible dynamic turned bloody on election day 1742. At about seven o'clock on the morning of October 1, several dozen sailors surrounded the Philadelphia courthouse (on Market Street between Second and Third), and several scuffles broke out. At ten o'clock, Isaac Norris, the Quaker Party's candidate for the Assembly, was elected. Almost immediately, the sailors began clubbing city residents, yelling, "Down with the plain clothes and broad brims!" an allusion to Germans and Quakers.[16] The sailors hefted bricks through the courthouse windows, showering voters with shards of broken glass.[17] Eventually, the crowd forced the sailors to flee, and the election continued without further incident. Despite the violence, the Quaker Party won, but the entire affair demonstrated the City of Brotherly Love's profound cultural and political cleavages.

In the half century after Penn's death, Philadelphia grew from a frontier settlement to the most important city in British North America, swelling from approximately five thousand inhabitants to nearly sixteen thousand by 1767, with twenty-five hundred more living in nearby Southwark and more than four thousand in Northern Liberties.[18] Peter Kalm, who visited Philadelphia in

1748, noted that the city was "now well filled with inhabitants of many nations, who in regard to their country, religion and trade are very different from one another."[19] Moreover, Pennsylvania was no longer the sparsely populated forest it had been when Penn arrived in 1682. By 1720, southeastern Pennsylvania was home to approximately thirty-seven thousand people, and by 1760, that number had risen to one hundred seventy-five thousand.[20] Consequently, the founding of new settlements and towns accelerated after 1740, with Europeans pushing farther west, exacerbating conflict with Native Americans.[21]

Immigration remained largely responsible for Philadelphia's population growth.[22] One immigrant in particular cast a long shadow over Philadelphia's history: Benjamin Franklin. Franklin was born in January 1706 in Boston, the son of Josiah and Abiah Franklin. Josiah could only afford to send Benjamin to school for two years; after that, Benjamin worked in Josiah's candle shop. When the boy was twelve, Josiah apprenticed Benjamin to James Franklin, Benjamin's older brother. James was a printer and newspaper publisher, and Benjamin relished the access to books that working in the printing trade provided. He did not, however, enjoy serving as his brother's apprentice, so he ran away to Philadelphia when he was seventeen, eventually becoming one of the city's leading citizens and a wealthy man. Aiding Franklin's ascent into wealth and influence was the fact that he was a newspaperman, though the *Pennsylvania Gazette* (the newspaper he bought in 1729) was not the city's only, or even oldest, newspaper. That honor fell to Andrew Bradford's *American Weekly Mercury* (founded 1719). Franklin managed the *Gazette* until 1748, when he "retired" to focus on public business and his scientific experiments.[23]

Another secret to Franklin's success was his judicious cultivation of powerful friends, who rewarded the young man with patronage and position: in 1736, he was selected to be the Assembly's clerk, holding the position until 1750. In 1748, Franklin was elected to the city's common council, and in 1751, he became one of Philadelphia's aldermen as well as a member of the Assembly (representing Philadelphia), which he held until losing his bid for reelection in 1764. William Allen, a Scotch-Irish Presbyterian then serving as chief justice of Pennsylvania's Supreme Court and a leading Penn family supporter, was instrumental in Franklin being appointed to the lucrative position of North America's postmaster general in 1753.[24] Until the Seven Years' War, Franklin managed to work with (and antagonize) both the Quaker and the Proprietary Parties (though he most often sided with the former); the war proved to be a turning point not only for Franklin but for Philadelphia, Pennsylvania, and Britain's North American colonies.[25]

Immigration shifted the colony's ethnic and religious makeup and, with it, its politics after 1720. Germans were the largest group of immigrants to the colony during this period. After 1727, German immigration increased rapidly, eventually peaking in the late 1740s before dropping off in the 1750s and 1760s.[26] All told, from 1682 to 1765, between sixty thousand and one hundred thousand Germans migrated to Pennsylvania, with perhaps as many as fifty thousand settling in Philadelphia, creating something of a German ghetto along the Delaware River north of Race Street.[27] The recent immigrants were poorer than the previous generations, relying more often on redemption to finance their trips across the Atlantic.[28] Like indentured servants, redemptioners relied on third parties to finance their trips across the Atlantic. The difference was that indentured servants negotiated their contracts prior to immigrating, whereas redemptioners negotiated contracts with potential masters upon arrival. This put them at a serious disadvantage: redemptioners could not leave the ship until someone purchased their contracts, a process that sometimes took weeks.[29] The influx of poor and sick immigrants alarmed government officials, and as early as 1717, Deputy Governor William Keith asked in a speech to the Assembly if it might be necessary to enact some "regulation . . . in regard to the unlimited numbers of these foreigners coming without licence from the King, or leave of the government."[30] In 1725, James Logan complained that the Germans immigrated "in crowds" and that "all these go on the best vacant lands, and seize upon them as common spoil."[31] In 1742, the Assembly passed legislation mandating seven years' residence in Pennsylvania before immigrants could naturalize. Because unnaturalized residents could not legally own land, many squatted, making it impossible for the proprietors to collect the quitrents due.[32]

Germans, who comprised between 50 and 60 percent of the colony's European population, were a key constituency in the colony's fractious political environment. They often allied with the Quakers in the late 1730s through the mid-1750s, allowing the Quakers (who made up about 20 percent the onset of the French and Indian War), to retain control of the colonial Assembly.[33] Quaker control of the Assembly ensured religious toleration, a pacifist policy toward Native Americans and other European powers, and (consequently) low taxes.[34] Meanwhile, the faction allied with the Penn family (known as the Proprietary Party, and after 1739 more aggressively antagonistic to the colony's Quaker elite) initially attempted to woo German voters, but their efforts were ham-handed and condescending (for example, advocating the establishment of charity schools designed to "Anglify" German immigrants).[35]

Anxiety about the Quakers' and Germans' unwillingness to pay for colonial defense contributed to Philadelphia's celebrated culture of volunteerism. During King George's War (1744–1748), Benjamin Franklin tried to organize a voluntary militia to defend the colony. To gin up support for the idea, he wrote a pamphlet, *Plain Truth: Or, Serious Considerations on the Present State of the City of Philadelphia and Province of Pennsylvania*, which was translated into German in order to encourage the colony's German inhabitants to break with their Quaker political allies and support the militia.[36] When the Germans failed to do this, Franklin turned his ire on them, demanding in 1751 to know "why should the Palatine Boors be suffered to swarm into our Settlements, and by herding together establish their Language and Manners to the Exclusion of ours? Why should Pennsylvania, founded by the English, become a Colony of Aliens, who will shortly be so numerous as to Germanize us instead of our Anglifying them, and will never adopt our Language or Customs, any more than they can acquire our Complexion?"[37] The city's Germans got the last laugh: in 1764, Franklin's political enemies widely circulated his disparaging comments among Philadelphia's German population, contributing to his defeat for reelection to the colonial Assembly.[38]

The next-largest group of immigrants to Pennsylvania during this period was the Irish. Philadelphia attracted approximately one-half of all Irish immigrants to British North America during the colonial period, with the total exceeding fifty-three thousand between 1729 and 1774.[39] Irish immigration to Philadelphia grew fivefold between 1730 and 1740, and though it temporarily dropped off for a few years thereafter, it quickly rebounded in the mid-1740s, spiking in the years just before the outbreak of the American Revolution.[40] Irish immigration to Pennsylvania alarmed some of the colony's leaders, such as James Logan, who in 1729 applauded the Assembly's efforts to limit Irish immigration and said of the Irish immigrants, "It is strange they thus crowd where they are not wanted."[41] Many Irish immigrants were actually Scotch-Irish, or the descendants of Scots who had settled in Ulster in Northern Ireland, comprising what one Quaker at the time ruefully called the "Scottish clan." Quakers were particularly concerned about growing numbers of Scotch-Irish Presbyterians immigrating to the colony.[42] Many settled in the colony's backcountry, but those who chose Philadelphia were heavily involved in the city's mercantile sector, becoming a visible segment of the city's economic and political elite closely allied with the Proprietary Party.[43] Most Irish immigrants were Presbyterians, with approximately one-quarter Quakers, followed by Anglicans and a relatively small number of Catholics (approximately 10 percent of the total).[44] Due to Scotch-Irish immigration to Pennsylvania, Philadelphia became a leading center of Presbyterianism in North America; in 1706, an Irish clergyman named Francis Makemie founded the first presbytery on the continent at Philadelphia, and eleven years later the city became home to the synod (overseeing the presbyteries of Philadelphia, Long Island, and New Castle).[45]

Despite Pennsylvania's celebrated religious toleration, anti-Catholicism remained a potent force in Pennsylvania politics even though the number of

Catholics remained relatively low in the colony (estimated at two thousand in 1756).[46] Anti-Catholicism was so thoroughly ingrained in English culture that when observers criticized Irish immigrants to Philadelphia, they did so by comparing Presbyterianism to Catholicism (a move that was particularly strange given the Presbyterians' antipathy toward Catholicism).[47] In a 1754 petition to Deputy Governor Robert Hunter Morris, several of Philadelphia's Germans emphasized their loyalty by pointing to their shared Protestantism. They asked rhetorically, "How, therefore, can any Man of due Reason think, much less say that [we] were any ways inclined to submit [ourselves] again under a Romish Slavery upheld by a French King?"[48] In 1733, the city's first Catholic church, St. Joseph's, opened on Willings Alley (between Third and Fourth just south of Walnut Street). Founded by a Jesuit priest, Father Joseph Greaton, the church proved controversial: in 1740, a mob of Presbyterians threatened to tear down the building and were dissuaded only by the pleas of a group of Quaker notables.[49] Thomas Penn, William's son, was aggressively anti-Catholic, trying unsuccessfully to prevent Mass from being conducted at St. Joseph's. Even Franklin was not above appealing to his readers' anti-Catholic sentiments to mobilize support for his projects. In *Plain Truth*, Franklin asserted that French Catholic missionaries to the Native Americans threatened to mobilize the newly converted Natives against the colony. More alarming, he prophesied the "invasion of a powerful French army, joined by Irish Catholics, under a bigoted Popish king!"[50] Despite the pervasive anti-Catholicism in Philadelphia, a second Catholic church, St. Mary's, opened on Fourth Street just above Spruce in 1763.

Pennsylvania also attracted a sizable stream of French immigrants, mostly Protestants fleeing persecution from the Catholic monarch. In 1685, King Louis XIV revoked the Edict of Nantes, which since 1598 had protected French subjects' freedom of conscience. This inaugurated a period of official persecution of Protestants, causing many to flee to Protestant countries in Europe or to North America. These French Protestants (called Huguenots) settled in substantial numbers in the Perkiomen Valley (present-day Montgomery County), in the Oley Valley (present-day Berks County), and at a settlement in Lancaster County on a large parcel of land given by William Penn to a Huguenot, Madame Marie Ferree, whose acquaintance he had made in England.[51] During the Seven Years' War, Great Britain forcibly relocated French neutrals (called Acadians) living in Nova Scotia; some of these ended up in Philadelphia, further adding to the city's ethnic diversity. One of these Huguenots was Anthony Benezet (born Antoine Bénézet), a Quaker who emigrated to Philadelphia in 1731 and played a leading role in the city's abolitionist community.

A small number of Jewish immigrants arrived in Philadelphia during the early eighteenth century. Jews had been in the Delaware Valley since the mid-seventeenth century, and the first documented Jew living in Philadelphia was Jonas Aaron (or Aarons), who arrived some time prior to 1703.[52] In 1738, Philadelphia's first Jewish cemetery opened between Eighth and Ninth Streets on Spruce. Beginning in 1740, several of Philadelphia's Jews met for services in private homes, and this group grew into the founding of Congregation Mikveh Israel. Jews (mostly from central and eastern Europe) began trickling into the city after 1740 because of Parliament's passing of the Plantation Act, which granted non-Brits living in the colonies the opportunity to naturalize after seven years' residence.[53] Interestingly, despite the long history of English anti-Semitism, at least some of Philadelphia's Jews joined such key institutions as the Library Company of Philadelphia (often known simply as the Library Company and the first subscription library in North America) and the city's Masonic lodge.[54]

Another reason for Pennsylvania's partisan rancor was a series of colonial wars during the first half of the eighteenth century that raised important challenges to the colony's Quaker identity. Largely forgotten today, the War of Jenkins' Ear (1739–1748) and the War of Austrian Succession (1740–1748) tested the colony's commitment to the Quaker ideal of pacifism and raised questions about its place in the British Empire, with consequences for Philadelphia. England went to war with Spain in 1739, and Spanish privateers (armed vessels owned by private individuals but licensed by the government to capture enemy shipping) raided ships sailing from or to Philadelphia. It was not unheard of for Spanish vessels to sail up the Delaware River during this period, threatening the city and its shipping.[55] Concerns over hostile ships were so severe that in 1747, Philadelphians constructed the colony's largest fortification, a grand battery (funded by a lottery) south of the city, complete with more than two dozen guns, though it received little financial support thereafter and largely fell into ruin.[56] These wars presented Pennsylvania's Quakers with an unappealing choice: support Britain against its enemies or remain true to their pacifism and risk the home country's ire. The Quaker-dominated Assembly chose a third option: authorizing money to support Britain's war effort while stipulating that those funds could not be used for military purposes. Naturally, once the funds were turned over to British officials, Pennsylvania's Assembly had no control over how the money was spent, but the ruse was enough to assuage the Quaker assemblymen's consciences and became a template for Pennsylvania's participation in Britain's colonial wars, at least for the time being.[57]

Another important, and related, change during this period was the souring of colonial-Native relations due to increased immigration and the Penn family's desire to make money.[58] Until the mid-1730s, the colony enjoyed more or less peaceful relations with Native Americans, and it was not unusual to see Natives in Philadelphia.[59] Things began changing in the 1730s, owing in large part to westward expansion and conflict between Pennsylvania and Maryland over the former's southern boundary.[60] In an effort to prevent Maryland from claiming the disputed territory, Pennsylvania officials encouraged settlement. Unfortunately, this violated long-standing promises to various Native American groups living in the region, particularly the Conestoga. Penn also reoriented the colony's policy to favor the Iroquois at the expense of other Native groups, antagonizing those groups and driving them into an alliance with the French. In 1736, Thomas Penn went so far as to recognize the Iroquois' supremacy over the Conestoga, a legal fiction that made it possible for the Iroquois to give the proprietor title to the land west of the Susquehanna River.[61] The following year Penn compounded this turnaround in the colony's policy toward Native Americans with the infamous Walking Purchase. While the Penn family held a grant to all of Pennsylvania from the English Crown, William Penn had only purchased from the Lenni Lenape a small portion of that area: roughly as far west as Lancaster County and as far north as the Tohickon Creek (just north of present-day Quakertown). To raise more money, the Penns needed to sell additional large tracts of land, but to do that they needed to first purchase those tracts from the colony's Native Americans.

Thus was born the Walking Purchase, an elaborate charade designed to give the Penns' land grab a veneer of legality.[62] Thomas Penn claimed to have a 1686 deed that obligated the Lenni Lenape to sell to the Penns a parcel of land defined by the length a man could walk in a day and a half. Using a variety of tricks, including a map that intentionally misrepresented the true scope of the territory at stake, James Logan (in his capacity as provincial secretary) persuaded the Lenni Lenape to acquiesce to the sale. That accomplished, Logan hired three runners and cleared a path through the territory, allowing the runners to cover approximately seventy miles, nearly twice the distance the Lenape had anticipated. Logan demanded the Lenape agree to sell more than one million acres, and the Delaware (who rightly felt they had been cheated) responded by decrying what they called "ye running walk."[63] When the Lenape turned for assistance to the Iroquois, the latter refused to intervene because of their agreement with the Penns. The short-term result was a substantial improvement in the Penn family's finances, but over the ensuing decades, the Penns' new policy—symbolized by the odious Walking Purchase—led to violent conflict between the colony's Natives and settlers that decisively reshaped Pennsylvania's prerevolutionary politics.[64]

Another trend that was reshaping colonial politics and society was the Enlightenment, a philosophical movement that espoused reason, rather than revealed truth, as the basis of knowledge and emphasized virtuous living (rather than strict doctrinal conformity) as the key to morality. Due to its size, influx of immigrants, and the diversity of its population, Philadelphia was a leading center of the Enlightenment. By the mid-eighteenth century, Philadelphia housed several learned societies, libraries, and educational institutions, and the influx of a wide range of immigrants ensured a steady flow of ideas. Adding to Philadelphia's importance, the city was also well on its way to becoming North America's leading printing center: in 1741, printer Andrew Bradford published the first magazine in North America, the *American Magazine* (Franklin's *General Magazine* appeared three days later). In 1743, Christopher (born Johann Christoph) Sauer, a German immigrant living in Germantown and the colonies' first German-language printer, published a German-language Bible, the first Bible published in North America. Three years later, he launched the first non-English-language newspaper in the colonies. In 1742, Franklin printed the first novel published in North America, Samuel Richardson's *Pamela; or, Virtue Rewarded.*[65]

The English clergyman and travel writer Andrew Burnaby, who visited Philadelphia as part of his tour of North America in 1759 and 1760, observed of the city that "philosophy seems not only to have made a considerable progress already, but to be daily gaining ground."[66] Local poet Elizabeth Graeme Fergusson assembled a salon of sorts that, at various times, included fellow poet Nathaniel Evans, composer and satirist Francis Hopkinson, and playwright Thomas Godfrey.[67] In 1728, naturalist John Bartram established his arboretum along the Schuylkill. The forty-five-acre preserve at the intersection of Fifty-Fourth Street and Lindbergh Boulevard is the continent's oldest extant botanical garden. By 1768, Philadelphia was home to several important learned societies, such as the American Philosophical Society (founded in 1743, though by 1746 it had lapsed into inactivity and was not revived until 1767) and the American Society for Promoting Useful Knowledge (founded in 1766). Philadelphia was also a leading center for medical and scientific education; in 1765, the Philadelphia College (which was connected to the Academy of Philadelphia and later became the University of Pennsylvania) opened the first medical school in North America. These institutions were not immune to political intrigue: the proprietor's supporters were well represented in the Library Company of Philadelphia, among the Pennsylvania Hospital's directors, and in the College and Academy of Philadelphia.[68] Sometimes political considerations were more important than scientific or cultural achievement when it came to membership in the American Philosophical Society.[69] Because of the political dimension to membership in these organizations, when the American Philosophical Society and the American Society for Promoting and Propagating Useful Knowledge merged in 1769, it required carefully balancing the officers of each organization.[70]

For the same reasons that the Enlightenment flourished in the City of Brotherly Love, Philadelphia was also a key site for the Great Awakening, a Christian evangelical revival that swept the colonies in the 1730s and 1740s. The Great Awakening was a reaction to the Enlightenment and to a perceived decline in religiosity. In 1739, George Whitefield, an evangelical English preacher who was one of Methodism's founders, visited Philadelphia.[71] According to Whitefield's traveling companion, William Seward, the revivalist spoke to several thousand people at various locations in Philadelphia and Germantown, which was "the largest Congregation we have yet had in *America*."[72] Whitefield's preaching was so popular that in 1740 he constructed a preaching house that was the city's largest building at the time and was funded entirely by donations. Located on Fourth Street between Arch and Market, the building served as both preaching house and schoolhouse for Black Philadelphians, although not for long; in 1749, the Academy of Philadelphia began operations in this building. Writing several decades later, Franklin recalled, "From being thoughtless or indifferent to religion, it seem'd as if all the world were growing religious, so that one could not walk thro' the town without hearing different psalms sung in different families of every street."[73] In Pennsylvania the Great Awakening emerged principally from the colony's Presbyterian churches, where "Old" and "New" Lights (opponents and supporters of the Great Awakening, respectively) battled for control. This was particularly a threat in Pennsylvania, which had no established church and where ministers were scarce.[74] Gottlieb Mittelberger, a Lutheran minister who lived in Pennsylvania for several years in the 1750s, claimed "there are many hundreds of adult persons who have not been and who do not even wish to be baptized. There are many who think nothing of the sacraments and the Holy Bible, nor even of God and his word. . . . In Pennsylvania everyone may not only believe what he will, but he may even say it freely and openly."[75]

Eighteenth-century Philadelphians enjoyed a reputation for plainness, frugality, and industry, though the city offered its share of unsavory pleasures, including liquor-fueled, multiday street fairs in May and November, bear and dogfighting, bullbaiting, and horse racing.[76] Drinking was extremely common in Philadelphia among men and women of all classes, which led to a minor social panic, so much so that in February 1733, a letter writer to the *Pennsylvania Gazette* disapprovingly clucked, "It is now become the practice of some otherwise discrete women . . . [to forgo food, opting instead for] two or three *drams* in the morning, by which their appetite for wholesome food is taken away."[77] At midcentury the city had more than one hundred licensed taverns, as well as "many Houses of Entertainment," which surely included at least a few brothels.[78] Many of these establishments were in an area known as Hell-Town that also housed many of the city's brothels.[79] Located north of Market Street along Water Street, Hell-Town was home to the city's most notorious tavern, the Three Jolly Irishmen.[80] In addition, nonmarital sex was common in Philadelphia (Benjamin Franklin fathered a son, William, out of wedlock in 1730).[81]

The prevalence of nonmarital sexuality points to the fact that in the decades before the Revolution, Philadelphians were renegotiating traditional relationships, part of a larger breakdown of deference to authority. Naturally, not all women were prostitutes or engaged in nonmarital sex, and women's experiences differed by class and race. Enslaved and poor women worked in and outside the home during this period, but even many wealthy women took on public roles.[82] For instance, the city's Quaker women were frequently among the most active dispensers of that sect's charity and public services.[83] That role often brought them into direct conflict with poor women who, by circumstance or choice, flouted traditional gender roles and hierarchies, making upper-class women among the primary enforcers of "appropriate" public behavior.[84]

While some Philadelphians may have frequented Hell-Town, most enjoyed more wholesome entertainments, including "dancing in the winter; and, in the summer, forming parties of pleasure upon the Schuylkill, and in the country."[85] In winter it was common for children to sled down the raised areas along Water Street or to skate on the various ponds that dotted Philadelphia, while in summer they swam in the Schuylkill.[86] Queen Anne's Place, an amusement park located on Third Street, even had a primitive merry-go-round.[87] Philadelphia and the surrounding area housed several subscription libraries and the first theater in North America (the Southwark Theatre, established 1766). Wealthy non-Quaker merchants organized the Dancing Assembly, which organized twice-monthly balls at which they could socialize. There were also temporary amusements, such as lectures and the public display of exotic animals, including leopards, lions, and camels.[88] Philadelphians of all social ranks placed small benches outside their houses; Minister Mittelberger recalled that the city's inhabitants sat "on [the benches] or promenade[ed] in front of them in the evening, when the weather is fine."[89] Fanny Salter recalled that her grandfather, who lived in Philadelphia in the mid-eighteenth century, "was in the habit of sitting on the porch at the street door, with a large silver tankard of punch . . . and a friend or two smoking and enjoying the punch."[90]

A visiting merchant named James Birket called Philadelphia "perhaps one of the best Laid out Citys in the world," while Lord Adam Gordon, a British Army officer and member of Parliament who visited there in the mid-1760s, described it as "one of the wonders of the World."[91] By midcentury, Philadelphia boasted the largest church building in British North America (Christ Church, constructed between 1727 and 1744 and located on Second Street between Arch and Market). Its tower, which was added in 1754 and offered "a clear and full view of the whole city and of [the] Delaware River," made it the tallest building in North America until the nineteenth century.[92]

Meanwhile, construction of the city's iconic Pennsylvania State House (known to later generations as Independence Hall) began in the early 1730s on Chestnut, between Fifth and Sixth (then on Philadelphia's western outskirts). The State House, built in the Georgian style then fashionable among Great Britain's elite, was one way of announcing Philadelphia's stature as the leading city in North America. Described by one visitor in 1774 as a "large handsome building," by the time of the Revolution it housed the Library Company of Philadelphia's books and had apartments for the building keeper and visiting delegations of Native Americans.[93] However, due to the Assembly's lack of money, it took nearly twenty years to complete the building. In 1752, the State House's bell arrived from England aboard the *Hibernia*, but it cracked when it was tested. The bell was melted down and recast by John Pass and John Stow at the latter's foundry on Second Street. When unveiled to the public, the sound was so awful that Pass and Stow had to melt down and recast the bell a second time. This bell (the third) was placed in the State House tower, later becoming famed as the Liberty Bell.

The city's growth led to continued deviations from Penn's plan for the city. Though by and large the grid plan existed into the twenty-first century (at least in the old part of the city) and became closely associated with Philadelphia, the large lots intended to make the city a "greene country towne" were quickly subdivided to allow developers to cram as many buildings into as small a space as possible. Even among the "first purchasers" there were speculators who bought lots and built several houses, and this trend accelerated in the eighteenth century. In part that was because colonial homes required several outbuildings (kitchens and outhouses, for instance) and because more space was needed for Philadelphia's growing population.[94] A good example of the impulse toward subdivision is the house Benjamin Franklin had built for himself in the early 1760s. Franklin acquired several more or less contiguous lots on a rectangle bounded by Market and Chestnut Streets on the north and south and Third and Fourth Streets on the east and west. His house was in the center of the rectangle, and on the property's Market Street face he constructed several rental buildings and a passageway to his house.[95]

Most building occurred along the Delaware River, leaving the area west of Seventh Street largely uninhabited.[96] Philadelphians preferred to live along the riverfront, spurring construction in Northern Liberties, Kensington (founded in 1730 by merchant Anthony Palmer), and Southwark (the area directly south of Cedar Street and officially created from the large Moyamensing tract south of the city in 1762) rather than westward toward the Schuylkill River.[97] In fact, the city's roads petered out west of Seventh Street, ending in a dense forest known as Governor's Woods, which stretched from High Street to South Street west of today's Broad Street (as a young man, Franklin and his friends would hike into the woods to read and discuss philosophy and literature).[98] The structure of the city's wards testified to this uneven development: all ten of Philadelphia's wards lay between Vine Street and Cedar (now South Street) and the Delaware River and Seventh Street. Ward divisions were not carried to the Schuylkill until 1785.[99] Within the developed areas, there were clear differences: houses in Upper Delaware Ward (the most desirable area, stretching between Vine and High Streets from the Delaware River to Front Street) were substantially more valuable and larger than those in Southwark.[100]

Philadelphia's growth created challenges that the corporation was ill-equipped to handle and the Assembly frequently unwilling to resolve. The city's municipal corporation was strongly allied with the Proprietary Party, making the Assembly unsympathetic, and therefore unresponsive, to Philadelphia's troubles.[101] The political struggle between the Assembly and the municipal corporation created real hardship for the city's residents. Franklin has been justly celebrated for his public spiritedness and his founding of several voluntary Philadelphia institutions and organizations, but the reality was that this was a response to the city government's inability to provide services concomitant with Philadelphia's needs, a fact that reflected choices made by the Assembly and the city's ruling elite not to grant the municipal corporation the powers it needed.[102] The municipal corporation's continued reliance on fees and rents made it nearly impossible to provide adequate services, and civic improvement projects were often financed by loans that the city corporation was unable to repay.[103] Another fundraising technique was lotteries, which became a staple of public funding by the 1740s, though the colony's Quakers opposed them, and the Assembly banned them in 1762.[104] Thus, while membership in the corporation still conveyed substantial prestige, the various boards of commissioners and wardens or other quasi-official organizations established by the Assembly did most of the actual governing.[105]

There were also inequities in the colony's political structure that worked to the city's detriment. The county was the main political unit in the colonial Assembly (a fact that distinguished Pennsylvania from the colonies in New England). The city, as a segment of Philadelphia County, was therefore at a disadvantage.[106] Based on its population by 1750, Philadelphia County (which included the city) was substantially underrepresented relative to Chester and Bucks Counties. The Assembly took no steps to remedy this problem by reforming representation to reflect immigration and settlement patterns more accurately. In fact, it went the other way: in order that the founding of new, non-Quaker majorities not dilute the Quaker Party's power in the Assembly, the counties of Lancaster (admitted 1729), York (1749), Cumberland (1750), Berks (1752), and Northampton (1752) were all allotted fewer representatives than the older counties.[107] The result was that by the early 1760s, the three counties nearest the city provided a majority of Assembly delegates, frustrating city residents and settlers in Pennsylvania's backcountry alike.[108]

Whereas Penn's original plan of awarding large purchasers city lots should have fostered a great deal of attachment between Philadelphia and the colonial elite, that did not happen.[109] Instead, those who grew wealthy tended to move out to the country, or at least summered in country manors in Point-No-Point (now called Bridesburg), Frankford, or the Falls of Schuylkill.[110] The corporation still had trouble finding people willing to serve as mayor because many still preferred to pay a fine rather than incur the expense of holding office. In one instance, an alderman went into hiding to avoid being mayor. In fact, fining men who refused to serve as mayor became an important source of municipal revenue by the 1760s.[111] In short (and not for the last time), political differences between the local and the colony-wide governments seriously challenged the city's ability to provide services to its inhabitants, leading Mittelberger to describe the colony as "the heaven of the farmers, the paradise of the mechanics, and the hell of the officials."[112]

One reason men were so reluctant to serve as mayor was the long list of problems facing Philadelphia, most caused or exacerbated by population growth. Fires were an ever-present danger in the city. As early as 1696, the colonial Assembly passed laws designed to lower the risk of fires, and in the late 1710s, Philadelphia's municipal corporation purchased a fire engine but, short on funds, failed to adequately maintain it.[113] In 1730, fire broke out on a docked ship and spread to nearby warehouses and several houses, causing an estimated £5,000 in damages.[114] Six years later, a fire seriously damaged several homes known as Budd's Long Row, which had the distinction of being the earliest known row houses in Philadelphia.[115] In 1736, Benjamin Franklin and several of his acquaintances organized the Union Fire Company, the first volunteer fire company in the colonies. In 1752, Franklin organized the Philadelphia Contributionship for the Insurance of Houses from Loss by Fire.[116] This organization insured buildings up to ten miles outside Philadelphia's city limits, and, in an era of weak municipal government, its underwriting standards became informal building codes that helped shape Philadelphia's development by encouraging the placement of kitchens in outbuildings and the use of brick and stone over wood.[117]

Ironically, though Philadelphia was a leading center of medical education, its status as a worldwide shipping center contributed to the frequent outbreak of illness. Smallpox closed the Pennsylvania Assembly in 1732, and four years later

it claimed the life of Franklin's four-year-old son, Francis.[118] In order to combat
the spread of illness, in early 1743 the city established a quarantine center, called
a pest house, on Fisher's Island (south of the city) to isolate sailors and immigrants found to have contagious diseases.[119] This did not completely address the
problem, so in 1751, a group of concerned citizens established the Pennsylvania Hospital to offer free medical treatment to the city's inhabitants (funded by
donations that were reluctantly matched by the colonial Assembly).[120] Here again
volunteerism was a pragmatic response to government failure. Unfortunately,
despite these precautions, disease remained endemic: there was an outbreak of
yellow fever in Philadelphia in 1754 among some of the city's Germans, waves of
smallpox in 1756 and 1757, and an outbreak of an "infectious distemper" among
a recently arrived shipment of enslaved people in 1762.[121] Unfortunately, the
prevalence of illness among the city's recent immigrants and poorest inhabitants
led to scapegoating: in 1754, Deputy Governor Robert Hunter Morris proposed
reducing German immigration to the colony in response to the yellow fever outbreak that year.[122]

One reason for epidemic outbreaks of disease was endemic pollution, which
was so bad that some residents and visitors called the city "Filthy-dirty," as
opposed to Philadelphia.[123] Dock Creek, which ran northwest between Spruce
and Walnut Streets, was essentially an open sewer for the city's tanners, who
strongly resisted any attempt to regulate what they could dump into the waterway.[124] In another move to alleviate illness, in 1744, Philadelphia provided every
house with its own well and constructed water pumps along the city streets. The
Assembly went further in 1762, establishing a Board of Street Commissioners
to work with the municipal corporation to pave the city's streets (previously
they were simply covered with gravel and were notoriously bad) and sidewalks
and to ensure the removal of refuse.[125] In 1769, the Assembly passed a spate
of ordinances designed to improve living conditions in Philadelphia, including
one that prohibited tossing "shavings, ashes, dung, or other filth or annoyance"
on the city's pavement and mandated that people sweep the walkways in front
of their dwellings at least once per week; prohibited soap makers, tanners, and
distillers from discharging waste into the region's waterways; and empowered
the city's aldermen to regulate the depth of wells, sinks, and privies.[126] Despite
these improvements, the city was still ravaged by periodic epidemics over the
ensuing decades.[127]

Crime was also a serious issue: Philadelphia was plagued by petty theft, rob-
bery, and even murder during this period.[128] Due to the prevalence of residents
discharging firearms in the city, in 1721, the Assembly prohibited the practice
and established a fine of five shillings for each offense.[129] Yet, idle gunfire continued: some Philadelphians celebrated New Year's Day by firing their weapons,

a practice that persists to this day.[130] The police force, such as it was, amounted to perhaps a half dozen constables who were supposed to be supported by the homeowners of the city's various wards. Those homeowners who chose not to participate could simply pay the constable six shillings per year. This system was rife with abuse and, in the best of circumstances, failed to provide adequate policing for a rapidly growing city.[131] Moreover, the constables were not on duty all night, so crimes committed after they made their rounds often went unsolved.[132] After years of complaint, the Assembly finally took action in 1750, establishing an independent force of "wardens of the watch," which represented another stopgap that eroded the corporation's authority.[133] In 1757, the Assembly passed a bill promoted by Benjamin Franklin (who was in London when it passed) subsidizing the erection of street lamps in Philadelphia, making it the first city in North America so equipped, though contemporaries remained concerned about the amount of crime.[134]

By the mid-eighteenth century, Philadelphia was the port of choice for a wide swath of territory stretching from northern New Jersey through Delaware and into northern Maryland.[135] In general, the city's merchants exported raw materials and agricultural produce all over the world (though trading with countries other than England was illegal under the Navigation Acts and thus led to a great deal of smuggling). Shallops, or light sailboats, moved agricultural produce along the region's waterways to Philadelphia, where it was loaded onto the fleet of ships anchored along the Delaware River.[136]

Beginning in 1730, Philadelphia entered a period of sustained economic growth unrivaled by any other city in North America.[137] Per capita exports more than doubled between 1730 and 1770, making Philadelphia the continent's largest port in British North America. Imports of finished goods grew even faster during this period, creating a veritable flood of consumer products.[138] James Birket marveled that the city had "the largest and best Market in America."[139] The city's growth led to the establishment of the "new" market (later known as Head House) in 1745, on Second Street between Pine and Lombard. In 1754, the city's famous London Coffee House opened for business at Front and Market Streets.[140] Owned by printer William Bradford and funded by the city's merchants, it quickly became a leading center for the dissemination of news, political meetings, and auctions of enslaved people.[141] In short, by the mid-eighteenth century, Philadelphia was a thriving, vibrant port city connected through commerce and immigration to a large portion of the world.

Yet there were winners and losers in the growing economy. Though it was comparatively easier to "make it" in Philadelphia than either New York or Boston between 1720 and 1750, that was little comfort to the thousands of Philadelphians living on the edge of penury.[142] One immigrant to Philadelphia in the mid-1720s claimed, "There are people who have been living here for 40 years and have not seen a beggar in Philadelphia," but the truth was more complicated.[143] By the 1720s, the city's richest 10 percent of inhabitants controlled a staggering 50 percent of Philadelphia's wealth.[144] Moreover, Philadelphia's integration into a regional and world economic system made it vulnerable to the booms and busts of the business cycle, resulting in a tenuous line between success and failure.[145] Because poverty relief in the early eighteenth century consisted of what was called "outdoor relief," or assistance (in the form of food, clothing, fuel, or cash) given directly to the impoverished, allowing them to remain in their houses, poverty in Philadelphia existed but was relatively inconspicuous (and this, despite the fact that after 1719, they were forced to wear a letter *P* on their shoulder to identify them as paupers).[146]

Poverty got worse, and became more visible, as the eighteenth century wore on: between 1709 and 1739, Philadelphia's population grew by more than 350 percent, but expenditures for the city's poor increased by over 500 percent, in part because of economic depressions in 1720 and 1728.[147] To put this in some perspective, Philadelphians spent substantially more per thousand inhabitants (£49) on poor relief during the 1730s than either New York (£21) or Boston (£31).[148] One immigrant wrote in 1728, "Such as came here twenty or thirty years ago have done well, as they could get acres of land for almost nothing, but now it is too late. . . . I would not advise any person to come to this country except . . . that they were poor and industrious persons, whose life in Europe had become unbearable."[149] Worse, the percentage of Philadelphians deemed too poor to pay their taxes more than doubled between 1740 and 1760 and then nearly doubled over the next fifteen years.[150]

As a result of growing poverty, in 1732, the Overseers of the Poor, a quasi-official group of reformers, opened the Philadelphia City Almshouse.[151] Encompassing an entire city block bordered by Third and Fourth Streets and Pine and Spruce Streets, the almshouse was designed to support approximately fifty of the city's most desperate "deserving" poor (children, widows, etc.). However, within thirty years it housed more than two hundred, necessitating a larger building: the Philadelphia Almshouse and House of Employment, which opened in 1767. Also encompassing an entire city block (between Tenth and Eleventh Streets and Spruce and Pine Streets) and colloquially known as the Bettering House, the new almshouse represented the drive toward building large-scale institutions to deal with Philadelphia's growing social problems.[152]

Compounding the problem was the fact that efforts to assist the impoverished were intentionally insufficient. The material success of Pennsylvania's economic elite depended on cheap labor, which is one of the reasons indentured servitude and enslavement were so pervasive in colonial Philadelphia. Though in later life Benjamin Franklin was an outspoken opponent of slavery, much of his wealth was derived from exploiting various forms of unfree labor.[153] And Franklin was hardly unique in that regard: Pennsylvania's economy relied more heavily on indentured and redemptioner servitude than that of any other colony in British North America, and the system lasted longer than in the other colonies.[154] Add enslavement to that mix, and you had an economy where nearly one-third of Philadelphia households exploited some type of unfree labor by the revolutionary period.[155] Voting in Pennsylvania's elections required being worth at least £50 (or owning a miniumum of fifty acres of property). That requirement ensured that few city workers or seamen could vote, given that in 1748, the average male laborer made between £16 and £20 per year. In short, alleviating poverty, ending unfree labor, or creating a more equitable distribution of profits would have threatened the colonial elite's control over the levers of power and there was simply no constituency for that in the Assembly.[156]

Indentured servants and enslaved people faced similar challenges in eighteenth-century Philadelphia's economy, frequently working side by side or in the same occupations. As Israel Acrelius, a Lutheran missionary and priest, noted in 1750, the colony's "laborers are generally composed of negroes (enslaved), partly of servants from Germany or Ireland bought for a term of years."[157] Indentured servant William Moraley referred to himself as a "voluntary slave."[158] Purchasers of servants' indentures frequently split up families, just as they did with their enslaved people.[159] Yet there were several key differences between indentured and redemptioner servants and enslaved Africans. Most importantly, indentured and redemption servitudes were not lifelong conditions.[160] In addition, indentured and redemptioner servants enjoyed all the rights of Englishmen except those specifically forfeited under their contracts; this was not the case for the enslaved.[161] To deter the development of common cause among enslaved Africans and indentured Europeans, Pennsylvania's Assembly enacted a series of racially discriminatory laws designed to stigmatize enslaved Africans. By 1760, enslaved people were to be tried in special courts without juries, could not drink alcohol, were not permitted to congregate in large groups or to be outdoors after nine o'clock at night, and were liable to harsher punishments than indentured servants.[162]

Though these laws exacerbated racial discrimination in the city, they also helped foster a distinctive Black community.[163] As early as 1740, George Whitefield (who opposed slavery) wanted to build a school in Philadelphia to educate the city's Black people, and by the 1750s, several schools appeared to educate the city's Black children (enslaved and free).[164] For twenty years prominent abolitionist Anthony Benezet conducted a school for Black students in his home near Third and Chestnut, and in 1770 he established the Negro School at Philadelphia at the intersection of Raspberry (now Hutchison) and Locust Streets. These separate institutions were necessitated by the widespread racism Black Philadelphians faced. Franklin noted in 1758 that "at present few or [no masters] give their Negro Children any Schooling, partly from a Prejudice that Reading and Knowledge in a Slave are both useless and dangerous; and partly from an Unwillingness in the Masters and Mistresses of common Schools to take black Scholars, lest the Parents of the white Children should be disgusted and take them away, not chusing to have their Children mix'd with Slaves in Education, Play, &c."[165] Even in death, racial discrimination predominated: Black people were buried in a segregated section of the Strangers' Burial Ground (located in Washington Square) called the Negroes Burying Ground.[166]

Enslavement had existed in the region since the 1630s, but after 1729 it became more important to the colony's economic growth.[167] In that year the Assembly lowered the duty on enslaved people from £5 to £2, and after 1731 it was often not even collected, leading abolitionist Ralph Sandiford to exclaim, "We have *negroes* flocking in upon us since the duty on them is reduced."[168] As a major shipping hub, Philadelphia became a key conduit for importing unfree labor (both enslaved and indentured).[169] Imports of enslaved people spiked in the 1730s and 1740s and during the late 1750s and early 1760s, when a series of conflicts (the War of Jenkins' Ear, the War of Spanish Succession, and the Seven Years' War, respectively) impeded European immigration to North America and tightened the labor market (British officials encouraged indentured servants to enlist in the military).[170] This was the peak of enslavement in Philadelphia; importation of enslaved people declined precipitously after 1764 because of a 1761 increase in (and more vigorous collection of) the duty to £10 per person, and the end of the Seven Years' War (which made available thousands of poor whites who had been otherwise occupied fighting).[171] Between 1720 and 1770, the percentage of Philadelphia's population that was enslaved fluctuated between approximately 7.5 percent and 10.5 percent.[172] In short, though fewer in number than other colonies, enslaved people constituted a sizable minority of the city's population and played a key role in its economy.[173]

Despite Israel Acrelius's declaration that "negroes are better treated in Pennsylvania than anywhere else in America," the reality of enslaved people's lives was harsh.[174] Contemporary advertisements for escaped slaves published during this period are unintentionally a catalog of scars, injuries, and deformities inflicted upon enslaved people by their enslavers.[175] William Moraley, who had firsthand knowledge of the vicissitudes of indentured servitude, called the condition of the enslaved "very bad," noting that there were "no Laws in Favour of these unhap[p]y Wretches."[176] Throughout this period, enslaved people from the West Indies (and later Africa) arrived in the region during the bitter winter months, sometimes without clothing. As a result, a significant number became ill, and some even died.[177] In fact, enslaved people in Philadelphia had a higher risk of death than whites of all social statuses and exhibited much lower fertility.[178] That being said, enslaved people were not monolithic, and slavery was not a static institution. Initially, most enslaved people imported into Pennsylvania came from the southern colonies or the West Indies. They typically spoke English, and many had already learned valuable skills. Moreover, they had been exposed to European and Caribbean diseases, making them less likely to become sick than enslaved people imported directly from Africa. By contrast, beginning in the late 1750s, Philadelphians began importing enslaved people directly from Africa because the Seven Years' War had created a labor vacuum in the city that traditional sources of enslaved people could not adequately fill.[179]

In addition to the city's population of enslaved Africans, a free Black population lived in Philadelphia. The evidence is fragmentary, but as early as 1717 there appear to have been at least some nonenslaved Black people, the result either of immigration, manumission, or self-purchase.[180] The growth of the city's free Black population alarmed city leaders, who feared that "free negroes . . . afford ill examples to other negroes."[181] The Assembly took steps to discourage manumission in 1726, though the number of free Black people grew after 1740.[182] Free Black people faced discrimination: marrying a white person would result in enslavement for life, while the white partner would be fined and sold into indentured servitude for seven years, a clear indication of the fact that many of the colony's whites feared the challenges to Pennsylvania's racial hierarchy.[183]

With its free Black community and Quaker heritage, Philadelphia became a key site of antislavery agitation. In 1729, Ralph Sandiford, an English Quaker who immigrated to Philadelphia as a boy, published *A Brief Examination of the Practice of the Times* (republished the following year as *The Mystery of Iniquity*). Sandiford's strident abolitionism won him several enemies; the Religious Society of Friends disowned him, and he eventually moved to a farm outside the city. Sandiford's fate did not deter Benjamin Lay, another Philadelphia Quaker abolitionist. In 1737, Lay, an eccentric and theatrical man, published the unambiguously titled *All Slave Keepers That Keep the Innocent in Bondage, Apostates*.[184] Lay was followed by several other abolitionists, including John Woolman and Anthony Benezet, who continued to press for an end to slavery. By the mid-1760s, due in part to their pressure, most local Quaker merchants had abandoned the slave trade, though enslavement itself persisted.[185]

A key turning point in Philadelphia's history was the French and Indian War (1754–1763).[186] By the mid-1740s, French officials in North America were growing concerned about the westward expansion of English-speaking settlers would push France off the continent. This fear was stoked by the fact that following the end of King George's War in 1748, Britain conferred upon the Ohio Company of Virginia's investors (including Virginia Governor Robert Dinwiddie) most of the area of present-day Ohio and a large portion of present-day western Pennsylvania, including the site of Pittsburgh. By 1752, representatives of the Ohio Company had completed a treaty with the Iroquois granting it the right to the land and to build a fort near present-day Pittsburgh. The French responded to this development by dispatching a small force of men to attack Native Americans as a reprisal for trading with the British. Then, in the spring of 1753, the French dispatched a two-thousand-man force to the region and built two forts, Fort Presque Isle and nearby Fort La Boeuf.

Naturally, increased French activity in what the Ohio Company considered its territory alarmed Governor Dinwiddie and the company's other investors. In October 1753, Dinwiddie sent a small party under the command of a twenty-one-year-old major in the Virginia militia, George Washington, into the territory to confront the French. Washington returned to Virginia in January 1754 with bad news: the French refused to vacate the area. Undaunted, that spring Dinwiddie dispatched Virginia militiamen under Washington's command into the area to reinforce a small outpost under construction at the confluence of the Allegheny and Monongahela Rivers. En route, Washington learned that the French had peaceably occupied the outpost, which they had renamed Fort Duquesne. On May 28, he confronted a French scouting party, and the two forces ended up in a short battle that led to the death of French commander Joseph Coulon de Villiers de Jumonville. Washington then retreated south and established Fort Necessity, a crude structure designed to protect his forces against the anticipated French counterattack. That attack came on July 3, when approximately six hundred French and Native soldiers captured the fort (they allowed Washington and his forces to evacuate it peacefully). The British and French governments, upon hearing news of these events, decided to send large military forces to the region, determined to assert control over the land. As a result, the French and Indian War, which metastasized into a worldwide conflict known as the Seven Years' War, had begun.

The war forced Pennsylvania's Assembly to make some hard choices about whether, and in what ways, to support Britain's military efforts. This debate quickly got bogged down in perennial conflict over the colony's relations with Native Americans, taxation, the Penns, and paper currency.[187] In 1754, prominent members of the Proprietary Party sought to use the war to their political advantage by petitioning the Crown to exclude Quakers from the Assembly during the war on the theory that the pacifists could not be expected to support military operations. There was some logic to that argument, and the war split the Assembly's Quakers, some of whom advocated total adherence to the sect's pacifist principles, while others saw the danger of antagonizing the Crown.[188] The elections that fall had a profound impact on the Assembly and on colonial politics. Six of the Assembly's Quakers (representing one-sixth of the body's delegates) decided to resign their seats rather than support efforts to provide economic aid to the Crown's military efforts. Non-Quaker opponents of the proprietors were elected to fill the seats, and four more Quakers resigned after the election, more than halving Quaker power in the Assembly (though Quakers regained some of these lost seats in the 1760s). The newly elected members of the Quaker Party were more antagonistic toward the proprietor (and, by extension, the deputy governor) than the men they had replaced.[189] In fact, members of the Assembly dispatched Franklin to London to persuade the Crown to rescind the Penns' charter; he departed Pennsylvania early the following year and stayed until 1762. Meanwhile, Quakers committed to pacifism formed the Friendly Association for Regaining and Preserving Peace with the Indians by Pacific Measures, outraging colonists in the backcountry.[190]

In the spring of 1755, an expedition under the command of General Edward Braddock set out from Maryland to retake Fort Duquesne, but his forces were decisively routed at the Battle of the Monongahela in early July. When news of Braddock's defeat reached Philadelphia, diarist Daniel Fisher recorded, "The Consternation of this City . . . is hardly to be expressed."[191] Alarm at the prospect of French forces marching east led the Assembly to debate a bill providing £50,000 to support England's war effort, but the Quakers refused to agree unless the money was raised by taxing all colonial estates, including the Penns', a condition that Deputy Governor Morris refused to accept. News of violent clashes between Europeans and Natives in the colony's western and middle regions again led to passage of a bill appropriating funds (this time £60,000) raised from taxing all estates (including the Penns'), but Morris refused to sign it. That spring brought news of additional clashes between Europeans and Natives west of the Susquehanna River, with outrages committed by both sides.[192] Ultimately, the Assembly passed a militia bill and worked out a compromise with the deputy governor under which the Penns would "donate" £5,000 (to be paid from quitrent arrears) in exchange for the Assembly dropping its demand to tax proprietary property, maintaining the fiction that the Assembly's Quakers were not actually funding the war.[193]

In addition to foisting upon the Quakers an unappealing choice between principle and pragmatism, the war exacerbated simmering political tensions. In 1756, Penn appointed William Denny as Pennsylvania's deputy governor, replacing Morris, who had resigned after only two years. When Denny arrived in Pennsylvania, expectations were high: he was escorted into town by a large and diverse group of Philadelphians, and the Assembly, eager to encourage

Denny's goodwill, feted the new governor at a sumptuous feast at the State House.[194] Things went downhill fast: when Denny asked the Assembly to provide funds for the British war effort, the body complied but on the condition that it, not the deputy governor, control the funds. Penn had ordered Denny to reassert proprietary control over the colony's funds, which the deputy governor did, albeit half-heartedly.

The Assembly's opposition to the proprietors and its pervasive antipathy toward Philadelphia was behind a fight over quartering British troops in the city during the fall of 1756. Under the terms of Parliament's Mutiny Act of 1689, inns or public houses were obligated to quarter and feed English troops, though the government would pay for those services. In 1755, faced with the need to provide winter quarters for British troops, the Pennsylvania Assembly passed a law that incorporated several elements of the Mutiny Act, but it was disallowed the following year because it incorporated a provision allowing subjects to refuse to quarter soldiers. Given the shortage of public houses in the colonies (relative to England), this provision threatened to literally leave British soldiers out in the cold. At the end of 1756, the Assembly passed essentially the same bill, thereby ensuring that private individuals could opt out of quartering soldiers. Denny refused to sign the bill (he eventually signed a modified version), but in the interim, British soldiers flooded into Philadelphia, where they were crammed into the city's relatively small number of public houses.[195] Due to overcrowding, conditions were miserable and contributed to an outbreak of smallpox.[196] Relations between Denny and the Assembly had been poisoned and never recovered.

At the same time, however, war was economically good for Philadelphia, at least initially. The British purchased lots of goods and material in Philadelphia during the war and ordered the construction of several buildings, fueling an economic boom that led to a more than fourfold expansion in the value of imports between 1757 and 1760.[197] The number of wholesalers (merchants who imported finished goods and sold them to retailers) more than doubled between 1750 and 1760.[198] Public outlays for poor relief dropped during this time, though the gap between the haves and the have-nots widened considerably after 1756.[199] During his visit in 1759, Andrew Burnaby found Philadelphia "in a very flourishing state, and inhabited by merchants, artisans, and persons of all occupations. . . . The streets are crowded with people, and the river with vessels."[200] It is no wonder why Philadelphians celebrated British victories by placing candles in their windows and, in at least one instance, by a large display of fireworks.[201]

The good times did not last. Though Burnaby did not know it at the time, he was seeing Philadelphia at the peak of its wartime prosperity. The city's economy contracted suddenly and dramatically after 1760, when North America stopped being an important theater of wartime operations. Lucrative military contracts disappeared, and more-effective British regulation of North American trade made it difficult for Philadelphia's merchants to conduct business with French merchants.[202] The sudden disappearance of British cash plunged the city into recession. Though wages recovered briefly in the mid-1760s, the overall trend was downward in the decade before the Revolution.[203] As a result, per capita public expenditures for the poor increased by nearly 50 percent, and the price of several necessities, inflated by the easy availability of cash, rose beyond the grasp of struggling workers.[204] Under pressure from British merchants, Parliament disallowed new issues of land bank currency in the colonies after 1760, and soon cash was, in the words of one contemporary, "monstrous scarce."[205] The city's merchants quickly spent all of their specie paying off their English creditors while selling their wares at fire sale prices, leading to a spate of bankruptcies.[206] Worse, Parliament vigorously cracked down on smuggling, further threatening merchants' finances and limiting the colonies' access to highly desirable goods. Writing to a friend in 1764, Philadelphia merchant Benjamin Marshall complained of two British navy ships patrolling Philadelphia shipping. According to Marshall, the captains of the ships were "so very strict that the smallest things don't escape their notice. . . . [T]hey search all Vessells very narrowly."[207] Parliament's aggressive new policies created a large group of disgruntled people blaming Great Britain and its supporters among the colonial elite, laying the groundwork for revolution in the following decade.

However, that was in the future. At the time, the French and Indian War was considered a triumph for Great Britain: under the terms of the Treaty of Paris (1763), Britain received all French territory in North America east of the Mississippi River and all of Canada. Unfortunately, these gains were costly. British relations with many Native American groups seriously deteriorated because of the war, forcing London to garrison troops on the North American frontier indefinitely. British fears of Native violence were well founded: at the war's end, British commanders in the Ohio Valley saw little reason to negotiate with the various local Native groups. British commanders discontinued the practice of giving Native leaders gifts (a necessary lubricant to diplomatic interactions) and tried to limit Native trade with white settlers. Dissatisfaction with British policies coalesced in Pontiac's Rebellion (1763), a three-year conflict that included the murders of white settlers in the region. A long-term, large-scale, essentially open-ended military commitment did not appeal to British policymakers, given that the Seven Years' War (of which the French and Indian War has been a front) had drained Britain's treasury.

The problem was that the alternatives were worse. The conflict between western Pennsylvanians and Natives radicalized many white settlers, who believed that the Pennsylvania Assembly cared more about the Natives than them. As a result, in mid-December 1763, a group of white settlers calling themselves the Paxton Boys murdered several Natives, including twenty peaceful and heavily Europeanized Conestoga living in Lancaster County just east of the Susquehanna River. Governor John Penn was disgusted and offered a reward of £200 (later increased to £600) for the scalps of the Paxton Boys.[208] In response, 250 or so Paxton Boys marched on Philadelphia, threatening violence against Natives who had taken refuge in the city and the Quakers, whose pacific policies they blamed for Pontiac's Rebellion. News of the Paxton Boys' approach sent shock waves through Philadelphia. Many of the city's inhabitants—including several young Quakers—took up arms to defend Philadelphia.[209] Trying to prevent bloodshed, a group of notables, including Benjamin Franklin, intercepted the Paxton Boys at Germantown and negotiated an end to the rampage. In early February, the Paxton Boys returned west, but that was not the end of the matter: both sides sought to turn these unsettling events to their gain. The Proprietary Party blamed the Quaker Party for Pontiac's Rebellion and the subsequent Paxton Boys affair.

Meanwhile, and in an example of supreme bad timing, in March 1764, Franklin's political ally, Assemblyman Joseph Galloway, renewed the effort to have the Crown revoke Penn's charter. Coming on the heels of Pontiac's Rebellion and the Paxton Boys scare, this was an unpopular move and became the election's key issue. The Proprietary Party skillfully capitalized on anti-Quaker sentiment and reminded voters about Franklin's anti-German comments in the 1750s. As a result, in the election of 1764 (which Benjamin Marshall called "the warmest and most close ever known here"), Franklin lost his bid for reelection to the Assembly, though control of the Assembly remained in Quaker hands.[210] Though no one could have known it in 1764, the French and Indian War had set in wide-ranging political, economic, and social changes that paved the way for revolution, which would dominate the next thirty-five years of Philadelphia's history and unleash profound social, political, and economic forces that decisively reshaped the city, the region, and the continent.

CHAPTER 4

The Revolutionary City, 1765–1800

Philadelphia played a leading role in national politics during the Revolution, hosting both the first and second Continental Congresses and acting as home to Congress during much of the Revolutionary War, the site of the Constitutional Convention in 1787, and the capital of the United States from 1790 to 1800. National and state-level politics played out in the city because it was the seat of both Pennsylvania's government and the national government. As a result, national and state politics shaped Philadelphia, but conditions in Philadelphia also influenced commonwealth and national politics.[1] Though the city left an imprint on the course of the Revolution, the departure of the national capital to Washington, DC, was the beginning of the end of Philadelphia's role as the United States' preeminent city. Moreover, the Revolution unleashed powerful democratizing forces that undermined traditional social hierarchies and reshaped the city's politics and culture.

Between 1767 and 1800, Philadelphia's population more than doubled, rising from just under sixteen thousand to approximately forty-one thousand inhabitants, with an additional eleven thousand people living in Northern Liberties and nearly ten thousand in Southwark.[2] Philadelphia was thus the largest city in North America and the second-largest city (behind London) in the British Empire.[3] Colonial women married younger and gave birth more frequently than women in Europe, though birth rates in North America began declining in the 1760s.[4] This growth, along with the exigencies of the Revolution, strained and then broke Philadelphia's municipal government. The patchwork of local agencies, volunteer organizations, and the municipal corporation was simply incapable of responding to the challenges posed by urban growth, economic change, and revolution, leading to the collapse of Philadelphia's government between 1776 and 1789.[5] The absence of municipal authority led to haphazard growth and changes to William Penn's plan for the city.

In the immediate aftermath of the Paxton Boys debacle, conditions in Pennsylvania appeared to return to normal. The Anti-Proprietary Party rebounded

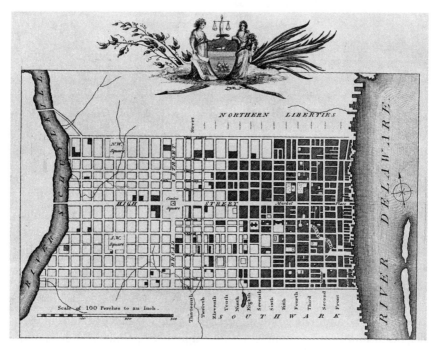

Figure 4. Scull and Heap's *A Plan of the City and Environs of Philadelphia*, 1777. Library of Congress, Geography and Map Division. On the eve of the American Revolution, Philadelphians preferred to live along the banks of the Delaware River. As a result, development occurred north and south along the river rather than west toward the Schuylkill.

quickly after its defeat in 1764, winning back all its lost seats in the Assembly by 1766. Consequently, Franklin's ally, Joseph Galloway, became speaker, a post he held until 1774.[6] Under Galloway's leadership, the Anti-Proprietary forces were an effective, well-oiled political machine.[7] In addition, Quakers now held nearly half (46 percent) of the Assembly's seats, an impressive resurgence from 1756, when resignations had dropped their numbers to less than one-third, ensuring that the Anti-Proprietary forces continued dominating the Pennsylvania Assembly.[8] This was all the more impressive when one considers that by the 1770s, Quakers represented a little over 10 percent of the colony's population. They thus exercised a disproportionate share of the political power, which did little to endear them to the colony's other inhabitants.[9] By contrast, the Proprietary Party remained a factitious coalition that could not compete with its better organized political opponents. In 1763, proprietor Thomas Penn appointed his nephew, John Penn, deputy governor of Pennsylvania. Thirty-four years old at the time of his appointment, John Penn had a rocky tenure as deputy governor; during the eight years of his first term, he faced Pontiac's Rebellion, the Paxton Boys uprising, and the conflict between the colonies and Great Britain. Recalled in 1771, John Penn returned in 1773, serving until Pennsylvania drafted a new constitution in 1776. During most of his first term as deputy governor, when in Philadelphia, Penn lived at what is now 242 South Third Street.

The French and Indian War set off wrenching political, economic, and social transformations, which is one reason why cities were fertile ground for revolution.[10] The cost of Britain's victory in the war was steep. Britain's national debt increased by nearly £60 million over the war's course, and the costs of protecting colonists whose relentless westward expansion caused ongoing conflict with the continent's Natives threatened to drain an already strained treasury.[11] In an attempt to limit these expenses, in October 1763, King George III issued a proclamation that, among other things, created a boundary between Britain's North American colonies and Native lands. The purpose of this provision was to improve Native-white relations by stopping the indiscriminate encroachment of Native lands by settlers. Naturally, this policy was unpopular among settlers and land speculators, who resented the limitations imposed on them. Exacerbating the situation, in 1764, Parliament promulgated the Currency Act, which extended to all Britain's North American colonies a prohibition against making paper money legal tender for private debts imposed on New England in 1751 and mandated that the colonies gradually remove existing currency from circulation. The result was a tightening of credit that hurt Pennsylvania's economy.[12]

Parliament also experimented with a variety of taxes to help retire its national debt and defray the costs of the ten thousand troops stationed in North America. For instance, in 1764, Parliament imposed the Sugar Act. Ironically, the Sugar Act reduced by half the tax imposed by an earlier act (the 1733 Molasses Act), but it provided for more-efficient collection, thereby effectively raising the price of sugar. Coming during the postwar economic depression, the act was unpopular, which led to some sporadic attempts to boycott British imports. The following year, Parliament promulgated the Stamp Act, which mandated that various official documents carry stamps, which were taxed at various levels. The act required colonists to pay for the stamps in specie, not paper currency, which was scarce and therefore hard to come by. The Stamp Act was extremely unpopular in the colonies, and in 1766, Parliament repealed it. But, concerned about the precedent this set, Parliament passed the Declaratory Act, which affirmed its authority "to make laws and statutes of sufficient force and validity to bind the colonies and people of America."[13]

British imperial policy became ensnared in the colony's existing partisan conflict.[14] The Anti-Proprietary Party's drive to make Pennsylvania a royal colony made it politically inexpedient for it to criticize the Stamp Act.[15] Joseph Galloway tepidly supported the act, while Benjamin Franklin (who advised "prudence and moderation" in responding to the act) arranged for his friend and political ally, John Hughes, to be appointed collector of the tax.[16] By contrast, the Proprietary Party opposed the Stamp Act mostly because its enemies—Franklin and Galloway—supported it.[17] Thus, the Stamp Act became a partisan issue, and in 1765, John Dickinson, a leader of the Proprietary faction, ran for election to the Assembly on a platform of resistance to the Stamp Act. The irony here is that the Proprietary Party, committed as it was to protecting the Penns' essentially feudal control over the colony, was evolving into an advocate of resistance to British imperial policy, a stance that pushed the colony toward revolution and the eventual abolition of proprietary government.

Following the Stamp Act's repeal in March 1766, business in Philadelphia seemed to return to normal, though of course in retrospect this was simply the calm before the storm.[18] In June 1766, Parliament passed the first of five laws collectively known as the Townshend Duties, the purpose of which was to raise revenue and create a more effective infrastructure for enforcing British trade and colonial policies.[19] The first act, the New York Restraining Act, prohibited that colony's colonial legislature from passing any laws until the colony provided quarters and food for British soldiers stationed in the colony (mandated under the 1765 Quartering Act, which New York resisted). The second of the Townshend Acts, the Revenue Act of 1767, taxed various building supplies (glass, lead, and paint) and, to crack down on smuggling, gave colonial agents broad authority to search private property. Crucially, the act also taxed paper, which alienated the city's newspapers, all of whom opposed the Townshend Duties and called for vigorous resistance.[20]

Another important element was the economic context. The number of taxpayers identified with titles like "gentleman" and "esquire" increased by approximately 300 percent in the two decades after the French and Indian War began. A related development was the increase in conspicuous consumption. By the last third of the eighteenth century, earlier moral concerns about luxury and consumption had, if not disappeared, at least been muted.[21] Now many people celebrated consumption as providing economic benefits to producers. In the 1760s and 1770s, the number of merchants in Philadelphia had increased steadily, as had the number and variety of imported goods available.[22]

Consumption often took the form of grander, more luxurious houses that broadcast their owners' affluence and wealth to passersby.[23] A good example of the new enthusiasm for conspicuous consumption is Benjamin Chew's country estate in Germantown, Cliveden. In 1763, Chew, then serving as the colony's attorney general, purchased eleven acres of land for £650, a huge amount given that most workers earned about £50 annually.[24] Over the next few years, Chew constructed his country seat, estimating the total cost to be more than £4,700.[25] Other examples include lawyer Andrew Hamilton's Bush Hill Estate (built in 1737 approximately where the Free Library of Philadelphia's Central Branch stands today) and privateer John Macpherson's Mount Pleasant (on the west bank of the Schuylkill River).[26]

In 1772, more than four dozen of Philadelphia's leading citizens subscribed £3,000 to build the City Tavern, allegedly the largest and most elegant tavern in British North America.[27] The tavern consciously aped British upper-class tastes and was unquestionably designed to be a space for the city's mercantile elite. It also became the unofficial archive of the city's shipping records.[28] Philadelphians dressed in British fashions, read British books, and drank that most British drink: tea. In October 1774, John Adams acidly noted, "Phyladelphia with all its Trade, and Wealth, and regularity is not Boston. The Morals of our People are much better, their Manners are more polite, and agreeable—they are purer English."[29] Consumption helped forge a unified British identity that bound the colonies more closely to Britain, but over the course of the eighteenth century, imperial policy impeded the colonists' ability to consume British goods by raising costs and making those goods more difficult to pay for.[30]

The economic good times were not good for everyone: wealthy merchants benefited to a far larger degree than the city's artisans, who remained excluded from power in the Assembly and the municipal corporation.[31] After 1750, it was simply harder to "make it" in Philadelphia than it had been earlier in the century, and the gulf between the city's haves and have-nots widened considerably as a result of the French and Indian War.[32] Prices for basic goods began steadily rising in the late 1760s, which disproportionately affected the city's poorest inhabitants.[33] Even a housing boom could not keep up with the city's expanding population, and Philadelphia's poorest residents were pushed to Northern Liberties and Southwark, creating concentrations of poverty that, for the first time in the city's history, led to the emergence of class-based residential segregation.[34] Physical and social distance bred contempt: writing to his brother in 1769, Alexander Mackraby, who visited Philadelphia during this period, complained of the quality of help in the city, asserting, "If you bring over a good [servant] he is spoilt in a month."[35] It was no coincidence that in 1767, the city's elite merchants opened a new and larger almshouse (referred to as the "Bettering House") occupying a city block bordered by Spruce and Pine and Tenth and Eleventh Streets; the goal was to instill "habits of industry" in the able-bodied poor.[36] In short, during the 1760s, there emerged a growing distance, both physical and economic, between the city's governing elite and most of its inhabitants that laid the groundwork for class conflict and revolutionary activity.[37]

Nor was it just the specific legislation or the local economic conditions that pushed Pennsylvania toward revolution. For instance, the Enlightenment, which discouraged attachment to hereditary government, corroded deference and thereby encouraged revolutionary agitation. The arguments mobilized by the proprietors' opponents in prior decades anticipated those made by the revolutionaries against King George III.[38] Additionally, the Scotch-Irish settlers in the colony's backcountry nursed age-old grievances against the monarchy that were newly fed by British attempts to limit westward expansion. Though these individuals remained underrepresented in Pennsylvania's colonial Assembly, the Paxton Boys affair demonstrated they had extralegal means at their disposal to influence policy.[39]

In addition, revolutionary rhetoric and the erosion of deference contributed to changes in the status of women. The most famous example is a letter by Abigail Adams to her husband, John, urging him and his fellow delegates to the Continental Congress to "remember the Ladies, and be more generous and favourable to them than your ancestors." Abigail Adams consciously appealed to her husband using revolutionary language ("Do not put such unlimited power into the hands of the Husbands. Remember all Men would be tyrants if they could. If particular care and attention is not paid to the Laidies we are determined to foment a Rebelion, and will not hold ourselves bound by any Laws in which we have no voice, or Representation") that mirrored the colonists' complaints about Parliament's actions, though John treated her letter as a joke.[40] While he and his fellow delegates ignored Abigail's plea, nevertheless the Revolution created opportunities for women to participate in the political sphere and to renegotiate their roles in society. For instance, as consumers, women could participate in revolutionary activities through boycotts of British goods.[41] Some women went further: Esther de Berdt Reed, who was born in London but moved to Philadelphia after marrying Joseph Reed, a prominent lawyer, penned a broadside, "The Sentiments of an American Woman," in which she called on American women to support the Patriot cause.[42] Reed's broadside inspired the Ladies Association of Philadelphia, an organization of women who went door to door in the city collecting money to support Washington's army.[43] In short, the corrosion of hierarchy by revolutionary sentiments helped spark a renegotiation of gender roles that would flower into the suffragist movement of the mid-nineteenth century.[44]

All of these factors coalesced to shape efforts to resist British imperial policy in the 1760s and 1770s. Between 1765 and 1770, Philadelphia's resistance to Parliament's actions was intermittent and essentially conservative.[45] Philadelphia's merchants, who led resistance efforts to British policy during this period, opposed what they saw as encroachments on their livelihoods but were not looking to overthrow the political or economic status quo.[46] Pennsylvania was hardly unique in this regard, and most of the mid-Atlantic colonies were less revolutionary than their New England counterparts.[47] Primarily, the struggle against Parliament's actions was carried on in Philadelphia's streets through mob action, vandalism, and violence, usually along preexisting partisan lines.[48] Members of the Proprietary Party encouraged a mob to attack the homes of Benjamin Franklin, Joseph Galloway, and other prominent Anti-Proprietary Party leaders. Galloway responded to the threats of mob violence by encouraging his own supporters to form a mob and protect the property of Anti-Proprietary Party leaders.[49] People viewed as insufficiently supportive of the Patriot cause could expect to have their windows smashed or suffer other forms of vandalism.[50] The fact that popular resistance to the Stamp Act nearly turned violent—mobs, spurred by supporters of the proprietors, nearly tore down prominent Quakers' houses—reinforced the merchants' essentially conservative outlook; after all, if this was revolution, they wanted no part, a fact that contributed to the restrained resistance to British policy in the late 1760s.[51]

Opponents of British policy used boycotts of British goods to great effect against the Townshend Duties in 1768 and 1769, though Philadelphia's merchants adopted these nonimportation protests six months after merchants in Boston and New York, and then only reluctantly.[52] Responding to the boycotts, in April 1770, Parliament repealed most of the Townshend Duties, retaining only the tax on tea (reinforced in the Tea Act of 1773). Once Parliament repealed most of the Townshend Duties, many of Philadelphia's merchants began trading again with merchants in Great Britain. However, a substantial minority (mostly Presbyterian and less wealthy) did not, and they seized control of the nascent yet inchoate revolutionary movement, instead allying with radical elements of the city's middling sort, thereby becoming a formidable force in Philadelphia's politics.[53]

Resistance to British policy turned more radical after 1770 as younger men eclipsed older, more-conservative merchants in the revolutionary movement's leadership.[54] Galloway led the more-conservative faction, while Charles Thomson led the more-radical camp. The Irish-born Thomson emigrated to North America in 1739 and became a Latin tutor at the the College and Academy of Philadelphia. Thomson opposed the Proprietary Party and strongly criticized the Stamp Act, eventually playing a leading role in Philadelphia's Sons of Liberty, an organization whose sole purpose was to oppose British efforts at taxing the colonies in the mid-1760s. Moreover, Philadelphia's newspapers remained committed to the revolutionary cause, making it difficult for conservatives like Galloway to reach a broad audience with their counterarguments.[55]

Revolutionary zeal was on full display in December 1773 during the Philadelphia Tea Party. Just as in Boston, Patriots in Philadelphia responded to the Tea Act by refusing to allow East India Company tea shipments to land in the city. On October 18, a public meeting of opponents of British trade policies adopted a series of resolutions opposing British policy generally and the Tea Act specifically. The resolves asserted "that whoever shall, directly or indirectly . . . or in anywise aid or abet in unloading, receiving, or vending the Tea sent, or to be sent by the East India Company, while it remains subject to the payment of the duty here, is an enemy of his country."[56] The following month word arrived in Philadelphia of the approach of a British merchant ship, the *Polly*, which carried East India Company tea consigned to the Philadelphia firm of James & Drinker. On November 27, the self-constituted Committee for Tarring and Feathering issued a handbill threatening to tar and feather both the *Polly*'s captain, Samuel Ayres, and any pilots who helped the ship navigate up the Delaware River.[57] Despite the threats, Ayres elected to sail to Philadelphia. When the *Polly* arrived, Ayres encountered an angry crowd waiting for the ship at the city's dock. A group of gentlemen escorted Ayres into the city, though his crew did not unload the tea. A mass meeting of Philadelphians convened in the yard of the State House on December 27 (the crowd being too large to fit inside the building and the largest crowd assembled in the colonies up to that point) and adopted a series of resolutions, including one that Ayres's cargo would not be landed. Ayres departed Philadelphia without having landed a single tea chest. Though far less dramatic than the better known Boston Tea Party (which took place December 16 but whose participants were inspired by the resolves adopted in Philadephia in October), these events demonstrated widespread resistance to Britain's policies in Philadelphia. Writing to John Adams in 1809, Benjamin Rush (one of the North America's best known physicians and a leading revolutionary figure) recalled, "I once heard you say that the *active* business of the American Revolution began in Philadelphia in the act of her citizens in sending back the tea ship, and that Massachusetts would have received her portion of the tea had not our example encouraged her to expect union and support in destroying it."[58]

Britain's response to the Boston Tea Party was severe: in the spring of 1774, Parliament passed a series of laws collectively known (to the revolutionaries, at least) as the Intolerable Acts. These closed Boston's port until the city's inhabitants paid for the destroyed tea, stripped Massachusetts of its charter, and authorized colonial governors to house British soldiers in unoccupied private buildings. Philadelphia escaped similar punishment, perhaps because its tea party did not result in the tea's destruction. When news of Britain's actions arrived in Philadelphia, the city's radicals formed a committee with some local merchants and successfully pressured many of the city's stores to close as an expression of solidarity with Boston.[59] A few days later, they asked Governor John Penn to call the Assembly into session to formulate a response to the Intolerable Acts. When Penn refused, saying he "cannot think such a step would be expedient or consistent with my duty," it pushed the committee members even further: they called a town meeting in which they denounced Britain's punishment of Boston and decided to participate in the Continental Congress, a meeting of delegates from most of the colonies called to develop a collective response to Great Britain's blockade of Boston Harbor.[60]

Philadelphia's size, location, and status made it the natural site to host the Continental Congress.[61] The fact that it was far less revolutionary than Boston was also an important consideration, because it would prevent opponents of revolutionary action from claiming that the Continental Congress spoke only for New England. Between September 5 and October 26, 1774, delegates met in Philadelphia's Carpenters' Hall. Governor Penn and the Assembly's more-conservative members, fearful of Parliament's wrath, assented to participation to soften whatever course of action the Congress adopted. As a result, Pennsylvania's delegation to the Continental Congress included both conservatives and radicals. The First Continental Congress's choice to assemble in Carpenters' Hall (on an alley off Chestnut Street between Third and Fourth Streets) was fraught with political significance: the members of the Carpenters' Company overwhelmingly supported aggressive resistance to Parliament's actions. The Congress published a plan for a comprehensive boycott designed to coerce British merchants into pressuring Parliament to change its policies. These boycotts proved more damaging to Britain's economy than those in the 1760s, in part because they were better coordinated, motivating some British merchants to pressure Parliament.[62]

However, King George III and Parliament refused to back down, deciding instead to crush the nascent rebellion. On April 19, 1775, local militia units in Massachusetts violently defied Britain's attempts to disarm them, leading to the Battles of Lexington and Concord. Once the firing began at Lexington and Concord, the last chance for compromise disappeared, which convinced many Philadelphians the time had come to forcibly resist the British government: within a week of the battles, thousands of Pennsylvanians volunteered for military service.[63] Formed into military companies, these "Associators" also served as a political organization, lobbying the Assembly to expand voting rights and fine Non-Associators.[64] The militia also used violence to intimidate and punish their opponents. For instance, militiamen tarred and feathered Dr. John Kearsley, a vocal Loyalist. According to Alexander Graydon, a Patriot living in Philadelphia at the time, Kearsley

> was seized at his own door by a party of the militia and in the attempt to resist them, received a wound in his hand from a bayonet. Being overpowered, he was placed in a cart provided for the purpose, and, amidst a multitude of boys and idlers, paraded through the streets to the tune of the rogues' march. I happened to be at the coffeehouse when the concourse arrived there. . . . Tar and feathers had been dispensed with, and, excepting the injury he had received in his hand, no sort of violence was offered by the mob to their victim.[65]

Kearsley was far from Philadelphia's only victim of mob violence, and the effect was to intimidate many would-be Loyalists into silence.[66]

Just under a month after the Battles of Lexington and Concord, representatives from twelve of the thirteen colonies convened the Second Continental Congress in Philadelphia to develop a unified response to the growing conflict. Galloway refused to serve in the Second Continental Congress and left the Assembly, retiring to his estate, Growden Mansion (near present-day Trevose, Pennsylvania).[67] For seven months, the Second Continental Congress met in the State House, creating a Continental Army (June 14) and promulgating a Declaration of Causes designed to explain the need to take up arms against the home country (July 6). In a last-ditch attempt to avoid war, conservatives in the Continental Congress got permission to dispatch the so-called Olive Branch Petition, drafted primarily by John Dickinson. It was designed to head off more conflict by proclaiming the colonies' loyalty and beseeching Parliament and the king to moderate Great Britain's policies. A copy of the petition reached Colonial Secretary Lord Dartmouth in London on August 21, but two days later, King George III (reacting to news of the Battle of Bunker Hill) proclaimed the colonies in rebellion. Now there was no turning back. Members of several local social organizations formed the First Troop Philadelphia City Cavalry (often simply called First City Troop), which participated in the battles of Trenton, Princeton, Brandywine, and Germantown.[68] In November 1775, the Continental Congress authorized Philadelphian Samuel Nicholas to raise two battalions of marines, which he did at a meeting held in Tun Tavern (on Front

Street between Chestnut and Walnut Streets); this marked the beginning of the US Marine Corps.

Many colonists remained ambivalent about or outright hostile to the Revolution.[69] In an effort to sway public opinion, in January 1776, a recently arrived English immigrant to Philadelphia named Thomas Paine published the most consequential pamphlet in US history. Titled *Common Sense* and published by Philadelphia printer Robert Bell, it asserted that the colonies should break with Great Britain. A phenomenal bestseller, the pamphlet was incredibly influential in marshaling support for independence: on May 15, 1776, the Continental Congress passed a resolution suggesting that colonies—now states—create new governments. In part this was a reaction to the large number of moderates and conservatives elected to the Pennsylvania Assembly on May 1. The delegates to the Continental Congress reasoned that Pennsylvania's existing government was an impediment to independence and decided to form a new one more favorable to the revolutionary cause.[70] At a mass meeting in the yard of the State House five days later, Philadelphia's mayor, John Bayard, read the Continental Congress's call for a new state government, which was met by loud cheers from the audience. This stood in stark contrast to the Pennsylvania Assembly, most of whose members opposed drafting a new constitution, rightly perceiving that such a step would likely deprive them of office.

Because of the Assembly's refusal to comply with the Continental Congress's request, it fell to the radical City Committee to arrange a convention to draft a new constitution for Pennsylvania.[71] The constitutional convention convened in July 1776 and elected Benjamin Franklin (who had recently returned from London and thrown in his lot with the revolutionaries) its president. Over the next few months, ninety-six delegates representing all of Pennsylvania's eleven counties drafted the most democratic state constitution in the United States. Under its terms each county and Philadelphia received six representatives (a total of seventy-two), though this was temporary: representation was due to be reapportioned following a census, which was completed in 1778. As a result of that census, the City of Philadelphia (which was combined with Philadelphia and Delaware County) lost a representative in the Assembly.[72] Pennsylvania's new constitution guaranteed suffrage for any freeman over twenty-one who paid any tax, eliminated property qualifications for the franchise, broke the representation imbalance that favored the eastern counties, divided executive power among the five members of the Supreme Executive Council, established a unicameral legislature elected annually, and prohibited holding office for more than four years in any seven.[73] In addition, the new constitution shifted the balance of political power—which had been maintained by the inequitable distribution of representatives among Pennsylvania's counties—from the eastern to the western counties, reversing the power structure that had existed prior to the Revolution.[74] The change was astonishing: before 1776, the Assembly was the most oligarchic in the colonies, with the smallest number of members, making the ratio between constituents and members the highest in North America; now it was the most representative of all the state governments.[75]

The reshaping of Pennsylvania's political system amounted to an "internal revolution," decisively ending the struggle between the Proprietary and Anti-Proprietary forces, reshuffling political alignments.[76] Later, in November 1779, the Assembly passed the Divestment Act, which confiscated the proprietors' unsold lands (the Penns were reimbursed for the land) and abolished quitrents. By ending the Penn family's ownership of Pennsylvania, it rendered moot the struggles between Proprietary and Anti-Proprietary forces, which had been the primary axis of political conflict. Seizing and auctioning the Penn family's land also opened hundreds of plots in Philadelphia, spurring construction in the city.[77]

Almost immediately, critics attacked the constitution, arguing that it lacked checks and balances and, because it was so democratic, endangered the commonwealth by enfranchising the mob. Several critics refused to take positions in the new state government created by the constitution.[78] The constitution's supporters were called Constitutionalists, and the document's opponents were known as Republicans; their rivalry became the basis for politics in Philadelphia until 1789.[79] Republicans were fearful of the fact that the new constitution specifically (and the Revolution's democratic aspects generally) threatened to overturn the established social hierarchy and that the "common people" might demand equality.[80]

Pennsylvania's new constitution also voided Philadelphia's municipal charter, creating a governmental vacuum in the city.[81] To fix the problem, in 1777, the Assembly passed an act creating justices of the peace, two of whom were to be elected from each ward. That March the Assembly empowered Philadelphia's justices of the peace to "do and perform certain matters and things formerly directed to be done and performed by the mayor, recorder and alderman." The act itself noted that due to the change in the commonwealth's government, "the powers of [Philadelphia's] mayor, recorder and aldermen have ceased and become void."[82] Those elected justices of the peace would be submitted to the Supreme Executive Council, and six of their number would be chosen. Despite this structure, municipal government more or less ceased to exist in Philadelphia for more than a decade.

Changes were afoot on the national level as well. Beginning in May 1776, various state assemblies authorized their representatives to the Continental Congress to declare independence from Great Britain. On June 7, Virginia delegate

Richard Henry Lee proposed a three-part resolution that included a declaration that the colonies were now "free and independent States." Congress voted to postpone discussion of the resolution for three weeks, during which several additional state assemblies (including Pennsylvania's) authorized their delegates to support a declaration of independence. On June 11, Congress created a five-person committee composed of John Adams, Benjamin Franklin, Thomas Jefferson, Roger Sherman, and Robert R. Livingston to draft a declaration laying out the colonies' grievances and rationale for declaring independence. The committee selected Jefferson to draft the document, which he did over a seventeen-day period in his room at the home of Jacob Graff Jr. on the southwest corner of Seventh and Market Streets. The committee presented the draft to Congress on Friday, June 28. The following Monday, Congress took up the issue of independence, with John Dickinson absenting himself from the vote. The following day, July 2, Congress adopted Richard Henry Lee's resolution and turned to editing Jefferson's declaration. On July 4, Congress voted to accept the amended document and sent it to the printer, though some members refused to sign it, fearing the consequences of independence. The most notable was John Dickinson, whose 1767 and 1768 *Letters from a Farmer in Pennsylvania* had proved instrumental in arousing opposition to the Townshend Duties. Despite his strong opposition to British policy, Dickinson believed independence to be a mistake, and he was not alone: many Philadelphians harbored doubts about the wisdom of declaring independence.[83]

The fact that Philadelphia hosted Congress and was the largest and most important city in British North America made it a natural target for British forces. As early as 1776, General Sir William Howe, the commander in chief of Britain's North American forces, proposed capturing Philadelphia, and by December of that year there was a widespread expectation that the British would move on the city.[84] Congress fled Philadelphia for Baltimore in mid-December, and the Pennsylvania Assembly placed Philadelphia under martial law, with General Israel Putnam acting as the city's military governor.[85] Patriots imprisoned the city's Loyalists and prepared local buildings for use as hospitals. The Pennsylvania Assembly created a state militia, and the units from the city were heavily Constitutionalists, who in turn used their power to punish their political enemies in the city.[86]

Though Howe's men failed to materialize in late 1776, Philadelphians remained on edge. Rumors of an impending invasion spread through the city in February 1777, though Congress did return from Baltimore in March.[87] In the summer of 1777, Howe made plans to occupy Philadelphia. Initially, Howe planned to sail his forces up the Delaware River and take the city. On reaching the Delaware Bay, Howe learned that navigating the Delaware was treacherous without a pilot and that the river was blocked by twin forts: Mifflin on the Pennsylvania bank of the Delaware and Mercer on the New Jersey side. Patriots had also placed iron-tipped spikes in the Delaware to prevent large ships from sailing upriver to Philadelphia. To avoid these obstacles, Howe sailed to northern Maryland and then marched north toward Philadelphia. His movements set off panic in Philadelphia; one contemporary recalled that by July, "the alarm was very great. The stores were moved out, the Militia called upon & harangued twice by Gen'l Mifflin, & attempts made to force out the unwiilling."[88] Fearing internal subversion from Loyalists in the city, in the fall of 1777, Congress expelled twenty-two men—the majority Quaker—from Philadelphia, sending them to Winchester, Virginia, for seven months.[89]

On September 11, 1777, Howe's forces confronted General George Washington's army near Chadds Ford, Pennsylvania, leading to the Battle of Brandywine, the war's longest single-day battle. The Battle of Brandywine was a Patriot defeat, and only luck prevented Washington's forces from being routed.[90] The battle was close enough to the city that Philadelphians could hear the firing "very distinctly," which touched off a panic in the city: one contemporary reported "a Man is at this very instant . . . parading through the City ringing a Bell and ordering all Houses to be immediately shut up, alarming the inhabitants that General Howe is advancing and that every man who can carry a Gun must appear on the Commons."[91] Howe did not advance on Philadelphia that day, but on September 16, Washington retreated in the face of superior numbers at the Battle of the Clouds (near Malvern, Pennsylvania). Washington left a force of 1,500 men in the area, crossed the Schuylkill, and marched his men through Philadelphia (which Quaker diarist Elizabeth Drinker described as causing "Great Confusion") en route to Reading, Pennsylvania, where he hoped to gather supplies.[92] According to James Allen, a lawyer in the city, "On Thursday [September] 18th The Congress and the city of Philadelphia were alarmed at midnight with an account that Gen'l Howe had crossed the River and would be there in a few hours; in consequence of which the Congress, all the publick boards, Officers, & all the Whigs in general left the City at midnight in the utmost consternation."[93] That rumor proved to be false, but on September 20, a British detachment conducted a surprise raid on the remnant of Washington's forces in the area, routing the Patriots at the Battle of Paoli.

Following that battle, Howe's men camped at Germantown on September 25. The following day, Lieutenant General Charles Cornwallis marched into Philadelphia with fifteen thousand men. To prevent the British from fortifying Philadelphia, on October 4, Washington attacked Howe's forces at Germantown, where the bulk of British forces remained encamped. The fighting was particularly intense, with some British soldiers barricading themselves in Cliveden and

Patriot forces shelling the house. The battle was a British victory, and Washington's forces entered winter quarters in Valley Forge, effectively conceding British control of Philadelphia. Famously, when told of the British occupation of Philadelphia, Benjamin Franklin quipped, "Instead of Howe taking Philadelphia, Philadelphia has taken Howe."[94] That was putting a brave face on a dire situation, and it did not match reality: one British soldier noted in his diary that the British entered the city "amidst the acclimation of some thousands of the inhabitants," a reflection of the strong Loyalist sentiment in the city.[95]

Howe had a difficult task ahead of him: on the one hand, he needed to defeat the Patriot forces, but on the other hand, he had to do so in a way that did not alienate the Loyalists and neutrals living in the territory he occupied. Howe commissioned a census and found that only twenty-three thousand of the city's approximately forty thousand inhabitants remained.[96] In a nod toward building goodwill, Howe guaranteed that Philadelphians who did not oppose his forces would remain unmolested, and he encouraged Loyalists to come to the city and conduct business in Philadelphia's vacant shops. The collapse of municipal services in 1776 had left the city mired in its own filth, and when Howe issued a proclamation mandating city residents to clean the streets in front of their properties, most ignored it.[97] It was incumbent upon Howe to reestablish city services, and he appointed Joseph Galloway as superintendent general of police and the Port of Philadelphia.[98] In addition to supporting the British by raising two companies of troops, Galloway worked to create a night watch, regulate the recently reopened markets, and operate the city's almshouse (part of which the British were using as a military hospital).[99] Galloway faced a daunting task that few Philadelphians were willing or able to assist with, and as a result, conditions in the city were grim. Inflation was rampant, and necessities, such as flour and salt, were scarce, particularly after the Continental Congress, in exile in York, Pennsylvania, decreed that anyone taking supplies to Philadelphia was liable to be executed if caught.[100] On November 1, 1777, Loyalist Sarah Logan Fisher wrote in her diary, "The prospect of suffering for want is such that it is dreadful to think what the distresses of the poor people are & must be. Everything is gone of the vegetable kind, plundered, great part of it, by the Hessians [German mercenaries employed by the British Army], as there can be nothing brought into the city."[101]

Nor did he just have civilians to worry about: after occupying the city and building fortifications, British forces had little else to do. Alcohol abuse and crime were rampant in the city, and desperation turned many of Philadelphia's women—who outnumbered men in the city by 30 percent during the occupation—into prostitutes.[102] The British worked to distract the army and the city's civilians. Occupied Philadelphia was alive with concerts, balls attended by the city's most fashionable ladies (at least the Loyalists who had not fled), cock-fights, horseraces, and at least one regatta on the Delaware.[103] The British also reopened the Southwark Theatre. Initially, the British had employed the vacant building as a hospital following the Battle of Germantown, but in early January 1778, it was used for theatrical presentations, perhaps as a rebuke to the commonwealth's constitution, which incorporated several of the so-called blue laws (legal prohibitions against activities on certain days, usually for religious reasons) that existed prior to the Revolution.[104] Major John André, who was later executed for his role in Benedict Arnold's treasonous plan to surrender the fort at West Point, New York, to the British, painted some of the theater's scenery.[105] Though these efforts provided a needed distraction to a tense army living in occupied territory, winning Philadelphians' hearts and minds would take more than cockfights and balls.

In fact, during the occupation, British soldiers showed little regard for either the city's citizens or their property, despite Howe's proclamation in February 1778 that his men would be punished for illegally seizing property.[106] The seizure and destruction of individual property was widespread and violent, eroding Philadelphians' goodwill toward the British Army and its allies.[107] On March 28, 1778, a resident of Kingsessing named Christiana Leach complained in her diary, "A party of rascals came to our house, sent by [Joseph] Galloway, and took our cattle and plundered our house, and also took father with them to the old prison. Our loss is at least £400."[108] British soldiers even destroyed a small natural history collection stored at the Colony in Schuylkill's clubhouse, the Castle.[109] On November 22, Loyalist Robert Morton criticized the British Army in his diary, writing:

> This morning about 10 o'clock the British set fire to Fair Hill Mansion House, Jon'a Mifflin's, and many others [amounting] to 11 besides houses, Barns, &c. The reason they assign for this destruction of their friends' property is on acco. of the Americans firing from these houses and harassing their Picquets . . . it is reasonable to conclude that men whose property is this wantonly destroyed under the pretence of depriving their enemy of a means of annoying y'm on their march, will soon be converted and become their professed enemies. . . . Here is an instance that Gen'l Washington's army cannot be accused of. There is not one instance to be produced where they have wantonly destroyed and burned their friends' property.[110]

The war transformed the city's environment, with the forest surrounding Philadelphia denuded of trees and turned into a barren patch of weed-choked

wilderness.[111] The devastation extended beyond the city's borders: British soldiers torched wide swaths of land in present-day Kensington and dammed
the Cohocksink Creek, turning the surrounding area into a nearly impassable
marshland.[112] The Marquis de Chastellux, who toured North America between
1780 and 1782, recalled, "The ruins of houses destroyed, or burnt, are the monuments the English have left behind them."[113] Ultimately, occupying Philadelphia did little to improve Britain's prospects in the war and probably made
them worse.

Following news of France's recognition of the United States (February 6,
1778) and Britain's declaration of war against France (March 17, 1778), British
officials decided to evacuate Philadelphia and return to New York. Galloway
opposed this move, no doubt fearing the consequences of the Patriots' return.[114]
That April, the British government notified Howe that his resignation (submitted the previous October) had been accepted, and he planned to sail for London on May 18. The week before departing, Howe threw a lavish party known
as the Meschianza at Walnut Grove, the abandoned country estate of Patriot
Joseph Wharton (near the current-day intersection of Fifth Street and Washington Avenue). The festivities included a mock joust and a massive fireworks
display. Many enslaved people saw their opportunity in the British evacuation
and escaped with the departing soldiers, as did several prominent Loyalists,
such as Galloway.[115]

Following the British evacuation, Patriots entered the city. According to
Peter S. Du Ponceau, a recent French emigrant who served as secretary to Baron
Friedrich Wilhelm von Steuben (the Prussian military officer who helped train
and professionalize Washington's army during the winter in Valley Forge) and
was among the Patriots who retook the city, Philadelphia "had been left by the
British, and Hessians, in the most filthy condition. . . . Such was the filth of the
City, that it was impossible for us to drink a comfortable dish of tea that evening.
As soon as our cups were filled, myriads of flies took possession of them."[116] The
Pennsylvania State House was near ruin, its steeple rotting and the stench of
trash and human waste inside and around the building overpowering.[117] A few
weeks after reentering the city, Washington's men celebrated the second anniversary of independence on a grand scale, firing thirteen cannons.[118] Despite the
pomp and ceremony, Patriot control of the city was no panacea for Philadelphia:
Patriot forces executed seven individuals for treason and seized more than one
hundred individuals' property.[119] Many British soldiers (who, like their counterparts in the Patriot army, were often poor) failed to settle their debts before
leaving the city, leaving merchants holding worthless letters of obligation.[120]
Washington appointed General Benedict Arnold the city's military commander.
Arnold declared martial law and ordered his men to search the city's houses for

weapons. His men seized any goods of military value owned by Loyalists and required military passes for travelers. Arnold quickly ran afoul of the Constitutionalists by his business decisions, his lavish entertainments, and his courtship of a prominent Loyalist, Peggy Shippen. In 1780, Philadelphians greeted news of Arnold's treason by burning effigies of the city's former military commander.[121]

The city faced several challenges. The men on both sides of the conflict needed to be fed, which caused shortages of food and other goods.[122] If that were not bad enough, lack of specie had led Congress to issue paper money that, coupled with the shortages of food, caused inflation, which eroded the value of tax receipts and made providing basic municipal services nearly impossible.[123] In May 1779, the Pennsylvania Assembly, dominated by members of the working class and radicals elected under the constitution of 1776, began imposing price controls to combat inflation. The Assembly's speaker, Constitutionalist Daniel Roberdeau, led the charge, proposing the creation of a committee of Philadelphians who would periodically publish, and constantly revise downward, prices for scarce goods. The idea was that community pressure (with its implicit threat of extralegal violence) would keep the city's merchants in line.[124] Roberdeau's plan was adopted, and the Assembly created committees to investigate the prices merchants charged for goods.[125]

The committees' investigations focused on Republican merchants' alleged malfeasance, particularly as the price controls system failed to deliver lower prices in July 1779. It is not surprising that the Constitutionalist-dominated Assembly used public anger about inflation as a cudgel with which to beat Republicans. Roberdeau and his supporters called a public meeting for July 26 and reaffirmed their commitment to price controls. Later that evening a mob of Roberdeau's supporters converged on the home of a prominent Republican, Whitehead Humphries, after he published a series of anti-Constitutionalist letters in a local paper. Only the arrival of Continental soldiers, dispatched by Benedict Arnold, prevented bloodshed.[126] These tactics were brutally effective: in an August 2 referendum on the price controls policy, the Constitutionalists banked their greatest electoral support in any election between 1776 and 1789, the pinnacle of their political strength.[127]

Yet prices continued climbing, arousing public anger toward the city's Republican merchants. On October 4, 1779, a group of militiamen met at Burns Tavern (on Tenth Street just south of Race Street). Fortified by alcohol and by the desire to do *something*, they marched through the city's streets, breaking up a Quaker meeting and capturing and humiliating some of Philadelphia's most prominent merchants. Republicans appealed to the Assembly for help against the mob, but the Constitutionalist-dominated Supreme Executive Council refused. Fearing for their safety, about two dozen prominent Republicans gathered at the home of James Wilson, the city's most prominent Republican lawyer. The Republicans barricaded themselves in Wilson's brick home on the corner of Third and Walnut, eventually exchanging gunfire with the militiamen as the latter tried to enter the house. The bloody standoff ended only when Joseph Reed, the president of the Supreme Executive Council, arrived with the First City Troop (generally considered pro-Republican) and forced the militia to leave the scene. The confrontation cost six lives and left seventeen people wounded.[128] Though price controls failed to stop or even slow inflation, in the spring of 1780, the Assembly invited representatives from the other states to Philadelphia to create a nationwide price control regimen. This was a fiasco from the beginning: only six states chose delegates, and only four states' delegates ever made it to Philadelphia, so nothing was accomplished.[129] The Constitutionalists' political fortunes declined: in 1780, Philadelphia elected Republicans to the Assembly, and the city's most prominent voluntary organizations and cultural institutions were overwhelmingly controlled by Republicans.[130]

After 1779, the center of military operations in North America moved south, relieving pressure on Philadelphia. Now out of danger, the city enjoyed some modest economic benefits of the war. Being cut off from British imports encouraged the city's industries, which, by the end of the century, were transforming the raw materials mined, produced, and grown in the region's hinterlands into finished products, putting Philadelphia on the road to becoming a leading industrial center.[131] In order to finance the war, in July 1780, the city's merchants established the continent's first bank, the Bank of Pennsylvania, to lend money to the Continental Congress. The following year it was superseded by the Bank of North America, the country's first commercial bank and the nation's de facto central bank. Located near the corner of Third and Chestnut, it initially operated out of its cashier's house.[132] The number of taxpayers in Philadelphia grew rapidly between 1779 and 1789. As a result, the commonwealth surveyed nearly two hundred new city blocks (each containing eight to twelve lots), fueling a building boom, with the number of structures within the city ballooning by nearly 66 percent between 1777 and 1790.[133] The growth in taxpayers was not evenly distributed throughout Philadelphia. Some wards (Walnut and Chestnut, for instance) experienced only modest increases in taxpayers, while others (such as Dock, Middle, and North) saw a huge uptick in the number of taxpayers.[134] In addition, housing in Philadelphia was scarce and rent prices high.[135] In fact, Philadelphia was one of the most expensive cities in the United States, a fact that members of Congress and even Presidents George Washington and John Adams grumbled about during the 1790s.[136]

Moreover, the hard feelings caused by the British occupation made the Patriot cause even more popular in Philadelphia. For instance, when Washington entered the city in late April 1780, he was greeted by a triumphal arch erected for his arrival.[137] In September 1781, Philadelphians showered flowers on the Patriot and French troops marching through the city. According to army chaplain Claude C. Robin, the soldiers "marched through the city, with military music playing before them . . . the streets were crowded with people, and the ladies appeared at the windows in the most brilliant attire."[138] The following month Cornwallis's forces surrendered to General George Washington at Yorktown, effectively ending the Revolution (though a treaty to the effect would not be signed until 1783). In celebration of Washington's victory, "the standard of the State was raised, and at twelve o'clock salutes were fired by the artillery in the State-House yard and by vessels in the harbor, which also displayed their colors. In the afternoon, Congress, the State Council . . . and others went into procession to the Dutch Lutheran Church, where a service of thanksgiving was performed by the Rev. Mr. [George] Duffield, one of the chaplains to Congress. In the evening there was a general illumination, and on the following evening a display of fireworks."[139]

Despite the American victory, the war's end raised some important challenges for the young nation. Demobilizing the army (which was composed largely of poor men) set off several confrontations over back pay owed to the soldiers.[140] The best known of these was the Newburgh Conspiracy of March 1783, and though Washington successfully defused that situation, it was far from the last. In June 1783, several hundred members of the Pennsylvania Line (a portion of the Continental Army) marched on Philadelphia and surrounded the State House, setting off a two-week confrontation. Robert Morris, the Philadelphia banker then serving as superintendent of finance (a position he had taken in 1781 in the aftermath of another mutiny over back pay), opposed paying the soldiers because of Congress's abysmal finances. On June 20, the soldiers surrounded the State House, intimidating congressmen, who in turn pushed through the crowd. The following day, members of Congress met with members of the Pennsylvania Executive Council to ask that the commonwealth do more to protect the federal government, but the council could not guarantee that the state militia would side with Congress against the mutineers.[141] As a result, Congress decamped for Princeton, New Jersey, staying until November.

Congress's exit did nothing to sate the soldiers' demands, and their numbers swelled over the next few days, terrorizing Philadelphians. Eventually, Washington dispatched 1,500 troops to Philadelphia to put down the mutiny. The entire event soured many members of Congress on Philadelphia; as a result, Congress migrated to Annapolis, Maryland, then to Trenton, New Jersey, before finally settling in Manhattan in January 1785. Though the Constitutional Convention met in Philadelphia in 1787 (it was still the largest and most important city in North America), and Congress eventually returned to the city in 1790, the entire experience convinced many members that it needed to create a federal district where it could guarantee its own security and aroused elite fears about the threat posed by the Revolution's democratic excesses.[142]

The war's end meant the resumption of trade with Great Britain, though the Royal Navy aggressively excluded American ships from trading with the British West Indies, causing a severe postwar depression that lasted into the 1790s. Moreover, the resumption of trade did not benefit Philadelphia as much as it did New York and Baltimore (both of which had more direct access to the Atlantic Ocean than Philadelphia, particularly in winter when the Delaware often froze).[143] As a result, Baltimore, which expanded markedly in the 1780s, directly challenged Philadelphia's position as a key port of entry and was more convenient for farmers in western Pennsylvania to reach than the City of Brotherly Love because of the steep Allegheny Mountains. To counter competition from Baltimore, a private company, the Company of the Pennsylvania and Lancaster Turnpike Road, built the first long-distance paved road in the United States. The road improved commerce by making it easier, cheaper, and faster to transport raw materials east to the city and finished products west to markets and was financed by charging users a fee. When it opened in 1795, it reduced the cost of transporting goods by more than 60 percent.[144]

In the mid-1780s, the Pennsylvania Assembly began altering the city's political structure to better reflect the realities created by the war and Philadelphia's subsequent population growth. In 1785, the Assembly extended Mulberry, North, Middle, and South Wards west from Seventh Street to the Schuylkill River. The Assembly also extended Dock Ward west but narrowed it, creating New Market Ward between Spruce and Cedar Streets and running between the rivers. In 1786, following a petition by the ward's inhabitants, the Assembly split Mulberry into two wards: North Mulberry (between Vine Street and Race and running from Front Street to the Schuylkill) and South Mulberry (between Race and Arch).[145] Population growth in Northern Liberties convinced the Assembly to divide it into eastern and western districts, apportioning each an accessor and two inspectors.[146] In 1800, bowing to Philadelphia's "increased population" and the "unequal distribution of the same into wards," the Assembly divided Philadelphia into fourteen wards: seven (Upper Delaware, Lower Delaware, High Street, Chestnut, Walnut, Dock, and New Market) began at the Delaware River and continued west to Fourth Street, while seven others (North Mulberry, South Mulberry, North, Middle, South, Locust, and Cedar) started at Fourth Street and continued west to the Schuylkill River.[147] During the 1790s, Middle Ward was home to some of the city's most famous residents, including Presidents George Washington and John Adams.[148] In addition, because of its close proximity to several key federal and state government buildings, Society Hill—which began as the center for the Free Society of Traders' mercantile activities—had become by the 1790s an exclusive neighborhood for Philadelphia's economic elite.[149] As always, development occurred close to the Delaware River, and as late as 1800, the city had few buildings west of Eighth Street.[150]

However, the collapse of municipal administration after 1776 meant there was little oversight of construction during this period. As a result, Philadelphians continued deviating from Penn's original grid plan by haphazardly constructing outbuildings (privies, kitchens, etc.), alleys, and other encroachments on the city's streets.[151] Conditions remained grim, with many homeowners forced to keep hogs for the sole purpose of eating refuse and the carcasses of dead animals.[152] Following the British Army's leveling of the city's woods, squatters flooded into the area. Thomas Twining, who visited the city in the 1790s, described the barren landscape this way: "Upon leaving the city, we entered immediately the country, the transition from streets to fields being abrupt, and not rendered gradual by detached houses and villas. . . . The fields, however, had nothing pleasing about them, being crossed and separated by the numerous intersections of the intended streets, and surrounded by rough-hewed rails, placed zig-zag instead of hedges."[153] Moreover, haphazard construction exacerbated the ever-present danger of fire.[154]

The need for improved city services dovetailed with the movement toward institutions for dealing with social problems. Nowhere was this more evident than in the shift in dealing with crime. Prior to the mid-eighteenth century, corporal punishment was the primary method of dealing with individuals convicted of crimes. Beginning in the mid-eighteenth century, Enlightenment thinkers such as the Italian criminologist and philosopher Cesare Beccaria argued for more humane methods of punishment. These theorists argued that incarceration (confining convicted people to prisons) was a more humane approach to punishment that gave society the time to rehabilitate convicts. In 1786, Pennsylvania mandated that inmates toil at public works in the city to defray the costs of their incarceration. This policy caused some problems (it gave inmates opportunities for causing mischief and receiving contraband from their friends and family) and was later abandoned.[155] Four years later, the Pennsylvania Assembly constructed a new cellblock for the Walnut Street Jail designed to segregate inmates from one another (prior to that convicted people shared a common room). Called the penitentiary house, it was the first such building in North America, making Philadelphia a leader in criminal justice reform for decades to come.[156]

In short, the American Revolution had upended hierarchies, corroded deference, and unleashed democratic impulses that reshaped society. In 1788, former
governor and proprietor John Penn, who remained in Pennsylvania after the
Revolution (except for a brief visit to England), described the commonwealth
(apparently without bitterness) as "this democratical country," abjuring the use
of his former honorifics.[157] Judith Sargent Murray, who visited Philadelphia in
the summer of 1790, described the spirit of equality that permeated the city's
inhabitants, an impression shared by other visitors during this period.[158] Elite
concern about the threats posed by democracy became an enduring feature of
American politics through at least the first half of the nineteenth century.[159]

Indeed, many Americans were alarmed by the democratic impulses unleashed
by the Revolution, fearing the mob violence that had characterized the opposition
to imperial policy during the 1760s and 1770s. Mob violence did not end with the
war: on May 5, 1787, a mob attacked an old woman known as Korbmacher who
lived near New Market. Apparently, the mob's members believed this woman to
be a witch, and two months later she died of her injuries. Persecution of so-called
witches was hardly unknown in Pennsylvania; after all, in 1683, William Penn
tried Margaret Mattson and Yeshro Hendrickson for witchcraft. A jury convicted
the women of "having the common fame of a witch," though not of practicing
witchcraft; they were released on bond for good behavior. A century later, witchcraft trials were rare (one newspaper that reported the attack on Korbmacher
denounced the "absurd and abominable notions of *witch-craft* and *sorcery*"), and
the specter of a mob murdering a woman on suspicion of being a witch without
any sort of due process must have appeared alarming indeed.[160]

As a result of this and the Revolution's other perceived democratic excesses,
a conservative counterrevolution emerged that reshaped the national, state,
and city governments.[161] This counterrevolution was rooted in both general
dissatisfaction with the efficacy of government at various levels and the concerns generated by violent uprisings like Shays's Rebellion, an armed uprising
in Massachusetts to protest state tax collection.[162] By the mid-1780s, the Constitutionalists' political support waned, to the point that in 1783 they won less than
40 percent of the Assembly's seats. After 1786, they never again won even that
many.[163] The weaknesses of the Articles of Confederation, which had governed
the nation since 1777, led to calls for a convention to amend the document. In
September 1786, delegates from five states—Delaware, New Jersey, New York,
Pennsylvania, and Virginia—met in Annapolis to discuss interstate trade, a discussion that turned to the Articles of Confederation's weaknesses. The Annapolis Convention sent to Congress a final report that, among other things, called
for a convention to meet the following summer to discuss amendments to the
Articles of Confederation.

That convention opened on May 25, 1787, in the Pennsylvania State House, and many delegates roomed together at the Indian Queen boarding house (on Third Street between Market and Chestnut), offering opportunities for discussions and compromises outside formal sessions.[164] Over the next four months, the convention moved from amending the Articles to drafting a new constitution, which was signed on September 17, 1787, though it took until June 1788 for enough states (nine) to ratify the document to make it official, thereby putting it into effect.[165] To celebrate ratification, the Constitution's supporters organized a massive parade through Philadelphia on July 4, 1788. Nearly five thousand people participated in the mile-and-a-half parade, which included floats celebrating the city's various trade organizations. An estimated seventeen thousand people watched the three-hour spectacle.[166] Despite these celebrations, the new federal Constitution was extremely controversial. Its opponents, a loosely organized coalition of individuals with a variety of concerns about the scope and breadth of federal power and the document's antidemocratic features, came to be called Anti-Federalists, while the Constitution's supporters were called Federalists. Pennsylvania's Constitutionalists tended to become Anti-Federalists, while the commonwealth's Republicans tended to become Federalists.[167]

Recognizing the serious problems caused by the collapse of Philadelphia's municipal government, in 1789, the Pennsylvania Assembly granted the city a new charter. In its preamble to the charter, the Assembly noted that "the administration of government in the City of Philadelphia is . . . inadequate to the suppression of vice and immorality, to the advancement of public health and order, and to the promotion of trade, industry, and happiness."[168] The charter defined Philadelphia as stretching from the Delaware River to the Schuylkill River and created a government of fifteen aldermen (elected every seven years) and a thirty-man common council (elected every three years). The aldermen selected from among their number the city's mayor. Municipal services improved markedly under the new charter, which empowered the city's commissioners to hire a superintendent of the nightly watch and several night watchmen. In 1798, the city even hired a "high constable," who could command the city's other constables, which represented an embryonic police force.[169] In 1796, the city established a fixed annual salary for the mayor of $1,000 (raised to $2,000 in 1805), ending the embarrassing unwillingness of the city's leading men to hold this office. Paying the mayor a fixed salary was possible because in 1790, the Assembly granted Philadelphia the right to impose and collect taxes.[170] In 1796, the Assembly revised the city's government, creating a bicameral legislature (a common council and a select council) that elected a mayor.[171] Despite expectations that the new charter would create a municipal government more responsive to the people's needs, in reality it was a political victory for Philadelphia's conservative prerevolutionary elite, who quickly came to dominate the city's government.[172] The first man elected as mayor under the new charter was Samuel Powel, the last man to serve as mayor under the original corporation's charter, a clear sign the prerevolutionary elite (including many opponents of independence) had returned to power.[173]

At about the same time as the Assembly granted Philadelphia a new charter, conservative opponents of the commonwealth's existing constitution launched a call for a convention to revise the document. On September 15, 1789 the Republican-dominated Assembly ordered the election of delegates to a constitutional convention, which met in Philadelphia that November. They drafted a constitution that established a bicameral legislature composed of a House of Representatives (elected annually) and a Senate (elected triennially) and a popularly elected governor who held office for three years. The new constitution enfranchised all white men who had lived in Pennsylvania for at least two years and paid either commonwealth or county taxes in the last six months.[174] In one respect, the 1790 constitution was more radical than its predecessor: it dropped the requirement that officeholders affirm the Old and New Testaments, thereby allowing Jews to serve in state government (obviously, atheists remained excluded).[175] This government came into being in September 1790 and met in Philadelphia.

Congress returned to Philadelphia in 1790, though only temporarily: the federal government planned on leaving the city permanently in 1800. Philadelphians aggressively tried to entice Congress to remain, and one way to do this was to construct buildings for the federal government.[176] Between 1787 and 1789, Philadelphia constructed Congress Hall, a two-story brick building at the intersection of Sixth and Chestnut Streets. Writing to Philadelphia's city and county commissioners in December 1790, Vice President John Adams commended Congress Hall as "commodious" and noted that the House of Representatives and the Senate "entertain a proper sense of the respect shown to the general government of the United States."[177] In addition, influential Philadelphians built a grand presidential mansion at Ninth and Market Street as an inducement for the government to remain in the city. Washington, who supported moving the federal capital south, never moved in, instead living in a rented house on Sixth and Market Streets owned by financier Robert Morris.[178] Washington affected an air of simplicity while president; one visitor recalled that "nothing in the exterior of the house . . . denoted the rank of its possessor. Next door was a hair-dresser."[179] Vice President Adams and several members of Congress lived in rented rooms in a house on South Fourth Street.[180] The would-be presidential mansion was later part of the University of Pennsylvania before being torn down in 1829.

One reason Philadelphians were so eager to retain the capital was that the federal government stimulated the local economy. In 1791, Congress chartered the Bank of the United States at the behest of Treasury Secretary Alexander Hamilton, who sought to improve the infant nation's financial situation and credit. Hamilton's plan called for the federal government to assume the states' war debts and to create a national bank. Hamilton's plan was designed to strengthen the federal government by giving it the power to craft unified fiscal and monetary policies.[181] Thomas Willing, a conservative Philadelphia merchant and former city mayor who had voted against the Declaration of Independence and had served as the Bank of North America's president since 1781, became the Bank of the United States' first president, serving until 1807. Initially, the Bank of the United States operated out of Carpenters' Hall, but in 1795, it moved to its new home: a neoclassical building on Third Street between Chestnut and Walnut. This encouraged allied activities, such as the founding of the continent's first official securities exchange, the Board of Brokers of Philadelphia, which operated out of the Merchants' Coffeehouse at the corner of Second and Walnut; it later became the Philadelphia Stock Exchange. In addition, in 1792, merchant Samuel Blodget convened a meeting of investors at the State House that formed the Insurance Company of North America, the country's oldest stock insurance company. Incorporated in 1794, the company provided shipping-, fire-, and life-insurance policies.[182]

Meanwhile, the outbreak of war between England and France in 1793 further stimulated Philadelphia's shipbuilding trade and fueled its import/export trade.[183] When Congress reestablished the US Navy in 1794 to protect US interests (American naval power had contracted severely in the decade after the war's end), it ordered the construction of six frigates, the first of which, the USS *United States,* was built in Philadelphia. As the seat of both the federal government and a worldwide shipping center, Philadelphia continued attracting a broad range of immigrants, leading one contemporary observer to describe it as "one great hotel or place of shelter for strangers."[184] After the war, the city's shippers, long connected to the West Indies and Britain, began trading in Asia.[185] A veritable flood of (mostly poor) Irish immigrants settled in Philadelphia during the 1780s (particularly in Northern Liberties, Southwark, and the North and South Mulberry wards).[186] Following the outbreak of revolution in Haiti in 1791, two thousand French refugees fled the island and settled in Philadelphia (often settling in the eastern portions of Middle, South, and Dock wards), swelling the city's already burgeoning population.[187] The French Revolution, which began in 1789, also drove French emigration to Pennsylvania. Several Frenchmen lived in Philadelphia, attracted by the city's cosmopolitanism and reputation for tolerance.[188] Throughout this period it was not unusual to see various groups of Native Americans in the city, particularly in Philadelphia's market.[189] Consequently, Philadelphia was, by the turn of the nineteenth century, among the world's most ethnically diverse cities.[190]

The revolutionaries' frequent invocation of "slaves" and "slavery" in their opposition to British imperial policy raised some challenging questions about enslavement in the colonies. The dyspeptic English essayist Samuel Johnson observed this contradiction in his 1775 pamphlet *Taxation no Tyranny* when he rhetorically asked, "How is it that we hear the loudest yelps for liberty among the drivers of negroes?"[191] Johnson had a point, but even as he made this remark, slavery in Pennsylvania was dying. In January 1773, nearly two hundred people, including some of Philadelphia's leading citizens, petitioned the Assembly to prohibit trading enslaved people within the commonwealth's borders. The Assembly failed to do this, but it did double the duty on importing enslaved people (to £20 per slave) and made the duty perpetual.[192] In 1776, the Quakers' Philadelphia Yearly Meeting took the momentous step of forcing its members, on pain of disownment, to free their enslaved people.[193] Though this move applied only to Quakers (whose political power was severely impacted by the American Revolution), the cumulative effect was dramatic: between 1767 and 1775, the number of enslavers in Philadelphia declined by more than one-third, while the number of enslaved people in the city fell by 50 percent.[194]

There was growing support to ban the import of enslaved people altogether. In 1775, twenty-four men (seventeen of whom were Quakers) formed the Society for the Relief of Free Negroes Unlawfully Held in Bondage, North America's first abolition society. It was reorganized in 1784 and renamed the Pennsylvania Society for Promoting the Abolition of Slavery and for the Relief of Free Negroes Unlawfully Held in Bondage. Several years later, the organization's president, Benjamin Franklin, petitioned Congress to ban slavery. In 1780, Pennsylvania's Assembly passed the Gradual Abolition Act, the first such law in the United States (Vermont had simply abolished slavery in its 1777 constitution). Under the act's terms, further importation of enslaved people into the commonwealth was illegal. Henceforth, any children born to enslaved mothers would themselves be bound as indentured servants to their mother's enslaver until age twenty-eight. The law's effect was profound: between 1790 and 1800, slavery nearly disappeared from Philadelphia.[195] The growing resistance to slavery spilled over into a decline in indentured servitude and a preference for paid servants (though as late as 1850, Pennsylvania was still home to at least a few enslaved people).[196]

Crucially, Pennsylvania's lawmakers recognized that the gradual emancipation law imperiled Philadelphia's chances of remaining the capital of the United States, so the act specifically exempted members of Congress.[197] The law was silent on members of the executive branch, so President George Washington scrupulously sent his enslaved people out of the commonwealth every few months (his attorney general, Edmund Randolph, failed to do so and saw his enslaved people emancipated under the law). Despite Washington's best efforts, he could not prevent one enslaved woman, twenty-two-year-old Ona Judge, from escaping to New Hampshire. Philadelphia's free Black community likely helped Judge and thousands of other escaped enslaved people make their way to freedom. Philadelphia was the largest and most important community of free Black people in the United States during the last decades of the eighteenth and the first decades of the nineteenth centuries, and several predominantly Black neighborhoods emerged during this period, including one along South Fifth Street.[198] Philadelphia's Black community was also ethnically and religiously diverse, including a substantial number of French-speaking refugees from Saint-Domingue (present-day Haiti), free or formerly enslaved Africans, and Black people born in the United States.[199]

The Black community's size and importance did not insulate its members from discrimination. Though Black Philadelphians were technically allowed to vote under Pennsylvania's constitution (the document did not explicitly limit the franchise to whites), few exercised the right, evidently afraid of potentially violent reprisals.[200] The year 1794 was crucially important for the city's Black community, for several reasons. First, Mother Bethel African Methodist Episcopal (AME) Church (the first independent Protestant denomination founded by Black people) opened on Sixth Street just north of Lombard to great fanfare. So did the African Episcopal Church of Saint Thomas, the nation's first Black Episcopal Church (the congregation itself had been founded two years before). An outgrowth of the Free African Society, a religious and mutual aid society founded in 1787 by the Reverend Richard Allen and the Reverend Absalom Jones, the church was a response to the pervasive discrimination Black people suffered at St. George's United Methodist Church.[201] Also that year, Philadelphia hosted the American Convention for Promoting the Abolition of Slavery, making the city a leading center of opposition to enslavement.

As home to both the commonwealth's and the nation's capitals, Philadelphia had an active season of dances, balls, and other entertainments, though attendance at these were usually restricted to the city's political and economic elite.[202] Philadelphia was also the young nation's undisputed intellectual capital in the last decade of the eighteenth century and was frequently called the "Athens of America." Johann David Schoepf, who visited Philadelphia just after the war, asserted that "the city, if not greatly beyond the others in North America in wealth and the number of houses, far surpasses them all in learning, in the arts, and public spirit."[203] In 1788, French visitor Jacques Pierre Brissot de Warville remarked that in Philadelphia "you find more well-educated men, more knowledge of politics and literature, more political and learned societies, than anywhere else in the United States."[204]

Philadelphia remained one of the world's leading publishing centers and had several subscription libraries, ensuring that its inhabitants had ready access to a wide variety of books, newspapers, and magazines.[205] In addition, as a publishing center, Philadelphia played a key role in shaping and disseminating ideas about culture, economics, and politics.[206] In 1782, Philadelphia printer and publisher Robert Aitken published the first complete English-language Bible in the United States in his shop on Market Street. In the mid-1780s, portrait painter and amateur scientist Charles Willson Peale opened to the public his Philadelphia Museum, a collection of natural history specimens located at Third and Lombard Streets. This was the first natural history museum in the United States, and it was designed to "to instruct the mind and sow the seeds of Virtue."[207] At various points the museum's collections were housed in the American Philosophical Society and the Pennsylvania State House. In 1793, English equestrian John Bill Ricketts established the country's first circus in Philadelphia, the Ricketts' Art Pantheon and Amphitheatre, at Sixth and Chestnut, which even President Washington attended (it burned down in 1799). In 1784, Philadelphians witnessed the country's first hot air balloon ascent. Taking off from the Walnut Street Jail's yard, balloonist Jean-Pierre Blanchard carried a letter written by George Washington that he delivered to the owner of the farm where the balloon eventually landed, the first instance of airmail in US history.[208]

The city continued offering seamier amusements, most including alcohol or sex.[209] Prostitution was highly visible in parts of Philadelphia, and by 1790, the city boasted more than two hundred licensed taverns, and laborers frequently drank during the workday.[210] Consequently, the Assembly reestablished many of Pennsylvania's blue laws in 1779, to the approval of several members of that body, though the provisions prohibiting the theater were repealed in 1789.[211] This was one front in a broader struggle to impose a certain vision of morality on an often reluctant working class and to constrain what some elites saw as out-of-control democracy.[212] In 1798, the Assembly went so far as to authorize Philadelphia's churches to string "so many chains across . . . streets, lanes or alleys . . . to hinder and obstruct all coaches . . . and all and every person or persons riding on horseback, from passing said churches or houses of religious worship during the time of divine services." The penalty for unlawfully removing the chains was fixed at thirty dollars, a considerable sum of money.[213]

Life in Philadelphia remained filled with unexpected deaths and random misfortunes. During the early stages of the Revolution, Patriots Clement Biddle and Alexander Graydon were practicing with their pistols when they accidentally shot a little boy.[214] Though the child was not seriously hurt, it was nonetheless a reminder that death from random gunplay remained a serious threat in Philadelphia. Far more seriously, in February 1784, a boy accidentally shot his friend while playing with a loaded gun, mortally wounding the child.[215] In addition, noted Jacques Pierre Brissot de Warville, "For some time there have been complaints of disorders and of robberies committed at night on the outskirts of Philadelphia by thieves who escaped from the prison."[216] Elizabeth Drinker recorded one unfortunate woman's fall into a privy, where she nearly drowned in her own feculence.[217]

As always, illness remained an ever-present threat.[218] A particularly vivid illustration of the hazards of urban life occurred in 1793, when the city suffered a devastating fire in mid-May followed by an outbreak of yellow fever in August. The disease killed quickly, and frequently, corpses were discovered because of the stench given off by decaying flesh. The yellow fever epidemic devastated the city, killing more than four thousand (including former mayor Samuel Powel).[219] Dauphin County prothonotary Alexander Graydon recalled that during this period, a "general gloom pervaded the country," while English traveller Henry Wansey described one grisly incident where, "in one house, an infant was found sucking at the dead body of its mother. Women [died] in the pains of child-bed, not having any living soul to come near them."[220] President Washington decamped for Germantown until the fall (where he lived in an elegant mansion owned by Revolutionary War colonel Isaac Franks), as did several other members of the executive branch. Those who could not flee the city—the poor, elderly, and disabled—were hardest hit by the epidemic.[221]

The yellow fever epidemic of 1793 was a turning point for public services in Philadelphia and highlighted the racism, bigotry, and political tensions that shaped the city's culture.[222] Though epidemic diseases had racked Philadelphia since its founding, this outbreak of yellow fever (which had not visited the city in more than a quarter century) was particularly horrific. It originated in Hell-Town in July, which helps explain why municipal authorities were slow to respond to the outbreak.[223] According to publisher Mathew Carey, "For a time [the yellow fever] was entirely confined to [Hell-Town]. . . . By degrees, it spread, owing to the want of precaution and to communion with the infected. Several persons were swept away before any great alarm was excited."[224] It took nearly a month for the city's leading physician, Dr. Benjamin Rush, to notify the public that a yellow fever epidemic had appeared in the city.

As the death toll rose, those who could leave (between one-third and one-half of Philadelphia's residents) fled the city, contributing to the collapse of municipal administration. As a result, the remaining city officials were forced to solicit volunteers for help in nursing the sick and disposing of the dead. The city's Black population played an especially important role in this regard. Many people, Black and white, believed (incorrectly, as it turned out) that Black people were immune to yellow fever. The Reverend Richard Allen and the Reverend Absalom Jones, along with other members of the Free African Society, stepped into the vacuum, providing medical care under the supervision of Dr. Rush. However, once the crisis passed, some whites claimed that Allen, Jones, and other Black Philadelphians only assisted with the sick and dying for financial reward. Carey went so far as to publish this assertion in a widely read pamphlet, *A Short Account of the Malignant Fever, Lately Prevalent in Philadelphia*. Allen and Jones responded with their own pamphlet, *A Narrative of the Proceedings of the Black People during the Late Awful Calamity in Philadelphia*, clapping back at their critics by saying, "We feel ourselves sensibly aggrieved by the censorious epithets of many, who did not render the least assistance in the time of necessity, yet are liberal of their censure of us, for the prices paid for our services."[225]

Yellow fever also aggravated xenophobia, which was subsumed in the struggle between the two political parties that had emerged: Federalists and Democratic-Republicans. Federalists tended to blame the epidemic on recently arrived refugees from Saint-Domingue, whose white ruling elite had been overthrown by the island's enslaved Black people in the only successful slave uprising that led to the creation of a free state. One reason for this was that the Democratic-Republicans were sympathetic to the French Revolution (which had broken out in 1789) and to France's revolutionary government, which was trying to reestablish control over Saint-Domingue. Moreover, in the lead-up to the outbreak of yellow fever in the nation's capital, Federalists were scandalized by France's recently arrived minister to the United States, Edmond Charles Genêt, whose outrageous antics infuriated President Washington and members of his cabinet.

This political background helps explain some of the steps the Pennsylvania Assembly took in the aftermath of the yellow fever epidemic. Noting the "increasing intercourse between the United States and foreign countries," in 1794, the Assembly established a health office dedicated to "securing the city and port of Philadelphia from the introduction of pestilential and contagious diseases, and for regulating the importation of German and other passengers."[226] Finding that insufficient, in 1798 the Assembly went further, establishing the Board of Health, which was empowered to collect taxes to underwrite projects designed to improve public health. Using these funds, the Board of Health erected the Lazaretto, a quarantine station, on a ten-acre tract along the Delaware in Tinicum Township. In 1799, the city's common council established the Watering Committee to devise a plan for providing city residents

clean water and even passed an ordinance authorizing Philadelphia to borrow $150,000 to implement the plan.[227] Opened in 1801, Philadelphia's Water
Works (housed in a neoclassical building in Center Square, where City Hall
stands today) was the nation's first steam-powered water-pumping machine.
Philadelphians could have clean water pumped into their homes by installing a
lead pipe to the wooden main and paying an annual fee of $5.[228] Philadelphia's
streets were also markedly cleaner by the late 1780s than they had been in the
decades leading up to the Revolution, though it remained common to see hogs
and other livestock roaming through the city eating refuse.

Unfortunately, the 1793 yellow fever epidemic increased calls for moving
the commonwealth's capital to another, less populous, and less expensive city.
Pennsylvania's 1793 Census of Taxables led to a greater number of western representatives in the Assembly, and over the next few years, they agitated to move
the capital to a more central location in the commonwealth.[229] In 1799, Pennsylvania's capital migrated first to Lancaster and then, in 1812, to Harrisburg.
The following year, the federal government decamped for Washington, DC,
marking the end of Philadelphia being the center of national and state governments. These departures reflected a pervasive antiurban bias that was characteristic of much of the revolutionary generation and that continued into the
nineteenth century.[230] The removal of the Pennsylvania and US capitals was the
end of an era for the city, though not the end of its history. Over the course of
the new century, Philadelphia would remake itself as an industrial engine powering America's growth into a world power. Yet Philadelphia's association with
the American Revolution cast a long shadow, driving a considerable amount of
tourism to the city during the decades that followed but eclipsing other epochs
in the city's history.

CHAPTER 5

The Athens of America, 1800–1854

The first half of the nineteenth century was a period of tumultuous change for the United States. Industrialization (the wide-scale development of machine-powered industry) and democratization (greater access to the vote), coupled with the persistence of ongoing social hierarchies, fomented political, social, and cultural conflict. Industrialization widened the gap between the haves and the have-nots, while democratization gave greater access to political power to some but not others, especially women and Black people. Elites tried to reinforce their social position through a variety of means, including institutions such as public schools and penitentiaries, as well as the manipulation of physical space, as in the creation of public parks. These trends were hardly unique to Philadelphia, which lost its status as the nation's preeminent shipping and banking city during the early nineteenth century. Increasingly, Philadelphia's businesses focused on industrial production for a regional market, which fostered an insular culture that continued into the twentieth century. The city's professional elite—lawyers, doctors, and bankers—eclipsed merchants as Philadelphia's cultural, political, and economic leaders, and the new economic system wrought by industrialization inaugurated a boom and bust cycle that, along with ethnic and racial tensions, contributed to pervasive urban violence in the 1830s, 1840s, and 1850s. One response to the violence was the 1854 consolidation of the municipalities within Philadelphia County into a single municipal entity, creating political boundaries that exist to the present.

Though more than a century old, Philadelphia in 1800 was only a kernel of the sprawling metropolis it later became. Largely undeveloped west of Eighth Street in 1800, the city by 1840 was thoroughly developed as far as Twelfth Street, with some sporadic construction as far west as the Schuylkill River.[1] According to the 1800 census, Philadelphia, Northern Liberties, and Southwark had a combined population approximately equal to New York City. Between 1790 and 1830, the United States' four key seaport cities—New York, Philadelphia, Baltimore, and New Orleans—experienced unprecedented growth.[2] In the half century

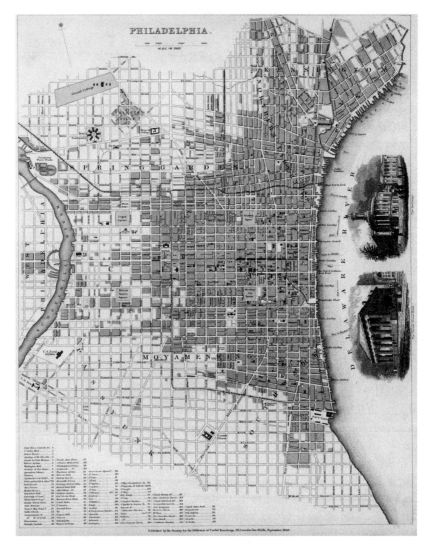

Figure 5. Philadelphia, 1840. David Rumsey Map Collection, David Rumsey Map Center, Stanford Libraries. The Industrial Revolution jumpstarted Philadelphia's growth and encouraged modifications to Penn's grid plan for the city.

from 1800 to the city's consolidation in 1854, Philadelphia's population grew by 300 percent, though it consistently lagged behind the Commonwealth of Pennsylvania's growth and the growth of the United States after 1800.[3] The population of Philadelphia County, which included the city and the fast-growing outlying districts, increased by more than 50 percent between 1800 and 1820, while over the succeeding twenty years it expanded by an additional 33 percent.[4] Writing in 1829, Deborah Norris Logan commented on "the extraordinary building activity which have appeared in the northern sections" that seemed to her "like the building of an entire city at once."[5] By the mid-1850s, Philadelphia was no longer the "walking city" it had been in Franklin's day.[6] In 1800, the Pennsylvania Assembly divided the city into fourteen wards. Seven—Upper Delaware, Lower Delaware, High Street, Chestnut, Walnut, Dock, and New Market—extended from the Delaware River to Fourth Street, while the remaining seven stretched from Fourth Street to the Schuylkill River. By 1825, expansion west of Fourth Street necessitated new political divisions. That year, the Assembly pushed the boundaries of these seven wards west to Seventh Street and split New Market into two wards (Pine and New Market, divided at Pine Street), bringing the total number to fifteen. Additional westward expansion necessitated the division of Cedar Ward (between Spruce and Cedar Streets, west of Seventh Street) into three wards in 1846: Lombard (Seventh to Twelfth), Spruce (Twelfth to Sixteenth), and Cedar (Sixteenth to the Schuylkill River).[7] Nor was population growth limited to the city proper: several outlying areas were incorporated during the first two decades of the nineteenth century, a nod to their growth. These included Moyamensing (incorporated in 1812), Spring Garden (1813), and Kensington (1820). Each was a corporation governed by a board of commissioners, which led to a patchwork of local regulations.[8] These new areas did not uniformly continue Philadelphia's grid plan, so streets veered off to accommodate natural landmarks, existing buildings, and local topography.

One consequence of the county's population growth was the large-scale settlement in what is now West Philadelphia. A permanent bridge across the river at Market Street that opened in 1805 made commuting from the area into the city substantially easier (prior to this commuters had to take a ferry), and it was joined by a second bridge (the world's longest single-arch bridge, dubbed "the Colossus of Fairmount") in 1812.[9] In 1804, anticipating the Market Street bridge's opening, William Hamilton began subdividing his Woodlands estate in West Philadelphia.[10] In 1813, his heirs sold off a significant portion of the estate, opening the land to residential development and spurring the growth of West Philadelphia as a suburb. During the 1830s, the Powel family sold off portions of their land in West Philadelphia, forming the basis of today's Powelton Village. By midcentury, West Philadelphia, which became a borough in 1844 and a district seven years later, had a large population of tradesmen and taverns, which reflected the fact that the region's roads were a vital pathway to Pennsylvania's interior and to Baltimore.[11] The area remained largely rural until the end of the century. In her autobiography, Florence Kelley, daughter of Congressman William D. Kelley, recalled an anecdote about life in West Philadelphia during the 1860s: "At Thanksgiving time, while I was a babe in her arms, my Mother called the members of the household to the front windows to see a flock of tur-keys being driven into town to market for the holiday."[12]

At the same time, many Philadelphians abandoned the city's older areas along the Delaware River, and the buildings were gradually converted into stores, warehouses, and tenements.[13] This was not uniform across the area. In 1830, Chestnut Ward (east of Seventh between Market and Chestnut Streets) had the highest average per person tax assessment of any city ward and was home to several key institutions, including the Bank of North America, the US Mint, as well as some of the city's most impressive mansions.[14] Between 1826 and 1856, the city's best hotel, the United States Hotel, stood on the north side of Chestnut Street opposite the Second Bank of the United States.[15] In general, however, the area along the Delaware transitioned from a residential to a com-mercial and mercantile district to such a degree that in 1845, the *Public Led-ger* complained that "Chestnut, Market and the other streets occupied by our wholesale mercantile firms now present a deserted appearance after five o'clock in the afternoon."[16]

Philadelphians' abandonment of the oldest parts of the city during the middle quarter of the nineteenth century was the culmination of several trends. These buildings were among Philadelphia's oldest, and as the city shifted from shipping to manufacturing, the attraction of being next to the Delaware neces-sarily diminished.[17] Many professionals, by contrast, no longer lived in the spaces where they worked, preferring to live in houses west of Broad Street or in the suburbs.[18] This was aided by several fleets of omnibuses, or large, horse-drawn carriages that linked Philadelphia's commercial center with the expand-ing districts to the north, south, and west.[19] Many omnibuses departed from the Merchants' Exchange Building (Third Street, just north of Walnut), one of the city's key buildings (it was the nation's first stock market), and transported passengers along routes throughout the city and surrounding districts. The omnibuses were incredibly expensive, which meant few working-class Phila-delphians could ride them.[20] As a result, Philadelphia's workers were forced to live within walking distance of their places of employment.[21]

Population growth led to the proliferation of that most Philadelphian of insti-tutions, the row house.[22] Though row houses had existed in Philadelphia since Wil-liam Penn's time, large-scale construction of these iconic buildings began around 1800. In 1791, financier Robert Morris bought an entire city block, bounded by Chestnut Street to the north, Walnut Street to the south, and Seventh and Eighth Streets to the east and west. He planned to build the largest mansion in North America.[23] Financial reversals prevented him from completing the building (Mor-ris ended up in debtors' prison), and developer William Sansom bought the land at a sheriff sale. Sansom demolished the incomplete mansion and bisected the property with a road he named for himself. Thomas Carstairs, a Scottish architect and builder who migrated to Philadelphia in the early 1780s, constructed a row of twenty-two houses along Sansom Street's south side between 1800 and 1802. Other row house developments—including York Row (Walnut Street west of Seventh) and Franklin Row (Ninth Street between Walnut and Locust)—soon followed.[24] Philadelphia's unique ground rent system—under which home builders leased unimproved lots for long periods at nominal rent, and the proliferation of building and loan organizations (the first of which was founded in Philadelphia in 1831)—encouraged the construction of houses and contributed to Philadelphia becoming, by the 1870s, the "City of Homes."[25] The first directory for a US city was published in Philadelphia in 1785. *Macpherson's Directory, for the City and Suburbs of Philadelphia* listed residents' houses by nearby cross streets. Within a decade, directories listed house numbers, implying that the practice of numbering houses began during this period, though the process was hardly standardized, with alleys and minor streets being especially problematic.[26]

Though tourists visited Philadelphia in the eighteenth century, during the nineteenth century the city became a bona fide tourist destination.[27] On the one hand, visitors wanted to see historic sites, particularly those connected to the American Revolution. Samuel Clemens (better known by his pen name, Mark Twain), who lived and worked in the city in 1853 and 1854, noted in a letter to his borther, "Philadelphia is rich in Revolutionary associations."[28] On the other hand, Philadelphia was also famous for its cutting-edge technological and architectural achievements.[29] One popular destination was the city's famed Water Works. In his will, Benjamin Franklin left the city money to help fund a system for providing the city with water, and in 1799, the city's Select and Common Councils created the Watering Committee. This became an incredibly powerful organization that operated largely independent of the councils. In fact, its annual expenditures often accounted for half or more of Philadelphia's budget because, for public health reasons, the committee provided the water below cost.[30] The city pumped water through wooden (later iron) pipes from a building in Center Square (current site of City Hall) designed by Benjamin Latrobe.[31] This infrastructure, while not always perfect, made Philadelphia's water system the best in the United States at the time, and the heretofore neglected square became a point of civic pride and a hub of activity.[32] The region's growth soon rendered the Water Works inadequate. In 1812, the Watering Committee began constructing a new one along the Schuylkill's eastern banks in Fairmount, which was outside the city's limits.[33] In order for it to work, the Watering Committee dammed the Schuylkill to create a pool behind the pump house; it was an engineering marvel, the largest dam in the United States at that time.[34]

The new gravity-fed pump house commenced operation in 1815, and in that same year, the Watering Committee closed Latrobe's pump house. Thereafter, Center Square fell into disuse, and in 1826, the city demolished the shuttered pump house.[35] Like its predecessor, the Fairmount Water Works became a popular recreational space.[36] In the late 1820s the Watering Committee backfilled the stone quarry that William Penn had ordered constructed and created a public park known as South Garden.[37] In 1844, Philadelphia purchased Lemon Hill, merchant Henry Pratt's estate in Fairmount (originally part of Robert Morris's three-hundred-acre estate, the Hills). Pratt died in 1838, and his heirs were bankrupted by the Panic of 1837 and the ensuing depression. Philadelphia's purchase of Lemon Hill made the Water Works the country's largest urban park.[38] The usually dyspeptic Englishwoman Frances Trollope marveled at the Water Works, writing in 1832: "At a most beautiful point of the Schuylkill River the water has been forced up into a magnificent reservoir, ample and elevated enough to send it through the whole city. The vast yet simple machinery by which this is achieved is open to the public, who resort in such numbers to see it, that evening stages run from Philadelphia to Fair Mount. . . . It is, in truth, one of the very prettiest spots the eye can look upon."[39] Additional pumping stations opened (Spring Garden in 1844 and Kensington along the Delaware in 1851), and Philadelphia was so well supplied with water that residents routinely used it to wash their steps and sidewalks, amazing tourists.[40]

Philadelphia was also renowned for its botanical gardens and public green areas. One well-known garden was at the Gray's Ferry Tavern on the Schuylkill's western bank. The tavern itself dated to the early eighteenth century and hosted several notable guests, including members of the Continental Congress and the Constitutional Convention. Its garden included a greenhouse and several picturesque walks, though it entered a period of rapid decline after 1800 and by midcentury had closed. In addition, Philadelphians could enjoy McArran's Garden. Owned by John McArran, an avid horticulturist, the garden (on what is now John F. Kennedy Boulevard between Seventeenth and Eighteenth Streets) included a greenhouse and aviary. McArran's Garden was a popular retreat; vendors sold ice cream, and there were often fireworks displays. Thomas Smith's Labyrinth Garden on Arch Street between Fifteenth and Sixteenth Streets was another popular recreational destination, complete with evening illumination and instrumental music. Another garden, the Old Lebanon, was at Tenth and South Streets and was notable for a well-attended celebration of President Andrew Jackson's inauguration that included a bear roast.[41]

A macabre aspect of the city's growth was the creation of one of Philadelphia's best-known landmarks, Laurel Hill Cemetery. In 1836, several prominent Philadelphians—druggist Frederick Brown, businessman Nathan Dunn, former mayor Benjamin Wood Richards, and local polymath John Jay Smith—purchased Laurel, the country estate of local merchant Joseph Sims, and hired architect John Notman to design what became known as Laurel Hill Cemetery. They wanted to create a tranquil resting place undisturbed by Philadelphia's transformation to an industrial metropolis, and it quickly became a popular destination for tourists and locals alike. Writing in December 1848, journalist George G. Foster described it as "one of the most exquisitely beautiful gardens of the dead which ever the heart of affection conceived or the hand of taste embellished."[42] Laurel Hill soon had competition: Monument Cemetery opened in 1837. Located on North Broad Street at what is now Temple University's campus, Monument Cemetery featured a Gothic gatehouse and broad avenues named for George Washington, Benjamin Franklin, and the Marquis de Lafayette. In the 1950s Temple University acquired Monument Cemetery, moved the bodies to Montgomery County, and built a parking lot. The cemetery's headstones were used as the foundation for the Betsy Ross Bridge, which was then under construction.[43]

The city also remained a center of scientific innovation and medical education. In preparing for their expedition across North America, Meriwether Lewis and William Clark visited Philadelphia to consult with some of the nation's leading experts, including Dr. Benjamin Rush, anatomist Caspar Wistar, and botanist Benjamin Smith Barton. Dr. Philip Syng Physick, the father of American surgery, was one of the nation's most-sought-after medical experts and practiced out of his home on Cypress Street just east of Fourth Street. University of Pennsylvania (later Swarthmore College) professor of anatomy Joseph Leidy was a leading scientist of the age and the first man to solve a murder using a microscope. In 1812, a group of Philadelphia naturalists founded the Academy of Natural Sciences, and within a decade it established itself as the country's preeminent institution for the study of the natural world. The Franklin Institute, founded in 1824, became a leading promoter of applied science and industrial innovation, winning the first monetary grant from the federal government for scientific research. Within a generation, Philadelphia's scientific landscape expanded to include the Spring Garden Institute (1850) and the Wagner Free Institute of Science (1855).

Medical education continued flourishing in Philadelphia. In 1821, several dozen apothecaries established the Philadelphia College of Pharmacy, the first such institution in North America, and in 1852, pharmacists meeting in the city established the American Pharmaceutical Association. In 1825, several local doctors, including George McClellan (father of famed Civil War general George B. McClellan), founded Jefferson Medical College. In 1832, Quaker merchant James Wills Jr. bequeathed more than $100,000 to the city, stipulating that the money be used to treat the blind, indigent, and lame. Two years later, the Wills Eye Hospital opened at Eighteenth and Race. In 1855, the nation's first hospital for children, Children's Hospital of Philadelphia, opened its doors. In 1858, well-known physician Thomas D. Mütter donated his extensive collection of medical specimens to the College of Physicians of Philadelphia to form the basis of a museum to educate the public about medical science.[44] In 1848, the Homeopathic Medical College of Pennsylvania began operation, and, extraordinarily, in 1850, the Female Medical College (renamed the Woman's Medical College of Pennsylvania in 1867), only the second institution in the United States intended to provide women with medical training, opened its doors on Arch Street between Sixth and Seventh. Perhaps it is no surprise that when President Andrew Jackson needed a new pair of glasses in 1831, he turned to noted Philadelphia oculist John M. McCallister & Company, which was at 48 Chestnut Street and was the first optical shop opened in North America.[45] Another mark of Philadelphia's prominence in medicine was the number of medical journals published in the city, including the *American Journal of the Medical Sciences*, the *North American Medical and Surgical Journal*, the *American Journal of Dental Science*, and the *American Journal of Pharmacy*.[46]

The efflorescence of scientific journals was also a function of the fact that Philadelphia remained an important publishing center and was home to several leading periodicals. One consequence was that the city attracted several important American writers, including Charles Brockden Brown and Edgar Allan Poe. The latter briefly worked as an editor and contributor at *Burton's Gentleman's Magazine and American Monthly Review* while living in Philadelphia between 1838 and 1844, and he wrote some of his most famous short stories, including "The Fall of the House of Usher," "The Masque of the Red Death," "The Gold-Bug," and "The Murders in the Rue Morgue" in the city. While living in Philadelphia, Poe corresponded with Henry Wadsworth Longfellow, whose epic 1847 poem *Evangeline* describes the eighteenth-century experiences of the Acadians who fled to the city. Author Sarah Josepha Buell Hale, who wrote the nursery rhyme "Mary Had a Little Lamb," lived in Philadelphia and edited *Godey's Lady's Book*, the most widely circulated magazine in the United States in the decades before the Civil War. Poet Frances E. W. Harper, among the first Black women to be published in the United States, moved to Philadelphia in the mid-1850s to advance the abolitionist cause, and she lived in the city, off and on, for the rest of her life. The emergence of cheap paper and steam-powered printing presses in the first half of the nineteenth century dropped the costs of printing newspapers, and by the 1830s, Philadelphia was home to several, including the *Philadelphia Inquirer* (begun in 1829), the *Public Ledger* (1836), and the *North American* (1839). No wonder the *Philadelphia Album and Ladies Literary Portfolio* boasted in May 1831 that "Philadelphia is truly the Athens of America."[47]

The region was home to several literary societies, libraries, musical organizations, and museums, the latter of which were among the best in the United States.[48] Several of these date to the eighteenth century, but many others came into being during the first half of the nineteenth. In 1838, Philadelphia merchant and philanthropist Nathan Dunn operated a museum of Chinese culture at Ninth and Sansom that, for three years, educated Philadelphians about one of the city's main trading partners. At one point it shared a building with Charles Willson Peale's Philadelphia Museum, which displayed a fully assembled mastodon skeleton.[49] The Musical Fund Hall (between Eighth and Ninth on Locust Street) presented concerts, lectures, and other entertainments throughout the period. By 1830, the Philadelphia region hosted at least nine libraries serving various constituencies and was home to such prominent artists as portraitist Thomas Sully, fresco painter Nicola Monachesi, William Rush (often considered the first important American sculptor), landscape painter Thomas Birch, and famed Black painter David Bustill Bowser, among others. In 1829, the Pennsylvania Horticultural Society hosted the first Philadelphia Flower Show, which remains as of this writing the longest-running such event in the United States. Elizabeth Taylor Greenfield, a formerly enslaved singer nicknamed "The Black Swan," won worldwide renown for her voice and lived in the city. In 1819, portrait painter Bass Otis published the nation's first lithograph (a print created using a metal or stone plate), and twenty years later, Joseph Saxton, an inventor and watchmaker who constructed a clock for Independence Hall's steeple, took the oldest surviving photograph in US history, a picture of Central High School. During the 1820s, theater flourished in Philadelphia at the Walnut Street Theatre and the Chestnut Street Theatre, to the dismay of those who objected to plays because of their alleged threat to public morals. Perhaps due to the blossoming of theater in Philadelphia, the city produced Edwin Forrest, one of the nation's leading actors (the Forrest Theatre on Walnut Street is named for him).

These wonders were the by-products of the Industrial Revolution (ca. 1760 to ca. 1840), as machines supplanted human and animal power in the production and transportation of goods. Powering this revolution was steam, and Philadelphia was a leading center of innovation in this new technology, due in no small measure to Pennsylvania's abundance of two key raw materials: coal and iron ore. Anthracite coal, which is almost pure carbon (meaning it has the highest energy density of all coal) and gives off little smoke when burned, was discovered in northeastern Pennsylvania in 1791. In 1820, it was arriving in the city by the boatload along an expanding network of canals, and by midcentury Philadelphia exported more coal than any US city, shipping 1.5 million tons of anthracite and a million tons of bituminous annually.[50] In addition, Pennsylvania led the nation in iron and later steel production, with Philadelphia-based firms producing nearly one-quarter of the latter by 1840.[51] In August 1787, John Fitch demonstrated to members of the Constitutional Convention the world's first viable steamboat, which cruised along the Delaware River. By the middle of the nineteenth century, steamboats plied the river, connecting Philadelphia to towns and cities north and south.

Few devices are more closely associated with the Industrial Revolution than trains, and Philadelphia was a leader in locomotive technology. In 1805, inventor Oliver Evans piloted the first steam–engine–powered vehicle down Philadelphia's streets, and the region was home to the Mars Iron Works (Ninth and Race), which was the country's leading steam engine manufacturer during the 1810s (the factory burned down in 1819).[52] In 1825, Matthias Baldwin established a locomotive factory at the southwest corner of Broad and Spring Garden Streets in Fairmount that eventually grew into the world's largest producer of railroad locomotives. Another key manufacturer was the Norris Locomotive Works (on the former Bush Hill Estate, near the current site of the Free Library of Philadelphia's Central Branch, and founded in 1832 as the American Steam Carriage Company). In 1843, a former member of the Pennsylvania House of Representatives, Charles B. Trego, boasted, "So eminent is the character of our locomotive steam engines, that they are not only sent to most parts of the United States . . . but when the traveler in Russia, Austria, and even in England, examines with admiration the locomotive engine which has drawn him . . . over the rail roads of those distant countries, he finds the word *Philadelphia* engraved upon its side."[53] In 1832, Philadelphia's first railroad opened, providing service between Germantown and a depot at Ninth and Green Streets; two years later, service was extended to Norristown. Meanwhile, a group of businessmen chartered the Philadelphia and Reading Railroad in 1833 to compete against canals for the lucrative coal-carrying trade. Railroad construction proliferated during the late 1830s. By midcentury, the Philadelphia, Wilmington, and Baltimore Railroad had a depot at Eleventh and Market, while the West Chester line terminated at Broad near Race, and the Southwark Railroad's depot was just a block off the Delaware River on Queen Street.[54] Railroads substantially changed American society, and nothing could stand in their way: in 1837, the city razed the High Street market house, one of the city's oldest and more celebrated landmarks, to make way for a railroad.[55]

By 1825, New York had eclipsed Philadelphia as the country's leading international shipping center, for several reasons.[56] One was geography: Manhattan was closer to the sea than Philadelphia, and navigating the Hudson River was easier than sailing up the Delaware. Another was federal government policy:

the Embargo Act of 1807, signed into law by President Thomas Jefferson, was designed to punish the British and French who were then at war with one another and menacing American shipping. This act and the subsequent Non-Intercourse Act drove the United States into recession and particularly hit seaport cities like Philadelphia. As a result, the value of goods, in both absolute numbers and in proportion to the nation's total imports, arriving in Philadelphia declined.[57] By restricting trading opportunities, the Embargo Act encouraged Philadelphians to invest money in local industry. Quaker merchant Thomas P. Cope noted in May 1808, "Money is abundant. The suppression of commerce has thrown large sums out of employment."[58] Redirecting into industry money previously invested in shipping helped turn Philadelphia into one of the country's most diverse manufacturing centers by 1860.[59] In general, the city's products were consumed locally or regionally, so Philadelphia was relatively less connected to the wider world than New York, fostering an insular and localist culture. Despite its declining international commerce, Philadelphia remained a key shipbuilding center. In 1801, the federal government established the Navy Yard, and in 1815 it launched its first ship, the USS *Franklin*. One visitor to Philadelphia noted that the city's Navy Yard was "one of the best" in the United States and "is celebrated for the excellence and superiority of the marine steamers built by her shipwrights."[60]

Another factor aiding New York's growth into the nation's economic capital was the Erie Canal, which connected New York City to towns along the state's northern edge as far as Lake Erie. Spurred by the War of 1812, which demonstrated the weakness of the United States' manufacturing and transportation infrastructures, enthusiasm for "internal improvements" (large-scale public works projects designed to improve the country's infrastructure) was high in the late 1810s and early 1820s.[61] The Erie Canal, the world's second-longest canal when it opened in 1825, cut the costs of transporting goods to New York City by more than 90 percent. The canal's effect on Philadelphia's economy was immediate and dramatic, with exports from the City of Brotherly Love dropping by nearly 50 percent over the next fifteen years.[62]

This is not to say that Philadelphians ignored canal building. As early as the 1790s, Philadelphians had proposed building canals to transport goods and crops more efficiently to and from Pennsylvania's hinterland. In 1815, the Union Canal Company began building locks and dams to make the Schuylkill navigable, eventually reaching Port Carbon in current-day Schuylkill County. The Schuylkill Navigation Company's construction of a canal, locks, and dam in 1818 on the river just north of Philadelphia spurred the growth of Manayunk (originally called Flat Rock), converting it nearly overnight into a manufacturing center of national importance. In 1819, John Towers established Manayunk's first mill, powered by water rushing through the canal, and by 1830, Philadelphia became the United States' leading textile manufacturing city.[63] Thus, by the 1820s, the Schuylkill River had become a key waterway for transporting raw materials to the Delaware Valley and conveying finished goods to the commonwealth's hinterlands.[64]

In addition, Pennsylvania expended considerable effort and money to counter the economic threat posed by the Erie Canal. In 1826, the Pennsylvania Assembly appropriated funding to construct the Main Line of Public Works, an east–west transportation network between Philadelphia and Pittsburgh composed of three canals and two railroad lines. The five sections—the Philadelphia and Columbia Railroad, the Eastern Division Canal, the Juniata Division Canal, the Allegheny Portage Railroad, and the Western Division Canal—opened between 1828 and 1834.[65] The Philadelphia and Columbia Railroad spurred the growth of Philadelphia's western suburbs (which became known as the Main Line). Yet for all the time and money spent, the Main Line of Public Works proved underwhelming. Although it more strongly connected Pittsburgh to Philadelphia, thereby unifying the state, it never seriously challenged New York's economic dominance. As one contemporary noted in 1852, many of Philadelphia's "most astute and enterprising merchants [have] removed to New York."[66] Unable to arrest New York's dominance of foreign commerce, Philadelphia transformed itself from an international shipping hub to a workshop converting raw materials from Pennsylvania's hinterland into finished products that served a mostly regional market.[67]

A related development was the fact that by midcentury, Philadelphia had lost its role as the hub of American banking. Though the city was still a center of American banking innovation (the nation's first savings bank, the Philadelphia Saving [later Savings] Fund Society, or PSFS, opened in 1816 on Sixth Street between Market and Chestnut), Philadelphia's status as the US financial capital was due in large part to the presence of the First Bank of the United States. However, the Democratic-Republicans (led by Thomas Jefferson) who dominated the federal government after 1800 made killing the bank one of their top priorities. When the charter of the First Bank of the United States expired in 1811, Vice President George Clinton broke a tie in the Senate, voting against a bill renewing it. Prominent Philadelphia merchant Stephen Girard purchased most of the institution's assets and opened what came to be known as Girard's (later Girard) Bank.

In 1812, the United States declared war on Great Britain, and Philadelphia played a key role in the conflict. Though political tension between the Federalist-dominated Select Council and the Democratic-Republican-controlled Common Council prevented the city from undertaking a coordinated defense, several

Philadelphians volunteered to fight, and Colonel Winfield Scott (later commanding general of the US Army) established a training camp in the northern
portion of West Philadelphia.[68] In addition, two local plumbers, Thomas Sparks
and John Bishop, produced lead shot for the federal government at their shot
tower. The two men dropped molten lead down the center of their 142-foot-tall
tower located at what is today 129-131 Carpenter Street. As the lead fell, it formed
perfectly round balls that could be fired from muskets. The city even housed
some British prisoners of war, though these escaped from the Arch Street Prison
in April 1814.[69]

While the War of 1812 spurred Philadelphia's economy, it was a disaster for
the United States: the British captured Washington, DC, and burned the city,
leading to widespread fears they would march on Philadelphia.[70] Moreover, the
country lacked a national bank that could effectively help the federal government raise needed money (despite Girard's and other local bankers' willing-
ness to sell bonds and lend the government huge sums of money). Cope acidly
noted in September 1814 that "the Bank of the U. States . . . had it not been put
down, could have afforded great facility to the fiscal concerns of the nation."[71]
Cope was not alone in this opinion; as a result, in 1816 Congress passed and
President James Madison (reluctantly) signed a bill chartering the Second Bank
of the United States for twenty years. Headquartered in Philadelphia, it could
not stave off a depression caused by the Panic of 1819, which only fueled criticism of the bank.[72]

A concomitant development was democratization, which reshaped America's
political, economic, and cultural landscape. The Revolution left a complicated
legacy that Americans were still grappling with in the early nineteenth century.[73] Associated with first the Jeffersonian Democratic-Republicans and then
the Jacksonian Democrats, democratization eroded the deference that lower-
class people had traditionally paid to upper-class people and increased calls for
more participation in government, alarming elites who sought to maintain their
social and political positions.[74] The trend toward democratization was undeniable: starting in 1839, Philadelphia's mayor was popularly elected, and in 1837, the
Pennsylvania Assembly convened a convention to draft a new, more democratic
state constitution. Philadelphia sent several delegates, including former member
of the House of Representatives John Sergeant, Philadelphia City Councilman
William M. Meredith, and journalist Thomas Earle. The new constitution, which
the commonwealth's voters approved in 1838, enfranchised free white men over
age twenty-one, but it also explicitly disenfranchised all Black voters. This was
no coincidence: democratization went hand in hand with racialization. Now,
instead of arguing that economic status qualified a man to vote, qualification
rested on race (white) and gender (male). Moreover, the new constitution limited

Philadelphia's representation in the state Senate to four members. As a result, Philadelphia, which accounted for one-fifth of Pennsylvania's population, was represented by only one-eighth of the commonwealth's senators.[75] This had much to do with the fact that Philadelphians tended to vote Federalist long after that party had ceased to exist nationally, which put the city at odds with most of the commonwealth.[76] In fact, during the so-called Era of Good Feelings (1815–1825), the United States was essentially a one-party system, with members of Jefferson's Democratic-Republicans filling nearly all federal offices.

This began changing in the mid-1820s with the emergence of what became called the Second Party System and is closely tied to the rise of Andrew Jackson. Jackson was a military hero whose victory at the Battle of New Orleans in 1815 earned him a national reputation and made him a serious candidate for the presidency. He was one of four men who ran in the presidential election of 1824, which splintered the Democratic-Republicans into two factions, the National Republicans and Jacksonian Democrats. None of the four candidates earned the requisite number of electoral votes, so the House of Representatives decided the election. The House selected Secretary of State John Adams despite the fact that he had won fewer popular votes than Jackson. Jackson was outraged by this and spent the next four years planning his campaign for the 1828 presidential election, which he won.

Jackson was a man of formidable passions, and he carried a grudge against the Bank of the United States for (he believed) causing the Panic of 1819, which had nearly ruined him. Jackson vetoed a bill rechartering the bank in 1832 and the following year tried to starve it of funds by depriving it of government money. Nicholas Biddle, president of the Second Bank, responded by calling in the bank's loans, which drained the economy of currency and triggered a recession.[77] This move, designed to prove the need for the bank, did little to earn it many admirers and only hardened Jackson's determination to see it destroyed. The Bank War thus became the crucible of attachment to the Democratic Party and crystallized Jackson's opponents into a political party, the Whigs. The Whig-controlled Senate censured Jackson in 1834 over his actions in the Bank War (the first time in US history that the Senate censured a sitting president), but he did not back down. In 1836, following the expiration of the Second Bank's federal charter, the Pennsylvania Assembly chartered it as a state bank, though this made it a far less powerful institution than it had been. During their period, Philadelphia occasionally elected Jacksonian Democrats, though the Bank War (and its threat to one of the city's leading institutions) meant Philadelphians usually preferred anti-Jacksonian candidates. By contrast, the fast-growing districts were overwhelmingly Democratic, which intensified antagonism between the city and its suburbs and helps explain the city's disenfranchisement.[78]

Jackson's policies culminated in the Panic of 1837, a financial crisis that sparked a catastrophic depression that lasted until the mid-1840s.[79] Banks in New York and Philadelphia stopped redeeming paper money for specie (that is, gold coin), an extremely unpopular move. In 1841, the Assembly mandated that banks resume specie redemptions or see their charters voided. This law forced the Bank of the United States into bankruptcy, resulting in its closure. That disrupted Pennsylvania's economy and shook Philadelphia's claim to being the nation's banking capital. Job R. Tyson, a Philadelphia lawyer and Whig politician, compared the event to an earthquake, claiming "the distress and dismay could not have been more painful and pervading."[80] British novelist Charles Dickens, who visited the city in 1842, said the bank's closure cast "a gloom on Philadelphia, under the depressing effect of which, it yet labored," while in 1844, Thomas P. Cope reflected, "When the Bank failed, our commerce & good name took forthwith a downward course—to rise, I fear, no more."[81]

These changes affected Philadelphia's social structure. As international shipping grew comparatively less important to Philadelphia's economy, the city's professionals—lawyers, doctors, and ministers—displaced merchants in controlling the levers of political power and cultural prestige in Philadelphia.[82] Descendants of the city's most prominent families were overrepresented in law, banking, medicine, and other professions, creating an almost unbreachable social and cultural divide that distinguished Philadelphia from its competitor cities and reinforced its insularity.[83] A nineteenth-century aphorism had it that Philadelphians asked about strangers, "Who was his grandfather?" while Bostonians asked, "How much does he know?" and New Yorkers asked, "How much is he worth?"[84] In *American Notes for General Circulation*, Dickens described an encounter with a Philadelphia Quaker that illustrates the truth of that aphorism: "I made acquaintance . . . with a mild and modest young quaker, who opened the discourse by informing me . . . that his grandfather was the inventor of cold-drawn castor oil. I mention the circumstance here, thinking it probable that this is the first occasion on which the valuable medicine in question was ever used as a conversational aperient."[85] Dickens went on to call Philadelphia "more provincial than Boston or New York."[86] The pace of life in Philadelphia struck visitors as slower than New York as well. Newspaperman George G. Foster noted in one of his "Philadelphia in Slices" columns, "In New-York every inhabitant goes as if an invisible somebody was after him with a sharp stick: in Philadelphia we take our time. We do not saunter, but we do not gallop. We are neither indolent nor insane."[87]

Meanwhile, the Industrial Revolution reshaped work, shifting production from home workshops to factories (which employed dozens or even hundreds of men), and eroded the traditional control over workers. A long-term process that took decades to complete, it was disconcerting and led to several confrontations between laborers and their employers.[88] It was not uncommon for factory employees to work twelve to fifteen hours per day, often in abysmal conditions, and many workers' wages declined during the 1830s and 1840s.[89] While life expectancy for Philadelphia's wealthy citizens improved during the first half of the nineteenth century because they were able to relocate to less densely inhabited areas of the city, the same could not be said of the region's poor.[90] Work-related deaths and injuries were common in the largely unregulated factories, leading one visitor to remark, "It would seem the *lame*, the *blind*, and *diseased* of all nations flock to Philadelphia. In walking the streets, you meet some with one arm, others with one eye, some with no eyes, some limping, some with wooden legs."[91] Industrialization also aggravated the residential segregation that emerged during the last third of the eighteenth century, fostering the proliferation of ethnic and racial ghettos.[92] Laborers lived at the edge of penury, and conditions in the city's poorer areas were awful and unsanitary, with high-population density and lack of facilities contributing to illness.[93] In 1830, New Market Ward (east of Seventh between Pine and South Streets) had the lowest average tax assessment ($81 per person) but the highest population of any of the city's wards. To put that in some perspective, the next lowest average per person tax assessment ($121) occurred in North Mulberry Ward (west of Seventh Street to the Schuylkill between Vine and Race Streets), and every other ward had average per person tax assessments at least double New Market Ward's.[94]

Philadelphia was at the forefront of labor organizing in the nineteenth century, in no small part because of the advanced state of its transformation to industrial capitalism.[95] In 1799, the city's journeymen shoemakers made the first attempt to collectively bargain with their employers and were locked out of their shops for the effort. In 1805, several journeymen shoemakers struck for seven weeks before being indicted by a grand jury for conspiracy. At the subsequent trial, the strikers were found guilty and each fined $80. This chilled labor activism in Philadelphia for more than a decade, but beginning in the 1820s, the region's workers regularly struck for higher wages and improved working conditions.[96] Between 1821 and 1840, workers in Philadelphia and the neighboring districts struck at least seventy-five times for higher wages and shorter work-days.[97] Sometimes these confrontations turned violent, as in the 1843 weavers' riot. In that case, striking weavers in Kensington violently attacked local weavers who refused to join them. When the sheriff arrived to restore order, the rioters beat him and his posse. The riot was only put down when the sheriff called out several companies of the local militia.[98] The agitation for employees' rights even led to the formation of the short-lived Working Men's Party in 1828, which ran candidates in local, state, and federal elections until 1831 and promoted "the interests and support[ed] the claims of the Working People."[99] Pennsylvania's workers won a major victory when, in March 1848, the Assembly passed a bill limiting workdays to ten hours. Yet tension between capitalists and workers remained, periodically flaring into violence.

The proliferation of factories led to increased air and water pollution. In 1832, Deborah Norris Logan described Manayunk, one of the region's premier industrial centers, as "littered, dirty, chaotic and with a manufacturing population."[100] Though laws against pollution existed, they were seldom enforced, in part because of the weakness of municipal government prior to the 1854 consolidation.[101] Deborah Norris Logan complained in 1829 that "the Third Street entrance into the city is particularly obnoxious . . . [due] to slaughter houses, blue dye and loose dirt and mud."[102] The city remained populated by animals, including hogs, pigs, dogs, goats, and, in at least one case, an orangutan, all of which did little for public health.[103] Indoor plumbing was rare during the first half of the nineteenth century, with most Philadelphians relying on outhouses (which contaminated groundwater) and chamber pots, which (when not simply dumped into the street) were emptied at several "poudrette pits" (essentially open pits for dumping human waste) outside the city.[104] While Philadelphia's declining role in international trade made the outbreaks of Caribbean diseases less frequent, there were several outbreaks of typhus (caused by contaminated drinking water) during this period.[105] In 1832, Philadelphia, like several cities across the globe, was ravaged by a cholera outbreak that killed nearly one thousand people, though the death rate in the City of Brotherly Love was substantially lower than in New York, likely because of the city's cleaner water supply.[106]

Fire remained a serious problem, with one visitor describing it as "very partial to Philadelphia."[107] Though the city and surrounding districts had several volunteer fire companies, these often contributed to the devastation caused by conflagrations. Writing in 1843, Cope despaired, "This volunteer system, once so efficient in the hands of respectable citizens, is found no longer to answer."[108] The city's fire companies, which had emerged in the eighteenth century to put out fires and provide conviviality for their (usually) upper-class members, became indistinguishable from gangs (which were rampant in the city and districts).[109] The companies competed with one another, and this competition often led to violent confrontations while the nearby buildings were engulfed by flames.[110] Noted folklorist and humorist Charles Godfrey Leland, recalling this era in his memoirs, described the firemen of the era as "fighting freely with pistols, knives, iron spanners, and slung shot, whatever they met, whether at fires or in the streets."[111] The problem was so acute that in 1848, the Assembly passed an act empowering the Court of Quarter Sessions (which had jurisdiction over minor complaints and all but the most serious criminal cases) to disband any fire company that rioted in Philadelphia County.[112] In 1870, Philadelphia's city councils eliminated the volunteer companies and organized a municipal fire department, which went into service the following year.[113]

The transition to industrial capitalism broke down the apprentice system, creating a large pool of unsupervised youths who were frequently unemployed and often poor, which contributed to the endemic violence in Philadelphia during the first half of the nineteenth century.[114] In 1800, it was not unheard of for young men to duel near the city, though this seems to have become less common by midcentury.[115]

Celebrating the New Year by firing guns remained a common practice, sometimes with catastrophic results.[116] Crime, ranging from petty theft to murder, remained a major preoccupation for Philadelphians during this period, with many perceiving that it was increasing.[117] The city was convulsed by several riots during the 1830s and 1840s.[118] Leland reflected in his memoirs, "Who shall ever write a history of Philadelphia from the Thirties to the end of the Fifties will record a popular period of turbulence and outrages so extensive as to now appear almost incredible."[119] An 1842 lithograph, "A View of the City of Brotherly Love," captured the tone of Philadelphia during this period: in the foreground, a Black woman viciously beats a white woman while their boys fight off to one side. On the left side of the panel, a volunteer fire company douses a group of citizens, ignoring the burning Pennsylvania Hall just across the street. The rest of the cartoon depicts various fights and drunken melees, all while William Penn looks down on the scene in disgust.[120] In 1844, the Pennsylvania Assembly mandated that the city and several surrounding suburbs create police forces with a ratio of at least one officer for every 150 residents. Philadelphia was not unique in this regard; New York and Boston created uniformed police forces in 1845 and 1846, respectively.[121] In 1854, the Assembly created a unified police force for Philadelphia and the various surrounding districts, which contributed to a sharp decline in the number of riots.[122]

One source of violence was the perennial tension between native-born Philadelphians and immigrants. Though Philadelphia continued attracting immigrants during the first half of the nineteenth century, New York, Boston, and even New Orleans became more attractive destinations for immigrants after 1800. As a result, by midcentury the proportion of Philadelphia's population that was foreign born was lower than the median percentage for American cities, though it remained an ethnically and racially heterogeneous city.[123] The largest group of immigrants to Philadelphia during the first half of the nineteenth century was Irish. Following Britain's crushing of the Irish Rebellion of 1798, many Irish people fled to the United States, with a great many settling in Philadelphia. During the 1840s, as famine overtook Ireland, Irish immigration to Philadelphia increased, and by 1860, Irish immigrants made up approximately 18 percent of the county's population (25 percent in some Southwark, Moyamensing, and Kensington wards).[124]

Irish immigrants faced considerable discrimination in Philadelphia. Cope belittled them, writing, "Trained in the sinks of vicious & hardened mendicity in [Ireland], they at once set to begging on their arrival here & often become a heavy charge on our charity, filling our streets with clamorous appeals & our alms houses with unproductive, haggard pauperism."[125] Irish immigrants were frequently forced to take the lowest-status and lowest-paid jobs, putting them in direct conflict with the region's Black population.[126] Antipathy toward Irish immigrants coalesced in the nativist movement, so called because its adherents, self-styled "native Americans" (white people born in the United States), sought to raise the bar for becoming a US citizen. In 1837, a group of nativists met in Germantown and formed an group to advocate for increasing to twenty-one years the waiting period for immigrants to become citizens. Seven years later, nativist and temperance advocate Lewis Charles Levin was elected to represent Pennsylvania's First Congressional District (which included a small portion of the city), a seat he held for three terms. Nativism was hardly new; in the eighteenth century, some Philadelphians deplored German immigrants' allegedly improper political influence. Democratization made these concerns more acute by increasing immigrants' access to voting and tying suffrage to race and gender rather than to property. Doing so increased their political influence, antagonizing some native-born Americans. In 1844, Cope sputtered to his diary, "The indigent poor & discontented of Europe are constantly arriving among us & exercise no small influence at our ballot boxes."[127] There were violent confrontations between Irish immigrants and so-called native Americans in 1828, 1831, 1842, 1843, and 1844. The last of these, the so-called Bible Riots of 1844, were the worst.[128]

Dovetailing with nativism was anti-Catholic bigotry, which had a long history among Protestants. Unlike in the eighteenth century, most Irish immigrants to the United States during the nineteenth century were Catholic, which led to the creation of new parishes, the construction of new churches, and in 1808 the establishment of the Catholic See of Philadelphia.[129] In the United States, anti-Catholic rhetoric reflected the fear that Catholicism, which was headed by a monarch (the pope), was inimical to republicanism and thus a threat to the country. The democratic impulses of the age magnified Catholic immigrants' political power, arousing some Protestants' fears of a Catholic plot to take over the country. In late 1842, several of the city's Protestant ministers formed the American Protestant Association, which committed itself to aggressively combating the "errors of Popery" and to "awaken the attention of the community to the dangers which threaten the liberties, and the public and domestic institutions, of these United States from the assaults of Romanism."[130]

Protestants responded with a variety of policies designed to "Americanize" Catholics, such as mandating that public school teachers read selections from the Bible to their classes. In 1838, Pennsylvania's legislature mandated that schools use the King James Bible. In November 1842, Philadelphia's Catholic bishop, Francis Kenrick, successfully persuaded the Board of Controllers of the Philadelphia Public Schools to allow Catholic students to read the Douay–Rheims Bible, a translation approved by the Catholic Church. This concession generated some nativist pushback but no violence. Approximately a year later, however, a rumor circulated through Kensington that a Catholic school director, Hugh Clark, was trying to abolish Bible readings altogether. Kenrick stoked the controversy by issuing a public statement asserting it was inconsistent with church law for Catholics to participate in religious exercises with non-Catholics, seemingly repudiating the concessions offered by the Board of Controllers in 1842. Cope, who was himself anti-Catholic, drolly noted, "There is a good deal of excitement on the subject."[131]

On May 3, 1844, members of the nativist American Republican Party (not to be confused with the Republican Party, which emerged in 1854) held a rally in Kensington and were attacked by a gang of Irish locals. Three days later, American Republicans convened another rally at a nearby market, and fighting broke out between nativists and Irish. The conflict devolved into a melee, with Kensington residents shooting at nativists from building windows, and the latter attacking several Catholics' houses and the Sisters of Charity seminary. On May 7, a mob of nativists marched into Kensington, again provoking armed conflict. The nativists burned several buildings and homes owned by Catholics, and the violence only ended when a division of the state militia marched into the area to quell the disorder. This, as it turned out, was only a break in the fighting, not the end: on May 8, nativists again attacked Catholic-owned buildings in Kensington, burning down St. Michael's Catholic Church, though they did not attack the nearby German Catholic church then under construction. Lawyer and essayist Sidney George Fisher called the riot "the most dangerous & violent we have had yet," but the violence abated, at least temporarily.[132]

That July, American Republicans planned a march through Southwark, ostensibly in celebration of Independence Day. Fearing violence, Governor David R. Porter authorized the stationing of militia troops around St. Philip Neri's Church (Queen Street just east of Second). There was no violence on July 4, but, incensed by the delivery of muskets from the Frankford Arsenal to the church, a large nativist mob gathered outside it on July 5. At the mob's behest, Sheriff Morton McMichael removed a dozen muskets from the church, but the mob was unsatisfied. McMichael acquiesced to their demands that they be allowed to search the church, whereupon several dozen additional firearms were discovered. Fearing the consequences of that news becoming public, just after midnight on May 6, General George Cadwalader of the state militia ordered the crowd to leave; when that did not happen, the sheriff dispatched a 150-man posse to forcibly disperse the mob. Thereafter, Cadwalader augmented his force, stationing three cannons outside the church. Cadwalader arrested former congressman Charles Naylor after the latter interfered with the militia's efforts to disperse the crowd. On July 7, a crowd formed around the church demanding Naylor's release and threatening the building with a cannon. After Naylor was released, the crowd attacked the church, even going so far as to cannonade the building. Militiamen shot at the crowd, causing it to disperse. That evening, reinforcements arrived with orders to clear the streets. Violent clashes broke out, with militiamen taking fire from windows and being cannonaded. Eventually, the militiamen got the upper hand and restored calm by the morning of July 8, but the cost was high: more than a dozen people lost their lives during the fight, and scores were injured.

Another source of violence was racism. By the outbreak of the Civil War, Philadelphia was home to the second-largest population of free Black people in the United States and the largest north of the Mason–Dixon Line.[133] In 1808, Black people accounted for approximately 11 percent of the city's population, though this declined to just over 7 percent by the mid-1830s.[134] Most Black Philadelphians lived in the vicinity of South and Water Streets, Sixth and Lombard, or in Southwark and Moyamensing, which by 1820 was 25 percent Black. In 1846, the Assembly divided Cedar Ward to create two predominantly Irish wards with a mostly Black ward in between.[135]

There was a small Black elite in Philadelphia that included men such as Francis Johnson, who earned a fortune and international fame as a composer and bandleader; Robert Bogle, a wealthy and respected caterer; and James Forten, a sailmaker and businessman who became one of the city's wealthiest residents (white or Black). In general, however, the region's Black people were extremely poor (and got poorer—and more visibly poor—during this period).[136] Black novelist Frank J. Webb, a grandson of former vice president Aaron Burr, depicted the deteriorating conditions of Philadelphia's Black community in his 1857 novel, *The Garies and Their Friends*, evoking the poverty, violence, and discrimination that confronted the city's Black residents.[137] Though fiction, its depiction of Black life in Philadelphia accurately reflected conditions. Cope noted in 1848 that Moyamensing's Black people were "huddled together in small rooms & are ragged, filthy & covered with vermin."[138] Members of Philadelphia's Black elite generally disdained poor Black people, in part because they believed poor Black people lived down to white Philadelphians' worst prejudices.[139] However, wealth and status could not shield elite Black people from the discrimination that was the rule in Philadelphia and that got worse in the first half of the nineteenth century.[140]

In absolute terms, the total number of free Black people in Philadelphia grew by about 30 percent (which was faster than the increase of Pennsylvania's Black population). That trend did not escape white Philadelphians' notice: in 1819, several petitioned the Pennsylvania Assembly begging for a legislative remedy to the fact that "the number of blacks has increased to an alarming extent" in Philadelphia.[141] Black people (wealthy and poor) were prohibited from riding the city's omnibuses (exceptions were made for servants), and they were often prohibited from attending public exhibitions or only permitted admittance during certain hours.[142] Beginning in 1828, caricaturist Edward W. Clay published a series of prints known as *Life in Philadelphia* that viciously mocked Black people's attempts to mimic upper-class dress and patterns of speech.[143] In 1838, Pennsylvania adopted a new constitution that limited voting to free white male citizens, depriving Black men of suffrage (women were already ineligible to vote under the constitution of 1790).[144] Under an 1854 law, the commonwealth's schools were segregated by race (this law was declared unconstitutional by the Court of Common Pleas in 1880 and amended to outlaw segregation).[145] Even the Pennsylvania Abolition Society did not admit Black members until 1842, a measure of the racism held even by white opponents of slavery, though other abolition societies, such as the Pennsylvania Anti-Slavery Society and the Philadelphia Female Anti-Slavery Society, included Black and white members.

That was far from the worst of it: in the 1830s and 1840s, white racists provoked several riots and committed myriad acts of anti-Black terrorism, such as the attempted burning of churches and of the city's Black orphanage.[146] In August 1834, a riot broke out when a small group of whites and Black people got into a fight over a carousel called the Flying Horses that had recently been erected near South and Seventh Streets. The following night, whites attacked Black people in the vicinity of the original fight, destroying the carousel, a Black church, and several homes.[147] In 1838, a white mob burned Pennsylvania Hall, a newly constructed venue for abolitionist speakers at Sixth and Haines Streets, because it hosted the second annual Anti-Slavery Convention of American Women.[148] In 1840, a Black man who was likely insane killed a night watchman in Southwark. The evening after the watchman's funeral, a mob of angry whites planned to riot in the Black neighborhood of southeastern Philadelphia and were only stopped because the city's mayor, John Swift, arrested the mob's ringleader.[149] In August 1842, a white mob rampaged for two days, attacking members of the Negro Moyamensing Temperance Society and torching several buildings. The mob attacked police officers trying to make arrests and were only stopped by the militia, which was belatedly dispatched to end the riot.[150] In mid-October 1849, members of a white gang known as the Killers torched the California House, a tavern at Sixth and St. Mary Streets owned by a Black man and his white wife. Apparently, the Killers believed that a Black person had shot one of the white men who was menacingly dragging a flaming cart through a Black neighborhood and decided to take their revenge on the California House, igniting a blaze that claimed several lives.[151]

Racism was not limited to overt acts of violence against Black Philadelphians and their property. Given Philadelphia's status as a leading center of scientific innovation and research, it is perhaps not surprising that the city would play a leading role in disseminating "race science," or the pseudoscientific study of racial differences and categories. One of the leading practitioners was Dr. Samuel George Morton, a Quaker physician who taught at the Philadelphia Medical College and amassed the world's largest collection of human skulls (chillingly called "American Golgotha"), which he used to "prove" intellectual differences between racial groups (who, he argued, represented different species).[152] Based on this grisly collection, in 1839 Morton published the first volume of *Crania Americana, or, A Comparative View of the Skulls of Various Aboriginal Nations of North and South America*, which concluded that white people were innately more intelligent than nonwhite people and led to him later being dubbed the "father of scientific racism."[153] Morton's research cast a long shadow: his collection was donated to the University of Pennsylvania in 1966, and some items from it were displayed in a Penn Museum classroom until 2020.[154]

Increasingly excluded from white society, Black people continued forming their own institutions, such as separate fraternal organizations and educational institutions.[155] One example was the Benjamin Banneker Institute, a debating and literary society founded in 1854. Headquartered on Eleventh Street just north of Lombard and named for the self-taught Black mathematician who helped survey Washington, DC, the institute provided elite Black people the opportunity to engage in intellectual activities.[156] There was also the Institute for Colored Youth (ICY), which later became Cheyney University. Founded in 1837 and located on Lombard Street west of Seventh, the ICY became the city's leading Black educational institution, offering a classical education to the children of Philadelphia's Black elite.[157] In 1844, Philadelphia's Black community established a lodge of the Grand United Order of Odd Fellows at Twelfth and Spruce Streets, only the third Black Odd Fellows lodge in the United States. Black Philadelphians also established separate churches, including the First

African Baptist Church in 1809, the First African Presbyterian Church (Seventh and Bainbridge), and in 1834, the first Black Lutheran congregation in the United States, St. Paul's Evangelical Lutheran. Black churches played an important role in the abolitionist movement: in 1830 Mother Bethel AME hosted the first Colored Convention, which sought to mobilize Black Americans to address issues facing the community. Though similar conventions were held in other cities, Philadelphia remained the movement's hub for several years, reflecting the importance of the city's Black community.

In the face of local and national racial tensions, Philadelphia played a leading role in the abolitionist movement. In 1827, several Philadelphia Quakers organized the Free Produce Society of Pennsylvania, which called for boycotting any goods produced by slave labor.[158] In 1833, a convention of Black and white abolitionists in Philadelphia formed the American Anti-Slavery Society, which was joined a few years later by the Pennsylvania State Anti-Slavery Society (PSAS). Almost immediately, the PSAS began publishing the *National Enquirer, and Constitutional Advocate of Universal Liberty*, an abolitionist newspaper that soon changed its name to the *Pennsylvania Freeman*, for which noted Quaker poet and abolitionist John Whittier Greenleaf briefly served as editor.[159] One reason Philadelphia was so attractive to abolitionists was the potent symbolism of the city's revolutionary history. On August 19, 1844, Frederick Douglass, who had escaped enslavement just six years before and was a rising star on the abolitionist speaking circuit, delivered his "Slaveholder's Sermon," a bitterly sarcastic attack on the position that the Bible justified enslavement, in the yard of Independence Hall.[160]

Douglass was no stranger to Philadelphia: he, like many other Black people escaping enslavement, transited through Philadelphia, which was a key stop on the Underground Railroad, a secret system of loosely connected safehouses, or "stations," along various routes from the South to the North.[161] As early as 1780, Philadelphia's Black community, aided by sympathetic whites, assisted enslaved people in escaping.[162] Pennsylvania's southern border, the Mason–Dixon Line, demarcated slave and free states, virtually guaranteeing that Philadelphia would become an important stop on the Underground Railroad. Several extant buildings, including Mother Bethel AME Church, St. George's United Methodist Church, Belmont Mansion (Fairmount Park), abolitionists William and Harriet Purvis's house (1601 Mount Vernon Street), and Samuel and Jennett Johnson's home (6306 Germantown Avenue) were Underground Railroad stops. As a key Underground Railroad site, Philadelphia saw several daring escapes, including that of Henry Box Brown, a Virginia slave who in 1849 arranged to have himself mailed in a wooden crate to members of the Philadelphia Vigilance Committee, a mixed-race group of abolitionists who assisted escapees with securing work and housing The Underground Railroad's most famous "engineer," Harriet Tubman, settled in Philadelphia in 1849 and used the city as a base for more than a dozen forays into the South to free enslaved Black people.[163]

With the success of the Underground Railroad, the kidnapping and enslavement of northern Black people increased dramatically. The legal prohibition of importing enslaved people into the United States after 1808 meant enslavers had to turn to other sources to meet their never-ending demand for labor.[164] Thus was born the internal slave trade, which was given official sanction in 1793, when Congress passed the Fugitive Slave Act, which created legal mechanisms for enslavers to recapture former enslaved people. Under the law's terms, enslavers or their agents could present escapees before "any Judge of the Circuit or District Courts of the United States, residing or being within the State, or before any magistrate of a county, city, or town corporate." The judge or magistrate then determined if the Black person in question was, in fact, an escaped slave.

As a result, Philadelphia's Black people enjoyed what one scholar has called a "precarious freedom," subject to the whims of local and commonwealth officials.[165] In 1826, the Assembly made it a crime to take Black people from Pennsylvania with the intention of enslaving them, though this seemed to have little effect: Philadelphia's newspapers remained filled with notices about missing Black people (many of them children) who had undoubtedly been kidnapped and enslaved.[166] Worse, in 1842, the US Supreme Court ruled Pennsylvania's law unconstitutional in *Prigg v. Pennsylvania*. In response, the Assembly passed a law in 1847 that essentially emancipated enslaved people brought into the Commonwealth and withdrew state support for recapturing escaped slaves. The following year, Philadelphia's Court of Common Pleas emancipated Lewis Pierce, an enslaved man from New Orleans brought to Philadelphia by his enslaver, Robert Tilghman. In response to this, Congress passed a new, more stringent Fugitive Slave Law in 1850 that made the federal government responsible for assisting in recapturing fugitives from enslavement, even if they were in a free state. Trials under this law, which were held in Independence Hall, aroused enormous fear among the city's Black people, who, whether born free or escaped from slavery, rightly feared being kidnapped and enslaved.[167]

Even white Philadelphians opposed to slavery were frequently hostile to abolitionists, who they saw as extremists. These individuals expressed a range of concerns, including fears of racial mixing and anxiety about the divisiveness of the conflict over slavery, which they blamed abolitionists for inflaming.[168] Deborah Norris Logan, who opposed slavery, nonetheless "exceedingly disapprove[d] of the conduct of some of the abolitionists and [felt] ashamed and provoked at the conduct of some of the women of the party," while Samuel Breck, who in 1821 sponsored a bill in the Pennsylvania House of Representatives to emancipate the

Commonwealth's remaining enslaved people, deplored "that the fanatical Abolitionists . . . persist in agitating the public by incendiary discourse, and practical
amalgamation with the Negroes."[169] The pervasive anti-abolitionism was partly
due to the fact that the city had deep economic and cultural ties to the South.
Abolitionist Charles Godfrey Leland claimed that in Philadelphia, "everything
Southern was exalted and worshipped."[170] Leland's statement was an exaggera-
tion to be sure, but it was nevertheless true that the city's textile industry converted southern cotton into finished materials, and so many wealthy South
Carolinians owned houses along Chestnut Street that it was called "Carolina
Row."[171] It was no coincidence that the Female Anti-Slavery Society decried in
1833 "the combination of interest which exists between the North and the South,
in their political, commercial, and domestic relations."[172]

The women's rights movement grew out of the abolitionist and moral reform
movements, and Philadelphia was a center of feminist advocacy. Though feminism existed prior to the early nineteenth century, the preponderance of women
in the abolitionist and social reform movements (women played key roles in both
movements but were frequently excluded from leadership positions and otherwise discriminated against) helped fuel demands for equality.[173] Lucretia Mott, an
organizer of the 1848 Seneca Falls Convention (the first women's rights convention), lived at 338 Arch Street in Philadelphia until 1857 and was heavily involved
in the abolitionist movement. She helped to found the Philadelphia Female Anti-
Slavery Society (PFASS) in 1833, the first racially integrated female abolitionist
society.[174] Among its other founders were several Black women, including James
Forten's wife, Charlotte, and their daughters, Margaretta, Harriet, and Sarah.[175]
Mary Grew was another prominent PFASS member who became a leading
advocate of women's suffrage.[176] Sarah and Angelina Grimké, two white South
Carolinian abolitionists, lived for a time in Philadelphia, attracted by its large
abolitionist community. Facing discrimination on account of their gender, both
became leaders in the women's rights movement, going so far as to compare white
women's status to slavery. The nascent women's rights movement scored a major
victory in 1848, when Pennsylvania passed a law that allowed women to keep
property they owned before marrying (previously, any property a single woman
owned became her husband's on their marriage), though wives still needed their
husbands' permission to sell even the women's own real estate.[177] In 1854, Philadelphia's Sansom Street Hall hosted the fifth National Women's Rights Convention, and the following year the paper *Woman's Advocate*, edited by Anne E.
McDowell and produced by an entirely female staff, appeared.

Continuing a trend that began in the late eighteenth century, elite Philadelphians turned to institutions to contain the social upheaval they saw all around
them.[178] By the 1830s these included dispensaries that provided free medical care

to the indigent, various almshouses, and several orphanages. The city's House of Industry, a shelter for the needy that forced residents to work, opened in 1846 at 714 Catharine Street. Sponsored by the Philadelphia Society for the Employment and Instruction of the Poor, it served mainly Irish and German immigrants, who made up the bulk of the city's foreign-born population. The most famous social-control institution was the Eastern State Penitentiary, located in Fairmount and opened in 1829. It was designed to reform inmates by rigorously segregating them from one another and from the corrupt world outside the institution's walls. Architect John Haviland's Gothic masterpiece revolutionized prison design throughout the world. All the cellblocks radiated from a central building (like spokes on a wheel), affording maximum surveillance with a relatively small guard force. The building's design allowed administrators to segregate the inmates from each other by keeping them in their cells twenty-three hours per day (one hour was spent in the attached exercise yard). Absolute silence was the rule, and inmates' contact with the outside world was strictly regulated.[179] This regimen required indoor plumbing and cells large enough to accommodate work equipment, making Eastern State Penitentiary the most expensive public works project in the United States at the time. Constructed with funds allocated by the Assembly but (at least initially) administered by members of the Philadelphia Society for Alleviating the Miseries of Public Prisons, Eastern State Penitentiary is a good example of the privatist tradition in Philadelphia and a model of the public-private partnerships that have characterized urban reform throughout the city's history. The penitentiary immediately became a popular tourist destination, attracting thousands of visitors each year, including British novelist Charles Dickens and French diplomat and political scientist Alexis de Tocqueville (author of *Democracy in America*). Dickens attacked the Pennsylvania system as "rigid, strict, and hopeless," believing its effects to be "cruel and wrong." Other visitors were less critical, and the Pennsylvania system soon became a model for penitentiaries around the world.[180]

Another institution for quieting social upheavals was the public school. Philadelphia was a national leader in public education. Though penitentiaries were undeniably institutions of social control, public schools were more ambiguous. They self-consciously inculcated values—patriotism, obedience, industry, and so on—to "Americanize" new immigrants. At the same time, calls for a more democratic government were matched by demands for greater access to education.[181] Support for public schools thus cut across party lines: among the leading advocates of public schooling were Philadelphians Roberts Vaux and John Sergeant, Democrat and Whig, respectively.[182] Urban public schools were sites of enormous expectations and thus controversy. The most significant riot of this period, the 1844 Bible Riots, were sparked by conflict over what was taught in the city's public schools. In 1818, Pennsylvania's Assembly passed an act creating the "First School District of Philadelphia." Under the law, Philadelphia County was divided into seven sections, each with its own directors. Though each section elected members to a central board called the Controllers of the Public Schools of the City and County of Philadelphia, in practice the system was decentralized and uncoordinated.[183] In 1834, the Assembly passed the Free School Act, which created a commonwealth-wide system of public schools and which Governor George Wolf signed into law. Two years later, the Assembly passed a bill allowing local officials to enroll students in publicly supported schools regardless of their parents' income.[184] In 1838, Central High School, the commonwealth's first public high school and the second oldest in the country, opened at the southeast corner of Penn Square. Ten years later, the Girls' Normal School, later reorganized as the Philadelphia High School for Girls and the commonwealth's first public secondary school for women, began operation. In 1848, journalist George G. Foster celebrated the city's public school system as "admirable and unrivaled," imparting a "thorough and practical knowledge of the English branches" that made the working classes behave themselves.[185]

Concern about the period's social upheavals and cultural conflicts was reflected in the city's architecture and urban planning, which evinced a desire to impose republican values on an unruly and diverse urban population.[186] Using physical space in this way was: William Penn's design for Philadelphia was explicitly intended to foster a "moral behavior." What had changed was that by the turn of the nineteenth century, architecture was developing into a professional field, and several institutions in the city (including the Carpenters' Company and the Franklin Institute) offered formal instruction in it. Philadelphia in the early nineteenth century was also home to several talented architects whose buildings self-consciously promoted republican values. The new vanguard of trained architects was led by British-born Benjamin Latrobe, who migrated to the United States in 1795.[187] Frequently called "the father of American architecture," Latrobe designed some of Philadelphia's most impressive buildings, including the Bank of Pennsylvania and the Center Square Water Works (on the site of today's City Hall), and thus played a key role in bringing Greek Revival-style architecture to the United States.[188] Latrobe's influence is visible in the work of his student William Strickland, who became one of the city's leading architects. Strickland designed the US Mint's second building (located at Chestnut and Juniper, opened in 1833, and demolished in the early twentieth century), and the city's Merchants' Exchange Building. Opened in 1834, the building housed the city's post office and served as a commercial center in much the same way that the London Coffee House had in the eighteenth century.[189]

Of course, the process of imposing values through architecture had a political aspect as well. Stephen Girard, who died in 1831, willed a large fortune to the City of Philadelphia to build and operate a free school for poor white male orphans. The resulting institution, Girard College, was founded in 1833 and opened its doors in 1848. Speaking in 1833 at the cornerstone-laying ceremony for the college, Nicholas Biddle, president of the Second Bank of the United States, celebrated the fact that its architecture reflected and reinforced the nation's values.[190] These values were hardly uncontested or universal, and the United States was then bitterly divided politically. Biddle was embroiled at that moment in a fight with President Jackson over the bank's future, and the college's Greek Revival design became a lightning rod of criticism from the region's Democrats.[191] Despite that, Girard College became a key tourist destination almost immediately, attracting visitors from around the world.[192]

One of the more interesting developments of the first half of the nineteenth century was various groups' attempts to mobilize Philadelphia's history and historical buildings in support of their political or social agendas.[193] The sense that the city's past was slipping away (symbolized by the 1810 toppling of the elm tree under which William Penn allegedly negotiated his first treaty with the Lenape) and that the revolutionary generation was passing from the scene (former presidents John Adams and Thomas Jefferson died on July 4, 1826) heightened nostalgia for the past.[194] Though this impulse was not unique to Philadelphia, as the site of so many key events of the Revolution, it was particularly strong in the region and resulted in the founding of the Historical Society of Pennsylvania and the renaming of Philadelphia's outlying squares after several prominent figures (Benjamin Franklin, James Logan, William Penn, and David Rittenhouse).[195] English historian Charles Richard Weld, who visited the city in 1855, concluded, "Probably there is no city in the United States more American than Philadelphia," though he did not mean it as a compliment.[196] Philadelphia's rich revolutionary history and sizable number of historic buildings, monuments, and artifacts made it a uniquely powerful political symbol.

To be sure, there was an element of revisionism and advocacy to these celebrations. When William Penn's grandson, Granville John Penn, visited Philadelphia in 1852, he was feted by the city councils and gave a large celebration at the Solitude, his Federal-style mansion built in 1785 along the Schuylkill River's east bank (now administered by the Philadelphia Zoo). Nary a word was spoken about the tense relations between the Penn family and city during the former's proprietorship, with everyone preferring to bask in the hazy glow of misty memories.[197] That was hardly incidental: the nostalgia for the (largely imaginary) past sprang in part from anxiety about the turbulent present. However, what elements of Philadelphia's past were remembered and celebrated was not a straightforward proposition: the region's workers invoked revolutionary rhetoric to demand higher wages and improved working conditions, while abolitionists and suffragists mobilized the city's history and historical buildings to promote their agendas.[198] In short, several groups sought to adopt and adapt the city's history and historic objects to weave for themselves a usable past that could be mobilized on behalf of their political and social agendas.

One site was central to this mythmaking process: Pennsylvania's State House (which people began calling Independence Hall in the mid-1820s).[199] Wilcocks A. Sleigh, who visited Philadelphia in 1853, noted, "There are many old buildings in the city, coeval with British possession, which are pointed out with great pride by the citizens. None, to my mind, was an object of greater interest, than the Old State-house, in Chestnut-street."[200] The city purchased the building from the commonwealth in 1816 to preserve it, though it continued fulfilling mundane tasks: voters cast their ballots at the building's first-floor windows, and during the 1830s and 1840s, it housed several courts, including Pennsylvania's Supreme Court, the federal district court, and the local Court of Common Pleas.[201] The building's basement hosted a dog kennel, and court proceedings were consistently interrupted by "the incessant howling of the imprisoned curs."[202] Despite this, it remained a powerful symbol and useful political prop: in 1848, former president John Quincy Adams's body lay in state at Independence Hall. Four years later, former senator and speaker of the House Henry Clay's body also lay in state there. In 1854, nativists (who had gained control of the city government that year) created a museum to the Founding Fathers on Independence Hall's ground floor designed to marshal support for anti-immigrant policies.[203]

As a cultural, intellectual, and publishing center with a heterogeneous population and a history of religious, ethnic, and racial strife, Philadelphia was the natural site for the broad-based, multifaceted reform movements that emerged in the early part of the nineteenth century and spawned the cultural wedge issues of the 1830s and 1840s. An important manifestation of the impulse for reform was the Second Great Awakening (ca. 1790 to ca. 1840), a Protestant religious revival that sought to counter a perceived decline in religiosity. That backdrop, combined with a perceived increase in crime and immorality, led to the creation of several reform organizations with explicitly religious missions.[204] For instance, in 1834, several local societies combined to form the American Sunday School Union, created to combat the allegedly rising incidents of crime, immorality, and vice. It was followed four years later by the Hebrew Sunday School Union. In one of the more notable instances of evangelization, the Churchmen's Missionary Association for Seamen of the Port of Philadelphia kept a boat—the Floating

Church of the Redeemer—moored at the foot of Dock Street, then Spruce Street, that could accommodate five hundred to six hundred worshippers.[205]

Reformers attacked all the old demons—crime, gambling, prostitution (which was so widespread that visitors to Philadelphia could purchase a guide listing brothels' addresses)—but one area of particular concern was alcohol, which played an important part in working-class leisure and sociability.[206] In fact, the United States' first lager beer was brewed in Philadelphia by John Wagner, a Bavarian immigrant who arrived in Philadelphia in 1840. During the first half of the nineteenth century, elite attitudes toward alcohol changed.[207] Factory labor, which involved more-routinized work patterns than preindustrial labor, required sobriety. Whereas once employers had routinely provided their workers alcohol, they now banned drinking on the job.[208] Dickens recalled the story of one man who, despite not having been convicted of any crime, asked to be incarcerated at Eastern State Penitentiary because the temptation to drink was overpowering.[209] Yet taverns remained key institutions for sociability, business, and leisure, particularly for America's working class. The city had hundreds of such institutions, many unlicensed and tucked away in alleys, and they competed against one another by offering attractions such as exotic animals.[210] The temperance movement scored significant success in Philadelphia, reducing the number of licensed taverns in the county by nearly two-thirds by midcentury. In 1849, the Assembly created the Board of Appraisers to issue licenses for taverns.[211] Reform sentiment resulted in nativist Robert T. Conrad being elected mayor in 1854 on a platform of enforcing Sabbath observance in the city.[212]

Voluntary reform organizations alone could not address the myriad challenges of industrialization and democratization. Widespread problems required coordinated government action, but the various district governments, the city's government, and the county government represented a "nightmare of conflicting jurisdictions" whose leaders feared losing power and influence in a consolidated government.[213] In fact, the Act of Consolidation, passed by the Assembly and signed into law by Governor William Bigler on February 2, 1854, was the culmination of nearly two decades of agitation that took on greater urgency following the Bible Riots of 1844.[214] The bill welded twenty-nine fiercely independent jurisdictions into the City of Philadelphia, making it coterminous with the county.[215] Overnight, Philadelphia expanded from a roughly two-mile footprint to a sprawling 130-mile behemoth divided into twenty-four wards, becoming the largest city by physical size in the United States. Consolidation represented a massive centralization of power in Philadelphia's municipal government; now, rather than several competing jurisdictions, there would be only the City of Philadelphia.[216] Paradoxically, consolidation also made the city government more democratic by making some formerly appointive offices (such as treasurer) elective for the first time in Philadelphia's history.[217] The mayor was elected every two years, ensuring he remained responsive to the voters' will.

Consolidation was not the panacea its boosters hoped: while instances of rioting declined, it never disappeared, and the city continued to be racked by crime, vice, and corruption well into the next century. The well-ordered city the boosters had hoped for, and that William Penn had long ago imagined, remained elusive. Moreover, the looming showdown over slavery placed Philadelphia, a northern city with strong economic and cultural ties to the South, in the center of the most divisive political issue of the time. The American Civil War and the period of Reconstruction that followed had a profound impact on what was, by 1861, an important industrial, financial, and transportation center. Though no longer the country's premier city, Philadelphia played a key role in the "Second American Revolution" and was transformed by the political, social, economic, and cultural changes it unleashed.

CHAPTER 6

Civil War and Reconstruction, 1854–1876

Without a doubt, the most important event in nineteenth-century US history was the American Civil War. Caused by the intractable conflict between enslavement and an allegedly free society, the devastating war had a major impact on Philadelphia, decisively reshaping its politics, culture, and economy. As a major industrial center in the southeastern corner of the southernmost northern state, Philadelphia was destined to play a key role in the war. In addition, the city's large Black population and array of historic sites and artifacts (such as Independence Hall and the Liberty Bell) had made Philadelphia a center of abolitionism, while the preponderance of textile manufacturers created close economic and cultural ties to the slaveholding South, so the increasingly ferocious conflict over slavery took place in the city's streets. The war forged a Republican majority that dominated city politics for nearly a century but proved ambivalent about the challenges raised by emancipation. Despite the abolition of slavery in the United States, racism remained a prominent feature of Philadelphia's cultural, economic, and political landscape well into the twentieth century.

The country's economy prospered during the early 1850s, in part because of the California Gold Rush, which led to an expansion of credit as banks issued paper currency against their burgeoning specie reserves. In addition, railroad construction boomed, creating a speculative bubble. By the mid-1850s, investors' concerns that the railroad bubble would pop contributed to a panic in August 1857. The following month, Philadelphia's Bank of Pennsylvania, which served as the commonwealth's unofficial banker, collapsed, causing a bank run.[1] As a result, several banks suspended specie payments, and ten thousand unemployed workers converged on Independence Hall to demand that the commonwealth create a jobs program. Fortunately, the Panic of 1857 did not produce the sort of extended recession that followed the Panic of 1837, and the twenty years after consolidation were largely a boom period for Philadelphia.[2] However, this was a near miss, as the events of the 1870s would show.

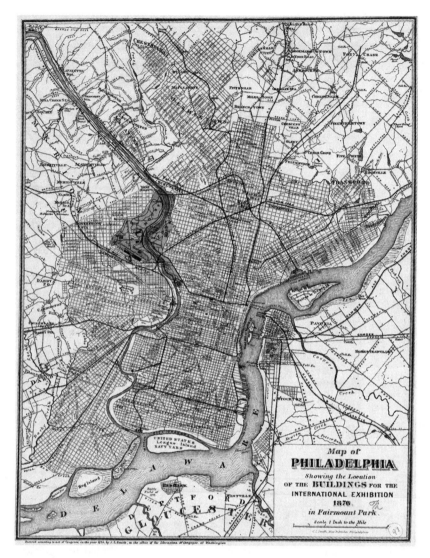

Figure 6. Philadelphia, 1876. American Geographical Society Library, University of Wisconsin-Milwaukee Libraries. By the centennial of American independence, Philadelphia was a sprawling metropolis beset by the challenges of rapid urbanization.

Between 1860 and 1900, Philadelphia's population more than doubled, expanding nearly 20 percent between 1860 and 1870 and then by approximately 25 percent each decade thereafter. Population growth and economic good times spurred a housing boom in Philadelphia in the late 1850s. To systematize the city's expanding housing stock, in August 1856, the city councils adopted an ordinance implementing what became known as the Philadelphia system of numbering buildings, which many visitors praised. Developed by inventor and council member John Mascher, the system quickly spread to other grid cities and continues to be used today.[3] The Civil War slowed new construction, but a second housing boom began in the late 1860s. Even during the depression-plagued 1870s, Philadelphians built new houses, to the point that in 1880, one-third of the city's dwellings were less than a decade old, and the boom continued into the early 1890s.[4] Visiting Philadelphia in the winter of 1873–1874, journalist Friedrich Ratzel was impressed by the city's housing stock, noting:

> The typical Philadelphia home dwelling, the model for about four-fifths of all the homes here, is a building constructed of exposed brick with the steps, sills, and door and window frames made out of some kind of cut stone which in the better and middle-class houses is actually white marble. The ground plots are generally long and rectangular, the house taking up the entire depth of the land except for one of the two rear corners which is used as a courtyard.[5]

The abundance of new housing reduced the city's overall population density, at least for native-born whites.[6]

This growth was not evenly distributed across the newly consolidated city, however. The former districts grew much more rapidly than the "old city" (what has come to be called Center City, a term that did not appear until later in the nineteenth century), which lost population during the 1860s and 1870s as it continued transitioning to a primarily financial and commercial area.[7] Moreover, the city's immigrant groups clustered together, though the communities they created were not ethnically homogeneous ghettos. Instead, there were small concentrations in otherwise heterogeneous communities. What bound these communities together tended to be shared employment—working-class Philadelphians usually lived close to their jobs—rather than ethnicity.[8] This was not the case for Philadelphia's Black population, whose members tended to live in racially segregated communities at this time. While residential density for white Philadelphians declined during this period, it increased for the city's Black community, which swelled in size because of the immigration of southern Black people after the Civil War.[9] At the war's outbreak, nearly one-third of Philadelphians had been born outside the United States, with the largest numbers coming from Ireland and Germany.[10]

Wealthy white people were able to live farther from their work because of the emergence of horse-drawn streetcars, which ran on railroad tracks on the streets.[11] These were faster and offered smoother rides than the omnibuses, which they quickly eclipsed. Writing in February 1859, Sidney George Fisher, a Philadelphia essayist and gentleman farmer, contrasted the "heavy, jolting, slow, and uncomfortable omnibus" with the "roomy ... clean, well cushioned and handsome" streetcars.[12] By the 1860s, there were even some steam-powered "dummies" (single-engine locomotives mounted with an enclosed sitting area for passengers) crisscrossing the city.[13] Streetcar lines connected Philadelphia's outer reaches to the old city and ran along major thoroughfares such as Germantown, Lancaster, Kensington, and Richmond Avenues; most lines connected travelers to recreational areas, including Fairmount Park.[14] One benefit to the proliferation of streetcars was the establishment in 1869 of the Philadelphia Fountain Society. Established by Dr. Wilson C. Swann, the society's purpose was to provide public watering fountains, ostensibly for horses but available to anyone who was thirsty.[15] By 1880, Philadelphia had more miles of horsecar rails than any city in the United States, though, like the rest of the country, the city was devastated by an outbreak of equine influenza in the fall of 1872. Known as the "Great Epizootic," the disease ravaged American cities, killing more than two thousand horses in Philadelphia alone.[16] Like the omnibuses they replaced, however, the streetcars were costly, and therefore few working-class Philadelphians rode them.[17]

During this period, the various railway lines serving southeastern Pennsylvania began consolidating, leading to the emergence of two large companies: the Pennsylvania Railroad (PRR, known as the "Pennsy") and the Philadelphia and Reading Railway (which became the Reading Railroad, usually called simply "the Reading"). By the time of the Centennial Exhibition in 1876, the PRR was an industrial behemoth that, in the words of Lincoln's former secretary of the navy, Gideon Welles, "controls Pennsylvania."[18] The City of Philadelphia held a substantial amount of PRR stock, meaning what was good for the railroad was good for Philadelphia, though not necessarily vice versa.[19] It was now feasible to live outside Philadelphia County but commute into the city for work, spurring the development of towns along the Main Line (the PRR purchased the Philadelphia and Columbia Railroad line in 1857), and traffic dramatically increased from 1860 through the centennial.[20] Philadelphia remained a leading site of locomotive production, though consolidation also characterized the industry: in 1873, the Baldwin Locomotive Works acquired the works of former local competitor Norris, which had gone out of business in 1866 despite being the United States' leading train manufacturer as recently as 1858.[21] Railroads spurred West Philadelphia's development: because city ordinances prevented steam locomotives from entering Philadelphia's downtown district, in 1864, the Pennsylvania Railroad opened a passenger depot at Thirtieth and Market Streets. Trains arrived at the station, were decoupled from the locomotives, then pulled across the bridge by oxen or horses (in 1876 this was replaced by a larger station at Thirty-Second and Market designed to handle crowds visiting the city for the Centennial Exhibition).[22]

Meanwhile, Philadelphia remained at the increasingly vitriolic center of the fight over slavery. Several factors account for this: Pennsylvania was the southernmost free state, and Philadelphia had a large free Black population, which made it an ideal place for enslaved people to escape toward and an ideal location for abolitionists' organizing. At the same time, the city was closely linked economically and culturally to the South (in 1859, Philadelphian Pierce Butler, who owned a forced labor camp in South Carolina, sold his enslaved people at the largest slave auction in US history).[23] The conflict was reaching a boiling point: since the early 1830s, Southerners had stopped referring to slavery as a "regrettable necessity" and begun arguing that it was a positive good. The Democratic Party took on a more pro-Southern orientation, becoming more strident in advocating the expansion of slavery. The Mexican-American War (1846–1848) exacerbated the tension over slavery in the United States because as a result of it, the country gained more than a half million acres of land from Mexico. On August 8, 1846, Congressman David Wilmot of Pennsylvania introduced a proviso to President James K. Polk's request for $2 million to buy the disputed area of Texas from Mexico. The proviso would have prohibited slavery in any territory purchased with the money. Though the amendment was defeated several times, it nonetheless demonstrated the growing sectionalism within the Democratic Party over the issue of slavery.

In 1850, Congress passed and President Millard Fillmore signed into law five bills collectively known as the Compromise of 1850. Taken together, the compromise was designed to settle the various issues raised by the Mexican-American War and the discovery of gold in California. In addition to settling the boundaries of various western territories, the bills replaced the Missouri Compromise (which had prohibited slavery above the 36°30' parallel, except in Missouri) with popular sovereignty, which enabled a territory's voters to decide whether to allow slavery. Another element of the compromise was the strengthened Fugitive Slave Act, which required government officials and citizens in free states to assist in recapturing escaped slaves. Naturally, this law particularly affected Pennsylvania, which had always been a key destination for Black people escaping enslavement. The Fugitive Slave Act led many northerners to conclude that slavery threatened their rights, and more than a few Pennsylvanians covertly or overtly resisted the law.[24] Several armed skirmishes, such as the Christiana Riot of 1851, broke out between Pennsylvanians and enslavers trying to kidnap Black people, which only heightened the sense that the commonwealth was under siege.

In mid-July 1855, a white abolitionist named Passmore Williamson and Black Underground Railroad conductor William Still helped three Black people, Jane Johnson and her two children, Daniel and Isaiah, escape enslavement. Their enslaver, John Hill Weaver, was the recently named US minister to Nicaragua, and he was headed to New York to board a steamship bound for his new post. Johnson and her children's escape infuriated Wheeler, though he was prevented from interfering by several Black dockhands. Williamson was incarcerated for several months in the Moyamensing Prison for his refusal to divulge the location of Johnson and her children, and the case received national attention. In 1855, the newly formed Republican Party nominated Williamson for canal commissioner despite (or perhaps because of) his imprisonment, though he was trounced in the election.[25] Founded the year before, the Republican Party was an amalgamation of antislavery individuals, ranging from conservatives (who sought only to prevent slavery's expansion into the territories) to radicals (who sought immediate abolition). Despite the concerns about the encroachments of slave states on free states' rights, abolitionism remained unpopular in Philadelphia. Novelist John Beauchamp Jones, who lived in the city off and on during the 1840s and 1850s and had even written a novel about Philadelphia (1851's *The City Merchant*) launched a weekly antiabolitionist newspaper, the *Southern Monitor*, in 1857. Headquartered in Goldsmith's Hall, just a block east of Independence Hall, the newspaper reviled abolitionists and aggressively disseminated pro-Southern propaganda.[26]

As a result, Republicans often expressed racist sentiments and downplayed their abolitionist views.[27] For instance, Sidney George Fisher, who opposed slavery, nonetheless complained to his diary in 1863, "The abolitionists . . . claim equality for the Negro race, the right of suffrage, &c. All of this is as absurd as it is dangerous."[28] Running for the Senate from Illinois in 1858, Abraham Lincoln said, "I will say then that I am not, nor ever have been, in favor of bringing about in any way the social and political equality of the black and white races—that I am not nor ever have been in favor of making VOTERS or jurors of negroes, NOR OF QUALIFYING THEM TO HOLD OFFICE, nor to intermarry with white people; and I will say in addition to this that there is a physical difference between the white and black races which I believe will forever forbid the two races living together on terms of social and political equality."[29] Nor was he the exception: the Republicans' 1860 platform specifically committed the party to "maintenance inviolate of the rights of the states, and especially the right of each state to order and control its own domestic institutions according to its own judgment exclusively."[30] Despite the Republicans' timidity on slavery, Philadelphia's Democrats aggressively demagogued on the issue, warning voters that their opponents sought to encourage interracial marriage. For this reason, Alexander Henry, the city's mayor from 1858 to 1865, was first elected as a member of the People's Party rather than as a Republican.[31]

In 1856, the Democrats nominated James Buchanan for president. Though a resident of Lancaster County, Buchanan was deeply connected to Philadelphia: his chief lieutenant, John W. Forney, was part owner of the *Pennsylvanian*, a Philadelphia paper of national reputation, and Buchanan's younger brother, the Reverend Edward Y. Buchanan, served as rector of Trinity Church in what is now Fox Chase. In addition, Robert Tyler, son of former president John Tyler and a leading Democratic Party operative in the commonwealth, lived in Philadelphia. The American Party (referred to as the Know-Nothings), a nativist party, held its nominating convention in Philadelphia's National Hall (Twelfth and Market Streets) and nominated former president Millard Fillmore.[32] Meanwhile, the Republican Party, to gin up support for its candidate, John C. Frémont, held its first national convention in Philadelphia's Musical Fund Hall at 808 Locust Street in mid-June 1856.

Buchanan won the election, the only Pennsylvanian to ever do so as of this writing. In 1856, 53 percent of Philadelphia's voters cast their ballots for Buchanan, while 36 percent voted for Fillmore (despite the fact that the proportion of immigrants in Philadelphia's population was lower than most other cities in the region, nativism remained a potent force in the city's politics).[33] Frémont won an anemic 11 percent of the city's vote, far below his showing nationwide and in the commonwealth.[34] Despite expectations that Buchanan would find a magical formula for uniting the country, he actually exacerbated sectional tension. Conflict over the growing encroachments by the Southern-dominated federal government on Northern states' rights led to conflict over fugitive slaves. This raised a legal question: did taking slaves into free states implicitly free those enslaved people? The most famous case involving a slave is of course *Dred Scott v. Sandford*, which the Supreme Court decided in 1857. In early April, a large group of Black Philadelphians protested the Supreme Court's decision.[35] Chief Justice Roger B. Taney's majority opinion asserted that "blacks had no rights which the white man was bound to respect," a statement that he (and President Buchanan) hoped would end the debate over slavery for good. Instead, the decision fueled conflict and propelled the country toward civil war.[36]

One flashpoint was Kansas, which was then a territory. Since the 1854 enactment of the Kansas–Nebraska Act, which had mandated that the territory's voters would decide whether Kansas would enter the Union a free or slave state, abolitionists and enslavers had violently fought for supremacy there. The 1856 Democratic Party platform pledged to honor the voters' decision, but Buchanan used his influence to support a proposed proslavery constitution for

Kansas that had only minority support.[37] This move, along with Buchanan's vindictive actions toward Democratic Senator Stephen A. Douglas of Illinois, fractured the Democratic Party, all but ensuring a Republican victory in the 1860 presidential election. When Buchanan failed to meet Forney's patronage demands, the latter started the Philadelphia *Press,* an anti-administration Democratic newspaper that later became the *War Press* (1861–1865) and the *Weekly Press* (1865–1877).

Tensions continued increasing around the country. On October 16, 1859, abolitionist John Brown and a small band of followers raided the federal arsenal in Harpers Ferry, Virginia (now West Virginia), to foment a slave uprising. After several days, US troops put down the raid and captured Brown, who was executed on December 2. The raid was a galvanizing event, provoking a backlash against abolitionism even among those nominally opposed to slavery.[38] Many Southerners viewed the raid as proof that most Northerners were committed to exterminating slavery.[39] Brown's supporters took his corpse "on tour," with a stop in Philadelphia. Mayor Alexander Henry was so alarmed at the prospect of a violent confrontation between abolitionists and Southern sympathizers that he ordered the police to surround the Philadelphia, Wilmington, and Baltimore Railroad station at Broad and Prime (now Washington Street) and even arranged a decoy coffin to draw the assembled crowd away from Brown's remains.[40] Two weeks later, fistfights broke out at a public meeting featuring abolitionist George William Curtis, and it was only the presence of Philadelphia police officers in large numbers that prevented further violence.[41]

Because of the factionalizing of the Democrats, the party could not agree on a nominee in 1860, and two men, Douglas and Vice President John C. Breckenridge, ran as Democrats, while a third, John Bell, was nominated by the newly formed Constitutional Union Party. Many of Philadelphia's Democratic leaders preferred Breckenridge, an avuncular, proslavery hardliner.[42] The clear winner was the Republican candidate; Abraham Lincoln won just over half of Philadelphians' votes, though this was well below his showing throughout the commonwealth.[43] Following Lincoln's election, several Southern states announced their secession from the Union. Supporters of conciliation rallied in Independence Hall in mid-December, calling on Northern states to accommodate Southern demands. Similar meetings convened in January, usually organized by the city's Democrats, while many business leaders (fearful of the economic consequences of conflict) counseled compromise.[44]

President-elect Lincoln was a master of mobilizing the nation's past on behalf of his agenda. He visited Philadelphia, a city rich with historical symbols, in late February 1861 on his way to Washington, DC, to be inaugurated the country's sixteenth president. Artist Joseph Boggs Beale described Lincoln's procession from the train station to the newly opened (and luxurious) Continental Hotel (Ninth and Chestnut Streets): "Mr. Lincoln kept his hat on & had a large bouquet in his left hand, & bowed to the people as they waved their handkerchiefs to him & saluted him with cheers & firing off pistols. The streets of the route were jammed as full of people as they could be."[45] Lincoln's visit to Philadelphia, coming amid the unprecedented secession crisis, was fraught with symbolism: on February 22 (George Washington's birthday) Lincoln went to Independence Hall and ceremonially raised the US flag on the building's flagpole. This act was a symbolic rebuke to the Southern states that claimed to have seceded in the wake of the recent presidential election.[46]

Yet patriotic symbolism and the pacific tones of Lincoln's inaugural address (he told the would-be secessionists that "though passion may have strained it must not break our bonds of affection") failed to assuage Southern fears. On the morning of April 12, South Carolina's militia fired on Fort Sumter, a US Army installation near Charleston. The firing on Fort Sumter changed the political calculus: despite Philadelphia's strong connection to the South, many Philadelphians (perhaps most) supported the federal government's efforts to enforce national law (though a small number did fight for the rebels).[47]

On April 13, Sidney George Fisher recorded seeing "immense crowds block up the streets in town at the newspaper and telegraph offices and the excitement is intense." Two days later he described the city "in a state of dangerous excitement."[48] According to Beale's diary for April 18, "The American flag is to be seen every where, of all sizes and quantities, all over the city, even the people in the street have little flags as badges, or Union rosettas, all the passenger cars & horses, drays, carriages etc. have the American flag displayed & many private residences have the flag flying from their windows."[49] A mob nearly destroyed the offices of the *Palmetto Flag*, a newly established weekly newspaper that promoted secession. Mobs also menaced the offices of several other pro-Southern newspapers and the homes of Collector of Customs Joseph B. Baker, a close Buchanan political ally, and former congressman William B. Reed, an unapologetic Confederate sympathizer.[50] Fisher noted in his diary on April 15, 1861, that "several well-known persons, who had openly expressed secession opinions, have been assaulted in the streets."[51] The Common Council, meeting six days after South Carolina batteries fired on Fort Sumter, passed a series of resolutions supporting the federal government's efforts to quell the rebellion.[52] On May 10, 1861, Colonel Robert Anderson, the commander of Fort Sumter, arrived in Philadelphia and was met by "an immense outpouring of the people of every class, condition, and age." The following morning he toured the city with First Lady Mary Todd Lincoln and in the afternoon held court at Independence Hall, meeting with a crowd of Philadelphians assembled to greet him.[53]

Following Lincoln's call on April 15 for seventy-five thousand volunteers to serve for three months to put down the rebellion, Pennsylvanians joined in large numbers, earning the commonwealth the distinction of being the first Northern state to respond to the president's call.[54] Philadelphians formed eight infantry units; these were later supplemented by several three-year regiments. However, when the first Philadelphia volunteers arrived in Baltimore, a prosecessionist mob pelted them with stones and stabbed one (George Leisenring) to death.[55] Members of the famous First City Troop saw action at the battles of Bull Run and Gettysburg.[56] By war's end, between eighty thousand and one hundred thousand Philadelphia men had served in uniform (25 to 33 percent of the city's male population at the time), with approximately ten thousand dying during the war.[57] Philadelphia's Rabbi Jacob Frankel (leader of Congregation Rodeph Shalom) became the US Army's first Jewish chaplain, and several city natives were leading Civil War generals.[58] Best known was George Brinton McClellan, son of famed Philadelphia physician Dr. George McClellan and Elizabeth Sophia Steinmetz Brinton. En route to Washington to be named commander of the Army of the Potomac, McClellan arrived in Philadelphia and was greeted by "shouts & cheers from a great crowd which had waited very long for him."[59] The following November, a delegation of Philadelphia's leading citizens presented McClellan with a ceremonial sword.[60] In addition, General George G. Meade, who commanded the Army of the Potomac at Gettysburg, lived for part of his childhood in Philadelphia and married into the city's politically prominent Sergeant family. After the war, Meade returned to Philadelphia, living for a time at 1836 Delancey Street and serving from 1866 to his death in 1872 as a Fairmount Park commissioner.[61] Major General Robert Patterson, commander of the Pennsylvania State militia, lived at 1300 Locust Street in what was then reputedly the city's largest private residence.[62] A prominent Democrat, Patterson was menaced by a mob of angry Philadelphians following the shelling of Fort Sumter, though he personally remained loyal to the United States.[63] In June 1860, while commanding Pennsylvania's volunteers, Patterson failed to prevent Confederate forces under Joseph E. Johnston's command from reinforcing P. G. T. Beauregard's Army of the Potomac (not to be confused with the US Army force of the same name) at the First Battle of Bull Run. As a result, Patterson was mustered out of the army in July 1861 and spent the rest of the war defending his actions to anyone who would listen.

Naturally, not all Philadelphians fell into line behind the war effort. Though John Beauchamp Jones shuttered the *Southern Monitor* and fled Philadelphia after the firing on Sumter, other pro-Southern propagandists stayed and worked to dampen support for the war effort. In fact, Albert Boileau, editor of the influential Democratic newspaper *Evening Journal*, was such a thorn in the Lincoln administration's side that he was arrested in January 1863 for publishing editorials "tending to the support and encouragement of the rebellion against the Government of the United States." His arrest quickly became a partisan affair, with Pennsylvania's Democrats denouncing both the Lincoln administration and Pennsylvania's Republican governor, Andrew G. Curtin. Even some Republicans were disgusted by the arrest and made their feelings known to the administration. As a result, after a few days in Baltimore's Fort McHenry, Boileau apologized for his actions and was released.[64] Soon after, Boileau sold the *Evening Journal* to Charles Pine, but it ceased publication soon after.[65] During the summer and fall of 1862, Philadelphia's Democrats campaigned vigorously against the Lincoln administration, claiming that the president's policies threatened white Philadelphians' civil liberties and warning that the war would result in the emancipation of enslaved people who might migrate to the city.[66] Speaking before a crowd at Independence Hall in August 1862, Charles J. Ingersoll, a former Democratic US representative, said:

> But what has been the whole object of the war previously? [A VOICE— "Free the nigger."] Has there been any other object, and if they accomplish that object; if they turn loose upon us four millions of negroes, are we to marry them? Are we to work with them? I will tell you what will be the result: These poor negroes, whom the Abolitionists love much less than you and I, would have their throats cut in a war of races, and that would be the end of this scheme of Mr. LINCOLN.[67]

This rhetoric was effective: Quaker Anna M. Ferris, who lived in Delaware but visited Philadelphia frequently, called the lead-up to the 1862 elections "by far the darkest period of the war" because "the North becomes more divided in sentiment & in strength as disasters and defeats multiply."[68] Republicans suffered losses in Congress, though Republican Charles O'Neill won Pennsylvania's Second District, a seat held by Democrat Charles J. Biddle (Nicholas Biddle's son).[69]

To marshal support for the war effort, in November 1862, several prominent Philadelphians organized the Union Club. The following month, this organization morphed into the Union League, whose members committed to using "every proper means in public and private" to support the war effort.[70] Initially headquartered at 1118 Chestnut Street, in May 1865, the Union League moved to its current building at the corner of Broad and Sansom Streets. A week after the Union League came into being, several prominent Democrats—Ingersoll and lawyers John C. Bullitt and George M. Wharton—founded the Central Democratic

Club, which took a hard-line position, declaring that "all power is inherent in the WHITE PEOPLE."[71] Racism was thus key to the Democrats' political appeals, but it failed them in 1863. In what was widely regarded as a referendum on the war, Governor Curtin defeated Democrat George W. Woodward in November 1863, and Democrats lost control of Philadelphia's city councils.[72] Naturally, not all of the city's Democrats were secessionists, but Unionists worked hard to make it seem that way.[73] In fact, one by-product of the war was that it created a decades-long Republican governing coalition in the city: between 1856 and 1903, the city's mayor was a Republican for all but eight years, and the Democratic Central Committee fizzled out in 1863.[74] Though the Democratic Party continued to exist in Philadelphia, its identification with secession tarnished it, and for the next seventy years, the city's political struggles took place primarily between factions of the Republican Party, not between Democrats and Republicans.[75]

The Civil War fueled an economic boom in Philadelphia. Secession caused a short recession, but the mass mobilization of troops boosted Philadelphia's manufacturing by 70 percent over the succeeding decade.[76] Philadelphia was home to two federal arsenals, Frankford (opened in 1816, at the intersection of Tacony and Bridge Streets) and Schuylkill (opened in 1800, at the intersection of Gray's Ferry and Washington Avenues). Philadelphia's William H. Horstmann and Sons produced many officers' uniforms, epaulets, and dress hats at the company's factory at the intersection of Fifth and Cherry Streets (currently the site of the US Mint), while William Whitaker & Sons Inc. produced blankets at its plant in Cedar Grove (one of the region's oldest textile factories). Pennsylvanians also contributed food and several raw materials, including the lion's share of iron, to the war effort.[77] The shipbuilding firm of William Cramp & Sons constructed the ironclad frigate *New Ironsides*, and the Navy Yard was abuzz with activity, building new warships and making others battle ready.[78] Following renovations, in 1863, Fort Mifflin was reactivated, serving as a prisoner of war camp for Confederates, and for Union soldiers accused or convicted of crimes. Philadelphian Jay Cooke, the United States' first investment banker, was instrumental in providing the federal government the money it needed to fund the war through a series of loans and by sales of government bonds. Cooke's innovative and aggressive marketing campaigns made these efforts a success and briefly returned Philadelphia to the center of American finance.[79]

Philadelphia was a key railroad hub, and soldiers often transited through the city. Among Union soldiers, Philadelphia quickly earned a reputation for hospitality.[80] The Union Volunteer Refreshment Saloon, which served warm meals and provided soldiers medical care, was funded by private donations to the US Sanitary Commission, a voluntary relief organization founded in June 1861. The saloon was at the Navy Yard on Washington and Swanson Avenues adjacent to the Philadelphia, Wilmington, and Baltimore Railroad station. In addition, the Cooper Shop Refreshment Saloon opened in May 1861 nearby, eventually expanding to the point it could feed one thousand soldiers per hour.[81] Given the city's privatist and volunteerist culture, it is no surprise that the managers of both saloons heavily advertised that they did their work "through the liberality of the citizens of Philadelphia, without any help whatever from the City, State or General Government."[82]

Moreover, Philadelphia's railroads and respected medical institutions made it an ideal location for treating sick and wounded soldiers. The first Civil War hospital opened on Christian Street just west of Ninth Street in May 1861. Here Drs. W. W. Kenn, George. R. Morehouse, and Silas W. Mitchell did groundbreaking work in treating soldiers' injuries. Following McClellan's campaign in the summer of 1862 in northern Virginia, patriotic Philadelphians organized the Citizens Volunteer Hospital (Broad Street near Washington Avenue) to treat wounded soldiers. Philadelphia was also home to two of the largest Civil War hospitals: Mower General, a sprawling, twenty-seven-acre complex in Chestnut Hill that opened in 1863, and Satterlee General, opened in 1862 on sixteen acres in West Philadelphia on the site of what is now Clark Park. By the war's end, two dozen hospitals had operated in Philadelphia, treating more than 150,000 soldiers wounded in the first "modern" war.[83] Meanwhile, a chapter of the Christian Commission, an organization started in New York and headquartered at 1011 Chestnut Street, dispensed aid (money, clothing, and food) and moral instruction to needy volunteer soldiers.[84]

Recognizing the Keystone State's importance to the war effort, Confederate forces made several incursions into Pennsylvania. For instance, forces under the command of James Ewell Brown "Jeb" Stuart entered south-central Pennsylvania in October 1862, raiding Mercersburg and Chambersburg and stoking fears they might burn Philadelphia.[85] Stuart did the same thing the following year, a prelude to the Battle of Gettysburg. In June 1863, following a triumphant victory against Union forces at Chancellorsville, Virginia, Robert E. Lee's troops invaded Pennsylvania to pressure the Union to end the war. Beginning in early June, Lee moved his forces north, causing considerable alarm and sending refugees—both Black and white—fleeing to Philadelphia.[86] In response to the Confederate threat, the Pennsylvania Assembly activated the Blue and Gray Reserves and organized a company of soldiers from the city's police force; in addition, the city councils allocated $500,000 to help defend the commonwealth.[87] The US War Department created the Departments of the Susquehanna and the Monongahela, comprising all of Pennsylvania east of Johnstown, including Philadelphia. Command of the Military District of Philadelphia passed to Major General Napoleon Jackson Tecumseh Dana, who was tasked with improving the city's fortifications. Dana worked with Mayor Henry to create a series of entrenchments around key transit areas, including the Falls of the Schuylkill and the Gray's Ferry Bridge. The arrival in Gettysburg of the Army of the Potomac under Meade's command ensured that the city's emergency troops saw little action.

The crisis in the summer of 1863 also galvanized the recruitment of Black soldiers into the US Army. From the outset, many Black men in Philadelphia sought to join the war effort but were denied the opportunity to serve until 1863 because President Lincoln feared antagonizing the four Border States (slave states that never seceded from the Union). In a bid to end the war, in late 1862, Lincoln announced that he would abolish slavery in any state still in rebellion on January 1, 1863. True to his word, on New Year's Day, the president issued the Emancipation Proclamation, which shifted the war's aims from preserving the Union to ending slavery. As a result, it became hard to deny the logic of allowing Black men to enlist, and Philadelphia became a center of Black recruitment and training.[88] On May 22, 1863, the War Department created the Bureau for Colored Troops, and the following month training began at a hastily constructed site in Montgomery County that came to be called Camp William Penn. Financier Cooke, who was an abolitionist, offered the use of his land in Cheltenham Township, Montgomery County, as a training camp for Black soldiers. Black recruits paraded through Philadelphia, marching out to the planned camp.[89] When Cooke's land proved unsuitable, the camp moved to nearby land (called Roadside) owned by abolitionist Lucretia Mott.[90] Though the Battle of Gettysburg ended before these troops were battle ready, Black Philadelphians played an important role in the war, and the city was even briefly home to the Free Military School for Applicants for Command of Colored Troops (1210 Chestnut Street), which trained white officers to command Black regiments.[91] Pennsylvania contributed one-fifth of the Union's Black soldiers, more than any other state (some even served with the famed Fifty-Fourth Massachusetts Regiment), and many of the recruits were from Philadelphia.[92] Despite valiant service in the war, however, Black soldiers faced considerable discrimination, including lower pay than their white counterparts.

For three weeks in June 1864, Philadelphia hosted the Great Central Fair, a fundraiser for the US Sanitary Commission. The Great Central Fair, the largest of all the Sanitary Commission's fundraising fairs, displayed manufactured goods, art, and curiosities in sixteen temporary buildings in the Logan Circle park. Anna M. Ferris, who attended the fair on June 9, gushed, "It is the most wonderful display of everything under the sun & in whole & in part admirabl[y] arranged."[93] According to Sidney George Fisher, who attended the fair on June 11, it was "well worth seeing." He noted, "The buildings are chiefly long

& lofty galleries with gothic roofs."[94] The fair's main exhibit hall was a two-hundred-thousand-square-foot building designed by William Strickland and Samuel H. Kneass. The event combined patriotic symbolism (the fair's main path was named Union Avenue) with undisguised appeals to US history.[95] For instance, the Historical Society of Pennsylvania lent the fair's organizers several artifacts connected to William Penn for the "Penn Parlor."[96] Moreover, the five-hundred-foot-long art gallery, which displayed more than one thousand paintings and sculptures (the largest art show in US history), featured several pieces with historical themes designed to arouse visitors' patriotism.[97] According to Fisher, "everything else was eclipsed . . . by the gallery of pictures. . . . The walls are covered with paintings large & small, none of them bad or mediocre, many admirable works of art, much the best I have ever seen."[98] The fair also featured a massive rotunda housing the horticultural department, which featured gas lighting and orchestral music, as well as thousands of rare plants and flowers.[99]

President Lincoln visited the fair on June 16 and, according to Sanitary Commission volunteer Mary A. Livermore, was nearly pressed to death by the enthusiastic crowd. Lincoln told Livermore:

> The police tried to open a way through the crowds for me, but they had to give it up; and I didn't know as I was going to get in at all. The people were everywhere; and, if they saw me starting for a place, they rushed there first, and stood shouting, hurrahing, and trying to shake hands. By and by the Committee hurried me along to a side door, which they suddenly opened, pushed me in, and then turned the key; and that gave me a chance to lunch, shake myself, and draw a long breath. That was the only quiet moment I had; for all the time I was in Philadelphia I was crowded, and jostled, and pulled about, and cheered, and serenaded, until I was more used up than I ever remember to have been in my life.[100]

Lincoln's experience was not terribly surprising: the fair was an unqualified success. On the opening day, fifteen thousand people attended the fair, and by the time it closed on June 28, a quarter million people—nearly half the city's population at the time—had purchased admission tickets. The fair raised $1 million for the Sanitary Commission, making it the organization's most successful fundraiser, though, like the abolitionist movement, to which it was closely connected, women provided most of the labor but were denied leadership positions.[101]

Meanwhile, 1864 was an election year, and it was clear that the presidential race would be a referendum on the war. The Democrats nominated disgruntled former general George B. McClellan. The election was raucous and bitterly contested, particularly in Philadelphia, which saw at least one fatality.[102]

Belgian scientist Jean-Charles Houzeau, who visited the city in October, noted the importance of winning Pennsylvania to Lincoln's reelection, telling his father, "Philadelphia is the home of McClellan, and it is on his own ground that his influence must be fought."[103] Contrary to many people's (including the president's) expectations, Lincoln decisively defeated McClellan, winning 2.2 million votes to his opponent's 1.8 million. Lincoln won Pennsylvania's twenty-six electoral votes, garnering just over half the commonwealth's votes, though the margin was higher in Philadelphia.[104] The *Press* described the scene on election night: "The Union men crowded Chestnut Street for a mile in length, cheering and shouting themselves hoarse. . . . This, with the music of the bands, made the time, though rain was now falling very fast, very lively and exciting."[105] Six months later, the war was over, but on the evening of April 14, 1865 (the same day Philadelphia's Common Council passed an ordinance relating to the planned celebrations of the war's end), John Wilkes Booth shot Lincoln; the president succumbed to his injuries early the following morning.[106] Lincoln's assassination had a tragic connection to Philadelphia: the small handgun Booth used, a Philadelphia derringer, was manufactured at Henry Deringer's gun shop in Northern Liberties (at the intersection of Green Street and Tamarind, an alley a half block west of Front Street).[107]

Philadelphia entered mourning: the city draped Independence Hall in black bunting, and Mayor Henry requested that all businesses in Philadelphia close out of respect for the slain president.[108] Lincoln's funeral train arrived in Philadelphia on April 22 on its way to Springfield, Illinois, and his body lay in state in Independence Hall, where more than eighty thousand citizens paid their final respects.[109] Emilie Davis, a Black Philadelphian, noted in her diary that "the coffin and hearse was beautiful this morning went down to see the President but could not due to the large crowd."[110] Despite the pall cast by Lincoln's death, that June Philadelphians rejoiced when hometown hero General George Meade marched his men along Ridge Avenue to be feted at the Union Volunteer Refreshment Saloon. Politically, the city had come a long way in four years: it was now Republican dominated and would be for nearly three quarters of a century.

The Civil War's end raised several thorny questions about how to "bind up the nation's wounds," as Lincoln so eloquently described it in his second inaugural address. His assassination elevated to the presidency former Democratic senator and Tennessee governor Andrew Johnson, who had been included with Lincoln on the ticket of the newly formed National Union Party (an election-specific party created by the merger of Lincoln supporters in the Republican Party, War Democrats, National Unionists, and other factions) as a way of demonstrating that the war was not a partisan affair. Thrust into the presidency and eager to build a political coalition that would allow him to win the

1868 presidential election, Johnson began pardoning high-ranking rebels and placing only minimal conditions on Southern states to rejoin the Union. This infuriated many Republicans, who rightly believed that Johnson was giving away all the gains the military had won on the battlefield. Philadelphia became the site of the showdown between Johnson's supporters and opponents in the summer of 1866. For three days in mid-August, Johnson's supporters held the National Union Convention at the Wigwam, a temporary building constructed for the event at Nineteenth and Girard Avenue. Approximately seven thousand of Johnson's supporters attended the conference, allegedly to "vindicate and restore" the Constitution.[111]

The following month, Johnson's opponents convened at Philadelphia's National Hall (at 1222–24 Market Street), which had opened in 1856. Officially called the Southern Loyalists Convention, it included delegates from around the country. Frederick Douglass was elected to represent New York at the convention. Many of his friends and political allies advised him not to go to Philadelphia, fearing that the presence of a Black man at the convention might be a boon for Johnson (or even provoke a riot in the city). Despite their pleas, Douglass went to the convention, where he was treated "as the ugly and deformed child of the family." However, he did march with the other convention attendees from Independence Hall along Chestnut Street and then up to National Hall. Douglass, who in 1862 had remarked, "There is not perhaps anywhere to be found a city in which prejudice against color is more rampant than Philadelphia," was delighted to be cheered by the Philadelphians lining the route, and he concluded that "the people [of Philadelphia] were more enlightened and had made more progress than their leaders had supposed."[112] At the polls that fall, voters rebuked Johnson, expanding Republicans' majority in Congress. Congressional Republicans asserted their control over Reconstruction, provoking a conflict with the president that concluded with Johnson being the first US president ever impeached. He was not removed from office, but he was not a viable presidential candidate in 1868, when voters elected war hero Ulysses S. Grant to the presidency.

Despite the warm reception Douglass received in Philadelphia in 1866, Black Philadelphians did not enjoy all the rights of citizenship. Pennsylvania, like several Northern states, did not allow Black men to vote, and city institutions were segregated.[113] In 1868, Philadelphians elected former Democratic Select Councilman Daniel M. Fox mayor. Fox ran on an avowedly racist platform, arguing that Republicans intended to enfranchise Black men.[114] Fox's election demonstrated how fragile the city's Republican apparatus was at this point and how deeply entrenched racism was in Philadelphia's politics.[115] Black Philadelphians did not take their second-class status lying down. Beginning in the late 1850s, Black Philadelphians challenged the city's companies to integrate their streetcars.[116] Once Blacks began serving in the US Army, the indignity of being denied access to most of the city's streetcar lines became even more difficult to bear, and Black Philadelphians redoubled their efforts to pressure the streetcar companies.[117] The companies obstinately refused, even going so far to poll their white riders in 1865 and then announce the easily predictable results, which only galvanized the movement to desegregate the cars. One of the leading figures of that movement was Octavius Catto. He was the scion of an elite Black Philadelphia family: the son of a Presbyterian minister and a leading figure during the war in the fight to allow Black volunteers.[118] A leader of the Pennsylvania State Equal Rights League (an organization founded to promote legal equality for Black people), Catto lobbied key Pennsylvania Republicans sympathetic to Black rights.[119] His efforts paid off when, in March 1867, the Assembly desegregated Philadelphia's streetcars. Catto's fiancée, Caroline LeCount, a Black Philadelphia public school teacher, tested the law by attempting to ride a streetcar. The streetcar operator refused to admit her, so LeCount complained to a magistrate, who in turn arrested and fined the streetcar operator.[120] As a result, the city's streetcar companies backed down and allowed Black Philadelphians to ride. Over the next decade, many other businesses dropped segregationist policies, eroding the barrier between Black and white Philadelphia.[121] In 1869, Pennsylvania ratified the Fifteenth Amendment to the Constitution, which forbade states and the federal government from abridging citizens' right to vote based on race; it went into effect the following year. It is telling that in the first election under the new policy, federal troops traveled to Philadelphia to protect Black voters, few of whom exercised the new right; some of those who tried were attacked by gangs of rock-throwing whites.[122] The following year, however, the absence of federal troops combined with a larger turnout of Black voters led to riots in several wards (now identified by numbers rather than names) that the local police failed to suppress, leading to the deaths of at least three Black citizens.[123] Most devastating for Philadelphia's Black community, a white man named Frank Kelly shot and killed Octavius Catto on Chestnut Street, dealing a serious blow to the movement toward full civil rights for Black Philadelphians.

While advancing civil rights, Pennsylvania's Republicans took steps to consolidate their control over all levels of government in the state. Following Fox's election as Philadelphia's mayor, the Pennsylvania Assembly passed a registration act, which mandated that Philadelphia and Pittsburgh create commissions to approve voters; unapproved citizens could not vote. The act was clearly designed to disenfranchise Democratic voters and thereby perpetuate Republican dominance of Philadelphia, and it worked: except for eight years, Republicans controlled Philadelphia's City Hall until 1952. Consequently, Philadelphia earned a considerable amount of attention from Republican politicians, including President Grant, who had a strong affinity for Philadelphia. In fact, after the war, Grant briefly considered settling in the city and commuting to Washington, so several leading Republican businessmen (including his future secretary of the navy, Adolph E. Borie, and Sanitary Commission President George H. Stuart) gifted the general a house at 2009 Chestnut Street (purchased with money raised by the Union League). Grant's responsibilities made it impossible for him to live in Philadelphia, so he ended up renting the house.[124] As president, Grant visited Philadelphia frequently, often meeting with the city's leading Republicans.[125] Around 1870, Grant gifted the cabin he used as his headquarters during the siege of Richmond to George H. Stuart, who reassembled it in Fairmount Park, where it stood until 1981.[126] In 1872, Republicans held their national convention in Philadelphia at the Academy of Music and nominated Grant for a second term. After leaving the presidency, Grant embarked on a worldwide tour, departing from Philadelphia in May 1877 and returning to the city on December 16, 1879. Future congressman William S. Vare recalled that when Grant paraded through Philadelphia, he stood in a crowd on Market Street and "helped to welcome the General back to his native country."[127]

Grant's two terms as president were not easy years for Philadelphia. The Panic of 1873 touched off a depression that was significantly worse than the one in 1857. As with the Panic of 1857, it had local roots: the failure of Jay Cooke & Company that September was a major factor. In the years after the Civil War, the United States experienced a railroad-building boom, spurred by the discovery of large deposits of silver in Nevada. However, the market for silver dried up in the early 1870s after Germany ceased minting silver coins in 1871 and President Grant signed into law the Coinage Act of 1873, which demonetized silver. Investors stopped purchasing long-term bonds issued by railroad companies. That September, Jay Cooke & Company, which was overextended and heavily invested in railroad construction projects, was unable to sell several million dollars of Northern Pacific Railroad bonds. Jay Cooke & Company was forced into bankruptcy, triggering a bank panic that pushed the United States into depression. Ironically, though a local firm triggered the depression, Philadelphia's banks weathered it substantially better than those in other cities.[128]

The same could not be said of Philadelphia's workers, the vast majority of whom lived on the edge of poverty.[129] Wages, which had increased because of labor shortages and economic growth during the 1860s, contracted, particularly for Black workers.[130] Philadelphia again played a key role in the organized labor movement, but with mixed success. For instance, in the summer of 1869, the National Labor Union (NLU), the country's first national labor federation, held its convention in Philadelphia, but the organization dissolved in

1873. The NLU's collapse created a vacuum that was filled by the Knights of Labor, founded in 1869 by a group of Philadelphia tailors. The depression of the 1870s spurred the organization's growth but posed significant challenges. For instance, in July 1877, the Baltimore & Ohio (B&O) Railroad cut its workers' wages for the third time in a year. To protest the cut, B&O workers in Martinsburg, West Virginia, began a strike, crippling the railroad. West Virginia Governor Henry M. Matthews dispatched the state militia, but they refused to fire on the strikers, so he appealed to the federal government for troops. Meanwhile, sympathy strikes broke out in several cities, including Philadelphia.[131] Mayor William Stokley supported the railroads, establishing a crisis headquarters at the Pennsylvania Railroad's West Philadelphia depot and threatening to use police force against strikers. When that proved insufficient, President Rutherford B. Hayes dispatched federal troops under the command of Pennsylvania native General Winfield S. Hancock to restore order. Not for the last time would federal troops be used to put down a strike in the United States.

The upheavals of the Civil War era fomented in many Americans nostalgia, particularly as the United States approached the one hundredth anniversary of the Declaration of Independence.[132] Philadelphia, with its rich revolutionary history, became a key site for meeting this need. Benjamin Franklin's grave, long neglected, became a must-see attraction during the 1850s, so Christ Church demolished a section of the brick wall surrounding its cemetery and replaced it with a fence that allowed passersby to see the grave. Philadelphia scientist Henry Seybert donated a thirteen-thousand-pound bell to be hung in Independence Hall's steeple; it contained metal from two Revolutionary War and two Civil War cannons and was rung for the first time on July 4, 1876.[133] In 1874, the city councils adopted a new coat of arms for Philadelphia that included several nods to the city's history. Designed by a local Presbyterian minister, the Reverend Dr. Henry C. McCook, it depicted the scales of justice over a shield emblazoned with a scythe and a sailing ship. Flanking the shield are two women, representing Peace and Plenty. Beneath them a scroll reads, "Philadelphia Maneto," usually translated as "Let brotherly love continue," derived from a biblical verse (Heb. 13:1).

The passion for history even led to the perpetuation of some famous myths, such as the story that seamstress Betsy Ross sewed the first US flag. According to the myth, George Washington and George Ross (who was Betsy's husband's uncle and a member of the Continental Congress) visited the seamstress and asked her to sew a flag for the recently independent United States. Allegedly, Ross made several suggestions to improve the design, including the substitution of five-pointed stars for six-pointed ones.[134] There is almost no contemporaneous evidence to support this assertion; it was first described by Ross's grandson, William J. Canby, in a paper delivered before the Historical Society of Pennsylvania (based largely on reminiscences of family members), and the story quickly attained the status of fact.[135] The Mund family, who operated a tavern in the house in which Ross supposedly sewed the nation's first flag, aggressively advertised the building's connection with this supposed event. In 1898, a group of concerned citizens calling themselves the American Flag House and Betsy Ross Memorial Association purchased the house (on Arch Street between Bread and Third) from the Munds and opened it as a museum. This moneymaking operation was still operating decades later; Ethel Alec-Tweedie, who visited Philadelphia in the early twentieth century, recalled meeting Betsy Ross's granddaughter, who was "selling trophies at the State House in Philadelphia, and seemed very proud of her descent."[136]

The clearest example of Americans' nostalgia was the 1876 Centennial Exhibition (officially, the International Exhibition of Arts, Manufactures, and Products of the Soil and Mine), the United States' first world's fair. Held in Fairmount Park, it was ostensibly a celebration of the Declaration of Independence's hundredth anniversary but was as much a celebration of the country's present and future as of its past.[137] As the anniversary of the Declaration of Independence approached, many perceived that a national celebration could aid in binding the country's still-raw wounds. Philadelphia, with its strong connection to the Revolution, was an ideal site for such an event, and in 1870, the Franklin Institute received the Philadelphia Select Council's permission to organize a celebration in Fairmount Park in 1876. Several organizations, including the Franklin Institute, the Fairmount Park Commission, and the Pennsylvania Academy of the Fine Arts, strongly lobbied Congress to select Philadelphia as the site. The Franklin Institute, one of the leading forces behind the Centennial Exhibition, described it as intended to "stimulate a pilgrimage to the Mecca of American Nationality, the Home of American Independence . . . as thereby may illustrate the unparalleled advancement in science and art, and all the various appliances, of human ingenuity, for the refinement and comfort of man," ably summarizing the event's dual purposes.[138] In fact, the exhibition looked backward and forward, mobilizing the city's history to create a forum for displaying the nation's rich industrial products and thus exposing the tensions of social, political, and economic change that had reshaped life in Philadelphia over the preceding one hundred years. In 1871, Congress passed and President Grant signed into law a bill calling for an exhibition and establishing the United States Centennial Commission. The Fairmount Park Commission offered 450 acres of land in West Philadelphia for the exhibition, and in 1874 construction began.[139] Philadelphia's enthusiasm for the centennial was so great that the construction site itself became a tourist attraction in the two years before the exhibition opened.[140]

On May 10, 1876, President Grant, accompanied by Brazil's emperor, Pedro II, opened the centennial to the public. Grant's remarks displayed a mixture of pride in and defensiveness about America's achievements. He noted, "Most of our schools, churches, libraries, [and] assylums [sic] have been established within an hundred years. Burthened by these great primal works of necessity which could not be [delayed], we have yet done what this exhibition will shew in the direction of rivaling older and more advanced nations in law, medicine, and theology—in science, literature, philosophy, and the fine arts. Whilst proud of what we have done, we regret that we have not done more."[141] Over the next five months, nearly ten million people (the equivalent of nearly 20 percent of the country's population at the time) traveled to Philadelphia to attend the exhibition. The Democratic and Republican presidential candidates, Samuel J. Tilden and Rutherford B. Hayes, visited, as did assorted celebrities. To accommodate the millions of people who came to the centennial, its grounds were flanked by several temporary structures designed to accommodate visitors' needs. Hotels ranged from the luxurious to the budget, which one visitor described as "a temporary wooden building, unpapered and unpainted inside and not at all proof against cold or wind. The beds with spring laths were barely covered and stuck into our sides considerably."[142] Elizabeth Cady Stanton, visiting Philadelphia that summer to advocate for women's suffrage, recalled that because of the Centennial Exhibition, "the city was crammed to its utmost capacity. With the crowd and the excessive heat, comfort was everywhere sacrificed to curiosity."[143]

Visitors willing to brave crowds and summer heat were not disappointed: the Centennial Exhibition was remarkable. Its main hall was the largest building by area in the world at the time, while the US Government Building, a 102,840-square-foot cruciform structure, educated exposition visitors about the federal government's bureaus and their functions.[144] Horticultural Hall was the world's largest botanical conservatory at the time, and the exhibition helped energize the "city beautiful" movement that would have a major impact on American municipalities in the coming decades, including Philadelphia.[145] Various states and countries from around the world contributed displays, providing Philadelphian Martha Garrett "an opportunity to compare our industrial products with those of other nations."[146] Most of the buildings were torn down after the exhibition closed, though several (including Memorial Hall, Horticultural Hall, and the Ohio Building) remain to this day.

The Centennial Exhibition's impact on Philadelphia lasted beyond the fair itself. The Philadelphia Museum of Art grew out of it. The exhibition's art gallery was located in what is now known as Memorial Hall, which was expected to be a permanent building. In 1877, the hall reopened as the Pennsylvania Museum of Art, which included the Pennsylvania Museum School of Industrial Art (it would later move to the Fairmount district and in 1938 was renamed the Phila-delphia Museum of Art). The centennial featured lots of public art with overtly political overtones, part of an attempt to use public space to inculcate patriotic values and bind the nation back together. This was largely due to the work of the Fairmount Park Art Association, a private nonprofit chartered in 1872 and committed to beautifying Fairmount Park by purchasing outdoor sculpture. Its first purchase, Edward Kemeys' *Hudson Bay Wolves Quarreling over the Carcass of a Deer*, was relocated to the Philadelphia Zoo in 1956.

Just as with the Great Central Fair, women played many of the key roles in organizing the Centennial Exhibition, and they were again denied a space in its main building to display their products, even though women made up nearly one-third of Philadelphia's industrial workforce. As a result, several promi-nent Philadelphia women, including Benjamin Franklin's great-granddaughter, Elizabeth Duane Gillespie, raised funds to construct their own building, called the Women's Pavilion.[147] One visitor noted, "Its special purpose was to contain exhibits of female work only, and thus be a means of pointing out occupations of usefulness and profit, adapted to women. The collection in this building rep-resented those pursuits for which women are specially adapted, [such] as sculp-ture, painting, literature, engraving, telegraphy, lithography, and education."[148] However, the National Woman Suffrage Association (NWSA) protested the cen-tennial because the Women's Pavilion organizers failed to advocate for women's suffrage. Intending to use the attention generated by the centennial, and tak-ing advantage of the symbolism of Independence Hall, on July 4, 1876, Susan B. Anthony and four other NWSA members strode, uninvited, onto the platform at the reading of the Declaration of Independence at Independence Hall and handed to the presiding officer, Senator Thomas W. Ferry, the "Declaration of the Rights of Women of the United States." According to Elizabeth Cady Stan-ton, "Senator Ferry's face paled as, bowing low, with no word, he received the Declaration, which thus became part of the day's proceedings." Anthony and the other NWSA members then walked around the building and mounted the bandstand and read the declaration to the assembled crowd.[149]

Perhaps not surprisingly, the centennial promoted an essentially nationalist and Eurocentric view of US history that failed to notice the contributions of the country's nonwhite citizens.[150] Interestingly, the organizers of the Women's Pavilion actively excluded Black women from leadership roles and responded with racial invective when the hypocrisy was pointed out.[151] Undeterred, Black Americans seized the chance to showcase their largely ignored contributions to the country's history and industrial progress. Philadelphia's African Methodist Episcopal (AME) Church pushed to erect a statue of its founder, Richard Allen, on the centennial grounds, though it only managed to briefly display Allen's bust shortly before the exhibition closed.[152] This was part of a larger postwar effort to preserve Black history and to leverage Black Union troops' wartime service to achieve the rights of full citizens.[153] For instance, in order to ensure that their contributions to the war effort were not forgotten, Black Civil War veterans created their own Grand Army of the Republic (GAR) lodges. Founded in April 1866, the GAR was a fraternal organization that lobbied on behalf of Civil War veterans. Philadelphia had three Black GAR posts: John W. Jackson (founded in 1867 and located on Eleventh Street just north of Lombard), Robert Bryan (founded in 1877 and located at the corner of Fifteenth and South), and Charles Sumner (located on Eleventh Street north of Girard Avenue).[154]

There is more than a little irony in the fact that the Centennial Exhibition, committed as it was to showcasing America's industrial growth, took place in Fairmount Park, which had been intended as a bucolic retreat from the industrial city.[155] Andrew Jackson Downing, the founder of American landscape architecture, expressed the prevailing sentiment in 1848 when he asserted that by constructing parks, gardens, libraries, and museums, cities could "soften and humanize the rude, educate and enlighten the ignorant, and give continual enjoyment to the educated."[156] Fairmount Park's growth was aided by a clause in the 1854 Act of Consolidation that required Philadelphia to create "within the limits of said city . . . areas of ground, convenient of access to all its inhabitants . . . as open public places, for the health and enjoyment of the people forever."[157] In 1857, the city acquired the Sedgeley Estate through eminent domain, which became part of Fairmount Park, and two years later, the city councils received a petition to expand the park onto the Schuylkill's west bank.[158] The following year, the councils invited proposals for developing the area into a public park. They selected cartographer and surveyor James C. Sidney's plan, but the outbreak of the Civil War ended work on the park.[159]

In 1867, the Pennsylvania Assembly established the Fairmount Park Commission, consisting of six ex officio members and ten citizens appointed to five-year terms by the District Court and the County Court of Common Pleas.[160] The commission used its powers to expand the park, and by 1900, Philadelphia had the second-highest number of acres devoted to parks of any city in the United States.[161] Mayor Morton McMichael was the commission's first president (his statue stands in the park near the intersection of Sedgley and Lemon Hill Drive), while General George Meade was vice president. The commission was joined in 1871 by a private organization, the Fairmount Park Association, which was fully in line with Philadelphia's privatist and volunteerist tradition.[162] By the mid-1870s, Fairmount Park comprised 2,500 acres, making it the nation's largest urban park at that time.[163] In 1874, the Philadelphia Zoological Gardens (later simply the Philadelphia Zoo) opened its doors. Though it had been chartered in 1859, the Civil War delayed its opening. Amazingly, the zoo acquired the Penn family's nearby former summer home, the Solitude, which served various purposes, including housing reptiles.

For many working-class Philadelphians, Fairmount Park remained largely inaccessible because of the cost of transportation. In 1884, the city councils authorized the creation of several small parks in the city, and in May 1888, a group of wealthy Philadelphians formed the City Parks Association to create and maintain parks.[164] By 1900, Philadelphia was second only to New York in the total acreage of its city parks, and because of its significantly smaller population, it enjoyed a higher amount of park space per capita than New York.[165] In cities across the United States (including Philadelphia), park administrators moved from conceiving parks as simply pastoral escapes from the industrial world to seeing them also as places of sporting recreation.[166] As part of this process, beginning in the 1890s, cities established municipal playgrounds. Up to this point, there were few places for children to play. George Wharton Pepper, who was born in 1867 to a wealthy and prominent Philadelphia family, recalled that when he was a child, "our playground was the street."[167] In 1895, the city councils appropriated money for the city's first playground, though playground development in the city really grew in the fifteen years after 1900. In July 1899, Smith Memorial Playground in Fairmount Park opened to the public. Funded by a bequest from Richard and Sarah Smith, whose family had made money in the typesetting business, the playground, which included a specially designed, sixteen-thousand-square-foot playhouse, was dedicated to the memory of their adult son, Stanfield, who died in 1890.

This drive took place as Reconstruction was winding down, a casualty of white ambivalence, Republican factionalism, Southern resurgence, and the ongoing economic depression. In 1870, Democrats won thirty seats in the US House of Representatives, and following the midterm elections of 1874, they took control of that body for the first time since before the war.[168] True to their campaign promises, they used their newfound power to hobble the Grant administration. In addition, Democrats gained control of the Pennsylvania House of Representatives and eroded the Republicans' majority in the state Senate. At both the national and state levels, Republican leaders concluded that additional civil rights legislation would only cost them politically and moved on to other priorities, like consolidating their power.[169]

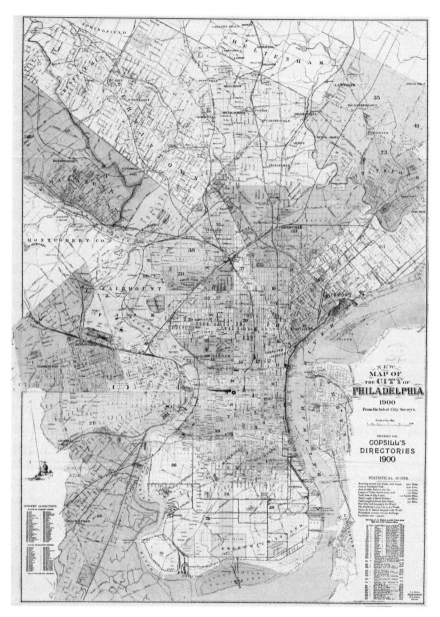

Figure 7. Philadelphia, 1900. Harvard Map Collection, Harvard University. By the turn of the twentieth century, Philadelphia had more or less assumed its modern form. Meeting the challenges posed by modernity, two wars, and the Great Depression radically altered the city's politics, economy, and culture.

CHAPTER 7

Corrupt and Contented, 1876–1901

In the quarter century following the Centennial Exhibition (a period called the Gilded Age), the trends visible since the turn of the century—industrialization, democratization, and immigration—continued reshaping Philadelphia's political, cultural, economic, and social landscape by opening opportunities and avenues of political participation and economic mobility for some people. The Second Industrial Revolution (c. 1870–c. 1914) created a middle class of clerks and salespeople in Philadelphia that enjoyed a dazzling array of consumer products and leisure activities even as many working-class Philadelphians lived in poverty. The city's industrial growth attracted a substantial number of immigrants (mostly Italians and Russian Jews) who created ethnic neighborhoods and changed the city's demographic profile, while factions of the Republican Party struggled for control of the city's government.[1]

Between 1880 and 1900, Philadelphia's population grew by 65 percent, expanding from approximately 850,000 to just under 1.3 million, though it was only the United States' third most populous city at the turn of the twentieth century, behind New York and Chicago. In addition, Philadelphia had a much lower number of immigrants than New York and Chicago.[2] Despite English journalist G. W. Steevens's claim in 1897 that he found in Philadelphia "the purest Anglo-Saxon citizen body among all the [United States'] large centres," that was rapidly changing because of the influx of the so-called new immigrants from Russia and Italy.[3] Nearly two decades before Ellis Island opened its doors, in 1873, the Philadelphia-based American Line, a naval shipping company, established the Washington Avenue Immigration Station (at Pier 51), which processed immigrants until 1915, when the building was demolished.[4]

One of the leading immigrant groups to Philadelphia during this period was Russian Jews fleeing anti-Semitic persecution. Philadelphia's small Jewish community dated to the early eighteenth century, and by the middle of the nineteenth century, the city was a center of American Judaism. In 1843, Isaac Leeser, a German-Jewish immigrant, established the United States' first English-language

Jewish publication, the *Occident and American Jewish Advocate*, which continued for more than a quarter century.[5] After the Civil War, Philadelphia was even home to the short-lived Maimonides College, a Jewish seminary located at the Hebrew Education Society Schoolhouse on Seventh Street just south of Callowhill.[6] Most of the approximately fifteen thousand Jews in Philadelphia at this time were descendants of German or central European immigrants.[7] In 1881, anti-Jewish pogroms broke out in various cities and towns in southwestern Russia (what is now Ukraine and Poland), a result of the assassination of Tsar Alexander II, which was blamed on Russia's Jews. On February 22, 1882, the SS *Illinois*, a Pennsylvania-class iron steamship constructed by Philadelphia shipbuilder William Cramp & Sons, arrived in the city with 225 Russian Jewish refugees, the start of a wave of Russian Jewish immigrants who came to Philadelphia. During that year alone, Philadelphia's tiny Jewish population grew by about 40 percent, and over the next decade, approximately forty thousand Russian Jews arrived at the Port of Philadelphia, and most remained in the city.[8]

New Jewish communities quickly developed, including a section of Port Richmond that came to be called "Jew Town."[9] Moreover, established communities developed a sizable Jewish presence: by the turn of the century, Society Hill had a large Russian Jewish population, and the James Forten School (the first public school in Philadelphia named for a Black man and originally known as Mary Street School, then Lombard Street Colored School) had an equal mix of Black and Jewish students.[10] By 1910, Eastern European Jews constituted Philadelphia's largest foreign-born population.[11] Philadelphia's Jewish community was far from homogeneous. Many of the city's native-born Jews feared that the influx of Jewish immigrants would arouse an anti-Semitic backlash, a reasonable fear given Philadelphia's long history of nativist and religious violence.[12] In an attempt to Americanize these new arrivals, Philadelphia's existing Jewish community created relief organizations and even established a newspaper, the *Jewish Exponent* (the second-oldest continuously published Jewish publication in the United States).[13]

Italian immigrants also began arriving in the United States in large numbers at the end of the nineteenth century, though Philadelphia had a small Italian community that dated to the eighteenth century. During the last three decades of the nineteenth century, Philadelphia's Italian population, which numbered a few hundred in 1870, exploded to eighteen thousand by 1900, with most immigrants settling in South Philadelphia's Second Ward.[14] The new immigrants settled in what had been the predominantly Black neighborhood around St. Mary Magdalen de Pazzi Church, the Italian Catholic church just west of Seventh Street on Montrose Street that was founded in 1852.[15] Almost immediately, Italian entrepreneurs began opening shops along Ninth Street, laying the groundwork for what eventually became one of Philadelphia's best-known landmarks, the Italian Market.[16] Other Italian communities sprang up in parts of the Northeast, in North and West Philadelphia, and in Manayunk. Like Philadelphia's Jewish community, the city's Italians were far from monolithic. Italy itself only unified as a country in 1861, and for many Italian immigrants, regional identity (Sicilian, Calabrian, etc.) was more important than being identified as Italian.[17] Crucially, many Americans did not consider these new immigrants white. Instead, late nineteenth- and early twentieth-century Americans often viewed immigrants from southern Europe as something between white and Black, and therefore many argued that these new arrivals were unfit for citizenship.[18]

One way to understand why some immigrants settled in Philadelphia and others did not has to do with "pull" factors. Because of the diversity of its industrial production and the highly skilled nature of many of its industries, Philadelphia was a more attractive destination for some immigrant groups than others. Those from urban areas (such as Russian Jews) or experienced in skilled industries (such as Italians) found employment opportunities in Philadelphia, while unskilled laborers and those from predominantly rural regions did not.[19] For instance, between 1870 and 1914, Pennsylvania attracted a larger number of Poles than any other state, and they tended to settle in the coalfields of northeastern Pennsylvania rather than in Philadelphia.[20] That is not to say that Philadelphia lacked a Polish community; far from it. In fact, Poles had lived in the Delaware Valley as far back as the seventeenth century, and several (most notably Tadeusz Kościuszko and Casimir Pulaski) served in the Continental Army during the Revolutionary War. In addition, Poles who arrived after 1870 did settle in Philadelphia, creating small Polish clusters in various places in the city. However, the coal, iron, and railroad companies employed large numbers of Poles, which helps explain why Polish immigrants tended to settle outside Philadelphia.[21] Over time this had a snowball effect, because kinship ties were a crucial method of securing work, eventually leading to some occupations being monopolized by certain ethnic groups.[22] Nor was that unique to Poles: for instance, the Italian *padrone* system, under which middlemen working on behalf of American employers recruited Italians to immigrate to the United States and found temporary housing on their arrival, funneled Italian immigrants into specific jobs. According to an 1897 US Department of Labor bulletin, Italians "have an exclusive claim on the work of keeping the streets of Philadelphia clean."[23] Moreover, the flood of eastern European immigrants into the city provided Philadelphia's wealthy, and even middle-class, residents with ready access to cheap domestic labor.[24]

In addition, there were substantial "push" factors at work when it came to immigration. For instance, a growing number of Asian immigrants moved to

Philadelphia during the last three decades of the nineteenth century, establishing the city's Chinatown. One reason Chinese people came to cities like Philadelphia is that they had been forced out of California. After the completion of the transcontinental railroad in 1869, Chinese laborers, who had played a crucial role in building the railroad, faced discrimination and violence on the West Coast. In 1882, Congress went so far as to pass the Chinese Exclusion Act, which banned Chinese laborers from coming to the United States. Chinese immigrants and Chinese Americans living on the West Coast migrated east.[25] In 1870, Lee Fong established Philadelphia's first Chinese laundry at 913 Race Street, which became the center of the city's Chinatown. Philadelphia's Chinatown grew quickly, eventually stretching for two blocks along Race Street by 1900 and adding to the city's ethnic and racial diversity.[26]

Meanwhile, Philadelphia's Black community expanded during the last decades of the nineteenth century, growing in absolute numbers by over 60 percent, partially owing to immigration of Black men and women from the upper South.[27] It remained the largest Black community of any northern city and the fourth largest in the United States (behind Baltimore, Washington, DC, and New Orleans) for several decades, though Black people accounted for a smaller proportion (between 3 and 4 percent) of Philadelphia's population than before the war.[28] During this period, Philadelphia's Black community remained economically diverse, including small upper and middle classes.[29] Southern Black people built substantial communities in Philadelphia's Fifth, Seventh, and Eighth Wards, which collectively spanned the rivers between Chestnut and South, and in the Fourth Ward, which ran from the Delaware River to Broad Street between South and Fitzwater Streets.[30] The best portrait of Philadelphia's late nineteenth-century Black population is famed sociologist W. E. B. Du Bois's landmark 1899 book, *The Philadelphia Negro*. In 1896 and 1897, Du Bois (the first Black man to earn a PhD from Harvard) lived in the city's Seventh Ward, and he surveyed people living in the ward's central area. He noted that pervasive discrimination kept Black Philadelphians overrepresented in the city's unskilled jobs and working as maids and servants.[31]

As with European immigrants, job prospects played a key role in shaping Philadelphia's Black community. The shortage of work for Black men in the city's industries led to a gender imbalance in Philadelphia's Black community, where women (who could find work as domestic servants) outnumbered men, and the percentage of Black female-headed households was nearly double that of white female-headed households.[32] One place that was willing to employ Black men was Midvale Steel, located in Nicetown along the Pennsylvania Railroad's tracks (near the intersection of present-day Roberts and Wissahickon Avenues). Beginning in 1890, Midvale began hiring Black men to work alongside whites at the steel plant, though the purpose was far from altruistic: the company's goal was to leverage white racism to arrest any attempts by the workers to unionize.[33] It is not coincidental that Midvale Steel was also known as a leading laboratory of the scientific efficiency movement. Frederick W. Taylor, a machinist who worked his way up to chief engineer of the works, developed a theory he called "scientific management," which was designed to increase labor productivity. After formulating the "best" way to produce an object, Taylor broke the production into constituent motions, timed workers performing each step, and developed rigid performance guidelines. Under scientific management, laborers were viewed as replaceable cogs in a machine, and ethnic or racial ties threatened their efficiency.

Working conditions in American factories were abysmal, labor was physically demanding and sometimes dangerous, wages were low, and workers suffered frequent periods of unemployment or underemployment.[34] The city's industrial base, located mostly in Kensington, Port Richmond, Frankford, Fairmount, and parts of South Philadelphia, was not dominated by any single industry.[35] Textile production, which covered a broad array of products, including clothes, rugs, and carpets, was the largest single employer: one in five Philadelphia factories produced textiles at the turn of the twentieth century, employing more than one-third of the city's workers and generating approximately 30 percent of the total value of the city's manufactured goods.[36] Another key Philadelphia industry was iron and steel products, a broad category that ranged from household goods to locomotives and ships. In fact, the half century after the Civil War was the peak of locomotive production in the city.[37] Philadelphia was also a leading center of leather production and remained one of the United States' key print production centers. Philadelphia was home to significant sugar-refining factories.[38] While Pennsylvania remained a leader in coal extraction, in 1859, the first commercial oil well was drilled in Titusville, and by the 1880s, clusters of oil refineries existed in Point Breeze and Girard Point; by the early 1890s, the Port of Philadelphia exported one-third of the country's petroleum output.[39]

These were filthy, physically demanding industries, and most Philadelphia workingmen did not earn enough to support their families, which was exacerbated when the city abolished "outdoor" (i.e. direct cash payments) relief in 1879.[40] Conditions like these helped reenergize the labor movement in Philadelphia and around the country, though with paltry results. In May 1886, twenty delegates from several labor unions met at Philadelphia's Donaldson Hall (Broad and Filbert Streets) and drafted a list of complaints about the Knights of Labor. When the Knights of Labor's leadership refused to address their concerns, forty-one delegates representing more than a dozen unions formed the American Federation of Labor (AFL). The AFL's leadership met again in Philadelphia in subsequent decades, often connecting its activities to the city's revolutionary past. At the organization's 1914 annual meeting, for instance, the AFL's president, Samuel Gompers, declared, "This is the third time our Federation has met in Philadelphia, once in old Donaldson Hall; the second time in Independence Hall, where the charter of America's independence was declared to the world, and here in 1914, in Horticultural Hall. And each of these occasions has been an epoch in the development of the spirit of the organized working people."[41] There were several important strikes during this period, including a work stoppage on the city's transit system during Christmas 1895. That year, several employees of the Union Traction Company (UTC) tried to form a union to secure better wages and a ten-hour workday. UTC management responded by firing the strikers and refused to recognize representatives of the Amalgamated Association of Street and Electric Railway Employees, who tried negotiating on the workers' behalf. Consequently, five thousand UTC employees walked off the job on December 17, virtually paralyzing the city the week before Christmas. The strikers enjoyed widespread support among Philadelphians, so Mayor Charles Warwick and several leading merchants (including John Wanamaker) pressured the UTC to settle. The UTC made some vague promises about improving conditions and hiring back the fired employees, neither of which it honored in the long run.[42] In 1903, striking workers shut down the city's textile industry, demanding a fifty-five-hour workweek. Mary Harris Jones, known as "Mother" Jones, marched an army of starving children who worked in the mills 125 miles, from Kensington to President Theodore Roosevelt's mansion in Oyster Bay, New York, to highlight the need for child labor laws. In general, Philadelphia's unions achieved little during this period, and the city, which had once been a leader in the labor movement, became known as the "graveyard of unionism."[43]

One reason the labor movement faltered in Philadelphia was the widespread availability of affordable housing, which dampened the sort of labor militancy that shook other American cities during this period. Philadelphia was much larger in terms of physical space than Manhattan, so land was more abundant and therefore cheaper. Consequently, Philadelphia had few of the high-rise tenements that dominated late nineteenth-century Manhattan. Moreover, in 1885, 1893, and 1895, Pennsylvania's legislature passed laws about apartment building construction that essentially made it impossible to construct the high-rise tenements (though existing buildings could still be converted into them).[44] Average population density in Philadelphia, which was lower than in most other cities, even fell during this period.[45] Averages can be deceptive, however: in some poorer neighborhoods, population density could be as high as two hundred people per acre.[46] Over the years, property owners had built tiny bandbox houses (two or three stories, with a single room on each floor) on what had been their own houses' backyards, leaving a rectangle of inward-facing houses surrounded by a rectangle of outward-facing houses. Philadelphia's Octavia Hill Association, founded in 1896 to alleviate some of the worst elements of the city's housing, noted that inward-facing houses were accessed by "a narrow passage-way from the street or court. This passage-way is also frequently the means by which the surface drainage is carried to the street or to an open sewer-connection at its entrance."[47] However, this reality was often invisible to the city's visitors (and even some residents), who confined themselves to the city's fashionable districts and historic sites.[48]

One attempt to address unsanitary living conditions was the settlement house movement, which began in London in the early 1880s. Staffed by women, most of whom were college-educated and middle or upper class, settlement houses provided not only stable housing for recent immigrants and Black people but also social services in the form of classes in literacy, cooking, and civics. Philadelphia's first settlement house opened at 617 St. Mary Street (now Rodman) Street in April 1892, and by the outbreak of World War I, the city had more than twenty of these institutions. To be sure, there was a paternalistic element to the settlement houses, and the women who worked in them (nearly all of whom were white) saw themselves as Americanizing and "reforming" the houses' residents. Despite that, settlement houses contributed to improving conditions for the city's poor, as did the public baths established by the Public Baths Association (PBA). Founded in 1895, the PBA tried to curtail the spread of disease by making available free baths. The first bathhouse opened in April 1898 at 410–12 Gaskill Street (between Lombard and South Streets). Five years later, the PBA opened a bathhouse for women across the street, and for the next four decades it provided "baths for everybody."[49]

Public health remained a concern, and horse-drawn streetcars caused a problem: namely, tons of horse dung on Philadelphia's streets. Though electric trolleys displaced horse-drawn streetcars at the end of this period, many Philadelphians kept animals, including chickens, goats, and horses, at or near their residences, creating tons of animal manure every day well into the twentieth century. Even upscale Chestnut Street was not immune; Mae Townsend Pease recalled that during the 1880s, "herds of cattle and flocks of sheep would be driven through the streets on their way to the slaughterhouse several blocks from our home. This was done at night or in the very early morning when the streets would be empty; there would be much commotion, and the shouting of the drovers could be heard above the protests of the unfortunate animals long before they came past the house."[50] Compounding the problem, it took several decades for Philadelphia to pave over the cobblestones in the myriad alleyways into which human and animal filth was trod and provided an ideal breeding ground for disease.[51]

Tha being said, the city took steps to improve public health by operating municipal swimming pools. In fact, Philadelphia was something of an innovator in this regard; though the first swimming pool in the United States was Boston's Cabot Street Bath (opened in 1868), Philadelphia built several "river baths" (swimming areas in the Delaware and Schuylkill) before constructing the first outdoor city pool in 1884, the Wharton Street Bath in South Philadelphia.[52] The city did not stop there: by 1892, Philadelphia had six outdoor pools operating in working-class neighborhoods across the city. That number had risen to eight by the turn of the century, meaning Philadelphia had more municipal pools than any other US city.[53] However, the city's pools left something to be desired: in 1898, Daniel Kearns, the secretary of Boston's bath commission, visited Philadelphia to investigate the city's baths. Kearns attacked the conditions of the pool houses, the cleanliness of the water, and the fact that the largely working-class clientele (men and women) failed to wear what he deemed to be appropriate swimsuits. Surprisingly, while the city's public pools were located exclusively in white working-class neighborhoods, they were not segregated by race: Kearns reported seeing both white and Black children bathing at the same time.[54]

One reason for the state of the city pools' water is that they drew from the rivers, which were hopelessly polluted. By the 1890s, Philadelphia had more water mains than any city in the United States, and Philadelphians were better supplied with water than New Yorkers, Chicagoans, and Bostonians. However, the Schuylkill, which provided almost all of the city's drinking water, was "far from satisfactory as to the quality of the water."[55] In 1851, the Pennsylvania Assembly mandated that the then independent districts of Kensington and Northern Liberties cooperate with Philadelphia in converting Cohocksink Creek into a storm sewer. In the 1870s, the city culverted the Cohocksink, in part to limit the amount of industrial waste dumped into the creek, which flows into the Delaware River.[56] Nor was this an isolated case: between 1869 and 1895, the city culverted Mill Creek, which drained much of rapidly growing West Philadelphia. In 1875, the Committee on Surveys and Regulations reported to Philadelphia's Common Council that "the Cohocksink sewer . . . is now filling up, and becoming filthy and highly prejudicial to the health of the neighborhood."[57] A decade later, only one-quarter of houses had indoor toilet facilities, with the rest relying on outdoor privies. In fact, Philadelphia had a relatively high ratio of citizens to sewer mains, meaning the city's sewer system carried a considerable amount of human waste.[58] Philadelphia had a "combined" sewer system, in which a single pipe carries storm water and wastewater to the treatment plant; when this system was overloaded by the runoff from heavy rains or snow melt, raw sewage backed up into the city's waterways, contaminating drinking water. Harriet Boyer recalled one instance where her traveling companion mistook a glass of drinking water for lemonade. Their hostess responded, "Oh, that isn't lemonade . . . the water always looks so, after a long rain. We Philadelphians are so used to the color we don't mind it, but I notice strangers always remark upon it."[59] Not coincidentally, typhoid fever killed a substantially greater percentage of Philadelphians than it did Bostonians or New Yorkers during the last quarter of the nineteenth century.[60]

A "Tenderloin" district (so called because you could get a "prime cut" of whatever your vice) emerged between Callowhill and Race Streets, stretching from Sixth to Thirteenth Streets. Here an ethnically and racially diverse population lived among brothels and saloons, as well as several dime museums, such as Colonel Wood's Oddity Museum (later Bradenbaugh's Museum at Ninth and Arch).[61] Several theaters, including the vaudevillian Bijou and the Lyceum (burlesque), provided entertainment, while the Star Theater on Eighth Street north of Race was simply described as "Merry-Go-Round."[62] In addition to there being rampant prostitution in the Tenderloin, its proximity to the city's emerging Chinatown meant it also housed several opium dens.[63] Though the Tenderloin was Philadelphia's best-known vice district, it was far from the only one; according to one visitor, along South Street "second hand stores of all descriptions alternate with low drinking places, and occupy forlorn and tumble-down tenements. All races, colors and sexes mingle here, and the man who [desires] missionary work need go no further than this quarter."[64]

As a result of the long-lasting depression caused by the Panic of 1873, cities around the United States adopted (or were forced to adopt) austerity measures that slowed the expansion of municipal services. In 1873, Pennsylvania's legislature severely restricted Philadelphia's ability to borrow money, and in 1879 it imposed a "pay as you go" act that applied only to Philadelphia and that made it illegal for the city to spend more than its estimated revenue.[65] The "pay as you go" mandate, which was intended to punish the wayward faction of the city's Republican machine, not only curtailed the patronage available, it made it difficult for the city to modernize its infrastructure, a problem compounded by the fact that taxes during the 1880s and 1890s were actually lower than during the 1870s, with many of the city's businesses paying little or nothing.[66] Here again the Assembly undermined the city: in an 1868 law that applied only to Philadelphia, the legislature decreed that farmland would be taxed at one-half and rural or suburban land at two-thirds, the rate assessed for the city's urban areas.[67] As a result, the city's poorest inhabitants paid a disproportionately high share of Philadelphia's taxes, which, in any event, the Pennsylvania Assembly kept artificially low, thereby stripping the city of the resources it could have used to mitigate these conditions.

In addition, the size, scope, and complexity of the modern industrial firm required office workers, clerks, and salespeople, who collectively formed an emerging middle class.[68] Nonmanual labor became an ever larger segment of employment during the fifty years after the Civil War, accounting for nearly one in five jobs in Philadelphia by 1920.[69] Though most new immigrants were shut out of the increasing number of white-collar jobs, the growth of such work created opportunities for native-born white women.[70] The proliferation of office work led to increased demand for higher education. In 1884, reflecting the important role that textiles played in the city's economy, businessman Theodore C. Search, president of the Philadelphia Association of Manufacturers of Textile Fabrics, opened the Philadelphia Textile School. In 1888, the commonwealth chartered Temple College of Philadelphia, an educational institution "intended primarily for the benefit of Working Men." Temple's founder, Baptist minister Russell H. Conwell, responded initially to requests from several individuals that he prepare them for ministerial careers, but the institution quickly came to serve impecunious students looking to advance their careers. In 1891, financier A. J. Drexel underwrote the establishment of the Drexel Institute of Art, Science, and Industry to educate students in the "practical arts and sciences."[71] The Drexel Institute's competitors included Union Business College (founded in 1865 and known now as Peirce College) and the Spring Garden Institute (founded in 1851 and since closed). All these institutions, but especially Temple and Drexel, responded to a particular perceived need: affordable, nonsectarian, and practical education designed to increase their students' social mobility.[72] In that regard they were successful; in 1906, Scottish travel writer John Foster Fraser noted, "In America, the technical schools, day and evening classes, are always crowded, and boys and girls, men and women, clamour for admission."[73]

Despite the appearance of new colleges, the University of Pennsylvania remained the city's preeminent institution of higher education; it underwent significant changes as well during this period. In 1872, Penn decamped from Ninth and Chestnut to its current location in West Philadelphia. The university's trustees bought ten and a half acres of the old Hamilton estate from the City of Philadelphia and in June 1871 laid the cornerstone of College Hall. Penn had been calling itself a "university" since 1779, but in the word's modern sense it only became so under the leadership of Provost William Pepper Jr., who served from 1881 to 1894. During Pepper's tenure, Penn opened the United States' first business school (later called Wharton after Joseph Wharton, who made a fortune in mining and contributed $100,000 toward the school's founding), established Penn's Graduate School of Arts and Sciences in 1882, and granted its first PhD (in physics) in 1889. In addition, the university grew: the graduating class of 1900 was eleven times larger than that of 1880, though Penn remained largely a commuter campus for the sons of well-to-do Philadelphia families during this period.[74]

This was also a time of expanded public elementary and high school education. Philadelphia enjoyed a reputation for having the "best [public education system] in the Union," though even this source noted it was "far from perfect."[75] According to one visitor, the city "pays its teachers [lower] salaries than most of the other cities, and the standard of the schools is not so high as it should be, in consequence."[76] This was despite the fact that in 1848, Philadelphia's Controllers of the Public Schools established the first municipal institute to train teachers.[77] Called a "normal" school, because it taught enrollees the norms of teaching, it prepared high school graduates to teach in elementary and high schools, a key step in the professionalization of education. Pennsylvania was also relatively late in passing a compulsory education law, and most working-class teenagers left school by fourteen and joined the labor force (though, ironically, due to pervasive hiring discrimination, Black youths tended to stay in school longer than their white counterparts).[78]

The growth of a middle class with some discretionary income spurred the growth of consumer products, many of which were manufactured in Philadelphia during this period. In 1866, William A. Breyer began producing and selling ice cream in his house. In 1882, he opened a store and ice cream factory at 2776 Frankford Avenue, where he stayed for fourteen years before moving the expanding company to 2103 Somerset Street. Hatmaker John B. Stetson moved to Philadelphia in 1865 and began manufacturing the "Boss of the Plains" style hat he had developed, better known as a "cowboy hat." He built a massive factory, opened in 1886, at Fourth and Montgomery, and constructed housing for his employees nearby. By 1910, Stetson was the nation's largest hat producer, operating from a sprawling, thirty-acre complex comprising twenty buildings, including an auditorium and a hospital.[79] These and other products made Philadelphia a byword for high-quality goods. In 1918, the city's Chamber of Commerce boasted that "Philadelphia [is] noted for the excellent workmanship."[80] In fact, Philadelphia became so associated with quality products that in 1880, some New York–based cream cheese manufacturers named their product after the city even though it was not even produced in Pennsylvania.

The ways Philadelphians bought products also changed during this period because of the emergence of the department store. In 1861, merchant John Wanamaker opened a small men's clothing store with his brother-in-law, Nathan Brown. The store was in a six-story building known as McNeill's Folly at Sixth and Market Streets (occupying the same site as Robert Morris's mansion, which served as the residence of Presidents George Washington and John Adams). Their enterprise proved to be incredibly successful, in no small measure because of its no-haggle policy and customers' ability to return goods for a refund. Following Brown's death, Wanamaker established a second store at

818 Chestnut Street, adjacent to the Continental Hotel. In 1876, Wanamaker opened his department store in the Pennsylvania Railroad's former freight sheds at Thirteenth and Market, showcasing a dazzling array of goods in one place.[81] Called the Grand Depot, it was the first store in the United States lit by electricity, and by 1900 it was the largest department store in the world.[82]

But Wanamaker had competition. In 1868, Quaker dry-goods merchants Justus Clayton Strawbridge and Isaac Hallowell Clothier opened their department store, Strawbridge & Clothier, in a three-story red brick building on the northwest corner of Eighth and Market Streets that Thomas Jefferson had used as his office while serving as secretary of state. In 1891, Rachel P. Lit opened a women's clothing shop. Two years later her brothers, Samuel and Jacob, joined her, and by 1907 the Lit Brothers' department store covered an entire city block (Market Street between Seventh and Eighth). In 1894, Isaac Gimbel opened Gimbel Brothers' second store at the southeast corner of Ninth and Market Streets (the first store was in Milwaukee). N. Snellenburg & Company was another well-known Philadelphia department store; at one point it was the world's largest clothing manufacturer. Founded in 1869 by Nathan Snellenburg, the company operated from 318 South Street before opening a much larger building that covered the triangle bounded by Fifth, South, Passyunk, and Bainbridge. In 1889, Snellenburg opened what became the growing company's flagship store on Market Street between Eleventh and Twelfth. Department stores offered convenience that changed commerce and reshaped the American city. Increasingly, downtown Philadelphia became not a place for residences but a center for working or purchasing goods and services.[83] Meanwhile, Chestnut Street, between Third and Fifth, became known as "Bank Row" for the number of banks that opened along it, while the country's first full-time commodities exchange, headquartered in the Bourse, opened on Fifth Street just north of Chestnut in 1890.[84]

The middle class had more leisure time than the working class and found a variety of ways to spend it. In the sprawling and anonymous metropolis of more than a million people by 1890, Philadelphians turned to clubs for a variety of reasons, including recreation, education, and political reform.[85] This was nothing new: the oldest private gentlemen's club, the Philadelphia Club, was founded in 1834. However, the sheer profusion of clubs during the late nineteenth century set this era apart. In 1902, various members of Penn's University Club founded the Franklin Inn Club, initially limiting its membership to authors. In 1892, the Stylus Club, Journalist Club, and Reporters Club merged to form the Pen & Pencil Club, the country's oldest continuously operating club for journalists. For artists, the city boasted the Philadelphia Society of Artists and the Plastic Club, while Philadelphia's architects joined the T Square Club.

The Acorn Club, opened in 1889, grew out of the New Century Guild, formed to assist working women.

A related development was the enthusiasm for organized sports. Boat races on the Schuylkill began during the mid-1830s, and in the following decade, the first boathouses of what would later be called Boathouse Row were constructed. In 1858, the Schuylkill Navy, an association of local rowing clubs, came into being, the nation's first body governing amateur athletics. Boat races on the Schuylkill were very popular, attracting thousands of spectators.[86] In 1895, the University of Pennsylvania began hosting the first Penn Relays, the oldest continuously run track and field competition in the United States.[87] In the early part of the nineteenth century, cricket was incredibly popular in the United States, and Philadelphia was home to the nation's first cricket club (the Philadelphia Cricket Club, established in 1854).[88] The club did not have an official home until 1883, when, through the generosity of Philadelphia industrialist Henry H. Houston, the club became established in Chestnut Hill. Its golf course, known as St. Martins, hosted the United States Open Championship in 1907, the first time the Philadelphia area hosted that event.[89]

However, cricket was soon eclipsed by the game that would become the great American pastime: baseball. The Civil War made baseball, which was largely a regional game before 1860, popular across the United States, and Philadelphia was no exception: by the late 1860s, Philadelphia had several white baseball teams and at least two Black ones, the Pythians (founded by Black educator Jacob White Jr. and captained by his friend and former classmate Octavius Catto) and the Excelsiors (later absorbed by the Pythians).[90] In 1869, the Pythians played the first interracial baseball game at the Jefferson Street Ballparks (Jefferson Street between Twenty-Fourth and Twenty-Fifth) against the all-white Olympics. Despite the advances toward equality made during the late 1860s, when the Pennsylvania State Convention of Baseball was founded in 1867, the organization excluded the Pythians, contributing to the 1884 formation of the National Colored Base Ball League.[91] Furthermore, in 1867, several Black Philadelphia women formed a baseball team, the Dolly Vardens, which scrimmaged against other female teams.[92] The Jefferson Street Ballpark was the Philadelphia Athletics' home field from 1871 to 1876, and it was the site of the inaugural National League game (April 22, 1876), which is generally credited as being the beginning of Major League Baseball. The Phillies ball club was founded in 1883, followed by the Philadelphia Athletics in 1901.

To get away from the squalid conditions around the city's factories, wealthy and middle-class white Philadelphians migrated west and north, spurring the development of West and North Philadelphia. The replacement of horse-drawn omnibuses by street railways made it easier and more convenient to traverse the sprawling metropolis, diminishing the need to locate industries near the city's waterways and making living near the Schuylkill River more attractive.[93] In 1892, the first electric trolley route opened in Philadelphia, and by 1900 all the city's streetcar lines had become electric trolley car lines. Electric trolleys charged lower fares, allowing Philadelphia's working class the opportunity to ride them, though middle-class Philadelphians were the real beneficiaries.[94] Walnut Street west of Broad became Philadelphia's most fashionable place to live, particularly in the stretch along Rittenhouse Square.[95] Initially settled during the colonial era and called "Goosetown" (because of the geese that congregated in the clay pits), Rittenhouse Square was populated by clay quarries and earthenware factories until the mid-nineteenth century. Though the square existed, it was hardly the bucolic park it is today: well into the nineteenth century, residents dumped their chamber pots in the square.[96] The first large-scale settlement occurred in the 1830s and 1840s, when Irish immigrants moved to the area to work in the various industries that had sprung up south of the square. Then, beginning in the 1850s, a few wealthy Philadelphians moved out to what was then the city's western edge, attracted by the quiet and relatively bucolic surroundings. Many were self-made men, and the mansions they built testified to their newly acquired wealth, though by the Centennial the square was home to a mix of new and old money families.[97]

Development also pushed on the Schuylkill River's west bank. West Philadelphia consisted of only two wards in 1875, the Twenty-Fourth and Twenty-Seventh, but by 1901 it comprised four (Twenty-Fourth, Twenty-Seventh, Thirty-Fourth, and Fortieth). In North Philadelphia, a similar story unfolded: between 1875 and 1901, the area north of Montgomery Avenue and west of Germantown Avenue swelled from three wards to six.[98] South Philadelphia, which was still largely farmland below Passyunk Avenue during the 1880s, underwent a building boom from the 1890s through the 1910s.[99] The ubiquity of railroads also made it possible for people to work in the city but live in the suburbs, spurring the development of towns along the old Main Line of Public Works; collectively, towns like Overbrook, Merion, Narberth, Wynnewood, Ardmore, Haverford, Bryn Mawr, and Paoli (known by the mnemonic "Old Maids Never Wed and Have Babies Period") are referred to as "the Main Line" to this day.[100] Another suburb, Elkins Park (just outside Philadelphia in Montgomery County), became a haven for massive estates owned by men such as Henry W. Breyer Sr., Jay Cooke, John Stetson, John Wanamaker, P. A. B. Widener, and William L. Elkins. The change could be disorienting; an 1891 publication noted, "No doubt many of the readers of this volume can remember when the public squares at Broad and Market streets were a Sunday afternoon's promenade from the city proper. . . . [A]ll of this is of the past. . . . Thousands of houses erected every year, thousands of new property-owners added to the records, thousands of new citizens given a positively personal interest in the city's welfare, is the history of landed interests here."[101]

According to Alexander McClure, a newspaper editor and former member of the Pennsylvania House of Representatives, the rapid accumulation of wealth, with its conspicuous display, "absolutely unsettled the whole social system of the city," pitting Philadelphia's established families against its nouveau riche.[102] This was not the first time rapid accumulation of wealth had upset the city's social order; a similar dynamic played out in the years leading up to the Revolutionary War. Just as at that time, the city's newly rich built ostentatious houses to broadcast their wealth and status, often along North Broad Street, Fairmount Avenue, Spring Garden Street, and Girard Avenue.[103] Frequently, these palatial mansions, which broadcast their owners' wealth and aspirations to status, were designed by Frank H. Furness, the go-to architect for the city's elite.[104] Furness was born in the city in 1839 and architecture while working in the office of architect John Fraser (not to be confused with the travel writer cited earlier) who designed the Union League of Philadelphia's building. After serving in the US Army during the Civil War (for which he won the Medal of Honor for bravery), Furness returned to Philadelphia, where he spent his entire career. During the 1870s, 1880s, and 1890s, in addition to residences, he built the Pennsylvania Academy of the Fine Arts (opened 1876), the Centennial National Bank (opened 1876, located at 3142 Market Street and now Drexel University's Paul Peck Alumni Center), and the Philadelphia Zoo's Gatehouses (1875). He also designed and built the University of Pennsylvania's library (now called the Fisher Fine Arts Library), dedicated in 1891. As the chief architect of the Pennsylvania Railroad (PRR), Furness supervised the expansion of the Broad Street Station in 1892–1893. Furness's work was underappreciated in the decades after his death (in part because of his association with the city's nouveau riche), though he was "rediscovered" in the mid-twentieth century.[105]

Sociologist E. Digby Baltzell's distinction between "upper class" and "elite" becomes useful for understanding Philadelphia's society and politics in this period. According to Baltzell, an upper class is "a group of *families* whose members are descendants of successful individuals . . . these families are at the top of the social class hierarchy." By contrast, elite simply means "those *individuals* who are . . . leaders in their chosen occupations or professions."[106] A person could be elite without being upper class (many were).[107] The distance between old and new money was embodied in the city's geography: the "right" people did not live north of Market Street.[108] Harriet Boyer, a New Yorker who lived in Philadelphia for several years, noted the prevailing belief among the city's old money that "a dozen or so vulgar people, who had made fortunes, as army contractors during the war, built some splendid mansions on a wide street. . . . Hundreds of nice, quiet people live there, in a nice, quiet, old-fashioned way, who have been steadily getting rich every year; whose grandchildren have had every advantage, are handsome, well bred, traveled, have enlarged ideas, and are well received everywhere; everywhere except South of Market Street, where they are socially ostracized."[109]

P. A. B. Widener II, grandson of the trolley line magnate who shared his name, complained in his autobiography about Philadelphia's exclusive social hierarchy, recalling that "the City of Brotherly Love, shrine of American liberty, was dedicated to the principles of snobbery more than any other American city."[110] In short, money alone did not open all of Philadelphia's doors: the city's most exclusive clubs and organizations remained largely closed to the nouveau riche elite and their immediate descendants.[111] In part due to this dynamic, Philadelphia was reputed to be sleepy, boring, and parochial relative to other American cities, which led to several popular jokes about it (one contemporary called Philadelphia "the joke-town of America").[112]

This was also a period of political corruption in cities across the United States, though for British Ambassador to the United States James Bryce, Philadelphia was "a peculiarly instructive instance of the evils which everywhere infect municipal government."[113] Muckraking journalist Lincoln Steffens went even further, calling Philadelphia both "corrupt and contented."[114] One reason for the corruption in city government was that Philadelphia was essentially a one-party town, though the Republican Party was riven by factions that often spent more time battling each other than the Democrats. William S. Vare, who enjoyed a long career in Philadelphia and Pennsylvania politics, recalled that in the 1880s, the city's Republicans were divided "into various factions . . . and the bickering between those elements . . . furnished the political strifes of the times."[115] On the one hand were the Stalwarts, who were committed to maintaining the party's political strength by constructing political "machines" through the distribution of patronage. Crucially, the Stalwarts were not a cohesive faction; competition for control of patronage led to conflict between various Stalwart factions and sometimes made for odd bedfellows politically. In opposition were the Half-Breeds—Republicans committed to ending the abuses of the machine politicians by enacting civil service reform. Often these were among Pennsylvania's industrial and commercial leaders frustrated by their relatively limited political influence with the machines.[116] For instance, Quakers played an outsized role in the political reform movements of the period, despite the sect's relatively limited political and cultural influence.[117] Conflict between the reformers and the machine politicians emerged during the 1860s, and it intensified during subsequent decades.[118]

A good example of the cost of corrupt government in Philadelphia was the debacle surrounding construction of the new city hall. The existing city hall, located at Fifth and Chestnut and housing not only municipal government but also the police and fire department's offices, was simply inadequate to the needs of the expanding municipal bureaucracy and was no longer in the middle of the city.[119] The economic growth of the Civil War years added to this pressure, so in 1870, the Pennsylvania Assembly created a public buildings commission to oversee the process of constructing a new city hall in Philadelphia. Part of the legislation gave Philadelphians the power to select, by referendum, one of two sites for the new building: Washington Square (on Walnut Street west of Sixth Street) or Penn Square (at the intersection of Broad and Market Streets). Select Council President William S. Stokley used his political influence to promote the Penn Square site because it was in his ward and would provide jobs and contracts he could use to build his political machine; the site won nearly 60 percent of votes cast.[120] Elected mayor in 1871, Stokley used his influence to steer construction contracts to his political allies. Originally projected to cost $10 million and take ten years to complete, building City Hall took until 1901 (though the building's exterior was finished in 1894) and cost $24 million.[121]

City Hall was designed by Philadelphia architect John MacArthur Jr. and Architect of the Capitol Thomas Ustick Walter in the Second Empire style that was then favored for public buildings in the United States from roughly the end of the Civil War to 1900. Named after architectural elements that were common in France during Napoleon III's reign (1852–1870), the Second Empire style featured mansard roofs and elaborate ornamentation. Philadelphia boasted several Second Empire buildings, though by far City Hall is its best known. Ornamented by 250 bronze and marble sculptures (including the thirty-seven-foot-tall statue of William Penn atop the main tower) created by Alexander Milne Calder, Philadelphia's City Hall was then the tallest habitable building in the world (a distinction it retained until 1908).

Building City Hall at Penn Square accelerated the westward migration of businesses, and there was a certain symbolism to the companies that surrounded it: railroads and department stores.[122] In 1881, the Pennsylvania Railroad opened the Broad Street Station on the northwest corner of Broad and Market Streets, just west of City Hall. No one could miss the symbolism of the PRR station sitting so close to Philadelphia's seat of government. The largest railroad terminal in the world at its construction, the building struck one visitor as "palatial in its appointments."[123] Trains entered the station through an elevated viaduct (called the "Chinese Wall") that ran for ten blocks west along Market Street toward the Schuylkill and discouraged development north of Market Street (it literally became the "wrong side of the tracks"), just as highways did during the mid-twentieth century.[124] Not to be outdone, the PRR's main competitor, the Reading Railroad, built its own grand terminal at Twelfth and Market Streets. Prior to the Reading Terminal's construction, the open-air Franklin Market and the Butchers' and Farmers' Market had operated on the site; these continued under the newly constructed train shed but became known as the Reading Terminal Market.

It was surely true that compaines like the PRR and the Reading Railroad bent Philadelphia's municipal government to their will, making it easy to view conflict over governmental reform through a "good versus evil" lens. However, the story is more complicated. Democratization allowed nonwealthy white men to vote and hold public office in greater numbers than ever before, and the reformers, many of whom came from privileged backgrounds, often looked down on politicians and on the voters who elected them, which limited the appeal of their movements.[125] One of the leading voices advocating reform was Philadelphia's *Public Ledger*, owned since 1864 by George W. Childs and A. J. Drexel (partner of investment firm Drexel & Co.). In 1872, several Philadelphia notables, including Childs, Drexel, Henry C. Lea, and Joshua B. Lippincott (founder of the publisher J. B. Lippincott Co.), organized the Reform Club for the purpose of "promoting the cause of municipal reform in the city of Philadelphia through mutual intercourse and discussion."[126] This was hardly new—volunteer-based reform organizations went back to Franklin's day—but the optics were terrible: the Reform Club met in a mansion on Chestnut Street. British Ambassador Bryce, who was sympathetic to the reformers, claimed "the local control and management of the party fell into the hands of obscure citizens . . . but who were valuable to the party because they *kept in power through their assiduous work among a lower class of voter* [my emphasis]."[127] The reformers did not stop there; they alleged that the machines "bought off" voters, asserting that

> those who are robbed . . . share in the proceeds of most of the robberies. . . . [I]t is some excuse for the large number of Philadelphians who have as yet failed to realize there is an urgent necessity for them to give time, labor and money, and to sacrifice many social and business interests in a probably unsuccessful effort to displace their present masters.[128]

However, antidemocratic sentiments like these could only alienate voters. Stalwarts were hardly committed democrats, but they did better than the reformers.[129] W. E. B. Du Bois pointed out that machine Republicans provided the city's Black men with jobs; reform would imperil the Black community's economic health. In what was clearly a dig at John Wanamaker, a leading Republican reformer whose store did not hire Black men and women, Du Bois noted that "these very reformers who want votes for specific reforms, will not themselves work beside Negroes, or admit them to positions in their stores or offices, or lend them friendly aid in trouble."[130]

Yet it is undeniable that the growth of industry and the flood of cash generated by the war created a generation of plutocrats who built a mutually beneficial series of relationships with elements of the Republican Party.[131] For instance, P. A. B. Widener, who was twenty-six at the war's commencement, won a lucrative contract to supply mutton to all federal soldiers within ten miles of Philadelphia.[132] Given that Philadelphia was a transit hub and the site of several hospitals, Widener's contract was enormously profitable, and he invested his profits in horse-drawn streetcars. His relationship to the Pennsylvania Republican political machine, in particular, ensured his financial success: in 1873, Philadelphia political boss Matthew S. Quay appointed Widener city treasurer, after the incumbent, Joseph Marcer, was convicted of larceny and imprisoned in Eastern State Penitentiary (Marcer's agent, Charles Tyson Yerkes, who was also convicted of larceny, served as the model for Frank Cowperwood in Theodore Dreiser's novels *The Financier*, *The Titan*, and *The Stoic*).[133] Widener used his office to purchase Philadelphia's various horsecar companies, and in 1883 Widener, William Kemble, and William L. Elkins formed the Philadelphia Traction Company, which monopolized Philadelphia's street railways and added to their political power.[134] For many Philadelphians, "good government" (as reformers defined it) was not in their economic interests.[135]

Whatever their qualms with machine politicians, many Republicans would not consider voting for a Democrat, for several reasons. One was Republicans' effectiveness in leveraging the memory of the Civil War and tarring Democrats as the party of secession (a tactic derided as "waving the bloody shirt").[136] Another had to do with the reformers' concerns about the effect that electing Democrats locally and statewide would have on the Republican Party in national elections. These merchants and manufacturers were particularly concerned about reductions in the tariff, or the tax assessed on imported goods, which made domestically produced goods more attractive to consumers.[137] This was a marked contrast to the so-called machine Republicans, one of whom rhetorically asked, "What do I care who is president, as long as I can carry my ward?"[138] In addition, Democrats were often no better than the Republicans they replaced. For instance, when Democrat Daniel M. Fox became mayor in 1869, he fired almost all of the city's police officers because most were Republican appointees. Fox's successor, William S. Stokley, in turn fired Fox's appointees, replacing them with Republicans.[139] Even when Democratic officeholders were not corrupt, as in the case of Robert Pattison, elected city comptroller in 1880, they exposed Republican malfeasance, injuring the party. The fact that Pattison used the city comptrollership as a stepping stone to two terms as Pennsylvania's governor (1883 to 1887 and 1891 to 1895), the only Democrat to win that office between 1861 and 1935, certainly did nothing to encourage Half-Breed Republicans to vote for Democrats. This kept the reform element in the Republican Party from achieving lasting gains.

One of the reformers' key goals was revising the commonwealth's constitution. Though less than four decades old, the 1838 constitution was ill-suited to the realities of Pennsylvania's new industrial economy. For instance, the state had no general incorporation law—the Assembly granted incorporations on a case-by-case basis through special legislation. This clogged the legislative process and created myriad opportunities for corruption.[140] The 1870 legislative session was a perfect illustration of what happened: in session for only sixty-five days, the Assembly passed and Governor John W. Geary signed into law nearly 1,500 bills.[141] A convention to revise the constitution met for ten months in 1873 at a variety of locations across the commonwealth, including at Philadelphia's Sixth Presbyterian Church near the corner of Sixth and Spruce Streets. The new constitution extended suffrage to all men (but not women, Black or white) over the age of twenty-one provided they were US citizens who had lived in Pennsylvania for at least a year, but it also had some antidemocratic features.[142] The constitution abolished the office of alderman, replacing it with magistrates.[143] This was a key development: aldermen were the elected officials closest to the voter; as a result, they were more reflective of their diverse constituents than mayors and more responsive to their constituents' needs.[144] By contrast, magistrates were elected at large, meaning they did not represent (and therefore had no ties to) the city's wards. Most of Philadelphia's aldermen did not come from old money families; instead, they were often the sort of "professional" politicians whom old-money Philadelphians disdained.[145] For upper- and middle-class reformers, the problem was that elected officials were too responsive to their constituents, and the reformers sought to make the process less democratic.[146] Strengthening the mayor and weakening the aldermen was, in their view, a way of ensuring only the "best people" were elected to office.[147]

Pennsylvania's new constitution further eroded Philadelphians' political power. Under the terms of the 1857 amendments to the constitution, Pennsylvania's legislature could set the number of senators in the Keystone State's upper house and apportion representation according to a district's taxable inhabitants, provided no city or county had more than four senators. Consequently, in 1860, Pennsylvania had twenty-eight state senators, with four (one-seventh) representing Philadelphia, even though the city accounted for nearly one-fifth of the commonwealth's population. Naturally, during the constitutional convention, Philadelphia's representatives sought to remedy this problem, but they failed.

In fact, the new constitution made the problem worse: each county received a single senator, regardless of population, and the legislature was prohibited from dividing counties, cities, towns, or boroughs into representative districts "unless absolutely necessary."[148]

While this was a blow to Philadelphia, it was a boon to the state-level Republican political machine. The Pennsylvania Assembly tended to defer to the representatives of communities when it came to framing legislation that affected those communities.[149] This placed fast-growing industrial cities, such as Allentown, at a disadvantage: though the cities tended to be dominated by Republicans, they were in counties controlled by Democrats. As a result, Democrats were able to impose their will on the city's Republicans. In fact, an 1870 meeting in Reading of so-called minority communities resolved "that the practice which has grown up in the Legislature of Pennsylvania of submitting all matters of local legislation to the exclusive control of local representatives has practically placed the local, political and business interests of minority constituencies requiring legislation at the mercy of the majority local representatives, and has afforded such a continued series of wrongs and petty oppression as loudly call for reform."[150] In other words, Pennsylvania's Republicans saw constitutional reform as an avenue for strengthening their political power in Pennsylvania's cities in counties controlled by Democrats. Looking at the matter this way, it becomes clear why, as early as 1867, Matthew S. Quay, who represented Philadelphia in the Pennsylvania House of Representatives (and who later succeeded J. Donald Cameron as head of the state Republican machine), advocated convening a convention to revise the commonwealth's constitution, even though Philadelphia, where the city and county were coterminous, did not have this problem.[151]

In 1880, believing "public affairs [were] in their worst stage of mismanagement, extravagance, and corruption," a group of 107 prominent Republican businessmen formed the Citizens' Committee of One Hundred, which was committed to maintaining the "purity of the ballot," "the nomination and election of a better class of candidates for office," and the promotion of "public service based upon character and capability alone."[152] The committee's key achievement was Philadelphia's new charter. Outlined in "An Act to Provide for the Better Government of Cities of the First Class in this Commonwealth," which the state legislature passed in the spring of 1885, that charter reorganized Philadelphia's government. Largely the work of Philadelphia lawyer John Christian Bullitt, the charter (which went into effect on April 4, 1887) established a bicameral legislating body composed of a forty-eight-member Select Council and a ninety-seven-member Common Council.[153] It also centralized municipal authority by consolidating the city's twenty-five bureaus into nine departments whose heads the city's mayor (now elected to a four-year term and prohibited

from seeking reelection for at least four years) appointed (though the appointments required the approval of the Select Council).[154] Strengthening the mayor
reversed the trend of the last several decades, which had seen the mayor's executive authority divided between boards and departments, curtailing the political
influence of organizations such as the Gas Trust (described below).[155] The Citizens' Committee of One Hundred, believing it had achieved its mission, thereafter dissolved, a good illustration of the stop-start approach that characterized
municipal reform in the 1870s and 1880s.[156]

However, the new city charter was far from the commanding victory the
municipal reformers hoped it would be. It is telling that the first mayor elected
under the new charter, Edwin H. Fitler, appointed as director of public safety
former mayor Stokley, which sent the message that it would be business as usual.
Matthew S. Quay, then serving as secretary of the commonwealth, supported the
new charter because he recognized it was useful to neuter the recalcitrant Gas
Trust boss, James (known as "King James") McManes. Gas illumination had first
occurred in Philadelphia in 1816. In 1835, the city councils passed an ordinance
authorizing the sale of $100,000 in stock to fund the construction and opera-
tions of the Philadelphia Gas Works (PGW). In 1841, the city took over control
of PGW, establishing a twelve-member board of trustees that would exist until
the gasworks' loans were paid off. In 1854, PGW purchased most of the county's gas plants, cementing a near monopoly on gas production in Philadelphia.[157]
The board of trustees continually replaced retired loans with new ones, thereby
perpetuating its existence.[158] The reason was simple: if the gasworks were under
trusteeship, it kept all the profits, which the trustees used to award sweetheart
deals to their political cronies. Though the trustees received no salary, they controlled nearly $2 million in annual contracts and approximately one thousand
jobs.[159] The result was the trustees used their influence to elect members of the
city councils, who in turn appointed members of PGW's board of trustees. Bryce
reprinted a letter from a Philadelphian who complained that

> aspirants for seats in the councils found it almost impossible to obtain
> either nomination or election without the favor of the trust. Thus the
> councils became filled with its henchmen or "heelers," submissive to its
> bidding, not only in the selection of trustees to fill the four yearly vacan-
> cies, but in every detail of city government with which the leaders of the
> trust desired to interfere.[160]

Until 1865, the board of trustees had Democratic and Republican members, but
that year the board came under total Republican control. Trustee McManes,
an Irish immigrant to Philadelphia, used the gasworks to build a formidable

political machine in Philadelphia, but he ran afoul of the statewide political machine run by Abraham Lincoln's former secretary of war, Simon Cameron.

Born into poverty in 1799, Cameron had built a fortune as a printer and later banker, which allowed him to establish himself as one of Pennsylvania's leading Democratic power brokers by 1840. When James Buchanan left the US Senate to become President James K. Polk's secretary of state in 1845, the Assembly picked Cameron to serve the remaining portion of Buchanan's Senate term. Defeated in his bid for a full Senate term in 1848, Cameron drifted away from the Democratic Party because of its increasingly Southern tilt. Cameron migrated into the nascent Republican Party by the mid-1850s, quickly establishing himself as a leader of one of its many factions. Because of Cameron's prominence in a politically important state, Lincoln appointed him secretary of war in 1861, a position the Pennsylvanian held only briefly. Lincoln fired Cameron in January 1862 because he vocally advocated allowing Black men to enlist into the Union army. After a brief stint as US minister to Russia, Cameron established himself as the political boss of Pennsylvania's Republican Party by the late 1860s. He used his power to engineer his reelection to the Senate, where he was a key Republican power broker for a decade.

The struggle over the gasworks was part of a larger conflict over the 1880 presidential election. In 1880, Cameron's machine promoted former general Ulysses S. Grant for president. Grant had already served two terms as president (1869–1877), during which Cameron (then a senator) had access to federal patronage that he used to reinforce his control of Pennsylvania's Republican Party. The election of Rutherford B. Hayes in 1876 essentially stripped Cameron of his access to federal patronage because, though a Republican, Hayes was committed to civil service reform and did not like Cameron personally. The former senator hoped that with Grant back in the White House, his machine would again have access to federal patronage. McManes, by contrast, promoted Ohio Representative James A. Garfield, who eventually received the Republican nomination and won the election. Furious at McManes, Cameron's supporters worked with the Citizens' Committee of One Hundred to temporarily depose McManes from PGW's board.[161] In addition, strengthening the mayor and providing him with the lion's share of the city's patronage actually contributed to the consolidation and entrenchment of a political machine.[162] Thus, by 1887, because of the reformers' efforts, the city's Republican machine was stronger and better organized than ever, and Philadelphia was a one-party town for nearly a half century. As one of Quay's lieutenants bragged to journalist Lincoln Steffens, "The [new] Charter was a great thing for us. It was the best, last throw of the reformers, and when we took that charter and went right on with our business, we took the heart out of reform forever."[163]

That being said, machine control of the city's government was never total or uncontested.[164] For instance, in 1894, the reformers in Philadelphia successfully pressured the city's Republicans not to nominate Boies Penrose, a state senator, for mayor. Penrose, a power broker closely allied with Matthew S. Quay (following Quay's death in 1904, he later assumed control of the Cameron political machine), had been photographed leaving a prostitute's house.[165] Beyond that, the tide of change was in the reformers' favor as, beginning in the 1870s, a national movement for civil service reform emerged. In 1883, President Chester A. Arthur signed into law the Pendleton Civil Service Reform Act, which mandated that the federal government hire people based on their skills and education, not their politics. Whereas the Jacksonians believed that any man could fulfill any government job and celebrated the idea of government agencies being run by political appointees, civil service reform rested on the assumption that governing required nonpartisan expertise. Over time this would erode, but never eliminate, the machine politicians' influence, though Pennsylvania's Republican machine managed to hobble civil service reform in the commonwealth well into the twentieth century.[166]

Despite the pervasive corruption of Philadelphia's government, the city remained a leading American cultural center. The Pennsylvania Museum and School of Industrial Art made Philadelphia a leading artistic center well into the twentieth century. The United States' oldest artists' club, the Philadelphia Sketch Club, opened in November 1860. Founded by several students at the Philadelphia Academy of the Fine Arts (PAFA), the Sketch Club's mission was to offer affordable drawing classes and create a space for local artists to display their work. One famous early member was Thomas Eakins, among the country's finest realist painters. His 1875 painting *The Gross Clinic*, considered one of the finest paintings by an American artist, was shown at the Centennial Exhibition, though in the US Army Post Hospital rather than the Art Department. Eakins was controversial: in 1886, he lost his position as PAFA's director after removing a male model's loincloth in a classroom that included female students. However, his influence was visible in the work of his pupils, a group that included painter Thomas P. Anshutz (who cofounded the Darby School and succeeded Eakins at PAFA), engraver and painter Alice Barber Stephens, painter and photographer Susan MacDowell (who married Eakins), and sculptor Frank Stephens. Noted German landscape artist Hermann Herzog immigrated to Philadelphia in the late 1860s. His painting of Yosemite's Sentinel Rock won a medal at the Centennial Exhibition.

Many of the city's most venerable cultural institutions moved west as well, though few crossed the Schuylkill River. In 1876, the Academy of Natural Sciences decamped from Broad and Sansom to Nineteenth and Race Streets. In

1880, the Library Company moved from Fifth and Chestnut to a new building (designed by Frank Furness) on the northwest corner of the intersection of Juniper and Locust Streets. Philadelphia also added several key cultural institutions during this period, most notably the Free Library of Philadelphia. Despite Benjamin Franklin's having started the continent's first subscription library and the city being a printing center, Philadelphia only belatedly established a municipal library.[167] In February 1891, the Free Library was chartered as "a general library which shall be free to all," distinguishing it from the subscription libraries that had existed in the city since the first third of the eighteenth century.[168] Funded by a bequest that Dr. William Pepper Jr. secured from his uncle, George S. Pepper, the Free Library was initially located at City Hall before moving to the Concert Hall at Twelfth and Chestnut, where it remained until 1910.

The city was home to several nationally prominent newspapers, including the *Public Ledger* and the *North American*.[169] In 1884, Black journalist Christopher J. Perry established the *Philadelphia Tribune*, the United States' oldest continuously published Black newspaper. The city was also home to several prominent late nineteenth-century writers, including Owen Wister, whose 1902 novel *The Virginian* is generally considered the first western ever published. Poet Walt Whitman lived in nearby Camden, New Jersey. Poet, playwright, and Union League co-founder George H. Boker lived in Philadelphia for most of his life (he served as US minister to Turkey and Russia during the 1870s). In 1889, Dutch-born author and editor Edward W. Bok moved to Philadelphia, in part attracted by the fact that the city was a major publishing center. He edited the *Ladies' Home Journal* and later married Mary L. Curtis, the daughter of publishing magnate Cyrus H. K. Curtis, whose Curtis Publishing Company produced iconic magazines such as the *Saturday Evening Post*. Agnes Repplier, the country's foremost essayist, lived in Philadelphia most of her life.

Philadelphians thought of the city as a leading center of American theater, and they were noted as being particularly enthusiastic playgoers.[170] The most notable Philadelphia actors of the period were the Barrymore family. British actor Maurice Barrymore married Philadelphian actress Georgiana Drew (who came from a well-established thespian family) in 1876, and they had three children, Lionel, Ethel, and John, all of whom became leading actors of their day. In fact, Ethel was considered the "First Lady of the American Theater." The city also played a small role in the emerging motion picture industry. Siegmund Lubin, a Polish Jewish immigrant to Philadelphia, began distributing films for Thomas Edison's New Jersey–based movie company in 1896. The following year, Lubin started producing his own films, eventually establishing a production facility at Twentieth Street and Indiana Avenue. Lubin later expanded, buying a 350-acre estate in Montgomery County called Betzwood, where he filmed hundreds of short films. Lubin's company folded in 1917, when US entry into World War I severely curtailed the European market for his films. However, during the 1920s, Philadelphia was home to the Colored Players Film Corporation, a short-lived, integrated movie studio that produced films that challenged stereotypes about Black people. The corporation was headquartered at 1337 Vine Street and released its best-known film, *Scar of Shame*, in 1927; two years later, the company went out of business.[171]

Philadelphia's historic sites and buildings remained popular tourist attractions, and a quick succession of national, regional, and local anniversaries— including the one hundredth anniversaries of Washington's winter in Valley Forge (1777–1778) and the drafting of the US Constitution (1787), as well as the two hundredth anniversary of Pennsylvania's founding (1682)—made the city a destination for American and European tourists.[172] Like the Centennial Exhibition, these celebrations usually mixed historical materials with pride in the city's industrial production.[173] Running just beneath the surface, however, was considerable tension: the upper class, alarmed at Philadelphia's changing demographics and the perceived epidemic of municipal corruption, sought to leverage the city's history to inculcate "American" values through a series of public celebrations.[174] As Mrs. E. D. Gillespie, who was active in several historical organizations, noted at the time, across the United States groups "were roused to work that the youth of the country should be more wise in their day and generation than we had been in ours. We were teaching them the value of the old landmarks and buildings made sacred through the presence of those who established the government of the country."[175]

Another aspect of these civic celebrations was the desire to unify the city. Consolidation did not immediately or neatly knit together the diverse, and previously independent, communities. Philadelphia remained, in the words of one visitor, "a string of villages," each characterized by "village gossip and village narrowness."[176] The civic celebrations, which emphasized the key events in the city's history, were designed to break down those provincial attachments, just as political reforms that shifted representation from the ward level to at-large were intended to do. One example of this attempt was the city's adoption in 1895 of a civic flag designed by local Presbyterian minister Henry C. McCook. It featured an azure blue background bisected by a vertical yellow stripe. Inside the stripe was the city's seal.[177] It was also visible in the substantial amount of public art commissioned in the years after the Civil War, much of which depicted Revolutionary War heroes, Union officers, and Republican politicians, a clear attempt to use public space to promote certain political values.[178] At the same time, other groups, including the city's Irish, German, Italian, and Black communities, also celebrated significant historical anniversaries in ways that reinforced their own distinctive histories and provided a counternarrative to the one promulgated by the city's elite.[179]

Yet, it is undeniable that the democratic and industrial forces unleashed in the first part of the nineteenth century had reshaped Philadelphia. With the city now a sprawling industrial behemoth, its government was a byword for corruption even as its manufactured goods were celebrated for their quality. As the country's third-largest city, Philadelphia remained a crucial center for American literature, theater, and scientific advancement even as vast swaths of its citizens toiled in poverty. Developing a responsive municipal government with the resources to address these issues became an overriding concern of the first half of the twentieth century, when progressive reformers and then the New Deal established the groundwork for what many would remember (nostalgically) as a golden age in the city's history.

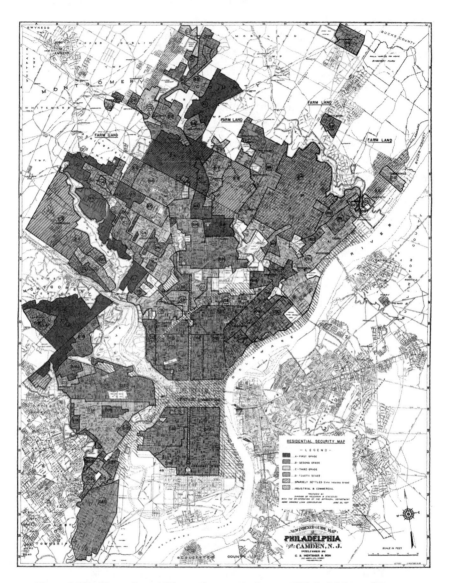

Figure 8. The Home Owners' Loan Corporation's map of Philadelphia, 1937. National Archives. As in many other US cities, Philadelphia banks and lenders discriminated against borrowers of color, creating disparities of wealth that persist to this day.

CHAPTER 8

Wars, Abroad and at Home, 1901–1945

Philadelphia's population reached its zenith by the mid-twentieth century, though as early as the mid-1920s, the first stirrings of deindustrialization were visible. At the dawn of the twentieth century, Philadelphia's population was just under 1.3 million, and in the fifteen years after the turn of the century, the city experienced its largest numerical increase of any fifteen-year period in its history.[1] Consistently the third-largest city in the United States during this period, in the 1940 census, Philadelphia's population registered a decline, though small (approximately 1 percent), and recovered in the next census.[2] World War I fueled a "great migration" of southern Black people to northern cities, including Philadelphia, while draconian laws passed during the 1920s effectively ended immigration to the United States, both of which reshaped the city demographically. These changes, along with the challenges posed by the Great Depression, eventually weakened the dominant Republican Party, setting in motion the end of its nearly century-long domination of the City of Brotherly Love. In addition, the New Deal and World War II expanded the definition of groups considered to be "white." These groups, who correctly perceived their claim to "whiteness" as precarious, often sought to reinforce their status through overt racism and discrimination, which had a devastating impact on the city's Black population that continues to this day.

Despite the reformers' efforts, Philadelphia's Republican political machines were stronger and more coherent in 1900 than at the end of the Civil War. One was led by a triumvirate of Israel W. Durham (who served at various times in the Pennsylvania Senate and as the state insurance commissioner), John Mack (owner of several paving companies that received municipal contracts at Durham's behest), and state Senator James P. "Sunny Jim" McNichol (who had interests in the Filbert Paving and Construction Company and the Penn Reduction Company). All were subservient to the state-level political machine controlled by Boies Penrose, which maintained discipline through the distribution of contracts and nearly ten thousand patronage jobs. In return, officeholders "donated" between 3 and 12 percent of their salaries to the machine. The Pennsylvania Assembly tried to curtail this practice by passing a law in February 1906 "prohibiting the solicitation, collection or receipt of, by or from officers or employees of cities of the first class," though this seems to have had little effect.[3] Durham's influence was so great that he was able to get his brother-in-law, Philip H. Johnson, named the city's official "architect in perpetuity." Johnson, who was a self-trained architect, received commissions on every building the city's Department of Health and Charities constructed between 1903 and 1933, a sum that eventually totaled $2 million. In addition, he designed several important buildings in Philadelphia, including the Municipal Auditorium (later known as the Civic Center, demolished in 2005) and the City Hall Annex (21 North Juniper Street, currently a hotel). In addition, he was one of several architects involved in the scandal-plagued construction of Pennsylvania's State Capitol, and he designed both the Pennhurst State Hospital and the Philadelphia Hospital for the Insane (later called Byberry State Hospital, 14000 Roosevelt Boulevard).[4]

Meanwhile, the Vare brothers—George, Edwin, and William S. (sometimes called the "Dukes of South Philadelphia")—consolidated a trash-hauling business into a Republican political machine that placed a family member in the Pennsylvania Senate every year from 1896 to 1928.[5] Initially, George ran the machine and served in the Pennsylvania House of Representatives and Senate until his death in 1908. Following George's death, Edwin took control of the machine, serving in the Pennsylvania House of Representatives until his death in 1922. Control then shifted to William, who served in the Pennsylvania and US Houses before running for the US Senate in 1926. The Vares' political machine drew its strength from the "river wards" (those closest to the Delaware River, comprising many of the city's poorest neighborhoods) and neutralized the anemic Democratic Party by offering its chairman, John O'Donnell, a few patronage posts in exchange for fielding weak candidates.[6] The Vares registered some of their own men as Democrats to ensure that O'Donnell was never seriously challenged in a primary and even paid the rent on the Democrats' headquarters.[7]

Durham's machine made a major misstep in 1905 with the so-called Gas War. Durham, who was in failing health, tried to set himself up for retirement by offering his friend and political ally Thomas Dolan's United Gas Improvement Company (UGIC) a sweetheart, seventy-five-year lease on the municipal gasworks.[8] The plan required UGIC to pay the city $25 million in exchange for the right to sell gas to the municipal gasworks' customers. The payment was a fraction of the lease's value but represented a massive infusion of quick cash that Durham could use to reward his political allies. Even for "corrupt and contented" Philadelphia, this was overreaching, and the city councils were deluged by angry complaints about the plan. Eventually, the councils agreed to open the lease to competitive bidding, though it was clear that in the end, UGIC would still win the contract. When the councils voted to award UGIC the lease, Mayor John Weaver threatened to veto the bill and fired several Durham allies from his administration. Eventually, Durham backed down, and the proposal was withdrawn.[9] Durham died in 1909, and control of the political machine passed to McNichol; its influence gradually declined.[10]

In response to the gas trust debacle, in 1905, political reformers from across Pennsylvania formed the Lincoln Party. Though its name was an allusion to a Republican president, the party welcomed Democrats. In that year's munici-pal elections, Lincoln Party candidates secured some impressive victories in Philadelphia and, during a special session of the legislature the following year, enactment of several key reforms (including a stronger civil service code). How-ever, little changed. Disgusted by the Republican and Democratic nominees for governor, dissidents from both parties met in Philadelphia in 1910 and founded the Keystone Party, which nominated businessman and former Pennsylvania state treasurer William H. Berry. He lost the election, but the following year, Philadelphia's Keystone Party nominated longtime reformer Rudolph Blanken-burg for mayor (the Democrats endorsed him too). Penrose promoted lawyer George H. Earle Jr. (father of future Pennsylvania governor George H. Earle III), who won the nomination after a bruising primary fight against William S. Vare. The primary split the Republican Party and allowed Blankenburg to win the election with 50.85 percent of the vote to Earle's 49.15 percent (a difference of just over four thousand votes).[11] While Blankenburg's administration achieved some reforms, he declined to seek a second term and was replaced by Thomas B. Smith, a Vare associate. The contrast between Blankenburg and Smith could not have been starker: in 1917, a melee between Penrose and Vare supporters turned violent, leading to the death of Philadelphia Police Officer George Eppley. Dis-trict Attorney Samuel Rotan indicted Mayor Smith for "conspiracy to commit murder," and though he was acquitted, this tarnished Smith's legacy.[12]

To defeat the Vares and thereby consolidate his control over the city, Penrose allied with the reformers, which led to a new city charter in 1919.[13] The new charter substantially weakened the mayor (a reversal of the 1885 Bullitt Charter) by placing much of the responsibility for governing with the now unicameral, twenty-one-member City Council.[14] The reason was simple: Penrose found it easier to control council members than mayors. For the first time, council members were paid—$5,000 annually, which one contemporary scholar described as "fairly large" when compared to other cities.[15] More impor-tantly, the city itself took on the tasks of trash removal, street cleaning, and paving, which had traditionally been contracted out to companies such as the

Vares'.[16] To fill those jobs, as well as the thousands of other positions in Philadelphia's government, the charter empowered the City Council to create the three-member Civil Service Commission. This system never worked as well as expected, but it was nevertheless step forward in stamping out corruption in Philadelphia's government.[17]

All of this took place against a backdrop of economic decline. The city's port remained one of the nation's busiest, exporting American agricultural produce and manufactured goods around the world.[18] However, leading industries, including textile production, moved south, while others consolidated and eliminated duplicative jobs.[19] A variety of factors—changing consumer tastes, the development of synthetic materials, and business owners' desire to shorten supply chains by moving closer to cotton production—battered Philadelphia's textile industry during the 1920s, a harbinger of postwar deindustrialization. Moreover, durable goods production, a mainstay of Philadelphia's industrial economy, shifted west, taking with it thousands of jobs.[20] While the two world wars slowed this process, they could not stop it.[21]

In addition, Philadelphia had a reputation as a low-wage city, a fact that cannot be separated from the reality that since the Civil War, regional employers had successfully thwarted labor organizing.[22] The Republican machines that controlled the city and the Commonwealth helped employers do that by deploying local and state law enforcement to assist employers in breaking up strikes.[23] In 1905, the state legislature created the Pennsylvania State Police, a paramilitary force originally intended to break strikes. Philadelphia's police department also broke up strikes, including one in the winter of 1909, when more than half of the city's mostly female shirtwaist (garment) workers struck.[24] A good example of law enforcement acting as strikebreakers occurred in 1909. Despite promising not to as part of the resolution of the 1895 transit strike, the Philadelphia Rapid Transit Company (PRT), aggressively stifled unionization among its employees. In 1909, the Amalgamated Association of Street and Electric Railroad Employees (AASERE) established a local and began a drive to unionize the PRT. When the PRT refused to recognize the local, meet its request for wage increases, or discuss the fact that the company required employees to buy their own uniforms, the local commenced a strike. As in 1895, public opinion sided with the strikers.[25] After five days, the PRT agreed to a wage increase of twenty-two cents per hour and to rehire workers fired during the strike, but the company did not recognize the union. In fact, the PRT went so far as to establish its own union, the Keystone Carmen, and aggressively pressured employees to join it.

The AASERE pushed back, noting that the PRT had failed to live up to its commitments; the company responded by firing more than 150 employees linked to the AASERE and importing scabs, or strikebreakers, to replace them.

Striking workers attacked the PRT's streetcars and property, leading Mayor John E. Reyburn to mobilize the city's police force on the company's behalf and deputize three thousand men to quell the violence.[26] When that failed, several hundred Pennsylvania State Police officers came to Philadelphia to help break the strike. Partially in response, other city unions staged sympathy strikes, crippling the city's industries. Unfortunately, this swung public opinion against these unions, and after a month, the sympathy strikes ended. All told, the strike cost more than two dozen lives, most killed during confrontations between strikers and scabs, though the company grudgingly acceded to many of their demands[27]

World War I (1914–1918) had a profound impact on Philadelphia, though it took place in Europe and the United States was not directly involved until nearly the end. On June 28, 1914, a nineteen-year-old Serbian nationalist named Gavrilo Princip assassinated Austrian Archduke Franz Ferdinand and his wife as a step toward ending Austro-Hungarian rule over Bosnia and Herzegovina. In response, Austria-Hungary issued several demands that Serbia almost certainly could not fulfill; the goal seems to have been to provoke a war, and on July 28, Austria-Hungary declared war on Serbia. Because of an elaborate series of treaty commitments between these two countries and the other European powers, Russia, Germany (which declared war on France), and Great Britain found themselves swept into one of the bloodiest wars in history. Initially, President Woodrow Wilson sought to keep the United States out of the war. In fact, in an address to naturalized citizens in Philadelphia's Convention Hall on May 10, 1915, Wilson told the assembled crowd, "The example of America must be the example not merely of peace because it will not fight, but of peace because peace is the healing and elevating influence of the world and strife is not. There is such a thing as a man being too proud to fight. There is such a thing as a nation being so right that it does not need to convince others by force that it is right."[28]

The administration's neutralist policies favored the Allies (Great Britain, France, and Russia). To deprive the Allies of American supplies, German submarines (U-boats) attacked all ships arriving in British ports. On May 7, 1915, a German U-boat torpedoed the RMS *Lusitania*, a British ocean liner with approximately two thousand people aboard. Just under twelve hundred of those aboard died (including at least fifteen Philadelphians), shifting American public opinion decisively against Germany.[29] As a result, Germany abandoned unrestricted submarine warfare, but the exigencies of the war made that policy unsustainable. In January 1917, Germany announced it would return to unrestricted submarine warfare, virtually guaranteeing that the United States would enter the war on the Allies' side. To weaken America before it could enter the war, the Germans encouraged Mexico to preemptively declare war against the United States. German's outrageous gambit became public when American

newpapers published German Foreign Secretary Arthur Zimmermann's intercepted January 1917 telegram to the German minister to Mexico proposing an
alliance of the two countries and promising the return of Mexican territory
ceded to the United States because of the Mexican-American War. The telegram further stoked American anger toward Germany and led the US Congress
to declare war against Germany on April 6, 1917.

World War I provided Philadelphia a much-needed economic boost, as
the value of exports departing the city's port nearly quintupled in the eighteen months following the war's outbreak.[30] Pennsylvania led the world in steel
output, and Philadelphia companies—including Midvale Steel, Baldwin Locomotive Works, and the various shipyards—churned out heavy machinery and
weapons for the US government.[31] Philadelphia's Edward G. Budd Manufacturing Company produced approximately one-half of all the helmets issued to US
soldiers, while the Remington Arms Company (located in nearby Eddystone)
produced approximately the same percentage of rifles issued to US personnel.[32]
Meanwhile, the city's textile firms produced uniforms, and even the inmates
at Eastern State Penitentiary contributed to the war effort, rolling bandages
and making socks for US soldiers.[33] In 1917, the federal government contracted
the American International Shipbuilding Corporation to construct a shipyard
on Hog Island, a small piece of land at the confluence of the Delaware and
Schuylkill Rivers. The two-and-a-half-mile-long shipyard, the largest in the
world at the time, produced 122 vessels (known as "Hog Islanders"). Local
journalist Christopher Morley predicted that Hog Island "will one day make
Philadelphia one of the world's greatest ports," but that proved untrue: the Hog
Island shipyard was demolished in 1921.[34] After the war, the US Army Corps of
Engineers filled the waterway separating the island from the mainland, and the
Pennsylvania National Guard began training pilots there. Though christened
the Philadelphia Municipal Airport in a 1927 ceremony conducted by famed
aviator Charles Lindbergh, its construction was slowed by the Depression, and
it did not open until 1940.

Despite the economic boost World War I generated, it contributed to a devastating public health crisis in Philadelphia with the spread of the H1N1 virus
(nicknamed the "Spanish flu" because of the erroneous belief that Spain was
particularly hard hit by the pandemic). The flu appeared in the Delaware Valley
in mid-September 1918, likely because of the transfer of several hundred infected
sailors from Boston to the Philadelphia Navy Yard.[35] On September 28, the city
held a twenty-three-block parade to drive the sales of bonds ("Liberty Loans")
that financed the United States' war effort, attracting an audience of approximately two hundred thousand and helping spread the disease.[36] One-quarter of
the city's population became ill over the next six months, with approximately

sixteen thousand dying, making Philadelphia the hardest hit US city.[37] The Comtesse Madeleine de Bryas, who visited Philadelphia during the outbreak, recalled, "We found the influenza was spreading its deathly germs over the city, and the people seemed rather frightened at its terrible effects."[38] Philadelphians were frightened with good reason; Mae Townsend Pease recalled, "Coffins piled up in the Railroad stations and in graveyards. The City became demoralized. The food stores closed. Hospitals were crowded and doctors had so many calls that they could not possibly attend to them all."[39]

The outbreak of Spanish flu was not the only public health crisis Philadelphia experienced during the first quarter of the twentieth century. Although the city was cleaner than ever before, thanks to the thousands of municipal workers who swept Philadelphia's streets and removed its garbage, there were still major public health issues.[40] Under pressure from Blankenburg's administration, the piggeries closed, and the stagnant pools of water near them were drained, though the combined sewer system dumped sewage into the Delaware and its tributaries, befouling the city's drinking water.[41] In addition, the city had a rat problem, particularly along the Delaware. Rats were believed to spread disease (an outbreak of bubonic plague in San Francisco from 1900 to 1904 was tied to rats), so Philadelphia adopted several measures to combat rodents, even going so far as to establish a "rat-receiving station" in 1914 at the Race Street Pier. Operated by the Bureau of Health, the station offered Philadelphians a bounty of five cents for every live rat they turned in and two cents for every dead one.[42] Periodic outbreaks of disease still sickened or killed many city residents. For instance, Philadelphia had a pneumonia outbreak in the winter of 1914–1915 and another the following year.[43] In 1916, the city suffered a tragic outbreak of polio that left dozens of people weakened or paralyzed. During the 1920s, the rate of infectious-disease deaths declined, in part because of better public health measures, though the city experienced a smallpox outbreak that claimed nearly two hundred lives in 1925.

While Philadelphia was, according to writer Algernon Sydney Logan, the country's most "war-bent" city, not everyone supported American entry into World War I.[44] Just after the United States declared war in April 1917, a small group of Philadelphia Quakers gathered to discuss how the impending draft (in May 1917, Congress passed the Selective Service Act, authorizing the federal government to conscript men twenty-one to forty-five into the US armed services) would impact so-called peace churches (Quakers, Amish, Brethren, and Mennonites). The organization they founded, the American Friends Service Committee (AFSC, located at 20 South Twelfth Street), provided manpower for humanitarian work in France and continues to exist. In 1947, the AFSC, along with the British Friends Service Council, won the Nobel Peace Prize for having "shown us that it is possible to carry into action something which is deeply rooted in the minds of many: sympathy with others; the desire to help others without regard to nationality or race; feelings which, when carried into deeds, must provide the foundations of a lasting peace."[45]

Socialists also opposed US entry into the war. Though some Americans founded socialist communities during the early nineteenth century, the first socialist party in the United States, initially called the Workingmen's Party of the United States and then the Socialist Labor Party of America (SLP), was founded in 1876. As its name suggests, it was closely tied to the labor union-ism movement and the labor upheavals of the last quarter of the nineteenth century. In 1901, dissidents from the SLP merged with the Social Democratic Party of America to form the Socialist Party of America (SPA). In 1904, the SPA nominated Eugene V. Debs for president of the United States (he had run in 1900 as the nominee of the Social Democratic Party of America). Debs lost in 1904, but the SPA nominated him again in 1908 and 1912; that year he won 6 percent of the popular vote, though no electoral votes. Clearly, the Socialist Party of America had a small but consequential following and was well repre-sented in the country's labor movement.[46] In Philadelphia, economic recessions in 1907–1908 and 1914–1915 likely added to the Socialist Party's numbers, and the University of Pennsylvania's Wharton School of Finance and Commerce even had a socialist economist on the faculty for several years (Dr. Scott Near-ing) until he was terminated in 1915 for agitating against child labor.[47]

In 1917, the Socialist Party's Philadelphia office (at 1326 Arch Street) mailed fifteen thousand leaflets to men who had been drafted under the recently passed Selective Service Act. The leaflets likened conscription to slavery and encour-aged recipients to sign a petition calling on Congress to repeal the act. Author-ities arrested two members of the executive board of Philadelphia's Socialist Party, Charles T. Schenck and Elizabeth Baer, for violating the Espionage Act of 1917, which prohibited interfering with the war effort; both were sentenced to six months in prison. They appealed their conviction to the US Supreme Court on the basis that the Espionage Act violated the First Amendment to the Con-stitution. In a landmark decision, the court ruled in 1919 that the Espionage Act did not violate the First Amendment. Nearing's termination and the *Schenck* case were two precursors of the first "Red Scare," an outbreak of nationwide anti-socialist and anti-communist hysteria that began in 1919. The Russian Rev-olution (1917–1923), in which Bolsheviks (members of a Marxist political party led by Vladimir Lenin) toppled the provisional government established follow-ing Tsar Nicholas II's abdication of the Russian throne, stoked American anx-iety about domestic revolutionary activity. In fact, the Russian Revolution led to a schism in the Socialist Party of America that resulted in the formation of the Communist Party of the United States of America in 1919. President Wilson even joined Great Britain and France in trying to prevent the Bolsheviks from consolidating control over Russia, a move that some historians have argued set in motion the Cold War.

One reason for the antipathy toward socialists was widespread fear of anarchism, which some observers found indistinguishable from socialism (despite the often bitter antagonism between these groups).[48] Both opposed US entry into World War I, but socialism advocated community ownership of the means of production, while anarchism called for abolishing state coercion and organizing society on a strictly voluntary basis. Probably the country's most famous anarchist during the late nineteenth and early twentieth centuries was Emma Goldman, a Russian-born Jew who immigrated to the United States in 1885. Radicalized by the 1886 Haymarket Square riot (when a confrontation between police and striking workers in Chicago turned violent), Goldman became a leading anarchist and women's rights advocate. In 1901 and 1909, Philadelphia police prevented Goldman from speaking in the city. This was hardly unusual; in addition to cracking striking workers' skulls, the Philadelphia Police Department routinely broke up so-called radical meetings, flagrantly violating Americans' civil rights.[49] Goldman and her former lover, Alexander Berkman (who served fourteen years in prison for trying to assassinate industrialist Henry Clay Frick), were later prosecuted under the Espionage Act, sentenced to two years in prison, and then deported.

Some anarchists responded to these repressive policies with terrorism. Just after Christmas in 1918, mail bombs heavily damaged the homes of Pennsylvania Supreme Court Justice Robert von Moschzisker, Municipal Court Judge Frank L. Gorman, Acting Superintendent of the Philadelphia Police William B. Mills, and Philadelphia Chamber of Commerce President Ernest T. Trigg. None were killed, but the *New York Times* breathlessly speculated that the bombings "are the start of terrorist plots planned to reach from one end of the country to the other."[50] That claim proved prophetic, because the following April, anarchists mailed bombs to several dozen key American political and industrial leaders; none injured its intended target, though the wife and servant of US Senator Thomas W. Hardwick of Georgia were severely injured. In June, anarchists planted eight more bombs, including three in Philadelphia. The bombings, coupled with strikes and race riots in several cities that year, provoked a conservative backlash. US Attorney General A. Mitchell Palmer, a Pennsylvania Democrat known as the "Fighting Quaker" and a target of the June bombing (the would-be assassin, an immigrant living in Philadelphia, accidentally killed himself in the blast), launched a series of raids designed to round up and deport left-leaning immigrants.[51] In December 1919, the USS *Buford* (nicknamed the

"Soviet Ark") carried 249 noncitizens expelled from the United States, including several members of Philadelphia's Russian community. That did little to assuage Americans' fears about subversion, and "communist" and "socialist" gradually morphed into all-purpose smears to attack people's political enemies.[52]

Another consequence of World War I for Philadelphia was the "Great Migration" of southern Black people to northern cities. At the war's outbreak, most Black people in the United States lived in the south. Once the United States entered World War I in 1917, millions of white men volunteered for or were conscripted into military service, creating a labor shortage that pushed up wages as economic conditions in southern agriculture faltered.[53] As a result, millions of Black people from all across the south moved to northern industrial cities, including Philadelphia, to take advantage of favorable economic conditions.[54] Between 1910 and 1920, the city's Black population increased by more than 50 percent, then grew by more than 100 percent over the next ten years. By 1930, Black people accounted for just over 11 percent of the city's population.[55] Yet Philadelphia's Black population was far from homogeneous, and the city's Black middle class tended to look down on poor Black people and the recent migrants.[56] This cultural divide was embodied in settlement patterns: many newly arrived Black migrants to Philadelphia settled in Society Hill, Queen Village, and Washington Square because they had the cheapest housing.[57] Meanwhile, Black Philadelphians with greater economic means moved to rapidly growing West Philadelphia, particularly in Morris Park, Overbrook, and Wynnefield; by 1930, over 60 percent of Black Philadelphians lived in West and Northwest Philadelphia.[58] A 1916 survey recorded clusters of Black-owned businesses in South Philadelphia around Broad Street, in West Philadelphia just south of Market Street, in North Philadelphia east and west of Broad Street, and in Germantown.[59] These settlement patterns were fueled by the departure of nearly fifty thousand white Philadelphians from the city to the suburbs (made possible by the proliferation of affordable public transit and automobiles), a precursor to the "white flight" of the 1950s and 1960s.[60]

Despite the tight labor market caused by the war, many Philadelphia employers refused to hire Black men and women. The few labor unions that existed in the city often excluded Black people, so if Philadelphia's Black men and women did secure jobs, they were often low wage and without opportunities for significant advancement.[61] Moreover, once white veterans returned from the war, they competed with the new migrants for jobs, further limiting Black workers' prospects for employment or advancement.[62]

Worse, many white Philadelphians used violence to intimidate Black people from moving into predominantly white neighborhoods.[63] On several occasions in the 1910s, white mobs attacked Black people who had recently purchased houses. One particularly well-known attack occurred on the evening of July 26, 1918, when a white mob attacked Adella Bond's home at 2936 Ellsworth Street, which had been previously occupied by a white family.[64] Bond, a municipal court probation officer, fired her revolver out her bedroom window to summon the police. The police arrived and arrested several white men, who were charged with rioting, but they also arrested Bond, who was charged with incitement to riot. Two days later, a white mob chased a Black man named Jesse Butler, who fired on the pursuing mob in an attempt to escape, killing a white man named Hugh Lavery. A similar event occurred that afternoon, when a white mob chased a Black man named Henry Huff into a house. When a plainclothes police officer tried to take Huff's gun, Huff fired, wounding that officer and another one. News of these events spread quickly through the city, and white mobs began attacking whatever Black people they encountered. The police flooded the city's streets to end the violence, but they often sided with the white mobs.[65] The following year, a white mob numbering about seventy-five tried to eject a Black family from the house they had recently purchased at 2535 Pine Street, and the situation turned into a melee. The police arrived and arrested all the Black people involved but almost none of the whites.[66] Chillingly, on October 7, 1922, Philadelphia became the first city to use tear gas on its own citizens, when police threw a gas grenade into a dress shop at 1530 Sansom Street to flush out two would-be thieves, both of whom were Black.[67] Even in allegedly integrated communities, Black residents faced discrimination. Alyce Jackson Alexander, a Black woman who grew up in Germantown during these years, recalled, "We were in a mixed neighborhood with Italians and Irish. . . . We weren't always allowed to go swimming [at the Waterview Playground]—only on certain days could the Black children go and swim."[68]

Philadelphia's Black community remained economically diverse, with small middle- and upper-class segments that made some notable progress during the first half of the twentieth century. For instance, in 1902, Julian F. Abele Jr. became the first Black man to graduate from the University of Pennsylvania's architecture department. Abele later joined prominent architect Horace Trumbauer's firm and played a role in designing some of Philadelphia's most prominent buildings, including the Free Library of Philadelphia's Central Branch and the Philadelphia Museum of Art. Celebrated Black philosopher and educator Alain LeRoy Locke (often called the "father of the Harlem Renaissance") was born in Philadelphia and went on to graduate from Central High School and attend the Philadelphia School of Pedagogy before becoming the world's first Black Rhodes Scholar and earning a PhD from Harvard University. In 1911, Philadelphia elected Republican Henry W. Bass to the Pennsylvania House of Representatives; Bass was the first Black man elected to either house of the Pennsylvania

Assembly. He was followed in 1920 by John C. Asbury and Andrew F. Stevens Jr., both Republicans, while Amos Scott became the city's first Black magistrate. In 1938, Philadelphia elected Democrat Crystal Bird Fauset to the Pennsylvania House, the first Black woman elected to any state legislature. In 1921, Sadie Tanner Mossell Alexander became the second Black woman in the United States to earn a PhD; six years later, she became the first Black woman to both graduate from the University of Pennsylvania's Law School and be admitted to the Pennsylvania Bar. Black men even served as police officers, patrolling areas with large Black populations (though in 1916 the South Street Businessmen's Association, which represented white businesses in the area, complained to the city's director of Public Safety about Black police officers, who routinely assisted Black customers in disputes with local business owners).[69] While racists often failed to recognize the nuanced class differences in the city's Black community, some middle- and upper-class Black Americans believed they could overcome discrimination and prejudice by distinguishing themselves from poor Black people. This belief, which found its best-known expression in elite educator Booker T. Washington's work, structured most of the Black agitation for civil and political rights well into the 1960s. In addition, Black migration to Philadelphia made the region more religiously diverse. In 1928, Prophet Noble Drew Ali, founder of the Moorish Science Temple of America (MSTA), established Temple Number 11. In 1943, Muhammad Ezaldeen (formerly of the MSTA) established the Addeynu Allahe Universal Arabic Association; one of his disciples, Imam Nasir Ahmed, established the region's first mosque, the International Muslim Brotherhood, on Christian Street in South Philadelphia. In 1954, the Nation of Islam's Malcolm X established that organization's Temple Number 12 in a building that had previously been a technical school and even briefly a synagogue, and which later became the Black Mafia's headquarters in the 1970s.

Immigrants still made up a smaller portion of Philadelphia's population (approximately 25 percent) than other large US cities, such as Boston, New York, and Chicago.[70] After World War I, Congress passed a series of draconian immigration laws, most notably the Immigration of Act of 1924, which heavily limited nonwhite immigration to the United States.[71] With immigration slowed, the intrastate migration of Black people became the largest driver of Philadelphia's population growth.[72] Yet some immigrants did arrive in Philadelphia during the first half of the twentieth century. Russians, most of whom were Jewish, made up the city's largest group of immigrants in 1920, and Italians were the second-largest foreign-born ethnic group.[73] The city's tiny Chinese community (centered mostly on Race Street between Ninth and Tenth) fluctuated between about nine hundred and about sixteen hundred during this period, in large part because, like the city's Italians, Philadelphia's Chinese residents tended to return to their homeland.[74] Because the Chinese did not see themselves as permanent settlers, they did not immigrate with their families, leading to a community where men vastly outnumbered women.[75] In addition, like the city's Black community, Philadelphia's Chinese population was subject to frequent harassment from the police department.[76] Since the nineteenth century, Philadelphia has had a small Spanish-speaking community composed largely of Spaniards and Cubans, augmented by Mexicans and a small number of Central and South Americans. Attracted by the city's cigar manufacturers (a key industry in Philadelphia), the city's Spanish-speaking population grew during the 1910s as migrants arrived in Philadelphia looking for work during World War I. Spanish-speaking Philadelphians built communities along the Delaware River in areas such as Northern Liberties and Southwark and in industrial areas such as Spring Garden.[77] Most new arrivals were Puerto Rican because, as American citizens, they were not affected by the racist immigration laws Congress passed after World War I.

Despite the persistent myth that immigrants quickly assimilated into the United States by learning English and adopting American culture, the reality is quite different. For instance, many of Philadelphia's Italian and Chinese immigrants only came to the United States to make money; their goal was to return to Italy and China respectively. Others cycled between the United States and their countries of origin seasonally. As late as 1920, only one-third of Italian-born Philadelphians were naturalized citizens.[78] Certainly, the fact that at this stage Italians were not considered "white" played a role: at several points Congress debated whether Italians were fit for American citizenship.[79] The imposition of restrictive immigration laws in the United States after World War I and the Italian Fascists' anti-immigration legislation of the 1920s ended the practice of Italians cycling between the United States and Italy.[80]

The war's end marked a turning point in US history. The upheavals of the Progressive Era (c. 1900 to c. 1920) and World War I led many Americans to yearn for a "return to normalcy," which was 1920 Republican presidential candidate Warren G. Harding's most important campaign promise. He won the election, presiding over the first part of a generally prosperous decade, the so-called Roaring Twenties. Despite Harding's campaign promises, there was no return to normalcy.[81] In fact, the social reform movements of the Progressive Era and the upheavals caused by World War I made any return to normalcy impossible. The ratification of the Nineteenth Amendment in 1920 granted to all American women the right to vote (though women of color were rarely able to exercise this right). Philadelphia and its revolutionary artifacts played an important role in the fight for women's suffrage: a copy of the Liberty Bell, a powerful symbol that had first been mobilized by abolitionists, toured Pennsylvania in 1915 in support of an amendment to the commonwealth constitution granting women the right to vote. Getting suffrage was a sea change for women in the United States, but it was part of a wider renegotiation of gender roles and social norms. In fact, though prevented from voting, American women played key roles in the abolitionist movement of the nineteenth century, and in the first half of the twentieth, Philadelphia's women broke down several long-standing barriers. For instance, Dr. Mary Engle Pennington, the first woman to earn a PhD from the University of Pennsylvania, was chief of the US Department of Agriculture's food research lab, while in 1935, ballerina and choreographer Catherine Little-field founded what later became the Philadelphia Ballet. Ora Mae Washington, a Black woman whose family came to Philadelphia as part of the Great Migration when she was just a child, became a world-famous tennis and basketball player and coach and is considered one of the country's greatest athletes.[82]

Her stature highlights the popularity of professional sports in the first half of the twentieth century. Baseball remained incredibly popular in Philadelphia. In fact, Philadelphian singer and songwriter Jack Norworth cowrote (along with Albert Von Tilzer) "Take Me Out to the Ball Game," which has been played at baseball games for decades.[83] Under Coach Connie Mack's leadership, the Philadelphia Athletics dominated the American League, capturing the pennant nine times between 1902 and 1931 and winning the World Series in 1910, 1911, 1913, 1929, and 1930. In 1909, they occupied the recently completed Shibe Park (Lehigh Avenue between Twentieth and Twenty-First Streets, and named for team owner Ben Shibe, who had patented the cork-center baseball), the major leagues' first reinforced concrete and steel stadium.[84] The Phillies played at National League Park (nicknamed the Baker Bowl after team owner William F. Baker) on Broad Street between Lehigh Avenue and Huntingdon Street until 1938, when they, too, began playing at Shibe Park.[85] It was at the Baker Bowl in 1915 that Woodrow Wilson became the first US president to attend the World Series (which the Phillies lost to the Boston Red Sox, four games to one). Major league baseball was segregated until 1947, but that did not stop Black athletes from playing the game. Across the Keystone State, Blacks formed teams, sometimes playing in one of the several Black professional baseball leagues that existed in the 1920s and 1930s. The best known of Philadelphia's Black professional baseball teams during this period was the Hilldale Athletic Club (previously known as the Darby Daisies), which won several pennants and the 1925 Colored World Series.[86] Baseball was so popular that the Philadelphia Athletics successfully pressured the Pennsylvania legislature to conduct a referendum on the state's blue laws. When the votes were tallied, most Pennsylvanians voted to repeal the laws, allowing the Athletics to legally play baseball on Sunday for the first time in the commonwealth's history.[87]

A related development was the emergence of professional football. In fact, the first professional football league was founded in Pennsylvania, and many baseball team owners saw the sport as a way of keeping their players in "fighting form" during the off-season.[88] The Philadelphia Eagles developed from the Frankford Athletic Association, a nonprofit sports club formed in 1899. In 1924, the National Football League (founded in 1920) made the team (then called the Frankford Yellow Jackets) a franchise. Because of the Depression, in 1931, the Yellow Jackets went bankrupt. In 1933, several ex–Yellow Jackets formed a new franchise, the Eagles (supposedly inspired by the National Recovery Administration's Blue Eagle logo).[89] Initially, the Eagles played their home games at the Baker Bowl, but in 1940, the team moved to Shibe Park. On December 19, 1948, the Eagles won the team's first championship game, beating the Chicago Cardinals 7 to 0.[90]

One reason for the popularity of professional sports was radio, which quickly became a staple of middle-class households, and Philadelphia was a leading radio manufacturing center.[91] For instance, the Atwater Kent Manufacturing Company, incorporated in 1919 by Arthur Atwater Kent Sr., became the world's largest radio manufacturer by the late 1920s. To meet the surging demand for radios, the company built a factory at 5000 Wissahickon Avenue that opened in 1924; the company eventually expanded it until it covered thirty-four acres. The Great Depression led to a drop in demand for Atwater Kent radios, so in 1936, the company sold the plant to another important local radio manufacturer, Philco, which had a sprawling manufacturing campus in Kensington.[92] Originally the Helios Electric Company and then the Philadelphia Storage Battery Company, Philco started making radios in 1928. Within a few years, Philco supplanted Atwater Kent as the country's leading radio manufacturer, a position it held into the 1950s. Philadelphia was also a leader in content creation, with more than one dozen radio stations operating by 1927. Philadelphia's first commercial radio station, WGL, began broadcasting in February 1922 from Thomas F. J. Howlett's mansion at 2303 North Broad Street. Within a few weeks, Howlett was joined on the air by Strawbridge & Clothier's station, WFI, and Gimbel Brothers' WIP (both started broadcasting on March 18, 1922). Later that year, Lit Brothers and Wanamaker's followed their competitors by launching WDAR (later WLIT) and WOO, respectively. These stations broadcast concerts and church services, as well as children's programs, though Wanamaker's ended its radio broadcasts in 1929, while WFI and WLIT consolidated in 1935 to become WFIL.[93] Programming became more sophisticated in the 1930s, a decade generally seen as radio's golden age. In 1933, WCAU opened the first building specifically designed to be a radio station. Located at 1618 Chestnut Street and constructed in the then-fashionable art deco style, WCAU's building housed several studios (including one that could accommodate the entire Philadelphia Orchestra).[94] WCAU was a Columbia Broadcasting System (CBS) affiliate, airing a mix of locally produced and syndicated programming, while WFIL affiliated with the National Broadcasting Company (NBC). In 1934, KYW moved to Philadelphia from Chicago and four years later opened its own studio at 1619 Walnut Street.

Not unrelated, Philadelphia was a leading city for various forms of music during the first half of the twentieth century. The Philadelphia Orchestra (founded in 1900) under conductor Leopold Stokowski, who led the orchestra from 1912 to 1936, was among the world's finest. With Stokowski's assistance, in 1924, Mary Louise Curtis Bok (heir to the Curtis Publishing Company fortune) founded the Curtis Institute of Music, one of the world's best music conservatories. The institute is at 1726 Locust Street, and its past directors include Efrem Zimbalist (who was Mary Louise Curtis Bok's second husband and the father of actor Efrem Zimbalist Jr.) and John S. de Lancie (father of actor John de Lancie, of the TV show *Star Trek: The Next Generation*). Philadelphia was also home to several generations of the Giannini family of musicians; father Ferruccio (a tenor) migrated to the United States and eventually settled in Philadelphia. His children were noted musicians and composers, and his daughter Eufemia taught at Curtis for several decades. Marc Blitzstein, a composer and lyricist, was a Philadelphia native who studied at Curtis and wrote the controversial musical *The Cradle Will Rock*. Lyricist, librettist, and theatrical producer Oscar Hammerstein even briefly operated an opera house at Broad and Poplar.[95]

Philadelphia was also home to a lively Black music scene. Bessie Smith, known as the Empress of the Blues, lived the last fourteen years of her life in the city, performing in local jazz clubs and theaters. Smith died in an automobile accident, and her funeral (which attracted thousands of mourners) was held at the O. V. Catto Elks Lodge (Sixteenth and Fitzwater). Famed contralto Marian Anderson was born in Philadelphia and sometimes performed in the city.[96] In addition, jazz pioneer Billie Holiday was born in the city in 1915 and lived for a time at 1409 Lombard Street. During the Depression, singer and actor Pearl Bailey (who gained considerable fame from the 1940s to the early 1970s) performed in Philadelphia's Black nightclubs. During the early 1940s, the Dixie Hummingbirds, a popular and influential gospel group, lived and performed in the city. Philadelphia was such an important center for Black music that it hosted the Second Annual National Negro Music Festival in May 1930, and its iconic poster featured the work of local printmaker Dox Thrash, coinventor of the carborundum printmaking process and one of the city's leading Black artists.[97] Denied membership in Local 77 of the American Federation of Musicians (AFM), the city's Black musicians in 1935 formed their own chapter (Local 274), which eventually grew into the second-largest Black AFM chapter.

Philadelphia's distinctive history and culture made it the perfect setting for several novels and plays during this period. In 1902, local novelist John Thomas McIntyre published *The Ragged Edge,* the first of his several novels about Philadelphia. In 1939, journalist Christopher Morley published *Kitty Foyle,* a steamy tale of love between the middle-class Kitty and the socialite Wyn Strafford; the book is peppered with observations about Philadelphia's culture. That same year, Philip Barry's comic play *The Philadelphia Story* (also about class boundaries and love) premiered at New York's Shubert Theatre. Several of the nation's most popular magazines—the *Saturday Evening Post,* the *Country Gentleman, Jack and Jill,* and the *Ladies' Home Journal*—were published in Philadelphia by the Curtis Publishing Company during this period, as was the evening paper with the country's largest circulation, the *Evening Bulletin.*[98] Famed artist Maxfield Parrish was born and grew up in Philadelphia. Parrish worked in several fields, including book and magazine illustration, but he also accepted commissions for murals, including *The Dream Garden* in the Curtis Center (601 Walnut Street).

Philadelphia was also home to several food innovations during this period. In 1888, George Renninger, an employee of the Wunderle Candy Company at 130 Pegg Avenue invented candy corn (originally called Chicken Feed). In 1902, restaurateurs Joseph Horn and Frank Hardart installed the country's first automat, a waiterless restaurant where customers could retrieve prepackaged food and drinks from vending machines, at 818 Chestnut Street. By 1941, Horn & Hardart was the world's largest restaurant chain. In 1914, Philip Bauer and Herbert Morris established Tasty Baking Company on Sedgley Avenue in Germantown and began producing Tastykakes, small, individually wrapped cakes. (The company later moved production to Hunting Park Avenue.) In 1917, the Goldenberg Candy Company (founded in 1890 by Romanian Jewish immigrant David Goldenberg in Kensington) developed Peanut Chews for the US Army as a protein-rich ration for soldiers. In 1895, Frank H. Fleer & Company, a confectioner founded ten years before and then located at 2343 Hamilton Street, introduced the world to Chiclets, or candy-coated gum. These were an instant success, and Fleer sold the company to Sen-Sen in 1909. Prevented by an article of the sale from competing with Chiclets, Fleer formed a new confectionery company, the Frank H. Fleer Corporation, and began looking for an alternative product. Located at Tenth and Diamond Streets, Fleer began issuing sports cards in 1923. In 1928, Fleer accountant Walter Diemer invented the first commercially successful bubble gum, which became a huge success for the company, which moved in 1930 to a larger factory at 5324 North Tenth Street. At roughly the same time, the cheesesteak—the iconic Philadelphia sandwich—was invented in South Philadelphia. Its exact origins are obscure; allegedly Pat and Harry Olivieri (who, among other things, ran a hot dog stand) first created the cheesesteak in 1930 and shortly thereafter established Pat's King of Steaks at the triangular intersection of Ninth Street, Wharton Street, and Passyunk Avenue. In 1932, the Girl Scouts of Greater Philadelphia baked and sold cookies at the Philadelphia Gas & Electric Company building at Broad and Arch Streets, starting a national fundraising tradition that continues to this day. Perhaps because of the proliferation of messy foods in Philadelphia during this period, in 1907, Arthur Scott, head of the Scott Paper Company (founded in 1879 and credited with being the first company to market toilet paper on a roll), invented paper towels, followed in 1930 by paper tissues.[99]

In 1920, Gimbels held the nation's first Thanksgiving Day parade in Philadelphia, a relatively small affair that included a few dozen marchers, fifteen cars, and firefighters dressed as Santa Claus; it became an annual tradition. In 1901, the Mummers marched for the first time along Broad Street, though the parade emerged from nineteenth-century neighborhood New Year's celebrations, which were disparaged by the city's upper class.[100] Though those celebrations drew on several ethnic traditions, the Mummers also embraced racist minstrel tropes that existed in American culture during the nineteenth century and continued to characterize the parade into the twenty-first century.[101] For instance, the Mummers' unofficial theme after 1903, "Oh, Dem Golden Slippers," was written in 1879 by James Bland, one of the country's leading minstrel song writers. Bland, who was Black, was born in New York but lived for a time in the Philadelphia area, where he died in 1911. William S. Vare, whose political machine drew its strength from South Philadelphia, was instrumental in the Mummers' transition to respectability, a reminder that whatever the city's upper class said, real power belonged to the political machines and was derived from appeasing their constituents.[102]

There were some who dissented from "normalcy," and the country experienced something of a culture war in the first three decades of the twentieth century. Because of a perceived increase in crime (particularly prostitution), the city formed the Vice Commission, whose 1913 report proclaimed, "There is no difficulty in locating street-walkers, houses of prostitution, hotels where no questions are asked, or saloons in which solicitation is permitted if not encouraged."[103] Part of the panic about prostitution was rooted in anxiety about changing gender roles. The war years contributed to a loosening of social restraints as women flocked to the cities to work jobs vacated by men serving in the military. Advocates for women's suffrage achieved a major victory in August 1920 with the ratification of the Nineteenth Amendment to the Constitution, guaranteeing women the right to vote in all states. (When Pennsylvania's men voted on the issue, thirty-three western and northern counties voted in favor, while Philadelphia voted against.)[104] In the 1920s, "flappers" (young women who dressed in short skirts and smoked in public) flouted traditional morals, while the proliferation of automobiles gave unmarried couples discrete places for sexual encounters away from the prying eyes of family and friends.[105] Camac Street, which runs from Walnut to Locust in between Twelfth and Thirteenth Streets, was celebrated as "Philadelphia's Greenwich Village" for its bohemian shops and speakeasies (today Camac is celebrated as the city's last remaining wood-paved street).[106] Despite all of this, the city still had a reputation for being provincial, insular, sleepy, conservative, and dull.[107]

The ratification of the Eighteenth Amendment (January 1919) and the enactment of the Volstead Act (October 1919) meant that as of January 17, 1920, it was illegal to manufacture, sell, or transport alcoholic beverages in the United States. On the one hand, Prohibition led to a massive decline in the per capita amount of alcohol Americans consumed. On the other hand, it contributed to the emergence of organized crime. Max "Boo" Hoff, born in 1892 to Russian Jewish immigrants living in South Philadelphia, built a successful gambling operation during the war and then, once Prohibition began, established himself as the city's leading bootlegger. He was far from the only one, however; others included Joseph Bruno, Mickey Duffy, and the Lanzetta brothers (Leo, Pius, Ignatius, Willie, Lucian, and Teo), and Salvatore Sabella. Their competition for territory turned violent, with several shootings and bombings rocking the city during the 1920s and early 1930s.[108] That, plus the growing number of automobiles, which made it possible for would-be lawbreakers to make a "quick getaway," strained Philadelphia's police force and led Philadelphians to demand law and order.[109]

Answering the voters' demands, the newly elected mayor, W. Freeland Kendrick, appointed Major General Smedley D. Butler as Philadelphia's director of the Department of Public Safety, which oversaw the city's police and fire departments.[110] Butler was an interesting choice: born in West Chester, Pennsylvania, he joined the US Marine Corps in 1898 and saw action all over the world, eventually winning the Medal of Honor twice. Butler (whom Kendrick had promised "absolute control" free from interference as a condition of the marine's taking the job) began raiding Philadelphia's speakeasies and cracking down on gambling and prostitution.[111] In order to stanch the flow of liquor into the city, he established checkpoints to search for alcohol. While Butler's tactics produced results, they also aroused the ire of public officials (particularly the Vares, who were involved in the vice trade and Kendrick's political patrons) and private citizens, who feared the encroachments on civil liberties.[112] At the end of 1925, President Calvin Coolidge refused to grant Butler a third year of leave to serve as Philadelphia's director of public safety (Butler was still on active duty and just being lent to the city). Consequently, Butler's tumultuous term came to an end, and the city returned to business as usual.[113]

The prosperity of the 1920s led to changes in the city's architecture as well. Between 1929 and 1933, the Pennsylvania Railroad built Thirtieth Street Station. In 1930, the company opened a new station and office building just north of City Hall at the intersection of Sixteenth Street and what is now called JFK Boulevard. Called Suburban Station, it served as the railroad's headquarters and was intended to replace the Broad Street Station, though the latter building continued operating until 1952. In 1931, the Terminal Commerce Building, an art deco structure that was then the East Coast's largest commercial building, opened on the northeast corner of Broad and Callowhill. The following year, the Pennsylvania Savings Fund Society (PSFS) opened its new headquarters, the first modern skyscraper in the United States. Designed by William Lescaze of the Philadelphia architectural firm Howe & Lescaze, it was the first building to have full air-conditioning and quickly became one of the defining elements of Philadelphia's skyline.[114]

At the same time, there was a national movement to preserve historically significant buildings. Inspired in part by the nostalgia and patriotism generated by the 1876 Centennial and in part by the growth of the tourism industry (which was stimulated by automobiles), organizations cropped up around the United States to ensure that the nation's historic buildings and battlefields were preserved. These organizations tended to be led by women. For instance, in 1899, the National Society of the Colonial Dames of America played a key role in preserving historically significant buildings in Philadelphia, including James Logan's country home (Stenton, at 4601 North Eighteenth Street) and the Laurel Hill Mansion (3487 Edgley Drive in East Fairmount Park).[115] Undoubtedly, one of the most important preservationists of this period was Frances Anne Wister. A descendant of James Logan, she was an active member of the National Society of the Colonial Dames, and as chairperson of the Women's Committee of the Philadelphia Orchestra, Wister was instrumental in derailing conductor Leopold Stokowski's campaign to relocate the orchestra from the Academy of Music on Broad Street to the Benjamin Franklin Parkway. As a result, the orchestra remained in its historic building, which was thus preserved. In 1931, with the assistance of her friends and acquaintances and in response to news that the Powel House (located at 244 South Third Street and the home of former mayor Samuel Powel) was slated for demolition to make way for a parking lot, she formed the Society for the Preservation of Landmarks. The society purchased the Powel House and a neighboring building, which was demolished to create a garden.[116] It went on to preserve several other historic houses, particularly those connected with the colonial period and the Revolution, including Grumbelthorpe (the Wister family home, at 5267 Germantown Avenue) and the Hill–Physick–Keith House (located at 321 South

Fourth Street and the residence of several prominent Philadelphia families at various times). Like most of the women who became involved in preserving Philadelphia's history at this time, Wister was wealthy and white, and her efforts were rooted in the belief that these buildings could help Americanize the city's many immigrants, a belief similar to Penn's faith that public space could cultivate moral behavior.[117]

The enthusiasm for historic preservation of colonial and revolutionary sites revived interest in the so-called Founding Fathers, which helped to keep Philadelphia in the spotlight.[118] Future president Warren G. Harding is credited with coining the term in 1916 (a variation of it appeared in his 1912 speech at the Republican National Convention), and it soon entered the American lexicon. Philadelphia liked to style itself "The City of Firsts" and the "most American of all the cities in America." As one visitor noted in 1908, "Philadelphia is even prouder of its culture and its antiquity than its riches."[119] That year, the city hosted a weeklong celebration of its 225th anniversary.[120] In the summer of 1926, Philadelphia celebrated the sesquicentennial (150th anniversary) of the signing of the Declaration of Independence. During that celebration, architect R. Brognard Okie (an 1897 graduate of the University of Pennsylvania's architecture program) designed and built a re-creation of the "President's House" (the Philadelphia mansion that George Washington lived in during his presidency), which the Daughters of the American Revolution used as their headquarters during the sesquicentennial celebrations. Over the next quarter century, Okie restored or reconstructed several historically significant buildings, including Pennsbury Manor (William Penn's manor house in Bucks County) and the Betsy Ross House.[121] However, unlike the 1876 Centennial Exhibition, the 1926 Sesquicentennial Exposition (which was a boondoggle for the Vare machine) was almost entirely backward looking and a total failure.[122] Lucretia L. Blankenburg, the widow of former mayor Rudolph Blankenburg, acidly noted in her 1928 memoir, "The less one says about the Sesqui-Centennial the better. It is over and may be recorded as the tragedy of 1926."[123]

Philadelphia also expanded its public transportation network in the first decades of the twentieth century, constructing elevated train lines and subways. In part, this was driven by merchants' desire to funnel people into Philadelphia's downtown shopping district.[124] The first underground railway opened in London in 1843, but the use of coal-burning locomotives made long lines impractical. The invention of electrical trains changed that. In 1890, London opened the first underground electrical train line (Charles Tyson Yerkes was involved in the financing and construction of London's electrical train lines). In 1897, Boston opened the United States' first underground train line, followed by New York in 1904 (overseen by Mayor George B. McClellan Jr.). In 1901, the Pennsylvania Assembly authorized cities to construct elevated and underground railways. In March 1907, the Philadelphia Rapid Transit Company (formerly the Union Traction Company) opened the Market Street subway line, eventually connecting Sixty-Ninth Street to Delaware Avenue. The city financed the Frankford Elevated Railway, designed to connect with the Market Street line and carry passengers to the city's Northeast section.[125]

The expansion of public transit spurred the development of outlying neighborhoods.[126] For instance, according to a 1912 survey, more than half of public transit users began their rides in West and North Philadelphia, and by the outbreak of World War I, nearly one-quarter of Philadelphia's population lived west of the Schuylkill River.[127] Builders constructed hundreds of identical row houses, which were relatively inexpensive and easy to erect.[128] For instance, John H. McClatchy built houses in West Philadelphia along the elevated train line and even constructed a shopping district adjacent to the Sixty-Ninth Street terminal (built in 1907). Fast growth came at a cost: between 1869 and 1895, the city enclosed various parts of Mill Creek, which snakes north and west through West Philadelphia from the Schuylkill River into Montgomery County. Developers then built houses and roads over the creek, but erosion combined with failure to maintain the underground cisterns led houses on the 4300 block of Walnut Street to collapse.[129]

Private automobiles, which reshaped American life, were becoming more abundant.[130] In 1894, mechanical engineer Henry G. Morris and chemist Pedro G. Salom built the Electrobat, one of the nation's first electric automobiles, and founded the United States' first electric car company in Philadelphia, Morris & Salom Electric Carriage and Wagon Company (located in the Drexel Building at Fourth and Chestnut).[131] The real turning point for autos in the United States occurred with the Ford Motor Company's introduction of the Model T in 1908, which went on to sell millions of units. Pennsylvania was a leading site for automobile manufacturing during this period: in 1914, Ford opened a factory at Broad and Lehigh, though in 1925, the company moved production to Chester County. Ford was far from the only car manufacturer in the area; others included the Ace Motor Corporation (1919–1924) and the Biddle Motor Car Company (1915–1922).[132] Most of the city's auto production, service, and sales companies were located along a two-mile stretch of Broad Street from Lehigh Avenue to Cherry Street.[133] Automobile production was such an important part of the city's industrial landscape that in 1902, the city hosted its first auto show, an event that continues to this day. Of course, all those cars needed to be serviced, so in 1921 four friends—W. Graham Jackson, Moe Radavitz, Emanuel Rosenfeld, and Maurice Strauss—founded Pep Auto Supply Company (later Pep Boys) at Sixty-Third and Market Streets, establishing a national brand.

To accommodate the proliferation of automobiles, the city built roads, which fueled the growth of suburbs and outer regions. In 1903, Mayor Samuel H. Ashbridge advocated a plan to build a road connecting Broad Street to Torresdale, a neighborhood in the city's Northeast. At the time, Torresdale was sparsely populated, but the Durham machine aggressively pushed for the road because of the possibility for profit (John Mack bought up much of the land surrounding the projected route through a shell company).[134] Originally called Torresdale Boulevard, then Northeast Boulevard when it was completed in 1914, it soon became known as Roosevelt Boulevard after ex-president Theodore Roosevelt. To connect Philadelphia to Camden (an important industrial city that was home to the Campbell Soup Company, the New York Shipbuilding Corporation, and the Radio Corporation of America, or RCA), New Jersey and Pennsylvania constructed the Delaware River Bridge. Renamed the Benjamin Franklin Bridge in 1956, it was the world's largest suspension bridge when it opened on July 1, 1926.

By far the most important road constructed during this period was the Benjamin Franklin Parkway. As early as 1871, some influential Philadelphians advocated the construction of a grand parkway designed to connect City Hall to Fairmount Park. In April 1892, the city councils passed an ordinance "to place upon the City plan a Park Boulevard from the City Hall to Fairmount Park," though the plan languished for a decade.[135] In 1902, several prominent Philadelphians formed the Parkway Association, and the following year that organization released a plan for the parkway. This plan proved controversial, but in March 1903, Mayor Ashbridge signed an ordinance placing the parkway on the city's plan and establishing some basic guidelines for its route.[136] In 1907, the Fairmount Park Art Association commissioned a comprehensive plan, designed by architects Paul P. Cret, Horace Trumbauer, and Clarence Zantzinger, which projected the parkway running from City Hall to the foot of the now-closed Fairmount Reservoir. In 1909, the city councils officially accepted this plan.[137] Over the next six years, the city acquired properties along the projected route (often through condemnation) and began demolishing buildings. In 1917, French landscape architect Jacques Gréber submitted a revised plan for the parkway to the Fairmount Park Commission (FPC); based on Paris's Avenue des Champs-Élysées, it became the blueprint for the parkway's construction.

Crucially, in 1910, the Pennsylvania Assembly granted the FPC the power to control the design and placement of all buildings within two hundred feet of the parkway.[138] This was incredibly important to the parkway's character because, from the beginning, the assumption had been that at least some of the city's cultural institutions would move to the parkway.[139] That assumption was rooted in the Fairmount Park Art Association's elitist belief that "the presence of objects of beauty is a great educator, and tends to refine the people and to cultivate their taste for the beautiful. In a manufacturing city this is especially desirable."[140] No building on the parkway was to be more central to its character than the Philadelphia Museum of Art. As early as 1902, creating an art museum along the parkway was central to the planning process, and many of the parkway's most vocal supporters (such as P. A. B. Widener) saw the two as inextricably linked. In fact, after Widener's death in 1915, his son Joseph promised to donate the industrialist's impressive art collection to the city provided Philadelphia built an art museum on the parkway.[141] A plan for the museum was finalized in 1917, but World War I slowed construction, and the museum did not open until March 26, 1928. Under the leadership of Fiske Kimball from 1925 to 1955, the Philadelphia Museum of Art established itself as one of the country's foremost art museums. It was later joined on the parkway by the Free Library of Philadelphia, the Rodin Museum, the Municipal Court, and the Franklin Institute, all housed in large, neoclassical buildings. In 1937, Philadelphia's City Council voted to rechristen it the Benjamin Franklin Parkway.[142] Extensive road construction and the growth of private automobile ownership paved the way for the outmigration of factories and other businesses to Philadelphia's suburbs, a process of deindustrialization that would devastate the city's economy.[143]

The Roaring Twenties ended abruptly in the fall of 1929 with the onset of the Great Depression. Though the stock market crash of late October 1929 is popularly associated with the Great Depression, signs of a crisis were visible earlier: six months before the crash, Philadelphia's unemployment rate was over 10 percent, with Black unemployment even higher.[144] Moreover, even before the stock market crash, Philadelphia's tax revenue had declined, and the number of properties sold at sheriff's sale increased.[145] A substantial portion of Philadelphia's occupied housing stock (much of it inhabited by Black people and recent immigrants) was unfit or nearly so, a fact highlighted by the devastating 1936 collapse of an apartment building at 519 South Fifteenth Street that killed a Black mother and her three children.[146]

Even for Philadelphians who prospered during the 1920s, structural changes in the US economy made them more vulnerable to an economic collapse. The 1920s "roar" was fueled in large part by the expansion of consumer credit. To purchase new and expensive items such as cars, radios, and washing machines, as well as real estate, individuals took out loans. In addition, the sales of bonds to finance the war drew more Americans into the country's banking system, where they deposited their paychecks into savings and checking accounts. US banks loaned Germany money so it could make good on the reparations mandated by the Treaty of Versailles, which had ended World War I; most countries suspended loan payments once the Depression started. Thus, when banks failed—as nearly one-third of Philadelphia's banks and savings and loans did between July 1930 and May 1931—they took with them a substantial portion of Philadelphians' savings.[147]

The Great Depression illustrated the limits of privatist approaches to poverty relief.[148] Initially, Philadelphia banker Horatio G. Lloyd chaired a committee that collected money for the unemployed and administered a soup kitchen and homeless shelter in the Baldwin Locomotive Works factory at Broad and Spring Garden Streets (closed since 1928 and later demolished by the Works Progress Administration in 1937).[149] Despite raising millions of dollars in donations and being lauded by President Herbert Hoover as a model for dealing with the Depression, private charity was unequal to the scale of need in Philadelphia: the homeless shelter in the former Baldwin works closed after less than a year. On April 11, 1932, the Community Council of Philadelphia distributed the last of its food supplies, at a time when unemployment stood at nearly 40 percent in Philadelphia and an additional 20 percent of workers could find only part-time work.[150] Meanwhile, Mayor J. Hampton Moore embraced austerity, firing more than three thousand city employees and cutting wages for those who remained.[151] The city was Philadelphia's largest single employer, so these firings and wage reductions created a ripple effect throughout the local and regional economy, worsening the Depression.[152] Moore later actively worked to ensure that Philadelphia missed out on federal money available from New Deal agencies because he opposed President Franklin D. Roosevelt, a fact that would damage Republicans politically.[153]

The Depression contributed to the growth of right-wing political parties and organizations, many of which predated the stock market crash. For instance, Pennsylvania during the 1920s had a large and very conspicuous Ku Klux Klan presence, even in urban areas like Philadelphia, and in 1921, members of Philadelphia's Italian community formed the city's first Fascist Club, before Benito Mussolini even seized power in Italy. [154] In 1931, Dino Grandi, Italy's minister for foreign affairs, visited the city and spoke to the Order of the Sons of Italy, which was broadcast on local radio.[155] Philadelphia's Friends of Italy nearly held a parade in support of Italy's invasion of Ethiopia in 1935, but city officials canceled the event at the last minute, fearing it would cause a race riot.[156] In the late 1930s, some Philadelphians of German descent enthusiastically joined the German-American Bund, a pro-Nazi organization.[157] The proliferation of fascist organizations pushed some antifascists into the American Communist Party, which peaked in influence during the mid-1930s.[158]

Perhaps the city's best-known fascist was Dr. Bessie Burchett. After attending Temple University, Burchett earned a PhD from the University of Pennsylvania, and she taught Latin for several decades in Philadelphia's public schools.[159] In May 1936, Burchett, then serving as head of the Foreign Languages

Department at South Philadelphia High School for Girls, publicly accused some of her colleagues of advocating communism, ridiculing patriotism, and trying to overthrow the government.[160] This caused an immediate sensation and made Burchett a celebrity among fascists and their fellow travelers. When pressed to expand on her charges, however, she only pointed to the fact that foreign language teachers may have (this was disputed) hung in their classrooms the flags of the countries whose languages they taught. Moreover, Burchett claimed, the schools were teaching "social justice" and failing to properly inculcate Christianity.[161] In response to her outrageous and ridiculous claims, the overwhelming majority of her colleagues at South Philadelphia High School for Girls (105 of 120) requested that she be fired; the school board responded by transferring her, but even this allowed Burchett to claim the mantle of victimhood. At a Nazi rally, she told listeners that she was being persecuted by Jews and communists, and she took to carrying two pistols (which she once brandished at a reporter), allegedly for "protection."[162] In the spring of 1939, students marched out of Burchett's class in West Philadelphia to protest her antics, though the Philadelphia police forced them back into the building.[163] In 1941, however, she went too far: in addition to being a white nationalist and an anti-Semite, Burchett was also a diehard Republican, and she defaced a school bulletin board, posting on it that President Roosevelt was a "murderer" and a "liar." The school board allowed her to resign (thereby preserving her pension), and she went on to write a book about her crusade against communism, *Education for Destruction*, publication of which was funded primarily by a local real estate broker and Catholic fascist named Joseph Gallagher, who was a leader in the local Coughlinite movement (followers of the anti-Semitic "radio priest," Father Charles Coughlin).[164]

Despite the proliferation of violent right-wing groups in the 1920s and early 1930s, Mayor Moore was more frightened of left-wing groups, so in the summer of 1932, he formed the Red Squad in the city's police department designed to infiltrate and disrupt left-wing organizations.[165] In practice, however, the Red Squad was often used to put down strikes and demonstrations by the unemployed, which proliferated during the Depression's first years.[166] When a column of approximately fifteen hundred marchers stopped to hear speakers at Reyburn Plaza, a block-long public park on North Broad Street between Arch and what is now JFK Boulevard that included a public band shell, Moore's director of public safety, Kern Dodge, ordered the city police to disband the peaceful demonstration. Officers waded into the crowd, beating and arresting hundreds of marchers, an event remembered as the "Battle of Reyburn Plaza."[167] Joseph F. Guffey, Pennsylvania's junior US senator during the mid-1930s, later remarked, "Violence and bloodshed along a national front marked the onset of the Depression."[168]

Mayor Moore's actions contributed to the Republicans' growing unpopularity in Philadelphia. They suffered several setbacks in the 1920s and 1930s, resulting in Philadelphia's transition to a Democratic city. Boies Penrose's death in 1921 left the Vare machine in control of Philadelphia.[169] Following Edwin Vare's death in 1922, William S. Vare took over control of the family's political machine and, in a bid to cement his control of the state-level Republican apparatus through federal patronage, ran for the US Senate in 1926. In a three-way primary that included Governor Gifford Pinchot and the incumbent, George Wharton Pepper, Vare emerged victorious and bested his Democratic challenger, William B. Wilson.[170] However, Wilson petitioned the US Senate to declare Vare's election fraudulent and prevent him from taking the seat, a move that Pinchot backed. For the next two and a half years, a Senate committee languidly investigated the matter, though there was little actual evidence to substantiate Wilson and Pinchot's charges. Would-be senator William Vare suffered a stroke in August 1928, and the following year the Senate voted not to admit him to the body. That blow was compounded by the fact that in November 1928, a substantial portion of the Vares' South Philadelphia constituents voted the Democratic ticket, headed by the United States' first major party Irish Catholic presidential nominee, Al Smith.[171] Meanwhile, Flora Vare (Edwin's widow), who had been elected to the Pennsylvania Senate in 1925 (making her the first woman to sit in that body), lost her reelection bid.[172] Though most voters returned to the Republican fold for the senatorial election of 1930 and the presidential election of 1932, the 1933 elections (the first genuinely competitive elections in decades) dealt the Vare machine another blow when its candidates for several offices lost.[173] William Vare's political power and influence declined, and he died of a second stroke in 1934, essentially ending the Vare political machine.[174] Deprived of access to municipal, state, or federal patronage, Philadelphia's would-be Republican machine builders found it difficult to consolidate their control over the city.[175] Meanwhile, as Black voters migrated toward the Democratic Party, some Republicans turned to race-baiting and outright racism as a way to attract white voters, a tactic that kept issues of race front and center in the city's politics.[176]

The New Deal also seriously wounded Pennsylvania's Republican machine, making the Democratic Party competitive in Philadelphia.[177] When President Hoover visited the city as part of his reelection campaign in October 1932, thirty thousand Philadelphians turned out to see him speak in Reyburn Plaza. He managed to carry the city, but that was the Republicans' last hurrah.[178] In 1930, Philadelphia had approximately 834,000 registered Democrats; by 1940, that number was 2,161,307, an increase of more than 250 percent. Though still outnumbered by registered Republicans, they were approaching parity.[179] In 1932, New York Governor Franklin D. Roosevelt won the presidency and launched his New Deal, a series of initiatives designed to restart the country's economy. The backbone of what came to be called the New Deal coalition was labor unions, white southerners, some Black people, and many ethnic minorities (Jews, Italians, and others), almost all of whom were the hardest hit by the Depression and therefore supported the administration's efforts to ameliorate its effects (white natives tended to remain Republicans).[180] Many of these were former Republican voters, but many were also groups (such as Italian immigrants) who had not voted in large numbers previously.[181]

It was a disparate coalition to be sure, held together in Philadelphia by John B. "Jack" Kelly Sr., (father of Academy Award–winning actress Grace Kelly) who became chairman of the Philadelphia Democratic Party (Vare ally John O'Donnell was ousted in 1934).[182] Like many Philadelphia Republicans during the 1930s, Kelly switched parties to become a Democrat. He ran for mayor of Philadelphia in 1935, and the election was an important turning point in the city's history. Though Kelly lost to Republican Samuel D. Wilson, he made a strong showing in a city that had been dominated by Republicans since the Civil War. Wilson could see the writing on the wall: despite being a Republican, Wilson abandoned Moore's opposition to Philadelphia receiving New Deal money, a clear indication of the shifting political winds.[183] In 1936, the Democratic National Convention met at the Philadelphia Convention Center (now demolished, it was at 3400 Civic Center Boulevard, just south of the University of Pennsylvania Museum) and nominated Roosevelt for a second term. The Democrats' choice of Philadelphia for the convention owed something to Mayor Wilson's assiduous courting of the party and probably contributed to Roosevelt's winning 60 percent of the city's votes in 1936.[184] While it would be inaccurate to call Philadelphia a Democratic city at this point, it was nonetheless true that the Republican machine was seriously weakened.

Federal spending during the Depression resulted in makeovers for City Hall and Independence Hall, a new custom house (Second and Chestnut), a new post office (Thirtieth and Market), a new naval hospital (Pattison Avenue between Broad and Twentieth Streets), and a Public Works Administration apartment complex in Juniata Park named after Carl Mackley, a local union hosiery worker killed by scabs during a strike at the H. C. Aberle and Company factory in Kensington in 1930.[185] However, the city's debts to the New Deal go much deeper. The National Industrial Recovery Act (NIRA), which became law in 1933, established employees' rights to form and belong to labor unions. Relatively few Philadelphia workers belonged to labor unions at the beginning of the Depression, mostly because employers did their level best to keep it that way, but the NIRA changed that.[186] In 1938, three thousand municipal workers in Philadelphia walked off the job in protest of layoffs and wage cuts. The eight-day strike, one of the first municipal workers' strikes in the nation's history, led to the formation of the American Federation of State, County, and Municipal Employees District Council 33 and a collective bargaining agreement for city employees.

In 1940, Roosevelt ran for an unprecedented third presidential term, and the Republican Party tried to recapture lost ground by hosting its national convention at the Philadelphia Convention Center. Attendee George Wharton Pepper later described it as a "free-for-all." The Republicans nominated businessman (and former Democrat) Wendell Willkie. It was the first national party convention broadcast live on television.[187] Willkie's stances were often indistinguishable from Roosevelt's, particularly regarding US involvement in the war in Europe. World War II broke out on September 1, 1939, when Germany invaded Poland; two days later, Great Britain and France declared war on Germany. Cynicism about US participation in World War I contributed to a sense among many Americans that the United States should remain as aloof as possible from World War II. Between 1934 and 1936, a Senate committee chaired by Gerald Nye of North Dakota examined allegations that US munitions manufacturers and financial interests manipulated the country into entering World War I. Though Roosevelt and Congress took some steps to mobilize the United States for what many saw as the country's inevitable entry into the war, public opinion did not support intervention. Ultimately, Roosevelt won the 1940 presidential election, though his popular vote total (55 percent) was significantly lower than four years before (60.8 percent). Just as in 1936, Roosevelt won Philadelphia County, though Willkie won a larger share of the popular vote than the party's 1936 nominee, Alfred Landon. Once Pennsylvania's most Republican county during the 1920s, Philadelphia in the 1930s was now among the commonwealth's least.[188]

On December 7, 1941, the Japanese attacked the US naval base at Pearl Harbor, near Honolulu, Hawaii; the following day, the United States declared war on Japan; three days later, Germany declared war on the United States. US entry into World War II ended the Great Depression, and Philadelphia contributed significantly to America's "Arsenal of Democracy." More than 15 percent of all federal government contracts for wartime matériel went to companies in the Philadelphia area, boosting the region's economy and lifting it out of the Depression.[189] Pennsylvania supplied nearly one-third of the country's steel output, which companies such as Baldwin Locomotive (now located in Eddystone) used to produce tanks and other vehicles.[190] Just as during the Civil War, prominent Philadelphians worked to establish hospitality services for military personnel visiting the city. In 1941, Philadelphia notables such as Edward G. Budd Sr. of Edward G. Budd Manufacturing Company, and William H. Harman, vice president of the Baldwin Locomotive Works, organized the Philadelphia United Service Organizations (USO), which maintained various lounges and clubs for uniformed personnel across the city.[191] Beginning in 1943, the US Army Ordnance Corps provided funding for the construction of what became the first electronic, programmable digital computer at the University of Pennsylvania. Known as the Electronic Numerical Integrator and Computer, or ENIAC, the machine (completed in late 1945) established Philadelphia as the birthplace of the computer (importantly, many of ENIAC's programmers were women). To mobilize support for the war, DC Comics leveraged one of Philadelphia's iconic historical artifacts, the Liberty Bell, in a new costumed superhero (Liberty Belle) that debuted in late 1942. By day a well-known radio columnist named Libby Lawrence, Liberty Belle was super strong and fast, and her powers were activated when her assistant, Tom Revere, rang the Liberty Bell. In this regard, DC continued a long tradition of mobilizing Philadelphia's history to support patriotic causes.

The flood of government contracts and the draft caused something of a manpower crisis by mid-1943, which led to extensive recruitment drives and set off the second wave of the Great Migration.[192] When Black migrants arrived in the city, however, they found it was far from the promised land. On the one hand, the flood of wartime contracts to companies in the region substantially reduced Black unemployment. On the other hand, some firms, such as the Sun Shipbuilding & Drydock Company (owned by the Pew Family, which was politically connected to the city's Republican establishment), strongly resisted any attempts to integrate its workforce.[193] This was just one of a set of challenges for Black people caused by the Depression and World War II. Even though Black voters were a crucial component of the New Deal coalition, legislation was often shaped to exclude them from reaping its benefits. Though Roosevelt had created an informal group of Black policy advisers (known as the "Black Cabinet") early in his presidency, the power of southern Democrats in Congress was such that the Roosevelt administration agreed to compromises that effectively shut Black people out of New Deal programs, creating long-lasting problems. Public housing constructed during the New Deal was segregated: "white" projects in "white neighborhoods" and "Black" projects in "Black neighborhoods."[194]

The best-known strike in Philadelphia during this period illustrates the ongoing racism Philadelphia's Black citizens faced. In 1941, Roosevelt created the Fair Employment Practices Commission (FEPC) to implement Executive Order 8802, which banned discriminatory practices by federal agencies and any contractors or unions doing war-related work. In 1944, the FEPC ordered the Philadelphia Transportation Company (PTC) to hire Black workers. Formed in 1940 following the Philadelphia Rapid Transit Company's dissolution in bankruptcy the year before, the PTC administered Philadelphia's various public transit lines. The PTC refused the FEPC's order, arguing that its in-house union, the Philadelphia Rapid Transit Employees Union (PRTEU), prevented it from firing existing employees and therefore it could not hire Black men.[195] That March a slim majority of PTC's workforce voted to have the Transit Workers Union (TWU), a Congress of Industrial Organizations (CIO) affiliate, represent them. The TWU favored hiring Black transit workers, but the PRTEU went out on strike, crippling the city's public transportation system. Incredibly, PTC's management supported the strike, seeing it as the better alternative to its workers being represented by the TWU.[196] Because the strike negatively impacted war production, President Roosevelt ordered US Army units to operate Philadelphia's public transportation system, and the strike collapsed after ten days. Following this action, the PTC employed an integrated workforce, but racism pervaded the city and its politics during the decades after the war.[197]

Just as with World War I, Americans sought a "return to normalcy" after Japan surrendered on September 2, 1945. The country had been battered by more than a decade and a half of economic depression and war. The long-term economic and demographic transformation of Philadelphia—deindustrialization, white flight, and population decline—set in motion changes that by the 1960s were collectively known as the "urban crisis." However, pervasive anti-urbanism and racism often left the city without the resources to adequately address these challenges.

Figure 9. *USGS 1:24000-scale Quadrangle for Philadelphia*, 1967. US Geological Survey. Postwar confidence in technocratic government led to changes in Philadelphia's skyline, roadways, and geography. Urban renewal and historical preservation benefited some Philadelphians but often at the expense of others.

CHAPTER 9

The Golden Age? 1945–1976

Americans greeted the end of World War II with both confidence and anxiety. The most destructive war in history left the United States one of the world's two superpowers, and federal government policies instituted during the New Deal created a period of unprecedented economic prosperity. However, Philadelphia faced a bleak future: what came to be called deindustrialization was already occurring in Philadelphia by the mid-1920s, and by one estimate, the city lost two-thirds of its industrial jobs in the half century after 1925, slipping from the nation's second to its fifth most important manufacturing center by 1958. Unemployment in the city was substantially higher than the national average as companies decamped for the suburbs.[1] Meanwhile, postwar attempts to renew cities like Philadelphia perfectly encapsulated many themes in the city's history: it pitted elite policymakers against ordinary citizens, exposed contradictory beliefs about which elements of Philadelphia's history were worth preserving, and reflected the pervasive racism and antiurbanism that had played key roles in the city's history since at least the eighteenth century.

Philadelphia's population peaked in 1950 at just over two million people. Over the next thirty years, it consistently declined, reaching 1,688,210 in 1980, a decline of more than 13 percent over the preceding ten years. In 1950, Philadelphia was the country's third-largest city; ten years later it had fallen to fourth place (behind Los Angeles), a position it held for the next thirty years. Population decline cost Philadelphia one-third of its representation in the US House of Representatives between 1953 and 1973, making it harder for the city to get much needed federal support.[2] Meanwhile, though deindustrialization began in the 1920s, it accelerated in the postwar period, with Philadelphia hemorrhaging perhaps 75 percent of its manufacturing jobs in the two decades after 1955.[3] Other cities faced similar challenges because federal, state, and local policies encouraged many whites to move to the rapidly growing suburbs (a process known as "white flight"). Yet those policies prevented Black people from moving to the suburbs, increasing their concentration in cities. Between 1940 and

1970, Philadelphia's Black population exploded from approximately 250,000 to more than 650,000, an increase of 260 percent, though the city's total population was nearly the same in 1970 as it was in 1940.[4] Not only did Philadelphia's Black population increase after World War II, but the percentage of Pennsylvania's Black population living in Philadelphia grew from 53.4 in 1940 to 61.1 by 1980.[5] Moreover, between 1950 and 1960, the concentration of Black Philadelphians living in majority Black wards went up, suggesting that they were becoming more spatially segregated.[6]

In addition, changes in US immigration policy altered Philadelphia's demographic makeup. The Immigration and Nationality Act of 1952 (cosponsored by Democratic US Representative Francis E. Walter of Pennsylvania) ended the practice of racial and ethnic discrimination in who could become citizens of the United States, and the Immigration and Nationality Act of 1965 (called the Hart–Celler Act) abolished the racist national-origins formula established in the 1920s (which capped immigration to the United States at 3 percent of the number of foreign-born people of each nationality already here). But for the first time, the law established a ceiling on the total number of immigrants the United States would admit and capped the number of legal immigrants from the Western Hemisphere.[7] As a result of this (and several failures of US foreign policy, notably in Korea and Southeast Asia), Asian immigration to the Delaware Valley substantially increased. Philadelphia's Chinatown expanded physically, spreading from Vine Street to Arch Street between Ninth and Eleventh Streets (though Asian immigrants also settled in other parts of the city).[8] Because of political pressure in the Soviet Union, many Russian Jews immigrated to the United States and, because of the preexisting Jewish community in Philadelphia, settled in the region.[9] For the first time in US history, Hart–Celler placed a cap on the number of Latin Americans who could immigrate to the United States. Because Puerto Ricans are American citizens, the anti-Latino cap did not affect them, and Philadelphia's Puerto Rican community grew by 700 percent between 1940 and 1960, becoming the mainland United States' third-largest Puerto Rican community (second-largest in 2010).[10] This was one reason Philadelphia became a leader in bilingual education in the 1970s. Dr. Eleanor Sandstrom, director of the city school district's Office of Foreign Languages, successfully secured federal funds for a program to teach English as a second language (ESL) and in 1969 even opened the Potter–Thomas Bilingual School (3001 North Sixth Street), which for a time was a national model for ESL education.[11] As a result, by the nation's Bicentennial celebration in 1976, Philadelphia was considerably more ethnically and racially diverse than the rest of Pennsylvania, a fact that had reshaped its politics and exacerbated conflict with the commonwealth.

At the end of the war, the most pressing issue facing cities around the country was the shortage of suitable housing for returning service members.[12] More than a decade of economic depression, followed by all-out war mobilization, meant that little housing had been constructed for more than fifteen years, while existing structures had often been allowed to deteriorate. To address this issue, policymakers advocated urban redevelopment, a process by which the city acquired (through the purchase or the use of eminent domain) supposedly "undesirable" privately owned properties and turned them over to developers.[13] This process, along with the federal government's funding parameters, helped exacerbate racial segregation in America's cities. In 1945, the Pennsylvania Assembly passed the Urban Redevelopment Law, designed "to promote elimination of blighted areas and supply sanitary housing in areas throughout the Commonwealth." It authorized the creation of local redevelopment authorities and borrowing money by issuing bonds to fund redevelopment activities.[14] The following year Philadelphia established the Redevelopment Authority, which used federal funds to acquire properties in areas identified for redevelopment by the City Planning Commission (CPC); the authority then resold the properties to developers below cost.[15]

One of the most important supporters of redevelopment was the Greater Philadelphia Movement (GPM), an organization of business and labor leaders, academics, and prominent Philadelphians created to "promote the social, economic, and governmental development of the Philadelphia Metropolitan Area."[16] Though technically bipartisan, most members were registered Republican, and "big-business, financial and legal interests" dominated the GPM and set the organization's priorities.[17] The GPM's members were separate from, and largely hostile to, the city's Republican political machine, and the organization's structure and purpose harked back to the "good government" reform parties of the Gilded Age. The fact that many members of the GPM did not live in the city and were thus less concerned about housing than arresting deindustrialization and attracting new businesses to the city helped shape redevelopment policies in Philadelphia during the 1950s.[18] The GPM sponsored the Better Philadelphia Exhibition, hosted from September 8 to October 15, 1947, by Gimbels department store at Eighth and Market Streets. The exhibit's goal was to present city planning in accessible and personal terms (the exhibition's theme was "What City Planning Means to You") to build popular support for redevelopment. *The American City* called the exhibition "the most significant thing that has happened to planning in nearly a score of years," predicting it would "stimulate general public education in city planning."[19] The exhibit, which garnered national attention, promoted a vision of what Philadelphia could be at the city's three hundredth anniversary in 1982. Nearly four hundred thousand people saw, free of charge, a two-floor exhibit at Gimbels that included a massive diorama of the city, as well as maps, a light show, and sculpture.[20] Despite this attempt to build public support for its agenda, just like earlier reform organizations, the GPM was elitist and adopted a top-down approach to reform that was often deaf to the concerns of members of local communities, laying the groundwork for the backlash that came in the decades that followed.[21]

The GPM was not the only organization concerned about housing and redevelopment: in 1948, Philadelphia was again in the national spotlight because the city hosted three presidential nominating conventions (Republican, Democratic, and Progressive), and each adopted platforms that included planks addressing the housing shortage. Between June 21 and 25, the Republican National Convention met at Convention Hall and Civic Center (Thirty-Fourth Street just south of Spruce Street). Republicans expected that the unpopular Democratic president, Harry S. Truman, would lose his bid for election in his own right (he had ascended to the presidency following Franklin D. Roosevelt's death in 1945). They nominated New York's governor, Thomas E. Dewey, and adopted a platform that among other things asserted, "Housing can best be supplied and financed by private enterprise; but the government can and should encourage the building of better homes at less cost. We recommend Federal aid to the States for local slum clearance and low-rental housing programs only where there is a need that cannot be met either by private enterprise or by the States and localities."[22] The following month, Democrats convened in the same building and nominated President Truman. Like the Republicans, the Democrats promised to "enact comprehensive housing legislation, including provisions for slum clearance and low-rent housing projects initiated by local agencies," though the platform also attacked Republicans for failing to pass legislation.[23]

Truman unexpectedly won the election, and the Democrats controlled both houses of Congress during the 1949–1951 sessions. Consequently, the first phase of postwar redevelopment policies reflected Democratic priorities. A good example is the Housing Act of 1949, which committed the federal government to alleviating the postwar housing shortage by encouraging the construction of residential units through public-private partnerships.[24] The goal was to provide every American with adequate affordable housing by deploying several strategies, including subsidized mortgages and the construction of public housing.[25] Republican Dwight D. Eisenhower won the presidency in 1952, and in 1954, Congress (now controlled by Republicans) amended the Housing Act of 1949, expanding it to include funding for industrial and commercial development but curtailing funds for public housing; the effect was to recast redevelopment as "urban renewal," shifting focus to slum clearance and commercial redevelopment, which Republicans favored.[26] Philadelphia architect and urban planner

Edmund Bacon, who directed the Philadelphia City Planning Commission (considered among the best planning commissions in the United States during this period) from 1949 until 1970, pushed back against wholesale "slum clearance" because he was committed to the idea that urban design could help ameliorate social ills.[27] Bacon helped create Philadelphia's Used House Program, in which the city rehabilitated existing homes for use as public housing.[28] In general, there was little he could do to prevent the reorientation of Philadelphia's urban renewal efforts, and as late as 1980, more than half of the city's housing stock had been built before World War II even as billions in federal aid had been spent on urban renewal.[29]

Of course, housing policy was closely related to race; after all, the city's nonwhite residents inhabited Philadelphia's worst housing stock.[30] The issue of racial discrimination was front and center during the presidential campaign of 1948. During the late 1940s, the Democratic Party seized the initiative to end racial discrimination, and though the 1948 Republican platform promised, among other things, a federal law against lynching and put the party on record as being opposed to segregation in the US armed forces, it was Democratic policymakers who actually delivered for Black voters. For instance, in 1946, President Truman convened a committee on civil rights to make "recommendations with respect to the adoption or establishment by legislation or otherwise of more adequate and effective means and procedures for the protection of the civil rights of the people of the United States."[31] The Democratic Party platform highlighted these efforts, commending Truman for his "courageous stand on the issue of civil rights" and asserting that "the Democratic Party is responsible for the great civil rights gains made in recent years in eliminating unfair and illegal discrimination based on race, creed or color." This was not mere rhetoric: on July 26, 1948, Truman issued Executive Order 9981, abolishing racial, ethnic, or religious discrimination in the United States' armed forces. However, Truman's bold actions on behalf of racial justice alienated several southern Democrats, who bolted the party and formed the short-lived States' Rights Democratic Party, or Dixiecrats.[32] In 1948, the Dixiecrats nominated South Carolina's governor, Strom Thurmond, for president; he attracted 2.4 percent of the popular vote and thirty-nine electoral votes. After the election, Thurmond returned to the Democratic Party, though he became a Republican following passage of the Civil Rights Act of 1964.

Racists were not the only ones disenchanted with Truman. Just over a week after the Democrats' national convention closed, the Progressive Party convened in Philadelphia at both Convention Hall and Shibe Park. The Progressives represented the Democratic Party's most liberal members; they felt Truman had not gone far enough toward racial justice. The Progressives nominated former vice president Henry Wallace for president and took aim at both parties in their platform, which read in part: "The old parties, acting for the forces of special privilege, conspire to destroy traditional American freedoms. They deny the Negro people the rights of citizenship. They impose a universal policy of Jim Crow and enforce it with every weapon of terror....They ignore the housing problem, although more than half the nation's families, including millions of veterans, are homeless or living in rural and urban slums."[33]

Members of the Progressive Party were also appalled by Truman's bellig-erent foreign policy toward the Soviet Union. During what came to be called the Cold War, American concerns about Soviet expansion abroad dovetailed with paranoia about communist subversion at home.[34] During the Depression and World War II, socialists and communists made in-roads in several import-ant organizations, including the labor movement and, to a lesser extent, pub-lic schools.[35] Antilabor politicians and business leaders used that fact to their advantage, asserting that labor unions were rife with "radical" ideas and a threat to the "American way of life," practice called "red-baiting." Red-baiting was both good politics and an old tactic; Woodrow Wilson's administration had success-fully used it during World War I to stifle opposition to US entry into the war, and anti–New Deal politicians adopted the tactic to weaken the New Deal coa-lition. The Republican sweep of Congress in the midterm elections of 1946 and the quick succession of communist "victories" (the so-called loss of China and the Soviet Union's test of a nuclear bomb in 1949 and North Korea's invasion of South Korea in 1950) gave anti–New Dealers renewed power. Yet it is import-ant to note that the anti-communist hysteria was a bipartisan affair; after all, it was President Truman, a Democrat, who decided to "scare the hell out of" the American people about the alleged threat of communist subversion to ensure that the United States remained engaged in world affairs after World War II.[36]

Scaring Americans about communism worked, and the anti-communist hysteria of the late 1940s and early 1950s had a palpable impact on Philadelphia. Philadelphia's Congress of Industrial Organizations (CIO) (which had a well-deserved reputation for conservatism) banned communists from membership, and the American Federation of Labor successfully pressured its affiliate, the American Federation of Teachers, to eject the Philadelphia local over alleged communist infiltration in 1941.[37] In 1947, the City of Philadelphia tried to block the Progressive Citizens of America (PCA) from holding a rally at Independence Hall in protest of the House Un-American Activities Committee's hearings into alleged communist influence in Hollywood. A federal judge later ruled that the city had to permit the rally, but spectators heckled the speakers, and fistfights broke out.[38] To combat the allegedly pervasive influence of communism in pub-lic schools and colleges, in 1951, the Assembly passed the Pennsylvania Loyalty

Act, a law demanding that teachers and public officials swear or affirm that they were not, and would not become, members of so-called subversive organizations. The law mandated that all state-aided institutions annually submit "a written report setting forth what procedures the institution has adopted to determine whether it has reason to believe that any subversive persons are in its employ and what steps, if any, have been or are being taken to terminate such employment."[39] In 1953, Temple University fired philosopher Barrows Dunham when he refused to answer questions posed by the Un-American Activities Committee, for which he was charged with contempt of Congress. Though Dunham was later acquitted, Temple did not rehire him. In 1955, the School District of Philadelphia dismissed more than two dozen teachers for their refusal to answer questions about their alleged communist affiliations.[40] Meanwhile, in 1954, nine members of the local Communist Party were convicted under the 1940 Smith Act, which prohibited advocating the violent overthrow of the US government; an appeals court vacated the convictions, and the Smith Act was declared unconstitutional.[41]

There were, however, active Soviet spies in Philadelphia. The most famous of these was Harry Gold, a Russian immigrant whose family had settled in South Philadelphia when he was a child. Radicalized by the Great Depression, Gold eventually became a Soviet spy. In 1950, physicist Klaus Fuchs, who had worked on the Manhattan Project, confessed to British intelligence officials that he had passed nuclear secrets to the Soviet Union through a courier, whom he identified as Harry Gold. When US officials arrested Gold, he confessed and named several individuals, including David Greenglass, brother of Ethel Rosenberg, and her husband, Julius. As a result, the Rosenbergs were convicted of espionage and became the first US citizens executed for that crime during peacetime. Gold served fourteen years in federal prison before being paroled for good behavior. He later returned to Philadelphia and worked as a pathologist at John F. Kennedy Memorial Hospital in the Northeast. Gold was one of the lucky ones: the Red Scare devastated many Americans' lives, weakened labor unions, and blunted support for the emerging civil rights movement, which racists claimed was supported by Moscow.[42] An odd bit of trivia is that Ian Fleming named his Cold War superspy James Bond after a Philadelphia ornithologist of that name who lived in Chestnut Hill and whose work was known to the author (Fleming was an avid birdwatcher).[43]

An offshoot of the Red Scare was the "Lavender Scare," a moral panic about gay people working in the federal government. World War II, which drew millions of men from rural areas and assembled them in single-sex environments far from home, helped foster the gay rights movement. Because of the general social disapproval of homosexuality and the fact that many states had

laws criminalizing it, gay men and lesbians usually hid their sexual orienta-
tions, which allegedly made them susceptible to blackmail. After the war, cities became particularly important spaces for gay life. Two American gay rights
organizations, the Mattachine Society (gay men) and the Daughters of Bilitis
(lesbians), were founded in 1950 and 1955, respectively, though these were not
the first such organizations: the Society for Human Rights was a gay rights
organization that briefly operated in 1924.[44] Antigay bigotry could reach absurd
heights, such as in 1955, when the Catholic Archdiocese of Camden protested
naming the bridge connecting Philadelphia and Gloucester, New Jersey, after
poet Walt Whitman (who had lived in Camden and is believed to have been
either gay or bisexual).[45] However, it was no laughing matter: gay sex was a criminal offense in Pennsylvania, and Philadelphia's police routinely harassed gay
people. This is one of the reasons gay bars and nightclubs were often connected
to the Mafia, which paid police protection money to be left alone, though this
did not always stop the police from raiding the bars.[46] "Cruising" for gay sex in
Washington Square (known as Philadelphia's "pervert park") or in Rittenhouse
Square (another favorite gay pickup spot) could get a gay man arrested, severely
beaten, or worse.[47]

Despite the pervasive anxiety of the 1950s, the decade is often recalled as
a "golden age" in Philadelphia's political history. Between 1951 and 1962, the
municipal government was led by Joseph S. Clark Jr. and Richardson Dilworth.[48] Often called "Damon and Pythias," a reference to the Greek myth
celebrating friendship and honor (though they were not friends), Clark and
Dilworth both came from wealth and represented the shared values and cultural assumptions associated with being white Anglo-Saxon Protestants.[49] In
1947, Richardson Dilworth, a recent convert to the Democratic Party, challenged Barney Samuel, a holdover from the Vare machine who had been mayor
since 1941; Clark, a Republican turned Democratic lawyer, managed Dilworth's
campaign.[50] Dilworth attacked corruption, specifically criticizing more than
one hundred city officials and ward leaders.[51] Samuel defeated Dilworth, eventually becoming Philadelphia's longest-serving, and last, Republican, mayor.
Opposition to corruption resonated with voters, particularly after Tennessee
US Senator Estes Kefauver's Special Committee to Investigate Crime in Interstate Commerce uncovered the fact that Philadelphia's organized crime families
paid members of the police department $150,000 per month to ignore their
criminal activities.[52] These stunning revelations prompted several officers and
city officials to kill themselves, and it helped usher in an era of Democratic control that continues to this day.[53]

Voters had had enough, and in 1951, Clark successfully ran for mayor, becoming the first Democrat to win since 1884. Meanwhile, Dilworth successfully ran

for Philadelphia district attorney and succeeded Clark (who had promised to serve only a single term) in 1956, holding the office until 1962. Both Clark and Dilworth wanted to keep the city's Democratic political establishment at arm's length.[54] Though Philadelphia's Democratic Party had made some impressive gains in the 1930s and early 1940s, it was by no means guaranteed at the war's end that it would dominate the city's politics. In fact, in 1946, Philadelphia was the last large city with a strong Republican machine, and its Democratic Party came perilously close to bankruptcy; at one point it was only due to a personal loan from Democratic City Committee Chairman Michael J. Bradley that the party could pay the rent on its headquarters and make its payroll.[55] That same year, Republicans were elected in all of Philadelphia's congressional districts, but this was the highwater mark of Republican influence in the city. After 1952, Democrats held all these seats, and Philadelphia's Republican Party "ceased to exist as a genuine contestant for power in the city."[56] This put the city at odds with the rest of the commonwealth: while Philadelphia was consistently among Pennsylvania's most Democratic counties, voting for the Democratic presidential nominee in the elections of 1948, 1952, and 1956, the Republican candidates in those years won a majority of the commonwealth's votes.[57] Moreover, in the forty-four years between 1943 and 1987, Pennsylvania had a Republican governor for twenty-eight, and Republicans often dominated the Assembly.[58] Put another way, there was an increasingly obvious political rift between Philadelphia and the rest of Pennsylvania, and it soured city–commonwealth relations during the coming decades.[59]

During their respective terms, Clark and Dilworth worked closely with the GPM, and they were aided while in office by the achievement of one of the organization's long-term goals: a new city charter.[60] Even before the ink had dried on the city's 1919 charter, Philadelphia's business community had sought to revise it.[61] Efforts in 1929 and 1931 failed, but in 1949, the Assembly passed the First Class City Home Rule Act, which gave "cities of the first class the right and power to frame, adopt and amend their own charters and to exercise the powers and authority of local self-government."[62] Two years later, Philadelphia became the commonwealth's first city to enact a home rule charter. The new charter sought to modernize, streamline, and systematize the city's sprawling municipal government, collapsed the distinction between city and county (eliminating most of the latter's offices), substantially increased the mayor's power, and created two new offices: finance director and managing director.[63] In addition, it created the Commission on Human Relations and the Parks and Recreation Department, an attempt to centralize control over the Fairmount Park Commission, which operated autonomously and had its own police force.[64] The overwhelming majority of voters approved the new charter despite the fact that most members of Philadelphia's Republican political machine vigorously opposed it, correctly recognizing that the end of county political offices would deprive them of much-needed patronage jobs.[65] The new charter helped push the city's Republican Party into political irrelevance.

One reason this period is remembered as a golden age in Philadelphia's political history is the unparalleled economic prosperity (at least for some): beginning around 1940 and continuing for about thirty-five years the gap in wages between the country's wealthiest and poorest wage earners collapsed, greatly expanding the country's middle class. The causes were complicated but included New Deal policies, the devastation of Europe because of World War II, massive government spending to fight the Cold War, and widespread unionism. Among the beneficiaries were the region's colleges and universities, which experienced massive growth after World War II because of increased federal and state economic support, coupled with a flood of new students, many of whom were only able to attend college because of the Servicemen's Readjustment Act of 1944, or the GI Bill, which paid veterans' college or vocational school tuition and provided them with money for living expenses.[66] In addition, the federal government funneled money to colleges and universities through the National Science Foundation, created in 1950 to support research and teaching in nonmedical science and engineering fields. To accommodate the massive influx of students, the University of Pennsylvania and Temple University undertook ambitious construction programs that relied to a greater or lesser extent on federal, state, and local assistance.

The economic boom of the 1950s and favorable government policies fueled an expanded consumer culture. Nothing symbolized this better than television, and, as with radio a generation before, Philadelphia was a leading center of hardware construction and content creation. In 1931, Philo T. Farnsworth, who invented electronic television, moved to Philadelphia to take a job at Philco. Things did not go smoothly for Farnsworth at Philco, so in 1933 he left and, the following year, established Farnsworth Television at 127 East Mermaid Lane in the Chestnut Hill neighborhood. That summer the Franklin Institute hosted the first public demonstration of Farnsworth's television, and within a few years he had established a station (W3XPF) in nearby Wyndmoor that broadcast programs to the approximately four dozen televisions in the region. Though W3XPF folded in 1939, television set production boomed after the war, and the number of stations proliferated; by 1950, the region had several stations, including WPTZ (one of the nation's earliest commercial television stations), WCAU-TV, and WFIL-TV. Philadelphia was also home to several nationally broadcast programs, including *The Mike Douglas Show*, a popular daytime talk show filmed at KYW (initially at 1619 Walnut and then at Fifth and Market Streets). Undoubtedly, the best-known television show produced in Philadelphia during this period was *American Bandstand*, which between 1957 and 1964 was broadcast nationally (for the five years prior it had been regionally broadcast). Filmed at WFIL's studio at Forty-Sixth and Market Streets, the show featured teenagers dancing to hit songs and musical performances by pop acts.[67] Coming amid the emergence of teen culture in the United States that was heavily tied to rock 'n' roll, *American Bandstand* played a key role in the music scene, with several homegrown pop stars such as Frankie Avalon, Chubby Checker, and Bobby Rydell scoring hits during the 1950s and 1960s. *Bandstand* also created several celebrities, including Jerry Blavat, who went on to host a show called *The Discophonic Scene*.[68]

As *American Bandstand* demonstrated, Philadelphia remained a center for music, though not just rock 'n' roll; tenor and movie star Mario Lanza was born in Philadelphia and got his start singing in opera productions put on by the local YMCA. Baritone, actor, professional athlete, and civil rights activist Paul Robeson lived at 4951 Walnut Street for a decade before his death in 1976. Noted saxophonist and jazz pioneer John Coltrane lived in Philadelphia during much of the 1940s and 1950s, owning a house at 1511 North Thirty-Third Street that is now a museum. Beginning in the mid-1960s, several music producers developed what was called "the Philadelphia sound," a combination of soul music and funk. In 1967, Kenneth Gamble and Leon Huff founded Philadelphia International Records (headquartered at 309 South Broad Street), which released music by Patti LaBelle, the O'Jays, and Lou Rawls. It was even memorialized in a hit song, MFSB's "T.S.O.P. (The Sound of Philadelphia)," which reached number one on the *Billboard* Hot 100 in 1974. Sigma Sound Studios (established in 1968 and located at 212 North Twelfth Street) attracted some of the best-known musical artists of the time, including Stevie Wonder and David Bowie. As a favor to his friend tennis star Billie Jean King, Elton John wrote "Philadelphia Freedom" (King then played for the World TeamTennis's Philadelphia Freedoms franchise); the song reached number one on the *Billboard* Hot 100 in 1975.

Despite the cheery images on television screens of clean-cut youths dancing joyfully, there was something of a moral panic about juvenile delinquency in the late 1940s and 1950s.[69] Movies like *Blackboard Jungle* and *Rebel Without a Cause* drove home the message that teenagers of the "Silent Generation" (born between 1925 and 1945) were hooligans.[70] In 1955, Philadelphia imposed a curfew on anyone under eighteen, but this did little to alleviate concerns about juvenile delinquency, and by the 1960s, Philadelphia was described (based on no apparent evidence) as the "youth gang capital of the United States."[71] Fear of a perceived increase in crime and favorable federal government policies encouraged many Philadelphians to move, either heading to the suburbs or out to the relatively bucolic Northeast.

Unlike many old cities, Philadelphia at the end of World War II had a considerable amount of undeveloped space. Under the terms of consolidation in 1854, the city extended as far north as Bucks and Montgomery Counties; much of this land in the Northeast was still rural. In 1958, the city government and the Chamber of Commerce for Greater Philadelphia formed the Philadelphia Industrial Development Corporation (PIDC), whose goal was to attract and retain businesses in the city by offering large parcels of land and low-cost financing to build new facilities, often in the Northeast.[72] In 1957, as a result of the Northeast's growth, the Thirty-Fifth Ward, a massive tract of land bounded by the Tacony Creek, Castor Avenue, and Frankford Avenue, extending north to Bucks County and west to Montgomery County, was divided into seven wards (the Thirty-Fifth and Fifty-Third through Fifty-Eighth). Meanwhile, by 1965, Center City had shrunk from six wards to two.[73] Nearby Bucks County experienced something of an industrial boom after the war because as automobiles proliferated, it was less important for factories to be located next to rail or water lines, while the construction of interstate highways made it economically feasible for manufacturers to move to suburban areas and build new, larger facilities.[74] Federal policy contributed to this development by heavily incentivizing the construction of highways with the Federal-Aid Highway Act of 1944, and it left a lasting impact on Philadelphia. In 1947, Philadelphia approved the construction of a limited-access highway connecting the city to the Pennsylvania Turnpike. Sections of what became known as the Schuylkill Expressway opened over the next thirteen years, with the last section opening in 1960.[75] Interstate 95 (I-95) was in the planning stages during the 1930s. The main north-south interstate highway on the East Coast, its stretch through Philadelphia was expected to connect the factories in the Northeast to the sea and airports in South Philadelphia.[76] These roads ultimately failed to achieve their designers' goals; the Schuylkill Expressway (which soon earned the dubious nickname the "SureKill Expressway") was outdated almost from the moment it opened, and Richardson Dilworth later called the decision to allow the expressway to cut through Fairmount Park the worst mistake of his administration. I-95, which was not completed until 1985, made it possible to bypass Philadelphia entirely, doing little to revitalize the city's economy.[77]

Concern about the exodus of businesses and white residents to the suburbs explains Clark's and Dilworth's enthusiastic embrace of urban renewal. The perceived need to retain white families in the city clearly drove many of these projects; after all, in 1958, Dilworth noted, "We have to give whites confidence they can live in town without being flooded [by Black people]."[78] Urban renewal succeeded insofar as it made Center City far whiter than the rest of Philadelphia's neighborhoods, but at a significant cost to the city's nonwhite residents.[79]

One of urban renewal's goals was to leverage Philadelphia's historic buildings to increase tourism to the city and thereby persuade businesses and white citizens not to leave. In other words, historic preservation was one element of urban renewal.[80]

This was not a new approach; Philadelphia's historic buildings had been must-see tourist attractions since at least the beginning of the nineteenth century. However, the officials in charge of Philadelphia's urban renewal had a limited sense of what counted as historic buildings, focusing primarily on eighteenth-century structures and sites directly connected to the Revolution.[81] No historic building was more iconic or famous than Independence Hall, of course, and it became the focus of massive urban renewal efforts in the 1950s. By the time Clark was elected mayor, Independence Hall was surrounded by what were considered "undesirable" neighborhoods. These included China-town and Philadelphia's Skid Row (described by one contemporary as "hobohemia" and "a reservoir of contagious disease which can quickly and insidiously penetrate the larger community"), which extended from Spring Garden Street to Market Street between the Delaware River and Thirteenth Street. Redeveloping the area surrounding Independence Hall had been a goal for at least forty years, but it had never gotten off the ground for a variety of reasons.[82] In 1939, following the completion of a new Customs House for Philadelphia, the Treasury Department transferred the current one (housed in the Second Bank of the United States building, just a short distance from Independence Hall) to the National Park Service (NPS).[83] In 1946, the Pennsylvania Assembly created a task force to investigate the feasibility of establishing a national park comprising Independence Hall and nearby historically significant buildings.[84] When the Better Philadelphia Exhibition opened at Gimbels the following year, its massive diorama depicted the proposed redevelopment of the area surrounding Independence Hall, an attempt to leverage the city's history to generate tourist income and encourage nearby companies not to decamp for the suburbs.[85] On January 2, 1951, the city formally transferred ownership of Independence Hall to the NPS. Two years later, the commonwealth began demolishing buildings to create the mall.

The drive to save Philadelphia's eighteenth-century buildings reached beyond Independence Hall and included the restoration of the Man Full of Troubles Tavern (125 Spruce Street), the Todd House (home of future First Lady Dolley Payne Todd Madison), and the creation of Franklin Court on the site of Benjamin Franklin's last home (322 Market Street). In addition, it led to some re-creations designed to look authentic, such as the American Philosophical Society Museum and Library at 104 South Fifth Street, which was built in 1958 but was a reconstruction of the organization's Library Hall building from 1789.

The enthusiasm for the city's historic buildings privileged eighteenth-century structures to the exclusion of other periods, in part because of the perennial faith that architecture and urban design could influence human behavior.[86] Unfortunately, the fetishization of eighteenth-century buildings led to the demolition of several buildings of national and local historical importance because they did not date to the eighteenth century (including a substantial portion of nearby Chinatown's houses and businesses).[87] Put another way, urban renewal privileged a moment in Philadelphia's history—the colonial and revolutionary periods—over most other eras, leading to the loss of historically significant structures from the nineteenth and early twentieth centuries.

One of the most important renewal projects during this period was the redevelopment of Society Hill. Since the second half of the nineteenth century, the oldest buildings in the city had become businesses or now housed recent immigrants and Black people, including those in Society Hill.[88] Edmund Bacon recalled that on a visit to Society Hill in 1940, he saw "signs up in the front yards of 18th-century houses 'For Sale for $400.' It showed the state to which [the neighborhood] had descended."[89] A 1956 Land Use Report created by the City Planning Commission showed virtually no residential properties between Vine Street and Walnut Street east of City Hall (and only small pockets of residential areas west of it).[90] Society Hill's proximity to Independence Hall made it a site of considerable redevelopment interest.[91] In 1955, Richardson Dilworth, running for mayor, advocated redevelopment of Society Hill, even going so far as to build a Colonial Revival–style mansion (designed by famed restoration architect G. Edwin Brumbaugh) in Society Hill on Sixth Street just east of Washington Square. C. Jared Ingersoll, scion of the Ingersoll family who served on the CPC, also moved to Society Hill.[92] As mayor, Dilworth fostered the creation of the Old Philadelphia Development Corporation.[93] This organization, which brought together a diverse coalition of business leaders, policymakers, academics, and labor leaders, was intended to locate and secure buyers for the Redevelopment Authority's Society Hill properties.[94] Ironically, despite the enthusiasm for eighteenth-century structures (real and re-created), one of the most important elements of Society Hill's renewal was the thoroughly modern Society Hill Towers, a complex of three thirty-one-story buildings designed by famed architect I. M. Pei. Society Hill's redevelopment was successful in that it transformed one of the city's poorest areas into one of its wealthiest.[95] As such, it was one of the earliest examples of gentrification (the displacement of an area's residents by individuals of higher socioeconomic status), a term that had not even been coined when the city began redeveloping Society Hill (it was invented in 1964 by British sociologist Ruth Glass to describe similar trends in London).[96]

Another significant redevelopment project was the area around the old Penn-sylvania Railroad's Broad Street Station. In 1948, the City Planning Commission declared the station and the surrounding area a redevelopment area. In 1953, both the Pennsylvania Railroad's Broad Street Station and the Chinese Wall were demolished, and the CPC redeveloped the four-block area as Penn Center. Bacon had high hopes for the site, selecting Kling & Associates, one of the region's bus-iest and most-respected architectural firms, to design Penn Center's buildings. The project failed to live up to Bacon's expectations: principal architect Vincent Kling designed five modernist slabs with few architectural flourishes, which one critic called "an uninspired compromise with real estate interests."[97] James Reich-ley, writing in *Harper's Magazine*, noted, "Penn Center is above all else the result of compromise, often between contending forces which conceived their interests to be diametrically opposed. That is much of its significance."[98]

In reaction to the buildings' unadorned aesthetic, in 1959, the City Coun-cil (since 1919 a unicameral body) passed ordinances mandating that devel-opers on Redevelopment Authority land and other Philadelphia construction projects devote at least 1 percent of their project's total cost to public art, the first such requirement in the United States.[99] In 1986, Mayor W. Wilson Goode established the Office of Arts and Culture to coordinate Philadelphia's public art, and in 1991 he established a formal procedure for accessioning and deacces-sioning public works of art.[100] Despite the widespread criticism, Kling went on to design some of Philadelphia's best-known municipal buildings, including the Municipal Services Building (1401 JFK Boulevard), a Brutalist masterpiece that won *Architect Magazine*'s 1962 Progressive Architecture Award.[101]

Nor was Kling the only important mid-twentieth-century architect in Phila-delphia. Perhaps the best known was Louis Kahn, who enjoyed a national repu-tation and helped develop a branch of modernist architecture sometimes called Philadelphia modernism. Kahn's family emigrated from what is today Estonia in 1906 and settled in Philadelphia, where he attended Central High and the University of Pennsylvania. Kahn worked on the Better Philadelphia Exhibition and in 1957 joined the University of Pennsylvania's faculty. Kahn had served as a consulting architect for the CPC from 1945 to 1954, where he was often in conflict with Bacon. The Museum of Modern Art called Kahn's design for the University of Pennsylvania's Alfred Newton Richards Medical Research Labo-ratories Building (1965) "probably the most consequential building constructed in the United States since the war."[102] He also designed the Esherick House, at 204 Sunrise Lane in Chestnut Hill, named for famed artist Wharton Esherick's niece, Margaret (Kahn and Wharton Esherick were close friends).

A related development was the reformation of the city's zoning code, which specified what types of buildings property owners could erect (and where) and limited the activities that could be conducted on a parcel of land.[103] New York City adopted the United States' first zoning code in 1916, and Philadelphia followed in 1933. Relying on maps created by the Works Progress Administration, the zoning code established thirteen classifications (seven residential, four commercial, and two industrial), reflecting existing conditions in the city. However, from the beginning, effective code enforcement was hampered because the city hired only two inspectors, so the department worked on the basis of complaints rather than proactive investigations. In addition, the Zoning Board of Adjustment, which heard applicants' appeals when a permit was denied, frequently issued variances, sapping the code's effectiveness.[104] Recognizing this, as well as the changes to the city's economic and demographic profile, in 1962, Philadelphia adopted a revised zoning code. The new code dramatically expanded the number of use codes for residential, commercial, and industrial properties, but, just as with the 1933 code, economic and demographic changes soon rendered it wieldy and obsolete, with variances legion and violations commonplace. The city's zoning code was updated in 1988 and rewritten in 2012.[105]

Despite policymakers' efforts to include Philadelphians in the planning process, urban renewal, historic preservation, and zoning reform sometimes took place against neighborhood residents' wishes.[106] Many of the GPM's members did not live in the city (novelist George Perry Sessions had famously said of Philadelphia that "those who own the city have abandoned it") and were more focused on economic growth than on quality-of-life issues, an echo of the nineteenth-century tension between democrats and technocrats described in chapter 4.[107] As a result, city planners and redevelopers sometimes grappled with substantial grassroots pushback. One case was the redevelopment of Eastwick, a semirural area of Southwest Philadelphia. Created from swampy land dredged to build the nearby Philadelphia International Airport, as late as the 1950s, some of the area's original homes lacked sewer access.[108] Urban redevelopment advocates saw Eastwick as a potential site for rehousing nearly twenty-five hundred families, most of them Black, displaced by redevelopment activities in North and West Philadelphia.[109] Eastwick's white residents pushed back, and subsequently, several Black residents reported Ku Klux Klan activity in the area. One Black family even had a cross burned on their lawn![110] A similar story unfolded in Whitman Park, a neighborhood in South Philadelphia. In 1956, the city planned to build four high-rise units of public housing intended for Black people displaced by urban renewal; later the plan changed to building townhomes. The site was just north of Oregon Avenue near a small, mostly Black neighborhood. Some of Whitman Park's white residents protested, and the project made little headway during the administration of Mayor James Tate. His successor, Frank Rizzo, halted the project by allowing a contract with Multicon (the company that would build the houses for low-income residents) to expire, a move for which he was successfully sued in federal court and that cost the city $626,000 in damages.[111] Eventually, the units were built under court order, and they opened in 1982 to little fanfare.[112] In general, white opposition to integration retarded the construction of public housing projects in Philadelphia.[113]

Yet even when residents won these battles, the victory was often pyrrhic. Such was the case of the Crosstown Expressway, an east-west highway connecting I-95 and the Schuylkill Expressway. In the early 1950s, various routes were considered, all cutting through majority Black and immigrant neighborhoods in South Philadelphia. Though it was never actually built, the expectation that it would be constructed depressed property values by persuading residents and businesses to leave the area and making lenders unwilling to give potential home buyers mortgages.[114] This dynamic depressed property values along the portion of South Street east of Broad Street, making it by 1963 the place where "all the hippest meet," according to the Orlons' hit song "South Street."

While federal government policy had generated widespread prosperity during the 1950s, there remained large swaths of poverty in the United States. Michael Harrington's classic 1962 book, *The Other America*, demonstrated that millions of Americans still lived in poverty. Though plenty of white families in the city and commonwealth were poor, Black families made up a disproportionately high number of Philadelphians living in poverty. One reason was that the various federal programs created during the New Deal (which fueled the widespread economic prosperity of the postwar decades) excluded Black Americans.[115] That was not incidental: southern Democrats had made sure that New Deal legislation was crafted in such a way as to prevent Black Americans from benefiting.[116] By the early 1960s, Black people held a disproportionately high share of civil service positions in Philadelphia (because the city's 1951 charter explicitly banned racial or religious discrimination in municipal hiring, and Clark's administration strongly enforced civil service regulation), but private sector jobs open to Black Philadelphians tended to be low-paid, low-status positions with little opportunity for advancement.[117] As a result, the average working-class Black family's income was just over half that of white working-class families, and Black Americans, including those living in Philadelphia, suffered higher rates of unemployment and poverty than whites; by one count, 20 percent of Black Philadelphia adults were unemployed in the early 1960s.[118]

In addition, perversions of some New Deal programs kept Black people from achieving homeownership.[119] The Great Depression spurred a wave of mortgage defaults, so in June 1933, Congress created the Home Owners' Loan Corporation (HOLC), which issued bonds and used the funds to purchase mortgages when the homeowners were struggling to make payments. The HOLC then refinanced the mortgages, usually for longer terms and at a lower interest rate than the original loans, which lowered homeowners' monthly payments. Beginning in 1935, the HOLC initiated the City Survey Program, which produced maps of more than two hundred US cities, assigning letter grades from A (First Grade) to D (Fourth Grade) to neighborhoods. The areas labeled D were outlined in red on the City Survey Program's maps, giving us the term "redlining," though it was not used at the time. HOLC assessments of neighborhoods considered race and immigrant status and rated neighborhoods with large Black and immigrant populations as undesirable.[120] For instance, the City Survey Map from 1937 identified South Philadelphia as either commercial or (with a very small exception near Rittenhouse Square) as D. In addition, almost all of West Philadelphia along the Schuylkill was either D or C, as was Spring Garden, Fairmount, Kensington, Frankford, and Bridesburg. By contrast, most tracts in far North Philadelphia and what would become the Northeast were rated A or B. Though by the time the HOLC created these maps, it had already issued most of its loans, they reflected existing lending practices.[121] The consequence was that though Philadelphia remained the "City of Homes," a substantially smaller proportion of the city's Black families owned their dwellings than the white families.[122] In 1953, the Commission on Human Relations found that, while 140,000 housing units had been recently built in Philadelphia, just over 1,000 were available to Black people.[123] As a result, these policies limited Black Philadelphians' opportunities to acquire wealth through homeownership, and they were unable to follow industrial jobs to the suburbs.[124]

It was not just federal government policy that disadvantaged Black Philadelphians; builders and realtors also played important roles. White people flocked to the Northeast, in part because Black people were largely excluded.[125] In nearby Bucks County, William J. Levitt, the famed developer of Levittown, had a strict whites-only policy in selling his homes. Amazingly, the Jewish Levitt also excluded Jews. In the ten years after World War II, Levitt mass-produced 145,000 low-cost homes in Northeast Philadelphia and the surrounding counties.[126] The NAACP sued Levitt, who coincidentally selected Dilworth, Paxson, Kalish, and Green (Richardson Dilworth's law firm) to represent him. William T. Coleman Jr., a prominent Black lawyer at the firm, worked out an agreement with Levitt by which the developer would end the whites-only policy. However, when Bill and Daisy Myers, a Black couple, purchased a Levittown house, local whites threw rocks at them and even threatened to bomb their home.[127]

Not all white developers excluded Black people; for instance, in 1956, Morris Milgram built Greenbelt Knoll in the Northeast, the city's first racially integrated planned development. Milgram required that 45 percent of the homes be sold to nonwhites.[128] Milgram himself lived in Greenbelt Knoll, as did several other prominent Philadelphians, including Robert N. C. Nix Sr., Pennsylvania's first Black member of the US House of Representatives.[129] This was the exception rather than the rule, however, and most new developments were explicitly or implicitly "whites only." That was a serious problem, because the Federal Housing Administration, which was created in 1934, offered mortgage insurance (which guaranteed mortgages against default and thereby made lenders more willing to loan money for longer terms, making it easier for buyers to purchase homes) only on new construction (a boon to housebuilders). Whites-only policies effectively prevented most would-be Black homebuyers from availing themselves of this program.[130]

Realtors also contributed to residential segregation: some refused to show Black would-be home buyers houses in so-called white neighborhoods. Others stoked white homeowners' fears of Black residents moving into the area in the hope that whites would sell their houses at below-market prices. These realtors could purchase the houses and sell them at a considerable profit to Black families; the process, known as "blockbusting," had a self-fulfilling logic that depressed the city's property values for the 1950s and 1960s.[131] This was not true of all Philadelphia neighborhoods, of course: Mount Airy, near Germantown, was integrated, a fact that many residents took great pride in.[132] In general, however, urban redevelopment, federal government policy, and homeowners' racism fueled an exodus of white people out of Philadelphia during the two decades after World War II, leaving the city surrounded by several predominantly white counties that former mayor Dilworth evocatively disparaged as a "white noose" around the city's neck.[133]

Racism combined with latent antiurbanism to place Philadelphia at a disadvantage relative to the commonwealth's other counties.[134] Joshua Eilberg, a member of the Pennsylvania House of Representatives from 1954 to 1966 and later a US congressman, recalled that he and his colleagues were "alert to the fact that the suburbs were resentful of Philadelphia. Any program that we wanted for Philadelphia, or involved Philadelphia institutions, frequently caused resentment or negative votes by upstate legislators."[135] The city was already underrepresented in both houses of the Pennsylvania legislature, but in 1962, the Assembly created new legislative districts. The map it devised for Philadelphia was designed to reduce the nonwhite population of each state Senate district, leading to a decline in the number of Black members in the Assembly.[136]

The pervasive and ongoing discrimination against Black people led to the modern civil rights movement beginning in the early 1950s. One element of the civil rights struggle was to redefine how white people perceived Black people, a practice known as "respectability politics."[137] This was one reason why civil rights organizations encouraged marchers to wear dress clothes. Local civil rights

activists criticized the annual Mummers parade, which had a long and troubling history of featuring white performers in blackface performing racist skits,
as perpetuating negative stereotypes about Black people. On December 19,
1963, Mummers parade director Elias Myers announced that participants
would no longer be permitted to wear blackface, the result of pressure by local
civil rights leaders. Several Mummers participants strongly objected and even
went so far as to picket Myers's house. Myers backpedaled, watering down the
ban on blackface, so the Congress of Racial Equality (CORE) and the NAACP
turned to the courts. On January 3, 1964, the Court of Common Pleas issued a
partial ban on blackface (the practice was banned on Broad Street) and prohibited CORE from picketing the parade, though some individuals continued the
practice of wearing blackface for decades.[138]

The civil rights movement was not monolithic, and there were several organizations in Philadelphia. The Student Nonviolent Coordinating Committee
(SNCC), which was founded in 1960 by young Black activists disenchanted
with the Reverend Dr. Martin Luther King Jr.'s Southern Christian Leadership
Conference, had an office in Philadelphia. Baptist minister Leon Sullivan (pastor of Zion Baptist Church, located on Broad Street just south of Erie Avenue,
and known as the "Lion of Zion"), joined by four hundred ministers, led a
"Don't buy where you don't work" campaign to leverage Black consumers' economic power to end discriminatory hiring practices.[139] Sullivan later founded
the Opportunities Industrialization Center, a nonprofit intended to provide
professional education and life-skills training to Black men and women to prepare them to enter the workforce. In 1968, Sullivan spearheaded the development of Sullivan Progress Plaza (1501 North Broad Street), the nation's first
shopping center built, operated, and owned by Black people. However, these
groups sometimes competed with one another, reflecting different ideologies
and approaches to achieving civil rights.[140]

Philadelphia's leading civil rights figure was attorney and president of the
local chapter of the NAACP Cecil B. Moore. Born in West Virginia in 1915,
Moore served in the Marine Corps during World War II and settled in Philadelphia in 1947. He used his GI Bill benefits to attend Temple University's
law school and built a successful practice defending his Black neighbors in
North Philadelphia. In 1963, he was elected president of the city's chapter of the
NAACP. Moore took a more confrontational approach than other civil rights
leaders.[141] At that time, Black people were a core constituency of the Democratic Party; after all, it was Black voters who helped deliver the city to the
Democrats in 1951.[142] Yet Black Philadelphians occupied few leadership positions in the party establishment, which meant it was often oblivious to Black
concerns.[143] Moore used his inaugural address as president of the NAACP in

January 1963 to put white Democrats on notice, saying, "No longer will the plantation system of white men [be] appointing our leaders ... in Philadelphia." He made good on that statement by encouraging Black Democrats to run for office.[144] Shortly after, Moore, in conjunction with Philadelphia's chapter of CORE, orchestrated a picketing campaign at the Municipal Services Building and other sites (including the Liberty Bell and the mayor's house) to highlight the building unions' discriminatory hiring practices.[145]

Moore's highest-profile campaign, by far, was the desegregation of Girard College, a private boys'school that admitted only whites but that was located in what was now a predominantly Black neighborhood. In the 1940s and 1950s, civil rights organizations had availed themselves of the court system to achieve goals, such as school desegregation, leading to landmark court decisions, most importantly 1954's *Brown v. Board of Education*. Yet a decade later, most Black students in Philadelphia still attended segregated and overcrowded schools.[146] In 1955, two prominent Black Philadelphia lawyers, Raymond Pace Alexander and Sadie Tanner Mossell Alexander, sued the Philadelphia City Trust (which administered Stephen Girard's will) to end Girard College's discriminatory admissions policy. Two years later, the US Supreme Court held that Girard College was an agency of the Commonwealth of Pennsylvania and therefore needed to admit Black students. However, to avoid being bound by that decision, the city transferred management of Girard College to a Board of City Trust, making the school a private institution.[147] There matters stood until Moore decided to change tactics and bring public (as opposed to legal) pressure to bear on the college's administrators. Beginning in May 1965, the NAACP, joined by other civil rights organizations, conducted daily marches outside Girard College's campus to protest the institution's discriminatory admissions policy.[148] In August 1965, Reverend King spoke to a crowd of thousands outside the college, telling them it was a "sad experience to stand in the city that has long been known as the cradle of liberty, that has in its midst a kind of Berlin Wall to keep the colored children of God out."[149] In 1967, the US District Court ruled that Girard College must admit Black students, and the following year, the Third Circuit Court of Appeals upheld the ruling and the US Supreme Court refused to intervene. As a result, Girard College began accepting Black boys and then transitioned to a coeducational institution in 1984.

Racist whites, who feared for their own status if they had to compete with Black people in a fair and equitable marketplace, responded with hostility and violence to the civil rights movement's modest demands.[150] In 1959, journalist and political scientist James Reichley noted that "smoldering hostility toward the Negroes is a sentiment present among all of [Philadelphia's] white groups."[151] Meanwhile, from the mid-1930s on, Republicans, who were trying to fracture the New Deal coalition, increasingly appealed to white voters through subtle (and not so subtle) racism.[152] During the 1959 mayoral campaign, Republican candidate Harrold Stassen (former governor of Minnesota and special assistant to President Dwight Eisenhower) accused Dilworth of encouraging southern Black people to migrate to Philadelphia to increase the number of Democratic voters.[153] Stoking white resentment for electoral gain reached its apotheosis during the 1968 presidential campaign in Richard Nixon's so-called southern strategy, which courted white Democratic voters by appealing to their resentment of Black people. Kevin Phillips, the architect of the strategy, observed in 1970, "The principal force which broke up the Democratic (New Deal) coalition is the Negro socioeconomic revolution and the liberal Democratic ideological inability to cope with it."[154] The white backlash dominated Philadelphia's politics in the 1960s and 1970s and was embodied in the figure of police commissioner (and later mayor) Frank Rizzo.

It is undeniable that many Americans perceived that incidents of violent crime were increasing in the country's cities. Though President Lyndon B. Johnson's Great Society programs are largely remembered as attempts to alleviate poverty, they laid the groundwork for the "war on crime" that followed. In fact, it was Johnson who, in 1965, declared a war on crime and promoted legislation that increased federal funding for, and helped militarize, law enforcement to a degree theretofore unprecedented in US history.[155] His successors, most notably Nixon, abandoned the Great Society's attempts to alleviate poverty and instead devoted even more resources to law enforcement, which promoted overpolicing and led to a greater number of negative interactions between officers and Black Philadelphians.[156] One reason Americans perceived that crime rates were going up was the salacious nature of local "action" news, a type of television reporting that was invented in Philadelphia. In 1965, KYW-TV's news director, Al Primo, developed the template for local television news reporting by sending the studio's reporters into the city to film dramatic or lurid events and interview witnesses. The program that developed, *Eyewitness News*, spanned several imitators (ABC's *Action News* premiered in 1970).[157] These programs overemphasized crime, which was, in the words of *Action News* correspondent Larry Kane, "cheap to cover." In 1974, he revealed to a local reporter that a survey of consumers a few years prior had indicated that crime was the number one topic viewers wanted to hear about.[158] Unfortunately, this type of reporting led many viewers to believe violent crime was much more prevalent than it really was, conditioning them to accept draconian tough-on-crime policies.[159]

There were several violent confrontations between police and Black Philadelphians during the early 1960s, due in no small part to the racism of many Philadelphia police officers. In October 1963, white Philadelphia police officer

John Tourigian shot and killed a twenty-four-year-old Black man, Willie Philyaw. According to Tourigian, Philyaw had stolen a watch from a drugstore and then attacked the officer with a knife (witnesses denied this account, pointing out that Philyaw had an injured leg and was epileptic). The shooting sparked outrage that nearly boiled over into a riot.

Importantly, it was not just white officers who held racist views; so did many Black officers. This dynamic reflected the several divisions in the Black community, including class and generation, and between those who clung to or rejected respectability politics.[160] On the evening of Friday, August 28, 1964, Odessa and Rush Bradford's car stalled on Columbia Avenue near Twenty-Second Street. Two police officers, one black and one white, approached the car., Following a verbal exchange, the two officers tried to forcibly remove Odessa Bradford from the car. The officers' aggressive behavior led to a confrontation between several witnesses and the police that escalated into three days of looting and vandalism.[161] Police Commissioner Howard Leary ordered his approximately six hundred men not to intervene, to the disgust of Deputy Commissioner Rizzo.[162] Rizzo believed in taking a hard line with Black protesters. For instance, during the Girard College protests in 1965, the police officers under Rizzo's command clubbed protesters, and in August 1966, he orchestrated a series of raids against the local SNCC chapter, which, among other things, had denounced the Philadelphia Police Department's racism and brutality. Stokely Carmichael, SNCC's new national chairman, denounced "Racist Rizzo" in particular.[163]

One of the most important confrontations between Philadelphia police officers and Black Philadelphians occurred on November 17, 1967. On that day, about thirty-five hundred high school students walked out of classes and picketed the school board's administration building on the Benjamin Franklin Parkway. These students demanded courses in Black history, the end to the school district's tracking system—which prevented most Black students from taking college preparatory classes—and the removal of police officers from the city's schools. Since the creation of public schooling in the nineteenth century, schools had been sites of political, social, and cultural conflict. The Philadelphia public school system was long controlled by a hidebound and conservative school board that prioritized balancing its budget over educational excellence, making it among the country's worst.[164] A documentary titled *High School* depicted an average day in the lives of the students, teachers, and administrators at Northeast High School. The film's depiction of the Philadelphia public school system was so devastating that various influential politicians essentially got the film banned in the city on its release in 1968.

In 1965, a supplement to Philadelphia's home rule charter reorganized the city's school board; the mayor, rather than the Court of Common Pleas, would now appoint members of the city's considerably smaller (nine members instead of fifteen) Board of Education.[165] In September 1965, Mayor James Tate appointed former mayor Richardson Dilworth president of the school board, inaugurating what many hoped would be a new era in public schooling in Philadelphia. That same year, the Philadelphia Federation of Teachers (founded after the American Federation of Teachers expelled the Philadelphia local in 1941 over fears of communist infiltration) won the right to collective bargaining, a turning point for the city's teachers. Until then, teachers' salaries across the commonwealth were lower than the national average and those paid in neighboring states, but that began to change as a result of collective bargaining.[166] In 1970, the Pennsylvania General Assembly passed Act 195, which allowed public employees to strike; over the next eleven years, Philadelphia's public school teachers struck six times, winning salary increases. However, improved pay and benefits for the city's public school teachers contributed to the school district's budget shortfalls that led to larger class sizes and deferred maintenance at schools.[167] During the protest at the school district's office, police officers under Rizzo's command provoked a riot, which they used as an excuse to beat the protesters, almost all of whom were teenagers. During the melee, Rizzo is alleged to have told his officers, "Get their black asses."[168] Many members of the city's Black community were horrified and demanded that Mayor Tate fire Rizzo, but the mayor had only narrowly won reelection ten days before after promising to retain the police commissioner.[169] Rizzo's actions during the school board protest cemented his reputation as the embodiment of Philadelphia's white backlash.

Racist whites' resistance to the civil rights movement led to the rejection of respectability politics among a younger group of Black activists and the elevation of more-aggressive leaders after 1965.[170] Cecil B. Moore, whom many whites at the time considered too pugnacious, is reported to have said, "If the white community thinks I am difficult to deal with, you should see what is coming behind me."[171] Nothing better represented this than the Black Panther Party (BPP), founded in Oakland, California, in 1966 and initially formed to aggressively push back against police brutality (the BPP soon began advocating for increased social programs to alleviate racial inequality). The BPP, which advocated Black men openly (and legally) carrying firearms, was so alarming to white policymakers in California that within months of the party's founding, the state legislature passed, and Governor Ronald Reagan signed, a bill repealing an earlier law that allowed the open carry of loaded firearms in the state. Named after California Assemblyman Don Mulford, a Republican then representing Oakland, the bill was supported by the National Rifle Association. Chapters of the BPP spread quickly to cities across the United States, including

Philadelphia, which hosted the Third National Conference on Black Power in 1968.[172] In September 1970, the Black Panther Party convened the Revolutionary People's Constitutional Convention (RPCC) in Philadelphia, one of the largest meetings of radical activists in US history. Ostensibly convened to draft a new version of the US Constitution, the RPCC was also an attempt to unify factions of the radical left, including the Native American, antiwar, Asian American, Chicano, gay rights, and feminist movements.

In fact, the civil rights movement midwifed those other liberation movements, and Philadelphia, as a racially diverse city with a deep bench of symbolically important buildings and artifacts, was a key site. For instance, just a year after the National Organization for Women (NOW), which was committed to ending discrimination against women, was founded in Washington, DC, in 1966, Ernesta Drinker Ballard established a Philadelphia chapter (though it was not incorporated until 1971).[173] Born in 1920, Ballard was descended from one of the city's most prominent families and married into another, though her status did not protect her from the sting of discrimination: when, as a little girl, she told her father she wanted to be a lawyer, her father dismissed that ambition.[174] Despite Ballard's elite pedigree, Philadelphia's chapter of NOW adopted a confrontational approach and took on some of the city's most venerable institutions. For instance, in 1973, it awarded the Union League, which banned women from membership, a "Barefoot and Pregnant" Award (under pressure from NOW, the Union League eventually began admitting women in 1986).[175]

Philadelphia's chapter of NOW was far more welcoming of lesbians than the national organization and was the first in the nation to have a lesbian president (Jan Welch).[176] Moreover, just as with the civil rights and the women's movements, Philadelphia had played an important role in the gay rights movement. On July 4, 1965, more than three dozen gay and lesbian activists marched around Independence Hall to advocate for gay rights, an event called a "reminder." The fourth and last reminder occurred just days after the Stonewall Riot in New York City, which inaugurated a more radical turn for the gay rights movement in the United States.[177] Philadelphia's first gay pride parade took place on July 11, 1972, starting at Rittenhouse Square, marching east along Chestnut Street, and culminating at Independence Hall. The following year, Giovanni's Room (located since 1984 at Twelfth and Pine Streets), the oldest still operating gay bookstore, opened. Several prominent gay rights activists lived in Philadelphia. For instance, Barbara Gittings, who helped found the New York chapter of the Daughters of Bilitis and edited that organization's magazine, *The Ladder*, led Philadelphia's "reminders" at Independence Hall. In 1972, Temple University professor of psychiatry Dr. John E. Fryer delivered a speech (in costume, to keep his identity secret) to the American Psychiatric Association conference that persuaded the organization to remove homosexuality from its list of mental illnesses the following year. Partially because of their activism, in 1982, the city passed an ordinance banning discrimination based on sexual orientation, and in 2007, it dedicated the first rainbow street signs in the Gayborhood, a region of Center City bounded by Walnut, Pine, Eleventh and Broad Streets.

The proliferation of protests and the cultural changes reshaping American society coincided with a fundamental shift in Philadelphia's politics. World War II had expanded who was considered "white" to include Italians, Jews, and other previously excluded groups, and the election of the Catholic John F. Kennedy to the presidency in 1960 indicated to many observers that anti-Catholicism was on the wane. As a result, in big cities across America, so-called white ethnics replaced white Anglo-Saxon Protestants (WASPs) in municipal government. Richardson Dilworth resigned as mayor in February 1962 to launch a bid for governor, and as of this writing, he is the last WASP elected Philadelphia's mayor.[178] He was replaced by the Irish Catholic City Council president, James Tate, who won election in his own right the following year. Unlike his predecessors Clark and Dilworth, Tate was cool to the GPM and drew his political support primarily from the city's working-class whites in South Philadelphia.[179] Tate served in the Pennsylvania House of Representatives between 1941 and 1946, then successfully sought election to Philadelphia's City Council in 1951, where he remained for a decade before ascending to the mayor's office.

However, that new inclusivity in American politics had a downside, in that white ethnic politicians often strengthened their claims to whiteness by denigrating Black people.[180] This helps explain one of Mayor Tate's most consequential decisions: appointing Frank Rizzo as police commissioner. Longtime member of the City Council Thacher Longstreth noted in his autobiography, "Tate was smart enough to realize the only way he could win [the 1967 election] was to endorse Rizzo without qualification, regardless of how much power Rizzo developed as a result. And his blank-check support gave Rizzo enough power and momentum so that he carried right on through to become the [Democratic mayoral] nominee in the '71 campaign."[181] Tate later claimed he saw the New Deal coalition breaking down because some white people believed that the Democrats were moving too fast on civil rights and promoted Rizzo's mayoral aspirations because "I felt [he] could bring the white working class back into the Democratic Party."[182] Tate's decision to promote Rizzo provided the latter a springboard to the mayor's office.[183]

When he ran for mayor in 1971, Rizzo proclaimed himself "the toughest cop in America," a dog whistle (a suggestive appeal to racism that is not explicitly racist) calculated to appeal to working-class whites and amplified by conservative media like Walter Annenberg's *Philadelphia Inquirer*.[184] Rizzo's opponent, perennial mayoral candidate Thacher Longstreth, could not have been more different: a Main Line WASP, he denounced police brutality against Black Philadelphians.[185] President Nixon declined to support Republican Longstreth's mayoral bid; the following year, Rizzo endorsed Nixon's reelection campaign, an illustration of the shifting alignments in American politics and Rizzo's fluid attachment to the Democratic Party (a former Republican, Rizzo switched parties in order to accept Tate's offer of police commissioner).[186] Rizzo's closeness to the Nixon administration paid dividends for Philadelphia, at least early on: Nixon visited the city during the 1972 campaign, signing the State and Local Fiscal Assistance Act of 1972 at Independence Hall.[187]

The popularity of New Deal policies had forced Republicans (reluctantly) to acquiesce to them. In 1954, President Dwight D. Eisenhower wrote to his brother, "Should any political party attempt to abolish social security, unemployment insurance, and eliminate labor laws and farm programs, you would not hear of that party again in our political history."[188] In the mid-1960s, Presidents Johnson and Nixon practiced what was being called "growth liberalism," a series of policies that included Great Society social programs and revenue sharing, under which the federal government "collects taxes, at which it is very effective, and shares a small part of them with state and local governments, which are more effective at identifying day-to-day needs. The corollary was that elected officials, not appointed bureaucrats, should decide where tax money ought to be spent."[189] Revenue sharing was particularly attractive to big-city mayors, who could use the funds to pay for basic services without tax increases, which appealed to both Tate and Rizzo (for obvious reasons) but made the city dependent on federal revenue. When that dried up, Philadelphia faced serious challenges.[190]

Like Nixon, Rizzo abused his authority and power, rewarding political allies and punishing enemies. For instance, in 1972, Rizzo's finance director, Lennox Moak, used his political influence to drive radio journalist Taylor Grant, a critic of Rizzo's administration, off the air.[191] The mayor also encouraged trade unionists to blockade the offices of the *Philadelphia Inquirer* after the newspaper published a critical column about Rizzo (the city's police officers did nothing to break up the blockade). More seriously, in 1973, Rizzo apparently tried to bribe the Philadelphia Democratic Party chairman, Peter J. Camiel, to settle a conflict over whom the party would endorse for district attorney. Camiel told the press about the alleged bribe, which Rizzo disputed, and both men eventually submitted to a lie detector test. Camiel passed, and Rizzo failed, which was widely reported in the local press and humiliated the "law and order" mayor. Rizzo got his revenge in 1976, when he successfully orchestrated Camiel's ouster as Democratic Party chairman. Philadelphia's police department remained corrupt and brutal: a 1974 report about it issued by the Pennsylvania Crime Commission totaled fourteen hundred pages and detailed dozens of instances of misconduct.[192] Police corruption and brutality were so bad under Mayor Rizzo that it was the subject of a 2000 television movie, *The Thin Blue Line*, starring Rob Morrow, Randy Quaid, and Paul Sorvino.

In early 1976, Rizzo's opponents began a drive to recall the mayor, then only a few months into his second term; former mayor Joseph Clark was the first signatory of the recall petition. The Rizzo administration challenged the validity of the recall petition's signatures, but when the Philadelphia County Common Pleas Court ruled the signatures were admissible, the city solicitor turned to the Pennsylvania Supreme Court, which ruled the city charter's recall provisions were unconstitutional. Rizzo was thus able to serve his second term, but the backlash led to the election of several anti-Rizzo candidates, including Edward G. "Ed" Rendell as district attorney in 1977. The following year, Rizzo pushed for a referendum to amend the city's charter to allow him to serve a third consecutive term as mayor, which was prohibited. Rizzo framed the issue in racial terms, telling his supporters to "vote white." The lopsided loss—about two-thirds of voters rejected the referendum—was a rebuke to Rizzo, but this obscured the fact that a substantially higher percentage of white Philadelphians voted for the proposed amendment, whereas some majority Black wards rejected it by a fifty-to-one ratio.[193] Antics like these led *Social Science Quarterly* to declare Rizzo the worst big-city mayor in the United States between 1960 and 1997.[194]

The 1970s were trying times for the United States, which entered a period of prolonged stagflation, or a recession with inflation (which reached double digits by the middle of the decade). The so-called City of Homes had fallen to fourth place among major cities for homeownership, lagging far behind the nearby suburbs.[195] At the same time, nearly two centuries of industrial activity had taken a considerable toll on the city's environment. Philadelphia had made some progress modernizing its sewer system, building waste treatment plants in the Northeast and South Philadelphia, and improving trash collection, but there was still considerable room for improvement.[196] In 1940, the Interstate Commission on the Delaware River declared the Delaware River (the source of much of the city's drinking water) "one of the most grossly polluted areas in the United States"; in 1946, journalist John Gunther ruefully noted that "Philadelphia drinks its own sewage, chlorinated."[197] Philadelphia was far from unique in this regard: on June 22, 1969, sparks ignited industrial debris and sewage floating on Cleveland's Cuyahoga River, causing a fire that caused thousands of dollars in damage and spurred calls for federal environmental legislation. A few months later, President Nixon signed into law the National Environmental Policy Act, the first of a spate of acts (the 1970 Clean Air Act, the Clean Water Act of 1972, the Safe Drinking Water Act of 1974, and the Resource Conservation and Recovery Act of 1976) designed to improve the country's environment and protect natural resources.

It was against this unpromising backdrop—protest, white backlash, stagflation, environmental degradation—that plans were made to celebrate the country's two hundredth birthday. As early as the late 1950s, Philadelphia's political leaders began considering the two hundredth anniversary of the signing of the Declaration of Independence as an opportunity to showcase the city.[198] In 1959, Edmund Bacon had looked forward to the Bicentennial as a moment when "the United States will receive the world in Philadelphia. . . . In this way, the reconsideration of the ideas of 1776 will occur in the place where they were originally formulated, and the world will determine, by observation . . . the actual reconstruction of Philadelphia as an unmatched expression of the vitality of American technology and culture."[199] Planning for the event during the 1960s, which was mired in political cronyism and growing cynicism about American institutions, did not live up to Bacon's rosy predictions, and the lack of enthusiasm of the Nixon administration (then embroiled in the Watergate scandal and trying to use federal funds for the Bicentennial to shore up political support) for the idea during the early 1970s hobbled planning.[200] Making the situation even worse, an outbreak of a mysterious respiratory ailment (later dubbed Legionnaires' disease) among attendees of the American Legion's annual conference at the Bellevue-Stratford in July 1976 brought the city unwanted attention during the Bicentennial summer; the hotel, one of the city's best known, went out of business as a result.

However, the Bicentennial was not entirely a failure: Philadelphia hosted Queen Elizabeth II of Great Britain and her husband, Prince Philip, for the first part of the couple's six-day tour of the United States. During the presidential campaign that fall, President Gerald Ford and Democratic nominee Jimmy Carter participated in the first presidential debates since 1960. The candidates met at the Walnut Street Theatre, but the event was marred by technical difficulties that left the two men standing awkwardly on the stage for twenty-seven minutes before audio was restored. In addition, though not directly related to the Bicentennial, in August 1976, Cardinal Karol Józef Wojtyła (soon to become Pope John Paul II) visited the city for the International Eucharistic Conference; as part of the proceedings, the Vatican raised the status of the city's cathedral to a basilica. The following year, the church canonized Philadelphia's own Bishop John Neumann (the first male American saint), who established the city's Catholic school system in the nineteenth century. In addition, several important museums opened in conjunction with the Bicentennial, including the Afro-American Historical and Cultural Museum (the first institution funded by a large city to interpret Black history and culture; in 1997 it was renamed the African American Museum in Philadelphia), the Declaration House, the Please Touch Museum, and the Mummers Museum.[201] In preparation for the Bicentennial, Philadelphia installed Robert Indiana's *LOVE* sculpture in John F. Kennedy Plaza. Originally intended to be temporary, the sculpture proved so popular that the city purchased it, and the park is now generally called LOVE Park. In short, the 1976 Bicentennial celebration, though neither the commanding success of its 1876 predecessor nor the abject failure of the 1926 Sesquicentennial Exposition, left a lasting impact on Philadelphia. However, as the city's three hundredth anniversary loomed, it was clear that Philadelphia had not realized the rosy expectations of the 1947 Better Philadelphia Exhibition.

CHAPTER 10

Crisis . . . and Renaissance?
Philadelphia Since 1976

As Philadelphia approached its three hundredth birthday in 1982, things were grim: crime was up, the city's population was down, and federal government support for America's cities was drying up. The so-called Reagan Revolution signaled the curtailment of New Deal programs in favor of neoliberalism, a series of policies that emphasized fiscal austerity, privatization, and market-oriented solutions to social problems. Neoliberalism, plus the "tough on crime" and "war on drugs" policies implemented by Republicans and Democrats, devastated American cities, including Philadelphia. Collectively, these developments combined with racism and antiurbanism to foster a sense of pessimism about cities that pervaded popular culture. Philadelphia's policymakers often turned to public-private partnerships to address the issues these policies created, which was consistent with neoliberalism and with Philadelphia's historical approach to dealing with social problems; the results were mixed. Yet during the first decade of the twenty-first century, there were glimmers of hope as Philadelphia registered its first population increase in a half century, leading some people to claim the city was experiencing a "renaissance."

Philadelphia's population shrank during the last three decades of the twentieth century, and it slipped from fourth- to fifth-most populous US city between 1980 and 1990, a position it held until 2020, when it slipped to sixth place. In fact, Philadelphia County had the dubious distinction of experiencing the nation's sharpest population decline during the 1990s.[1] This trend reversed slightly in the twenty-first century, due largely to increased immigration to the United States, even as the city's white population shrank by nearly one-third between 1990 and 2010.[2]

The aggregate numbers do not tell the whole story, however. While Philadelphia's overall white population declined between 1990 and 2010, the populations of Center City, Fairmount, Brewerytown, and Northern Liberties grew

Figure 10. Philadelphia
from outer space, 2013.
NASA Earth Observa-
tory. Nearly three and
a half centuries after
William Penn founded
the city, it has grown and
evolved beyond even his
wildest dreams.

by more than 10 percent. This contrasted sharply with such neighborhoods
as Frankford, Olney, Nicetown, Logan, and Oak Lane, which saw their white
populations decline by more than 50 percent. In South Philadelphia, the overwhelming majority of census tracts had concentrations of either white or Black
people higher than 75 percent in 1980.[3] Black people moved into these areas,
with Frankford and Olney experiencing more than 20 percent growth in their
respective Black populations between 1990 and 2010.[4] Philadelphia's Black community was not homogeneous: middle-class Black families tended to cluster
in Mount Airy and Germantown, and poorer Black Philadelphians located in
North, South, and West Philadelphia.[5] By 2008, Philadelphia had significant
immigrant communities in pockets of Center City, South Philadelphia, and
the Northeast. The Brookings Institution reported in 2008 that even "among
its peer regions, metropolitan Philadelphia had the largest and fastest growing
immigrant population."[6] Aided by changes in US immigration law (including

the 1980 Refugee Act and the 1986 Immigration Reform and Control Act), Philadelphia became home to significant communities of non–US born residents after 1990 (mostly Asian and Latino, though including Africans and other groups), and the city officially became "majority minority" in the early twenty-first century.[7] Philadelphia's Asian community grew by more than 125 percent between 1990 and 2010, while the city's Latino community grew by 110.3 percent over the same period, aided by a significant influx of Mexican immigrants who settled in the region after the mid-1980s (though Puerto Ricans remained the largest single Latino group in Philadelphia).[8] This turn of events was a substantial change from the first half of the twentieth century, when the city was home to a much smaller immigrant population than other big American cities. Philadelphia's majority minority status also contrasted sharply with the rest of the commonwealth's population, which was more than 85 percent white in 2000.[9] In short, though incredibly ethnically and racially diverse, Philadelphia was simultaneously among the United States' most segregated cities.[10]

Of course, these demographic changes were reflected in the city's political history. Unsuccessful in his attempt to amend the city charter's prohibition on anyone serving a third consecutive term as mayor, Frank Rizzo left office in 1980, leaving his successor, William J. "Bill" Green III, with a massive deficit. Green was descended from local political royalty: he had served in the US House of Representatives, following the death of his father, William J. Green Jr.[11] First elected to Congress in 1944, Green Jr. was defeated in the Republican landslide of 1946 but won back the seat two years later, holding it until his death in 1963, when Green III succeeded him.[12] The younger Green was more liberal than his father and a political reformer but lacked his father's political skills, which he would need to navigate the complex challenges facing the city.

Green tried to mitigate many of the city's festering racial problems, with mixed success. For instance, under his administration, the Philadelphia Police Department adopted its first firearms policy, specifying in what situations guns could be used; this contributed to a precipitous decline in police-involved shootings and citizen complaints against the department, though police brutality remained common.[13] However, one of the most divisive incidents in Philadelphia's recent history, the murder of Philadelphia Police Officer Daniel Faulkner apparently by Mumia Abu-Jamal, occurred at the end of Green's second year in office. Abu-Jamal, a former Black Panther, was working part time as a radio journalist and moonlighting as a cabdriver. Just before 4:00 a.m. on December 9, 1981, Faulkner pulled over Abu-Jamal's younger brother, William Cook, near the intersection of Thirteenth and Locust Streets; the two men apparently became involved in a physical altercation. Abu-Jamal, who was driving his cab that night, happened to be in the area and observed Cook and Faulkner struggling.

Abu-Jamal parked his cab nearby and ran toward Cook and Faulkner, carrying his legally registered gun; apparently, Abu-Jamal and Faulkner exchanged gunfire. Faulkner died at the scene, and Abu-Jamal was seriously wounded. At trial, prosecutors alleged that Abu-Jamal confessed at the hospital to shooting Faulkner, but contemporaneous reports and witness statements contradict that assertion. Nevertheless, a majority white jury convicted Abu-Jamal of murder and sentenced him to death. This inflamed racial tension, especially given Judge Albert F. Sabo's proclaimed disinterest in procedure, documented bias toward prosecutors, and proclivity for imposing the death penalty (by 1995, he had sentenced more defendants to death than any other judge in the United States at that time).[14] As a result, Abu-Jamal remains a cause célèbre, with Amnesty International claiming in 2000 that "the proceedings used to convict and sentence Mumia Abu-Jamal to death were in violation of minimum international standards that govern fair trial procedures and the use of the death penalty."[15]

Green made progress on the city's finances, but his term was marked by bitter conflict with the City Council (which he claimed was "the worst legislative body in the free world") and Philadelphia's municipal employees.[16] In his inaugural address, Green told the audience "the city is fiscally sick" and "stern measures will be in order"; a month later he laid off 1,300 municipal employees, which did little to endear him to city residents.[17] In 1982, the City Council passed an ordinance over Green's veto requiring that at least 15 percent of city contracts go to firms owned by minorities and another 10 percent to firms owned by women; Green responded by refusing to appoint members to the committee the council created to oversee the ordinance's enforcement.[18] Also in 1982, the mayor sued local WCAU-TV reporter Larry Kane for defamation after he inaccurately claimed that Green had taken kickbacks; Kane and the station quickly settled.[19] Green unexpectedly declined to seek reelection in 1983, becoming Philadelphia's first one-term mayor in more than a quarter century.

After a bruising, racially divisive contest for the Democratic nomination against former mayor Frank Rizzo, Managing Director W. Wilson Goode went on to win the general election, becoming the city's first Black mayor.[20] Race was front and center during the campaign: Rizzo attacked civil rights leader and politician Jesse Jackson and even endorsed Bernard Epton, the white Republican candidate for mayor of Chicago, who was running against Harold Washington, a Black Democrat; like Goode, Washington won the race, becoming Chicago's first Black mayor.[21] In short, Rizzo tried to mobilize white resentment to win the election, just as he had done in the 1970s, but white flight, which increased the proportion of Black voters in the city, made this an untenable strategy.[22]

Goode was just one of several local Black politicians elected in the late 1970s and early 1980s; others included former member of the Pennsylvania House

Lucien Blackwell and civil rights attorney Cecil B. Moore (who had admonished Philadelphia's Democratic Party about taking Black votes for granted in 1963), both elected to the City Coucil in 1975. Nor was it just Black men winning elective office: in 1975, Dr. Ethel D. Allen won an at-large seat on the council, the first Black woman elected to that body.[23] At the state level, Roxanne Jones won election to the Pennsylvania Senate from Philadelphia in 1984, becoming the first Black woman to serve in that body in the commonwealth's history.[24] Naturally, Philadelphia's emerging Black political leaders were not homogeneous, but the racist backlash of the late 1960s and 1970s helped galvanize the Black community and persuaded many to seek political office.[25] In 1968, West Philadelphia political activist John White Sr. established the Black Political Forum (BPF), which was designed to help Black people win political office. The BPF helped several Black candidates, and it won White the nickname "Godfather of Black Politics."[26] Meanwhile, Philadelphia's Latino community also achieved some political clout in the 1970s, 1980s, and 1990s. For instance, in 1984, Angel Ortiz became the first Latino elected to City Council. In fact, between 1975 and 1990, the percentage of council members who were Black or Hispanic more than doubled.[27] In 1999, John White Sr. observed to a reporter from *Al Día*, the local Spanish-language newspaper, "the black and the brown, if we unite, we're going to control this city."[28]

In addition to enjoying widespread support from Philadelphia's Black community, Goode— who had won 98 percent of Black voters' ballots but only 22 percent of those cast by white voters—had impressed Philadelphia's business community, which shaped his policy agenda.[29] For instance, Goode appointed key business leaders (including prominent members and officers of the Chamber of Commerce for Greater Philadelphia) to his cabinet, which gave the administration a decidedly pro-business character.[30] This was on full display in July 1986, when nearly thirty thousand municipal workers struck to avoid a city audit of their unions' medical and welfare funds' books. Trash piled up and rotted in the sweltering heat as city residents were locked out of municipal swimming pools and recreation centers. Goode threatened to fire workers who refused to end the strike, a move that would have thrown between thirteen hundred and seventeen hundred municipal workers (mostly Black men) out of work. The *Philadelphia Inquirer* and the city's business community cheered Goode on, and the union eventually capitulated, giving the city access to its books. When the contract expired two years later, Goode preemptively threatened to privatize trash collection service.[31]

So-called "pro-business" policies spurred an office-building boom in Philadelphia, leading to major changes in its skyline even as the rest of the city languished.[32] In 1984, real estate developer Willard G. Rouse III announced his intention to build a sixty-one-story skyscraper called One Liberty Place. This plan was controversial because of a gentleman's agreement not to construct buildings higher than City Hall's statue of William Penn, but it also reflected the tensions created by the neoliberal policies then in vogue. The growth of financial services and insurance in the early 1980s spurred the construction of new office buildings in Center City. Edmund Bacon, who was no stranger to controversy, opposed One Liberty Place, saying, "Once [the gentlemen's agreement not to build a building higher than the William Penn statue is] smashed, it's gone." He asserted that architecture and space cultivated certain values that One Liberty Place threatened: "I think it's very, very destructive that he [Rouse] . . . has chosen to destroy a historical tradition that set a very fine and disciplined form for the city."[33] Despite this strong criticism, and the fact that his "mail ran a thousand to one against the project," Goode strongly supported it, later saying the pushback against One Liberty Place was "symbolic of what was wrong with this city" (it did not hurt that Rouse was a member of Goode's economic roundtable).[34] In retrospect, One Liberty Place has been described as an "outstanding" example of postmodern architecture, a catchall term that emphasizes reaction to modernism rather than shared stylistic elements. Other examples of local postmodern architecture include the Guild House (711 Spring Garden Street) and the Vanna Venturi House in Chestnut Hill, both designed by local architect Robert Venturi, a leading postmodern architect and student of Louis Kahn's. Venturi's work was whimsical and ornate, in stark contrast to the austere modernism that dominated the mid-twentieth century, which is reflected in the imaginative (and controversial) restoration work he did at Franklin Court. Rather than reconstruct Benjamin Franklin's house, Venturi elected to create "ghost structures" of the buildings and to use different colored pavement to demarcate the buildings' various rooms.[35]

Rouse was also involved in the decades-long attempt to revitalize Penn's Landing. Deindustrialization ended Philadelphia's role as a major port; by 1960, only a small portion of the city's nearly two dozen piers were still active. In 1961, as part of its urban renewal efforts, the City Planning Commission undertook an ambitious project to backfill part of the river and redevelop it as a residential, commercial, and entertainment space. Progress was slow, and later in the decade the commission handed the project off to the Old Philadelphia Development Corporation, which in turn spun it off to a newly formed nonprofit, the Penn's Landing Corporation (PLC), in 1970. Controversy over the construction of Interstate 95 inhibited the PLC's ability to make progress on the site, which largely languished, though by 1986, the site's Great Plaza had been completed. At about that time, Rouse & Associates expressed interest in building a $70 million mixed use complex at Penn's Landing. City Councilman Leland M. Beloff (who represented Old City) and Philadelphia Mafia boss Nicodemo "Little

Nicky" Scarfo tried to extort $1 million (and a free apartment for Beloff's mistress) from Rouse. Scarfo had risen to boss after a violent and bloody four-year struggle for control of the city's mob, sometimes called the "First Philadelphia Mafia War," that began in March 1980 following the murder of Angelo "the Docile Don" Bruno. Rouse turned the tables on them by notifying the FBI, which eventually led to Scarfo and Beloff going to prison.[36] Scarfo's 1988 conviction created a power vacuum that led to the outbreak of the "Second Philadelphia Mafia War" (1991–1995), which ended with the elevation of Ralph Natale to boss. Natale's arrest and subsequent decision to cooperate with authorities led to Joseph Salvatore "Skinny Joey" Merlino allegedly becoming boss of the city's crime family, a position he allegedly still holds. Meanwhile, the redevelopment of Penn's Landing, though later promoted by Mayors Ed Rendell, John Street, and Michael Nutter, never came to fruition.[37]

Goode implemented several important programs and policies designed to reduce poverty and address quality of life issues.[38] Among the more notable was the Philadelphia Anti-Graffiti Network (PAGN), which Goode's administration founded in January 1984 to combat graffiti and thereby fulfill a campaign pledge.[39] Ironically, Philadelphia is usually cited as the birthplace of modern graffiti, with an artist named Cornbread (birth name Darryl Alexander McCray) pioneering the use of spray paint (invented in 1949) to "tag" buildings and other structures.[40] One of the PAGN's most notable programs was Mural Arts, which built on the success of a similar Philadelphia Museum of Art program that had ended the year before. This program reflected assumptions about the power of public space to influence people's behavior, though Mural Arts actively involved community members at all stages of the planning process. Though originally planned to be a temporary program, it was widely popular and continues as of this writing, earning the city national (and even international) acclaim: in 1991, the Ash Center for Democratic Governance and Innovation at Harvard University recognized Philadelphia with its prestigious Innovations in American Government Award for the success of the Mural Arts Project, and in 2007, Britain's Prince Charles and his wife, Camilla, the Duchess of Cornwall, visited the city, in part to better understand the Mural Arts program and see if it could be duplicated in London. As a result of the thousands of murals the program has created, Philadelphia has been called the "City of Murals."[41]

Despite these successes, Mayor Goode was severely hampered by the Reagan and Bush administrations' evisceration of federal funding programs.[42] The economic challenges of the 1970s, coupled with the social and cultural upheavals of those years, led some policymakers to abandon growth liberalism in favor of the so-called Reagan Revolution, which unabashedly embraced neoliberalism, an ideology that promoted reflexive privatization of government services, deregulation of industry, and substantial cuts to public assistance programs. Powered by unquestioning faith in the market, neoliberals advocated deregulation of industry, privatization, and austerity, which over the succeeding decades exacerbated the gap between the wealthy and the poor in the United States and eroded the social services available, particularly in the country's cities.[43] In some ways, neoliberalism resembled the privatism that had characterized Philadelphia in the eighteenth and nineteenth centuries; certainly, this is what Vice President George H. W. Bush had in mind in 1988 when he called for substituting private nonprofit organizations for the government in providing social services (though the "thousand points of light" he had promised never materialized).[44]

It was not incidental that neoliberal policies would disproportionately hurt cities and people of color; racism and antiurbanism were part of the Republican Party's electoral appeal and had been since the New Deal. Republicans aggressively attacked the welfare state, which it associated (using dog whistles) with cities and Black people. Reagan perfected this technique; in his failed 1976 campaign for the Republican presidential nomination, he stirred up his predominantly white audiences with lurid allegations about "welfare queens," or women who defrauded the welfare system. These exaggerated and often false anecdotes included racist dog whistles designed to stoke white resentment and erode popular support for government assistance programs, and they worked: Reagan won the presidency in 1980 and 1984, and his vice president, George H. W. Bush, won the presidential election of 1988.

Neoliberalism devastated Philadelphia, where unemployment rates were higher than the national average, median wage growth was anemic, the percentage of Philadelphians who owned their homes (while still higher than other cities) dropped, and a substantial percentage of the city's population lived in poverty. Federal and state aid to Philadelphia, which began declining under President Jimmy Carter, bottomed out during the 1980s, dropping from nearly 26 percent of revenue in 1979 to just over 7 percent in 1988.[45] Meanwhile, Pennsylvania's legislature, which was politically hostile to Philadelphia, did nothing to backfill the loss; from 1963 to 1990, Philadelphians received nearly 40 percent less money per capita from the commonwealth than the average Pennsylvanian.[46] Declining federal revenue and low commonwealth support forced Philadelphia to rely more heavily on tax revenue than other large American cities. That, combined with a shrinking population, starved the city for revenue. Compounding the problem was that Philadelphia's status as both a county and a city imposed substantial additional strains on municipal finances.[47] Finally, median household income in Philadelphia was less than three-quarters of the region's at the end of Rizzo's term and fell by more than 6 percentage points over the ensuing twenty years (in 2017, Philadelphia was the nation's poorest big city).[48]

Several iconic Philadelphia businesses disappeared, including Lit Brothers (1977), the *Bulletin* (1982), the Philadelphia Savings Fund Society (1992), Wanamaker's (1995), and Strawbridge & Clothier (2006). In an attempt to revive the city's declining role as a retail center, in 1977, the Gallery at Market East opened, but it could not compete with the nearby suburban King of Prussia mall, which was the largest shopping mall in the United States when it opened in 1963. Philadelphia continued hemorrhaging jobs, and those that remained tended to be low-wage jobs in the services industry (which grew by 47 percent in the city between 1970 and 1990).[49] In 1982, Chaka Fattah, an up-and-coming Black Democrat then running for the Pennsylvania House of Representatives, bluntly told the *Philadelphia Tribune* that "the manufacturing . . . is gone, and for all intents and purposes, it's not coming back. [Philadelphia] is a service center, a tourist center, and we need to understand it . . . [and] start training kids for those jobs."[50] In reality, what emerged was a great separation between a relatively limited amount of very-high-wage work and the proliferation of low-wage jobs in what one 1995 observer described as "a stagnant real economy with a shrinking job base."[51]

The city faced a significant public health crisis in the 1980s and 1990s: HIV (human immunodeficiency virus) and AIDS (acquired immunodeficiency syndrome). Doctors became aware of Philadelphia's first case of AIDS in September 1981 (though that term would not be used until the following summer), just three months after the US Centers for Disease Control issued a warning about a rare form of pneumonia then appearing among Los Angeles's gay men. Though President Reagan did not first mention AIDS until 1985 (more than four years into his presidency), Philadelphia's local political establishment was more responsive: in the spring of 1983, the city appointed its first coordinator for issues related to AIDS, and that fall Mayor Green issued a proclamation recognizing AIDS Awareness Month (despite having refused to sign an August 1982 ordinance prohibiting antigay discrimination in housing, employment, and public accommodations). Goode went even further than Green, banning discrimination against individuals with AIDS in March 1986 and establishing the AIDS Activity Coordinating Office the following year.

However, as the number of HIV infections grew over the next few years, it became clear that Philadelphia's gay community had to advocate for itself. In 1987, activists formed two groups, We the People with AIDS/HIV and the AIDS Coalition to Unleash the Power (ACT UP), to mobilize government resources to find a cure.[52] Though founded in New York, ACT UP chose Philadelphia as the site of several demonstrations: members marched in front of the Liberty Bell just days before the two hundredth anniversary of the signing of the US Constitution; a few weeks before, nearly six hundred demonstrators had protested at Independence Hall, where two hundred US representatives and senators had gathered to celebrate the two hundredth anniversary of the Constitution.[53] In

July 1992, Mayor Ed Rendell legalized needle exchange (a program whereby people could exchange their used syringes for clean ones, thus obviating the need to reuse or share these items). His executive order noted, "HIV/AIDS presents a significant risk to the health of the citizens of Philadelphia, and the rate of HIV infection is increasing at an alarming rate."[54] Though other cities were devastated by the AIDS crisis, the release in 1993 of the film *Philadelphia*, which is loosely based on the stories of attorneys Geoffrey Bowers and Clarence B. Cain, indelibly linked the city with the AIDS crisis.[55] On July 4, 2005, Elton John held the Philadelphia Freedom Concert, a fundraising event in support of HIV/AIDS awareness. Named for his 1975 hit song "Philadelphia Freedom," the concert was held on the Benjamin Franklin Parkway; it featured performances from Bryan Adams, Patti LaBelle, the Philly Pops, and John himself.

Many Americans at this time believed that crime rates had spiked in the late 1960s, which resulted in widespread white support for several racist law enforcement policies that devastated big cities like Philadelphia and contributed to the mass incarceration of Black people.[56] For instance, University of Pennsylvania criminologist Marvin Wolfgang, who was once dubbed "the most influential criminologist in the English-speaking world," argued (along with coauthors Robert M. Figlio and Thorsten Sellin) in *Delinquency in a Birth Cohort* (1972) that most violent crime was committed by a small number of offenders. This understanding of crime and delinquency became a justification for lengthening sentences, limiting parole, and adopting draconian "three strikes" laws, which mandated judges impose life sentences on individuals convicted of three felonies.[57] Another devastating policy was "broken windows" policing, which was widely adopted by police departments across the country and dramatically increased negative interactions between police and urban Black people. Derived from a 1982 article written by political scientist James Q. Wilson and criminologist George L. Kelling and published in the *Atlantic Monthly*, "broken windows" theorists asserted that policymakers should aggressively punish petty crime as a way of deterring more serious offenses.

In 1995, a Wilson protégé, John J. Dilulio Jr. (then at Princeton, and, as of this writing, at the University of Pennsylvania), predicted the arrival of "superpredators," or young men with "vacant stares and smiles and . . . remorseless eyes" who would commit unspeakable acts of "impulsive violence."[58] These overheated, apocalyptic, and, as it turned out, inaccurate predictions appealed to "law and order" voters (First Lady Hillary Clinton even used the term "superpredator" in drumming up support for a draconian crime bill her husband, then President Bill Clinton, was promoting in 1996), but the policies they led to dramatically increased the number of incarcerated men of color, devastating America's cities.[59] Another devastating policy was the so-called war on drugs,

which President Richard Nixon declared in June 1971, and which became a key
policy of the Ronald Reagan and George H. W. Bush administrations. The war
on drugs served Republicans' political objectives, namely, criminalizing their
political opponents and stoking their base's racist fears. In 1994, John Ehrlich-
man, Nixon's former assistant to the president for domestic affairs, told journalist Dan Baum, "The Nixon campaign in 1968, and the Nixon White House after
that, had two enemies: the antiwar left and black people. You understand what
I'm saying? We knew we couldn't make it illegal to be either against the war
or black, but by getting the public to associate the hippies with marijuana and
blacks with heroin, and then criminalizing both heavily, we could disrupt those
communities. We could arrest their leaders, raid their homes, break up their
meetings, and vilify them night after night on the evening news. Did we know
we were lying about the drugs? Of course we did."[60]

While the war on drugs was a constant during these decades, the fight
shifted from methamphetamines to crack cocaine to opioids. In the late 1970s
and 1980s, methamphetamine flooded Philadelphia's streets and was so ubiquitous that Peter F. Vaira, the US attorney for the Eastern District of Pennsylvania, told the House of Representatives Select Committee on Narcotics Abuse
and Control that "Philadelphia is the meth capital of the country."[61] There are
reasons to question Vaira's assertion (which reinforced the widespread percep-
tion of the city as crime ridden and dangerous), though it is certainly true that
the K&A gang (an Irish and Jewish organized crime outfit located in Northeast Philadelphia) was heavily involved in selling meth.[62] Beginning in the early
1980s, the country suffered a so-called crack epidemic. Crack, a rock form of
cocaine, was cheaper than powder cocaine (though pharmacologically indistinguishable) and, because of that, was widely associated with poor and Black
users. In 1986, Congress passed the Anti-Drug Abuse Act, which introduced
mandatory minimum sentences for drug possession and more heavily sanc-
tioned possession of crack than powder cocaine. This contributed to the disproportionately higher rates of incarceration among communities of color. An
open-air drug market even emerged in an area of North Philadelphia reputed
at the time to have the highest per capita sales of heroin and cocaine in the
United States.[63] The so-called Badlands, bounded by Kensington Avenue, Broad
Street, Hunting Park Avenue, and York Street, was named by novelist and former *Philadelphia Inquirer* columnist Steve Lopez. In August 1995, the area
received national attention when the *Nightline* television program reported
on the Badlands and interviewed two local heroin users.[64] Crack cocaine was
enormously profitable, but it also led to violence: in 1990, 605 people were murdered in the city, compared with 356 in 2019 (which itself was incredibly high
by recent standards).[65] By the turn of the century, Philadelphia had earned the

dubious nickname "Killadelphia" because of the high rates of homicide. On December 28, 2000, the city witnessed the deadliest mass murder in its history, the so-called Lex Street Massacre, which cost ten lives and received national headlines.[66]

The latest drug epidemic involves opioids. In 1995, the US Food and Drug Administration approved Purdue Pharma's OxyContin, which combined oxycodone (an opioid derived from poppy plants) with a time-release agent, claiming this would provide users with sustained pain relief. Perdue downplayed the risks of addiction to OxyContin while aggressively pushing doctors to prescribe it. The combination of falsehoods about OxyContin's addictiveness and pressure on doctors to prescribe made it widely available; as a result, it captured a massive share of the market for prescription painkillers and was often abused. As it became clear that Perdue had lied about the drug's addictiveness, the federal government filed charges against it and aggressively tried to dissuade doctors from prescribing OxyContin. As a result, OxyContin became harder to get, so some users turned to heroin. The country witnessed a nearly 300 percent increase in heroin-related overdoses in the decade after 2002, spiking rapidly after 2010, but that was only the beginning: around 2013, fentanyl (a synthetic opioid like morphine but up to one hundred times stronger), originally developed in 1960, began finding its way into other street drugs, such as cocaine and heroin. In 2016, Philadelphia County registered the second-highest overdose death rate of all US counties with over one million inhabitants (Allegheny County, which includes Pittsburgh, was number one), and the preponderance of those involved opioids.[67] In 2019, what commentators dubbed the "opioid epidemic" actually contributed to the first decline in Americans' life expectancy.[68] President Donald Trump called opioid addiction and overdose death a "public health emergency" in 2017, though William M. McSwain, the US attorney for the Eastern District of Pennsylvania, aggressively opposed a safe injection site in Kensington proposed by the nonprofit Safehouse that would have likely reduced overdose deaths. McSwain sued Safehouse in 2019, and in January 2021, the US Court of Appeals for the Third Circuit ruled that a safe injection site would violate federal law.

In a sense, McSwain was simply running down a path blazed by Philadelphia's district attorneys, who since the mid-1960s had often taken harsh and punitive approaches to charging defendants, particularly those of color. This trend was certainly visible during the two decades that Arlen Specter and Ed Rendell held the office, but it reached its apotheosis under Lynne Abraham.[69] Abraham, who served as Philadelphia's district attorney for nineteen years, earned the nicknames "Deadliest DA" and "Queen of Death" because of how frequently and aggressively she sought the death penalty for defendants.

Abraham's office won 108 death sentences (though several were overturned), and by 1995, the country's sixth-largest city had the third-largest death row. Several critics at the time and since have seen evidence of racial bias in Abraham's charging decisions, especially after she told a reporter she believed Black people committed 85 percent of the city's crime and aggressively opposed President Bill Clinton's nomination of Philadelphia Common Pleas Court Judge Frederica Massiah-Jackson (a Black woman) to the federal bench on the grounds that Jackson was allegedly "pro-criminal."[70]

The pervasive get-tough-on-crime impulse (and its racial undertones) contributed to one of the most tragic events in the city's recent history, the deadly confrontation between the Philadelphia Police Department and MOVE. MOVE was founded by West Philadelphia native John Africa, born Vincent Leaphart. After a stint in the US Army during the Korean conflict, Africa married and adopted a fairly conventional lifestyle, but in 1972, he founded a movement that, in the words of one reporter, "melded the revolutionary ideology of the Black Panthers with the nature- and animal-loving communalism of 1960s hippies."[71] In 1973, a white MOVE member named Donald Glassey purchased a home in Powelton Village at 309 North Thirty-Third Street and invited several other members of the organization to live there; the house became MOVE's unofficial headquarters.[72] MOVE members clashed with local residents, who complained about unleashed dogs, garbage in the backyard that attracted rodents, and other nuisances. In addition, members of MOVE began protesting at sites that included the Board of Education and the Philadelphia Zoo.

However, it was aggressive protests over endemic police brutality that made MOVE a target of police ire: in 1974 and 1975, members of MOVE had been arrested a total of 150 times and incurred $15,000 in fines.[73] At a party in March 1976 to celebrate the release of several MOVE members from jail, members clashed with police officers, with both sides blaming the other for the violence. (MOVE claimed the police had killed a member's baby, though they produced no evidence to substantiate this charge.) This event was a turning point in the group's history; John Africa told his followers that while MOVE was committed to nonviolence, they nonetheless had a right and a responsibility to protect themselves. Consequently, MOVE's members began fortifying the Powelton Village house, building an eight-foot-high wall around the backyard. In late May 1977, members appeared on the house's porch brandishing firearms, alarming neighbors, who called the police. The city began a fifteen-month blockade of MOVE that ended up generating support for the organization in some quarters. Authorities shut off utilities to the house and surrounded it with barricades made of sandbags and snow fencing. At 6:00 a.m. on August 8, 1978, the police ordered the members of MOVE to surrender. Then, according to *Philadelphia*

Daily News reporter Kitty Caparella, who was on the scene, "bulldozers shoved away the parapet where for 15 months MOVE had threatened a showdown if four of their members weren't released from prison. Using a battering ram, flak-jacketed cops rammed the front, side, and basement windows . . . deluge tanks were positioned close to the house, where they discharged columns of water directly into the basement."[74] The gunfight cost the life of Police Officer James Ramp and resulted in injuries to officers, firefighters, and members of MOVE. After clearing the house, the city demolished it. On August 4, 1981, a jury convicted nine MOVE members of third-degree murder; they were sentenced to decades in prison. Three police officers filmed beating MOVE member Delbert Africa were acquitted the following February, demonstrating to many people that the city's police could and would brutalize Philadelphians with impunity.[75]

In 1981, several members of MOVE relocated to 6221 Osage Avenue, a house owned by John Africa's sister, Louise James. It was not long before neighbors began complaining of the same issues that had troubled MOVE's Powelton Village neighbors. By the middle of 1984, city officials were looking for a way to evict MOVE from the Osage Avenue house, but with little luck. In early May 1985, neighbors reported seeing MOVE members installing a five-gallon gasoline tank on the house's roof. On May 7, Mayor Goode authorized the police to forcibly evict MOVE and arrest some of its members. By May 12, the city had acquired search and arrest warrants, and police evacuated Osage Avenue residents. Officers did not, however, prevent the children of MOVE members from returning to the house even though the operation was planned for early the next morning. At 5:35 a.m. on May 13, Police Commissioner Gregore J. Sambor used a bullhorn to demand that several MOVE members in the Osage Avenue house surrender within fifteen minutes. At 5:50 police fired tear gas and smoke bombs at the house in preparation for a forcible entry; MOVE members responded by firing their guns at police. In response, police officers returned fire, enfilading the house with ten thousand rounds over the next ninety minutes. Though police used explosives to blast open the front door, they were unable to penetrate fortifications that MOVE members had constructed in the house. At 3:45 p.m. Goode told a press conference he would use "any means" to take the house, and shortly after, police concocted a plan to drop an explosive on the house to shatter a bunker on the roof. At 5:27 a helicopter dropped the bomb, which ignited the nearby gasoline can. Sambor allowed the building to burn for an hour; firefighters did not turn their hoses on until 6:32 p.m.[76] Firefighters did not contain the flames until nearly midnight, by which time the fire had consumed nearly two square blocks. Worse, the fire claimed the lives of eleven inhabitants of the Osage Avenue house, including five children. Ramona Africa, the only adult in the MOVE house to survive the bombing, was convicted of riot and conspiracy and spent seven years in prison. James Berghaier, one of the Philadelphia police officers at the scene, recalled decades later, "Five kids died and the neighbors lost everything. We failed, and it bothers me."[77]

In the aftermath, the mayor's office and the Police and Fire Departments blamed each other for the fiasco.[78] Compounding the tragedy was the city's almost comical attempt to make amends. In March 1986, Goode promised that Philadelphia would rebuild the sixty-one houses destroyed by the bombing and fire by that Christmas. Ernest Edwards Jr. and Oscar Harris, the contractors that the Goode administration initially picked, were convicted of stealing thousands of dollars in city funds; that July the city hired a second contractor, but the homes they built were later deemed substandard, repurchased by the city, and stood vacant for many years.[79] The MOVE bombing left lasting scars that, decades later, still had not completely healed.[80] During the 1990s, juries awarded several MOVE members and their families multimillion-dollar settlements.[81] In November 2020, following a series of protests and demonstrations about the death of George Floyd at the hands of Minneapolis Police Officer Derek Chauvin, the Philadelphia City Council voted to apologize for the MOVE bombing. The mishandling of the MOVE episode forever tarnished Goode's legacy: widely considered a rising star in the Democratic Party before 1985, he is today ranked among the country's worst big-city mayors since 1960.[82]

Meanwhile, violent demonstrations by racist whites in Southwest Philadelphia convinced Goode to declare a state of emergency on November 22, 1985. On November 3, a Black couple, Charles Williams and Marietta Bloxom, moved into a house on the 2500 block of Sixty-First Street. Nearby, a mixed-race couple, Gerald and Carol Fox, moved into a house at Sixty-Fourth Street and Buist Avenue. Almost immediately, crowds of angry white people, often numbering several hundred, gathered in front of the couples' houses, often throwing bottles through windows or shooting BBs at the houses. Newspaper coverage framed the whites' concerns as rooted in economic anxiety (property values in the neighborhood had consistently declined for nearly thirty years), but one white woman in her twenties told the *Philadelphia Inquirer*, "Once a black family moves in, [some white residents'] tolerance is so low because of what they have seen and what they fear. It's almost an innate fear of blacks."[83] Goode, who had grown up in the area, called the situation a "ticking time bomb," which is why he declared the state of emergency; four days later, fed up with the threats to their lives, Williams and Bloxom announced they would move (Gerald and Carol Fox announced they intended to stay).[84] The protests continued and even attracted members of the Ku Klux Klan, who distributed literature to the white mob.[85] Goode ended the state of emergency two days after Christmas, but by then the damage had been done: on December 12, four white people burned Williams and Bloxom's house, which was allegedly under twenty-four-hour police surveillance at the time; though fortunately no one was in it, the fire consumed the family's possessions.[86] A nascent secessionist movement emerged in the Northeast (sometimes called "Rizzoland") fueled by white residents who complained that the Black mayor treated them as second-class citizens.[87] Writing in the *Chicago Tribune*, Philip Lentz opined that 1985 had been "sobering and humbling" for Goode, noting, "After an unusually long honeymoon with the press and public that attracted national attention, Philadelphia's first black mayor finds himself questioned, attacked and very much on the defensive."[88]

The generally dismal mood was reflected in popular entertainment, which usually presented Philadelphia as dirty, dilapidated, corrupt, and (crucially) heavily Black.[89] Few films are more closely associated with Philadelphia than 1976's *Rocky*, which won the Academy Award for Best Picture and spawned several sequels. The film is the perfect depiction of Philadelphia in the mid-1970s. Sylvester Stallone, who wrote the film, stars as Rocky Balboa, an amateur boxer and leg breaker for a local loan shark, Tony Gazzo. Balboa's life changes when the reigning world heavyweight champion, Apollo Creed (played by Carl Weathers), announces he wants to fight an unknown boxer on New Year's Day 1976 at the Spectrum. Rocky trains hard and, the day of the fight, puts up an incredible fight. The match ends in a split decision in Creed's favor, allowing him to retain his title. In a city racked by racial conflict, it escaped no one's notice that Rocky is an Italian American forced to take demeaning and illegal work because of a lack of opportunity. His opponent, Apollo Creed, is by contrast a pugnacious, wealthy, and flamboyant Black man who does not train nearly as hard as Rocky but still manages to keep his title, implicitly suggesting that Black people have it "easier" than whites. In case anyone missed the point, Creed chooses to fight Rocky because of the latter's Italian heritage, remarking, "Who discovered America? Columbus, right? What better way to celebrate its two hundredth birthday than [for a Black man] to get it on with one of his descendants?"

Rocky was far from the only film that depicted Philadelphia as corrupt and broken. Perhaps the best known (after *Rocky*) is 1985's *Witness*, which stars Harrison Ford as Philadelphia police detective John Book, who must protect a young Amish boy named Samuel after he witnesses the murder of an undercover police officer at Thirtieth Street Station. It turns out that the murderer was another Philadelphia police officer, James McFee (played by Danny Glover), who killed the undercover cop because he knew that McFee was selling seized chemicals to drug dealers for use in making amphetamines. The film climaxes with Book killing McFee and another corrupt Philadelphia cop, Sergeant Leon

Ferguson (played by Angus MacInnes), with help from the Amish community with whom he has sought refuge. The 1981 film *Blow Out*, directed by Philadelphia native Brian De Palma, starred John Travolta as a Philadelphia-based sound technician who stumbles onto a plot to assassinate a presidential candidate. In this cynical film, Travolta is unable to stop the plot and ends up profiting from the murder of his love interest, played by Nancy Allen. The following year Tom Skerritt starred in *Fighting Back* as John D'Angelo, a South Philadelphia deli owner turned vigilante who forms a group to patrol his neighborhood after violent incidents and is later encouraged by the police commissioner to murder a pimp named Eldorado because the police are "too busy." After murdering Eldorado, D'Angelo is elected to the City Council. On a lighter note, 1990's *Downtown* starred Anthony Edwards as a suburban police officer named Alex Kearney who is transferred to "Downtown" after running afoul of a Main Line businessman. He is partnered with a streetwise police sergeant, Dennis Curren (played by Forest Whitaker). Initially a by-the-book cop, Kearney goes rogue (much to Curren's delight) when his friend is murdered. The message was clear: Philadelphia's institutions were too feckless or corrupt to address the city's apparent social and moral collapse, leaving it up to Hollywood rogue cops and vigilantes to restore order, usually through violence against people of color.

In the 1987 Democratic primary, Goode faced a serious challenge from District Attorney Ed Rendell. Besting Rendell, Goode faced former mayor Frank Rizzo, who had returned to the Republican Party and won its nomination. Rizzo went even further in race-baiting during this campaign than he had four years before, outrageously comparing Goode to Louis Farrakhan, the anti-Semitic and racist leader of the Nation of Islam.[90] Goode, who had retained the business community's support (particularly members of the Greater Philadelphia First Corporation), won reelection but in 1988 revealed a budget deficit of nearly $100 million.[91] He asked the City Council to increase taxes, but it responded with a package of small tax increases and substantial cuts to social services, neither of which did much to improve the city's finances. In 1990, the city government proposed borrowing $375 million, a nearly 100 percent increase over the previous year's bond issue. Investigative reporting uncovered the fact that the additional money was needed to cover $73.8 million in accumulated deficits from the previous six years and a projected shortfall in excess of $130 million for 1991.[92] As a result of these revelations, the various credit-rating agencies downgraded Philadelphia's bonds, scaring potential investors and making them unwilling to lend.[93] Consequently, at the end of Goode's term in 1991, the city was on the brink of bankruptcy.

To make Philadelphia's municipal bonds more attractive to investors, in the spring of 1991 (and at the behest of Philadelphia City Council member John

Street) Pennsylvania Governor Robert Casey signed into law a bill creating the Pennsylvania Intergovernmental Cooperation Authority (PICA). The legislation allowed Philadelphia to issue bonds secured by an additional 1 percent above Pennsylvania's 6 percent sales tax but empowered PICA to withhold revenue if the majority of its five-member board rejected the city's five-year fiscal plan.[94] This gave PICA enormous power over Philadelphia's budget, and because the governor, the president pro tempore of the Pennsylvania Senate, the Pennsylvania Senate minority leader, and the majority and minority leaders of the Pennsylvania House of Representatives each appointed one of the members. PICA's creation was, in short, an enormous transfer of power from the city to the commonwealth, which was then placed in the hands of a nondemocratically accountable organization that was the creation of an often-hostile Pennsylvania legislature.[95]

As Goode's second term came to an end, Rendell again sought the Democratic nomination, besting several other candidates in the primary, including former City Council member Lucien Blackwell. Rizzo again successfully sought the Republican nomination but died on July 16, less than two months before the election. The Republicans quickly nominated Democrat-turned-Republican Joseph M. Egan Jr., who lost the election in a landslide.[96] Support for Rizzo did not die with the man; in 1998, his family, friends, and political supporters donated to the city a ten-foot-tall bronze statue of the former mayor sculpted by Zenos Frudakis. The statue, which was always controversial, became the focus of protesters' ire in the summer of 2020 following a series of highly publicized killings of Black men and women by the police. On June 3, 2020, the city removed the statue from the stairs of the Municipal Services Building. Four days later, a mural of Rizzo at Ninth and Montrose Streets in South Philadelphia (which had been the city's "most defaced piece of public art") was painted over.[97]

Rendell began his administration with a stark assertion: "Philadelphia stands on the brink of total disaster." His prescription? Neoliberalism.[98] Rendell was an early example of a "New Democrat," or self-styled socially liberal fiscal conservative. Tired of being denied the White House, by the late 1980s, some Democrats enthusiastically espoused neoliberal policies, resulting in what historians have dubbed the "neoliberal consensus." The quintessential New Democrat was Bill Clinton, who won the presidency in 1992 promising a slew of neoliberal policies. Rendell was personally close to the Clintons, defending Bill Clinton at various times during the latter's presidency and aggressively campaigning on Hillary Clinton's behalf in 2008 and 2016.[99] Rendell also had a flair for self-promotion, inviting journalist Buzz Bissinger to spend the next several years shadowing him in what the mayor described as his "fight to save the city." The resulting book, the borderline hagiographical *A Prayer for the City*, helped burnish Rendell's image as a tough New Democrat willing to make hard choices to do what few others could or would.[100] No wonder Clinton's vice president, Al Gore, dubbed Rendell "America's Mayor" in 1997.[101]

For many of Rendell's critics, however, the mayor's interest in Philadelphia stopped at Center City's borders. Focusing on Center City as the key to revitalizing Philadelphia was nothing new; after all, this had been Clark's and Dilworth's strategies, and Wilson Goode had called Center City "the heart in the body."[102] Rendell took it to new heights, becoming what one prominent Democrat described as the "mayor of Center City".[103] Rendell's policies won Philadelphia some additional federal funds and made it more attractive to businesses, but little of this "trickled down" to the city's poor.[104] Between 1990 and 2000, median income fell, while the percentage of Philadelphians living in poverty grew: by 2017, more than one in four Philadelphians earned less than the federal poverty level, the highest such rate of the United States' ten largest cities.[105] At the same time, Philadelphia demolished more than twenty public housing towers, encouraging builders to redevelop the areas with lower-density, higher-cost middle-class housing.[106] Meanwhile, Philadelphia's declining tax base starved the city's public school system of much-needed revenue, which created a "push" factor that sent families fleeing to the suburbs (even as poverty spread there as well).[107] In January 2002, the Commonwealth of Pennsylvania effectively took over control of the city's public school system when it replaced the Board of Education with the five-member School Reform Commission (SRC). Though the city appointed two members, the commonwealth appointed the other three, and the SRC contracted with outside organizations (including private companies) to administer some of Philadelphia's public schools. Privatization, which was a key neoliberal goal, was not limited to public schools; under Rendell, the city privatized several services, reversing a key Progressive-era reform designed to combat corruption.[108] Austerity eroded services for city inhabitants, diminishing their quality of life. Appropriations for the city's park system, for instance, fell from more than 2 percent of Philadelphia's budget in 1960 to just over 0.3 percent in 2009, even as the commonwealth imposed financial obligations on the city while not providing additional revenue.[109]

During his administration, Rendell worked closely with City Council President John Street, who succeeded Cecil B. Moore in representing the city's Fifth District, which covered a broad swath of territory stretching from North Philadelphia through Rittenhouse Square.[110] In 1999, Street won the Democratic primary and successfully (though very narrowly) bested Republican candidate Sam Katz in the general election. Though Street had strongly supported neoliberal policies while on City Council, the new mayor took steps to address quality-of-life issues for Philadelphians living outside Center City. For instance, he aggressively towed the tens of thousands of abandoned cars in Philadelphia and in 2001 launched the Neighborhood Transformation Initiative (NTI), an antiblight program that used public funds to acquire and demolish abandoned houses and then redevelop the properties. The scale of the problem was daunting: the "City of Homes" had an estimated fifty-seven thousand vacant houses, of which more than 10 percent were considered "imminently dangerous."[111] Funded by a $295 million bond issue, the program had some notable successes, including the redevelopment of the famed Divine Lorraine Hotel (Broad Street just south of Fairmount) and Bartram's Garden near Kingsessing. Yet there remained considerably more work to do, with one North Philadelphia resident in 2017 describing his neighborhood as "just blocks and blocks of abandoned houses."[112]

For all his good work, however, Street could never quite escape the suspicion that he was corrupt. In 2003, Street ran for reelection, winning the Democratic primary by more than 99 percent, and again facing off against Republican nominee Sam Katz. On October 7, twenty-three days before the election, Philadelphia police officers discovered an FBI listening device—a bug—in Street's office. The FBI was investigating an alleged involvement in a "pay to play" scheme involving Ronald A. White, a former gang member who had become one of the city's leading attorneys and was a well-known fundraiser for Street. The discovery threw the mayor's race into chaos; Street's campaign claimed that as a prominent big-city mayor and a Black man, he had been targeted by the George W. Bush administration, which hoped to throw the election to Katz. Ultimately, Street won reelection, and the FBI never discovered any evidence that he had done anything illegal. However, White and eleven other individuals (including City Treasurer Corey Kemp) were indicted; prosecutors eventually secured twenty-four convictions.[113] In 2006, these events were chronicled in the documentary *The Shame of a City*, whose title self-consciously referenced muckraker Lincoln Steffen's 1904 book *The Shame of the Cities*, in which he called Philadelphia "corrupt and contented." In 2007, former City Council member Michael Nutter ran for the Democratic nomination for mayor on a reform platform ("crime and corruption"), even though crime rates were declining and there was no evidence that Street had done anything illegal. Nevertheless, according to Nutter, Street's era was "an environment in Philadelphia that raised serious ethical concerns about how decisions were made."[114]

Despite his awareness of the long history of police racism, Nutter supported so-called "tough-on-crime" policies (such as stop and frisk, in which police officers detained citizens and questioned or even searched them based only on a suspicion the person might be involved in a crime) that had characterized his recent predecessors' approach to governing and had disproportionately harmed people of color.[115] Astonishingly, after Nutter left office, he defended stop and frisk even while admitting he had been stopped by police multiple times (including while serving on the City Council and after he left City Hall).[116] While Nutter called being mayor "the best job in politics," Nutter's mayoralty was in part defined by the Great Recession (December 2007 to June 2009), which placed limits on his ability to formulate and implement policies.[117] Nevertheless, in 2007, newly elected Mayor Nutter pledged to turn Philadelphia into America's "greenest city." Four years later, his administration released Philadelphia2035, a bold, comprehensive plan that described itself as "an aspirational, yet realistic vision for the City" built on three themes: Thrive, Connect, and Renew.[118] Another interesting element of Philadelphia2035 was its invocation of William Penn's design for Philadelphia. "It began with a plan," the report's authors tell us, as if to validate their plan (and planning in general) by referencing his. The faith that carefully curated public spaces could shape citizens' behavior is a bedrock belief that has pervaded Philadelphia's history for more than three centuries. That Penn had a plan for Philadelphia is undeniable, but, as the preceding pages make clear, he was often frustrated in its implementation, as were his successors. Penn, like many of them, sought to influence human behavior through manipulation of space and form, which never worked as well as they hoped. Yet, that faith in the transformative power of curated space remains undiminished to this day.

Meanwhile, at the dawn of the twenty-first century, city boosters sought to leverage Philadelphia's unique history to increase tourism.[119] Between July 31 and August 3, 2000, Philadelphia hosted the Republican National Convention, the first presidential nominating convention in the city since 1948. The Republicans chose Texas Governor George W. Bush, who explicitly referenced the city's history in his speech, tying it to his aspirations in seeking the presidency. According to Bush, "Together, we will renew America's purpose. Our founders first defined that purpose here in Philadelphia. Ben Franklin was here, Thomas Jefferson and, of course, George Washington, or, as his friends called him, George W." In 2009, the city even adopted a new tagline ("Life, Liberty, and You") accompanied by the Liberty Bell's silhouette, a demonstration of how closely tied the city's revolutionary past was to its economic future.[120]

As always, Philadelphia's historical "meaning" was contested and could be leveraged in a variety of ways. In March 2008, while pursuing the Democratic nomination for president, US Senator Barack Obama of Illinois delivered a nationally televised speech from the Constitution Center. In his speech, titled "A More Perfect Union," Obama explored racism and Black anger while just yards away from two powerful historical symbols—Independence Hall and the Liberty Bell—that politicians and activists had leveraged for centuries. In July

2016, the Democrats held their presidential nominating convention in Phila-delphia at the Wells Fargo Center, choosing former secretary of state Hillary Clinton (who lost the general election to Donald Trump).

One controversy in particular, that over the so-called President's House, high-lights the ongoing and perennial fight over how to define and preserve Philadel-phia's history, especially when it involves tourism and race. Historians had long known that as president, George Washington and John Adams had rented Robert Morris's mansion on Market Street between Fifth and Sixth, though the building itself was largely torn down in the first third of the nineteenth century.[121] However, no one "forgot" that Washington and Adams had lived on Market Street (even if the specific location of the building was in doubt), and the National Park Service (NPS) briefly considered including that portion of the street in what would later become Independence National Historical Park, though it ultimately chose not to do so. This was a colossal blunder, because portions of the house still existed until they were demolished as part of the process of building the park.[122] As a result, few visitors to the park realized that Washington and Adams lived a block north of Independence Hall, even after 1976, when the NPS moved the Liberty Bell to a specially constructed pavilion just a few hundred feet from where the Morris mansion stood. In fact, by that point, a public restroom stood on a portion of the site that the mansion had once occupied.

In 1997, the NPS began planning a multimillion-dollar redevelopment of the park with a particular focus on constructing a new building to house the Liberty Bell. The NPS decided to demolish the public bathroom near the cor-ner of Sixth and Market and replaced it with the new Liberty Bell Center. This placed the Liberty Bell Center not only on the site of the President's House but put the entrance to the building directly over the space where Washington housed his enslaved people while president. It was no secret that Washington had enslaved people or that as president, he had skirted Pennsylvania's Gradual Abolition Act of 1780 by cycling enslaved people back to his home at Mount Vernon, in Virginia. All in all, at least nine enslaved people—Austin, Giles, Hercules, Joe, Moll, Ona Judge, Paris, Richmond, and Christopher Sheels—spent time in bondage at the President's House. Of these nine, only Ona Judge and Hercules managed to escape and elude recapture.[123]

None of this was unknown or secret so much as it was being ignored. How-ever, that began changing when historian Edward Lawler Jr. published a ninety-page scholarly article in the *Pennsylvania Magazine of History and Biography* about the President's House that established both its location and floor plan, calling into question the NPS's plans for the new Liberty Bell Center. Lawler had shared his findings with the NPS before the article was published, and his work was widely reported in the press.[124] Lawler's article galvanized historians

Gary B. Nash and Randall Miller and later *Philadelphia Inquirer* columnist Acel Moore to pressure the NPS to modify the designs for the Liberty Bell Center and to revise its interpretive plan to include both a discussion of the President's House and the presence of enslaved people at the site.[125] The NPS was reluctant to do this, eventually offering to create a single sign. The NPS's reluctance, as well as (unfounded) rumors that the site contained enslaved people's remains, led Philadelphia attorney Michael Coard to form the Avenging The Ancestors Coalition (ATAC), an organization dedicated to "to compel the National Park Service (NPS) and Independence National Historical Park (INHP) to [create] . . . a prominent Slavery Memorial . . . to honor primarily the nine African descendants enslaved by President George Washington at the President's House."[126] ATAC and other groups pressured the NPS to modify its designs and found powerful allies in US Representative Chaka Fattah of Pennsylvania and Mayor John Street.[127] As a result of their efforts, the NPS constructed an open-air partial re-creation of the President's House that explicitly foregrounds the history of American slavery by including several interactive exhibits chronicling the experiences of the people Washington enslaved, including Ona Judge.[128]

Despite Philadelphia's undeniable symbolic power, antiurbanism (usually fueled by racism) remains. Americans' ambivalence about cities generally, and toward Philadelphia in particular, is illustrated in President Trump's shameless lies about voter fraud during the 2020 presidential election, such as telling his mostly white supporters that "bad things happen in Philadelphia," an assertion that amused Philadelphians quickly adopted for T-shirts and bumper stickers. Though widely derided, Trump's assertion about "bad things" happening in Philadelphia, a majority-minority city, suggests that racism and antiurbanism remain obstacles to progress. Moreover, even as the city's population grew slightly in the twenty-first century, Pennsylvania's population shrank, eroding the commonwealth's representation in Congress and thereby potentially imperiling federal aid to the region. As this book made its way toward publication, Philadelphia's voters elected Cherelle Parker the city's one hundredth mayor. She is the first Black female to hold the mayoralty, and she campaigned on raising the minimum wage in the city, promoting green policies, and hiring more police officers. How well her administration will achieve these goals is unknowable (she will have been in office less than a year when this book is published), but it is my hope that she and other policymakers will learn from the city's long history to successfully craft policies that promote equitable growth and improved quality of life for all Philadelphians.

Conclusion

A Symbol and a Place

One of the stranger aspects of this project is leaving the story in medias res. My prior books have all explored institutions (Eastern State Penitentiary) or people (Lincoln's secretary of war, Simon Cameron) whose stories ended neatly by closure or death. Philadelphia's history continues to be written even as I type these words. The observation that led to this book—that Philadelphia does a terrible job remembering its own history—sprang from my own experience, having spent most of my life in the Philadelphia metropolitan area (though, as many Philadelphians would be quick to point out, not in the city itself). It was a little humbling to realize that the entirety of my life span is covered by less than a single chapter in this book. At several dozen points during the years-long process of researching and writing this book, I (a Delaware Valley native, avid museumgoer, and professional historian who has written several books about Pennsylvania), said, "I never knew that!"

Because there is no history without the historian, it is useful to consider my own relationship with Philadelphia. Born in 1980, I grew up absorbing the anti-urban assumptions and attitudes that characterized life in nearby Montgomery County. Fed by sensationalist imagery on the local news and movies like *Rocky* and *Witness*, I thought of Philadelphia as an exotic but potentially dangerous place you went to visit historic sites like Independence Hall or museums like the Franklin Institute. Once I got to high school, the exotic and forbidden air of the city made it seductive; I spent many weekend nights prowling South Street with my friends, believing myself more sophisticated than I actually was because I was "downtown."

Philadelphia has changed substantially in the intervening years. In her 2020 book, *Becoming Philadelphia*, Inga Saffron, the *Philadelphia Inquirer*'s Pulitzer Prize–winning architecture critic, described the city as having undergone an "astounding comeback" since 1998.[1] That sense of optimism is clearly visible in the city's current comprehensive plan, Philadelphia2035, which offers a vision of the city as composed of vibrantly "diverse, authentic neighborhoods."[2] Saffron's dating of Philadelphia's "comeback" as beginning in 1998 resonates with me on a personal level: that was the year I graduated from high school. My generation—Generation X, xennial, or millennial, depending on whom you ask—has contributed to the city's recent population bump. Yet the growth in Philadelphia's population, spurred by the popularity of such neighborhoods as Fairmount, Fishtown, and Manayunk, has led to concerns about gentrification, or the process by which wealthy (usually white) people move into a neighborhood, often displacing poor (typically Black) residents.

One of this book's themes is that Philadelphians have consistently tried to use public space, through architecture and public art, to shape citizens' behavior and beliefs. This has met with limited success, as citizens pushed back against attempts to control where they lived and how they used the city's space. Yet generations of urban planners have left their imprint on the city and its landscape: from the grid layout to the Benjamin Franklin Parkway and public housing, we live with the legacy of efforts to use public space to promote specific values and behaviors. Of course, the mobilization of space to foster and promote certain standards of conduct is also related to Philadelphians' long history of leveraging the city's historical buildings and objects for economic, political, and social purposes. Almost from its creation, Philadelphia offered a rich tapestry of unique experiences and sights. Advancements in transportation, which coincided with nostalgia for the revolutionary era, made the city a tourist destination in the nineteenth century. As this book demonstrates, Philadelphia had more to offer than its large collection of colonial and revolutionary buildings and artifacts, but these played a key role in how the city defined itself. The process of deciding what stories are worth telling and what objects or buildings are worth preserving has never been uncontroversial. As *Philadelphia: A Narrative History* illustrates, divergent and sometimes antagonistic groups have tried to enlist the city's buildings, artifacts, and symbols on behalf of their agendas, a phenomenon described in the introduction as forging a usable history.

Of course, that process needs to be understood against two pervasive (and related) impulses that have played an important role in Philadelphia's history: antiurbanism and bigotry (particularly racism). Antiurbanism is "as American as apple pie," and even William Penn's designs for Philadelphia reflected certain antiurban biases. However, in recent years, antagonism toward cities seems to be getting worse: political scientists have identified a growing divide between rural and urban voters, with the former becoming more uniformly Republican and the latter more strongly Democratic. In fact, geographic location and proximity to a city have become some of the best correlates of political identity and ideology, even when controlling for other variables.[3]

In part, this may reflect the different experiences between urban and rural dwellers: Republicans have, for nearly a century, opposed government programs designed to create a social safety net or more-equitable conditions, arguing that if these things are going to be done at all, they should be done by private non-profits, an ideology that resonates with Philadelphia's strong privatist tradition. However that tradition was usually wholly inadequate to the challenges the city faced, with the result being substantial human misery. The Progressive Era, the New Deal, and the Great Society can be understood as attempts, however imperfect, to address these challenges, but the United States abandoned many of those reforms' most notable policies beginning in the 1970s, turning instead toward austerity and neoliberalism. Recently, a growing number of Americans are pushing back on what has been dubbed the neoliberal consensus, though policies that took decades to implement will take years to reform or replace. In short, while neoliberalism has fallen out of favor among some policymakers, it is by no means dead.

One cause of Americans' long-standing (and in some places growing) antiur-banism is racism and bigotry. These ugly and destructive ways of thinking touch nearly every aspect of Philadelphia's history, and reckoning with that legacy is a fraught and ongoing process with profound social, political, and economic costs. As of this writing, Philadelphia is the second most racially segregated city (behind Chicago), developing large pockets of Black and Latino communities that over the last few years have become poorer.[4] Gentrification, which has spurred the city's first population growth in decades, has contributed to the increase in segregation by pushing up rental prices beyond what many people can afford.[5]

While these are large-scale challenges, none of them just happened: they are the outcomes (sometimes accidental but more often intentional) of policies adopted at various levels of government and of decisions made by millions of individuals over the past four centuries. My hope is that this book will demonstrate to readers the role that contingency and agency have played in driving Philadelphia's history and in shaping its condition. Nothing about contemporary Philadelphia and the challenges it faces are inevitable or preordained. Recognizing that fact leads to the inescapable conclusion that the city's future is not set in stone. In short, if you want to see better, more just outcomes, you must first understand the steps that led us here, and I hope that *Philadelphia: A Narrative History* has helped you do that.

NOTES

Introduction

1. Richard R. Beeman, *The Varieties of Political Experience in Eighteenth-Century America* (Philadelphia: University of Pennsylvania Press, 2004), 247.

2. Julius Rubin, "Urban Growth and Regional Development," in *The Growth of Seaport Cities, 1790–1825,* ed. David T. Gilchrist (Charlottesville: University of Virginia Press, 1967), 4. See also Edwin Wolf 2nd, "The Origins of Philadelphia's Self-Deprecation, 1820–1920," *Pennsylvania Magazine of History and Biography,* 104, no. 1 (January 1980): 60.

3. Washington to Lafayette, 28 July 1791, *FoundersOnline,* accessed December 2, 2022, https://founders.archives.gov/documents/Washington/05-08-02-0260; Jefferson to Rush, 23 September 1800, *FoundersOnline,* accessed April 7, 2021, https://founders.archives.gov/documents/Jefferson/01-32-02-0102.

4. *Official Proceedings of the Democratic National Convention* (Logansport, IN: Wilson, Humphreys, 1896), 234; Theodore Roosevelt, "The City in Modern Life," in *The Works of Theodore Roosevelt,* vol. 12, *Literary Essays* (New York: National Edition, 1926), 226.

5. Charles Nelson Glaab and Andrew Theodore Brown, *A History of Urban America* (New York: Macmillan, 1983), 302.

6. Historian William W. Cutler III describes the prevailing sentiment as favoring "grand boulevards and pretentious public buildings." William W. Cutler III, "The Persistent Dualism: Centralization and Decentralization in Philadelphia, 1854–1975," in *The Divided Metropolis: Social and Spatial Dimensions of Philadelphia, 1800–1920,* ed. William W. Cutler III and Howard Gillette Jr. (Westport, CT: Greenwood Press, 1980), 257.

7. Thomas Wirth, "Urban Neglect: The Environment, Public Health, and Influenza in Philadelphia, 1915–1919," *Pennsylvania History,* 73, no. 3 (Summer 2006): 323–24; Robert P. Armstrong, "Green Space in the Gritty City: The Planning and Development of Philadelphia's Park System, 1854–1929" (PhD diss., Lehigh University, 2012), 145; Paul Boyer, *Urban Masses and Moral Order in America, 1820–1920* (Cambridge, MA: Harvard University Press, 1992), 221.

8. Van Wyck Brooks, "On Creating a Usable Past," *Dial* (April 11, 1918): 339.

9. Robert Penn Warren, *All the King's Men* (New York: Harcourt, 2002), 604.

Chapter 1

1. Sally Schwartz, "Society and Culture in the Seventeenth-Century Delaware Valley," *Delaware History,* 20, no. 2 (Fall 1982): 105. According to historian Mark L. Thompson, "Over time nonnative settler communities crafted national identities that were more communal and less state orient[ed] than they were in previous incarnations. . . . [T]hese

reinvented 'nations' preserved their autonomy by acting as loyal, obedient subjects, as most of their members chose to do. Demonstrating fidelity to their new masters enabled aliens to gain access to the rights, privileges, and *power* that accrued to the individuals with the official status of subjects." Mark L. Thompson, *The Contest for the Delaware Valley: Allegiance, Identity, and Empire in the Seventeenth Century* (Baton Rouge: Louisiana State University Press, 2013), 9.

2. Kurt W. Carr and Roger W. Moeller, *First Pennsylvanians: The Archeology of Native Americans in Pennsylvania* (Harrisburg: Pennsylvania Historical and Museum Commission, 2015), 49–51; Daniel K. Richter, "A Framework for Pennsylvania Indian History," *Pennsylvania History*, 57, no. 3 (July 1990): 237.

3. Carr and Moeller, *First Pennsylvanians*, 127.

4. Carr and Moeller, *First Pennsylvanians*, 142; Richter, "Framework," 237; and Marshall J. Becker, "Lenape Culture History: The Transition of 1600 and Its Implications for the Archeology of the Final Phase of the Late Woodland Period," *Journal of Middle Atlantic Archeology* 27 (2012): 54.

5. Jean R. Soderlund, "The Lenape Origins of Delaware Valley Peace and Freedom," in *Quakers and Native Americans*, ed. Ignacio Gallup-Diaz and Geoffrey Plank (Boston: Brill, 2019), 18; Robert S. Grumet, *Historic Contact: Indian People and Colonists in Today's Northeastern United States in the Sixteenth Through Eighteenth Centuries* (Norman: University of Oklahoma Press, 2021), 231.

6. Daniel K. Richter, *Native Americans' Pennsylvania* (University Park: Pennsylvania Historical Association, 2005), 26; Grumet, *Historic Contact*, 211; Robert S. Grumet, *The Lenapes* (New York: Chelsea House, 1989), 25, 52.

7. Gunlög Fur, *A Nation of Women: Gender and Colonial Encounters Among the Delaware Indians* (Philadelphia: University of Pennsylvania Press, 2012), 6; Jean R. Soderlund, *Lenape Country: Delaware Valley Society Before William Penn* (Philadelphia: University of Pennsylvania Press, 2016), 7.

8. Amy C. Schutt, *Peoples of the River Valleys: The Odyssey of the Delaware Indians* (Philadelphia: University of Pennsylvania Press, 2007), 9.

9. Marshall J. Becker, "The Boundary Between the Lenape and the Munsee: The Forks of the Delaware as a Buffer Zone," *Man in the Northeast*, 26 (Fall 1983): 3.

10. Soderlund, "Lenape Origins," i, 18; Richter, "Framework," 237; Marshall J. Becker, "Lenape Population at the Time of European Contact: Estimating Native Numbers in the Lower Delaware Valley," *Proceedings of the American Philosophical Society*, 133, no. 2 (June 1989): 113. A contemporary visitor to the region estimated the population of Lenape at eight hundred. See Beauchamp Plantagenet, *A Description of the Province of New Albion* (London: G. P. Humphrey, 1648), 15.

11. On the diversity of Lenape buildings, see Schutt, *Peoples of the River Valleys*, 16.

12. Richter, *Native Americans' Pennsylvania*, 21.

13. Richter, *Native Americans' Pennsylvania*, 28.

14. In some cases, the sachem was "last among equals." William Penn described a scenario in which, having received some goods, a Lenape sachem "sub-divideth it in like manner among his Dependants, they hardly leaving themselves an Equal share with one of their Subjects." *A Letter from William Penn, Proprietary and Governour of Pennsylvania*

in America, to the Committee of the Free Society of Traders of That Province, Residing in London (London: Andrew Sowle, 1683), 6. Carr and Moeller note that the position was frequently more of a burden than anything else. See *First Pennsylvanians*, 27; Carol Barnes, "Subsistence and Social Organization of the Delaware Indians: 1600 A.D.," *Bulletin of the Philadelphia Archeological Society*, 1, no. 1 (November 1968): 24.

15. Richter, *Native Americans' Pennsylvania*, 26; Fur, *Nation of Women*, 16–18.

16. Schutt, *Peoples of the River Valleys*, 22; Grumet, *Lenapes*, 14; Soderlund, *Lenape Country*, 24.

17. Historian Daniel K. Richter goes so far as to describe these bands as "collections of people generally at peace with one another who recognized strong affinities of marriage, trade, and language." Richter, "Framework," 239. See also Soderlund, *Lenape Country*, 12.

18. Robert Child, 24 December 1645, *Publications of the Colonial Society of Massachusetts*, 38 (April 1947): 50–53.

19. Adriaen van der Donck, *Remonstrance of New Netherland and Occurrences There*, trans. E. B. O'Callaghan (Albany, NY: Weed, Parsons, 1856), 22.

20. Thomas J. Sugrue, "The Peopling and Depeopling of Early Pennsylvania: Indians and Colonists, 1680–1720," *Pennsylvania Magazine of History and Biography*, 116, no. 1 (January 1992): 11.

21. Johannes de Laet, "From the 'New World,' by Johan de Laet, 1625, 1630, 1633, 1640," in *Narratives of New Netherland*, ed. J. Franklin Jameson (New York: Charles Scribner's Sons, 1909), 38.

22. Thomas Yong, "Thomas Yong's Voyage to Virginia and Delaware Bay and River in 1634," in *Collections of the Massachusetts Historical Society*, vol. 9, 4th ser. (Boston: John Wilson and Son, 1871), 119. See also Richter, "Framework," 242, and Daniel K. Richter, *Trade, Land, Power: The Struggle for Eastern North America* (Philadelphia: University of Pennsylvania Press, 2013), 3, 54–55, 100.

23. Soderlund, *Lenape Country*, 25–34.

24. Historian Daniel K. Richter argues this reflected deep divisions "over whether its North American holdings were to be trading outposts or settlement colonies." Richter, *Trade, Land, Power*, 97.

25. Soderlund, "Lenape Origins," 21; Soderlund, *Lenape Country*, 53; Richter, *Trade, Land, Power*, 6.

26. Soderlund, *Lenape Country*, 17.

27. Carr and Moeller, *First Pennsylvanians*, 206; Richter, "Framework," 242; Richter, *Native Americans' Pennsylvania*, 37.

28. David Pietersz de Vries, "Korte Historiael Ende Journaels Aenteyckeninge," in *Narratives of New Netherland, 1609–1664*, ed. J. Franklin Jameson (New York: Charles Scribner's Sons, 1909), 231.

29. Marshall Joseph Becker, "Lenape Maize Sales to the Swedish Colonists: Cultural Stability During the Early Colonial Period," in *New Sweden in America*, ed. Carol E. Hoffecker, Richard Waldron, Lorraine E. Williams, and Barbara E. Benson (Newark: University of Delaware Press, 1995), 121, 125.

30. Schutt, *Peoples of the River Valleys*, 33; Soderlund, "Lenape Origins," 18; Fur, *Nation of Women*, 31–32. Jean R. Soderlund makes clear that the Europeans were aware of

the Lenape's understanding of these transactions and periodically gave the Natives gifts to remain in their good graces. See Soderlund, *Lenape Country*, 78.

31. Soderlund, *Lenape Country*, 4–5; Richter, *Trade, Land, Power*, 7.

32. C. A. Weslager, *The English on the Delaware* (New Brunswick, NJ: Rutgers University Press, 1967), 6.

33. "Relation of Thomas Yong, 1634," in *Narratives of Early Pennsylvania, West New Jersey, and Delaware, 1630–1707*, ed. Albert Cook Myers (New York: Charles Scribner's Sons, 1912), 44.

34. Jeffrey M. Dorwart, *Invasion and Insurrection: Security, Defense, and War in the Delaware Valley, 1621–1815* (Newark: University of Delaware, 2008), 29; Jean R. Soderlund and Claude Epstein, "Lenape-Colonist Land Conveyances in West New Jersey: Evolving Expectations in Space and Time," *New Jersey Studies: An Interdisciplinary Journal*, 4, no. 2 (Summer 2018): 197.

35. Edward C. Carter II and Clifford Lewis III, "Sir Edmund Plowden and the New Albion Charter, 1632–1785," *Pennsylvania Magazine of History and Biography*, 83, no. 2 (April 1959): 154.

36. Gregory Bernard Keen, *The Descendants of Jöran Kyn of New Sweden* (Philadelphia: Swedish Colonial Society, 1913), inset map.

37. William W. Comfort, "William Penn's Religious Background," *Pennsylvania Magazine of History and Biography*, 68, no. 4 (October 1944): 343; John E. Pomfret, "The First Purchasers of Pennsylvania, 1681–1700," *Pennsylvania Magazine of History and Biography*, 80, no. 2 (April 1956): 138.

38. Christopher Ward, *New Sweden on the Delaware* (Philadelphia: University of Pennsylvania Press, 1938), 36.

39. Schwartz, "Society and Culture," 109; Soderlund, *Lenape Country*, 7.

40. Jasper Danckaerts, *The Journal of Jasper Danckaerts, 1679–1680*, ed. Bartlett B. James and J. Franklin Jameson (New York: Charles Scribner's Sons, 1913), 98.

41. Ward, *New Sweden*, 72.

42. The exception to this pattern was the Finns, who tended to migrate in families; their wives and daughters provided a small measure of natural increase in the colony. Evan Haefeli, "The Revolt of the Long Swede: Transatlantic Hopes and Fears on the Delaware, 1669," *Pennsylvania Magazine of History and Biography*, 130, no. 2 (April 2006): 154.

43. This number comes from Peter Stebbins Craig, ed., *The 1693 Census of the Swedes on the Delaware* (Winter Park, FL: SAG Publications, 1993), 1. Lower estimates can be found in Marshall Joseph Becker, "Pre-Penn Settlements of the Delaware Valley: Lenape, Dutch, and Swedes in the Delaware Valley in the Seventeenth Century," *Pennsylvania Geological Magazine*, 32, no. 3 (1982): 232. Karen Ordahl Kupperman claims the number is a dozen in "Scandinavian Colonies Confront the New World," in *New Sweden in America*, ed. Carol E. Hoffecker, Richard Waldron, Lorraine E. Williams, and Barbara E. Benson (Newark: University of Delaware Press, 1995), 94.

44. Kupperman, "Scandinavian Colonies," 102.

45. John Winthrop, *The Journal of John Winthrop, 1630–1649*, ed. Richard S. Dunn, James Savage, and Laetitia Yeandle (Cambridge, MA: Belknap Press of Harvard University Press, 1996), 480.

46. Weslager, *English on the Delaware*, 71.

47. Becker, "Lenape Maize Sales," 130.

48. Ward, *New Sweden*, 54–55.

49. Winthrop, *Journal*, 616.

50. Ward, *New Sweden*, 87.

51. Richter, *Trade, Land, Power*, 102.

52. Kupperman, "Scandinavian Colonies," 102.

53. Ward, *New Sweden*, 73.

54. Carl E. Bridenbaugh, "The Old and New Societies of the Delaware Valley in the Seventeenth-Century," *Pennsylvania Magazine of History and Biography*, 100, no. 2 (April 1976): 154; Richter, *Trade, Land, Power*, 99.

55. Quoted in Weslager, *English on the Delaware*, 109.

56. Weslager, *English on the Delaware*, 120–29.

57. Grumet, *Historic Contact*, 234; Soderlund, *Lenape Country*, 7.

58. Thompson, *Contest for the Delaware Valley*, 7; Soderlund, *Lenape Country*, 5.

59. Soderlund, "Lenape Origins," 16; Becker, "Pre-Penn Settlements," 232.

60. Schwartz, "Society and Culture," 106.

61. Weslager, *English on the Delaware*, 135.

62. Van Tienhoven to Stuyvesant, 9 November 1648, in *Documents Relative to the Colonial History of the State of New York*, vol. 12 (Albany, NY: Parson, Weed, 1881), 46. Writing to John Witherspoon in 1651, an English seaman named Thomas Doxey reported on his visit to the Delaware Valley, saying, "Here is a grete difference beetxite the Swede and the Dutch/Bouthe of them striving for to bee Masters of the River and Soe by that meanes the trad is much hindered and Detes hard for to gette." Thomas Doxey, "Thomas Doxey's Letter from the Delaware Valley, 1651," *Delaware History*, 8 (1958): 52.

63. Quoted in Amandus Johnson, *The Swedish Settlements on the Delaware: Their History and Relation to the Indians, Dutch, and English, 1638–1664*, vol. 1 (Philadelphia: University of Pennsylvania Press, 1911), 435.

64. Norris Stanley Barratt, *Colonial Wars in America: Address Before the Society of Colonial Wars in the Commonwealth of Pennsylvania, March 13, 1913* (Lancaster, PA: New Era Printing, 1913), 26.

65. Soderlund, *Lenape Country*, 77–78.

66. Soderlund, *Lenape Country*, 77–80.

67. Quoted in Johnson, *Swedish Settlements*, 448.

68. Johnson, *Swedish Settlements*, 445–46.

69. Ward, *New Sweden on the Delaware*, 186.

70. Johan Risingh, *The Rise and Fall of New Sweden: Governor Johan Risingh's Journal 1654–1655 and Its Historical Context*, ed. Stellan Dahlgren and Hans Norman (Stockholm: Almqqvist & Wiksell International, 1988), 151, 165.

71. *Rise and Fall of New Sweden*, 151.

72. Quoted in Amandus Johnson, "Johan Classon Risingh, the Last Director of New Sweden, on the Delaware," *Pennsylvania Magazine of History and Biography*, 39, no. 2 (1915): 134.

73. *Rise and Fall of New Sweden*, 193.

74. Soderlund, *Lenape Country*, 170–71.

75. Peter Stebbins Craig notes that when Stuyvesant tried to enlist Swedes living in the Delaware Valley to assist with a military raid on a Native settlement in present-day Kingston, New York, they refused. Craig, *1693 Census*, 5.

76. Samuel W. Pennypacker, "The Settlement of Germantown, and the Causes Which Led to It," *Pennsylvania Magazine of History and Biography*, 4, no. 1 (1880): 35; Christopher Ward, *The Dutch and Swedes on the Delaware, 1609–1664* (Philadelphia: University of Pennsylvania Press, 1930), 362.

77. Peter Stebbins Craig, ed., *The 1671 Census of the Delaware* (Philadelphia: Genealogical Society of Pennsylvania, 1999), vii, 1.

78. Haefeli, "Revolt of the Long Swede," 140.

79. Thompson, *Contest for the Delaware Valley*, 3–5.

Chapter 2

1. Jean R. Soderlund, *Lenape Country: Delaware Valley Society before William Penn* (Philadelphia: University of Pennsylvania Press, 2015), 4–5.

2. Marshall Joseph Becker, "Pre-Penn Settlements of the Delaware Valley: Lenape, Dutch, and Swedes in the Delaware Valley in the Seventeenth Century," *Pennsylvania Geological Magazine*, 32, no. 3 (1982): 232; Peter S. Craig, *The 1693 Census of the Swedes on the Delaware* (Winter Park, FL: SAG Publications, 1993), 7.

3. For instance, historian Michael W. Zuckerman argues, "From the first, the people of Pennsylvania, New Jersey, and New York acted under conditions of cultural pluralism that only came to characterize the rest of the country in the nineteenth century." Introduction, in *Friends and Neighbors: Group Life in America's First Plural Society*, ed. Michael W. Zuckerman (Philadelphia: Temple University Press, 1982), 5.

4. John Smolenski, *Friends and Strangers: The Making of a Creole Culture in Colonial Pennsylvania* (Philadelphia: University of Pennsylvania Press, 2010), 4.

5. Jessica Chopin Roney, *Governed by a Spirit of Opposition: The Origins of American Political Practice in Colonial Philadelphia* (Baltimore: Johns Hopkins University Press, 2014), 1.

6. Katherine Gerbner, "Antislavery in Print: The Germantown Protest, the 'Exhortation,' and the Seventeenth-Century Quaker Debate on Slavery," *Early American Studies*, 9, no. 3 (Fall 2011): 557.

7. Margaret Hope Bacon, "Quaker Women in Overseas Ministry," *Quaker History*, 77, no. 2 (Fall 1988): 93; Kenneth L. Carroll, "Some Thoughts on George Fox's Visit to America in 1672," *Quaker History*, 61, no. 2 (Autumn 1972): 82.

8. Johan Winsser, "Quieting Mary Dyer: Edward Burrough and Dyer's Letter to the Massachusetts General Court, 26 October 1659," *Quaker History*, 105, no. 1 (Spring 2016): 43; Marie Balsley Taylor, "Apostates in the Woods: Quakers, Praying Indians, and Circuits of Communication in Humphrey Norton's New-England's Ensigne," in *Quakers and Native Americans*, ed. Ignacio Gallup-Diaz and Geoffrey Plank (Boston: Brill, 2019), 30–31.

9. John E. Pomfret, *Colonial New Jersey: A History* (New York: Charles Scribner's Sons, 1973), 31.

10. Wayland F. Dunaway, "English Settlers in Colonial Pennsylvania," *Pennsylvania Magazine of History and Biography*, 52, no. 4 (October 1928): 319–20; John F. Watson, *Annals of Philadelphia and Pennsylvania, in the Olden Times*, vol. 1 (Philadelphia: Elijah Thomas, 1857), 10.

11. John W. Reps, "William Penn and the Planning of Philadelphia," *Town Planning Review*, 27, no. 1 (April 1956): 27–28; Pomfret, *Colonial New Jersey*, 35–37; John E. Pomfret, *The Province of East New Jersey, 1609–1702: The Rebellious Proprietary* (New York: Octagon Books, 1981), 110–11.

12. John E. Pomfret, "The First Purchasers of Pennsylvania, 1681–1700," *Pennsylvania Magazine of History and Biography*, 80, no. 2 (April 1956): 139; Susan E. Klepp, "Encounter and Experiment: The Colonial Period," in *Pennsylvania: A History of the Commonwealth*, ed. Randall M. Miller and William A. Pencak (University Park:Pennsylvania State University Press, 2002), 63–64; Craig W. Horle, *The Quakers and the English Legal System, 1660–1688* (Philadelphia: University of Pennsylvania Press, 2008), 102; Andrew R. Murphy, *William Penn: A Life* (New York: Oxford University Press, 2018), 67.

13. Murphy, *William Penn*, 37–40.

14. William W. Comfort, "William Penn's Religious Background," *Pennsylvania Magazine of History and Biography*, 68, no. 4 (October 1944): 346; Murphy, *William Penn*, 138–39.

15. "Charter for the Province of Pennsylvania—1681," Avalon Project: Documents in Law, History and Diplomacy, accessed November 17, 2018, http://avalon.law.yale.edu /17th_century/pa01.asp; Richard S. Dunn, "William Penn and the Selling of Pennsylvania, 1681–1685," *Proceedings of the American Philosophical Society*, 127, no. 5 (October 1983): 322.

16. Gary B. Nash, *Quakers and Politics: Pennsylvania, 1681–1726* (Boston: Northeastern University Press, 1993), 10.

17. Pomfret, "First Purchasers," 147; Dunn, "William Penn and the Selling of Pennsylvania," 324; Nash, *Quakers and Politics*, 13.

18. Pomfret, "First Purchasers," 147.

19. William E. Lingelbach, "William Penn and City Planning," *Pennsylvania Magazine of History and Biography*, 68, no. 4 (October 1944): 402. Historian Gary B. Nash called it "an alluring plan of land allocation" for Penn's investors. Nash, *Quakers and Politics*, 18.

20. Matthew A. Zimmerman, "First Purchasers of Pennsylvania," *Encyclopedia of Greater Philadelphia*, n.d., accessed November 25, 2018, https://philadelphiaencyclopedia .org/archive/first-purchasers-of-pennsylvania/.

21. Wayland F. Dunaway, "Early Welsh Settlers of Pennsylvania," *Pennsylvania History*12, no. 4 (October 1945): 254; E. Digby Baltzell, *Puritan Boston and Quaker Philadelphia: Two Protestant Ethics and the Spirit of Class Authority and Leadership* (Boston: Beacon Press, 1982), 115.

22. Samuel W. Pennypacker, "The Settlement of Germantown, and the Causes Which Led to It," *Pennsylvania Magazine of History and Biography*, 4, no. 1 (1880): 5.

23. Marianne S. Wokeck, "German and Irish Immigration to Colonial Philadelphia," *Proceedings of the American Philosophical Society*, 133, no. 2 (June 1989): 128.

24. Soderlund, *Lenape Country*, 171.

25. This belt was donated to the Historical Society of Pennsylvania in 1857 by Penn's great-grandson, Granville Penn, though doubts have been raised about the authenticity of the belt and its provenance. Frank G. Speck and William Orchard, *The Penn Wampum Belts*, vol. 4. (New York: Museum of the American Indian, 1925), 9.

26. Frederick D. Stone. "Penn's Treaty with the Indians: Did It Take Place in 1682 or 1683," *Pennsylvania Magazine of History and Biography*, 6, no. 2 (1882): 218.

27. On the mythical/legendary nature of this event, see Dawn G. Marsh, *A Lenape Among the Quakers: The Life of Hannah Freeman* (Lincoln: University of Nebraska Press, 2014), 58, and Soderlund, *Lenape Country*, 170.

28. William A. Pencak, "Pennsylvania's Early Defense Policy, 1682–1730," in *Pennsylvania: A Military History*, ed. William Pencak, Christian B. Keller, and Barbara A. Gannon (Yardley, PA: Westholme, 2016), 7.

29. *Annals of Pennsylvania, 1609–1682: From the Discovery of the Delaware*, ed. Samuel Hazard (Philadelphia: Hazard & Mitchell, 1850), 137; John F. Watson, *Annals of Philadelphia and Pennsylvania, in the Olden Times*, vol. 2 (Philadelphia: Edwin S. Stuart, 1891), 101–2.

30. "Extracts from the Minutes of the Council," in *Annals of Pennsylvania, 1609–1682*, 94; Watson, *Annals of Philadelphia and Pennsylvania*, 2:31. According to the 2020 census, approximately fourteen thousand Native Americans—representing .33 percent of the city's population—live in Philadelphia. Laura Benshoff, 'We're a Living Presence': Philly Celebrates First Officially Recognized Indigenous Peoples Day. Whyy.org, October 11, 2011. https://whyy.org/articles/were-a-living-presence-philly-celebrates-first-officially-recognized-indigenous-peoples-day/. Charles P. Keith, "The Bishop of London and Penn's Indian Policy," *Pennsylvania Magazine of History and Biography*, 31, no. 4 (1907): 389.

31. Pencak, "Pennsylvania's Early Defense Policy," 8.

32. Edward Corbyn Obert Beatty, *William Penn as Social Philosopher* (New York: Columbia University Press, 1939), 280.

33. Justus F. Sachse, ed., "The Missive of Justus Falckner, of Germantown, Concerning the Religious Condition of Pennsylvania in the Year 1701," *Pennsylvania Magazine of History and Biography*, 21, no. 2 (1897): 218.

34. Samuel Guldin, "Diary of Samuel Guldin, Relating to His Journey to Pennsylvania, June to September 1710 (Continued)," ed. William J. Hinke, *Journal of the Presbyterian Historical Society*, 14, no. 2 (June 1930): 69.

35. Frederick D. Stone, "A Vindication of William Penn by Philip Ford, and Other Papers Relating to the Settlement of Pennsylvania," *Pennsylvania Magazine of History and Biography*, 6, no. 2 (1882): 175.

36. Stone, "Vindication of William Penn," 178.

37. The fortieth parallel cuts through present-day Philadelphia right above Indiana Avenue in North Philadelphia, about three and a half miles north of City Hall.

38. "The Charter of Maryland: 1632," Avalon Project: Documents in Law, History and Diplomacy, accessed November 17, 2018, http://avalon.law.yale.edu/17th_century/ma01.asp.

39. Walter B. Scaife, "The Boundary Dispute Between Maryland and Pennsylvania," *Pennsylvania Magazine of History and Biography*, 9, no. 3 (October 1885): 242–43. For

additional examples, see Sally Schwartz, "Society and Culture in the Seventeenth-Century Delaware Valley," *Delaware History*, 20, no. 2 (Fall 1982): 98.

40. Irma Corcoran, "William Penn and His Purchasers: Problems in Paradise," *Proceedings of the American Philosophical Society*, 138, no. 4 (December 1994): 477.

41. *Annals of Pennsylvania, 1609–1682: From the Discovery of the Delaware*, ed. Samuel Hazard (Philadelphia: Hazard & Mitchell, 1850), 575.

42. A. Karl Yergey, "The Frontier in Doubt: The Maryland-Pennsylvania Border Dispute, 1681–1767," *Mid-America: A Historical Review*, 80, no. 1 (Winter 1998): 61.

43. Each colony had three counties, so they were evenly matched in the Assembly. Many Pennsylvanian delegates thought that Delaware's delegates diminished their authority and threatened Pennsylvania's Quaker character, while Delaware's delegates feared that Pennsylvania's rapid growth would mean the creation of additional counties in Pennsylvania and a consequent diminution of Delaware's political power in the Assembly. As a result, Penn eventually granted Delaware a separate colonial government in 1701.

44. William Penn, "Rough Draft of Declaration Agt. Lord Baltimore, 1684," in *Pennsylvania Archives*, ser. 1, vol. 1, ed. Samuel Hazard (Philadelphia: Joseph Severns, 1852), 89.

45. "Charter of Maryland: 1632," Avalon Project.

46. Yergey, "Frontier in Doubt," 67.

47. Soderlund, *Lenape Country*, 161.

48. Joan de Lourdes Leonard, "The Organization and Procedure of the Pennsylvania Assembly, 1682–1776," *Pennsylvania Magazine of History and Biography*, 72, no. 3 (July 1948): 233.

49. Hermann Wellenreuther, "The Political Dilemma of the Quakers in Pennsylvania, 1681–1748," *Pennsylvania Magazine of History and Biography*, 94, no. 2 (April 1970): 136–37.

50. James T. Lemon, *The Best Poor Man's Country: A Geographical Study of Early Southeastern Pennsylvania* (New York: W. W. Norton, 1972), 25. Historian Michael W. Zuckerman asserts, "The politicians of the Middle Atlantic provinces operated in partisan environments unparalleled in America." Zuckerman, "Introduction," *Friends and Neighbors*, 5.

51. "Charter for the Province of Pennsylvania–1681," Avalon Project: Documents in Law, History and Diplomacy, accessed November 17, 2018, http://avalon.law.yale.edu/17th _century/pa01.asp.

52. Richard Alan Ryerson, "William Penn's Gentry Commonwealth: An Interpretation of the Constitutional History of Early Pennsylvania, 1681–1701," *Pennsylvania History*, 61, no. 4 (October 1994): 408.

53. John Smolenski observes, "Penn regarded the role of the Assembly as limited but not insignificant." Smolenski, *Friends and Strangers*, 69.

54. Leonard, "The Organization and Procedure of the Pennsylvania Assembly," 221. For instance, in 1695, the Assembly met in the Whitpan house on Front Street just below Walnut Street. The following year, it met in Samuel Carpenter's house. Watson, *Annals of Philadelphia and Pennsylvania*, 1:57.

55. Ryerson, "William Penn's Gentry Commonwealth," 410; Roney, *Governed by a Spirit of Opposition*, 6; Richard R. Beeman, *The Varieties of Political Experience in Eighteenth-Century America* (Philadelphia: University of Pennsylvania Press, 2004), 211.

56. Penn to James Logan, 8 July 1701, *Correspondence Between William Penn and James Logan, and Others, 1700–1750,* vol. 1 (Philadelphia: J. B. Lippincott, 1870), 56.

57. Oddly, the governor's council continued to exist, despite having no official role in government. Chester R. Young, "The Evolution of the Pennsylvania Assembly, 1682–1748," *Pennsylvania Magazine of History and Biography,* 35, no. 2 (April 1968): 149; Thomas Wendel, "The Keith–Lloyd Alliance: Factional and Coalition Politics in Colonial Pennsylvania," *Pennsylvania Magazine of History and Biography,* 92, no. 3 (July 1968): 292.

58. *Votes and Proceedings of the House of Representatives of the Province of Pennsylvania,* vol. 1: December 4, 1682–September 26, 1776, ed. Gertrude McKinney and Charles F. Hoban (Harrisburg, PA: State Printer, 1931), 311.

59. Watson, *Annals of Philadelphia and Pennsylvania,* 1:25. However, there were dangers, particularly from pirates and privateers who plied the Atlantic and occasionally sailed up the Delaware. For more information, see William M. Mervine, "Pirates and Privateers in the Delaware Bay and River," *Pennsylvania Magazine of History and Biography,* 32, no. 4 (1908): 459–70.

60. Watson, *Annals of Philadelphia and Pennsylvania,* 1: 97. Interestingly, Lowdon at one point owned one of the lots on which Independence Hall was later built. Clarence H. Browning, "The State House Yard, and Who Owned It First After William Penn," *Pennsylvania Magazine of History and Biography,* 40, no. 1 (1916): 98.

61. Watson, *Annals of Philadelphia and Pennsylvania,* 2:273.

62. Murphy, *William Penn,* 220. James T. Lemon asserts, "The significant achievements of Penn and his sons were the founding of Philadelphia and the establishment of several county towns that became the chief points of political, economic, and social interaction in the region." Lemon, *Best Poor Man's Country,* 26,

63. Elizabeth Milroy, *The Grid and the River: Philadelphia's Green Places, 1682–1876* (University Park: Pennsylvania State University Press, 2016), 4; Elizabeth Gray Kogen Spera, "Building for Business: The Impact of Commerce on the City Plan and Architecture of the City of Philadelphia, 1750–1800" (PhD diss., University of Pennsylvania, 1980), ix; Lemon, *Best Poor Man's Country,* 125.

64. Pencak, "Pennsylvania's Early Defense Policy," 7.

65. Watson, *Annals of Philadelphia and Pennsylvania,* 1:147–49. According to Watson, the Svensons' house was located just north of Gloria Dei (Old Swedes') Church on Swanson Street between Christian Street and Queen Street.

66. Gary B. Nash, "City Planning and Political Tension in the Seventeenth Century: The Case of Philadelphia," *Proceedings of the American Philosophical Society,* 112, no. 1 (February 1968): 59; John W. Reps, "William Penn and the Planning of Philadelphia," *Town Planning Review,* 27, no. 1 (April 1956): 31–32.

67. William Penn, *A Letter from William Penn, Proprietary and Governor of Pennsylvania in America, to the Committee of the Society of Freed Traders* (London: Andrew Sowle, 1683), 10.

68. According to historian Gary B. Nash, "William Penn believed that the success of the 'holy experiment' depended on an orderly pattern of taking up land, on economic regulation, and on firm lines of authority." Gary B. Nash, *The **Urban Crucible: Social Change, Political Consciousness and the Origins of the American Revolution*** (Cambridge, MA:

Harvard University Press, 1986), 3. See also Lemon, *Best Poor Man's Country*, 50; *The Charters of the Province of Pennsylvania and the City of Philadelphia* (Philadelphia: B. Franklin, 1744), 23; Murphy, *William Penn*, 5.

69. William Penn, "Instructions Given by Me," in *William Penn and the Founding of Pennsylvania: A Documentary History*, ed. Jean R. Soderlund (Philadelphia: University of Pennsylvania Press, 1983), 85.

70. William Penn, "Direction and Information to Such Persons as Are Inclined to America," *Pennsylvania Magazine of History and Biography*, 4, no. 3 (1880): 334.

71. Nancy M. Heinzen, *The Perfect Square: A History of Rittenhouse Square* (Philadelphia: Temple University Press, 2009), 9.

72. Hannah Benner Roach, "The Planting of Philadelphia: A Seventeenth-Century Real Estate Development: 2," *Pennsylvania Magazine of History and Biography*, 92, no. 2 (April 1968): 178.

73. William Penn, "A Further Account of the Province of Pennsylvania," in *Narratives of Early Pennsylvania, West New Jersey, and Delaware, 1630–1677*, ed. Albert Cook Myers (New York: Charles Scribner's Sons, 1912), 261, 269.

74. Penn's eldest son, John, was born in the house in January 1700, earning him the sobriquet "The American." Watson, *Annals of Philadelphia and Pennsylvania*, I:, 163.

75. Sachse, "Missive of Justus Falckner," 216; Oswald Sidensticker et al., "The Hermits of the Wissahickon," *Pennsylvania Magazine of History and Biography*, 11, no. 4 (January 1888): 427. As late as 1728, the hermits still lived along the Wissahickon. Anonymous, *Diary of a Voyage from Rotterdam to Philadelphia in 1728*, trans. Justus F. Sachse (Lancaster: Pennsylvania-German Society, 1909), 24.

76. Harry Kyriakodis and Joel Spivak, *Underground Philadelphia: From Caves and Canals to Tunnels and Transit* (Charleston, SC: History Press, 2019), 19.

77. Nash, "City Planning and Political Tension," 61.

78. Nash, "City Planning and Political Tension," 66.

79. Wendel, "The Keith–Lloyd Alliance," 291.

80. James Claypoole, who was the society's treasurer, boasted that his lot (on Walnut Street between First Street and Second Street) was "one of the [best] in the city." James Claypoole to Edward Claypoole, 2 October 1683, in *James Claypoole's Letter Book: London and Philadelphia, 1681–1684*, ed. Marion Balderston (San Marino, CA: Huntington Library, 1967), 223.

81. Corcoran, "William Penn and His Purchasers," 485; Nash, "City Planning and Political Tension," 62. See Hannah Benner Roach, "The Planting of Philadelphia: A Seventeenth-Century Real Estate Development 1" *Pennsylvania Magazine of History and Biography*, 92, no. 1 (January 1968): 43.

82. Roach, "Planting of Philadelphia:1," 47.

83. Nash, "City Planning and Political Tension," 62.

84. "Philadelphia in 1682," *Pennsylvania Magazine of History and Biography*, 13, no. 2 (July 1889): 228.

85. The Blue Anchor was hard to miss; it was directly in front of the area's main wharves. Roach, "Planting of Philadelphia:2," 182; Watson, *Annals of Philadelphia and Pennsylvania*, 1:44.

86. Watson, *Annals of Philadelphia and Pennsylvania*, 1:171.

87. "Philadelphia in 1682," 229.

88. William Penn, "Letter from William Penn to the Committee of the Free Society of Traders, 1683," in *Narratives of Early Pennsylvania, West Jersey, and Delaware, 1630–1707*, ed. Albert C. Myers (New York: Charles Scribner's Sons, 1912), 226.

89. Daniel B. Shumway, "A Rare Dutch Document Concerning the Province of Pennsylvania in the Seventeenth Century," *Pennsylvania Magazine of History and Biography*, 49, no. 2 (April 1925): 100.

90. Susan E. Klepp goes so far as to call the city's early history a "demographic disaster." "Demography in Early Philadelphia, 1690–1860," *Proceedings of the American Philosophical Society*, 133, no. 2 (June 1989): 95–98.

91. Gabriel Thomas, *An Historical and Geographical Account of the Province and County of Pennsilvania and of Weft New Jersey in America* (London: A. Baldwin, 1698), 36.

92. Susan E. Klepp, "Demography in Early Philadelphia," 93.

93. Quoted in Murphy, *William Penn*, 158.

94. Lemon, *Best Poor Man's Country*, 220. "To a considerable extent the growth of [Philadelphia] and the expansion of [its] economy during this period was dictated by the development of the hinterlands to which they were commercially linked." Nash, *Urban Crucible*, 33.

95. Dunn, "William Penn and the Selling of Pennsylvania," 327; Nash, *Quakers and Politics*, 56–57. Crucially, Thomas M. Doerflinger noted that Philadelphia's merchant community was far from homogeneous.See *A Vigorous Spirit of Enterprise: Merchants and Economic Development in Revolutionary Philadelphia* (New York: W. W. Norton, 1992), 15.

96. Marion V. Brewington, "Maritime Philadelphia, 1609–1837," *Pennsylvania Magazine of History and Biography*, 63, no. 2 (April 1939): 103.

97. Watson, *Annals of Philadelphia and Pennsylvania*, 1:93.

98. Brewington, "Maritime Philadelphia," 97.

99. *Penn, Letter from William Penn*, 10.

100. Thomas, *Historical and Geographical Account*, 38–39.

101. Benjamin Franklin, "A Modest Inquiry into the Nature and Necessity of a Paper Currency," in *Colonial Currency Reprints*, vol. 2, ed. Andrew McFarland Davis (Boston: John Wilson & Son, 1911), 338.

102. Nash, *Urban Crucible*, 64; Carl Bridenbaugh and Jessica Bridenbaugh, *Rebels and Gentlemen*, (New York: Reynal & Hitchcock, 1942), 13; Sam Bass Warner, *The Private City: Philadelphia in Three Periods of Its Growth*, 2nd ed. (Philadelphia: University of Pennsylvania Press, 1987), 6.

103. Curtis Nettles, "The Economic Relations of Boston, Philadelphia, and New York, 1680–1715," *Journal of Economic and Business History*, 3, no. 2 (February 1931): 209–11.

104. Penn had intended the east side of Front Street to be a common area and promenade for all city inhabitants. Watson, *Annals of Philadelphia and Pennsylvania*, 1:166–67.

105. *A Digest of the Ordinances of the Corporation of the City of Philadelphia and of the Acts of the Assembly Relating Thereto* (Philadelphia: J. Crissy, 1841), 419–20.

106. Penn to Logan, 1 October 1703, *Correspondence Between William Penn and James Logan*, 1:277; George Thomas, "To the Assembly Concerning the Bill for the Better

Raising of Money on the Inhabitants of Philadelphia," *Pennsylvania Archives*, 4th series, vol. 1: 1681–1747, ed. George Edward Reed (Harrisburg, PA: Wm. Stanley, 1900), 703.

107. Harry Kyriakodis, *Philadelphia's Lost Waterfront* (Charleston, SC: History Press, 2011), 129; Milroy, *Grid and the River*, 25.

108. Nash, *The Urban Crucible*, 18.

109. Thomas Lloyd, "The First Charter of the City of Philadelphia, 1691," *Pennsylvania Magazine of History and Biography*, 18, no. 4 (1894): 504. Curiously, this charter was lost for several decades until being discovered in 1887 among the papers of Clement Biddle, a Revolutionary War Patriot and Quaker who organized the city's "Quaker Blues," a volunteer regiment. Edward Allinson and Boies Penrose, *Philadelphia, 1681–1887: A History of Municipal Government* (Philadelphia: Allen, Lane & Scott, 1887), xlv.

110. Ernest S. Griffith, *History of American City Government: The Colonial Period* (New York: De Capo Press, 1972), 16–19.

111. Griffith, *History of American City Government*, 55.

112. *The Charters of the Province of Pennsylvania and the City of Philadelphia* (Philadelphia,: B. Franklin, 1744), 29.

113. Daniel Johnson, "'What Must Poor People Do?': Economic Protest and Plebeian Culture in Philadelphia, 1682–1754," *Pennsylvania History*, 79, no. 2 (Spring 2012): 121.

114. Allinson and Penrose, *Philadelphia, 1681–1887*,12.

115. Judith M. Diamondstone, "Philadelphia's Municipal Corporation, 1701–1776," *Pennsylvania Magazine of History and Biography*, 90, no. 2 (April 1966): 187–91. Quoting from the City Council's minutes from 1704 to 1776, John F. Watson noted that in 1714 Philadelphia's mayor expended his own funds in celebration of the proclamation of George I king of England. Watson, *Annals of Philadelphia and Pennsylvania*, 1:60.

116. Watson, *Annals of Philadelphia and Pennsylvania*, 1:59–60.

117. Benjamin L. Carp, *Rebels Rising: Cities and the American Revolution* (New York: Oxford University Press, 2007), 174.

118. Diamondstone, "Philadelphia's Municipal Corporation," 196.

119. Quoted in Watson, *Annals of Philadelphia and Pennsylvania*, 1:78.

120. Johnson, "'What Must Poor People Do?,'" 121.

121. Nettles, "The Economic Relations of Boston, Philadelphia, and New York," *Journal of Economic and Business History*, 3, no. 2 (February 1931): 198; Wendel, "The Keith–Lloyd Alliance," 295.

122. Allinson and Penrose, *Philadelphia, 1681–1887*, 28–29.

123. Watson, *Annals of Philadelphia and Pennsylvania*, 1:97.

124. Watson, *Annals of Philadelphia and Pennsylvania*, 1:356.

125. This building was located on the southwest corner of Third and Market (then called High) streets. Watson, *Annals of Philadelphia and Pennsylvania*, 1:360.

126. Howard M. Jenkins, "The Family of William Penn. 8: William Penn, Junior (Continued)," *Pennsylvania Magazine of History and Biography*, 21, no. 2 (1897): 145–46.

127. Deborah Mathias Gough, "The Roots of Episcopalian Authority Structures: The Church of England in Colonial Philadelphia," in Zuckerman, *Friends and Neighbors*, 92–94.

128. Watson, *Annals of Philadelphia and Pennsylvania*, 1:351

129. Allinson and Penrose, *Philadelphia, 1681–1887*, 37.

130. Susan E. Klepp, "Demography in Early Philadelphia," 95; Billy G. Smith, "Death and Life in a Colonial Immigrant City: A Demographic Analysis of Philadelphia," *Journal of Economic History*, 37, no. 4 (December 1977): 874.

131. Watson, *Annals of Philadelphia and Pennsylvania*, 1:38, 433–44, 495.

132. Howard W. Lloyd, ed., "Philadelphia in 1698," *Pennsylvania Magazine of History and Biography*, 18, no. 2 (1894): 247.

133. Smith, "Death and Life in a Colonial Immigrant City," 875.

134. "Philadelphia in 1682," *Pennsylvania Magazine of History and Biography*, 13, no. 2 (July 1889): 230.

135. Andreas Sandel, "Extracts from the Journal of Rev. Andreas Sandel, Pastor of 'Gloria Dei' Swedish Lutheran Church, 1702–1719," *Pennsylvania Magazine of History and Biography*, 30, no. 3 (1906): 298. There was apparently a significant outbreak of "the Barbados distemper" in 1699, which claimed several lives. Watson, *Annals of Philadelphia and Pennsylvania*, 2:370. In volume 1, Watson noted that in 1705, "the city of Philadelphia was visited by sickness in the spring." 96.

136. Watson, *Annals of Philadelphia and Pennsylvania*, 2:33.

137. Watson, *Annals of Philadelphia and Pennsylvania*, 1:96.

138. Chapter 104, *Statutes at Large of Pennsylvania from 1682–1700*, vol. 1, ed. Robert L. Cable (Harrisburg, PA: Legislative Reference Bureau, 2001), 206; *Philadelphia: A Chronological and Documentary History, 1615–1970*, ed. Adrienne Siegel (Dobbs Ferry, NY: Oceana Publications, 1975), 6. See also Charles R. Barker, "Philadelphia in the Late 'Forties," *Philadelphia History*, vol. 2 (Philadelphia: City History Society of Philadelphia, 1931), 258.

139. Built between 1698 and 1700, Gloria Dei (or Old Swedes' Episcopal Church) was the site of the first Lutheran ordination in the Western Hemisphere. Sandel, "Extracts from the Journal of Rev. Andreas Sandel," 292.

140. Andreas Sandel, "Extracts from the Journal of Rev. Andreas Sandel, Pastor of 'Gloria Dei' Swedish Lutheran Church, 1702–1719 (continued)," *Pennsylvania Magazine of History and Biography*, 30, no. 4 (1906): 448–49.

141. Watson, *Annals of Philadelphia and Pennsylvania*, 1:447.

142. Smolenski, *Friends and Strangers*, 9. According to historian Gary B. Nash, this was not unique to William Penn; he asserts that "the Quaker personality had two sides, one that emphasized control, hierarchy, and community and another that celebrated freedom, individualism, and nonconformity." Nash, *The Urban Crucible*, 31. Nor was he alone in making this observation; according to historian Susan S. Forbes, "The basic precept of Quakerism is the presence of an Inner Light within each individual, given by a merciful God who wished to present to man his means of salvation. But because of the individualistic, antinomian thrust of this theology soon disclosed a prospect of anarchy, early Quakers were impelled to emphasize the spiritual authority of the group." Susan S. Forbes, "Quaker Tribalism," in Zuckerman, *Friends and Neighbors*, 5.

143. Patrick Spero, "The Conojocular War: The Politics of Colonial Competition, 1732–1737," *Pennsylvania Magazine of History and Biography*, 136, no. 4 (October 2012): 375.

144. William Penn, "The Frame," *Minutes of the Provincial Council of Pennsylvania*, vol. 1 (Harrisburg, PA: Theophilus Penn, 1838), xxiii; Milroy, *Grid and the River*, 25; J. T. Jable, "Pennsylvania's Early Blue Laws: A Quaker Experiment in the Suppression of Sport and Amusements, 1682–1740," *Journal of Sport History*, 1, no. 2 (Fall 1974): 107.

145. Agnes Repplier, *Philadelphia: The Place and the People* (New York: Macmillan, 1904), 34.

146. Josiah G. Leach, "Colonial Mayors of Philadelphia," *Pennsylvania Magazine of History and Biography*, 18, no. 4 (1894): 424.

147. J. William Frost, "Pennsylvania Institutes Religious Liberty, 1682–1860," *Pennsylvania Magazine of History and Biography*, 112, no. 3 (July 1988): 324–25; Alan Tully, "Quaker Party and Policies: The Dynamics of Politics in Pre-Revolutionary Pennsylvania, 1730–1775," in *Power and Status: Officeholding in Colonial America*, ed. Bruce C. Daniels (Middletown, CT: Wesleyan University Press, 1986), 76–77; Alan Tully, *William Penn's Legacy: Politics and Social Structure in Provincial Pennsylvania, 1726–1755* (Baltimore: Johns Hopkins University Press, 1977), 145.

148. Pomfret, "First Purchasers of Pennsylvania," 149.

149. Sachse, "Missive of Justus Falckner," 218.

150. William Penn to his Son, 2 November 1700, *Pennsylvania Archives: Series 2, Papers Relating to Provincial Affairs in Pennsylvania, 1682–1750*, vol. 7, ed. John B. Linn and William H. Egle (Harrisburg, PA: Pennsylvania General Assembly, 1878), 12.

151. Soderlund, *Lenape Country*, 163.

152. Moreover, Penn himself had a history of expressing anti-Catholic sentiments, though this had moderated by 1685. Paul Douglas Newman, " 'Good Will to All Men . . . From the King on the Throne to the Beggar on the Dunghill': William Penn, the Roman Catholics, and Religious Toleration," *Pennsylvania History*, 61, no. 4 (October 1994): 457.

153. Penn to Logan, 29 February 1708. *Correspondence Between William Penn and James Logan*, vol. 2 (Philadelphia: J. B. Lippincott, 1872), 294.

154. Sachse, "Missive of Justus Falckner," 221.

155. Francis D. Pastorius, "Circumstantial Geographical Description of Pennsylvania," in *Narratives of Early Pennsylvania, West Jersey, and Delaware, 1630–1707*, ed. Albert C. Myers (New York: Charles Scribner's Sons, 1912), 381.

156. Smolenski, *Friends and Strangers*, 168; Forbes, "Quaker Tribalism," 150–51.

157. Nash, *Urban Crucible*, 30–31; J. William Frost, *A Perfect Freedom: Religious Liberty in Pennsylvania* (University Park: Pennsylvania State University Press, 1990), 19; Murphy, *William Penn*, 216–20; Jon Butler, "Notes and Documents: The Records of the First 'American' Denomination—The Keithians of Pennsylvania, 1694–1700," *Pennsylvania Magazine of History and Biography*, 120, no. 1/2 (January and April 1996): 90–91.

158. Beverly C. Tomek, *Slavery and Abolition in Pennsylvania* (Philadelphia: Temple University Press, 2021), 8–9; Jean R. Soderlund, "Black Importation and Migration into Southeastern Pennsylvania, 1682–1810," *Proceedings of the American Philosophical Society*, 133, no. 2 (June 1989): 144, 146; Pennypacker, "Settlement of Germantown," 25; Gary B. Nash, *Forging Freedom: The Formation of Philadelphia's Black Community, 1720–1840* (Cambridge, MA: Harvard University Press, 1988), 8; William H. Williams, *Slavery and Freedom in Delaware, 1639–1865* (Lanham, MD: SR Books, 1996), xii–xv.

159. In October 1683 James Claypoole wrote to his brother in London expressing unhappiness at the latter's failure to send "4 Blacks, viz., a man, a woman, a boy, a girl." Though Claypoole does not use the term "slaves," this is surely what he meant. Claypoole to Edward Claypoole, 2 October 1683, *James Claypoole's Letter Book*, 223.

160. According to Jean R. Soderlund, "Most of the Quakers who controlled Philadelphia Yearly Meeting before 1730 brought Black slaves from the West Indies and Africa to serve in their homes, shops, and fields." She goes on to note, "Early in the colonial period, before 1711, the majority of slave owners (as represented in the probate records) were merchants, professionals, and men who styled themselves gentlemen." Jean R. Soderlund, *Quakers and Slavery: A Divided Spirit* (Princeton, NJ: Princeton University Press, 1985), 54–63. For a discussion of the composition of Philadelphia's slave population, see Soderlund, "Black Importation," 147. According to historian Gary B. Nash, by the 1690s, nearly 7 percent of Philadelphia families enslaved Africans. Nash, *Urban Crucible*, 7. See also Tomek, *Slavery and Abolition*, 9.

161. Nicholas P. Wood and Jean R. Soderlund point out that Quaker leaders criticized the institution as early as the 1670s. Nicholas P. Wood and Jean R. Soderlund, "'To Friends and All Whom It May Concerne': William Southeby's Rediscovered 1696 Antislavery Protest," *Pennsylvania Magazine of History and Biography*, 141, no. 2 (April 2017): 180–81. However, according to Martha Paxson Grundy, "A few friends had begun speaking out against the evil of race-based chattel slavery as soon as they encountered it in the Caribbean in the 1650s." Martha Paxson Grundy, "David Ferris: Arguments Against Quaker Slaveholding," *Quaker History*, 103, no. 2 (Fall, 2014): 18. J. William Frost notes that while the Quakers did encounter slavery in the Caribbean in the 1650s, that encounter "is notable for one phenomenon: neglect of any mention of the institution with no great concern for the enslaved." J. William Frost, "Quaker Antislavery: From Dissidence to Sense of the Meeting," *Quaker History*, 103, no. 1 (Spring 2012): 13. Katherine Gerbner has asserted that many of these early antislavery Quakers (most notably George Fox) were "all operating under a worldview that fundamentally accepted slavery." Gerbner, "Antislavery in Print," 553. See also Brontë Short, "'It is a Terror . . . That men Should be Handled So in Pennsylvania.' Early Quaker Reasoning, Debate, and the Abolitionist Influence of the *Germantown Friends' Protest Against Slavery*." *Pennsylvania History*, 90, no. 1 (Winter, 2023): 105, and Tomek, *Slavery and Abolition*, 26–27.

162. Soderlund, *Quakers and Slavery*, 18; Jason Daniels, "Protest and Participation: Reconsidering the Quaker Slave Trade in Early Eighteenth-Century Philadelphia," *Pennsylvania History*, 85, no, 2 (Spring 2018): 245.

163. "Germantown Quaker Protest Against Slavery," Haverford College Special Collections, 990 B-R, accessed December 12, 2018, http://triptych.brynmawr.edu/cdm/compoundobject/collection/HC_QuakSlav/id/11.

164. The consensus is that Keith wrote this document, though Katherine Gerbner has argued that he merely facilitated its publication. Gerbner, "Antislavery in Print," 554–55.

165. Edwin Wolf 2nd, *Philadelphia: Portrait of an American City* (Philadelphia: Camino Books, 1990), 31; Soderlund, *Quakers and Slavery*, 18.

166. Sidensticker et al., "Hermits of the Wissahickon," 439–40.

167. Thomas E. Drake calls Southeby "the leading antislavery Friend of the day." Thomas E. Drake, "Cadwalader Morgan, an Early Antislavery Friend," *Bulletin of Friends' Historical Association*, 23, no. 2 (Autumn 1934): 97. See also Wood and Soderlund, "'To Friends,'" 178–79; Tomek, *Slavery and Abolition*, 31.

168. Cadwalader Morgan, "Quaker Protest Against Slavery, Merion (Pa.) 1696," *Quakers and Slavery, Haverford College*, accessed January 22, 2022, https://digitalcollections .tricolib.brynmawr.edu/object/hc135386; Daniels, "Protest and Participation," 245.

169. Watson, *Annals of Philadelphia and Pennsylvania*, 2:262; Henry J. Cadbury, ed., "Another Early Quaker Anti-Slavery Document." *Journal of Negro History*, 27, no. 2 (April 1942): 211. On the one hand, Thomas E. Drake celebrates the Philadelphia Yearly Meeting's "first official stand against slavery." Drake, "Cadwalader Morgan," 97. On the other hand, according to Jean R. Soderlund, the Meeting's agreement was unsatisfactory because "it had no teeth for discipling slave owners and traders." Soderlund, *Quakers and Slavery*, 19.

170. Darold D. Wax, "Negro Import Duties in Colonial Pennsylvania," *Pennsylvania Magazine of History and Biography*, 97, no. 1 (January 1973): 23–24; Daniels, "Protest and Participation," 243.

171. Daniels, "Protest and Participation," 255; Soderlund, *Quakers and Slavery*, 58.

172. Quoted in Darold D. Wax, "Quaker Merchants and the Slave Trade in Colonial Pennsylvania," *Pennsylvania Magazine of History and Biography*, 86, no. 2 (April 1962):156–57.

173. Watson, *Annals of Philadelphia and Pennsylvania*, 2:263.

174. Wax, "Negro Import Duties," 23–24; Wood and Soderlund, "'To Friends,'" 186.

175. Soderlund, "Black Importation," 145. See also Tomek, *Slavery and Abolition*, 31–33.

176. Lloyd, "Philadelphia in 1698," 248. Historian James T. Lemon has validated this assertion, concluding that "if the 'holy experiment' did not bring bounty for all, it allowed many to improve their material lot." Lemon, *Best Poor Man's Country*, 13. See also Nash, *Urban Crucible*, 11.

Chapter 3

1. Daniel Johnson, "'What Must Poor People Do?': Economic Protest and Plebeian Culture in Philadelphia, 1682–1754," *Pennsylvania History*, 79, no. 2 (Spring 2012): 121; Gary B. Nash, *Quakers and Politics: Pennsylvania, 1681–1726* (Boston: Northeastern University Press, 1993), 63; Gary B. Nash, *The Urban Crucible: Social Change, Political Consciousness and the Origins of the American Revolution* (Cambridge, MA: Harvard University Press, 1986), 29.

2. Anonymous, *Diary of a Voyage from Rotterdam to Philadelphia in 1728*, trans. Justus F. Sachse (Lancaster: Pennsylvania-German Society, 1909), 23.

3. Katie A. Moore, "America's First Economic Stimulus Package: Paper Money and the Body Politic in Colonial Pennsylvania, 1715–1730," *Pennsylvania History*, 83, no. 4 (Autumn 2016): 543–34. There was some basis for Logan's fears; after all, when the first land-bank currency was issued in 1723, it was pegged at £1.34 Pennsylvania to £1 sterling, but by 1739 it had depreciated to £1.7 Pennsylvania to £1 sterling. Theodore Thayer, "The Land-Bank System in the American Colonies," *Journal of Economic History*, 13, no. 2

(Spring 1953): 151. Benjamin Franklin recalled, "About this time there was a cry among the people for more paper money. . . . The wealthy inhabitants oppos'd any addition, being against all paper currency, from an apprehension that it would depreciate, as it had done in New England, to the prejudice of all creditors." Benjamin Franklin, *The Autobiography of Benjamin Franklin* (New York: Houghton Mifflin, 1906), 67. See also Mary M. Schweitzer, *Custom and Contract: Household, Government, and the Economy in Colonial Pennsylvania* (New York: Columbia University Press, 1987), 125; Ronald Schultz, "The Small-Producer Tradition and the Moral Origins of Artisan Radicalism in Philadelphia, 1720–1810," *Past and Present*, 127, no. 1 (May 1990): 96–98.

4. Hermann Wellenreuther, "The Quest for Harmony in a Turbulent World: The Principle of 'Love and Unity' in Colonial Pennsylvania Politics," *Pennsylvania Magazine of History and Biography*, 107, no. 4 (October 1983): 550.

5. Gottlieb Mittelberger, *Journey to Pennsylvania in the Year 1750*, trans. Carl T. Eben (Philadelphia: John Jos. McVey, 1898), 88. See also Thayer, "Land-Bank System," 145–55; James H. Hutson, "Benjamin Franklin and Pennsylvania Politics, 1751–1755: A Reappraisal," *Pennsylvania Magazine of History and Biography*, 93, no. 3 (July 1969): 325–27.

6. Stephen Brobeck, "Revolutionary Change in Colonial Philadelphia: The Brief Life of the Proprietary Gentry," *William and Mary Quarterly*, 33, no. 3 (July 1976): 419.

7. Benjamin H. Newcomb, "Effects of the Stamp Act on Colonial Pennsylvania Politics," *William and Mary Quarterly*, 23, no. 2 (April 1966): 259.

8. Alan Tully, "Quaker Party and Policies: The Dynamics of Politics in Pre-Revolutionary Pennsylvania, 1730–1775," in *Power and Status: Officeholding in Colonial America*, ed. Bruce C. Daniels (Middletown, CT: Wesleyan University Press, 1986), 101.

9. Rosalind L. Branning, *Pennsylvania Constitutional Development* (Pittsburgh: University of Pittsburgh Press, 1960), 10–11; Richard R. Beeman, *The Varieties of Political Experience in Eighteenth-Century America* (Philadelphia: University of Pennsylvania Press, 2004), 208–9.

10. Wellenreuther, "Quest for Harmony," 551.

11. Newcomb, "Effects of the Stamp Act," 266.

12. Joan de Lourdes Leonard, "Elections in Colonial Pennsylvania," *William and Mary Quarterly*, 11, no. 3 (July 1954): 385; Gary B. Nash, "The Transformation of Urban Politics, 1700–1765," *Journal of American History*, 60, no. 3 (December 1973): 606.

13. John F. Watson, *Annals of Philadelphia and Pennsylvania in the Olden Times*, vol. 1 (Philadelphia: Elijah Thomas, 1857), 79. In a later volume, Watson noted that, over a three-day period leading up to this election, Philadelphians consumed 4,500 gallons of beer. John F. Watson, *Annals of Philadelphia and Pennsylvania in the Olden Times*, vol. 3 (Philadelphia: Edwin S. Stuart, 1884), 344.

14. Alan Tully, "Englishmen and Germans: National-Group Contact in Colonial Pennsylvania, 1700–1755," *Pennsylvania History*, 45, no. 3 (July 1978): 242.

15. William T. Parsons, "The Bloody Election of 1742," *Pennsylvania History*, 36, no. 3 (July 1969): 293; Beeman, *Varieties of Political Experience*, 220.

16. William Thomas Johnson, "Some Aspects of the Relations of the Government and German Settlers in Colonial Pennsylvania, 1683–1754 (Part One)," *Pennsylvania History*, 11, no. 2 (April 1944): 101–2.

17. Parsons, "Bloody Election of 1742," 298.

18. Marc L. Harris, "What Politeness Demanded: Ethnic Omissions in Franklin's *Autobiography*," *Pennsylvania History*, 61, no. 3 (July 1994): 289; Gary B. Nash and Billy G. Smith, "The Population of Eighteenth-Century Philadelphia," *Pennsylvania Magazine of History and Biography*, 99, no. 3 (July 1975): 366; Aaron Sullivan, "'That Charity Which Begins at Home': Ethnic Societies and Benevolence in Eighteenth-Century Philadelphia," *Pennsylvania Magazine of History and Biography*, 134, no. 4 (October 2010): 310.

19. Peter Kalm, *Peter Kalm's Travels in North America: The English Version of 1770*, ed. Adolph B. Benson (New York: Dover Publications, 1964), 32.

20. Susan E. Klepp, "Demography in Early Philadelphia, 1690–1860," *Proceedings of the American Philosophical Society*, 133, no. 2 (June 1989): 95.

21. James T. Lemon, "Urbanization and the Development of Eighteenth-Century Southeastern Pennsylvania," *William and Mary Quarterly*, 24, no. 4 (October 1967): 529; Frederick B. Tolles, *Meeting House and Counting House: The Quaker Merchants of Colonial Philadelphia, 1682–1763* (New York: W. W. Norton, 1848), 19.

22. Klepp, "Demography in Early Philadelphia," 96; Susan E. Klepp, *Revolutionary Conceptions: Women, Fertility, and Family Limitation in America, 1760–1820* (Chapel Hill: University of North Carolina Press, 2009), 26.

23. Charles E. Clark and Charles E. Wetherell, "The Measure of Maturity: The *Pennsylvania Gazette*, 1728–1765," *William and Mary Quarterly*, 46, no. 2 (April 1989): 286, 292. Joan de Lourdes Leonard, "The Organization and Procedure of the Pennsylvania Assembly, 1682–1776. 2: The Legislative Process," *Pennsylvania Magazine of History and Biography*, 72, no. 4 (October 1948): 378. This is further reinforced by Fanny Salter's recollection that her grandfather, who had lived in Philadelphia during this time, later claimed "he knew not only every gentleman in town, but every gentleman's Black servant, and dog." "Fanny Salter's Reminiscences of Colonial Days in Philadelphia," *Pennsylvania Magazine of History and Biography*, 40, no. 2 (1916): 187.

24. Hutson, "Benjamin Franklin and Pennsylvania Politics," 307.

25. John J. Zimmerman, "Benjamin Franklin and the Quaker Party, 1755–1756," *William and Mary Quarterly*, 17, no. 1 (July 1960): 296. James H. Hutson describes Franklin as an "independent," but he apparently means only that during this period, Franklin did not consistently affiliate with either political party. Hutson, "Benjamin Franklin and Pennsylvania Politics," 304. Alan Tully notes that Franklin "was a Quaker ally on most questions." Tully, "Englishmen and Germans," 246. In his autobiography, Franklin recalled, "It was thought by some of my friends that, by [advocating for colonial defense], I should offend [the Quakers], and thereby lose my interest in the Assembly of the province, where they formed a great majority." Franklin, *Autobiography*, 118.

26. Marianne S. Wokeck, "German and Irish Immigration to Colonial Philadelphia," *Proceedings of the American Philosophical Society*, 133, no. 2 (June 1989): 132, and Donald E. Harpster, "Americanization of the Philadelphia German Reformed Community in the Era of the Revolution, 1775–1801," *Pennsylvania History*, 90, no. 1 (Winter 2023): 2. Alan Tully points out that the constant influx of newly arrived immigrants in the city likely fueled Philadelphians' prejudices against Germans, noting, "When members of Philadelphia's elite looked westward, they saw not the hard-working apolitical German farmer that

their country counterparts saw the immigrant become, but the unpropertied, strange, and unassimilated refuge from the Rhineland who had just stepped off the boat." Tully, "Englishmen and Germans," 248.

27. Farley Grubb, "The Market Structure of Shipping German Immigrants to Colonial America," *Pennsylvania Magazine of History and Biography*, 111, no. 1 (January 1987): 28; John B. Frantz, "Franklin and the Pennsylvania Germans," *Pennsylvania History*, 65, no. 1 (Winter 1998): 21; Klepp, "Demography in Early Philadelphia," 95; Harris, "What Politeness Demanded," 289.

28. Wokeck, "German and Irish Immigration," 129; Michael Bradley McCoy, "Absconding Servants, Anxious Germans, and Angry Sailors: Working People and the Making of the Philadelphia Election Riot of 1742," *Pennsylvania History*, 74, no. 1 (Autumn 2007): 438.

29. Farley Grubb, "Redemptioner Immigration to Pennsylvania: Evidence on Contract Choice and Profitability," *Journal of Economic History*, 46, no. 2 (June 1986): 409; Kalm, *Peter Kalm's Travels*, 16; Otto Pollak, "German Immigrant Problems in Eighteenth Century Pennsylvania as Reflected in Trouble Advertisements," *American Sociological Review*, 8, no. 6 (December 1943): 675–76; Mittelberger, *Journey to Pennsylvania*," 37. On the nature of redemption, see Farley Grubb, "The Auction of Redemptioner Servants, 1771–1804: An Economic Analysis," *Journal of Economic History*, 48, no. 3 (September 1988): 584; Robert O. Heavner, "Indentured Servitude: The Philadelphia Market, 1771–1773," *Journal of Economic History*, 38, no. 3 (September 1978): 703.

30. Quoted in Robert Proud, *The Hiftory of Pennsylvania, in North America*, vol. 2 (Philadelphia: Zachariah Poulson, 1798), 100.

31. William Beidelman, *The Story of the Pennsylvania Germans: Embracing an Account of their Origin, Their History, and Their Dialect* (Easton, PA: Express Book Print, 1898), 52.

32. Watson, *Annals of Philadelphia and Pennsylvania*, II259; Tully, "Englishmen and Germans," 247.

33. Johnson, "Some Aspects," 99–100; Wolfgang Splitter, "The Germans in Pennsylvania, 1758–1790: A Quantitative Analysis," *Pennsylvania Magazine of History and Biography*, 122, no. 1/2 (January–April 1998): 47; Brontë Short, "'It is a Terror . . . That Men Should be Handled So in Pennsylvania': Early Quaker Reasoning, Debate, and the Abolitionist Influence of the *Germantown Friends' Protest Against Slavery*," *Pennsylvania History*, 90, no. 1 (Winter, 2023): 105; Peter Brock, *Pioneers of the Peaceable Kingdom: The Quaker Peace Testimony from the Colonial Era to the First World War* (Princeton, NJ: Princeton University Press, 1968), 118; Beeman, *Varieties of Political Experience*, 206. Crucially, not all Germans allied with the Quakers; while those of the Pietistic sects tended to support the Quakers, Lutherans and Reformed Germans often supported the Proprietary Party. Robert Daiutolo Jr., "The Role of Quakers in Indian Affairs During the French and Indian War," *Quaker History*, 77, no. 1 (Spring 1988): 2; Richard Alan Ryerson, "Portrait of a Colonial Oligarchy: The Quaker Elite in the Pennsylvania Assembly, 1729–1776," in *Power and Status: Officeholding in Colonial America*, ed. Bruce C. Daniels (Middletown, CT: Wesleyan University Press, 1986), 108.

34. Frantz, "Franklin and the Pennsylvania Germans," 23.

35. Parsons, "Bloody Election of 1742," 292; and Hermann Wellenreuther, "The Political Dilemma of the Quakers in Pennsylvania, 1681–1748," *Pennsylvania Magazine of History and Biography*, 94, no. 2 (April 1970): 157; Hutson, "Benjamin Franklin and

Pennsylvania Politics," 306. Some of Franklin's allies suggested going even further by suppressing the printing of German-language books in Pennsylvania and by preventing German speakers from holding office unless they and their children could speak English "intelligibly." Whitfield J. Bell, "Benjamin Franklin and the German Charity Schools," *Proceedings of the American Philosophical Society*, 99, no. 6 (December 1955): 381.

36. Jared Sparks, Introduction to *Plain Truth: Or, Serious Considerations on the Present State of the City of Philadelphia and Province of Pennsylvania*, in *The Works of Benjamin Franklin*, vol. 3, ed. Jared Sparks (Chicago: Townsend Mac, 1882), 3.

37. Benjamin Franklin, "Observations Concerning the Increase of Mankind, 1751," in *Observations on the Late and Present Conduct of the French, With Regard to Their Encroachments Upon the British Colonies in North America*, ed. William Clarke (Boston: William Clarke, 1755), 53.

38. Beeman, *Varieties of Political Experience*, 244. Historian Erika Lee cites Franklin's behavior as the genesis of the pernicious "they keep coming" myth about immigrants to the United States. This myth asserts that "immigration is nothing less than a hostile invasion of the nation" and accounts for many of the nativist and racist immigration laws the United States would implement in the nineteenth and twentieth centuries that would in turn shape Philadelphia's demographic character. Erika Lee, "Immigration," in *Myth America: Historians Take on the Biggest Legends and Lies About Our Past*, ed. Kevin M. Kruse and Julian E. Zelizer (New York: Basic Books, 2022), 57.

39. Wokeck, "German and Irish Immigration," 128; Marianne S. Wokeck, "Irish Immigration to the Delaware Valley before the American Revolution," *Proceedings of the Irish Academy: Archeology, Culture, History, Literature*, 98C, no. 5 (1996): 120.

40. Wokeck, "German and Irish Immigration," 141; Wokeck, "Irish Immigration to the Delaware Valley," 103.

41. Quoted in T. P. Meyer, "The Germans of Pennsylvania: Their Coming and Conflicts with the Irish," *Pennsylvania-German: A Popular Magazine of Biography, History, Genealogy, Folklore, Literature, etc.*, 11 (1910): 44. This sentiment was hardly universal; in 1729, Franklin's *Pennsylvania Gazette* decried the "Disrespect and Aversion . . . [that the Irish] every where meet among the inhabitants of the Plantations, and the Hardships they must necessarily undergo before they can be well settled." "Affairs of Ireland," *Pennsylvania Gazette*, November 20, 1729.

42. Thomas Wendel, "The Keith–Lloyd Alliance: Factional and Coalition Politics in Colonial Pennsylvania," *Pennsylvania Magazine of History and Biography*, 92 no. 3 (July 1968): 292–93; Thomas M. Doerflinger, "Commercial Specialization in Philadelphia's Merchant Community, 1750–1791," *Business History Review*, 57, no. 1 (Spring 1983): 215.

43. Brobeck, "Revolutionary Change," 421.

44. Wokeck, "Irish Immigration to the Delaware Valley," 109, 114.

45. Randall H. Balmer and John R. Fitzmier, *The Presbyterians* (Westport, CT: Greenwood Press, 1993), 194.

46. "The State of Religion in America: Report of Bishop Challoner of the London District to Rome in 1756," *American Catholic Historical Researches*, 13, no. 1 (January 1896): 35.

47. Benjamin Bankhurst, "A Looking-Glass for Presbyterians: Recasting a Prejudice in Late Colonial Pennsylvania," *Pennsylvania Magazine of History and Biography*, 133, no 4

(October 2009): 333–34; Joseph J. Casino, "Anti-Popery in Colonial Pennsylvania," *Pennsylvania Magazine of History and Biography*, 105, no. 3 (July 1981): 296.

48. "Address to the German Protestants—1754," *Pennsylvania Archives*: Series 2, vol. 2, ed. John B. Linn and Wm. H. Egle (Harrisburg, PA: E. K. Meyers, 1890), 592.

49. Casino, "Anti-Popery," 294–95.

50. Franklin, *Plain Truth*, 8, 19.

51. Wayland F. Dunaway, "The French Racial Strain in Colonial Pennsylvania," *Pennsylvania Magazine of History and Biography*, 53, no. 4 (1929), 331.

52. Abraham S. Wolf Rosenbach, "Notes on the First Settlement of Jews in Pennsylvania, 1655–1703," *Publications of the American Jewish Historical Society*, no. 5 (1897): 191.

53. Toni Pitock, "Commerce and Community: Philadelphia's Early Jewish Settlers, 1736–1776," *Pennsylvania Magazine of History and Biography*, 140, no. 3 (October 2016): 272; William A. Pencak, "Jews and Anti-Semitism in Early Pennsylvania," *Pennsylvania Magazine of History and Biography*, 126, no. 3 (July 2002): 369.

54. Pencak, "Jews and Anti-Semitism," 371; Edwin Wolf 2nd and Maxwell Whiteman, *The History of the Jews of Philadelphia: From Colonial Times to the Age of Jackson* (Philadelphia: Jewish Publication Society of America, 1956), 14.

55. In fact, the appearance of a Spanish privateer in the Delaware River in 1744 is, according to Jared Sparks, the impetus behind Franklin's *Plain Truth*. Sparks, *Works of Benjamin Franklin*, 3:1.

56. Traveling through the region in 1759 and 1760, English clergyman Andrew Burnaby noted that the battery "is in a state of decay." Andrew Burnaby, *Burnaby's Travels Through America: Reprinted from the Third Edition of 1798* (New York: A. Wessels, 1904), 90.

57. William A. Pencak and Christian B. Keller, "Wars in Pennsylvania, 1731–1748," in *Pennsylvania: A Military History*, ed. William A. Pencak, Christian B. Keller, and Barbara A. Gannon (Yardley, PA: Westholme, 2016), 13–14; Tolles, *Meeting House*, 24.

58. Quoted in Proud, *Hiftory of Pennsylvania*, 100. See also Beeman, *Varieties of Political Experience*, 205.

59. Anonymous, *Diary of a Voyage*, 21–22; John F. Watson, *Annals of Philadelphia and Pennsylvania, in the Olden Times*, vol. 2 (Philadelphia: Edwin S. Stuart, 1891), 34; and Colin G. Calloway, *"The Chiefs Now in This City": Indians and the Urban Frontier in Early America* (New York: Oxford University Press, 2021), 4.

60. There were still conflicts and periodic outbreaks of violence, including an instance in 1728 when two white settlers killed a Native; these men were later hanged for the crime. Anonymous, *Diary of a Voyage*, 21. In addition, James H. Merrell asserts that the transformation in European-Native relations in Pennsylvania happened in the late 1720s. James H. Merrell, *Into the American Woods: Negotiators on the Pennsylvania Frontier* (New York: W. W. Norton, 1999), 36.

61. Patrick Spero, "The Conojocular War: The Politics of Colonial Competition, 1732–1737," *Pennsylvania Magazine of History and Biography*, 136, no. 4 (October 2012): 397.

62. Francis Jennings, "The Scandalous Indian Policy of William Penn's Sons: Deeds and Documents of the Walking Purchase," *Pennsylvania History*, 37, no. 1 (January 1970): 22–25.

63. Merrell, *Into the American Woods*, 36.

64. The change was not dramatic or immediate: as late as 1750, it was not uncommon for Native groups to come into Philadelphia to trade or to meet with the colony's deputy governor. Mittelberger, *Journey to Pennsylvania*, 84.

65. According to Gottlieb Mittelberger, who visited Philadelphia in 1750, the city was home to two of the colony's four printing offices (the others being in Germantown and Lancaster). This is almost surely inaccurate, as he claimed that two of the four (one in Philadelphia and one in Germantown) were German-language publishers. Were this the case, it would make Benjamin Franklin the only English-language printer in Philadelphia. Mittelberger, *Journey to Pennsylvania*, 101.

66. Burnaby, *Burnaby's Travels*, 96.

67. Edwin Wolf 2nd, *Philadelphia: Portrait of an American City* (Philadelphia: Camino Books, 1990), 44.

68. Hutson, "Benjamin Franklin and Pennsylvania Politics," 307–8; Ann Uhry Abrams, "Benjamin West's Documentation of Colonial History: William Penn's Treaty with the Indians," *Art Bulletin*, 64, no. 1 (March 1982): 64. Historian G. B. Warden went so far as to call the Academy of Pennsylvania a "training ground for younger Proprietary men" under the provostship of the Reverend Dr. William Smith. G. B. Warden, "The Proprietary Group in Pennsylvania, 1754–1764," *William and Mary Quarterly*, 21, no. 3 (July 1964): 374.

69. Harold E. Taussig, "Deism in Philadelphia During the Age of Franklin," *Pennsylvania History*, 37, no. 3 (July 1970): 219.

70. Brooke Hindle, "The Quaker Background and Science in Colonial Philadelphia," *Isis*, 46, no. 3 (September 1955): 246.

71. Carl Bridenbaugh and Jessica Bridenbaugh, *Rebels and Gentlemen: Philadelphia in the Age of Franklin* (New York: Reynal & Hitchcock, 1942), 19.

72. William Seward, *Journal of a Voyage from Savannah to Philadelphia, and from Philadelphia to England* (London: J. Oswald, 1740), 6.

73. Franklin, *Autobiography*, 110.

74. Martin E. Lodge, "The Crisis of the Churches in the Middle Colonies, 1720–1750," *Pennsylvania Magazine of History and Biography*, 95, no. 2 (April 1971), 199.

75. Mittelberger, *Journey to Pennsylvania*, 32. Nor was Mittelberger the only one to raise this concern: as early as 1720, the Reverend John Philip Boehm complained of the religious independence of Philadelphia's inhabitants. See Boehm to the Classis of Amsterdam, 12 November 1730, in *Life and Letters of the Reverend John Philip Boehm*, ed. William J. Hinke (Philadelphia: Sunday School Board of the Reformed Church of the United States, 1916), 205. In 1731, the Reverend William Beckett of Lewes, Delaware, went so far as to condemn Philadelphia as "the greatest sink of Quakerism and Infidelity in all of English America." See Beckett to Humphreys, 7 February 1731, in *Calendar of Letters from Canada, Newfoundland, Pennsylvania, Barbados, and the Bahamas, 1721–1793, Preserved at the United Society for the Propagation of the Gospel* (London: Swift, 1972), 76. Despite this hyperbole, Pennsylvania was hardly the religious free-for-all that these men claimed; Mittelberger himself reported the fact that retailers who conducted business on the Sabbath were fined for doing so under a law passed in 1749.

76. Burnaby, *Burnaby's Travels*, 104; Mittelberger, *Journey to Pennsylvania*, 56. According to Alexander Graydon, who grew up in Philadelphia during this period, the horses

"were kept in the Widow Nichols' stables, which, from her house (the Indian Queen, at the corner of Market Street), extended, perhaps, two-thirds or more, of the way to Chestnut Street." Alexander Graydon, *Memoirs of a Life Chiefly Passed in Pennsylvania within the Last Sixty Years* (Edinburgh, UK: William Blackwood, 1822), 36. Watson, *Annals of Philadelphia and Pennsylvania*, 1:277–79. See also Eric Foner, *Tom Paine and Revolutionary America* (New York: Oxford University Press, 1977), 50; Clare A. Lyons, *Sex Among the Rabble: An Intimate History of Gender and Power in the Age of Revolution, Philadelphia, 1730–1830* (Chapel Hill: University of North Carolina Press, 2006), 1.

77. "To The Printer of the *GAZETTE*," *Pennsylvania Gazette*, February 8, 1733. John F. Watson claimed that in 1728, 224,500 gallons of rum were imported into Philadelphia, an astonishing amount of alcohol given that the city and surrounding area contained fewer than ten thousand people. Watson, *Annals of Philadelphia and Pennsylvania*, 2:415. William Moraley offers a detailed description of the various alcoholic drinks available in Philadelphia in 1729 in *The Infortunate: The Voyage and Adventures of William Moraley, an Indentured Servant*, ed. Susan E. Klepp and Billy G. Smith (University Park: Pennsylvania State University Press, 1992), 104.

78. Moraley, *Infortunate*, 68. In his visit to the city, William Black described the centrality of drinking to everyday interactions; see William Black, "Journal of William Black, 1744 (continued)," ed. R. Alonzo Brock, *Pennsylvania Magazine of History and Biography*, 1, no. 3 (1877): 244–46, and William Black, "Journal of William Black, 1744 (continued)," ed. R. Alonzo Brock, *Pennsylvania Magazine of History and Biography*, 1, no. 4 (1877), 404–5.

79. Watson, *Annals of Philadelphia and Pennsylvania*, 1:277.

80. J. T. Jable, "Pennsylvania's Early Blue Laws: A Quaker Experiment in the Suppression of Sport and Amusements, 1682–1740," *Journal of Sport History*, 1, no. 2 (Fall 1974): 111; Lyons, *Sex Among the Rabble*, 83.

81. Lyons, *Sex Among the Rabble*, 74.

82. Lyons, *Sex Among the Rabble*, 31–32.

83. Jean R. Soderlund, "Women's Authority in Pennsylvania and New Jersey Quaker Meetings, 1680–1760," *William and Mary Quarterly*, 44, no. 4 (October 1987): 736.

84. Lyons, *Sex Among the Rabble*, 213.

85. Burnaby, *Burnaby's Travels*, 97, 117, 140; Johann David Schoepf, *Travels in the Confederation* (Philadelphia: William J. Campbell, 1911), 97.

86. Graydon, *Memoirs of a Life*, 53; Watson, *Annals of Philadelphia and Pennsylvania*, 1:170.

87. Watson, *Annals of Philadelphia and Pennsylvania*, 1:278–79; and Rebecca H. Davis, "Old Philadelphia," *Harper's New Monthly Magazine*, 52, no. 311 (April 1876): 717.

88. Advertisement, *Pennsylvania Gazette*, October 25, 1744; Elizabeth Drinker, *The Diary of Elizabeth Drinker: The Life Cycle of an Eighteenth-Century Woman*, ed. Elaine Forman Crane (Boston: Northeastern University Press, 1994), 12; Watson, *Annals of Philadelphia and Pennsylvania*, 2:482–83; William S. Dye Jr., "Pennsylvania Versus the Theatre," *Pennsylvania Magazine of History and Biography*, 55, no. 4 (1931): 352.

89. Mittelberger, *Journey to Pennsylvania*, 120; Watson, *Annals of Philadelphia and Pennsylvania*, 1:174.

90. "Fanny Salter's Reminiscences," 187; Watson, *Annals of Philadelphia and Pennsylvania*, 1:174. Nor was Salter's grandfather unusual in this regard; several visitors to Philadelphia during the eighteenth century described Philadelphians' habit of sitting on small benches outside their houses. See François-Jean de Chastellux, *Travels in North America in the Years 1780–81–82*, trans. George Grieve (New York, 1828), 79; Edward D. Seeber, ed. and trans., *On the Threshold of Liberty: Journal of a Frenchman's Tour of the American Colonies in 1777* (Bloomington: Indiana University Press, 1959), 20; and J. P. Brissot de Warville, *New Travels in the United States of America, 1788*, ed. Durand Echeverria (Cambridge, MA: Harvard University Press, 1964), 254.

91. James Birket, *Some Cursory Remarks Made by James Birket in His Voyage to North America, 1750–1751* (New Haven, CT: Yale University Press, 1916), 63, and Adam Gordon, "Journal of Lord Adam Gordon," in *Travels in the American Colonies*, ed. Newton D. Mereness (New York: Macmillan, 1916), 410.

92. John Adams, Diary, 8 September 1774, Founders Online, National Archives, accessed August 13, 2019, https://founders.archives.gov/documents/Adams/01-02-02 -0004-0006-0009.

93. John W. Jordan, ed., "A Description of the State-House, Philadelphia, in 1774," *Pennsylvania Magazine of History and Biography*, 23, no. 4 (1899): 418. See also Charlene Mires, *Independence Hall in American Memory* (Philadelphia: University of Pennsylvania Press, 2002), 12.

94. "Behind each house is a little court or garden, where usually are the necessaries." Schoepf, *Travels in the Confederation*, 60; Sharon V. Salinger, "Spaces, Inside and Outside, in Eighteenth-Century Philadelphia," *Journal of Interdisciplinary History*, 26, no. 1 (Summer 1995): 2.

95. Edward M. Riley, "Franklin's Home," *Transactions of the American Philosophical Society*, 43, no. 1 (1953): 148–49; Watson, *Annals of Philadelphia and Pennsylvania*, 1:163; Schultz, "Small-Producer Tradition," 89; Carole Shammas, "The Space Problem in Early United States Cities," *William and Mary Quarterly*, 57, no. 3 (July 2002): 528.

96. Several visitors remarked on this. Birket, *Some Cursory Remarks*, 64. Thomas Pownall, who later served as governor of Massachusetts Bay, predicted Philadelphia would never stretch from river to river. "Governor Thomas Pownall's Description of the Streets and the Main Roads about Philadelphia, 1754," *Pennsylvania Magazine of History and Biography*, 18, no. 2 (1894), 211.

97. According to John F. Watson, the number of houses in Northern Liberties grew nearly ninefold between 1749 and 1769. Watson, *Annals of Philadelphia and Pennsylvania*, 3:239. The fact that the Schuylkill had many large rocks in it prevented ships from sailing up it, thereby making land along its banks less desirable and retarding growth. Samuel Guldin, "Diary of the Rev. Samuel Guldin, Relating to His Journey to Pennsylvania, June to September 1710 (continued)," ed. William J. Hinke, *Journal of the Presbyterian Historical Society*, 14, no. 2 (June 1930): 68. Peter Kalm also noted these impediments to development, writing, "The cataracts . . .of the Schuylkill at some distance from Philadelphia make [this river] useless in regard to the conveyance of goods either from or to Philadelphia." Kalm, *Peter Kalm's Travels*, 27.

98. Watson, *Annals of Philadelphia and Pennsylvania*, 1:231; Franklin, *Autobiography*, 38According to Anthony Johnson, whom Watson interviewed for his *Annals*, "a large bear came across the road in daytime ... he has seen an abundance of wild turkeys and has often heard the wolves howl at night near his father's house." Watson, *Annals of Philadelphia and Pennsylvania*, 2:35.

99. John Daly and Allen Weinberg, *Genealogy of Philadelphia County Subdivisions*, 2nd ed. (Philadelphia: Philadelphia Department of Records, 1966), 56–57.

100. Salinger, "Spaces," 9. In his *Annals*, John Watson prints a 1749 count of the total number of houses in each ward; it shows Mulberry as the highest (488), followed by Dock (245) and then Middle (238). The rest have 200 or fewer houses. Watson, *Annals of Philadelphia and Pennsylvania*, 1:236.

101. Judith M. Diamondstone, "Philadelphia's Municipal Corporation, 1701–1776," *Pennsylvania Magazine of History and Biography*, 90, no. 2 (April 1966): 196–97.

102. Carole Shammas, "The Female Social Structure of Philadelphia in 1775," *Pennsylvania Magazine of History and Biography*, 107, no. 1 (January 1983): 70; Jessica Chopin Roney, *Governed by a Spirit of Opposition: The Origins of American Political Practice in Colonial Philadelphia* (Baltimore: Johns Hopkins University Press, 2014), 3.

103. Diamondstone, "Philadelphia's Municipal Corporation," 190.

104. Watson, *Annals of Philadelphia and Pennsylvania*, 1:383. The battery constructed south of the city in the late 1740s was financed by a lottery, and there was a lottery the following year to finance street paving. Franklin, *Autobiography*, 120; Watson, *Annals of Philadelphia and Pennsylvania*, 2:25; Harrold E. Gillingham, "Lotteries in Philadelphia Prior to 1776," *Pennsylvania History*, 5, no. 2 (April 1938): 95; Asa Earl Martin, "Lotteries in Pennsylvania Prior to 1833," *Pennsylvania Magazine of History and Biography*, 47, no. 4 (1923): 313.

105. Brobeck, "Revolutionary Change," 412; Ernest S. Griffith, *History of American City Government: The Colonial Period* (New York: Da Capo Press, 1972), 20; Sam Bass Warner, *The Private City: Philadelphia in Three Periods of Its Growth*, 2nd ed. (Philadelphia: University of Pennsylvania Press, 1987), 10.

106. Wayne L. Bockelman, "Local Government in Colonial Pennsylvania," in *Town and Country: Essays on the Structure of Local Government in the American Colonies*, ed. Bruce C. Daniels (Middletown, CT: Wesleyan University Press, 1978), 216, 233; Tully, "Quaker Party and Policies," 76–77; E. Digby Baltzell, *Puritan Boston and Quaker Philadelphia: Two Protestant Ethics and the Spirit of Class Authority and Leadership* (Boston: Beacon Press, 1982), 120.

107. C. H. Lincoln, "Representation in the Pennsylvania Assembly Prior to the Revolution," *Pennsylvania Magazine of History and Biography*, 23, no. 1 (1899): 27–28.

108. Warden, "Proprietary Group in Pennsylvania," 385; J. Philip Gleason, "A Scurrilous Colonial Election and Franklin's Reputation," *William and Mary Quarterly*, 18, no. 1 (January 1961): 71.

109. Griffith, *History of American City Government*," 58–59; Hannah Callender Sansom, *Diary of Hannah Callender Sansom: Sense and Sensibility in the Age of the American Revolution*, ed. Susan E. Klepp and Karin Wulf (Ithaca, NY: Cornell University Press, 2010), 17.

110. Point-No-Point got its name from an optical illusion at the cape of the Frankford Creek. Tolles, *Meeting House*, 16. A. Michal McMahon, "'Small Matters': Benjamin Franklin, Philadelphia, and the 'Progress of Cities,'" *Pennsylvania Magazine of History and Biography*, 116, no. 2 (April 1992): 166; Elizabeth Milroy, *The Grid and the River: Philadelphia's Green Places, 1682–1876* (University Park: Pennsylvania State University Press, 2016), 4; Margaret B. Tinkcom, "Cliveden: The Building of a Philadelphia Countryseat1763–1767," *Pennsylvania Magazine of History and Biography*, 88, no. 1 (January 1964): 3.

111. Griffith, *History of American City Government*, 58–59. 176–77.

112. Mittelberger, *Journey to Pennsylvania*, 63.

113. Watson, *Annals of Philadelphia and Pennsylvania*, 3:405–6. Watson also recounts, without specifics, a story about ice skaters who set fire to an abandoned tavern on Water Street. Watson, *Annals of Philadelphia and Pennsylvania*, 2:470. On the challenges Philadelphia's municipal corporation faced, see Judith M. Diamondstone, "The Government of Eighteenth-Century Philadelphia," in *Town and Country: Essays on the Structure of Local Government in the American Colonies*, ed. Bruce C. Daniels (Middletown, CT: Wesleyan University Press, 1978), 255.

114. Watson, *Annals of Philadelphia and Pennsylvania*, 1:497.

115. Budd's Long Row was actually two rows of houses along Front Street between Walnut and Dock. William J. Murtagh, "The Philadelphia Row House," *Journal of the Society of Architectural Historians*, 16no. 4 (December 1957): 8.

116. Though Franklin's organization is often called the first property insurance company in the colonies, John F. Watson described a 1721 advertisement for insurance printed in Andrew Bradford's newspaper. Watson, *Annals of Philadelphia and Pennsylvania*, 2:490.

117. Salinger, "Spaces," 3. Gottlieb Mittelberger claimed that when he visited the city in 1750, "All the houses are built of stone or brick up to the fourth story, and roofed with shingles of cedar wood." Mittelberger, *Journey to Pennsylvania*, 49. These regulations helped but did not completely alleviate the problem. Drinker, *Diary*, 8. Philadelphia was not completely devoid of regulations governing construction. In 1721, the Assembly mandated that builders consult with city-appointed "surveyors and regulators" before starting construction. In 1731, the Assembly mandated that coopers and bakers practice their occupations in stone or brick buildings with earthen floors and plastered ceilings. *A Digest of the Ordinances of the Corporation of the City of Philadelphia and the Acts of the Assembly Relating Thereto* (Philadelphia: J. Crissy, 1841), 5, 311.

118. Calloway, *"Chiefs Now in This City,"* 95.

119. Watson, *Annals of Philadelphia and Pennsylvania*, 3:333.

120. Foulke, Samuel, "Fragments of a Journal Kept by Samuel Foulke, of Bucks County, While a Member of the Colonial Assembly of Pennsylvania, 1762–3–4," ed. Howard M. Jenkins, *Pennsylvania Magazine of History and Biography*, 5, no. 1 (1881): 63. See also Gary B. Nash, "Poverty and Poor Relief in Pre-Revolutionary Philadelphia," *William and Mary Quarterly*, 33, no 1. (January 1976): 7.

121. Foulke, "Fragments of a Journal," 63; Calloway, *"Chiefs Now in This City,"* 95.

122. Robert Hunter Morris, "To the Assembly Concerning the Bill for Preventing the Importation of German or Other Passengers," in *Pennsylvania Archives*, 4th ser, vol. 2:

1747–1759, ed. George Edward Reed. (Harrisburg, PA: Wm. Stanley Ray, 1901), 335. Penn appointed two doctors, Thomas Graeme and Thomas Bond, to investigate the outbreak. In their report, Graeme and Bond blamed the Assembly for failing "to make the necessary Regulations to prevent malignant Diseases being generated by these people, after they Come into Port," proof that, even in cases of public health, politics played a large role. "A Colonial Health Report of Philadelphia, 1754," *Pennsylvania Magazine of History and Biography*, 36, no. 4 (1912): 479.

123. Watson, *Annals of Philadelphia and Pennsylvania*, 1:101.

124. McMahon, "Small Matters," 168–69. The fact that William Hudson, who owned several of the tanneries, was well-connected politically (he served as mayor in 1725–1726) may account for some of the difficulty in preventing the dumping of toxic runoff into Dock Creek. Diamondstone, "Philadelphia's Municipal Corporation," 194.

125. "Governor Thomas Pownall's Description of the Streets and Main Roads about Philadelphia, 1754," *Pennsylvania Magazine of History and Biography*, 18, no. 2 (1894): 65, 212. During this period, the roads in and around the city were treacherous. John F. Watson printed one man's recollection: "The road before it was turnpiked was extremely clayey and mirey, and in some places, especially at Penn's creek, there was fearful quicksand." Watson, *Annals of Philadelphia and Pennsylvania*, 2:33; Diamondstone, "Government of Eighteenth-Century Philadelphia," 252–53. The Assembly even authorized a lottery to pay for paving the city's streets. See Charles S. Olton, "Philadelphia's First Environmental Crisis," *Pennsylvania Magazine of History and Biography*, 98, no. 1 (January 1974): 93. According to Gary Nash, this program functioned as a sort of "make work" project that provided employment for the growing number of unemployed inhabitants. Gary B. Nash, "Up from the Bottom in Franklin's Philadelphia," *Past and Present*, no. 77 (November 1977): 79.

126. *Digest of the Ordinances*, 62, 226, 244–45, 284.

127. Drinker, *Diary*, 27.

128. John F. Watson notes that in 1738, one of Franklin's friends printed an advertisement offering a reward for a watch that had been stolen from him. Watson, *Annals of Philadelphia and Pennsylvania*, II122. In addition, he paraphrases an advertisement that printer Andrew Bradford produced "for apprehending John Jones . . . who stole five or six sheets of the 5 shilling and 20 shilling bills, which Bradford was printing." Watson, *Annals of Philadelphia and Pennsylvania*, 2:417. In her diary, Hannah Callender Sansom recounted two sensational murders that occurred within weeks of one another in 1760. Sansom, *Diary*, 141, 144. See also John Penn, "Proclamation of Reward for the Apprehension of the Perpetrators of Certain Highway Robberies and the Murder of Henry Hamilton," *Pennsylvania Archives*, 4th ser., vol. 3: 1759–1785, ed. George Edward Reed (Harrisburg, PA: Wm. Stanley Ray, 1901), 239; John Penn, "Proclamation of Reward for the Apprehension of the Perpetrators of Certain Burglaries and Robberies in the City of Philadelphia," *Pennsylvania Archives*, 4th series, vol. 3: 1759–1785, ed. George Edward Reed (Harrisburg, PA: Wm. Stanley Ray, 1901), 320. See also Advertisement, *Pennsylvania Gazette*, June 16, 1737; August 6, 1741; December 14, 1744.

129. *Digest of the Ordinances*, 119–20.

130. Jean R. Soderlund, "Black Women in Colonial Pennsylvania," *Pennsylvania Magazine of History and Biography*, 107, no. 1 (January 1983): 56; Watson, *Annals*

of Philadelphia and Pennsylvania, 2:483. The practice of firing guns on New Year's Day continued despite this ordinance, necessitating the passage of another in December 1774, which raised the fine to ten shillings. *Digest of the Ordinances*, 120–21. As of this writing, this asinine practice remains regrettably common, frequently resulting in death or injury.

131. Franklin, *Autobiography*, 108; Diamondstone, "Government of Eighteenth-Century Philadelphia," 250.

132. Watson, *Annals of Philadelphia and Pennsylvania*, 1:211.

133. "Order of the Mayor and Alderman Concerning the Constabulary and Watch," *Pennsylvania Gazette*, July 7, 1752; Diamondstone, "Government of Eighteenth-Century Philadelphia," 251.

134. These street lamps were called Franklin lamps, named after their inventor and composed of four panes of glass. These were cheaper to make and replace than the ornate globes used in streetlamps in London. Harry Kyriakodis and Joel Spivak, *Underground Philadelphia: From Caves and Canals to Tunnels and Transit* (Charleston, SC: History Press, 2019), 48.

135. John F. Walzer, "Colonial Philadelphia and Its Backcountry," *Winterthur Portfolio*, 7 (1972), 161.

136. Victor L. Johnson, "Fair Traders and Smugglers in Philadelphia, 1754–1763." *Pennsylvania Magazine of History and Biography*, 83, no. 2 (April 1959): 125; Doerflinger, "Commercial Specialization," 214.

137. Nash, *Urban Crucible*, 75.

138. David E. Dauer, "Colonial Philadelphia's Intraregional Transportation System: An Overview," *Working Papers from the Regional Economic History Research Center*, 2, no. 3 (1979): 4; T. H Breen, "'The Baubles of Britain': The American Consumer Revolutions of the Eighteenth Century," *Past and Present*, no. 119 (May 1988): 74.

139. Birket, *Some Cursory Remarks*, 69. This was also Daniel Fisher's impression when he visited Philadelphia in 1755. Daniel Fisher, "Extracts from the Diary of Daniel Fisher, 1755," *Pennsylvania Magazine of History and Biography*, 17, no. 3 (1893): 266. This sentiment was echoed by William Black, who visited the city in 1744; he claimed that Philadelphia's market "is allowed by Foreigners to be the best of its bigness in the known World, and undoubtedly the largest in America." Black, "Journal," 1, no. 4 (1877): 405.

140. Ezra Stiles, "Diary of Ezra Stiles," *Proceedings of the Massachusetts Historical Society*, 2nd ser., vol. 7 (1891–1892): 341.

141. Frederick B. Tolles, ed., "The Twilight of the Holy Experiment: A Contemporary View," *Bulletin of Friends' Historical Association*, 45, no. 1 (Spring 1956): 35; Watson, *Annals of Philadelphia and Pennsylvania*, 1:102, 394.

142. Nash, *Urban Crucible*, 45, 76.

143. Johann Christopher Sower, "An Early Description of Pennsylvania: Letter of Christopher Sower, Written in 1724," *Pennsylvania Magazine of History and Biography*, 45, no. 3 (1921): 250–51.

144. Schultz, "Small-Producer Tradition," 93.

145. Billy G. Smith, "Introduction: 'The Best Poor Man's Country?'" in *Down and Out in Early America*, ed. Billy G. Smith (University Park: Pennsylvania State University Press, 2004), xviii.

146. Watson, *Annals of Philadelphia and Pennsylvania*, 2:482; Karin Wulf, "Gender and the Political Economy of Poor Relief in Colonial Philadelphia," in *Down and Out in Early America*, ed. Billy G. Smith (University Park: Pennsylvania State University Press, 2004), 165; McCoy, "Absconding Servants," 428.

147. Nash, "Poverty and Poor Relief," 9; Moore, "America's First Economic Stimulus Package," 532, 545.

148. Billy G. Smith, "Poverty and Economic Marginality in Eighteenth-Century America," *Proceedings of the American Philosophical Society*, 132, no. 1 (March 1988): 88. This average is also misleading; according to Gary B. Nash, who has studied Philadelphia poverty in great depth, in 1739, Philadelphians spent £83 per 1,000 residents on poor relief, a substantially greater number than the average (£49) for the decade. Nash, "Poverty and Poor Relief," 9.

149. Anonymous, *Diary of a Voyage*, 18.

150. Billy G. Smith, "The Material Lives of Laboring Philadelphians, 1750–1800," *William and Mary Quarterly*, 38, no. 2 (April 1981): 189–90; and Nash, "Up from the Bottom," 66.

151. Institutionalization was what led Gottlieb Mittelberger to claim "beggars are nowhere to be seen" in Philadelphia. This was literally true—they were housed in the almshouse and thus were inconspicuous. Mittelberger, *Journey to Pennsylvania*, 67. Sam Bass Warner described this as "privatism," a process by which city dwellers would "cooperate . . . in public tasks that promised mutual material benefit" without upsetting the existing social and economic hierarchies. Warner, *Private City*, xii.

152. Sullivan, "'That Charity,'" 311.

153. Gary B. Nash, "Franklin and Slavery," *Proceedings of the American Philosophical Society*, 150, no 4 (December 2006): 621.

154. Heavner, "Indentured Servitude,": 702.

155. Shammas, "Space Problem," 530.

156. McCoy, "Absconding Servants," 433; Beeman, *Varieties of Political Experience*, 208; Kalm, *Peter Kalm's Travels*, 204. These wages paled in comparison to those paid to missionaries sent to the colonies, who could expect to earn £50 per year. According to William Moraley, the deputy governor earned approximately £2,500 per year. Moraley, *Infortunate*, 80, 103. Thomas Wendel noted, "The fifty-acre property qualification for the vote was not particularly restrictive, although the fifty-pound property qualification in the city perhaps worked a greater hardship there." Wendel, "Keith–Lloyd Alliance," 295. See also Morton Keller, "The Personality of Cities: Boston, New York, Philadelphia," *Proceedings of the Massachusetts Historical Society*, 3rd ser., vol. 97 (1985): 6.

157. Israel Acrelius, *A History of New Sweden; or, the Settlements on the River Delaware* (Philadelphia: Historical Society of Pennsylvania, 1874), 168.

158. Moraley, *Infortunate*, 64.

159. McCoy, "Absconding Servants," 439.

160. Susan E. Klepp, "Seasoning and Society: Racial Differences in Mortality in Eighteenth-Century Philadelphia," *William and Mary Quarterly*, 51, no. 3 (July 1994): 474; Ira V. Brown, "Pennsylvania's Antislavery Pioneers," *Pennsylvania Magazine of History and*

Biography, 55, no. 2 (April 1988): 60; Wokeck, "Irish Immigration to the Delaware Valley," 116; Watson, *Annals of Philadelphia and Pennsylvania*, 2:266.

161. Heavner, "Indentured Servitude," 701.

162. John F. Watson notes that just as Philadelphia's slave population began climbing in the 1730s, complaints to the city government about the city's Black people became more frequent. Complaints included "frequent and tumultuous meetings" that involved "gaming, cursing, [and] swearing." Watson, *Annals of Philadelphia and Pennsylvania*, 1:62.

163. Brown, "Pennsylvania's Antislavery Pioneers," 60.

164. Frank J. Klingberg, "The African Immigrant in Colonial Pennsylvania and Delaware," *Historical Magazine of the Protestant Episcopal Church*, 11, no. 2 (June 1942): 141; Soderlund, "Black Women," 64; Gary B. Nash, *Forging Freedom: The Formation of Philadelphia's Black Community, 1720–1840* (Cambridge, MA: Harvard University Press, 1988), 22. In fact, Whitefield converted several Black Philadelphians during his 1740 visit to the city, at least according to his traveling companion, William Seward. Seward, *Journal of a Voyage*, 6.

165. Franklin to John Waring, 3 January 1758, *Founders Online*, National Archives, last modified June 13, 2018, http://founders.archives.gov/documents/Franklin/01-07-02 -0147.

166. Drinker, *Diary*, 15.

167. William H. Williams, *Slavery and Freedom in Delaware, 1639–1865* (Lanham, MD: SR Books, 1996), xii.

168. Ralph Sandiford, *Mystery of Iniquity*, 2nd ed. (London: Ralph Sandiford, 1730), 5; Darold D. Wax, "Negro Import Duties in Colonial Pennsylvania," *Pennsylvania Magazine of History and Biography*, 97, no. 1 (January 1973): 24.

169. Farley Grubb, "Servant Auction Records and Immigration into the Delaware Valley, 1745–1831: The Proportion of Females Among Immigrant Servants," *Proceedings of the American Philosophical Society*, 133, no. 2 (June 1989): 156.

170. Jean R. Soderlund, "Black Importation and Migration into Southeastern Pennsylvania, 1682–1800," *Proceedings of the American Philosophical Society*, 133, no. 2 (June 1989): 145–46.

171. Harris, "What Politeness Demanded," 289; Wax, "Negro Import Duties," 28; Brown, "Pennsylvania's Antislavery Pioneers," 60.

172. Soderlund, "Black Importation,"147; Klepp, "Seasoning and Society," 476; Mittelberger, *Journey to Pennsylvania*, 106.

173. Wax, "Negro Import Duties," 22.

174. Acrelius, *History of New Sweden*, 168. Acrelius was hardly the only person to make this assertion; J. Hector St. John de Crèvecœur in his *Letters from an American Farmer* claimed that slaves "enjoy as much liberty as their masters, they are as well clad, and as well fed; in health and sickness they are tenderly taken care of; they live under the same roof, and are, truly speaking, a part of our families." J. Hector St. John de Crèvecœur, *Letters from an American Farmer* (Belfast: James Magee, 1783), 146.

175. For examples of the scars, injuries, and deformities that enslavers inflicted upon the enslaved, see Billy G. Smith and Richard Wojtowicz, eds., *Blacks Who Stole Themselves:*

Advertisements for Runaways in the Pennsylvania Gazette, 1728–1790 (Philadelphia: University of Pennsylvania Press, 1989).

176. Moraley, *Infortunate*, 94.

177. Darold D. Wax, "Quaker Merchants and the Slave Trade in Colonial Pennsylvania," *Pennsylvania Magazine of History and Biography*, 86, no. 2 (April 1962): 153–54, 159; Soderlund, "Black Women," 57.

178. Klepp, "Seasoning and Society," 474, 476.

179. Kalm, *Peter Kalm's Travels*, 207; Darold D. Wax, "Africans on the Delaware: The Pennsylvania Slave Trade, 1759–1765," *Pennsylvania History*, 50, no. 1 (January 1983): 40–41. John F. Watson quoted one Philadelphian who recalled seeing slaves auctioned at the London Coffeehouse; this man claimed he "never saw any arrive direct from Africa, but enough came round by Barbadoes, &c." Watson, *Annals of Philadelphia and Pennsylvania*, 1:102. However, in the second volume, Watson quoted a 1762 ad for "one hundred and seventy negroes just arrived from the Gold Coast." Watson, *Annals of Philadelphia and Pennsylvania*, 2:264,

180. Gary B. Nash, "Slaves and Slaveowners in Colonial Philadelphia," *William and Mary Quarterly*, 30, no. 2 (April 1973): 240.

181. "An Act for the Better Regulating of Negroes in this Province," Commonwealth of Pennsylvania Legislative Reference Bureau, accessed January 3, 2019, https://www.palrb .gov/Preservation/Statutes-at-Large/View-Document/17001799/1726/0/act/0292.pdf

182. Soderlund, "Black Women," 51.

183. Edward Raymond Turner, "Slavery in Colonial Pennsylvania," *Pennsylvania Magazine of History and Biography*, 35, no. 2 (1911): 144–47; Brown, "Pennsylvania's Antislavery Pioneers," 61; Nash, *Forging Freedom*, 35.

184. Marcus Rediker, *The Fearless Benjamin Lay: The Quaker Dwarf Who Became the First Revolutionary Abolitionist* (Boston: Beacon Press, 2017), 86.

185. Wax, "Quaker Merchants," 159. See also Geoffrey Plank, *John Woolman's Path to the Peaceable Kingdom: A Quaker in the British Empire* (Philadelphia: University of Pennsylvania Press, 2012), 168; Jon R. Kershner, "'Come Out of Babylon, My People': John Woolman's (1720–72) Anti-Slavery Theology and the Transatlantic Economy," in *Quakers and Their Allies in the Abolitionist Cause, 1754–1808*, ed. Maurice Jackson and Susan Kozel (New York: Taylor & Francis, 2016), 86; Maurice Jackson, "'What Shall Be Done with the Negroes?' Anthony Benezet's Legacy: Then and Now," in *Quakers and Their Allies in the Abolitionist Cause, 1754–1808*, ed. Maurice Jackson and Susan Kozel (New York: Taylor & Francis, 2016), 57.

186. Sansom, *Diary*, 37.

187. Zimmerman, "Benjamin Franklin and the Quaker Party," 300.

188. It is worth noting that at least one historian has calculated that Quakers accounted for approximately 13 percent of Philadelphia's population in 1769. Hindle, "Quaker Background and Science," 247.

189. Ryerson, "Portrait of a Colonial Oligarchy," 129; Zimmerman, "Benjamin Franklin and the Quaker Party," 311; John J. Zimmerman, "Governor Denny and the Quartering Act of 1756," *Pennsylvania Magazine of History and Biography*, 91, no. 3 (July 1967): 272.

190. Theodore Thayer, "The Friendly Association," *Pennsylvania Magazine of History and Biography*, 67, no. 4 (October 1943): 456; Daiutolo, "Role of Quakers," 29–30.

191. Fisher, "Extracts from the Diary," 273.

192. "List of Pennsylvania Settlers Murdered, Scalped and Taken Prisoner by Indians, 1755–1756," *Pennsylvania Magazine of History and Biography*, 32, no. 8 (1908): 309–19.

193. Daiutolo, "Role of Quakers," 4.

194. Nicholas B. Wainwright, "Governor William Denny in Pennsylvania," *Pennsylvania Magazine of History and Biography*, 81, no. 2 (April 1957): 172.

195. In a letter to Penn, Denny admitted he was aware that the city lacked enough accommodations for the troops. William Denny, "Memoir of His Excellency Colonel William Denny, Lieutenant-Governor of Pennsylvania, etc.," *Pennsylvania Magazine of History and Biography*, 44, no. 2 (1920): 112.

196. Zimmerman, "Governor Denny," 277–80.

197. Harry D. Berg, "Economic Consequences of the French and Indian War for Philadelphia Merchants," *Pennsylvania History*, 13, no. 3 (July 1946): 186.

198. Doerflinger, "Commercial Specialization," 22.

199. Billy G. Smith, "Inequality in Late Colonial Pennsylvania: A Note on Its Nature and Growth," *William and Mary Quarterly*, 41, no. 4 (October 1984): 634.

200. Burnaby, *Burnaby's Travels*, 90–91.

201. Watson, *Annals of Philadelphia and Pennsylvania*, 2:494; Sansom, *Diary*, 65.

202. Johnson, "Fair Traders," 143.

203. Smith, "Material Lives," 183.

204. Nash, "Poverty and Poor Relief," 9–13.

205. Thomas Stewardson, ed., "Extracts from the Letter-Book of Benjamin Marshall, 1763–1766," *Pennsylvania Magazine of History and Biography*, 20, no. 2 (1896): 208.

206. Berg, "Economic Consequences," 190.

207. Stewardson, "Extracts," 207. See also Thayer, "Land-Bank System," 145–55. Thomas M. Doerflinger has noted that the city's merchant community was not monolithic and that the recession affected certain types of merchants more than others. That being said, the overall point—that the end of the French and Indian War negatively impacted Philadelphia's economy—is true. Thomas M. Doerflinger, "Philadelphia Merchants and the Logic of Moderation, 1760–1775," *William and Mary Quarterly*, 40, no. 2 (April 1983): 203.

208. Jeremy Engels, "'Equipped for Murder': The Paxton Boys and the 'Spirit of Killing All Indians' in Pennsylvania, 1763–1764," *Rhetoric and Public Affairs*, 8, no. 3 (Fall 2005): 369.

209. Carp, *Rebels Rising*, 184; Nathan Kozuskanich, "'Falling under the Domination Totally of the Presbyterians': The Paxton Riots and the Coming of the Revolution in Pennsylvania," in *Pennsylvania's Revolution*, ed. William Pencak (University Park: Pennsylvania State University Press, 2010), 12.

210. Stewardson, "Extracts," 207; Engels, "'Equipped for Murder,'" 374; Glenn Weaver, "Benjamin Franklin and the Pennsylvania Germans." *William and Mary Quarterly*, 14, no. 4 (October 1957): 552.

Chapter 4

1. Benjamin H. Irvin, "The Streets of Philadelphia: Crowds, Congress, and the Political Culture of Revolution, 1774–1783," *Pennsylvania Magazine of History and Biography*, 129, no. 1 (January 2005): 9, 17.

2. "Notes and Documents: The Population of Eighteenth-Century Philadelphia," ed. Gary B. Nash and Billy G. Smith, *Pennsylvania Magazine of History and Biography*, 99, no. 3 (July 1975): 366.

3. Carl Bridenbaugh and Jessica Bridenbaugh, *Rebels and Gentlemen: Philadelphia in the Age of Franklin* (New York: Reynal & Hitchcock, 1942), 4. Crucially, it was a distant second; several Londoners who visited Philadelphia found the city wanting. Owen S. Ireland, *Sentiments of a British-American Woman: Esther Deberdt Reed and the American Revolution* (University Park: Pennsylvania State University Press, 2017), 99.

4. Susan E. Klepp, *Revolutionary Conceptions: Women, Fertility, and Family Limitation in America, 1760–1820* (Chapel Hill: University of North Carolina Press, 2009), 10, 29.

5. George Winthrop Geib, "A History of Philadelphia, 1776–1789" (PhD diss., University of Pennsylvania, 1969), 56.

6. Alan Tully, "Quaker Party and Proprietary Policies: The Dynamics of Politics in Pre-Revolutionary Pennsylvania, 1730–1775," in *Power and Status: Office Holding in Colonial America*, ed. Bruce C. Daniels (Middletown, CT: Wesleyan University Press, 1986), 79–80.

7. Benjamin H. Newcomb, "Effects of the Stamp Act on Colonial Pennsylvania Politics," *William and Mary Quarterly*, 23, no. 2 (April 1966), 266–67.

8. Richard Alan Ryerson, "Portrait of a Colonial Oligarchy: The Quaker Elite in the Pennsylvania Assembly, 1729–1776," in *Power and Status: Officeholding in Colonial America*, ed. Bruce C. Daniels (Middletown, CT: Wesleyan University Press, 1986), 131–32.

9. Ryerson, "Portrait of a Colonial Oligarchy," 108; Robert F. Oaks, "Philadelphians in Exile: The Problem of Loyalty During the American Revolution," *Pennsylvania Magazine of History and Biography*, 96, no. 3 (July 1972): 299; Richard R. Beeman, *The Varieties of Political Experience in Eighteenth-Century America* (Philadelphia: University of Pennsylvania Press, 2004), 206.

10. Charles S. Olton, "Philadelphia's Mechanics and the First Decade of Revolution, 1765–1775," *Journal of American History*, 59, no. 2 (September 1972): 314–15; Benjamin L. Carp, *Rebels Rising: Cities and the American Revolution* (New York: Oxford University Press, 2007), 4; Carl Bridenbaugh, *Cities in Revolt: Urban Life in America, 1743–1776* (New York: Oxford University Press, 1971), 425; Gary B. Nash *The Urban Crucible: Social Change, Political Consciousness and the Origins of the American Revolution* (Cambridge, MA: Harvard University Press, 1986), ix.

11. Edmund S. Morgan and Helen M. Morgan, *The Stamp Act Crisis: Prologue to Revolution* (Chapel Hill: University of North Carolina Press, 1995), 21.

12. Jack P. Greene and Richard M. Jellison, "The Currency Act of 1764 in Imperial-Colonial Relations, 1764–1776," *William and Mary Quarterly*, 18, no. 1 (October 1961): 489; Thomas M. Doerflinger, "Philadelphia Merchants and the Logic of Moderation, 1760–1775," *William and Mary Quarterly*, 40, no. 2 (April 1983): 206.

13. "1766: 6 George 3 c.12: American Colonies Act," n.d., The Statutes Project, accessed March 5, 2019, http://statutes.org.uk/site/the-statutes/eighteenth-century/1766-6 -george-3-c-12-securing-america/.

14. Beeman, *Varieties of Political Experience*, 248.

15. Carp, *Rebels Rising*, 189.

16. "From Benjamin Franklin to John Hughes, 9 August 1765," Founders Online, National Archives, accessed April 11, 2019, https://founders.archives.gov/documents /Franklin/01-12-02-0123. See also John E. Ferling, "Joseph Galloway: A Reassessment of the Motivations of a Pennsylvania Loyalist," *Pennsylvania History*, 39, no. 2 (April 1972): 168.

17. John J. Zimmerman, "Charles Thomson, 'The Sam Adams of Philadelphia,'" *Mississippi Valley Historical Review*, 45, no. 3 (December 1958): 469.

18. Newcomb, "Effects of the Stamp Act," 269.

19. Nash and Smith, "Notes and Documents," 367; Doerflinger, "Philadelphia Merchants," 210.

20. Arthur M. Schlesinger, "Politics, Propaganda, and the Philadelphia Press, 1767–1770," *Pennsylvania Magazine of History and Biography*, 60, no 4 (October 1936): 314; Nathan Kozuskanich, "'Falling Under the Domination Totally of the Presbyterians': The Paxton Riots and the Coming of the Revolution in Pennsylvania," in *Pennsylvania's Revolution*, ed. William Pencak (University Park: Pennsylvania State University Press, 2010), 20.

21. Clare A. Lyons, *Sex Among the Rabble: An Intimate History of Gender and Power in the Age of Revolution, Philadelphia, 1730–1830* (Chapel Hill: University of North Carolina Press, 2006), 61; Kenneth Hafertepe, "Banking Houses in the United States: The First Generation, 1781–1811," *Winterthur Portfolio*, 35, no. 1 (Spring 2000): 2; Beeman, *Varieties of Political Experience*, 268–69. Writing in 1781, Claude C. Robin, a French abbot who served as chaplain to Washington's army during the American Revolution and visited Philadelphia in 1781, complained, "But by the increase of inhabitants, by the flocking in of strangers, and its becoming a commercial settlement, the fortunes of individuals were enlarged, luxury was introduced, the manners of the people were indelibly changed, and that *golden age*, which was here realized, was soon considered as nothing but a brilliant meteor, which blazed out in a moment to the astonished world, and disappeared forever." Claude C. Robin, *New Travels Through North-America* (Philadelphia: Robert Bell, 1783), 46. See also Caleb Cresson, *Diary of Caleb Cresson, 1791–1792*, ed. Ezra Townsend Cresson and Charles Caleb Cresson (Philadelphia: self-pub., 1877), 125.

22. Dr. Robert Honeyman, who visited Philadelphia in 1775, described the city as "famous for its extensive trade." Robert Honeyman, *Colonial Panorama, 1775: Dr. Robert Honeyman's Journal for March and April*, ed. Philip Padelford (Freeport, NY: Books for Libraries Press, 1939), 14. Solomon Drowne, a medical student who arrived in Philadelphia in 1774, marveled at the broad range of products available in the city, saying, "There is scarce anything a Person can mention but can be got here, i.e., for Money." Solomon Drowne, "Dr. Solomon Drowne," ed. Harold E. Gillingham, *Pennsylvania Magazine of History and Biography*, 48, no. 3 (1924): 236. As early as 1765, one visitor to Philadelphia commented on the number of "very rich merchants in this City." "Journal of a French Traveler in the Colonies, 1765, II," *American Historical Review*, 27, no. 1 (October 1921): 79. Another visitor who arrived around the same time asserted, "Every body in Philadelphia

deals more or less in trade." Henry Gordon, "Journal of Captain Harry Gordon's Journey from Pittsburg down the Ohio and the Mississippi to New Orleans, Mobile, and Pensacola," in *Travels in the American Colonies*, ed. Newton D. Mereness (New York: Macmillan, 1916), 412. In 1791, Ferdinand M. Bayard, who visited Philadelphia that year, complained, "This population of the cities, divided by wealth and monarchical prejudices, is drawn together by luxury." Ferdinand M. Bayard, *Travels of a Frenchman in Maryland and Virginia with a Description of Philadelphia and Baltimore in 1791*, trans. and ed. Ben C. McCary (Ann Arbor, MI: Edwards Brothers, 1950), 130. See also John Mair, "Journal of John Mair, 1791," *American Historical Review*, 12, no. 1 (October 1906): 81; Judith Sargent Murray, *From Gloucester to Philadelphia in 1790*, ed. Bonnie Hurd Smith (Cambridge, MA: Judith Sargent Murray Society, 1998), 108; J. P. Brissot de Warville, *New Travels in the United States of America, 1788*, ed. Durand Echeverria (Cambridge, MA: Harvard University Press, 1964), 199; Michelle L. Craig, "Grounds for Debate? The Place of the Caribbean Provisions Trade in Philadelphia," *Pennsylvania Magazine of History and Biography*, 128, no. 2 (April 2004): 172; Anne Bezanson, "Inflation and Controls, Pennsylvania, 1774–1779," *Journal of Economic History*, 8, suppl. (1948): 3; Edwin Wolf 2nd, *Philadelphia: Portrait of an American City* (Philadelphia: Camino Books, 1990), 39.

23. Murray, *From Gloucester*, 163. Even the Quakers were not immune. Médéric Louis Élie Moreau de Saint-Méry, a French visitor to Philadelphia in the 1790s, complained, "One sees the coquetry of the young Quakeress, who know how to combine their affected simplicity with very worldly tastes, which this sect would wholly eradicate." Moreau de Saint-Méry, "An Eighteenth Century Frenchman on American Quakerism in Pennsylvania," *Bulletin of Friends' Historical Society of Philadelphia*, 9, no. 3 (May 1920): 129. See also Billy G. Smith, "Inequality in Late Colonial Philadelphia: A Note on Its Nature and Growth," *William and Mary Quarterly*, 41, no. 4 (October 1984): 643–64; Grant Miles Simon, "Houses and Early Life in Philadelphia," *Transactions of the American Philosophical Society*, 43, no. 1 (1953): 280; Steve Rosswurm, "Class Relations, Political Economy, and Society in Philadelphia," in *Shaping a National Culture: The Philadelphia Experience, 1750–1800*, ed. Catherine E. Hutchins (Winterthur, DE: Henry Francis Du Pont Winterthur Museum, 1994), 46; David L. Barquist, "'The Honours of a Court' or 'The Severity of Virtue': Household Furnishings and Cultural Aspirations in Philadelphia," in *Shaping a National Culture: The Philadelphia Experience, 1750—1800*, ed. Catherine E. Hutchins (Winterthur, DE: Henry Francis Du Pont Winterthur Museum, 1994), 314.

24. *The Infortunate: The Voyage and Adventures of William Moraley, an Indentured Servant*, ed. Susan E. Klepp and Billy G. Smith (University Park: Pennsylvania State University Press, 1992), 80, 103.

25. Margaret B. Tinkcom, "Cliveden: The Building of a Philadelphia Countryseat, 1763–1767," *Pennsylvania Magazine of History and Biography*, 88, no. 1 (January 1964): 4, 34. On the growth of the city's gentry during this period, see Stephen Brobeck, "Revolutionary Change in Colonial Philadelphia: The Brief Life of the Proprietary Gentry," *William and Mary Quarterly*, 33, no. 3 (July 1976): 425–26. For a first-hand description of the relative differences between Philadelphians' houses, see Edward D. Seeber, ed. and trans., *On the Threshold of Liberty: Journal of a Frenchman's Tour of the American Colonies in 1777* (Bloomington: Indiana University Press, 1959), 150.

26. Wolf, *Philadelphia*, 57.

27. Bridenbaugh and Bridenbaugh, *Rebels and Gentlemen*, 21.

28. Henry Wansey, *The Journal of an Excursion to the United States of North America in the Summer of 1794* (Salisbury, UK: J. Easton, 1796), 111. See also Irvin, "Streets of Philadelphia," 20; Lynn Matluck Brooks, "Emblem of Gaiety, Love, and Legislation: Dance in Eighteenth-Century Philadelphia," *Pennsylvania Magazine of History and Biography*, 115, no. 1 (January 1991): 63, 67.

29. John Adams, *The Works of John Adams, Second President of the United States*, vol. 2, ed. Charles Francis Adams (Boston: Charles C. Little & James Brown, 1850), 395.

30. In a 1769 letter to the Committee of Merchants in London, Philadelphia's merchant community specifically cited the rights of Englishmen as the reason behind their opposition to Parliament's actions. Dan Benezet et al. "Letter from a Committee of Merchants in Philadelphia to the Committee of Merchants in London, 1769," *Pennsylvania Magazine of History and Biography*, 27, no. 1 (1903): 86. See also Eric Foner, *Tom Paine and Revolutionary America* (New York: Oxford University Press, 1977), 25; J. T. Jable, "The Pennsylvania Sunday Blue Laws of 1779: A View of Pennsylvania Society and Politics During the American Revolution," *Pennsylvania History*, 40, no. 4 (October 1973): 421; Jane T. Merritt, "Tea Trade, Consumption, and the Republican Paradox in Prerevolutionary Philadelphia," *Pennsylvania Magazine of History and Biography*, 128, no. 2 (April 2004): 118–19; Kate Haulman, "Fashion and the Culture Wars of Revolutionary Philadelphia," *William and Mary Quarterly*, 3rd ser., 62, no. 4 (October 2005): 629; Ireland, *Sentiments of a British-American Woman*, 102; Beeman, *Varieties of Political Experience*, 247.

31. Ronald Schultz, "The Small-Producer Tradition and the Moral Origins of Artisan Radicalism in Philadelphia, 1720–1810," *Past and Present*, no. 127 (May 1990): 99. A good illustration of this dynamic can be found in Ireland, *Sentiments of a British-American Woman*, 111.

32. Smith, "Inequality, 634.

33. Gary B. Nash, "Up from the Bottom in Franklin's Philadelphia," *Past and Present*, no. 77 (November 1977): 74.

34. Henry Wansey, who visited Philadelphia in 1794, noted, "Mr. Bingham told me that, in the year 1783, he bought a piece of land adjoining Philadelphia, for eight hundred and fifty pounds, which now yields eight hundred and fifty pounds per annum, and he has never laid out twenty pounds upon it." Wansey, *Journal*, 137. See also Billy G. Smith, "The Material Lives of Laboring Philadelphians, 1750–1800," *William and Mary Quarterly*, 38, no. 2 (April 1981): 177; Ronald Schultz, "God and Workingmen: Popular Religion and the Formation of Philadelphia's Working Class, 1790–1830," in *Religion in a Revolutionary Age*, ed. Ronald Hoffman and Peter Albert (Charlottesville: University of Virginia Press, 1993), 128.

35. Mackraby to Mackraby, 2 December 1770, "Philadelphia Society Before the Revolution (Concluded)," *Pennsylvania Magazine of History and Biography*, 11, no. 4 (January 1888): 492.

36. Lyons, *Sex Among the Rabble*, 63.

37. "Meffieurs HALL and SELLERS," *Pennsylvania Gazette*, September 27, 1770. See also Brobeck, "Revolutionary Change," 426; Aaron Sullivan, "'That Charity Which Begins at Home': Ethnic Societies and Benevolence in Eighteenth-Century Philadelphia,"

Pennsylvania Magazine of History and Biography, 134, no. 4 (October 2010): 319; Rosswurm, "Class Relations," 52; Smith, "Inequality," 636; Richard G. Miller, *Philadelphia, the Federalist City: A Study of Urban Politics, 1789–1801* (Port Washington, NY: Kennikat Press, 1976), 5; Bezanson, "Inflation and Controls," 1; Foner, *Tom Paine*, 62.

38. In 1756, a Philadelphia tradesman complained to a friend, "I am sorry to acquaint you, that the Honest endeavors of the present Assembly to preserve the Liberties of their Countrymen have been so basely represented at Home, by a Set of Men whose principle [sic] Aim seems to be nothing less than engrossing sole Power of our Properties and Persons. Our Properties by taxing us freely and our Persons by ordering us to Duties in Military Stations—which latter must and will Depend upon the Caprice of one Man, the Supreme Magistrate of *Pensilvania* for the time being." Frederick B. Tolles, ed., "The Twilight of the Holy Experiment: A Contemporary View," *Bulletin of Friends' Historical Association*, 45, no. 1 (Spring 1956): 35.

39. Doerflinger, "Philadelphia Merchants," 215.

40. Abigail Adams to John Adams, 31 March–5 April 1776, Adams Family Papers, Massachusetts Historical Society, Boston, accessed July 21, 2022, https://www.masshist.org /digitaladams/archive/doc?id=L17760331aa.

41. Susan Branson, *These Fiery Frenchified Dames: Women and Political Culture in Early National Philadelphia* (Philadelphia: University of Pennsylvania Press, 2001), 11; Lyons, *Sex Among the Rabble*, 3.

42. Esther de Berdt Reed, "The Sentiments of an American Woman," *Pennsylvania Magazine of History and Biography*, 18, no. 3 (1894): 363–64.

43. Ireland, *Sentiments of a British-American Woman*, 126.

44. Jean R. Soderlund, "Women in Eighteenth-Century Pennsylvania: Toward a Model of Diversity," *Pennsylvania Magazine of History and Biography*, 115, no. 2 (April 1991): 171–72; Lyons, *Sex Among the Rabble*, 67.

45. Carp, *Rebels Rising*, 191.

46. Doerflinger, "Philadelphia Merchants," 197–98; Merritt, "Tea Trade," 132; James Farley, "The Ill-Fated Voyage of the *Providentia*: Richard Vaux, Loyalist Merchant, and the Trans-Atlantic Mercantile World in the Late Eighteenth Century," *Pennsylvania History*, 62, no. 3 (Summer 1995): 367.

47. James E. Gibson, "The Pennsylvania Provincial Conference of 1776," *Pennsylvania Magazine of History and Biography*, 58, no. 4 (1934): 314; Donald F. Johnson, "Ambiguous Allegiances: Urban Loyalties During the American Revolution," *Journal of American History*, 104, no. 3 (December 2017): 610.

48. Beeman, *Varieties of Political Experience*, 270.

49. "To Benjamin Franklin from Joseph Galloway, 18 [July] 1765," Founders Online, National Archives, accessed April 11, 2019, https://founders.archives.gov/documents /Franklin/01-12-02-0111. See also Newcomb, "Effects of the Stamp Act," 269.

50. Judith Van Buskirk, "They Didn't Join the Band: Disaffected Women in Revolutionary Pennsylvania," *Pennsylvania History*, 62, no. 3 (Summer 1995): 306; Wendy Lucas Castro, "'Being Separated from My Dearest Husband, in This Cruel Manner': Elizabeth Drinker and the Seven-Month Exile of Philadelphia Quakers," *Quaker History*, 100, no. 1 (Spring 2011): 42; Kozuskanich, "Falling Under the Domination," 22.

51. Doerflinger, "Philadelphia Merchants," 216; Carp, *Rebels Rising*, 192.

52. Merritt, "Tea Trade," 134.

53. Robert Gough, "Can a Rich Man Favor Revolution? The Case of Philadelphia in 1776," *Pennsylvania History*, 48, no. 3 (July 1981): 238; Farley, "Ill-Fated Voyage," 366; Foner, *Tom Paine*, 60. Some historians have found other forces at work as well. For instance, there appears to have been a difference in the ways dry-goods merchants (importers of paper, furniture, ceramics, etc.) responded to British policy when compared to provisions merchants (i.e., importers of coffee and sugar). Craig, "Grounds for Debate?," 171–72.

54. Alexander Graydon, *Memoirs of a Life, Chiefly Passed in Pennsylvania within the Last Sixty Years* (Edinburgh, UK: William Blackwood, 1822), 115. See also Richard Alan Ryerson, "Political Mobilization and the American Revolution: The Revolutionary Movement in Philadelphia, 1765–1776," *William and Mary Quarterly*, 31, no. 4 (October 1974): 577; Robert F. Oaks, "Philadelphia Merchants and the First Continental Congress," *Pennsylvania History*, 40, no. 2 (April 1973): 159; Gough, "Can a Rich Man Favor Revolution?," 240; Richard Alan Ryerson, "Republican Theory and Partisan Reality in Revolutionary Philadelphia: Toward a New View of the Constitutionalist Party," in *Sovereign States in an Age of Uncertainty*, ed. Ronald Hoffman and Peter Albert (Charlottesville: University of Virginia Press, 1982), 117.

55. Carp, *Rebels Rising*, 193; Schlesinger, "Politics," 321.

56. Thomas B. Taylor, "The Philadelphia Counterpart of the Boston Tea Party," *Bulletin of Friends' Historical Society of Philadelphia*, 2, no. 3 (November 1908): 103; Frederick D. Stone, "How the Landing of Tea Was Opposed in Philadelphia by Colonel William Bradford and Others in 1773," *Pennsylvania Magazine of History and Biography*, 15, no. 4 (1891): 388.

57. Stone, "How the Landing of Tea Was Opposed," 389–90.

58. Rush to Adams, 14 August 1809, *Letters of Benjamin Rush*, vol. 2: 1793–1813, ed. Lyman Henry Butterfield (Princeton, NJ: Princeton University Press, 1951), 1013.

59. Christopher Marshall, *Passages from the Diary of Christopher Marshall*, ed. William Duane (Philadelphia: Hazard & Mitchell, 1849), 6.

60. Marshall, *Passages*, 7; Graydon, *Memoirs*, 127. See also Kozuskanich, "Falling Under the Domination," 24.

61. As Joseph Reed, a member of the Continental Congress and future president of Pennsylvania's Supreme Executive Council, noted in 1774, "The Weight of Influence of this Province and City . . . [is] considerable." Joseph Reed, *Life and Correspondence of Joseph Reed*, vol. 1, ed. William B. Reed (Philadelphia: Lindsay & Blackiston, 1847), 70.

62. Craig, "Grounds for Debate?," 172.

63. Ireland, *Sentiments of a British-American Woman*, 126.

64. John Gilbert McCurdy, "Taxation and Representation: Pennsylvania Bachelors and the American Revolution," *Pennsylvania Magazine of History and Biography*, 129, no. 3 (July 2005): 302; William A. Pencak and Barbara A. Gannon, "Pennsylvania in the American Revolution," in *Pennsylvania: A Military History*, ed. William A. Pencack, Christian B. Keller, and Barbara A. Gannon (Yardley, PA: Westholme, 2016), 60; Kozuskanich, "Falling Under the Domination," 25.

65. Graydon, *Memoirs*, 122–23.

66. In addition to relating this incident, Clement Biddle described the tarring and feathering of "a very genteel young man" that occurred about the same time. Clement Biddle, *Autobiography of Clement Biddle* (Philadelphia: E. Claxton, 1883), 72.

67. Joseph Galloway, "Some Letters of Joseph Galloway, 1774–1775," *Pennsylvania Magazine of History and Biography*, 21, no. 4 (1897): 477–78. See also Paul Leicester Ford, "The Adoption of the Pennsylvania Constitution of 1776," *Political Science Quarterly*, 10, no. 3 (September 1895): 432–33.

68. Michael J. Lewis, *Philadelphia Builds: Essays on Architecture* (Philadelphia: Paul Dry Books, 2021), 224.

69. James Allen, "Diary of James Allen, Esq., of Philadelphia, Counsellor-at-Law, 1770–1778 (continued)," *Pennsylvania Magazine of History and Biography*, 9, no. 3 (1885): 278; Marshall, *Passages from the Diary of Christopher Marshall*, 75.

70. Measuring the actual amount of support for independence in Philadelphia at any given time during this period is incredibly difficult, as the record is contradictory. For instance, James Allen claimed, "Yesterday the Resolve of Congress was read by Bradford at the Coffee-house. One man only huzzaed; in general it was ill received. . . . This step of Congress, just at the time peace commissioners are expected to arrive, was purposely contrived to prevent overtures of peace." Allen, "Diary," 187. Writing in May 1775, Loyalist Samuel Curwen claimed, "Philadelphia is wholly American, strong friends to congressional measures." Samuel Curwen, *Journal and Letters of the Late Samuel Curwen* (New York: C. S. Francis, 1842), 29. Dr. John Berkenhout, a peace commissioner dispatched in 1778 by the British government to negotiate with the Continental Congress, claimed, "Most Americans with whom I conversed, on my Journey through the Jerseys and at Philadelphia, lamented their separation from the Mother Country, disapproved the declaration of independence, and detested their French alliance." John Berkenhout, "Journal of an Excursion from New York to Philadelphia in the Year 1778," in *Travels in the American Colonies*, ed. Newton D. Mereness (New York: Macmillan, 1916), 577. Dr. James Clitherall, who visited Philadelphia in 1776 in the company of the wives of two members of the Continental Congress, claimed, "The body of the people were for Independency." James Clitherall, "Extracts from the Diary of James Clitherall, 1776," *Pennsylvania Magazine of History and Biography*, 22, no. 4 (1898): 469. See also Pencak and Gannon, "Pennsylvania in the American Revolution," 61.

71. Gibson, "Pennsylvania Provincial Conference," 319–20.

72. Wayne L. Bockelman and Owen S. Ireland, "The Internal Revolution in Pennsylvania: An Ethnic-Religious Interpretation," *Pennsylvania History*, 41, no. 2 (April 1974): 151; James M. Aldrich, "A Quantitative Reassessment of the Effects of Sectionalism in Pennsylvania During the War for Independence," *Pennsylvania History*, 39, no. 3 (July 1972): 341.

73. McCurdy, "Taxation and Representation," 303. According to John Gilbert McCurdy, the new constitution enfranchised approximately 75 percent of white men in Pennsylvania's rural areas and 90 percent of white men in Philadelphia. John Gilbert McCurdy, "The Origins of Universal Suffrage: The Pennsylvania Constitution of 1776," *Pennsylvania Legacies*, 8, no. 2 (November 2008): 11.

74. Rosalind L. Branning, *Pennsylvania Constitutional Development* (Pittsburgh: University of Pittsburgh Press, 1960), 12; Brooks, "Emblem of Gaiety," 72; William Pencak, Introduction, in *Pennsylvania's Revolution*, ed. William Pencak (University Park: Pennsylvania State University Press, 2010), 3.

75. Ryerson, "Portrait of a Colonial Oligarchy," 108; Charles D. Russell, "Islam as a Danger to Republican Virtue: Broadening Religious Liberty in Revolutionary Pennsylvania," *Pennsylvania History*, 76, no. 3 (Summer 2009): 256–57; Joseph S. Foster, "The Politics of Ideology: The Pennsylvania Convention of 1789–90," *Pennsylvania History*, 59, no. 2 (April 1992): 124; Beeman, *Varieties of Political Experience*, 273. Historian John Gilbert McCurdy has asserted, "While this shift may seem less than radical two centuries later, it marks the origins of universal suffrage in the United States and the belief that all citizens should be allowed a voice in the selection of their leaders." McCurdy, "Origins of Universal Suffrage," 8.

76. Bockelman and Ireland, "Internal Revolution," 127; Nash, *Urban Crucible*, 240.

77. Donna J. Rilling, *Making Houses, Crafting Capitalism: Builders in Philadelphia, 1790–1850* (Philadelphia: University of Pennsylvania Press, 2001), 4; Elizabeth Milroy, *The Grid and the River: Philadelphia's Green Places, 1682–1776* (University Park: Pennsylvania State University Press, 2016), 43.

78. Graydon, *Memoirs*, 302. See also Irvin, "Streets of Philadelphia," 21; Jable, "Pennsylvania Sunday Blue Laws," 416; Carp, *Rebels Rising*, 210.

79. Graydon, *Memoirs*, 348. See also Geib, "History of Philadelphia," 5; Miller, *Philadelphia*, 21.

80. Even some Patriots were concerned about the democratic and antihierarchical implications of revolutionary action. For instance, Alexander Graydon deplored the militia's tarring and feathering of Dr. John Kearsley, noting, "I was shocked at seeing a lately respected citizen so cruelly vilified." Graydon, *Memoirs*, 123. Other contemporaries were more explicit in condemning the Revolution as the work of a democratic "mob." Robert Morton, a young Philadelphia Loyalist, described the Patriots as "a licentious mob" exercising "lawless power." Robert Morton, "Diary of Robert Morton," *Pennsylvania Magazine of History and Biography*, 1, no. 1 (1877): 4. Dr. James Clitherall, who visited the city in 1776, perceived this tension, noting how those opposed to independence "have now retired into the country disgusted at the present proceedings, fearful of the people, and railing at men in office on account of their low birth and little fortune." Clitherall, "Extracts from the Diary," 469. A good example of such a person was lawyer James Allen, who disparaged the "Associators" and claimed, "The madness of the multitude is but one degree better than the submission to the Tea-Act." Allen, "Diary," 186. Alexander Graydon, who lived in Philadelphia during the Revolution, recalled, "Mr. James Allen was also suspected of having no very cordial affection for the cause, although he shouldered a musket in the ranks of the militia." Graydon, *Memoirs*, 116.

81. Miller, *Philadelphia*, 20.

82. James Mitchell and Henry Flanders, eds., *Statutes at Large of Pennsylvania from 1681 to 1801*, vol. 9: 1776–1779 (Harrisburg, PA: Wm. Stanley Ray, 1903), ch. 746, 64–65.

83. Alexander Graydon described the Declaration of Independence as "the great cause of schism" between moderate and radical opponents of Britain's policies. Graydon, *Memoirs*, 300.

84. Allen, "Diary," 190; Sarah Logan Fisher, "'A Diary of Trifling Occurrences': Philadelphia, 1776–1777," ed. Nicholas B. Wainwright, *Pennsylvania Magazine of History and Biography*, 82, no. 4 (October 1958): 414.

85. Fisher, "Diary," 416; Ireland, *Sentiments of a British-American Woman*, 138.

86. Geib, "History of Philadelphia," 58–62.

87. Allen, "Diary," 278; Fisher, "Diary," 422.

88. Allen, "Diary," 284. Several Quakers, writing to Quakers in Ireland, complained of the dire situation that December, noting, "On the apprehension of the British forces intending to attack this city, Congress, and the powers who act with them, ordered all the provisions out of the city, except what would serve the consumption of its inhabitants a very short time, and have prevented supplies from coming, except in small parcels." "Letter of Friends in Philadelphia to Friends in Ireland, Soliciting Aid During the Occupation of Philadelphia by the British," *Pennsylvania Magazine of History and Biography*, 20, no. 1 (1896): 125.

89. Fisher, "Diary," 444; Elizabeth Drinker, *The Diary of Elizabeth Drinker: The Life Cycle of an Eighteenth-Century Woman*, ed. Elaine Forman Crane (Boston: Northeastern University Press, 1994), 60–61; Castro, "'Being Separated,'" 40.

90. William Eddis, *Letters from America, Historical and Descriptive* (London, 1777), 437.

91. Biddle, *Autobiography*, 101. See also Margaret Stedman, "Excitement in Philadelphia on Hearing of the Defeat at Brandywine," *Pennsylvania Magazine of History and Biography*, 14, no. 1 (April 1890): 64–65.

92. Drinker, *Diary*, 62. Drinker was not the only person to chronicle the disorder in Philadelphia; Margaret Stedman also described the aftermath of the Battle of Brandywine as leaving Philadelphia "all in confusion." Stedman, "Excitement," 66. See also Castro, "'Being Separated,'" 43.

93. Allen, "Diary," 290.

94. Franklin was not the only person to predict this. James Allen noted in his diary that "Howe's situation will be distressed cooped up there." Allen, "Diary," 290. On September 23, Washington wrote to John Hancock, then serving as president of the Continental Congress, claiming that "the acquisition of Philadelphia may, instead of his good fortune, prove his Ruin." George Washington, *The Writings of George Washington*, vol. 6: 1777–1778, ed. Worthington Chauncey Ford (New York: G. P. Putnam's Sons, 1890), 83. A Frenchman who visited the city prior to Howe's occupation claimed, "But the ease with which Philadelphia can be conquered is no proof of the usefulness and advantage of possessing it. The Congress can flee in one direction while the enemy is entering from another; the city has no important arsenals, no warehouses stocked with provisions, and no facilities for having any; moreover, if the neighboring rivers and bays should perchance freeze over, it would become, for any Royalists imprudent enough to quarter themselves there, what the fields of Saratoga were for General Burgoyne." Seeber, *On the Threshold of Liberty*, 147.

95. William S. Baker, ed., "Itinerary of General George Washington from June 15, 1775, to December 23, 1783," *Pennsylvania Magazine of History and Biography*, 14, no. 2

(July 1890): 269; Fisher, "Diary," 413. See also Oaks, "Philadelphians in Exile," 308; Drinker, *Diary*, 64; Owen S. Ireland, "The Ethnic-Religious Dimension of Pennsylvania Politics, 1778–1779," *William and Mary Quarterly*, 30, no. 3 (July 1973): 426.

96. Graydon, *Memoirs*, 299. See also Geib, "History of Philadelphia," 58–76.

97. Darlene Emmert Fisher, "Social Life in Philadelphia During the British Occupation," *Pennsylvania History*, 37, no. 3 (July 1970): 242.

98. Grace Growden Galloway, "Diary of Grace Growden Galloway," ed. Raymond C. Werner, *Pennsylvania Magazine of History and Biography*, 55, no. 1 (1931): 33.

99. Geib, "History of Philadelphia," 78–79.

100. Willard O. Mishoff, "Business in Philadelphia During the British Occupation, 1777–1778," *Pennsylvania Magazine of History and Biography*, 61, no. 2 (April 1937): 166–168, 177; Louis J. Zanine, "Brigadier General John Lacey and the Pennsylvania Militia in 1778," *Pennsylvania History*, 48, no. 2 (April 1981): 129.

101. Fisher, "Diary," 414; Allen, "Diary," 424; John M. Coleman, "Joseph Galloway and the British Occupation of Philadelphia," *Pennsylvania History*, 30, no. 3 (July 1963): 291.

102. Irvin, "Streets of Philadelphia," 24.

103. Ireland, *Sentiments of a British-American Woman*, 161–62.

104. J. William Frost, "Pennsylvania Institutes Religious Liberty," *Pennsylvania Magazine of History and Biography*, 112, no. 3 (July 1988): 336; Fisher, "Social Life," 245; Jable, "Pennsylvania Sunday Blue Laws," 421; Heather S. Nathans, "Forging a Powerful Engine: Building Theaters and Elites in Post-Revolutionary Boston and Philadelphia," *Pennsylvania History*, 66 (1999): 114.

105. William S. Dye Jr., "Pennsylvania Versus the Theatre," *Pennsylvania Magazine of History and Biography*, 55, no. 4 (1931): 359; Fred Lewis Pattee, "The British Theater in Philadelphia in 1778," *American Literature*, 6, no. 4 (January 1935): 381; Morton, "Diary," 4; Allen, "Diary," 432; Meredith H. Lair, "Redcoat Theater: Negotiating Identity in Occupied Philadelphia, 1777–1778," in *Pennsylvania's Revolution*, ed. William Pencak (University Park: Pennsylvania State University Press, 2010), 196; Townsend Ward, "South Second Street and Its Associations," *Pennsylvania Magazine of History and Biography*, 4, no. 1 (1880): 45; Irvin, "Streets of Philadelphia," 22.

106. Fisher, "Social Life," 242.

107. Anthony Cuthbert, "Assessment of Damages Done by the British Troops During the Occupation of Philadelphia, 1777–1778," *Pennsylvania Magazine of History and Biography*, 25, no. 3 (1901): 323–35; Hugh Jones Jr., "Assessment of Damages Done by the British Troops During the Occupation of Philadelphia, 1777–1778 (continued)," *Pennsylvania Magazine of History and Biography*, 25, no. 4 (1901): 544–59. See also Fisher, "Diary," 464.

108. Christiana Leach, "Selections from the Diary of Christiana Leach, of Kingsessing, 1765–1796," ed. Robert H. Hinckley, *Pennsylvania Magazine of History and Biography*, 35, no. 3 (1911): 345. Following Howe's departure from the city, James Allen condemned the general, saying, "His conduct has given little satisfaction either here or in England. He has . . . offended all the friends of the Government by neglect of them & suffering their property to be destroyed." Allen, "Diary," 438.

109. Johann David Schoepf, *Travels in the Confederation* (Philadelphia: William J. Campbell, 1911), 86.

110. Morton, "Diary," 30.

111. "The want of fuel obliged the [British] army to burn all the Woods and fences about the City." Allen, "Diary," 427–28. See also Geib, "History of Philadelphia," 136, 165–66; John W. Jackson, *With the British Army in Philadelphia, 1777–1778* (San Rafael, CA: Presidio Press, 1979), 191.

112. Rich Remer, "Old Kensington," *Pennsylvania Legacies*, 2, no. 2 (November 2002): 11.

113. François-Jean de Chastellux, *Travels in North America in the Years 1780–81–82*, trans. George Grieve (New York, 1828), 89.

114. Morton, "Diary," 8. See also Coleman, "Joseph Galloway," 296.

115. Mishoff, "Business in Philadelphia," 178; Galloway, "Diary," 34. See also Charles R. Peterson, "Carpenters' Hall," *Transactions of the American Philosophical Society*, 43, no. 1 (1953): 102.

116. Peter S. Duponceau, "Autobiographical Letters of Peter S. Duponceau," *Pennsylvania Magazine of History and Biography*, 40, no. 2 (1916): 184.

117. Milroy, *Grid and the River*, 40.

118. Lewis Nicola to Horatio Gates, 3 July 1778, "Unpublished Letters of Colonel Nicola, Revolutionary Soldier," ed. Howard R. Marraro, *Pennsylvania History*, 13, no. 4 (October 1946): 277; Drinker, 78.

119. Samuel Rowland Fisher, "Journal of Samuel Rowland Fisher, of Philadelphia, 1779–1781," *Pennsylvania Magazine of History and Biography*, 41, no. 2 (1917): 170; Van Buskirk, "They Didn't Join," 319; Johnson, "Ambiguous Allegiances," 613.

120. Mishoff, "Business in Philadelphia," 179; Laird, "Redcoat Theater," 199.

121. Geib, "History of Philadelphia," 150; Foner, *Tom Paine*, 55.

122. Mary M. Schweitzer, "The Economy of Philadelphia and Its Hinterland," in *Shaping a National Culture: The Philadelphia Experience, 1750–1800*, ed. Catherine E. Hutchins (Winterthur, DE: Henry Francis Du Pont Winterthur Museum, 1994), 112.

123. Geib, "History of Philadelphia," 157.

124. Geib, "History of Philadelphia," 98–99.

125. Geib, "History of Philadelphia," 100–101.

126. Geib, "History of Philadelphia," 112–13.

127. Geib, "History of Philadelphia," 116.

128. Geib, "History of Philadelphia," 123–30; Thomas P. Slaughter, "Crowds in Eighteenth-Century America: Reflections and New Directions," *Pennsylvania Magazine of History and Biography*, 115, no. 1 (January 1991): 11.

129. Geib, "History of Philadelphia," 131–33.

130. Geib, "History of Philadelphia," 239–41.

131. Thomas C. Cochran, "Philadelphia: The American Industrial Center, 1750–1850," *Pennsylvania Magazine of History and Biography*, 106, no. 3 (July 1982): 326.

132. Foner, *Tom Paine*, 27.

133. Geib, "History of Philadelphia," 174.

134. Geib, "History of Philadelphia," 169.

135. Smith, "Material Lives," 176.

136. In 1774, medical student Solomon Drowne, who marveled at the quality of Philadelphia's markets, nonetheless conceded that "things bear a high price" in the city. Drowne, "Dr. Solomon Drowne," 236. See also Mair, "Journal," 80. Edward M. Riley, "Philadelphia: The Nation's Capital, 1790–1800," *Pennsylvania History*, 20, no. 4 (October 1953): 377; Patrick M'Robert, "Patrick M'Robert's 'Tour Through Part of the North Provinces of America," ed. Carl Bridenbaugh, ed., *Pennsylvania Magazine of History and Biography*, 59, no. 1 (April 1935): 166. In March 1793, the Pennsylvania Assembly voted itself a 50 percent raise because its members could not afford to live in Philadelphia, but this provoked such an outcry that it convinced many members to consider moving the commonwealth's government to a different location. Leonard J. Sneddon, "From Philadelphia to Lancaster: The First Move of Pennsylvania's Capital," *Pennsylvania Magazine of History and Biography*, 38, no. 4 (October 1971): 351; Carole Shammas, "The Space Problem in Early United States Cities," *William and Mary Quarterly*, 57, no. 3 (July 2002): 536.

137. Brooks, "Emblem of Gaiety," 82.

138. Robin, *New Travels*, 44; Pencak and Gannon, "Pennsylvania in the American Revolution," 97.

139. Anna Rawle and William Brooke Rawle, "A Loyalist's Account of Certain Occurrences in Philadelphia After Cornwallis's Surrender at Yorktown," *Pennsylvania Magazine of History and Biography*, 16, no. 1 (April 1892): 103–4; Drinker, *Diary*, 91.

140. Pencak and Gannon, "Pennsylvania in the American Revolution," 88; McCurdy, "Origins of Universal Suffrage," 7.

141. Kenneth R. Bowling, "New Light on the Philadelphia Mutiny of 1783: Federal-State Confrontation at the Close of the War for Independence," *Pennsylvania Magazine of History and Biography*, 101, no. 4 (October 1977): 427.

142. Bowling, "New Light," 449.

143. Geib, "History of Philadelphia," 216.

144. Cochran, "Philadelphia," 328.

145. James T. Mitchell and Henry Flanders, eds., *Statutes at Large of Pennsylvania from 1681 to 1801*, vol. 12: 1785–1787 (Harrisburg, PA: Harrisburg Publishing, 1906), ch. 1223, 220.

146. James T. Mitchell and Henry Flanders, eds., *Statutes at Large of Pennsylvania from 1681 to 1801*, vol. 15: 1794–1797 (Harrisburg, PA: C. M. Aughinbaugh, 1911), ch. 1812, 251.

147. James T. Mitchell and Henry Flanders, eds., *Statutes at Large of Pennsylvania from 1681 to 1801*, vol. 16: 1798–1801 (Harrisburg, PA: C. M. Aughinbaugh, 1911), ch. 2110, 421; John Daly and Allen Weinberg, *Genealogy of Philadelphia County Subdivisions*, 2nd ed. (Philadelphia: Philadelphia Department of Records, 1966), 57–59.

148. Cornelius William Stafford, *The Philadelphia Directory for 1798: Containing the Names, Occupations, and Places of Abode of the Citizens* (Philadelphia: William W. Woodward, 1798), 13.

149. Nathans, "Forging a Powerful Engine," 125.

150. Brissot de Warville, *New Travels*, 173; Shammas, "Space Problem," 539.

151. Geib, "History of Philadelphia," 166.

152. Geib, "History of Philadelphia," 184.

153. Thomas Twining, *Travels in America 100 Years Ago* (New York: Harper & Brothers, 1894), 60.

154. Geib, "History of Philadelphia," 229.

155. In her diary, Ann Warder noted, "At first the prisoners were much averse to this shameful exposure, and preferred death to it. Two things I think need regulation, suffering people to talk to them and to prevent their receiving money." Ann Warder, "Extracts from the Diary of Ann Warder (Concluded)," *Pennsylvania Magazine of History and Biography*, 18, no. 1 (1894): 61.

156. In *A Book of Remembrance*, Benjamin Franklin's great-granddaughter recalled getting her shoes made at the Walnut Street Jail as a child. Elizabeth Duane Gillespie, *A Book of Remembrance* (Philadelphia: J. B. Lippincott, 1901), 9.

157. John Penn, "John Penn's Journal of a Visit to Reading, Harrisburg, Carlisle, and Lancaster, in 1788," *Pennsylvania Magazine of History and Biography*, 3, no. 3 (1879): 284.

158. Murray, *From Gloucester*, 189–200; Brissot de Warville, *New Travels*, 153.

159. Alfred F. Young, *The Shoemaker and the Tea Party: Memory and the American Revolution* (Boston: Beacon Press, 2001), 92.

160. "Philadelphia, May 9," *Independent Gazetteer*, May 9, 1787. See also Edmund S. Morgan, "The Witch & We, the People," *American Heritage*, 34, no. 5 (August/September 1983): 8; Richard Beeman, *Plain, Honest Men: The Making of the American Constitution* (New York: Random House, 2009), 226.

161. Chastellux, *Travels*, 94. See also Ronald Schultz, "Small-Producer Thought: The Argument About Capitalism," in *Life in Early Philadelphia: Documents from the Revolutionary and Early National Periods*, ed. Billy G. Smith (University Park: Pennsylvania State University Press, 1995), 265.

162. Fisher, "Journal," 275.

163. Ryerson, "Republican Theory," 127; Miller, *Philadelphia*, 22.

164. Manasseh Cutler, "New York and Philadelphia in 1787," *Pennsylvania Magazine of History and Biography*, 12, no. 1 (April 1888): 103.

165. "Some of the best informed told me, they did not believe a single member [of the convention] was *perfectly* satisfied with the Constitution, but they believed it was the best they could ever agree upon, and that it was infinitely better to have such a one than to break up without fixing on some form of government." Biddle, *Autobiography*, 217. See also R. Carter Pittman, "Jasper Yeates's Notes on the Pennsylvania Ratifying Convention, 1787," *William and Mary Quarterly*, 22, no. 2 (April 1965): 303.

166. Laura Rigal, "Grand Federal Procession," *Encyclopedia of Greater Philadelphia*, n.d., accessed, July 8, 2019, https://philadelphiaencyclopedia.org/archive/grand-federal-procession/.

167. Ryerson, "Republican Theory," 118.

168. James T. Mitchell and Henry Flanders, eds., *Statutes at Large of Pennsylvania from 1681 to 1801*, vol. 13: 1787–1789 (Harrisburg, PA: Harrisburg Publishing, 1908), ch. 1794, 193.

169. Edward Allinson and Boies Penrose, *Philadelphia, 1681–1887: A History of Municipal Development* (Philadelphia: Allen, Lane & Scott, 1887). 99–100.

170. Allinson and Penrose, *Philadelphia*, 84.

171. Mitchell and Flanders, *Statutes at Large*, vol. 15, ch. 1759, 462–63; Geib, "History of Philadelphia," 294–95; Miller, *Philadelphia*, 26.

172. Writing in 1791, visitor Ferdinand M. Bayard complained, "In Philadelphia, the merchant class is the leading class, and the inhabitants devote themselves to mercantile affairs with all the ardor which can be prompted by vanity, long credit and the prospect of acquiring, easily and quickly, a very large fortune." Bayard, *Travels*, 125. See also Whitney Martinko, *Historic Real Estate: Market Morality and the Politics of Preservation in the Early United States* (Philadelphia: University of Pennsylvania Press, 2020), 43.

173. Schultz, "Small-Producer Tradition," 109; Milroy, *Grid and the River*, 43; Wolf, *Philadelphia*, 98.

174. Miller, *Philadelphia*, 29; Foster, "Politics of Ideology," 123.

175. Frost, "Pennsylvania Institutes Religious Freedom," 337.

176. Miller, *Philadelphia*, 35; Riley, "Philadelphia," 360.

177. Adams to City and County Commissioners of Philadelphia, 9 December 1790, Founders Early Access, n.d., accessed July 7, 2019, https://rotunda.upress.virginia.edu /founders/default.xqy?keys=FOEA-search-1-2&expandNote=on#match1.

178. Riley, "Philadelphia," 360; Dennis C. Kurjack, "The 'President's House' in Philadelphia," *Pennsylvania History*, 20, no. 4 (October 1953): 382.

179. Twining, *Travels*, 60. This was in keeping with Washington's style as president. John Mair, who visited the president in Philadelphia in 1791, noted that "he observes great simplicity of manner." Mair, "Journal," 81.

180. Owned by John Francis, who was listed in 1793 as a "hotel keeper," the house was at 13 South Fourth Street. James Hardie, *The Philadelphia Directory and Register* (Philadelphia: T. Dobson, 1793), 48; Twining, *Travels*, 31–34.

181. Roland M. Bauman, "'Heads I Win, Tails You Lose': The Public Creditor and the Assumption Issue in Pennsylvania, 1790–1802," *Pennsylvania History*, 44, no. 3 (July 1977): 197; David J. Cowen, "The First Bank of the United States and the Securities Market Crash of 1792," *Journal of Economic History*, 60, no. 4 (December 2000): 1041.

182. Wolf, *Philadelphia*, 102.

183. Smith, "Material Lives," 190, 193.

184. Samuel Hazard, ed., *The Register of Pennsylvania: Devoted to the Preservation of Facts and Documents, and Every Other Kind of Useful Information Respecting the State of Pennsylvania*, vol. 3 (Philadelphia: W. F. Gedden, 1829), 22.

185. Craig, "Grounds for Debate?," 154; Brewington, "Maritime Philadelphia," 114.

186. Miller, *Philadelphia*, 115; Edward C. Carter II, "A 'Wild Irishman' Under Every Federalist's Bed: Naturalization in Philadelphia, 1789–1806," *Pennsylvania Magazine of History and Biography*, 94, no. 3 (July 1970): 342; Billy G. Smith and Paul Sivitz, "Identifying and Mapping Ethnicity in Philadelphia During the Early Republic," *Pennsylvania Magazine of History and Biography*, 140, no. 3 (October 2016): 406.

187. John Davies, "Saint-Dominguan Refugees of African Descent and the Forging of Ethnic Identity in Early National Philadelphia," *Pennsylvania Magazine of History and*

Biography, 134, no. 2 (April 2010): 115; Wayland Fuller Dunaway, "The French Racial Strain in Colonial Pennsylvania," *Pennsylvania Magazine of History and Biography*, 53, no. 4 (1929): 336.

188. Graydon, *Memoirs*, 383. See also John L. Earl III, "Talleyrand in Philadelphia, 1794–1796," *Pennsylvania Magazine of History and Biography*, 91, no. 3 (July 1967): 282; Branson, *These Fiery*, 57.

189. Honeyman, *Colonial Panorama*, 16; Cresson, *Diary*, 141; Murray, *From Glouces-ter*, 165, 189; Carroll Frey, "Indian Chiefs View 'Penn's Treaty,'" *Bulletin of Friends' His-torical Society Association*, 40, no. 2 (Autumn 1951): 103; Colin G. Calloway, *"The Chiefs Now in This City": Indians and the Urban Frontier in Early America* (New York: Oxford University Press, 2021), 136.

190. Smith and Sivitz, "Identifying," 398.

191. Samuel Johnson, *Taxation No Tyranny; an Answer to the Resolutions and Address of the American Congress* (London: T. Cadell, 1775), 89. Lawyer James Allen confided to his diary, "My inducement principally to join them is that a man is suspected who does not." Allen, "Diary," 185. See also Zachary McLeod Hutchins, "The Slave Narrative and the Stamp Act, or Letters from Two American Farmers in Pennsylvania," *Early American Literature*, 50, no. 3 (2015): 645.

192. Wax, "Negro Import Duties," 24, 37.

193. Galloway, "Diary," 45. See also Hermann Wellenreuther, "The Quest for Har-mony in a Turbulent World: The Principle of 'Love and Unity' in Colonial Pennsylvania Politics," *Pennsylvania Magazine of History and Biography*, 107, no. 4 (October 1983): 543.

194. Gary B. Nash, *Forging Freedom: The Formation of Philadelphia's Black Commu-nity, 1720–1840* (Cambridge, MA: Harvard University Press, 1988), 33. On Quaker politi-cal strength and the American Revolution, see Jean R. Soderlund, "Women's Authority in Pennsylvania and New Jersey Quaker Meetings, 1680–1760," *William and Mary Quarterly*, 44, no. 4 (October 1987): 722.

195. Warville, *New Travels*, 228. See also Smith and Sivitz, "Identifying," 409.

196. Smith and Sivitz, "Identifying," 405; Lyons, *Sex Among the Rabble*, 31.

197. Paul Finkelman, "The Pennsylvania Delegation and the Peculiar Institution: The Two Faces of the Keystone State," *Pennsylvania Magazine of History and Biography*, 112, no. 1 (January 1988): 53.

198. Smith and Sivitz, "Identifying," 409; Nash, *Forging Freedom*, 2.

199. Davies, "Saint-Dominguan Refugees," 110.

200. Julie Winch, "Free Men and 'Freemen': Black Voting Rights in Pennsylvania, 1790–1870," *Pennsylvania Legacies*, 8, no. 2 (November 2008): 14.

201. Dee E. Andrews, "Religion and Social Change: The Rise of the Methodists," in *Shaping a National Culture: The Philadelphia Experience, 1750–1800*, ed. Catherine E. Hutchins (Winterthur, DE: Henry Francis Du Pont Winterthur Museum, 1994), 151; Billy G. Smith, "Black Family Life in Philadelphia from Slavery to Freedom, in *Shaping a National Culture: The Philadelphia Experience, 1750–1800*, ed. Catherine E. Hutchins (Winterthur, DE: Henry Francis Du Pont Winterthur Museum, 1994), 83.

202. Nancy Shippen, *Nancy Shippen: Her Journal Book*, ed. Ethel Armes (Philadel-phia: J. B. Lippincott, 1935), 102, 166, 188.

203. Schoepf, *Travels*, 57. See also Chastellux, *Travels*, 111.

204. Warville, *New Travels*, 253.

205. Warville, *New Travels*, 258.

206. Branson, *These Fiery*, 21–24.

207. "It is not yet so extensive as the Leverian Museum in London, but every day increasing." Wansey, *Journal*, 135. For descriptions of Peale's collection in 1787, see Cutler, "New York and Philadelphia," 106; Murray, *From Gloucester*, 165.

208. Drinker, *Diary*, 98.

209. Geib, "History of Philadelphia," 290; Ric Northup Caric, "Blustering Brags, Dueling Inventors, and Corn-Square Geniuses: Artisan Leisure in Philadelphia, 1785–1825," *American Journal of Semiotics*, 12, no. 1–4 (1998): 327–28; Schultz, "God and Workingmen," 127; Lyons, *Sex Among the Rabble*, 61.

210. Miller, *Philadelphia*, 15; Calloway, *"Chiefs Now in This City,"* 137.

211. Theatergoing remained a controversial activity despite its legality. Judith Sargent Murray, who visited Philadelphia in the summer of 1790, faced considerable opposition to her desire to see a theatrical performance and had to disguise herself to attend a performance. Murray, *From Gloucester*, 174. See also Jable, "Pennsylvania Sunday Blue Laws," 413. These attempts mirrored efforts by Congress to prevent "every species of extravagance and dissipation." Brooks, "Emblem of Gaiety," 71.

212. Schultz, "God and Workingmen," 127; Nathans, "Forging a Powerful Engine," 114.

213. Mitchell and Flanders, *Statutes at Large*, vol. 16, ch. 1889, 106; Miller, *Philadelphia*, 6.

214. Graydon, *Memoirs*, 121.

215. Shippen, *Nancy Shippen*, 179–80.

216. Warville, *New Travels*, 254.

217. Drinker, *Diary*, 107.

218. Calloway, *"Chiefs Now in This City,"* 99–100.

219. Miller, *Philadelphia*, 57.

220. Graydon, *Memoirs*, 384; Wansey, *Journal*, 138. Scenes like this were repeated in subsequent outbreaks. See "Extracts from a Diary Kept During the Yellow Fever Plague in Philadelphia, PA. in 1798," *Records of the American Catholic Historical Society of Philadelphia*, 13, no. 4 (December 1902): 492–93. See also Biddle, *Autobiography*, 256.

221. Susan E. Klepp, "Malthusian Miseries and the Working Poor in Philadelphia, 1780–1830: Gender and Infant Mortality," in *Down and Out in Early America*, ed. Billy G. Smith (University Park: Pennsylvania State University Press, 2004), 71.

222. Graydon, *Memoirs*, 35.

223. Billy G. Smith, *Ship of Death: A Voyage that Changed the Atlantic World* (New Haven, CT: Yale University Press, 2013), 187.

224. Matthew Carey, *A Short Account of the Malignant Fever, Lately Prevalent in Philadelphia* (London: J. Johnson, 1794), 20.

225. Carey, *Short Account, 11*; Richard Allen and Absalom Jones, *A Narrative of the Proceedings of the Black People During the Late Awful Calamity in Philadelphia* (Philadelphia: William W. Woodward, 1794), 5.

226. Mitchell and Flanders, *Statutes at Large*, vol. 15, ch. 1759, 119.

227. Allinson and Penrose, *Philadelphia*, 91.

228. Harry Kyriakodis and Joel Spivak, *Underground Philadelphia: From Caves and Canals to Tunnels and Transit* (Charleston, SC: History Press, 2019), 29–31.

229. Sneddon, "From Philadelphia to Lancaster," 353.

230. David Schuyler, *The New Urban Landscape: The Redefinition of City Form in Nineteenth-Century America* (Baltimore: Johns Hopkins University Press, 1993), 24.

Chapter 5

1. William Russell Birch, "Plan of the City of Philadelphia, 1800," in *The City of Philadelphia, in the State of Pennsylvania North America: As It appeared in the Year 1800* (Springland Cottage, PA: W. Birch, 1800); "Philadelphia" (London: Society for the Diffusion of Useful Knowledge, 1840).

2. George Rogers Taylor, Comment, in *The Growth of Seaport Cities, 1790–1825*, ed. David T. Gilchrist (Charlottesville: University of Virginia Press, 1967), 44; Ernest S. Griffith and Charles R. Adrian, *A History of American City Government: The Formation of Traditions, 1775–1870* (Washington, DC: University Press of America, 1983), 27.

3. Carole Shammas, "The Space Problem in Early United States Cities," *William and Mary Quarterly*, 57, no. 3 (July 2000): 509; Everett S. Lee and Michael Lalli, "Population," in *The Growth of Seaport Cities, 1790–1825*, ed. David T. Gilchrist (Charlottesville: University of Virginia Press, 1967), 29.

4. Edwin Wolf 2nd, *Philadelphia: Portrait of an American City* (Philadelphia: Camino Books, 1990), 123, 152; Elizabeth Milroy, *The Grid and the River: Philadelphia's Green Places, 1682–1876* (University Park: Pennsylvania State University Press, 2016), 182.

5. Marleen S. Barr, "The 'Worthy' and the 'Irrelevant': Deborah Norris Logan's Diary" (PhD diss., State University of New York, Buffalo, 1980), 545–56.

6. Sam Bass Warner, *The Private City: Philadelphia in Three Periods of Its Growth*, 2nd ed. (Philadelphia: University of Pennsylvania Press, 1987), 50; Priscilla Ferguson Clement, *Welfare and the Poor in the Nineteenth-Century City: Philadelphia, 1800–1854* (Cranbury, NJ: Fairleigh Dickinson University Press, 1985), 24.

7. John Daly and Allen Weinberg, *Genealogy of Philadelphia County Subdivisions*, 2nd ed. (Philadelphia: Philadelphia Department of Records, 1966), 60–61.

8. Charles R. Barker, "Philadelphia, 1836–9: Transportation and Development," In *Philadelphia History*, vol. 2 (Philadelphia: City History Society of Philadelphia, 1933), 353.

9. Thomas H. Keels, *Forgotten Philadelphia: Lost Architecture of the Quaker City* (Philadelphia: Temple University Press, 2007), 112.

10. Roger Miller and Joseph Siry, "The Emerging Suburb: West Philadelphia, 1850–1880," *Pennsylvania History*, 47, no. 2 (April 1980): 107.

11. Miller and Siry, "Emerging Suburb," 106; Henry Leffman, "The Consolidation of Philadelphia," in *Philadelphia History: Consisting of Papers Read Before the City History Society of Philadelphia* (Philadelphia: City History Society of Philadelphia, 1917), 28.

12. Florence Kelley, *The Autobiography of Florence Kelley: Notes of Sixty Years*, ed. Kathryn Kish Sklar (Chicago: Charles H. Kerr, 1986), 34.

13. Elizabeth M. Geffen, "Violence in Philadelphia in the 1840s and 1850s," *Pennsylvania History*, 36, no. 4 (October 1969): 404; Howard Gillette Jr., "The Emergence of the

Modern Metropolis: Philadelphia in Its Age of Consolidation," in *The Divided Metropolis: Social and Spatial Dimensions of Philadelphia, 1800–1975*, ed. William W. Cutler III and Howard Gillette Jr. (Westport, CT: Greenwood Press, 1980), 10; Alan N. Burstein, "Immigrants and Residential Mobility: The Irish and Germans in Philadelphia, 1850–1880," in *Philadelphia: Work, Space, Family, and Group Experience in the 19th Century*, ed. Theodore Hershberg (New York: Oxford University Press, 1981), 199.

14. George G. Foster, "Philadelphia in Slices," *Pennsylvania Magazine of History and Biography*, 93, no 1 (January 1969): 29; Barr, "'Worthy,'" 168; Hugo Reid, *Sketches in North America* (London: Longman, Green, Longman, & Roberts, 1861), 224. See also William Sullivan, *The Industrial Worker in Pennsylvania, 1800–1840* (New York: Johnson Reprint, 1972), 194; William S. Hastings, "Philadelphia Microcosm," *Pennsylvania Magazine of History and Biography*, 91, no. 2 (April 1967): 169–70. This was reinforced by the Market Street Railroad, which congested its namesake and thereby made Chestnut Street that much more attractive. Jeffrey P. Roberts, "Railroads and the Downtown: Philadelphia, 1830–1900," in *The Divided Metropolis: Social and Spatial Dimensions of Philadelphia, 1800–1975*, ed. William W. Cutler III and Howard Gillette Jr. (Westport, CT: Greenwood Press, 1980), 29.

15. A. Rugbaean, *Transatlantic Rambles* (London: George Bell, 1852), 44.

16. Quoted in Charles R. Barker, "Philadelphia in the Late 'Forties," in *Philadelphia History*, vol. 2 (Philadelphia: City History Society of Philadelphia, 1931), 256.

17. Hastings, "Philadelphia Microcosm," 177; William W. Cutler III and Howard Gillette Jr., Preface, in *The Divided Metropolis: Social and Spatial Dimensions of Philadelphia, 1800–1975*, ed. William W. Cutler III and Howard Gillette Jr. (Westport, CT: Greenwood Press, 1980), xiv.

18. Shammas, "Space Problem," 528; Theodore Hershberg et al., "The 'Journey-to-Work': An Empirical Investigation of Work, Residence and Transportation, Philadelphia, 1850 and 1880," in *Philadelphia: Work, Space, Family, and Group Experience in the 19th Century*, ed. Theodore Hershberg (New York: Oxford University Press, 1981), 146.

19. Robert A. Slaney, *Short Journal of a Visit to Canada and the States of America in 1860* (London: Hatchard, 1861), 53. Chandler to Howell, 2 September 1833 and Howell to Evans, 15 May 1834, Elizabeth Margaret Chandler, *Remember the Distance that Divides Us: The Family Letters of Philadelphia Quaker Abolitionist and Michigan Pioneer Elizabeth Margaret Chandler, 1830–1842*, ed. Marcia J. Heringa Mason (East Lansing: Michigan State University Press, 2004), 196, 237. See also Roberts, "Railroads," 34; Hershberg et al., "'Journey-to-Work,'" 141, 147.

20. Martha H. Garrett, *Memoirs of Philadelphia in the Nineteenth Century* (Philadelphia: self-pub., 1910), 26. See also Hershberg et al., "'Journey-to-Work,'" 146.

21. Milroy, *Grid and the River*, 237; Diane Lindstrom, *Economic Development in the Philadelphia Region, 1810–1850* (New York: Columbia University Press, 1978), 1; David R. Johnson, "Crime Patterns in Philadelphia, 1840–70," in *The Peoples of Philadelphia: A History of Ethnic Groups and Lower-Class Life, 1790–1940*, ed. Allen F. Davis and Mark H. Haller (Philadelphia: University of Pennsylvania Press, 1998), 90; Hershberg et al., "'Journey-to-Work,'" 166.

22. Michael J. Lewis, *Philadelphia Builds: Essays on Architecture* (Philadelphia: Paul Dry Books, 2021), 5.

23. Thomas P. Cope described Morris's house as an "uncouth & expensive edifice." Thomas P. Cope, *Philadelphia Merchant: The Diary of Thomas P. Cope, 1801–1851* (South Bend, IN: Gateway Editions, 1978), 63.

24. Kenneth Ames, "Robert Mills and the Philadelphia Row Home," *Journal of the Society of Architectural Historians*, 27, no. 2 (May 1968): 143.

25. Donna J. Rilling, *Making Houses, Crafting Capitalism: Builders in Philadelphia, 1790–1850* (Philadelphia: University of Pennsylvania Press, 2001), 45–52, 186; John F. Sutherland, "Housing the Poor in the City of Homes: Philadelphia at the Turn of the Century," in *The Peoples of Philadelphia: A History of Ethnic Groups and Lower-Class Life, 1790–1940*, ed. Allen F. Davis and Mark H. Haller (Philadelphia: University of Pennsylvania Press, 1998), 176; Dennis Clark, *The Irish in Philadelphia: Ten Generations of Urban Experience* (Philadelphia: Temple University Press, 1973), 50.

26. For the earlier practice, see Francis White, *The Philadelphia Directory* (Philadelphia: Young, Stewart & McCulloch, 1785). For a directory containing house numbers, see James Hardie, *The Philadelphia Directory and Register* (Philadelphia: T. Dobson, 1793). See also Hastings, "Philadelphia Microcosm," 173. Historian Charles R. Barker described the house-numbering system as "execrable" and "a pot-pourri of systems." Barker, "Philadelphia, 1836–9," 357. See also Gillette, "Emergence," 11; Bruno Giberti, *Designing the Centennial: A History of the 1876 International Exhibition in Philadelphia* (Lexington: University Press of Kentucky, 2002), 22–23.

27. Edwin Wolf 2nd, "The Origins of Philadelphia's Self-Deprecation, 1820–1920," *Pennsylvania Magazine of History and Biography*, 104, no. 1 (January 1980): 62; Daniel Kilbride, *An American Aristocracy: Southern Planters in Antebellum Philadelphia* (Columbia: University of South Carolina Press, 2006), 128. For an example, see William Rees, "From Indiana to North Carolina in 1854: The Diary of William Rees," *Quaker History*, 59, no. 2 (Autumn 1970): 69–70.

28. Samuel L. Clemens, *Mark Twain's Letters: Volume 1: 1853–1866*, ed. Edgar Marquess Branch, Michael B. Frank, and Kenneth M. Sanderson (Berkeley: University of California Press, 1988), 23. See also Whitney Martinko, *Historic Real Estate: Market Morality and the Politics of Preservation in the Early United States* (Philadelphia: University of Pennsylvania Press, 2020), 9.

29. W. Barksdale Maynard, "'Best, Lowliest Style!' The Early-Nineteenth-Century Rediscovery of American Colonial Architecture," *Journal of the Society of Architectural Historians*, 59, no. 3 (September 2000): 338–41.

30. Milroy, *Grid and the River*, 159; Warner, *Private City*, 105.

31. Barr, "'Worthy,'" 285. See also Griffith and Adrian, *History of American City Government*, 73.

32. Milroy, *Grid and the River*, 48; James McClelland and Lynn Miller, *City in a Park: A History of Philadelphia's Fairmount Park System* (Philadelphia: Temple University Press, 2016), 11; Fritz Redlich, "Notes and Documents: The Philadelphia Water Works in Relation to the Industrial Revolution in the United States," *Pennsylvania Magazine of History and Biography*, 69, no. 3 (July 1945): 248. Philadelphia's superiority in providing municipal water was a point of civic pride. Merchant Thomas P. Cope, who served on the Watering Committee, noted in his diary in September 1820 that he was "continually reminded of the

advantages which [Philadelphia] enjoys" over other cities "in the article of water." Cope, *Philadelphia Merchant*, 383.

33. Arthur S. Marks, "Palladianism on the Schuylkill: The Work of Frederick Graff at Fairmount," *Proceedings of the American Philosophical Society*, 154, no 2 (June 2010): 212.

34. McClelland and Miller, *City in a Park*, 14.

35. Milroy, *Grid and the River*, 164.

36. David Crockett, *The Autobiography of David Crockett* (New York: Charles Scribner's Sons, 1923), 148.

37. McClelland and Miller, *City in a Park*, 18.

38. Warner, *Private City*, 106. On the purchase itself, see Cope, *Philadelphia Merchant*, 415.

39. Frances Milton Trollope, *Domestic Manners of the Americans: Complete in One Volume* (London: Whittakers, Treacher, 1832), 211. Nor was Trollope the only one impressed by the Water Works; several diarists and letter writers noted its beauty. See Sidney George Fisher, *A Philadelphia Perspective: The Diary of Sidney George Fisher Covering the Years 1834–1871*, ed. Nicholas B. Wainwright (Philadelphia: Historical Society of Pennsylvania, 1967), 221; Barr, "'Worthy,'" 413; Nathaniel T. W. Carrington, "A Barbados Planter's Visit to Philadelphia in 1837: The Journal of Nathaniel T. W. Carrington," ed. James C. Brandow, *Pennsylvania Magazine of History and Biography*, 106, no. 3 (July 1982): 416; Clara Bromley, *A Woman's Wanderings in the Western World* (London: Saunders, Otley, 1861), 38. 363; Wilcocks A. Sleigh, *Pine Forests and Hackmatack Clearings; or, Travel, Life, and Adventure, in the British North American Provinces* (London: Richard Bentley, 1853), 315–16. See also Michal McMahon, "Makeshift Technology: Water and Politics in 19th-Century Philadelphia," *Environmental Review*, 12, no. 4 (Winter 1988): 24. George G. Foster, by contrast, looked down on the working-class men and women who used the area for recreation. Foster, "Philadelphia in Slices," 65–67.

40. Dickens noted that "Philadelphia is most bountifully provided with fresh water, which is showered and jerked about, and turned on, and poured off, everywhere." Charles Dickens, *American Notes for General Circulation* (Paris: A. and W. Galignani, 1842), 122. See also Reid, *Sketches*, 225; Frederick Marryat, *A Diary in America, with Remarks on Its Institutions* (Philadelphia: Carey & Hart, 1839), 147–48; Michael P. McCarthy, *Typhoid and the Politics of Public Health in Nineteenth-Century Philadelphia* (Philadelphia: American Philosophical Society, 1987), 6.

41. John F. Watson, *Annals of Philadelphia, and Pennsylvania, in the Olden Time*, vol. 3 (Philadelphia: Edwin S. Stuart, 1899), 401–2; Thomas H. Keels, *Forgotten Philadelphia*, 91; Harry Kyriakodis, "Pleasure Gardens, Without Worry, in the City," Hidden City Philadelphia, March 19, 2014, accessed December 10, 2019, https://hiddencityphila.org/2014/03/pleasure-gardens-without-worry-in-the-city/.

42. Foster, "Philadelphia in Slices," 45. He was not the only one impressed with Laurel Hill; Samuel Breck noted in 1840, "The cemetery [is] divided by handsome ornamental railings, and ornamented with mausoleums, vaults, columns, etc. Sir Walter Scott and Old Mortality at the entrance, sculpted by Thom, is of exquisite truth and beauty." Samuel Breck, "The Diary of Samuel Breck, 1839–1840," *Pennsylvania Magazine of History and Biography*, 103, no. 4 (October 1979): 517.

43. Keels, *Forgotten Philadelphia*, 102.

44. Cristin O'Keefe Aptowicz, *Dr. Mütter's Marvels: A True Tale of Intrigue and Innovation at the Dawn of Modern Medicine* (New York: Avery Publishing Group, 2015), x.

45. John McAllister & Co. to Andrew Jackson, October 13, 1831. Andrew Jackson papers, 1775–1874. Library of Congress.

46. *Philadelphia in 1830–1: Or, a Brief Account of the Various Institutions and Public Objects in This Metropolis* (Philadelphia: E. L. Carey and A. Hart, 1830), 120; R. A. Smith, *Philadelphia As It Is, in 1852* (Philadelphia: Lindsay & Blakiston, 1852), xi.

47. "The Prospects of Our City," *Philadelphia Album and Ladies Literary Portfolio*, 5, no. 20 (May 14, 1831).

48. Frederick Marryat, who visited the United States in the late 1830s, found the city's museums "far superior to most in the states." Marryat, *Diary in America*, 147–48.

49. Fisher, *Philadelphia Perspective*, 65–66; A. R. Beck, "Notes of a Visit to Philadelphia, Made by a Moravian Sister in 1810," *Pennsylvania Magazine of History and Biography*, 36, no. 3 (1912): 358; David R. Brigham, *Public Culture in the Early Republic: Peale's Museum and Its Audience* (Washington, DC: Smithsonian Institution Press, 1996), 64–66; Wolf, *Philadelphia*, 175.

50. One English visitor to Philadelphia claimed that "the shipment of coal, brought down the railway from the great Pennsylvania coal-fields, seem to be conducted on so large a scale, that a Northumbrian might be deceived into the idea that he was on the banks of the Tyre." William Chambers, *Things as They Are in America* (London: William & Robert Chambers, 1854), 307. See also Milroy, *Grid and the River*, 204.

51. Wolf, *Philadelphia*, 150.

52. Thomas C. Cochran, "Philadelphia: The American Industrial Center, 1750–1850," *Pennsylvania Magazine of History and Biography*, 106, no. 3 (July 1982): 331.

53. Charles B. Trego, *A Geography of Pennsylvania* (Philadelphia: Edward C. Biddle, 1843), 325.

54. Wolf, "Origins of Philadelphia's Self-Deprecation," 68; Charles R. Barker, "Philadelphia in the Late 'Forties," 248.

55. Barker, "Philadelphia, 1836–9," 357.

56. Chambers, *Things as They Are*, 320. Herman Krooss, "Financial Institutions," in *The Growth of Seaport Cities, 1790–1825*, ed. David T. Gilchrist (Charlottesville: University of Virginia Press, 1967), 104.

57. Lindstrom, *Economic Development*, 30; Clement, *Welfare*, 26.

58. Cope, *Philadelphia Merchant*, 228.

59. Morton Keller, "The Personality of Cities: Boston, New York, Philadelphia," *Proceedings of the Massachusetts Historical Society*, 3rd ser., 97 (1985): 10.

60. Sleigh, *Pine Forests*, 324.

61. Edward J. Gibbons and Edward S. Gibbons, "The Building of the Schuylkill Navigation System, 1815–1828," *Pennsylvania History*, 57, no. 1 (January 1990): 15.

62. Wolf, *Philadelphia*, 165.

63. Samuel Breck, "The Diary of Samuel Breck, 1823–1827," *Pennsylvania Magazine of History and Biography*, 103, no. 1 (January 1979): 87; Lindstrom, *Economic Development*, 42.

64. Samuel Breck, "The Diary of Samuel Breck, 1814–1822," *Pennsylvania Magazine of History and Biography*, 102, no. 4 (October 1978): 500; Breck, "Diary, 1823–1827," 103. See also Rilling, *Making Houses*, 25; Lindstrom, *Economic Development*, viii; Sullivan, *Industrial Worker*, 6–7.

65. Joseph A. Stausbaugh, "The Influence of the Pennsylvania Mainline of Public Works," *Gettysburg Historical Journal*, 5, article 4 (2006): 18–19.

66. Job R. Tyson, *Letters, on the Resources and Commerce of Philadelphia* (Philadelphia: Inquirer Job Press, 1851), 3.

67. Diane Lindstrom, "Demand, Markets, and Eastern Economic Development: Philadelphia, 1815–1840," *Journal of Economic History*, 35, no. 1 (March 1975): 272.

68. Edward Burd to Jasper Yeates, 19 April 1813, *The Burd Papers: Selections from Letters Written by Edward Burd, 1763–1828*, ed. Lewis Burd Walker (self-pub., 1899), 221. See also J. St. George Joyce, *Story of Philadelphia* (Philadelphia: Rex Printing House, 1919), 205–7.

69. Breck, "Diary, 1814–1822," 474–75.

70. Cope, *Philadelphia Merchant*, 272, 296; Breck, "Diary, 1814–1822," 476.

71. Cope, *Philadelphia Merchant*, 299.

72. Clement, *Welfare*, 27.

73. Albrecht Koschnik, "Political Conflict and Public Contest: Rituals of National Celebration in Philadelphia, 1788–1815," *Pennsylvania Magazine of History and Biography*, 118, no. 3 (July 1994): 247–48.

74. Sidney GeorgeFisher, recalling a debate, said in his diary, "a large portion of the educated men in the country were opposed to democracy & its influences, [and] considered that all the evil & none of the good we enjoy were ascribable to it." Fisher, *Philadelphia Perspective*, 151. In 1839, after noting that the city recorder was formerly a blacksmith, Samuel Breck opined, "The truth is that the intelligence of this country is excluded from all public stations." Breck, "Diary, 1839–1840," 502. Englishman Sir Henry Keating, who visited Philadelphia in 1830, observed, "A strong aristocratick feeling pervades the wealthy part of this community." "Philadelphia in 1830: An English View," ed. Russell M. Posner, *Pennsylvania Magazine of History and Biography*, 95, no. 2 (April 1971): 243. Another visitor, Frederick Marryat, opined, "Philadelphia has claimed for herself the most aristocratic city in the Union." Marryat, *Diary in America*, 146. See also Sullivan, *Industrial Worker*, 37; Alan M. Zachary, "Social Disorder and the Philadelphia Elite Before Jackson," *Pennsylvania Magazine of History and Biography*, 99, no. 3 (July 1973): 293; Francis W. Hoeber, "Drama in the Courtroom: Philadelphia's Irish Riot of 1831," *Pennsylvania Magazine of History and Biography*, 125, no. 3 (July 2001): 196; Kilbride, *American Aristocracy*, 2.

75. Rosalind L. Branning, *Pennsylvania Constitutional Development* (Pittsburgh: University of Pittsburgh Press, 1960), 71.

76. Clement, *Welfare*, 26.

77. Howell to Evans, 20 January 1834 and Chandler to Howell, 27 January 1834, Chandler, *Remember*, 220, 225; Sullivan, *Industrial Worker*, 53; John Runcie, "'Hunting the Nigs' in Philadelphia: The Race Riot of August 1834," *Pennsylvania History*, 39, no. 2 (April 1972): 201–2.

78. Sullivan, *Industrial Worker*, 199; Andrew Heath, *In Union There Is Strength: Philadelphia in the Age of Urban Consolidation* (Philadelphia: University of Pennsylvania Press, 2019), 21.

79. Barr, "'Worthy,'" 893–94; Clement, *Welfare*, 28.

80. Tyson, *Letters*, 15.

81. Dickens, *American Notes*, 122; Cope, *Philadelphia Merchant*, 429; Heath, *In Union*, 19. See also Fisher, *Philadelphia Perspective*, 77, 134; Howell to Chandler, 22 May 1842, Chandler, *Remember*, 342.

82. Wolf, *Philadelphia*, 127; Gordon C. Bjork, "Foreign Trade," in *The Growth of Seaport Cities, 1790–1825*, ed. David T. Gilchrist (Charlottesville: University of Virginia Press, 1967), 56–57; Zachary, "Social Disorder," 290; Warner, *Private City*, 82.

83. Wolf, "Origins of Philadelphia's Self-Deprecation," 60.

84. Sidney Fisher reflected this attitude in his diary in 1837 when he contrasted Philadelphia's culture with New York's, describing the former as "unpretending, elegant, cordial & friendly containing many persons not rich, but few whose families have not held the same station for several generations." Fisher, *Philadelphia Perspective*, 21. See also Keller, "Personality of Cities," 2; Zachary, "Social Disorder," 292; Kilbride, *American Aristocracy*, 3.

85. Dickens, *American Notes*, 121.

86. Dickens, *American Notes*, 123.

87. Foster, "Philadelphia in Slices," *New York Tribune*, 28William Chambers noted that Philadelphia offered "the attractions usually sought for by a class of emigrants whose aim goes beyond mere money-making or the ordinary necessities of existence." Chambers, *Things as They Are*, 321. The counterpoint to these assertions was Nathaniel Carrington's 1837 observation: "There is by no means the bustle and quantity of business [in Philadelphia] that there is in New York. I think as much is done in the latter city in one week as in a month here." Carrington, "Barbados Planter's Visit," 415.

88. Bruce Laurie and Mark Schmitz, "Manufacture and Productivity: The Making of an Industrial Base, Philadelphia, 1850–1880," in *Philadelphia: Work, Space, Family, and Group Experience in the 19th Century*, ed. Theodore Hershberg (New York: Oxford University Press, 1981), 43, 50.

89. William A. Sullivan, "The Industrial Revolution and the Factory Operative in Pennsylvania," *Pennsylvania Magazine of History and Biography*, 78, no. 4 (October 1954): 483.

90. Chandler to Howell, n.d., Chandler, *Remember*, 128. See also Shammas, "Space Problem," 525; Susan E. Klepp, "Demography in Early Philadelphia, 1690–1860," *Proceedings of the American Philosophical Society*, 133, no. 2 (June 1989): 97; Louis Kantrow, "Life Expectancy of the Gentry in Eighteenth and Nineteenth-Century Philadelphia," in *The Demographic History of the Philadelphia Region, 1600–1860, Proceedings of the American Philosophical Society*, 133, no. 2 (June 1989): 320; Sullivan, *Industrial Worker*, 32; Clark, *Irish in Philadelphia*, 48.

91. Anne Royall, *Mrs. Royall's Pennsylvania: Or, Travels Continued in the United States*, vol. 1 (Washington, DC: self-pub., 1829), 85. See also Barr, "'Worthy,'" 647, 650, 662.

92. Clement, *Welfare*, 25; Hershberg et al., "'Journey-to-Work,'" 165.

93. Barr, "'Worthy,'" 151, 534; Sutherland, "Housing the Poor," 179.

94. Sullivan, *Industrial Worker*, 194.

95. Heath, *In Union*, 49–50.

96. Andrew Heath calls Philadelphia "a center of labor organizing" in this period. Heath, *In Union*, 50.

97. Sullivan, *Industrial Worker*, 221–30.

98. Joyce, *Story of Philadelphia*, 28–29.

99. Sullivan, *Industrial Worker*, 171.

100. Barr, "'Worthy,'" 764.

101. Milroy, *Grid and the River*, 205–7; McMahon, "Makeshift Technology," 29.

102. Barr, "'Worthy,'" 547.

103. Howell to Chandler, 23 June 1834, Chandler, *Remember*, 187.

104. Adam Levine, "Sewers, Pollution, and Public Health in Philadelphia," *Pennsylvania Legacies*, 10, no. 1 (May 2010): 16; Sullivan, "Industrial Revolution," 477.

105. Klepp, "Demography in Early Philadelphia," 97; Clement, *Welfare*, 28.

106. Barr, "'Worthy,'" 124–25; Howell to Evans, 25 July 1832, and Chandler to Howell, n.d., Chandler, *Remember*, 125–28. See also Wolf, *Philadelphia*, 167; John B. Osborne, "Preparing for the Pandemic: City Boards of Health and the Arrival of Cholera in Montreal, New York, and Philadelphia in 1832," *Urban History Review*, 36, no. 2 (Spring 2008): 30.

107. Rugbaean, *Transatlantic Rambles*, 45. Many Philadelphians cataloged outbreaks in their diaries and letters. See Barr, "'Worthy,'" 236, 274, 580; Sinkler to Wharton, 18 July 1850, *Between North and South: The Letters of Emily Wharton Sinkler, 1842–1865*, ed. Anne Sinkler Whaley LeClerq (Columbia: University of South Carolina Press, 2001), 132.

108. Cope, *Philadelphia Merchant*, 417.

109. Beginning in the mid-1820s and continuing for the next thirty years, Philadelphia and the surrounding districts were menaced by several gangs, including the Bouncers, the Blood Tubs, the Fluters, the Killers, the Rats, and the Skinners. Barker, "Philadelphia in the Late 'Forties," 260; Runcie, "'Hunting,'" 204–5; Griffith and Adrian, *History of American City Government*, 90; Bruce Laurie, "Fire Companies and Gangs in Southwark: The 1840s," in *The Peoples of Philadelphia: A History of Ethnic Groups and Lower-Class Life, 1790–1940*, ed. Allen F. Davis and Mark H. Haller (Philadelphia: University of Pennsylvania Press, 1998), 78; Johnson, "Crime Patterns," 98–99.

110. Barker, "Philadelphia, 1836–9," 355.

111. Charles Godfrey Leland, *Memoirs*, 2nd ed. (London: William Heinemann, 1894), 216–17; Fisher, *Philadelphia Perspective*, 175; Howell to Chandler, 25 September 1841, Chandler, *Remember*, 337. George G. Foster considered the firemen's reputations as undeserved, drawing a distinction between gangs and fire companies, but with little evidence. Foster, "Philadelphia in Slices," 34–35.

112. *Ordinances of the Corporation of, and Acts of the Assembly Relating to, the City of Philadelphia* (Philadelphia: Crissy & Markley, 1851), 316–17.

113. Allinson and Penrose, *Philadelphia, 1681–1887*, 205.

114. Heath, *In Union*, 36.

115. Cope, *Philadelphia Merchant*, 127, 132; Barr, "'Worthy,'" 576; Breck, "Diary, 1823–1827," 234. See also Runcie, "'Hunting,'" 188.

116. Barr, "'Worthy,'" 603.

117. Cope, *Philadelphia Merchant*, 79, 181, 221, 310, 424, 450, 592; Fisher, *Philadelphia Perspective*, 65; Barr, "'Worthy,'" 576; Breck, "Diary, 1814–1822," 497; Breck, "Diary, 1823–1827," 238; Chandler, *Remember*, 198; Isaac Mickle, *A Gentleman of Much Promise: The Diary of Isaac Mickle, 1837–1845*, ed. Philip English Mackey, vols. 1 and 2 (Philadelphia: University of Pennsylvania Press, 1977), 164, 179, 277, 424.

118. Keller, "Personality of Cities," 11; Michael Feldberg, "Urbanization as a Cause of Violence: Philadelphia as a Test Case," in *The Peoples of Philadelphia: A History of Ethnic Groups and Lower-Class Life, 1790–1940*, ed. Allen F. Davis and Mark H. Haller (Philadelphia: University of Pennsylvania Press, 1998), 55.

119. Leland, *Memoirs*, 216. Others also observed that this period appeared particularly lawless. Barr, "'Worthy,'" 512, 585. See also Runcie, "'Hunting,'" 187; Zachary M. Schrag, *The Fires of Philadelphia: Citizen-Soldiers, Nativism, and the 1844 Riots over the Soul of a Nation* (New York: Pegasus Books, 2021), 58.

120. "A View of the City of Brotherly Love" (New York: H. R. Robinson, 1842), Historical Society of Pennsylvania large graphics collection (#V65). See also Johnson, "Crime Patterns," 100–101; Griffith and Adrian, *History of American City Government*, 58; Schrag, *Fires of Philadelphia*, 58.

121. Griffith and Adrian, *History of American City Government*, 87.

122. Barker, "Philadelphia in the Late 'Forties," 258; Geffen, "Violence," 404; Michael P. McCarthy, "The Philadelphia Consolidation of 1854: A Reappraisal," *Pennsylvania Magazine of History and Biography*, 110, no. 4 (October 1986): 535–37; Griffith and Adrian, *History of American City Government*, 58. See also Joyce, *Story of Philadelphia*, 239–40; Foster, "Philadelphia in Slices," 36; Cope, *Philadelphia Merchant*, 518, 581.

123. Barr, "'Worthy,'" 101, 153; Wolf, "Origins of Philadelphia's Self-Deprecation," 65; Lee and Lalli, "Population," 33; Allen F. Davis, Introduction, in *The Peoples of Philadelphia: A History of Ethnic Groups and Lower-Class Life, 1790–1940*, ed. Allen F. Davis and Mark H. Haller (Philadelphia: University of Pennsylvania Press, 1998), 9; Clement, *Welfare*, 25.

124. Clark, *Irish in Philadelphia*, 29; Warner, *Private City*, 139; J. Matthew Gallman, *Receiving Erin's Children: Philadelphia, Liverpool, and the Irish Famine Migration, 1845–1855* (Chapel Hill: University of North Carolina Press, 2000), 6; Richard A. Warren, "Displaced 'Pan-Americans' and the Transformation of the Catholic Church in Philadelphia, 1789–1850," *Pennsylvania Magazine of History and Biography*, 128, no. 4 (October 2004): 348.

125. Cope, *Philadelphia Merchant*, 409–10. Nor was he the only one who expressed these sentiments; Sidney George Fisher called Irish immigrants "the refuse of Europe" and complained that they voted for Democrats. Fisher, *Philadelphia Perspective*, 177.

126. Barr, "'Worthy,'" 405; John Modell and Lynn H. Lees, "The Irish Countrymen Urbanized: A Comparative Perspective on the Famine Migration," in *Philadelphia: Work, Space, Family, and Group Experience in the 19th Century*, ed. Theodore Hershberg (New York: Oxford University Press, 1981), 351; Emma Jones Lapsansky, "'Since They Got Those Separate Churches': Afro-Americans and Racism in Jacksonian Philadelphia," *American Quarterly*, 32, no. 1 (Spring 1980): 56, 61; W. E. B. Du Bois, *The Philadelphia Negro* (Philadelphia: University of Pennsylvania Press, 1996), 26; John F. Quinn, "The Rise and Fall of Repeal: Slavery and Irish Nationalism in Antebellum Philadelphia," *Pennsylvania*

Magazine of History and Biography, 130, no 1 (January 2006): 50; Joseph Wilson, *The Elite of Our People: Joseph Wilson's Sketches of Black Upper-Class Life in Antebellum Philadelphia*, ed. Julie Winch (University Park: Pennsylvania State University Press, 2000), 12.

127. Cope, *Philadelphia Merchant*, 437. Deborah Norris Logan complained in 1834, "The wretched hordes of low foreigners who come among us are the great enemies of our peace and comfort." Barr, "'Worthy,'" 811.

128. Milroy, *Grid and the River*, 234; Amanda Beyer-Purvis, "The Philadelphia Bible Riots of 1844: Contest over the Rights of Citizens," *Pennsylvania History*, 83, no. 3 (Summer 2016): 366.

129. Richard N. Juliani, "The Parish as an Urban Institution: Italian Catholics in Philadelphia," *Records of the American Catholic Historical Society of Philadelphia*, 96, no. 1/4 (March–December 1985): 52.

130. *Address of the Board of Managers of the American Protestant Association* (Philadelphia: James C. Haswell, 1843), 7.

131. Cope, *Philadelphia Merchant*, 428.

132. Fisher, *Philadelphia Perspective*, 165. See also Mickle, *Gentleman*, 441–45.

133. Theodore Hershberg, "Free Blacks in Antebellum Philadelphia: A Study of Ex-Slaves, Freeborn, and Socioeconomic Decline," in *Philadelphia: Work, Space, Family, and Group Experience in the 19th Century*, ed. Theodore Hershberg (New York: Oxford University Press, 1981), 368; Du Bois, *Philadelphia Negro*, 26; Julie Winch, "Philadelphia and the Other Underground Railroad," *Pennsylvania Magazine of History and Biography*, 111, no. 1 (January 1987): 8.

134. Wolf, *Philadelphia*, 141; Geffen, "Violence," 385; Winch, "Philadelphia," 8. There's reason to believe this is a low estimate; after all, Philadelphia was home to many escaped slaves who would have avoided calling attention to themselves. Julie Winch, "Self-Help and Self-Determination: Black Philadelphians and the Dimensions of Freedom," in *Antislavery and Abolition in Philadelphia: Emancipation and the Long Struggle for Racial Justice in the City of Brotherly Love*, ed. Richard Newman and James Mueller (Baton Rouge: Louisiana State University Press, 2011), 75.

135. Gillette, "Emergence," 7.

136. Marryat, *Diary in America*, 149; Lapsansky, "'Since They Got,'" 57; Hershberg, "Free Blacks," 370–74; Clement, *Welfare*, 33; Nash, *Forging Freedom*, 173. Elizabeth Geffen points out that Black people were overrepresented in the population of the city's almshouse. Geffen, "Violence," 385.

137. Mary Mallard, "'Faithfully Drawn from Real Life': Autobiographical Elements in Frank J. Webb's *The Garies and their Friends*," *Pennsylvania Magazine of History and Biography*, 137, no. 3 (July 2013): 262.

138. Cope, *Philadelphia Merchant*, 548. In 1830, Deborah Norris Logan described the heartbreaking scene of a "maudlin colored woman with a sick child" asking for alms. Logan "did not like her but pitied the baby and would have recommended her to the overseers of the poor to put it under medical care." The baby died that evening. Barr, "'Worthy,'" 576–77.

139. Beverly C. Tomek, *Slavery and Abolition in Pennsylvania* (Philadelphia: Temple University Press, 2021), 56–57.

140. Nash, *Forging Freedom*, 177.

141. Ira Berlin, "Slavery, Freedom, and Philadelphia's Struggle for Brotherly Love, 1685 to 1861," in *Antislavery and Abolition in Philadelphia: Emancipation and the Long Struggle for Racial Justice in the City of Brotherly Love*, ed. Richard Newman and James Mueller (Baton Rouge: Louisiana State University Press, 2011), 26; *Journal of the Twenty-Ninth House of Representatives of the Commonwealth of Pennsylvania* (Harrisburg, PA: James Peacock, 1819), 139.

142. Richard Cobden, *The American Diaries of Richard Cobden*, ed. Elizabeth Hoon Cawley (Princeton, NJ: Princeton University Press, 1952), 91; Eyre Crowe, *With Thackeray in America* (New York: Charles Scribner's Sons, 1893), 105; Chambers, *Things as They Are*, 321.

143. Frederick Marryat observed, "Singular is the degree of contempt and dislike which the free Blacks are held in all the free states of America." Marryat, *Diary in America*, 149. See also Lapsansky, "'Since They Got,'" 65; Edward Clay, "*Life in Philadelphia Collection*," Library Company of Philadelphia, accessed December 10, 2019, https://digital.librarycompany.org/islandora/object/Islandora%3ALINP1?f%5B0%5D=RELS_EXT_isMemberOfCollection_uri_ms%3A%22info%5C%3Afedora%5C/Islandora%5C%3ALINP1%22.

144. Roy H. Akagi, "The Pennsylvania Constitution of 1838," *Pennsylvania Magazine of History and Biography*, 48, no. 4 (1924): 329. Though technically able to vote before 1838, most free Black Philadelphians did not do so, in large measure because of procedural barriers created by racist whites and in part out of fear of arousing whites' animosity. See Van Gosse, *The First Reconstruction: Black Politics in America from the Revolution to the Civil War* (Chapel Hill: University of North Carolina Press, 2021), 103–4.

145. Barker, "Philadelphia in the Late 'Forties," 264.

146. Barker, "Philadelphia, 1836–9," 364; Howell to Chandler, 29 May 1838, Chandler, *Remember*, 318.

147. Runcie, "'Hunting,'" 190.

148. Elizabeth Cady Stanton, *Eighty Years and More* (New York: European Publishing, 1898), 89.

149. Wolf, *Philadelphia*, 157.

150. Mickle, *Gentleman*, 314. See also Geffen, "Violence," 387.

151. "A Terrible Riot," *Jeffersonian Republican*, October 18, 1849; *Life and Adventures of Charles Anderson Chester* (Philadelphia: 1850), 30.

152. Khalil Gibran Muhammad, *The Condemnation of Blackness: Race, Crime, and the Making of Modern Urban America* (Cambridge, MA: Harvard University Press, 2019), 22; George M. Fredrickson, *The Black Image in the White Mind: The Debate on African-American Character and Destiny, 1817–1914* (New York: Harper Torchbooks, 1972), 74; Emily Renschler and Janet Monge, "The Samuel George Morton Cranial Collection." *Expedition Magazine*, 50, no. 3, 31; Harriet A. Washington, *Medical Apartheid: The Dark History of Medical Experimentation on Black Americans from Colonial Times to the Present* (New York: Penguin Random House, 2008), 90.

153. Ari Kelman, "Vanishing Indians," in *Myth America: Historians Take on the Biggest Legends and Lies About Our Past*, ed. Kevin M. Kruse and Julian E. Zelizer (New York: Basic Books, 2022), 45.

154. Peter Crimmins, "Penn Museum Apologizes for 'Unethical Possession of Human Remains,'" NPR.org., accessed December 12, 2022, https://www.npr.org/2021/04/27 /988972736/penn-museum-apologizes-for-unethical-possession-of-human-remains.

155. Emma Jones Lapsansky, "'Discipline to the Mind': Philadelphia's Banneker Institute, 1854–1872," *Pennsylvania Magazine of History and Biography*, 117, no. 1–2 (1993): 86; Dee E. Andrews, "From Natural Rights to National Sins: Philadelphia's Churches Face Antislavery," in *Antislavery and Abolition in Philadelphia: Emancipation and the Long Struggle for Racial Justice in the City of Brotherly Love*, ed. Richard Newman and James Mueller (Baton Rouge: Louisiana State University Press, 2011), 187; Wilson, *Elite of Our People*, 33; Tomek, *Slavery and Abolition*, 58; Nash, *Forging Freedom*, 183; Frederick Douglass, *Life and Times of Frederick Douglass: Written by Himself* (Hartford, CT: Park Publishing, 1882), 308.

156. Foster, "Philadelphia in Slices," 60–61; Lapsansky, "'Since They Got,'" 58.

157. Judith Giesburg, Introduction, in *Emilie Davis's Civil War: The Diaries of a Free Black Woman in Philadelphia, 1863–1865,* ed. Judith Giesburg (University Park: Pennsylvania State University Press, 2014), 8.

158. Norman B. Wilkinson, "The Philadelphia Free Produce Attack upon Slavery," *Pennsylvania Magazine of History and Biography*, 66, no. 3 (July 1942): 298–99.

159. Tomek, *Slavery and Abolition*, 78–83.

160. "Meeting in the State House Yard," *Pennsylvania Freeman*, August 22, 1844.

161. Douglass, *Life and Times*, 249.

162. Nilgün Anaolu-Okur, "Underground Railroad in Philadelphia, 1830–1860," *Journal of Black Studies*, 25, no. 5 (1995): 542.

163. Okur, "Underground Railroad," 546–47.

164. Isaac Hopper, *Kidnappers in Philadelphia: Isaac Hopper's Tales of Oppression, 1780–1843*, ed. Daniel E. Meaders (New York: Routledge, 2019), 55; Tomek, *Slavery and Abolition*, 70.

165. Elliott Drago, "A Precarious Freedom: The 1820 Philadelphia Kidnapping Crisis," *Pennsylvania Magazine of History and Biography*, 145, no. 2 (April 2021): 120–21.

166. Winch, "Philadelphia," 7; Frankie Hutton, *The Early Black Press in America: 1827 to 1860* \(Westport, CT: Greenwood, 1993), 152.

167. Cope, *Philadelphia Merchant*, 602; Charlene Mires, "Slavery, Nativism, and the Forgotten History of Independence Hall," *Pennsylvania History*, 67, no. 4 (Autumn 2000): 488.

168. Elizabeth M. Geffen, "Philadelphia Protestantism Reacts to Social Reform Movements Before the Civil War," *Pennsylvania Magazine of History and Biography*, 30, no. 2 (April 1963): 197.

169. Barr, "'Worthy,'" 923; Samuel Breck, "The Diary of Samuel Breck, 1834–1835, 1838," *Pennsylvania Magazine of History and Biography*, 103, no. 3 (July 1979): 370; Howell to Evans, 21 January 1835, and Evans to Howell, 5 March, 1835, Chandler, *Remember*, 268.

170. Leland, *Memoirs*, 136.

171. Zachary, "Social Disorder," 301; Michael Feldberg, "The Crowd in Philadelphia: A Comparative Perspective," *Labor History*, 15, no. 3 (June 1974): 326; Lindstrom, "Demand," 272; Kilbride, *American Aristocracy*, 5.

172. "Resolutions: First Anti-Slavery Convention of American Women," in *Feminist Manifestos: A Global Documentary Reader*, ed. Penny A. Weiss with Megan Brueske (New York: New York University Press, 2018), 58.

173. Ira V. Brown, "The Women's Rights Movement in Pennsylvania, 1848–1873," *Pennsylvania History*, 32, no. 2 (April 1965): 154; Ira V. Brown, "'Am I Not a Woman and a Sister?' The Anti-Slavery Convention of American Women, 1837–1839." *Pennsylvania History*, 50, no. 1 (January 1983): 1; Margaret Hope Bacon, "Antislavery Women Find a Voice," *Pennsylvania Legacies*, 5, no. 2 (November 2005): 10; Thelma M. Smith, "Feminism in Philadelphia, 1790–1850," *Pennsylvania Magazine of History and Biography*, 68, no. 3 (July 1944): 245.

174. *McElroy's Philadelphia Directory, 1856* (Philadelphia: Edward C. & John Biddle, 1856), 465.

175. Emily Hatcher, "The Philadelphia Female Anti-Slavery Society and the Civil War," *Pennsylvania Magazine of History and Biography*, 135, no. 4 (October 2011): 528.

176. Ira V. Brown "Cradle of Feminism: The Philadelphia Female Anti-Slavery Society, 1833–1840," *Pennsylvania Magazine of History and Biography*, 102, no. 2 (April 1978): 152.

177. Brown, "Women's Rights Movement," 155.

178. Lee L. Schreiber, "Bluebloods and Local Societies: A Philadelphia Microcosm," *Pennsylvania History*, 49, no. 3 (July 1981): 252.

179. Fisher, *Philadelphia Perspective*, 9; Chambers, *Things as They Are*, 310.

180. Dickens, *American Notes*, 123. By contrast, English judge Sir Henry S. Keating observed after his visit to Eastern State Penitentiary that if the Pennsylvania system delivered on its promises, "it would indeed be . . . a most happy thing." Posner, "Philadelphia in 1830," 241. See also Slaney, *Short*, 51; Rugbaean, *Transatlantic Rambles*, 309.

181. Akagi, "Pennsylvania Constitution," 317.

182. Zachary, "Social Disorder," 295; Griffith and Adrian, *History of American City Government*, 77.

183. *Ordinances of the Corporation*, 112.

184. Breck, "Diary, 1834–1835, 1838," 366.

185. Barker, "Philadelphia in the Late 'Forties," 265; Foster, "Philadelphia in Slices," 32; Chambers, *Things as They Are*, 314–15.

186. David Brain, "Practical Knowledge and Occupational Control: The Professionalization of Architecture in the United States," *Sociological Forum*, 6, no. 2 (June 1991): 243; Milroy, *Grid and the River*, 227; Heath, *In Union*, 8.

187. Jeffrey A. Cohen, "Building a Discipline: Early Institutional Settings for Architectural Education in Philadelphia, 1804–1890," *Journal of the Society of Architectural Historians*, 53, no. 2 (June 1994): 140–41; Brain, "Practical Knowledge," 245; Lewis, *Philadelphia Builds*, 22; Martinko, *Historic Real Estate*, 9–10.

188. Talbot Hamlin, "Some Greek Revival Architects of Philadelphia," *Pennsylvania Magazine of History and Biography*, 65, no. 2 (April 1941): 122.

189. Agnes Addison Gilchrist, "The Philadelphia Exchange: William Strickland, Architect," *Transactions of the American Philosophical Society*, 43, no 1 (1953): 87.

190. Nicholas Biddle, "The Girard College," in *Journal of the Franklin Institute*, vol. 12, ed. Thomas P. Jones (Philadelphia: Franklin Institute, 1833), 230.

191. Gillette, "Emergence," 4; Laurie, "Fire Companies," 73.

192. Robert A. Slaney, commenting on the building in 1860, claimed, "Almost half the bequest must have been expended in a magnificent but almost useless building, and unless so directed by the will, it was wrong to do so." Slaney, *Short*, 55. See also Alexander Marjoribanks, *Travels in South and North America* (London: Simpkin, Marshall, 1853), 429–30.

193. Gary B. Nash, *First City: Philadelphia and the Forging of Historical Memory* (Philadelphia: University of Pennsylvania Press, 2006), 17.

194. Cope, *Philadelphia Merchant*, 251; Barr, "'Worthy,'" 359. This was hardly unique to Philadelphia; see Alfred F. Young, *The Shoemaker and the Tea Party: Memory and the American Revolution* (Boston: Beacon Press, 2001), 181–84.

195. Anna Verplanck, "Making History: Antiquarian Culture in Mid-Nineteenth-Century Philadelphia," *Pennsylvania Magazine of History and Biography*, 138, no. 4 (October 2014): 399.

196. Charles R. Weld, *A Vacation Tour in the United States and Canada* (London: Longman, Brown, Green & Longmans, 1855), 339. William Chambers echoed this sentiment, noting, "Philadelphia is somehow associated, *par excellence*, in the minds of the English with the idea of America. When we think of the history of that great country, or of its statesmen, or patriots, up comes the notion of Philadelphia in a very remarkable way." Chambers, *Things as They Are*, 318.

197. Joyce, *Story of Philadelphia*, 243–44. See also Martinko, *Historic Real Estate*, 88–90.

198. Feldberg, "Urbanization," 58; Verplanck, "Making History," 397; Berlin, "Slavery, Freedom," 35.

199. Charlene Mires, *Independence Hall in American Memory* (Philadelphia: University of Pennsylvania Press, 2002), 71.

200. Sleigh, *Pine Forests*, 323.

201. Foster, "Philadelphia in Slices," 72; Fisher, *Philadelphia Perspective*, 104; Chambers, *Things as They Are*, 308. See also Wolf, *Philadelphia*, 142; Bjork, "Foreign Trade," 60; Martinko, *Historic Real Estate*, 54–55.

202. Quoted in Barker, "Philadelphia in the Late 'Forties," 268.

203. Charlene Mires, "Independence Hall," *Encyclopedia of Greater Philadelphia*, accessed November 17, 2019, https://philadelphiaencyclopedia.org/archive/independence-hall/.

204. Griffith and Adrian, *History of American City Government*, 65; Gallman, *Receiving Erin's Children*, 18; Geffen, "Philadelphia Protestantism," 197; Schreiber, "Bluebloods," 251.

205. Keels, *Forgotten Philadelphia*, 116.

206. *A Guide to the Stranger, or Pocket Companion for the Fancy, Containing a List of the Gay Houses and Ladies of Pleasure in the City of Brotherly Love and Sisterly Affection* (Philadelphia: n.p., 1849). On alcohol, see Ric Northrup Caric, "Blustering Brags, Dueling Inventors, and Corn-Square Geniuses: Artisan Leisure in Philadelphia, 1785–1825," *American Journal of Semiotics*, 12, no. 1–4 (1995), 325; Edith Jeffrey, "Reform, Renewal, and Vindication: Irish Immigrants and the Catholic Total Abstinence Movement in Antebellum Philadelphia," *Pennsylvania Magazine of History and Biography*, 112, no. 3 (July 1988): 407.

207. Cope, *Philadelphia Merchant*, 435; Barr, "'Worthy,'" 577; Breck, "Diary, 1823–1827," 111; Breck, "Diary, 1834–1835, 1838," 356; Bromley, *Woman's Wanderings*, 34; Wilson, *Elite of Our People*, 100–101. See also Matthew Warner Osborn, "A Detestable Shrine: Alcohol Abuse in Antebellum Philadelphia," *Journal of the Early Republic*, 29, no. 1 (Spring 2009): 104–5.

208. Sullivan, "Industrial Revolution," 479.

209. Dickens, *American Notes*, 136.

210. Barker, "Philadelphia, 1836–9," 367; Foster, "Philadelphia in Slices," 49; Griffith and Adrian, *History of American City Government*, 103; Marcia Carlisle, "Disorderly City, Disorderly Women: Prostitution in Ante-Bellum Philadelphia," *Pennsylvania Magazine of History and Biography*, 110, no. 4 (October 1986): 552.

211. Barker, "Philadelphia in the Late 'Forties," 259.

212. Gillette, "Emergence," 9; Mires, "Slavery, Nativism," 95.

213. Quoted in Barker, "Philadelphia in the Late 'Forties," 256. See also Allinson and Penrose, *Philadelphia*, 141–42; Milroy, *Grid and the River*, 218; Heath, *In Union*, 21.

214. Leffman, "Consolidation," 28; Russell F. Weigley, "'A Peaceful City': Public Order in Philadelphia from Consolidation Through the Civil War," in *The Peoples of Philadelphia: A History of Ethnic Groups and Lower-Class Life, 1790–1940*, ed. Allen F. Davis and Mark H. Haller (Philadelphia: University of Pennsylvania Press, 1998), 156.

215. *The City and County of Philadelphia: A Discussion of Their Legal Relations* (Philadelphia: Bureau of Municipal Research of Philadelphia, 1923), 12; Heath, *In Union*, 9.

216. Gillette, "Emergence," 12; Geffen, "Violence," 407; *City and County of Philadelphia*, 17.

217. McCarthy, "Philadelphia Consolidation," 533; Heath, *In Union*, 11.

Chapter 6

1. Sidney George Fisher, *A Philadelphia Perspective: The Diary of Sidney George Fisher, Covering the Years 1834–1871* (Philadelphia: Historical Society of Pennsylvania, 1967), 279.

2. Bruce Laurie and Mark Schmitz, "Manufacture and Productivity: The Making of an Industrial Base, Philadelphia: 1850–1880," in *Philadelphia: Work, Space, Family, and Group Experience in the 19th Century*, ed. Theodore Hershberg (New York: Oxford University Press, 1981), 67; Austin E. Hutchinson, "Philadelphia and the Panic of 1857," *Pennsylvania History*, 3, no. 2 (July 1936): 193.

3. *Journal of the Common Council of the City of Philadelphia Beginning May 12 and Ending November 16, 1856* (Philadelphia: Town's Printing Office, 1856), 161. On praise for the system, see Alfred Falk, *Trans-Pacific Sketches: A Tour Through the United States and Canada* (Melbourne, Australia: George Robertson, 1877), 169; Henry Latham, *Black and White: A Journal of Three Months' Tour in the United States* (London: Macmillan, 1867), 15; James Horatio Booty, *Three Months in Canada and the United States* (London: self-pub., 1862), 16.

4. Theodore Hershberg et al., "The 'Journey-to-Work': An Empirical Investigation of Work, Residence and Transportation, Philadelphia, 1850 and 1880," in *Philadelphia: Work, Space, Family, and Group Experience in the 19th Century*, ed. Theodore Hershberg (New York: Oxford University Press, 1981), 154.

5. Friedrich Ratzel, "Philadelphia on the Eve of the Nation's Centennial: A Visitor's Description in 1873–74," ed. Stewart A. Stehlin, *Pennsylvania History*, 44, no. 1 (January 1977): 31.

6. Hershberg et al., "'Journey-to-Work,'" 157–58. Visitors commented on the low population density; for instance, see Latham, *Black and White*, 16.

7. Howard Gillette Jr. "The Emergence of the Modern Metropolis: Philadelphia in the Age of Its Consolidation," in *The Divided Metropolis: Social and Spatial Dimensions of Philadelphia, 1800–1975*, ed. William W. Cutler III and Howard Gillette Jr. (Westport, CT: Greenwood Press, 1980), 15; Jeffrey P. Roberts, "Railroads and the Downtown: Philadelphia, 1830–1900," in *The Divided Metropolis: Social and Spatial Dimensions of Philadelphia, 1800–1975*, ed. William W. Cutler III and Howard Gillette Jr. (Westport, CT: Greenwood Press, 1980), 38.

8. Sam Bass Warner, *The Private City: Philadelphia in Three Periods of Its Growth*, 2nd ed. (Philadelphia: University of Pennsylvania Press, 1987), 50; Maxwell Whiteman, "Philadelphia's Jewish Neighborhoods," in *The Peoples of Philadelphia: A History of Ethnic Groups and Lower-Class Life, 1790–1940*, ed. Allen F. Davis and Mark H. Haller (Philadelphia: University of Pennsylvania Press, 1998), 233; Alan N. Burstein, "Immigrants and Residential Mobility: The Irish and Germans in Philadelphia, 1850–1880," in *Philadelphia: Work, Space, Family, and Group Experience in the 19th Century*, ed. Theodore Hershberg (New York: Oxford University Press, 1981), 180–83; Stephanie W. Greenberg, "Industrial Location and Ethnic Residential Patterns in an Industrializing City: Philadelphia, 1880," in *Philadelphia: Work, Space, Family, and Group Experience in the 19th Century*, ed. Theodore Hershberg (New York: Oxford University Press, 1981), 224; Theodore Hershberg et al., "A Tale of Three Cities: Blacks, Immigrants, and Opportunity in Philadelphia, 1850–1880, 1930, 1970," in *Philadelphia: Work, Space, Family, and Group Experience in the 19'h Century*, ed. Theodore Hershberg (New York: Oxford University Press, 1981), 469; Dennis Clark, "The Philadelphia Irish: Persistent Presence," in *The Peoples of Philadelphia: A History of Ethnic Groups and Lower-Class Life, 1790–1940*, ed. Allen F. Davis and Mark H. Haller (Philadelphia: University of Pennsylvania Press, 1998), 137.

9. Greenberg, "Industrial Location," 226; Theodore Hershberg, "Free Blacks in Antebellum Philadelphia: A Study of Ex-Slaves, Freeborn, and Socioeconomic Decline," in *Philadelphia: Work, Space, Family, and Group Experience in the 19th Century*, ed. Theodore Hershberg (New York: Oxford University Press, 1981), 374.

10. William Dusinberre, *Civil War Issues in Philadelphia, 1856–1865* (Philadelphia: University of Pennsylvania Press, 1965), 20; Hershberg et al., "Tale of Three Cities," 467.

11. Martha H. Garrett, *Memoirs of Philadelphia in the Nineteenth Century* (Philadelphia: self-pub., 1910), 2–3.

12. Fisher, *Philadelphia Perspective*, 316.

13. Fisher, *Philadelphia Perspective*, 432.

14. Garrett, *Memoirs*, 6; Joseph Boggs Beale, "Education of an Artist: The Diary of Joseph Boggs Beale, 1856–1862," ed. Nicholas B. Wainwright, *Pennsylvania Magazine of History and Biography*, 97, no. 4 (October 1973): 490; Ratzel, "Philadelphia on the Eve," 36. See also Hershberg et al., "'Journey-to-Work,'" 148.

15. *Journal of the Select Council of the City of Philadelphia from January 1, 1872, to July 1, 1872* (Philadelphia: E. C. Markley & Son, 1872), 361; Harry Kyriakodis and Joel Spivak, *Underground Philadelphia: From Caves and Canals to Tunnels and Transit* (Charleston, SC: History Press, 2019), 38–39.

16. Gunther Barth, *City People: The Rise of Modern City Culture in Nineteenth-Century America* (New York: Oxford University Press, 1980), 54.

17. Burstein, "Immigrants," 177; Gillette, "Emergence of the Modern Metropolis," 18.

18. Gideon Welles, *Diary of Gideon Welles*, vol. 3 (Boston: Houghton Mifflin, 1911), 505–6. On the role of the PRR in Pennsylvania, see Albert J. Churella, *The Pennsylvania Railroad*, vol. 1: *Building an Empire, 1846–1917* (Philadelphia: University of Pennsylvania Press, 2012), 327.

19. Andrew Heath, "The Public Interest of the Private City: The Pennsylvania Railroad, Urban Space, and Philadelphia's Economic Elite, 1846–1877," *Pennsylvania Magazine of History and Biography*, 79, no 2 (Spring 2012): 188.

20. Beale, "Education of an Artist," 488; Fisher, *Philadelphia Perspective*, 327. See also Roberts, "Railroads and the Downtown," 37–40; William W. Cutler III, "The Persistent Dualism: Centralization and Decentralization in Philadelphia, 1854–1975," in *The Divided Metropolis: Social and Spatial Dimensions of Philadelphia, 1800–1920*, ed. William W. Cutler III and Howard Gillette Jr. (Westport, CT: Greenwood Press, 1980), 253; David R. Contosta, "Suburban Quasi Government in Chestnut Hill, Philadelphia," *Pennsylvania Magazine of History and Biography*, 116, no. 3 (July 1992): 260.

21. Kyriakodis and Spivak, *Underground Philadelphia*, 126.

22. Kyriakodis and Spivak, *Underground Philadelphia*, 80; Domenic Vitello, "Engineering the Metropolis: William Sellers, Joseph W. Wilson, and Industrial Philadelphia," *Pennsylvania Magazine of History and Biography*, 126, no. 2 (April 2002): 276.

23. Malcolm Bell, *Major Butler's Legacy: Five Generations of a Slaveholding Family* (Athens: University of Georgia Press, 1989), xxi.

24. Joseph S. Elkinton, *Selections from the Diary and Correspondence of Joseph S. Elkinton, 1830–1905* (Philadelphia: self-pub., 1913), 11; Charlotte L. Forten, *The Journal of Charlotte L. Forten: A Free Negro in the Slave Era*, ed. Ray Allen Billington (New York: W. W. Norton, 1953), 127.

25. Oliver L. Pflug, "Pennsylvania Politics, 1854–1860" (master's thesis, University of Montana, 2002), 40–41.

26. *McElroy's Philadelphia Directory for 1859* (Edward C. and John Biddle, 1859), 360; J. B. Jones, *A Rebel War Clerk's Diary: At the Confederate States Capital*, vol. 1 (Philadelphia: J. B. Lippincott, 1866), 2.

27. Robert L. Bloom, "Morton McMichael's 'North American,'" *Pennsylvania Magazine of History and Biography*, 77, no. 2 (April 1953): 174; Judith Giesburg, Introduction, *Emilie Davis's Civil War: The Diaries of a Free Black Woman in Philadelphia, 1863–1865*, by Emilie Davis (University Park: Pennsylvania State University Press, 2014), 8.

28. Fisher, *Philadelphia Perspective*, 456.

29. "Mr. Lincoln and Negro Equality," *New York Times*, December 28, 1860, 4.

30. "Republican Party Platform of 1860," American Presidency Project, https://www.presidency.ucsb.edu/node/273296. See also Elwyn B. Robinson, "The 'North American':

Advocate of Protection," *Pennsylvania Magazine of History and Biography*, 64, no. 3 (July 1940): 348.

31. Robinson, "'North American,'" 347.

32. Dusinberre, *Civil War Issues*, 39.

33. Laurie and Schmitz, "Manufacture and Productivity," 43.

34. J. Matthew Gallman, *Mastering Wartime: A Social History of Philadelphia During the Civil War* (Philadelphia: University of Pennsylvania Press, 2000), 2.

35. Dusinberre, *Civil War Issues*, 63.

36. Fisher, *Philadelphia Perspective*, 269.

37. "1856 Democratic Party Platform," American Presidency Project, https://www.presidency.ucsb.edu/node/273169.

38. N. Orwin Rush, "Lucretia Mott and the Philadelphia Antislavery Fairs," *Bulletin of Friends Historical Association*, 35, no. 2 (Autumn 1946): 72.

39. Fisher, *Philadelphia Perspective*, 334. See also Dusinberre, *Civil War Issues*, 84.

40. Russell F. Weigley, "'A Peaceful City': Public Order in Philadelphia from Consolidation Through the Civil War," in *The Peoples of Philadelphia: A History of Ethnic Groups and Lower-Class Life, 1790–1940*, ed. Allen F. Davis and Mark H. Haller (Philadelphia: University of Pennsylvania Press, 1998), 158; Winnifred K. MacKay, "Philadelphia During the Civil War, 1861–1865," *Pennsylvania Magazine of History and Biography*, 70, no. 1 (January 1946): 16.

41. Fisher, *Philadelphia Perspective*, 341. See also Russell F. Weigley, "The Border City in the Civil War, 1854–1865," in *Philadelphia: A 300-Year History*, ed. Russell F. Weigley (New York: W. W. Norton, 1982), 390.

42. Irwin F. Greenberg, "Charles Ingersoll: The Aristocrat as Copperhead," *Pennsylvania Magazine of History and Biography*, 93, no. 2 (April 1969): 194.

43. Gallman, *Mastering Wartime*, 86; Christian B. Keller, "Pennsylvania's War for the Union, 1861–1863," in *Pennsylvania: A Military History*, ed. William A. Pencak, Christian B. Keller, and Barbara A. Gannon (Yardley, PA: Westholme, 2016), 143; J. Matthew Gallman, "Preserving the Peace: Order and Disorder in Civil War Philadelphia," *Pennsylvania History*, 55, no. 4 (October 1988): 204.

44. Christian B. Keller, "Keystone Confederates: Pennsylvanians Who Fought for Dixie," in *Pennsylvania's Civil War*, ed. William Blair and William Pencak (University Park: Pennsylvania State University Press, 2001), 3.

45. Beale, "Education of an Artist," 498. For descriptions of the Continental Hotel, see John Walter, *First Impressions of America* (London: self-pub., 1867), 72.

46. Joseph George Jr., "Philadelphians Greet Their President-Elect—1861," *Pennsylvania Magazine of History and Biography*, 29, no. 4 (October 1962): 384–86.

47. Dusinberre, *Civil War Issues*, 96; Gallman, *Mastering Wartime*, 4; Keller, "Keystone Confederates," 8; Clark, "Philadelphia Irish," 141; Weigley, "'Peaceful City,'" 163; Gallman, "Preserving the Peace," 202.

48. Fisher, *Philadelphia Perspective*, 384–85. See also Sarah Butler Wister, "Sarah Butler Wister's Civil War Diary," *Pennsylvania Magazine of History and Biography*, 102, no. 3 (July 1978): 273.

49. Beale, "Education of an Artist," 499; Sidney George Fisher described similar scenes; see Fisher, *Philadelphia Perspective*, 385.

50. Dusinberre, *Civil War Issues*, 117–18; Weigley, "Border City," 394. See also "Sarah Butler Wister's Civil War Diary," 276.

51. Fisher, *Philadelphia Perspective*, 385.

52. *Journal of the Common Council of the City of Philadelphia, Beginning November 15, 1860 and Ending June 27, 1861* (Philadelphia: King & Baird, 1861), 244.

53. Arrival of Col. Robert Anderson," *Press*, May 13, 1861; Beale, "Education of an Artist," 500.

54. Keller, "Pennsylvania's War," 144; MacKay, "Philadelphia," 11.

55. Wister, "Sarah Butler Wister's Civil War Diary," 279; Anna M. Ferris, "The Civil War Diaries of Anna M. Ferris," ed. Harold B. Hancock, *Delaware History*, 9, no. 3 (April 1961): 229. See also MacKay, "Philadelphia," 9.

56. Michael J. Lewis, *Philadelphia Builds: Essays on Architecture* (Philadelphia: Paul Dry Books, 2021), 224.

57. Gallman, *Mastering Wartime*, 16–18.

58. Jacob Frankel Chaplaincy Certificate, March 2, 1864, Rodeph Shalom Papers, Temple University Special Collections Research Center; Sidney B. Hoenig, "The Orthodox Rabbi as a Military Chaplain: A Bicentennial Retrospective," *Tradition: A Journal of Orthodox Jewish Thought*, 16, no. 2 (Fall 1976): 36.

59. Beale, "Education of an Artist," 490.

60. George B. McClellan, *McClellan's Own Story* (New York: Charles L. Webster, 1887), 174. 655; *Journal of the Common Council of the City of Philadelphia: January 6, 1862 to July 3, 1862* (Philadelphia: McLaughlin Brothers, 1862), 62; *Journal of the Common Council of the City of Philadelphia: July 10, 1862 to January 3, 1863* (Philadelphia: McLaughlin Brothers, 1863), 122.

61. *McElroy's Philadelphia Directory, 1867* (Philadelphia: A. McElroy, 1867), 581; Edward G. Longacre, ed., "'Come Home Soon and Dont Delay': Letters from the Home Front, July 1861," *Pennsylvania Magazine of History and Biography*, 100, no. 3 (July 1976): 395.

62. *McElroy's Philadelphia Directory, 1860* (Philadelphia: E. C. & J. Biddle, 1860), 769. Regarding the assertion that his was the city's largest private residence, see George Randolph Snowden, "Home to Franklin: Excerpts from the Civil War Diary of George Randolph Snowden," ed. Charles H. Ness, *Western Pennsylvania Historical Magazine*, 54, no. 2 (April 1971): 160.

63. Wister, "Sarah Butler Wister's Civil War Diary," 276.

64. "The Case of Mr. Boileau," *New York Times*, February 3, 1863, 5.

65. Arnold Shankman, "Freedom of the Press During the Civil War: The Case of Albert D. Boileau," *Pennsylvania History*, 42, no. 4 (October 1975): 312–14.

66. Dusinberre, *Civil War Issues*, 151.

67. "The Democratic Mass Meeting in Philadelphia," *New York Times*, August 26, 1862. See also Dusinberre, *Civil War Issues*, 157; Greenberg, "Charles Ingersoll," 197.

68. Ferris, "Civil War Diaries," 239.

69. Greenberg, "Charles Ingersoll," 202; Nicholas B. Wainwright, "The Loyal Opposition in Civil War Philadelphia," *Pennsylvania Magazine of History and Biography*, 88, no. 3 (July 1964): 297.

70. Quoted in Barbara J. Mitnick, "The Union League of Philadelphia and the Civil War," *Pennsylvania Legacies*, 13, no. 1–2 (June 2013): 34. See also Fisher, *Philadelphia Perspective*, 445.

71. Quoted in Greenberg, "Charles Ingersoll," 203. See also Fisher, *Philadelphia Perspective*, 451.

72. Fisher, *Philadelphia Perspective*, 459.

73. Gallman, *Mastering Wartime*, 179; Greenberg, "Charles Ingersoll," 194; Wainwright, "Loyal Opposition," 294; Gallman, "Preserving the Peace," 209; Nash, *First City*, 233.

74. Greenberg, "Charles Ingersoll," 208.

75. Dusinberre, *Civil War Issues*, 102.

76. On the recession, see Ferris, "Civil War Diaries," 228, 228, 231. For the recovery, see Gallman, *Mastering Wartime*, 255; Domenic Vitello, *Engineering Philadelphia: The Sellers Family and the Industrial Metropolis* (Ithaca, NY: Cornell University Press, 2013), 115.

77. William Blair, Introduction, in *Pennsylvania's Civil War*, ed. William Blair and William Pencak (University Park: Pennsylvania State University Press, 2001), 141.

78. Gallman, *Mastering Wartime*, 281; MacKay, "Philadelphia," 15.

79. Weigley, "Border City," 405.

80. Charles J. Stille, *Memorial of the Great Central Fair for the U.S. Sanitary Commission* (Philadelphia: US Sanitary Commission, 1864), 11; Wister, "Sarah Butler Wister's Civil War Diary," 280; John J. Brady, "Journal of John J. Brady, Color Corporal Twelfth Regiment N.Y.S.V.," in *Documents of the Assembly of the State of New York: Ninety-First Session—1868*, vol. 40–148 (Albany, NY: C. Van Benthuysen & Sons, 1868), 439; John M. Gould, *History of the First-Tenth-Twenty-Ninth Maine Regiment* (Portland, ME: Stephen Berry, 1871), 35; D. L. Day, *My Diary of Rambles with the 25th Mass. Volunteer Infantry* (Milford, MA: King & Billings, 1884), 9; *History of the Fifth Massachusetts Battery* (Boston: Luther E. Cowles, 1902), 96; Wilbur Fisk, *Anti-Rebel: The Civil War Letters of Wilbur Fisk* (Croton-on-Hudson, NY: Emil Rosenblatt, 1983), 55–56, 152–53; John Haley, *The Rebel Yell and the Yankee Hurrah: The Civil War Journal of a Maine Volunteer*, ed. Ruth L. Silliker (Camden, ME: Down East Books, 1985), 30–31, 281.

81. Gallman, *Mastering Wartime*, 129.

82. Fisk, *Anti-Rebel*, 340.

83. Gallman, *Mastering Wartime*, 130; MacKay, "Philadelphia," 25; Nash, *First City*, 242–43.

84. MacKay, "Philadelphia," 27.

85. Ferris, "Civil War Diaries," 239.

86. On refugees, see Emilie Davis, *Emilie Davis's Civil War: The Diaries of a Free Black Woman in Philadelphia, 1863–1865*, ed. Judith Giesburg (University Park: Pennsylvania State University Press, 2014), 8. See also Gallman, *Mastering Wartime*, 7; William L. Calderhead, "Philadelphia in Crisis: June–July 1863," *Pennsylvania History*, 28, no. 2 (April 1961): 143.

87. Gallman, *Mastering Wartime*, 21; MacKay, "Philadelphia," 32–33; Edward Coddington, "Pennsylvania Prepares for Invasion, 1863," *Pennsylvania History*, 31, no. 4 (April 1964): 165.

88. Fisher, *Philadelphia Perspective*, 455; White to Bustill, 19 August 1862, "Letters of Negroes, Largely Personal and Private [Part 1]," *Journal of Negro History*, 11, no. 1 (January 1926): 62. See also Nash, *First City*, 228.

89. Weigley, "'Peaceful City,'" 168.

90. John C. Brock and Eric Ledell Smith, "The Civil War Letters of Quartermaster Sergeant John C. Brock, 43rd Regiment, United States Colored Troops," in *Pennsylvania's Civil War*, ed. William Blair and William Pencak (University Park: Pennsylvania State University Press, 2001), 144; Henry Yates Thompson, *An Englishman in the American Civil War: The Diaries of Henry Yates Thompson*, ed. Christopher Chancellor (London: Sidgwick & Jackson, 1971), 88. See also Jeffrey D. Wert, "Camp William Penn and the Black Soldier," *Pennsylvania History*, 46, no. 4 (October 1979): 335.

91. *Free Military School for Applicants for Command of Colored Troops* (Philadelphia: King & Baird, 1864). See also Frederick M. Binder, "Philadelphia's Free Military School," *Pennsylvania History*, 17, no. 4 (October 1950): 290; Zachery A. Fry, "Philadelphia's Free Military School and the Radicalization of Wartime Officer Education, 1863–1864," *Pennsylvania Magazine of History and Biography*, 141, no. 3 (October 2017): 276.

92. James Henry Gooding, *On the Altar of Freedom: A Black Soldier's Letters from the Front*, ed. Virginia M. Adams (Amherst: University of Massachusetts Press, 1999), 14; Hope to Faith, "Letters of Negroes," 83; Letter 10, in *A Grand Army of Black Men*, ed. Edwin S. Redkey (Cambridge: Cambridge University Press, 1993), 22. See also Dusinberre, *Civil War Issues*, 165; Binder, "Philadelphia's Free Military School," 291–92; Emma Jones Lapsansky, "Friends, Wives, and Strivings: Networks and Community Values Among Nineteenth-Century Philadelphia Afroamerican Elites," *Pennsylvania Magazine of History and Biography*, 108, no. 1 (January 1984): 3.

93. Ferris, "Civil War Diaries," 252.

94. Fisher, *Philadelphia Perspective*, 473. See also Suzanne Colton Wilson, ed., *Column South* (Flagstaff, AZ: J. F. Colton, 1960), 162–63.

95. Richard S. Newman, "All's Fair: Philadelphia and the Sanitary Fair Movement During the Civil War," *Pennsylvania Legacies*, 13, no. 1–2 (June 2013): 58; Nash, *First City*, 247.

96. *Philadelphia Sanitary Fair Catalogue and Guide* (Philadelphia: Magee Stationer, 1864), 28. Anna M. Ferris noted in her diary, "Old Revolutionary trophies also appear, more gratifying to our national pride & awakening no unpleasant feelings of sorrow & dread." Ferris, "Civil War Diaries," 252. See also Nash, *First City*, 248.

97. Elizabeth Milroy, "Avenue of Dreams: Patriotism and the Spectator at Philadelphia's Great Central Sanitary Fair," in *Pennsylvania's Civil War*, ed. William Blair and William Pencak (University Park: Pennsylvania State University Press, 2001), 45. This see Stille, *Memorial*, 11.

98. *Philadelphia Perspective*, 474. See also Davis, *Emilie Davis's Civil War*, 110; Samuel Whitaker Pennypacker, *The Autobiography of a Pennsylvanian* (Philadelphia: John C. Winston, 1918), 83.

99. MacKay, "Philadelphia," 30.

100. Mary A. Livermore, *My Story of the War: A Woman's Narrative of Four Years Personal Experience* (Hartford, CT: A. D. Worthington, 1892), 579–80.

101. Nash, *First City*, 241; Gallman, *Mastering Wartime*, 150–59.

102. Emilie Davis noted that "the Democrats had the rowdy [procession]." Davis, *Emilie Davis's Civil War*, 128. See also Gallman, "Preserving the Peace," 205.

103. David Rankin, ed., "Political Parades and American Democracy: Jean-Charles Houzeau on Lincoln's 1864 Reelection Campaign," *Civil War History*, 30, no. 4 (December 1984): 328.

104. MacKay, "Philadelphia," 35.

105. "The City," *Press*, November 9, 1864, 2.

106. *Journal of the Common Council of the City of Philadelphia for the Year 1865*, vol. 1 (Philadelphia: King & Baird, 1865), 392.

107. *McElroy's Philadelphia Directory, 1866* (Philadelphia: A. McElroy, 1866), 190; Samuel L. Smedley, *Atlas of the City of Philadelphia* (Philadelphia: J. B. Lippincott, 1862), sec. 11.

108. Fisher, *Philadelphia Perspective*, 493; MacKay, "Philadelphia," 47.

109. Garrett, *Memoirs*, 21–22; Ferris, "Civil War Diaries," 262; Fisher, *Philadelphia Perspective*, 494. See also Edwin Wolf 2nd, *Philadelphia: Portrait of an American City* (Philadelphia: Camino Books, 1990), 221.

110. Davis, *Emilie Davis's Civil War*, 158. See also Florence Kelley, *The Autobiography of Florence Kelley: Notes of Sixty Years*, ed. Kathryn Kish Sklar (Chicago: Charles H. Kerr, 1986), 24–25.

111. *Proceedings of the National Union Convention Held at Philadelphia, August 14, 1866* (Washington, DC: National Union Executive Committee, 1866), 1.

112. Frederick Douglass, *Douglass' Monthly*, February 1862; Frederick Douglass, *Life and Times of Frederick Douglass: Written by Himself* (Hartford, CT: Park Publishing, 1882),472–76. See also Philip S. Foner, "The Battle to End Discrimination Against Negroes on Philadelphia's Streetcars (Part 1): Background and Beginning of the Battle," *Pennsylvania History*, 40, no. 3 (July 1973): 262; Nash, *First City*, 232. Even some white people understood that white Philadelphians were especially hostile to Black people. See Fisher, *Philadelphia Perspective*, 256; Richard Cobden, *The American Diaries of Richard Cobden*, ed. Elizabeth Hoon Cawley (Princeton, NJ: Princeton University Press, 1952), 176.

113. Nick Salvatore, *We All Got History: The Memory Books of Amos Webber* (Urbana: University of Illinois Press, 2007), 19–21; Jacques Offenbach, *Orpheus in America: Offenbach's Diary of His Journey to the New World* (Bloomington: Indiana University Press, 1957), 128–29. See also Theodore Hershberg and Henry Williams, "Mulattoes and Blacks: Intra-group Color Differences and Social Stratification in Nineteenth-Century Philadelphia," in *Philadelphia: Work, Space, Family, and Group Experience in the 19th Century*, ed. Theodore Hershberg (New York: Oxford University Press, 1981), 425; Lapsansky, "Friends, Wives," 4.

114. Andrew Diemer, "Reconstructing Philadelphia: African Americans and Politics in the Post-Civil War North," *Pennsylvania Magazine of History and Biography*, 133, no. 1 (January 2009): 47.

115. Nash, *First City*, 250.

116. Diemer, "Reconstructing Philadelphia," 35; Geoff D. Zylstra, "Whiteness, Freedom, and Technology: The Racial Struggle over Philadelphia's Streetcars, 1859–1867,"

Technology and Culture, 52, no. 4 (October 2011): 695; Foner, "Battle to End Discrimination," 276.

117. Letter 94, in Redkey, *Grand Army*, 219; Reginald H. Pitts, "'Let Us Desert This Friendless Place': George Moses Horton in Philadelphia—1866," *Journal of Negro History*, 80, no. 4 (Autumn 1995): 148.

118. Harry C. Silcox, "Nineteenth Century Philadelphia Black Militant: Octavius V. Catto (1839–1871)," *Pennsylvania History*, 44, no. 1 (January 1977): 54–60.

119. Hugh Davis, "The Pennsylvania State Equal Rights League and the Northern Black Struggle for Legal Equality, 1864–1877," *Pennsylvania Magazine of History and Biography*, 126, no. 4 (October 2002): 612.

120. Wolf, *Philadelphia*, 217; Silcox, "Nineteenth Century," 65.

121. Brian E. Alnutt, "'The Negro Excursions': Recreational Outings Among Philadelphia African Americans, 1876–1926," *Pennsylvania Magazine of History and Biography*, 129, no. 1 (January 2005): 79.

122. Edward Price, "The Black Voting Rights Issue in Pennsylvania, 1780–1900," *Pennsylvania Magazine of History and Biography*, 100, no. 3 (July 1976): 368.

123. Silcox, "Nineteenth Century," 73; Price, "Black Voting Rights," 369.

124. Jean Edward Smith, *Grant* (New York: Simon & Schuster, 2001), 419; Ronald C. White, *American Ulysses: A Life of Ulysses S. Grant* (New York: Random House, 2016), 425.

125. Bloom, "Morton McMichael's 'North American,'" 170. See also William C. Borlase, *Sunways: A Record of Rambles in Many Lands* (Plymouth, MA: W. Brendon & Son, 1878), 69.

126. George W. Childs, *Recollections* (Philadelphia: J. B. Lippincott, 1890), 86–87. See also David Gerald Orr, "Work in Progress: The City Point Headquarters Cabin of Ulysses S. Grant," *Perspectives in Vernacular Architecture*, 1 (1982): 196.

127. William S. Vare, *My Forty Years in Politics* (Philadelphia: Roland Swain, 1933), 39.

128. Weigley, "Border City," 432.

129. Bruce Laurie et al. "Immigrants and Industry: The Philadelphia Experience in *Philadelphia: Work, Space, Family, and Group Experience in the 19th Century*, ed. Theodore Hershberg (New York: Oxford University Press, 1981), 99.

130. Fisher, *Philadelphia Perspective*, 505; Philip S. Foner, "Black Participation in the Centennial of 1876," *Phylon*, 39, no. 4 (1978): 288.

131. Andrew B. Arnold, "Mother Jones and the Panics of 1873 and 1893," *Pennsylvania Legacies*, 11, no. 1 (May 2011): 18.

132. Nash, *First City*, 254.

133. Arthur H. Frazier, "Henry Seybert and the Centennial Clock and Bell at Independence Hall," *Pennsylvania Magazine of History and Biography*, 102, no. 1 (January 1978): 53.

134. William J. Canby, The History of the Flag of the United States: paper delivered before the Historical Society of Pennsylvania, Philadelphia, March 14, 1870. (Philadelphia: Historical Society of Pennsylvania, 1870).

135. J. Franklin Riegart, *The History of the First United States Flag* (Philadelphia, PA: Lane S. Hart, 1878).

136. Ethel Alec-Tweedie, *America as I Saw It* (London: Hutchison, 1913), 142.

137. Kimberly Orcutt, "H. H. Moore's *Almeh* and the Politics of the Centennial Exhibition," *American Art*, 21, no. 1 (Spring 2007): 35.

138. *Preliminary Report of Joint Special Committee on Celebration of Centennial Anniversary of American Independence* (Philadelphia: E. C. Markley & Son, 1870), 5. See also Philip B. Hawk, *My Mother's Diary and I* (P. B. Hawk, 1951), 39; Laurie and Schmitz, "Manufacture and Productivity," 44.

139. J. St. George Joyce, *Story of Philadelphia* (Philadelphia: Rex Printing House, 1919), 276.

140. Ratzel, "Philadelphia on the Eve," 35; Borlase, *Sunways*, 77. The construction site remained an attraction even after the Centennial closed; see H. Hussy Vivian, *Notes of a Tour in America* (London: Edward Stanford, 1878), 59; Charles Beadle, *A Trip to the United States in 1887* (London: J. S. Virtue, 1887), 39; S. Reynolds Hole, *A Little Tour in America* (London: Edward Arnold, 1892), 256; George Campbell, *The American People: The Relations Between the White and the Black* (New York: Worthington, 1899), 243; Winifred, Lady Howard of Glossop, *Journal of a Tour of the United States, Canada, and Mexico* (London, 1897), 324.

141. "Address," in *The Papers of Ulysses S. Grant*, vol. 27, January 1–October 31, 1876, ed. John Y. Simon (Carbondale: Southern Illinois University Press, 2005), 107.

142. James L. Broderick, *The Character of the Country: The Iowa Diary of James L. Broderick, 1876–1877*, ed. Loren N. Horton (Iowa City: Iowa State Historical Department, 1976), 27.

143. Elizabeth Cady Stanton, *Eighty Years and More* (New York: European Publishing, 1898), 307. See also Ellis R. Shipp, *The Early Autobiography and Diary of Ellis Reynolds Shipp, M.D.* (Salt Lake City, UT: Deseret News Press, 1962), 216.

144. James McClelland and Lynn Miller, *City in a Park: A History of Philadelphia's Fairmount Park System* (Philadelphia: Temple University Press, 2016), 54; Judy Braun Zegas, "North American Indian Exhibit at the Centennial Exposition," *Curator*, 19, no. 2 (June 1976): 162.

145. McClelland and Miller, *City in a Park*, 59–62.

146. Garrett, *Memoirs*, 23. See also Longacre et al., "Come Home Soon," 407; Falk, *Trans-Pacific Sketches*, 177–93; Broderick, *Character of the Country*, 28.

147. Laurie and Schmitz, "Manufacture and Productivity," 46; Newman, "All's Fair," 59; Rachel Filene Seidman, "'We Were Enlisted for War': Ladies' Aid Societies and the Politics of Women's Work During the Civil War," in *Pennsylvania's Civil War*, ed. William Blair and William Pencak (University Park: Pennsylvania State University Press, 2001), 62–63, 69.

148. Falk, *Trans-Pacific Sketches*, 211.

149. Stanton, *Eighty Years*, 312–13. See also Mary Frances Cordato, "'Toward a New Century': Women and the Philadelphia Centennial Exhibition, 1876," *Pennsylvania Magazine of History and Biography*, 107, no. 1 (January 1983): 130–31.

150. Zegas, "North American Indian Exhibit," 163.

151. Foner, "Black Participation," 287; Newman, "All's Fair," 62.

152. Mitch Kachun, "Before the Eyes of All Nations: African-American Identity and Historical Memory at the Centennial Exhibition of 1876," *Pennsylvania History*, 65, no. 3 (Summer 1998): 308–18.

153. Diemer, "Reconstructing Philadelphia," 29–30; Nash, *First City*, 238–39.

154. Barbara A. Gannon, "Sites of Memory, Sites of Glory: African-American Grand Army of the Republic Posts in Pennsylvania," in *Pennsylvania's Civil War*, ed. William Blair and William Pencak (University Park: Pennsylvania State University Press, 2001), 173; "National GAR Records Program—Historical Summary of the Grand Army of the Republic (GAR) Posts by State: Pennsylvania," Sons of Union Veterans of the Civil War, accessed February 14, 2020, updated August 14, 2019, http://www.suvcw.org/garrecords /garposts/pa.pdf.

155. Lewis, *Philadelphia Builds*, 44–47.

156. Andrew Jackson Downing, "A Talk About Public Parks and Gardens," *Horticulturalist: Journal of Rural Art and Rural Taste*, 3, no. 4 (October 1848): 156. See also David Schuyler, *The New Urban Landscape: The Redefinition of City Form in Nineteenth-Century America* (Baltimore: Johns Hopkins University Press, 1993), 28.

157. *A Further Supplement to an Act Entitled "An Act to Incorporate the City of Philadelphia," Passed January 31, 1854* (Philadelphia: Crissy & Markley, 1856), 37.

158. McClelland and Miller, *City in a Park*, 38.

159. Lewis, *Philadelphia Builds*, 47–48.

160. Jon C. Teaford, *The Unheralded Triumph: City Government in America, 1870–1900* (Baltimore: Johns Hopkins University Press, 1984), 69.

161. Teaford, *Unheralded Triumph*, 253.

162. Michael J. Lewis, "The First Design for Fairmount Park," *Pennsylvania Magazine of History and Biography*, 130, no. 3 (July 2006): 291.

163. Milroy, "Avenue of Dreams," 54.

164. Robert P. Armstrong, "Green Space in the Gritty City: The Planning and Development of Philadelphia's Park System, 1854–1929" (PhD diss., Lehigh University, 2012), 113–18.

165. Teaford, *Unheralded Triumph*, 253.

166. Schuyler, *New Urban Landscape*, 187; Barth, *City People*, 39.

167. George Wharton Pepper, *Philadelphia Lawyer: An Autobiography* (Philadelphia: J. B. Lippincott, 1944), 22.

168. J. Kent Follmar, "Reaction to Reconstruction: Pennsylvania Republicans in the Forty-Second Congress, 1871–1873," *Western Pennsylvania Historical Magazine*, 61, no. 3 (July 1978): 204, 218.

169. Fisher, *Philadelphia Perspective*, 491. See also Salvatore, *We All Got History*, 19–21; Offenbach, *Orpheus in America*, 213–14; Edward J. Price Jr. "School Segregation in Nineteenth-Century Pennsylvania," *Pennsylvania History*, 43, no. 2 (April 1976): 132–33; Price, "Black Voting Rights," 365; Davis, "Pennsylvania State," 622; Philip S. Foner, "The Battle to End Discrimination Against Negroes on Philadelphia's Streetcars (Part 2): The Victory," *Pennsylvania History*, 40, no. 4 (December 1973): 357.

Chapter 7

1. Caroline Golab, "The Immigrant and the City: Poles, Italians, and Jews in Philadelphia, 1870–1920," in *The Peoples of Philadelphia: A History of Ethnic Groups and Lower-Class Life, 1790–1940*, ed. Allen F. Davis and Mark H. Haller (Philadelphia:

University of Pennsylvania Press, 1998), 204–5; Gunther Barth, *City People: The Rise of Modern City Culture in Nineteenth-Century America* (New York: Oxford University Press, 1980), 8.

2. Nathaniel Burt and Wallace E. Davies, "The Iron Age: 1876–1905," in *Philadelphia: A 300-Year History*, ed. Russell F. Weigley (New York: W. W. Norton, 1982), 488; Caroline Golab, "The Polish Experience in Philadelphia: Migrant Laborers Who Did Not Come," in *The Ethnic Experience in Pennsylvania*, ed. John E. Bodnar (Lewisburg, PA: Bucknell University Press, 1973), 39; John F. Sutherland, "Housing the Poor in the City of Homes: Philadelphia at the Turn of the Century," in *The Peoples of Philadelphia: A History of Ethnic Groups and Lower-Class Life, 1790–1940*, ed. Allen F. Davis and Mark H. Haller (Philadelphia: University of Pennsylvania Press, 1998), 180; Howell John Harris, *Bloodless Victories: The Rise and Fall of the Open Shop in the Philadelphia Metal Trades, 1890–1940* (New York: Cambridge University Press, 2000), 24; Tera W. Hunter, "The 'Brotherly Love' for Which This City Is Proverbial Should Extend to All," in *W. E. B. Du Bois, Race, and the City: The Philadelphia Negro and Its Legacy*, ed. Michael B. Katz and Thomas J. Sugrue (Philadelphia: University of Pennsylvania Press, 1998), 129; John F. Sutherland, "The Origins of Philadelphia's Octavia Hill Association: Social Reform in the 'Contented' City," *Pennsylvania Magazine of History and Biography*, 99, no. 1 (January 1975): 22.

3. G. W. Steevens, *The Land of the Dollar* (London: William Blackwood & Sons, 1897), 115; James H. Adams, *Urban Reform and Sexual Vice in Progressive-Era Philadelphia: The Faithful and the Fallen* (Lanham, MD: Lexington Books, 2015), 33.

4. J. Murphy, *Real Philly History, Real Fast: Fascinating Facts and Interesting Oddities About the City's Heroes and Historic Sites* (Philadelphia: Temple University Press, 2021), 39–42.

5. Murray Friedman, "Introduction: The Making of a National Jewish Community," in *Jewish Life in Philadelphia, 1830–1940*, ed. Murray Friedman (Philadelphia: American Jewish Committee, 1983), 4.

6. David U. Todes, "The History of Jewish Education in Philadelphia, 1782–1873" (PhD diss., Dropsie College, 1953), 104.

7. Edwin Wolf 2nd, "The German-Jewish Influence in Philadelphia's Charities," in *Jewish Life in Philadelphia, 1830–1940*, ed. Murray Friedman (Philadelphia: American Jewish Committee, 1983), 125; Maxwell Whiteman, "The Fiddlers Rejected: Jewish Immigrant Expression in Philadelphia," in *Jewish Life in Philadelphia, 1830–1940*, ed. Murray Friedman (Philadelphia: American Jewish Committee, 1983), 80; Thomas H. Keels, *Forgotten Philadelphia: Lost Architecture of the Quaker City* (Philadelphia: Temple University Press, 2007), 137.

8. Burt and Davies, "Iron Age," 488–89; Maxwell Whiteman, "The European Jew Comes to Philadelphia," in *The Ethnic Experience in Pennsylvania*, ed. John E. Bodnar (Lewisburg, PA: Bucknell University Press, 1973), 297.

9. Maxwell Whiteman, "Philadelphia's Jewish Neighborhoods," in *The Peoples of Philadelphia: A History of Ethnic Groups and Lower-Class Life, 1790–1940*, ed. Allen F. Davis and Mark H. Haller (Philadelphia: University of Pennsylvania Press, 1998), 232–33.

10. Sutherland, "Housing the Poor," 180–81; John A. Lukacs, *Philadelphia: Patricians and Philistines, 1900–1950* (New York: Farrar, Straus & Giroux, 1981), 22; Gary B. Nash,

First City: Philadelphia and the Forging of Historical Memory (Philadelphia: University of Pennsylvania Press, 2006), 283.

11. Golab, "Polish Experience," 40; Golab, "Immigrant and the City," 205.

12. Philip Goodman, *Franklin Street* (New York: Alfred A. Knopf, 1942), 3; Whiteman, "European Jew," 293; Whiteman, "Philadelphia's Jewish Neighborhoods," 234; Robert Tabak, "Orthodox Judaism in Transition," in *Jewish Life in Philadelphia, 1830–1940*, ed. Murray Friedman (Philadelphia: American Jewish Committee, 1983), 48; Evelyn Bodek Rosen, *The Philadelphia Fels, 1880–1920: A Social Portrait* (Madison, NJ: Fairleigh Dickinson University Press, 2000), 45; Nash, *First City*, 283.

13. Friedman, "Introduction," 10.

14. The exact number of Italians in Philadelphia in 1900 is hard to determine. For various estimates, see Burt and Davies, "Iron Age," 490; Richard N. Juliani, "The Origin and Development of the Italian Community in Philadelphia," in *The Ethnic Experience in Pennsylvania*, ed. John E. Bodnar (Lewisburg, PA: Bucknell University Press, 1973), 237; Sutherland, "Housing the Poor," 180–1; Joan Y. Dickinson, "Aspects of Italian Immigration," *Pennsylvania Magazine of History and Biography*, 90, no. 4 (October 1966): 457; M. Agnes Gertrude, "Italian Immigration into Philadelphia," *Records of the American Catholic Historical Society of Philadelphia*, 58, no. 2 (June 1947): 133.

15. Edwin Wolf 2nd, *Philadelphia: Portrait of an American City* (Philadelphia: Camino Books, 1990), 249.

16. Murphy, *Real Philly History*, 81–82.

17. Juliani, "Origin and Development," 242.

18. David R. Roediger, *Working Toward Whiteness: How America's Immigrants Became White* (New York: Basic Books, 2018), 6–7.

19. Golab, "Polish Experience," 60; Golab, "Immigrant and the City,": 207; Juliani, "Origin and Development," 244–45; Walter Licht, *Getting Work: Philadelphia, 1840–1950* (Philadelphia: University of Pennsylvania Press, 1999), 14.

20. Matthew S. Magda, *Polish Presence in Pennsylvania* (University Park: Pennsylvania Historical Association, 1992), 21.

21. Magda, *Polish Presence*, 20–22.

22. Licht, *Getting Work*, 31; Ken Fones-Wolf, *Trade Union Gospel: Christianity and Labor in Industrial Philadelphia, 1865–1915* (Philadelphia: Temple University Press, 1989), 19; Dickinson, "Aspects of Italian Immigration," 454; Magda, *Polish Presence*, 26.

23. John Koren, "The Padrone System and Padrone Banks," *Bulletin of the Department of Labor*, no. 9 (March 1897): 123. See also Gertrude, "Italian Immigration," 140.

24. Mae Townsend Pease, *Reminiscences from Lamplight to Satellite* (Philadelphia: Dorrance, 1960), 3; Goodman, *Franklin Street*, 7. See also Wolf, *Philadelphia*, 252; Sutherland, "Housing the Poor," 180; Hunter, "'Brotherly Love,'" 131; Margaret Lynch-Brennan, "Bridget in Philadelphia: The Irish Servant Girl, 1840–1930," *Pennsylvania Legacies*, 14, no. 2 (Fall 2014): 14.

25. Dongzheng Jin, "The Sojourners' Story: Philadelphia's Chinese Immigrants, 1900–1925" (PhD diss., Temple University, 1997), 104.

26. Kathryn E. Wilson, "From Bachelor Enclave to Urban Village: The Evolution of Early Chinatown," *Pennsylvania Legacies*, 12, no. 1 (May 2012): 12–14; Clem Harris, "Old

Philadelphians, The Great Migration and the Irony of Progressive Politics," in *If There Is No Struggle There Is No Progress: Black Politics in Twentieth-Century Philadelphia*, ed. James Wolfinger (Philadelphia: Temple University Press, 2022), 13.

27. Burt and Davies, "Iron Age," 491; Sutherland, "Housing the Poor," 179–80; Golab, "Immigrant and the City," 209; Barth, *City People*, 16.

28. W. E. B. Du Bois, *The Philadelphia Negro: A Social Study* (Philadelphia: University of Pennsylvania Press, 1996), 49.

29. Roger Lane, *William Dorsey's Philadelphia and Ours: On the Past and Future of the Black City in America* (New York: Oxford University Press, 1991), xiii; Roger Lane, *Roots of Violence in Black Philadelphia, 1860–1900* (Cambridge, MA: Harvard University Press, 1989), 6.

30. Du Bois, *Philadelphia Negro*, 58–59; John Daly and Allen Weinberg, *Genealogy of Philadelphia County Subdivisions*, 2nd ed. (Philadelphia: Philadelphia Department of Records, 1966), 77.

31. Golab, "Immigrant and the City," 208–9; Harris, *Bloodless Victories*, 19; Nash, *First City*, 286; Hunter, "'Brotherly Love,'" 127.

32. Du Bois, *Philadelphia Negro*, 53–55, 60; Hunter, "'Brotherly Love,'" 130; Harris, "Old Philadelphians," 14.

33. Harris, *Bloodless Victories*, 20; Jacqueline Jones, "'Lifework' and Its Limits: The Problem of Labor in *The Philadelphia Negro*," in *W. E. B. Du Bois, Race, and the City: The Philadelphia Negro and Its Legacy*, ed. Michael B. Katz and Thomas J. Sugrue (Philadelphia: University of Pennsylvania Press, 1998), 108.

34. John F. Fraser, *America at Work* (London: Cassell, 1906), 43; Ellis Reynolds Shipp, MD, *The Early Autobiography and Diary of Ellis Reynolds Shipp, M.D.*, ed. Ellis Shipp Musser (Salt Lake City: Deseret News Press, 1962), 227. See also Dennis Clark, "'Ramcat' and Rittenhouse Square: Related Communities," in *The Divided Metropolis: Social and Spatial Dimensions of Philadelphia, 1800–1920*, ed. William W. Cutler III and Howard Gillette Jr. (Westport, CT: Greenwood Press, 1980), 131–32; Licht, *Getting Work*, 16; Sherri Broder, *Tramps, Unfit Mothers, and Neglected Children: Negotiating the Family in Late Nineteenth-Century Philadelphia* (Philadelphia: University of Pennsylvania Press, 2002), 14–15; Jones, "'Lifework,'" 115; James Wolfinger, *Running the Rails: Capital and Labor in the Philadelphia Transit Industry* (Ithaca, NY: Cornell University Press, 2016), 42; Harry C. Silcox, "William McMullen, Nineteenth-Century Political Boss," *Pennsylvania Magazine of History and Biography*, 110, no. 3 (July 1986): 390.

35. Stuart M. Blumin, *The Emergence of the Middle Class: Social Experience in the American City, 1760–1900* (New York: Cambridge University Press, 1989), 259; Licht, *Getting Work*, 4; Fones-Wolf, *Trade Union Gospel*, 4.

36. Fraser, *America at Work*, 71; Burt and Davies, "Iron Age," 481; Golab, "Polish Experience," 55; Maxwell Whiteman, "Out of the Sweatshop," in *Jewish Life in Philadelphia, 1830–1940*, ed. Murray Friedman (Philadelphia: American Jewish Committee, 1983), 65–66; Hunter, "'Brotherly Love,'" 128.

37. Fraser, *America at Work*, 40; E. Digby Baltzell, *Philadelphia Gentlemen: The Making of a National Upper Class* (Philadelphia: University of Pennsylvania Press, 1979), 110–12.

38. Burt and Davies, "Iron Age," 482; Golab, "Immigrant and the City," 212.

39. Samuel Whitaker Pennypacker, *The Autobiography of a Pennsylvanian* (Philadelphia: John C. Winston, 1918), 115; George Randolph Snowden, "Home to Franklin: Excerpts from the Civil War Diary of George Randolph Snowden," ed. Charles H. Ness, *Western Pennsylvania Historical Magazine*, 54, no. 2 (April 1971): 159; William S. Vare, *My Forty Years in Politics* (Philadelphia: Roland Swain, 1933), 40. See also Burt and Davies, "Iron Age," 483.

40. Pease, *Reminiscences*, 16. What charity there was available often came with a heaping side of condescension; for an example, see Helen Parrish, "Reform and Uplift Among Philadelphia Negroes: The Diary of Helen Parrish, 1888," ed. Allen F. Davis and John F. Sutherland, *Pennsylvania Magazine of History and Biography*, 94, no. 4 (October 1970): 500–17. See also Fones-Wolf, *Trade Union Gospel*, 10–12; Broder, *Tramps*, 144; Eudice Glassberg, "Work, Wages, and the Cost of Living: Ethnic Differences and the Poverty Line, Philadelphia, 1880," *Pennsylvania History*, 46, no. 1 (January 1979): 53.

41. *Report of the Proceedings of the Thirty-Fourth Annual Convention of the American Federation of Labor, 1914* (Washington, DC: Law Reporter Printing, 1914), 3.

42. "A Complete Tie-up of the Union Traction," *Philadelphia Inquirer*, December 18, 1895, 1; "Settling Affairs After the Strike," *Philadelphia Inquirer*, December 28, 1895, 2; William Z. Foster, *From Bryan to Stalin* (New York: International Publishers, 1937), 15. See also Wolfinger, *Running the Rails*, 60–63.

43. Charles W. Ervin, *Homegrown Liberal: The Autobiography of Charles W. Ervin* (New York: Dodd, Mead, 1954), 38. See also Lloyd M. Abernathy, "Progressivism: 1905–1919," in *Philadelphia: A 300-Year History*, ed. Russell F. Weigley (New York: W. W. Norton, 1982), 526; Licht, *Getting Work*, 178; Peter Cole, *Wobblies on the Waterfront: Interracial Unionism in Progressive-Era Philadelphia* (Urbana: University of Illinois Press, 2007), 79; Thomas H. Coode and John F. Bauman, *People, Poverty, and Politics: Pennsylvanians During the Great Depression* (Lewisburg, PA: Bucknell University Press, 1981), 53; James Wolfinger, *Philadelphia Divided: Race and Politics in the City of Brotherly Love* (Chapel Hill: University of North Carolina Press, 2007), 26–27; Gladys L. Palmer, *Philadelphia Workers in a Changing Economy* (Philadelphia: University of Pennsylvania Press, 1956), 29; Nash, *First City*, 287.

44. *Laws of the General Assembly of the Commonwealth of Pennsylvania Passed at the Session of 1895* (Harrisburg, PA: Clarence M. Busch, 1895), 178. John Koren noted in 1897, "The Italian quarter contains only a few tenement houses of considerable size, smaller homes being the rule, many owned by the occupants." Koren, "Padrone System," 123. See also Willard Glazier, *Peculiarities of American Cities* (Philadelphia: Hubbard Brothers, 1885), 387; Emily W. Dinwiddie, *Housing Conditions in Philadelphia* (Philadelphia: Octavia Hill Society, 1904), 3; Sutherland, "Origins," 21; Adams, *Urban Reform*, 34–35.

45. Sutherland, "Housing the Poor," 182.

46. Dickinson, "Aspects of Italian Immigration," 461.

47. Octavia Hill Association, "Certain Aspects of the Housing Problem in Philadelphia," *Annals of the American Academy of Political and Social Science*, 20 (July 1902): 117. See also Dinwiddie, *Housing Conditions*, 11; Goodman, *Franklin Street*, 4.

48. Lady Duffus Hardy, *Through Cities and Prairie Lands* (Chicago: Belford, Clarke, 1882), 297; P. A. B. Widener II, *Without Drums* (New York: G. P. Putnam's Sons, 1940), 7.

Even some who visited the city's slums downplayed the amount of misery poor Philadelphians endured. For instance, see Glazier, *Peculiarities*, 398.

49. Murphy, *Real Philly History*, 34–36.

50. Pease, *Reminiscences*, 5.

51. Hardy, *Through Cities*, 300; Fannie de C. Miller, *Snap Notes from an Eastern Trip* (San Francisco: S. Carson, 1892), 99; Harriet Boyer, *North of Market Street: Being the Adventures of a New York Woman in Philadelphia* (Philadelphia: Avil Printing, 1896), 10. See also Sutherland, "Housing the Poor," 185; Whiteman, "Philadelphia's Jewish Neighborhoods," 245; Hunter, "'Brotherly Love,'" 141.

52. Vincent Fraley, "Diving into Philly's History of Swimming Pools," *Philadelphia Inquirer*, June 15, 2017. accessed December 12, 2022, https://www.inquirer.com/philly/opinion/commentary/diving-into-phillys-history-of-swimming-pools-20170615.html; Zoe Greenberg, "Ghosts in the Water," *Philadelphia Inquirer*, July 26, 2022.Accessed December 12, 2022, https://www.inquirer.com/news/inq2/more-perfect-union-swimming-pools-philadelphia-segregation-funding-racism-20220726.html.

53. Fraley, "Diving into Philly's History"; Jeff Wiltse, *Contested Waters: A Social History of Swimming Pools in America* (Chapel Hill: University of North Carolina Press, 2010), 24–25.

54. *Reports of the Proceedings of the City Council of Boston for the Year Commencing January 3, 1898, and Ending December 31, 1898* (Boston: Municipal Printing Office, 1899), 619.

55. John Russell Young, *Memorial History of the City of Philadelphia*, vol. 1 (New York: New-York History, 1895), 562.

56. "An Act to Provide for the Construction of a Culvert Along Cohocksink Creek, in the County of Philadelphia," *Laws of the General Assembly of the Commonwealth of Pennsylvania Passed at the Session of 1851* (Harrisburg, PA: Theo. Fenn, 1851), 92; Harry Kyriakodis and Joel Spivak, *Underground Philadelphia: From Caves and Canals to Tunnels and Transit* (Charleston, SC: History Press, 2019), 21.

57. *Journal of the Common Council of the City of Philadelphia for the Year 1875*, vol. 2 (Philadelphia: King & Baird, 1875), 138; James Bryce, *The American Commonwealth*, vol. 1 (Chicago: Charles H. Sergel, 1914), 606.

58. H. W. Sanborn, *Eighty-Fourth Annual Report of the Chief Engineer of the Philadelphia Water Department for the Year 1885* (Philadelphia: Dunlap & Clarke, 1886), 10; Jon C. Teaford, *The Unheralded Triumph: City Government in America, 1870–1900* (Baltimore: Johns Hopkins University Press, 1984), 219.

59. Boyer, *North of Market Street:*, 21–22.

60. Beatrice Webb, *Beatrice Webb's American Diary, 1898*, ed. David Shannon (Madison: University of Wisconsin Press, 1963), 47. See also Young, *Memorial History*, 1:562; Sutherland, "Housing the Poor," 188; Teaford, *Unheralded Triumph*, 221.

61. For a description of Bradenbaugh's Museum, see Frank M. Trexler, "The Diary of Frank M. Trexler," ed. Edwin Baldrige, in *Proceedings of the Lehigh County Historical Society*, vol. 35 (Allentown, PA: Lehigh County Historical Society, 1982), 195–96.

62. William E. Meehan, *Rand, McNally & Co.'s Handy Guide to Philadelphia and Environs* (Chicago: Rand, McNally, 1896), 42–43.

63. Adams, *Urban Reform*, 33.

64. Glazier, *Peculiarities*, 379. See also Goodman, *Franklin Street*, 45.

65. *Laws of the General Assembly of the Commonwealth of Pennsylvania Passed at the Session of 1879* (Harrisburg, PA: Lane S. Hart, 1879), 130; Teaford, *Unheralded Triumph*, 288.

66. Peter McCaffery, *When Bosses Ruled Philadelphia: The Emergence of the Republican Machine, 1867–1933* (University Park: Pennsylvania State University Press, 1993), 71; Teaford, *Unheralded Triumph*, 291; Sam Alewitz, "Sanitation and Public Health: Philadelphia, 1870–1900" (PhD diss., Case Western Reserve University, 1981), iv.

67. *Laws of the General Assembly of the Commonwealth of Pennsylvania Passed at the Session of 1868* (Harrisburg, PA: Singerly & Myers, 1868), 443–44; Bryce, *American Commonwealth*, 1:606–7. See also Teaford, *Unheralded Triumph*, 302–3.

68. Jeffrey P. Roberts, "Railroads and the Downtown: Philadelphia, 1830–1900," in *The Divided Metropolis: Social and Spatial Dimensions of Philadelphia, 1800–1920*, ed. William W. Cutler III and Howard Gillette Jr. (Westport, CT: Greenwood Press, 1980), 38; Deborah C. Andrews, "Bank Buildings in Nineteenth-Century Philadelphia," in *The Divided Metropolis: Social and Spatial Dimensions of Philadelphia, 1800–1920*, ed. William W. Cutler III and Howard Gillette Jr. (Westport, CT: Greenwood Press, 1980), 77; Blumin, *Emergence*, 267.

69. Jerome P. Bjelopera, *City of Clerks: Office and Sales Workers in Philadelphia, 1870–1920* (Urbana: University of Illinois Press, 2005), 13.

70. Bjelopera, *City of Clerks*, 21–29; Jones, "'Lifework,'" 104.

71. E. Digby Baltzell, *Puritan Boston and Quaker Philadelphia: Two Protestant Ethics and the Spirit of Class Authority and Leadership* (Boston: Beacon Press, 1982), 234.

72. Bjelopera, *City of Clerks*, 18–19.

73. Fraser, *America at Work*, 79.

74. Baltzell, *Puritan Boston*, 253; Nash, *First City*, 289. On the relationship between Penn and the other Ivy League institutions, see Pepper, *Philadelphia Lawyer*, 31.

75. William C. Borlase, *Sunways: A Record of Rambles in Many Lands* (Plymouth, MA: W. Brendon & Son, 1878), 74.

76. Glazier, *Peculiarities*, 390.

77. Teaford, *Unheralded Triumph*, 265.

78. Levi J. Coppin, who served as Mother Bethel AME's minister in the late-1870s, recalled, "None of the various industries of Philadelphia . . . would take a colored apprentice." Levi J. Coppin, *Unwritten History* (Philadelphia: A.M.E. Book Concern, 1919), 359. See also Licht, *Getting Work*, 29, 44; Baltzell, *Puritan Boston*, 269. On leaving school to work, see Vare, *My Forty Years*, 37.

79. *Atlas of the City of Philadelphia* (New York: G. W. Bromley, 1910), plate 15. See also Keels, *Forgotten Philadelphia*, 138–39.

80. Philadelphia Chamber of Commerce, *1918–1919 Philadelphia Year Book* (Philadelphia: Ware Bros., 1918), 8.

81. Elizabeth Milroy notes that the Sanitary Fair was a "proto-shopping mall," while Bruno Giberti describes the Centennial Exhibition as "the equivalent of a shopping center." Elizabeth Milroy, "Avenue of Dreams: Patriotism and the Spectator at Philadelphia's Great

Central Sanitary Fair," in *Pennsylvania's Civil War*, ed. William Blair and William Pencak (University Park: Pennsylvania State University Press, 2001), 35; Bruno Giberti, *Designing the Centennial: A History of the 1876 International Exhibition in Philadelphia* (Lexington: University Press of Kentucky, 2002), 105.

82. Keels, *Forgotten Philadelphia*, 147–48.

83. Roberts, "Railroads," 39; Clark, "'Ramcat,'" 131; Blumin, *Emergence*, 277.

84. Glazier, *Peculiarities*, 378; *Official Handbook of City Hall Philadelphia* (Philadelphia: City Publishing, 1901), 114. See also Andrews, "Bank Buildings," 72; Keels, *Forgotten Philadelphia*, 143. See also Barth, *City People*, 29–30.

85. Burt and Davies, "Iron Age," 520; Barth, *City People*, 53.

86. Joseph Boggs Beale, "Education of an Artist: The Diary of Joseph Boggs Beale, 1856–1862," ed. Nicholas B. Wainwright, *Pennsylvania Magazine of History and Biography*, 97, no. 4 (October 1973): 493; James McClelland and Lynn Miller, *City in a Park: A History of Philadelphia's Fairmount Park System* (Philadelphia: Temple University Press, 2016), 41.

87. Brian Startare and Kevin Reavy, *This Day in Philadelphia Sports* (New York: Sports Publishing, 2019), 109.

88. Jerrold Casway, "Octavius Catto and the Pythians of Philadelphia," *Pennsylvania Legacies*, 7, no. 1 (May 2007): 6. See also Pepper, *Philadelphia Lawyer*, 27.

89. Startare and Reavy, *This Day*, 168.

90. On the Civil War and baseball in Philadelphia, see Adam S. Johnston, *The Soldier Boy's Diary Book* (Pittsburgh, 1866), 132; Barth, *City People*, 161. On Black teams, see Casway, "Octavius Catto," 5.

91. Harry C. Silcox, "Nineteenth-Century Philadelphia Black Militant: Octavius V. Catto (1839–1871)," *Pennsylvania History*, 44, no. 1 (January 1977): 67–68; Casway, "Octavius Catto," 8; Karen Guenther, *Sports in Pennsylvania* (Harrisburg, PA: Huggins Printing, 2007), 51.

92. Startare and Reavy, *This Day*, 137.

93. Bobbye P. Burke, Otto Sperr, and Trina Vaux., *Historic Rittenhouse: A Philadelphia Neighborhood* (Philadelphia: Historic Rittenhouse, 1985), 20; Lukacs, *Philadelphia*, 52–53.

94. Meredith Savory, "Instability and Uniformity: Residential Patterns in Two Philadelphia Neighborhoods, 1880–1970," in *The Divided Metropolis: Social and Spatial Dimensions of Philadelphia, 1800–1920*, ed. William W. Cutler III and Howard Gillette Jr. (Westport, CT: Greenwood Press, 1980), 197; Teaford, *Unheralded Triumph*, 236, 239; Barth, *City People*, 54–55; Bjelopera, *City of Clerks*, 143–45.

95. Baltzell, *Philadelphia Gentlemen*, 185–86.

96. Burke et al., *Historic Rittenhouse*, 7.

97. Nancy M. Heinzen, *The Perfect Square: A History of Rittenhouse Square* (Philadelphia: Temple University Press, 2009), 38–44; Baltzell, *Philadelphia Gentlemen*, 183–84.

98. Daly and Weinberg, *Genealogy*, 72–80; Lukacs, *Philadelphia*, 14.

99. Anne E. Krulikowski, "'Farms Don't Pay': The Transformation of the Philadelphian Metropolitan Landscape, 1880–1930," *Pennsylvania History*, 72, no. 2 (Spring 2005): 201–5; "Philadelphia in 1886," map (Philadelphia: Burk & McFetridge, 1886), Library of Congress, accessed December 12, 2022 https://www.loc.gov/item/76695290/.

100. Burt and Davies, "Iron Age," 477; David Schuyler, *The New Urban Landscape: The Redefinition of City Form in Nineteenth-Century America* (Baltimore: Johns Hopkins University Press, 1993), 165–66.

101. *Philadelphia and Popular Philadelphians* (Philadelphia: North American, 1891), 221.

102. Alexander McClure, *Old Time Notes of Pennsylvania*, vol. 2 (Philadelphia: John C. Winston, 1905), 247. See also Barth, *City People*, 20; Friedman, "Introduction," 11; Lukacs, *Philadelphia*, 6. Philadelphia's snobbery could reach comical heights, as when one prominent Philadelphia lady exclaimed, "I don't see why they make such a fuss about that man Franklin; he was not a Philadelphian." Francis Biddle, *A Casual Past* (Garden City, NY: Doubleday, 1961), 153.

103. George E. Thomas, "Architectural Patronage and Social Stratification in Philadelphia Between 1840 and 1920," in *The Divided Metropolis: Social and Spatial Dimensions of Philadelphia, 1800–1920*, ed. William W. Cutler III and Howard Gillette Jr. (Westport, CT: Greenwood Press, 1980), 93; Baltzell, *Puritan Boston*, 323; Baltzell, *Philadelphia Gentlemen*, 192; Keels, *Forgotten Philadelphia*, 134.

104. Andrews, "Bank Buildings," 73; Thomas, "Architectural Patronage," 102; Clark, "'Ramcat,'" 134–35; George E. Thomas, *Frank Furness: Architecture in the Age of the Great Machines* (Philadelphia: University of Pennsylvania Press, 2018), 2.

105. Andrews, "Bank Buildings," 73; George B. Tatum, *Penn's Great Town* (Philadelphia: University of Pennsylvania Press, 1961), 111; Baltzell, *Puritan Boston*, 329; Keels, *Forgotten Philadelphia*, 127; Michael J. Lewis, *Philadelphia Builds: Essays on Architecture* (Philadelphia: Paul Dry Books, 2021), 247.

106. Baltzell, *Philadelphia Gentlemen*, 6–7.

107. Fraser, *America at Work*, 76.

108. See also Widener, *Without Drums*, 10.

109. Boyer, *North of Market Street*, 47.

110. Widener, *Without Drums*, 9.

111. Baltzell, *Puritan Boston*, 239.

112. Fraser, *America at Work*, 76; Max O'Rell, *A Frenchman in America: Recollections of Men and Things* (New York: Cassell, 1891), 215. See also George E. Vickers, *Philadelphia: The Story of an American City* (Chicago: World's Columbian Exposition, 1893), 224; Glazier, *Peculiarities*, 379; Burt and Davies, "Iron Age," 474; Thomas, "Architectural Patronage," 112; Heinzen, *Perfect Square*, 86; James A. Kehl, *Boss Rule in the Gilded Age: Matt Quay of Pennsylvania* (Pittsburgh: University of Pittsburgh Press, 1981), 70; Baltzell, *Puritan Boston*, 249; Lukacs, *Philadelphia*, 9.

113. James Bryce, *The American Commonwealth*, vol. 2 (Chicago: Charles H. Sergel, 1914), 423.

114. McCaffery, *When Bosses Ruled*, 158.

115. Vare, *My Forty Years*, 46. See also Webb, *Beatrice Webb's American Diary*, 44; McCaffery, *When Bosses Ruled*, 36.

116. For instance, according to E. Digby Baltzell, "One way of looking at the political leadership of urban America in the twentieth century is to see it as a dialectical contest between the reforming forces of class authority, on the one hand, and personal loyalties

to the boss of the political machine, on the other." Baltzell, *Puritan Boston*, 377. See also McCaffery, *When Bosses Ruled*, 51; Domenic Vitello, *Engineering Philadelphia: The Sellers Family and the Industrial Metropolis* (Ithaca, NY: Cornell University Press, 2013), 110, 117.

117. Baltzell, *Puritan Boston*, 328; Philip S. Benjamin, *The Philadelphia Quakers in the Industrial Age, 1865–1920* (Philadelphia: Temple University Press, 1976), viii. Though Philadelphia was widely known as the "Quaker City," Quakers made up less than 1 percent of its population at the time of the Centennial Exhibition, and by the turn of the century, it had declined even further, yet fully 25 percent of the Committee of One Hundred's members were Quakers. Burt and Davies, "Iron Age," 474; McCaffery, *When Bosses Ruled*, 70; Philip S. Benjamin, "Gentlemen Reformers in the Quaker City, 1870–1912," *Political Science Quarterly*, 85, no. 1 (March 1970): 61; Lukacs, *Philadelphia*, 42. On the decline of Quaker influence, see Alfred Falk, *Trans-Pacific Sketches: A Tour Through the United States and Canada* (Melbourne, Australia: George Robertson, 1877), 174; David Macrae, *The Americans at Home*, vol. 1 (Edinburgh, UK: Edmonston & Douglas, 1870), 88; Amelia M. Murray, *Letters from the United States, Cuba, and Canada* (New York: G. P. Putnam, 1856), 158.

118. McCaffery, *When Bosses Ruled*, 47.

119. Howard Gillette Jr., "Philadelphia's City Hall: Monument to a New Political Machine," *Pennsylvania Magazine of History and Biography*, 97, no. 2 (April 1973): 233.

120. Wolf, *Philadelphia*, 222.

121. *Official Handbook of City Hall* , 6.

122. Glazier, *Peculiarities*, 377. See also Roberts, "Railroads," 42; Marion L. Bell, *Crusade in the City: Revivalism in Nineteenth-Century Philadelphia* (Lewisburg, PA: Bucknell University Press, 1977), 213.

123. Glazier, *Peculiarities*, 388.

124. Baltzell, *Puritan Boston*, 395; Keels, *Forgotten Philadelphia*, 150–51.

125. Ernest S. Griffith, *A History of American City Government: The Conspicuous Failure, 1870–1900* (New York: Praeger, 1974), 64; Teaford, *Unheralded Triumph*, 3; McCaffery, *When Bosses Ruled*, 48; Vitello, *Engineering Philadelphia*, 120; Benjamin, *Philadelphia Quakers*, 73–74.

126. *Weekly Notes of Cases Argued and Determined in the Supreme Court of Pennsylvania*, vol. 4: May 1877 to January 1878 (Philadelphia: Kay & Brother, 1878), 33. See also Benjamin, *Philadelphia Quakers*, 77.

127. Bryce, *American Commonwealth*, 2:406. Beatrice Webb, who visited both city councils, condescendingly described the members of Philadelphia's municipal government as a "low looking lot." Webb, *Beatrice Webb's American Diary*, 44.

128. Charles Richardson, "The Philadelphia Situation," in *Proceedings of the Boston Conference for Good Government*, ed. Clinton R. Woodruff (Philadelphia: National Municipal League, 1902), 162.

129. Baltzell, *Puritan Boston*, 378.

130. Du Bois, *Philadelphia Negro*, 27.

131. Sidney George Fisher, *A Philadelphia Perspective: The Diary of Sidney George Fisher, Covering the Years 1834–1871* ed. Nicholas B. Wainwright (Philadelphia: Historical Society of Pennsylvania, 1967), 488. See also Russell F. Weigley, "'A Peaceful City':

Public Order in Philadelphia from Consolidation Through the Civil War," in *The Peoples of Philadelphia: A History of Ethnic Groups and Lower-Class Life, 1790–1940*, ed. Allen F. Davis and Mark H. Haller (Philadelphia: University of Pennsylvania Press, 1998), 160; Morton Keller, "The Personality of Cities: Boston, New York, Philadelphia." *Proceedings of the Massachusetts Historical Society*, 3rd ser., vol. 97 (1985), 14; Edwin Wolf 2ⁿᵈ, "The Origins of Philadelphia's Self-Deprecation, 1820-1920." *Pennsylvania Magazine of History & Biography*, vol. 104, no. 1 (January 1980), 71; McCaffery, *When Bosses Ruled*, 25; Baltzell, *Philadelphia Gentlemen*, 126.

132. Widener, *Without Drums*, 20.

133. Robert Forrey, "Charles Tyson Yerkes: Philadelphia-Born Robber Baron," *Pennsylvania Magazine of History and Biography*, 99, no. 2 (April 1975): 228.

134. Widener, *Without Drums*, 22. See also Wolfinger, *Running the Rails*, 23–27; Harold E. Cox and John F. Meyers, "The Philadelphia Traction Monopoly and the Pennsylvania Constitution of 1874: Prostitution of an Ideal," *Pennsylvania History*, 35, no. 4 (October 1968): 411; Baltzell, *Puritan Boston*, 241–42.

135. Webb, *Beatrice Webb's American Diary*, 43.

136. Algernon Sydney Logan, *Vistas from the Stream*, vol. 1 (Philadelphia: National Publishing, 1934), 400. For an example of this in practice, see George Campbell, *The American People: The Relations Between the White and the Black* (New York: Worthington, 1899), 244.

137. Logan, *Vistas*, 1:401. See also Harold Zink, *City Bosses in the United States: A Study of Twenty Municipal Bosses* (New York: AMS Press, 1968), 203; Vitello, *Engineering Philadelphia*, 122; Maxwell Whiteman, *Gentlemen in Crisis: The First Century of the Union League, 1862–1962* (Philadelphia: Union League of Philadelphia, 1975), 145; Arthur P. Dudden, "Lincoln Steffens's Philadelphia," *Pennsylvania History*, 31, no. 4 (October 1964): 455.

138. Quoted in Zink, *City Bosses*, 208. See also Kehl, *Boss Rule*, 61; Baltzell, *Puritan Boston*, 405.

139. Teaford, *Unheralded Triumph*, 168–69.

140. Rosalind L. Branning, *Pennsylvania Constitutional Development* (Pittsburgh: University of Pittsburgh Press, 1960), 37–38; Cox and Meyers, "Philadelphia Traction Monopoly," 406.

141. Mahlon H. Hellerich, "The Origin of the Pennsylvania Constitutional Convention of 1873," *Pennsylvania History*, 34, no. 2 (April 1967): 159; Teaford, *Unheralded Triumph*, 103.

142. *Constitution of the Commonwealth of Pennsylvania* (Harrisburg, PA: William Stanley Ray, 1902), 24–25.

143. Boies Penrose and Edward Allinson, *Philadelphia, 1681–1887: A History of Municipal Development* (Philadelphia: Allen, Lane & Scott, 1887), 160.

144. Teaford, *Unheralded Triumph*, 25; Kehl, *Boss Rule*, 71–72; Silcox, "William McMullen," 395, 401.

145. Teaford, *Unheralded Triumph*, 99.

146. Teaford, *Unheralded Triumph*, 104.

147. Teaford, *Unheralded Triumph*, 187–88.

148. *Constitution of the Commonwealth*, 8. See also Branning, *Pennsylvania Constitutional Development*, 56.

149. Teaford, *Unheralded Triumph*, 88.

150. *Debates of the Convention to Amend the Constitution of Pennsylvania*, vol. 7 (Harrisburg, PA: Benjamin Singerly, 1873), 71.

151. Hellerich, "Origin of the Pennsylvania Constitutional Convention," 167; Kehl, *Boss Rule*, 56.

152. George E. Vickers, *The Fall of Bossism: A History of the Committee of One Hundred and the Reform Movement in Philadelphia and Pennsylvania*, vol. 1 (Philadelphia: A. C. Bryson, 1883), 3; Young, *Memorial History*, 1:545; Griffith, *History of American City Government*, 104.

153. Harry A. Barth, "The Philadelphia City Council," *National Municipal Review*, 13, no. 5 (May 1924): 294.

154. *Laws of the General Assembly of the Commonwealth of Pennsylvania Passed at the Session of 1885* (Harrisburg, PA: Edwin K. Meyers, 1885), 39–54; *Official Handbook of City Hall*, 13; Griffith, *History of American City Government*, 108.

155. Teaford, *Unheralded Triumph*, 23; McCaffery, *When Bosses Ruled*, 39.

156. Political columnist and historian Paul B. Beers noted, "Reform has always worked better in Pennsylvania as an issue-based effort rather than a broad political movement." Paul B. Beers, *Pennsylvania Politics Today and Yesterday: The Tolerable Accommodation* (University Park: Pennsylvania State University Press, 1980), 30.

157. Kyriakodis and Spivak, *Underground Philadelphia*, 52–53; McCaffery, *When Bosses Ruled*, 18–19.

158. *A Digest of the Ordinances of the Corporation of the City of Philadelphia and of the Acts of the Assembly Relating Thereto* (Philadelphia: J. Crissy, 1841), 146.

159. Zink, *City Bosses*, 195.

160. Bryce, *American Commonwealth*, 2:373.

161. Kehl, *Boss Rule*, 75.

162. McCaffery, *When Bosses Ruled*, 73, 98.

163. Lincoln Steffens, *The Autobiography of Lincoln Steffens*, vol. 1 (New York: Harcourt, Brace, 1958), 412. See also Baltzell, *Puritan Boston*, 403.

164. Jack M. Treadway, *Elections in Pennsylvania: A Century of Partisan Conflict in the Keystone State* (University Park: Pennsylvania State University Press, 2005), 11.

165. Baltzell, *Puritan Boston*, 409; Lukacs, *Philadelphia*, 50.

166. Beers, *Pennsylvania Politics*, 28.

167. Teaford, *Unheralded Triumph*, 261.

168. *First Annual Report, Free Library of Philadelphia* (Philadelphia: Edward Stern, 1896), 23.

169. In 1885, Willard Glazier claimed "the newspapers of Philadelphia rank second only to those of New York." Glazier, *Peculiarities*, 389.

170. Joseph Hatton, *Henry Irving's Impressions of America, Narrated in a Series of Sketches, Chronicles, and Conversations* (London: Sampson Low, Marston, Searle & Rivington, 1884), 143; Logan, *Vistas*, 327.

171. "Letter: Macon, Georgia to the Colored Players Film Corporation, Philadelphia, Pennsylvania, 1927 Oct. 28," Theater Records Series, Charles Henry Douglass Jr. Business Records, 1906-1967, Middle Georgia Archives, presented in the Digital Library of Georgia, accessed December 12, 2022. https://dlg.usg.edu/record/dlg_dtrm_dbr036?canvas=0&x= 1278&y=1649&w=9251; S. Torriano Berry and Venise T. Berry, *The 50 Most Influential Black Films: A Celebration of African-American Talent, Determination, and Creativity* (New York: Kensington, 2001), 39.

172. Hardy, *Through Cities*, 300.

173. Glazier, *Peculiarities*, 396; Trexler, "Diary," 37–38.

174. Nash, *First City*, 313; David Glassberg, "Public Ritual and Cultural Hierarchy: Philadelphia's Civic Celebrations at the Turn of the Twentieth Century," *Pennsylvania Magazine of History and Biography*, 107, no. 3 (July 1983): 421.

175. Elizabeth Duane Gillespie, *A Book of Remembrance* (Philadelphia: J. B. Lippincott, 1901), 389.

176. Boyer, *North of Market Street*, 65. Nor was she the only person to make this observation; see also Pepper, *Philadelphia Lawyer*, 22.

177. *Official Handbook of City Hall*, 58.

178. Fairmount Park Art Association, *Twenty-Fifth Annual Report* (Philadelphia: Fairmount Park Art Association, 1897), I; Penny Balkin Bach, *Public Art in Philadelphia* (Philadelphia: Temple University Press, 1992), 216.

179. Nash, *First City*, 291–300; Glassberg, "Public Ritual," 425.

Chapter 8

1. Lloyd M. Abernathy, "Progressivism: 1905–1919," in *Philadelphia: A 300-Year History*, ed. Russell F. Weigley (New York: W. W. Norton, 1982), 526.

2. Paul B. Beers, *Pennsylvania Politics Today and Yesterday: The Tolerable Accommodation* (University Park: Pennsylvania State University Press, 1980), 17; Gladys L. Palmer, *Philadelphia Workers in a Changing Economy* (Philadelphia: University of Pennsylvania Press, 1956), 22.

3. *Laws of the General Assembly of the Commonwealth of Pennsylvania Passed at the Session of 1905* (Harrisburg, PA: Wm. Stanley Ray, 1906), 29. See also Abernathy, "Progressivism," 539; Lloyd M. Abernathy, "Insurgency in Philadelphia, 1905," *Pennsylvania Magazine of History and Biography*, 87, no. 1 (January 1963): 3–4; Walter Licht, *Getting Work: Philadelphia, 1840–1950* (Philadelphia: University of Pennsylvania Press, 1992), 203; Peter McCaffery, *When Bosses Ruled Philadelphia: The Emergence of the Republican Machine, 1867–1933* (University Park: Pennsylvania State University Press, 1993), 83; Francis M. Ryan, *AFSCME's Philadelphia Story: Municipal Workers and Urban Power in the Twentieth Century* (Philadelphia: Temple University Press, 2011), 1.

4. Sandra Tatman, "Johnson, Philip H. (1868–1933)," Philadelphia Architects and Buildings, Athenaeum of Philadelphia, accessed September 6, 2022, https://www .philadelphiabuildings.org/pab/app/ar_display.cfm/25016; Adrian Trevisan, "Philip H. Johnson: The Architect That Swindled the City," *Hidden City Philadelphia*, August 20, 2021, accessed September 6, 2022, https://hiddencityphila.org/2021/08/philip-h-johnson -the-architect-that-swindled-the-city/.

5. Beers, *Pennsylvania Politics*, 61–63.

6. Thomas H. Coode and John F. Bauman, *People, Poverty, and Politics: Pennsylvanians During the Great Depression* (Lewisburg, PA: Bucknell University Press, 1981), 177; James Wolfinger, *Philadelphia Divided: Race and Politics in the City of Brotherly Love* (Chapel Hill: University of North Carolina Press, 2007), 28.

7. Jack M. Treadway, *Elections in Pennsylvania: A Century of Partisan Conflict in the Keystone State* (University Park: Pennsylvania State University Press, 2005), 12–13; Stefano Luconi, "Machine Politics and the Consolidation of the Roosevelt Majority: The Case of Italian Americans in Pittsburgh and Philadelphia," *Journal of American Ethnic History*, 15, no. 2 (Winter 1996): 34; Stefano Luconi, "Bringing Out the Italian-American Vote in Philadelphia," *Pennsylvania Magazine of History and Biography*, 117, no. 4 (October 1993): 264; Beers, *Pennsylvania Politics*, 64; Irwin F. Greenberg, "Philadelphia Democrats Get a New Deal: The Election of 1933," *Pennsylvania Magazine of History and Biography*, 97, no. 2 (April 1973): 210.

8. William Bayard Hale, "An Empire of Illusion and Its Fall," *American Illustrated Magazine*, 60 (May–October 1905): 454.

9. Abernathy, "Insurgency," 9.

10. Ellen C. Leichtman, "The Machine, the Mayor, and the Marine: The Battle over Prohibition in Philadelphia, 1924–1925," *Pennsylvania History*, 82, no. 2 (Spring 2015): 112–14.

11. Donald W. Disbrow, "Reform in Philadelphia Under Mayor Blankenburg, 1912–1916," *Pennsylvania History*, 27. no. 4 (October 1960): 381; Bonnie R. Fox, "The Philadelphia Progressives: A Test of the Hofstadter–Hays Thesis," *Pennsylvania History*, 34, no. 4 (October 1967): 378.

12. Historian Ernest S. Griffith asserts that Smith's election was the end of the Progressive Era in Philadelphia. Ernest S. Griffith, *A History of American City Government: The Progressive Years and Their Aftermath, 1900–1920* (Westport, CT: Praeger, 1974), 134–35.

13. Beers, *Pennsylvania Politics*, 55.

14. *The New Charter of Philadelphia* (Philadelphia: The Mayor, 1920), 1; Clinton R. Woodruff, "Progress in Philadelphia," *American Journal of Sociology*, 26, no. 3 (November 1920): 316; Harry A. Barth, "The Philadelphia City Council," *National Municipal Review*, 13, no. 5 (May 1924): 294. See also Charles R. Adrian, *A History of American City Government: The Emergence of the Metropolis, 1920–1945* (Lanham, MD: University Press of America, 1987), 371. See also Abernathy, "Insurgency," 12; Committee of Seventy, *The Charter: A History* (Philadelphia: Committee of Seventy, 1980), 3; Leichtman, "Machine," 121–22.

15. Adrian, *History*, 489; J. St. George Joyce, *Story of Philadelphia* (Philadelphia: Rex Printing House, 1919), 300; Barth, "Philadelphia City Council," 294.

16. Abernathy, "Progressivism," 564.

17. Licht, *Getting Work*, 205–8.

18. Peter Cole, *Wobblies on the Waterfront: Interracial Unionism in Progressive-Era Philadelphia* (Urbana: University of Illinois Press, 2007), 11.

19. Abernathy, "Progressivism," 533; Adrian, *History*, 371.

20. Palmer, *Philadelphia Workers*, 49.

21. Gladys L. Palmer, *Recent Trends in Employment and Unemployment in Philadelphia* (Philadelphia: Philadelphia Labor Market Studies, 1937), 3. See also Licht, *Getting Work*, 10–11; Coode and Bauman, *People, Poverty*, 52–53; Palmer, *Philadelphia Workers*, 33.

22. Charles W. Ervin, *Homegrown Liberal: The Autobiography of Charles W. Ervin*, ed. Jean Gould (New York: Dodd, Mead, 1954), 38. See also Abernathy, "Progressivism," 526; Licht, *Getting Work*, 178; Cole, *Wobblies*, 79; Coode and Bauman, *People, Poverty*, 53; Wolfinger, *Philadelphia Divided*, 26–27; Palmer, *Philadelphia Workers*, 29.

23. Cole, *Wobblies*, 40–47.

24. Bill Lynskey, "'I Shall Speak in Philadelphia': Emma Goldman and the Free Speech League," *Pennsylvania Magazine of History and Biography*, 133, no. 2 (April 2009): 179.

25. Joyce, *Story of Philadelphia*, 307; William B. Richter, *North of Society Hill* (North Quincy, MA: Christopher Publishing House, 1970), 14.

26. Ervin, *Homegrown Liberal*, 39.

27. Abernathy, "Progressivism," 549–50; Daniel Sidorick, "The 'Girl Army': The Philadelphia Shirtwaist Strike of 1909–1910," in *Pennsylvania History: Essays and Documents*, ed. Jeffrey A. Davis and Paul D. Newman (Upper Saddle River, NJ: Prentice Hall, 2010), 251; Joyce, *Story of Philadelphia*, 307; McCaffery, *When Bosses Ruled*, 64–88.

28. Woodrow Wilson, "Address to Naturalized Citizens at Convention Hall, Philadelphia," May 10, 1915, American Presidency Project, accessed August 3, 2020, https://www.presidency.ucsb.edu/node/206560. See also Disbrow, "Reform in Philadelphia," 393.

29. Barbara A. Gannon, "Pennsylvania in the First War to End All Wars," in *Pennsylvania: A Military History*, ed. William A. Pencak, Christian B. Keller, and Barbara A. Gannon (Yardley, PA: Westholme, 2016), 213; Griffith, *History*, 260–61.

30. Cole, *Wobblies*, 65; J. Frederic Dewhurst and Ernest A. Tupper, *Social and Economic Character of Unemployment in Philadelphia: April, 1929* (Washington, DC: Government Printing Office, 1930), 1. See also Disbrow, "Reform in Philadelphia," 387; Howell John Harris, *Bloodless Victories: The Rise and Fall of the Open Shop in the Philadelphia Metal Trades, 1890–1940* (New York: Cambridge University Press, 2000), 202.

31. Gannon, "Pennsylvania," 220; Treadway, *Elections*, 8; Jeffrey A. Davis and Paul D. Newman, "World War I and 1920s Pennsylvania," in *Pennsylvania History: Essays and Documents*, ed. Jeffrey A. Davis and Paul D. Newman (Upper Saddle River, NJ: Prentice Hall, 2010), 262.

32. Pennsylvania War History Commission, "Pennsylvania's Contributions in War Munitions (1917–1918)," in *Pennsylvania History: Essays and Documents*, ed. Jeffrey A. Davis and Paul D. Newman (Upper Saddle River, NJ: Prentice Hall, 2010), 280–81; Harris, *Bloodless Victories*, 208.

33. Joyce, *Story of Philadelphia*, 339.

34. Madeleine de Bryas and Jacqueline de Bryas, *A French Woman's Impressions of America* (New York: Century, 1920), 79; Christopher Morley, *Travels in Philadelphia* (Philadelphia: David McKay, 1921), 77. See also Gannon, "Pennsylvania," 220; Thomas H. Keels, *Forgotten Philadelphia: Lost Architecture of the Quaker City* (Philadelphia: Temple University Press, 2007), 105.

35. Jim Higgins, "An Epidemic's Strawman: Wilmer Krusen, Philadelphia's 1918–1919 Influenza Epidemic, and Historical Memory," *Pennsylvania Magazine of History and Biography*, 144, no. 1 (January 2020): 62–63.

36. Higgins, "Epidemic's Strawman," 77.

37. Thomas Wirth, "Urban Neglect: The Environment, Public Health, and Influenza in Philadelphia, 1915–1919," *Pennsylvania History*, 73, no. 3 (Summer 2006): 331–32; Christine Stetler, "The 1918 Spanish Influenza: Three Months of Horror in Philadelphia," *Pennsylvania History*, 84, no. 4 (Autumn 2017): 462.

38. Bryas and Bryas, *French Woman's Impressions*, 261.

39. Mae Townsend Pease, *Reminiscences from Lamplight to Satellite* (Philadelphia: Dorrance, 1960), 57. For similar reminiscences, see Richter, *North of Society Hill*, 16; Mary Wickham Bond, *Ninety Years "At Home" in Philadelphia* (Philadelphia: Dorrance, 1988), 10; Constance O'Hara, *Heaven Was Not Enough* (Philadelphia: J. B. Lippincott, 1955), 129–30.

40. Ryan, *AFSCME's Philadelphia Story*, 15–16.

41. Lucretia L. Blankenburg, *The Blankenburgs of Philadelphia* (Philadelphia: John C. Winston, 1928), 62; *Report on Collection and Treatment of the Sewage of the City of Philadelphia* (Philadelphia: City of Philadelphia, 1914), 5.

42. Harry Kyriakodis and Joel Spivak, *Underground Philadelphia: From Caves and Canals to Tunnels and Transit* (Charleston, SC: History Press, 2019), 47.

43. Higgins, "Epidemic's Strawman," 71.

44. Algernon Sydney Logan, *Vistas from the Stream*, vol. 2 (Philadelphia: National Publishing, 1934), 296. See also Pease, *Reminiscences*, 52; Bond, *Ninety Years*, 8.

45. "American Friends Service Committee," in *The Cambridge Companion to Quakerism*, ed. Stephen W. Angell and Pink Dandelion (Cambridge: Cambridge University Press, 2018), 93.

46. Griffith, *History*, 14–15; Cole, *Wobblies*, 81; Coode and Bauman, *People, Poverty*, 53.

47. For contemporary perspectives on Nearing, see George Wharton Pepper, *Philadelphia Lawyer: An Autobiography* (Philadelphia: J. B. Lippincott, 1944), 109; Rexford G. Tugwell, *To The Lesser Heights of Morningside* (Philadelphia: University of Pennsylvania Press, 1982), 15, 25, 67; Ervin, *Homegrown Liberal*, 61–63. See also Disbrow, "Reform in Philadelphia," 391; Joyce, *Story of Philadelphia*, 311; Lynskey, "'I Shall Speak,'" 167; Harris, *Bloodless Victories*, 199.

48. Paul Lyons, *Philadelphia Communists, 1936–1956* (Philadelphia: Temple University Press, 1982), 34; Chaim Leib Weinberg, *Forty Years in the Struggle: The Memoirs of a Jewish Anarchist*, ed. Robert P. Helms (Duluth, MN: Litwin Books, 2008), 81.

49. Lynskey, "'I Shall Speak,'" 175–78; Lyons, *Philadelphia Communists*, 31; Elizabeth Gurley Flynn, *The Rebel Girl: An Autobiography* (New York: International Publishers, 1973), 122.

50. "Scent Nation-Wide Terrorist Plot," *New York Times*, January 1, 1919.

51. Flynn, *Rebel Girl*, 257.

52. Morley, *Travels in Philadelphia*, 101; Kelley to Dirksen, 11 February 1931, *The Selected Letters of Florence Kelley, 1869–1931*, ed. Kathryn Kish Sklar and Beverly Wilson Palmer (Urbana: University of Illinois Press, 2009), 467.

53. Frederic Miller, "The Black Migration to Philadelphia: A 1924 Profile," in *African Americans in Pennsylvania: Shifting Historical Perspectives*, ed. Joe William Trotter Jr. and Eric Ledell Smith (University Park: Pennsylvania State University Press, 1997), 294–95.

54. "Geneva E. Edney," *Germantown Crier*, 56, no. 2 (Fall 2006): 58. See also Robert Gregg, *Sparks from the Anvil of Oppression: Philadelphia's African Methodists and Southern Migrants, 1890–1940* (Philadelphia: Temple University Press, 1993), 151.

55. Margaret B. Tinkcom, "Depression and War, 1929–1946," in *Philadelphia: A 300-Year History*, ed. Russell F. Weigley (New York: W. W. Norton, 1982), 602; Caroline Golab, "The Immigrant and the City: Poles, Italian, and Jews in Philadelphia, 1870–1920," in *The Peoples of Philadelphia: A History of Ethnic Groups and Lower-Class Life, 1790–1940*, ed. Allen F. Davis and Mark H. Haller (Philadelphia: University of Pennsylvania Press, 1998), 209; Miller, "Black Migration," 288–89; V. P. Franklin, "The Philadelphia Race Riot of 1918," in *African Americans in Pennsylvania: Shifting Historical Perspectives*, ed. Joe William Trotter Jr. and Eric Ledell Smith (University Park: Pennsylvania State University Press, 1997), 317; Cole, *Wobblies*, 20; John F. Bauman, "Black Slums/Black Projects: The New Deal and Negro Housing in Philadelphia," *Pennsylvania History*, 41, no. 3 (July 1974): 314; Coode and Bauman, *People, Poverty*, 202; Marcus Anthony Hunter, *Black Citymakers: How* The Philadelphia Negro *Changed Urban America* (New York: Oxford University Press, 2013), 84; Ryan, *AFSCME's Philadelphia Story*, 25; Lisa Levenstein, *A Movement Without Marches: African American Women and the Politics of Poverty in Postwar Philadelphia* (Chapel Hill: University of North Carolina Press, 2009), 9.

56. Sadie Tanner Mossell, "The Standard of Living Among One Hundred Negro Migrant Families in Philadelphia," *Annals of the American Academy of Political and Social Science*, 98 (November 1921): 173; Alice Dunbar-Nelson, *Give Us Each Day: The Diary of Alice Dunbar-Nelson*, ed. Gloria T. Hull (New York: W. W. Norton, 1984), 27. See also Coode and Bauman, *People, Poverty*, 202; Hunter, *Black Citymakers*, 79.

57. Richter, *North of Society Hill*, 34; Margaret S. Marsh, "The Impact of the Market Street 'El' on Northern West Philadelphia: Environmental Change and Social Transformation, 1900–1930," in *The Divided Metropolis: Social and Spatial Dimensions of Philadelphia, 1800–1920*, ed. William W. Cutler III and Howard Gillette Jr. (Westport, CT: Greenwood Press, 1980), 182; John F. Bauman, "Public Housing in the Depression: Slum Reform in Philadelphia Neighborhoods in the 1930s," in *The Divided Metropolis: Social and Spatial Dimensions of Philadelphia, 1800–1920*, ed. William W. Cutler III and Howard Gillette Jr. (Westport, CT: Greenwood Press, 1980), 235–37; Sam Bass Warner, *The Private City: Philadelphia in Three Periods of Its Growth*, 2nd ed. (Philadelphia: University of Pennsylvania Press, 1987), 171.

58. *Vital Statistics of Philadelphia* (Philadelphia: City of Philadelphia, 1916), 11–15. See also Marsh, "Impact," 182–83; Warner, *Private City*, 182, 194; Miller, "Black Migration," 298–99; Hunter, *Black Citymakers*, 15; Wolfinger, *Philadelphia Divided*, 415, 88; Kenneth Finkel, *Insight Philadelphia: Historical Essays Illustrated* (New Brunswick, NJ: Rutgers University Press, 2018), 63.

59. *The Negro in Business in Philadelphia* (Philadelphia: Armstrong Association of Philadelphia, 1917), 1.

60. Richter, *North of Society Hill*, 18; Charles Pete Banner-Haley, "*The Philadelphia Tribune* and the Persistence of Black Republicanism During the Great Depression," in *Pennsylvania History: Essays and Documents*, ed. Jeffrey A. Davis and Paul D. Newman (Upper Saddle River, NJ: Prentice Hall, 2010), 286; Wolfinger, *Philadelphia Divided*, 20; William W. Cutler III, "In Search of Influence and Authority: Parents and the Politics of the Home-School Relationship in Philadelphia and Two of Its Suburbs, 1905–1935," *Pennsylvania History*, 63, no. 3 (Summer 1996): 369.

61. "John 'Archie' Clark," *Germantown Crier*, 56, no. 2 (Fall 2006): 48; "Edney," *Germantown Crier*, 55; "Charles Cauthorn," *Germantown Crier*, 56, no. 2 (Fall 2006): 62–63. See also Licht, *Getting Work*, 45–51, 121–31; Cole, *Wobblies*, 15; Wolfinger, *Philadelphia Divided*, 25–26; Ryan, *AFSCME's Philadelphia Story*, 9; Sharon McConnell-Sidorick, *Silk Stockings and Socialism: Philadelphia's Radical Hosiery Workers from the Jazz Age to the New Deal* (Chapel Hill: University of North Carolina Press, 2017), 6.

62. Miller, "Black Migration," 302.

63. V. P. Franklin, "'Voice of the Black Community': The *Philadelphia Tribune*, 1912–1941," *Pennsylvania History*, 51, no. 4 (October 1984): 266; Bauman, "Black Slums," 311; Coode and Bauman, *People, Poverty*, 203; Wolfinger, *Philadelphia Divided*, 2.

64. Finkel, *Insight Philadelphia*, 256.

65. Franklin, "Philadelphia Race Riot," 317–25; Cole, *Wobblies*, 97. For similar incidents, see Khalil Gibran Muhammad, *The Condemnation of Blackness: Race, Crime, and the Making of Modern Urban America* (Cambridge, MA: Harvard University Press, 2019), 214–15.

66. Hunter, *Black Citymakers*, 75; Finkel, *Insight Philadelphia*, 257. Nor was this an isolated incident; see Muhammad, *Condemnation*, 249.

67. Finkel, *Insight Philadelphia*, 194–95; Daniel P. Jones, "From Military to Civilian Technology: The Introduction of Tear Gas for Civil Riot Control," *Technology and Culture*, 19, no. 2 (April 1978): 161; "Gas Bombs Prove Nemesis to Bandits," *Philadelphia Inquirer*, October 8, 1922.

68. "Alyce Jackson Alexander," *Germantown Crier*, 56, no. 2 (Fall 2006): 46.

69. Franklin, "Voice," 267; Hunter, *Black Citymakers*, 37–41.

70. Arthur P. Dudden, "The City Embraces 'Normalcy,'" in *Philadelphia: A 300-Year History*, ed. Russell F. Weigley (New York: W. W. Norton, 1982), 587; Golab, "Immigrant and the City," 203–4; Treadway, *Elections*, 2.

71. Cole, *Wobblies*, 103; Disbrow, "Reform in Philadelphia," 393; Victor Vázquez-Hernández, "Pan-Latino Enclaves in Philadelphia and the Formation of the Puerto Rican Community," in *Global Philadelphia: Immigrant Communities Old and New*, ed. Ayumi Takenaka and Mary Johnson Osirim (Philadelphia: Temple University Press, 2010), 78. For one Philadelphian's reaction, see Cyrus Adler, *Selected Letters*, vol. 2, ed. Ira Robinson (Philadelphia: Jewish Publication Society, 1985), 108–9.

72. Dudden, "City Embraces 'Normalcy,'" 591; Franklin, "Voice," 265.

73. Austin F. MacDonald, "The Democratic Party in Philadelphia: A Study in Political Pathology," *National Municipal Review*, 14 (1925): 295; Sandy Hingston, "What Two Centuries of Census Records Taught Us About Philadelphia," *Philadelphia Magazine*, January 18, 2020, accessed August 3, 2020, https://www.phillymag.com/news/2020/01

/18/philadelphia-census-records/; Luconi, "Machine Politics," 34; Stefano Luconi, "The Changing Meaning of Ethnic Identity Among Italian Americans in Philadelphia During the Inter-War Years," *Pennsylvania History*, 63, no. 4 (Autumn 1996): 561; Kenneth J. Heineman, "A Tale of Two Cities: Pittsburgh, Philadelphia, and the Elusive Quest for a New Deal Majority in the Keystone State," *Pennsylvania Magazine of History and Biography*, 132, no. 4 (October 2008): 315.

74. Dongzheng Jin, "The Sojourners' Story: Philadelphia's Chinese Immigrants, 1900–1925" (PhD diss., Temple University, 1997), 65; Kathryn E. Wilson, *Ethnic Renewal in Philadelphia's Chinatown: Space, Place, and Struggle* (Philadelphia: Temple University Press, 2015), 24.

75. Jin, "Sojourners' Story," 2.

76. Jin, "Sojourners' Story," 130–33; Wilson, *Ethnic Renewal*, 30.

77. Victor Vázquez, "Tobacco, Trains, and Textiles: Philadelphia's Early Spanish-Speaking Enclaves, 1920–1936," *Pennsylvania Legacies*, 3, no. 2 (November 2003): 12; Víctor Vázquez-Hernández, "From Pan-Latino Enclaves to Community: Puerto Ricans in Philadelphia, 1910–2000," in *Puerto Rican Diaspora: Historical Perspectives*, ed. Carmen Whalen and Victor Vázquez-Hernández (Philadelphia: Temple University Press, 2005), 89–90; Vázquez-Hernández, "Pan-Latino Enclaves in Philadelphia," 77–79.

78. Luconi, "Bringing Out," 257–59.

79. David R. Roediger, *Working Toward Whiteness: How America's Immigrants Became White* (New York: Basic Books, 2018), 59–67.

80. Luconi, "Changing Meaning," 564.

81. Pease, *Reminiscences*, 59. See also Bond, *Ninety Years*, 13.

82. Pamela Grundy, "Ora Washington," in *Out of the Shadows: A Biographical History of African American Athletes*, ed. David K. Wiggins (Fayetteville: University of Arkansas Press, 2008), 80.

83. Brian Startare and Kevin Reavy, *This Day in Philadelphia Sports* (New York: Sports Publishing, 2019), 121.

84. Startare and Reavy, *This Day*, 163; Keels, *Forgotten Philadelphia*, 184.

85. Startare and Reavy, *This Day*, 100.

86. Karen Guenther, *Sports in Pennsylvania* (Harrisburg, PA: Huggins Printing, 2007), 64–65; Startare and Reavy, *This Day*, 161–62; Neil Lanctot, "Fair Dealing and Clean Playing: Ed Bolden and the Hilldale Club, 1910–1932," *Pennsylvania Magazine of History and Biography*, 117, no. 1–2 (January–April 1993): 41.

87. John A. Lucas, "The Unholy Experiment: Professional Baseball's Struggle Against Pennsylvania Sunday Blue Laws, 1926–1934," *Pennsylvania History: A Journal of Mid-Atlantic Studies*, 38, no. 2 (April 1971): 174.

88. Guenther, *Sports in Pennsylvania*, 64–65.

89. Startare and Reavy, *This Day*, 185.

90. Keels, *Forgotten Philadelphia*, 185.

91. Palmer, *Recent Trends*, 26.

92. Keels, *Forgotten Philadelphia*, 194–95.

93. Alan Boris, *Philadelphia Radio* (Charleston, SC: Arcadia, 2011), 11–17.

94. Boris, *Philadelphia Radio*, 22.

95. George Barton, *Little Journeys Around Old Philadelphia* (Philadelphia: Peter Reilly, 1926), 30–31. See also John A. Lukacs, *Philadelphia: Patricians and Philistines, 1900–1950* (New York: Farrar, Straus & Giroux, 1981), 176.

96. Geneva E. Edney recalled that when she was a child, her parents took her to see Anderson in concert in South Philadelphia. "Edney," *Germantown Crier*, 56.

97. Dunbar-Nelson, *Give Us Each Day*, 301.

98. Keels, *Forgotten Philadelphia*, 182.

99. Bob Batchelor, *The 1900s* (Westport, CT: Greenwood Press, 2002), 56–57.

100. Patricia Anne Masters, *The Philadelphia Mummers: Building Community Through Play* (Philadelphia: Temple University Press, 2007), 4.

101. Masters, *Philadelphia Mummers*, 26–27.

102. William S. Vare, *My Forty Years in Politics* (Philadelphia: Roland Swain, 1933), 41–42.

103. Vice Commission of Philadelphia, *A Report on Existing Conditions with Recommendations to the Honorable Rudolph Blankenburg, Mayor of Philadelphia.* (Philadelphia: Vice Commission of Philadelphia, 1913), 4. See also Richter, *North of Society Hill*, 15–16; Hale, "Empire of Illusion," 453. On Progressive concerns about prostitution more generally, see Paul Boyer, *Urban Masses and Moral Order in America, 1820–1920* (Cambridge, MA: Harvard University Press, 1992).

104. Jeffrey A. Davis and Paul D. Newman, eds., "Suffrage Facts in Black and White," in *Pennsylvania History: Essays and Documents* (Upper Saddle River, NJ: Prentice Hall, 2010), 258.

105. Bond, *Ninety Years*, 13; O'Hara, *Heaven*, 150. See also McConnell-Sidorick, *Silk Stockings*, 75.

106. According to Christopher Morley, Camac Street's boosters also styled it "The Greatest Little Street in the World." Morley, *Travels in Philadelphia*, 142.

107. Morley, *Travels in Philadelphia*, 56; Dora Knowlton Thompson Ranous, *Diary of a Daly Debutante* (New York: Duffield, 1910), 182; Arnold Bennett, *Your United States: Impressions of a First Visit* (New York: Harper & Brothers, 1912); 69; Henry James, *The American Scene* (New York: Harper & Brothers, 1907), 265; William Archer, *America To-Day: Observations and Reflections* (London: William Heinemann, 1900), 31; Clare Sheridan, *My American Diary* (New York: Boni & Liveright, 1922), 123–28; Elizabeth Robins Pennell, *Our Philadelphia* (Philadelphia: J. B. Lippincott, 1914), 10, 19; Liu Hung Chang, *Memoirs*, ed. William Francis Mannix (New York: Houghton Mifflin, 1913), 199–205; Frank Brookhouser, *Our Philadelphia: A Candid and Colorful Portrait of a Great City* (Garden City, NY: Doubleday, 1957), 11; O'Hara, *Heaven*, 109.

108. Dudden, "City Embraces 'Normalcy,'" 580; Luconi, "Changing Meaning," 566; Dennis Clark, *The Irish in Philadelphia: Ten Generations of Urban Experience* (Philadelphia: Temple University Press, 1973), 155; Finkel, *Insight Philadelphia*, 262–63.

109. Abernathy, "Progressivism," 568; Tinkcom, "Depression and War," 629.

110. Fred D. Baldwin, "Smedley D. Butler and Prohibition Enforcement in Philadelphia, 1924–1925," *Pennsylvania Magazine of History and Biography*, 84, no. 3 (July 1960): 353.

111. Baldwin, "Smedley D. Butler," 354; Leichtman, "Machine," 110.

112. Beers, *Pennsylvania Politics*, 74–75; Leichtman, "Machine," 109.

113. Dudden, "City Embraces 'Normalcy,'" 579; Adrian, *History*, 257; McConnell-Sidorick, *Silk Stockings*, 3.

114. Finkel, *Insight Philadelphia*, 118–19; William H. Jordy, "PSFS: Its Development and Its Significance in Modern Architecture," *Journal of the Society of Architectural Historians*, 21, no. 2 (May 1962): 47.

115. Harold Donaldson Eberlein and Horace Mater Lippincott, *The Colonial Homes of Philadelphia and Its Neighbourhood* (Philadelphia: J. B. Lippincott, 1912), 132, 212; "Stenton, 4601 North 18th Street, Philadelphia, Philadelphia County, PA," Historic American Landscapes Survey (Library of Congress), accessed September 4, 2022, https://www.loc.gov/pictures/item/pa4148/; "Laurel Hill, Edgeley Point Lane, Philadelphia, Philadelphia County, PA," Historic American Landscapes Survey (Library of Congress), accessed September 4, 2022, https://www.loc.gov/pictures/item/pa0757/.

116. *Philadelphia: A Guide to the Nation's Birthplace* (Philadelphia: Pennsylvania Historical Commission, 1939), 346; Roger W. Moss, *Historic Houses of Philadelphia; A Tour of the Region's Museum Houses* (Philadelphia: University of Pennsylvania Press, 1998), 18.

117. Marguerite S. Shaffer, *See America First: Tourism and National Identity, 1880–1940* (Washington, DC: Smithsonian Institution Press, 2001), 4.

118. Davis and Newman, "World War I," 242.

119. George Morgan, *The City of Firsts: Being a Complete History of the City of Philadelphia from Its Founding in 1682, to the Present Time* (Philadelphia: Historical Publication Society, 1926), 3; Barton, *Little Journeys*, 25; Vay de Vaya, *The Inner Life of the United States* (New York: E. P. Dutton, 1908), 88.

120. Joyce, *Story of Philadelphia*, 309.

121. John R. Vile, *The American Flag: An Encyclopedia of the Stars and Stripes in U.S. History, Culture, and Law* (Santa Barbara, CA: ABC-Clio, 2018), 21.

122. Beers, *Pennsylvania Politics*, 74; David Glassberg, "Public Ritual and Cultural Hierarchy: Philadelphia's Civic Celebrations at the Turn of the Twentieth Century," *Pennsylvania Magazine of History and Biography*, 107, no. 3 (July 1983): 432–33; Finkel, *Insight Philadelphia*, 199; Bruce J. Evensen, "'Saving the City's Reputation': Philadelphia's Struggle over Self-Identity, Sabbath-Breaking, and Boxing in America's Sesquicentennial Year," *Pennsylvania History*, 60, no. 1 (January 1993): 7.

123. Blankenburg, *Blankenburgs of Philadelphia*, 151.

124. Joyce, *Story of Philadelphia*, 302; John F. Bauman, "Downtown Versus Neighborhood: Focusing on Philadelphia in the Metropolitan Era, 1920–1960," *Pennsylvania History*, 48, no. 1 (January 1981): 6.

125. A. Merritt Taylor, "Philadelphia's Transit Problem," *Annals of the American Academy of Political and Social Science*, 57 no. 1 (January 1915): 29–30.

126. Robert P. Armstrong, "Green Space in the Gritty City: The Planning and Development of Philadelphia's Park System, 1854–1929," (PhD diss., Lehigh University, 2012), 137.

127. Abernathy, "Progressivism," 532; M. Agnes Gertrude, "Italian Immigration into Philadelphia," *Records of the American Catholic Historical Society of Philadelphia*, 58, no. 2 (June 1947): 138; Marsh, "Impact," 174; Warner, *Private City*, 192.

128. Marsh, "Impact," 181.

129. Kyriakodis and Spivak, *Underground Philadelphia*, 23.

130. Dudden, "City Embraces 'Normalcy,'" 605.

131. "Some American Autocars" and "The Chicago Autocar Road Trial," *Autocar*, November 9, 1895, 22–23.

132. Beers, *Pennsylvania Politics*, 17.

133. Kevin McMahon and Logan Ferguson, "Automobile Row Thematic Historic District," Preservation Alliance for Greater Philadelphia, accessed August 17, 2020, https://www.phila.gov/media/20200117144730/Historic-District-Automobile-Row.pdf. See also W. Thacher Longstreth with Dan Rottenberg, *Main Line WASP* (New York: W. W. Norton, 1990), 36.

134. McCaffery, *When Bosses Ruled*, 91–92.

135. *Ordinances of the City of Philadelphia: From January 1 to December 31, 1892* (Philadelphia: Dunlap Printing, 1893), 211–12. See also Fairmount Park Art Association, *An Account of Its Origins and Activities from Its Foundation in 1871. Issued on the Occasion of Its Fiftieth Anniversary* (Philadelphia: Fairmount Park Art Association, 1922), 246; David B. Brownlee, *Building the City Beautiful: The Benjamin Franklin Parkway and the Philadelphia Museum of Art* (Philadelphia: Philadelphia Museum of Art, 1989).

136. *Ordinances of the City of Philadelphia: From January 1 to December 31, 1903* (Philadelphia: Dunlap Printing 1904), 53–55.

137. David B. Brownlee, *Making a Modern Classic: The Architecture of the Philadelphia Museum of Art* (Philadelphia: Philadelphia Museum of Art, 1997), 59–63.

138. Armstrong, "Green Space," 177.

139. Morley, *Travels in Philadelphia*, 64–65. See also Finkel, *Insight Philadelphia*, 110–11.

140. Fairmount Park Art Association. *Twenty-Fifth Annual Report*. Philadelphia: Fairmount Park Art Association, 1897, 1.

141. Brownlee, *Making a Modern Classic*, 75.

142. Brownlee, *Making a Modern Classic*, 115.

143. Palmer, *Philadelphia Workers*, 54; Susan G. Davis, *Parades and Power: Street Theater in Nineteenth-Century Philadelphia* (Berkeley: University of California Press, 1988), 169.

144. Dewhurst and Tupper, *Social and Economic Character*, 1–2. See also Banner-Haley, "*Philadelphia Tribune*," 288; Vázquez, "Tobacco, Trains," 15; Bonnie R. Fox, "Unemployment Relief in Philadelphia, 1930–1932: A Study of the Depression's Impact on Volunteerism," *Pennsylvania Magazine of History and Biography*, 93, no. 1 (January 1969): 88.

145. Coode and Bauman, *People, Poverty*, 178.

146. Franklin Klein Fretz, "The Furnished Room Problem in Philadelphia" (PhD diss., University of Pennsylvania, 1912), 5, 10; Frank A. Craig, *A Study of the Housing and Social Conditions in Selected Districts of Philadelphia* (Philadelphia: Henry Phipps Institute, 1915), 6. See also Adrian, *History*, 190–93; Wirth, "Urban Neglect," 326–27; Bauman, "Black Slums," 312–16; Coode and Bauman, *People, Poverty*, 200–201; Hunter, *Black Citymakers*, 69.

147. R. Daniel Wadhwani, "Soothing the People's Panic: The Banking Crisis of the 1930s in Philadelphia," *Pennsylvania Legacies*, 11, no. 1 (May 2011): 26; Hunter, *Black City-makers*, 23.

148. Warner, *Private City*, 204; Adrian, *History*, 132–33; Palmer, *Philadelphia Workers*, 14–15. Political bosses had also provided some ad hoc assistance to citizens, but their waning political power and the Depression's scope made this unfeasible. See John T. Salter, "Party Organization in Philadelphia: The Ward Committeeman," *American Political Science Review*, 27, no. 4 (August 1933): 618; Griffith, *History*, 142; Beers, *Pennsylvania Politics*, 63; Committee of Seventy, *Charter*, 2; Coode and Bauman, *People, Poverty*, 177; Fox, "Unemployment Relief," 87.

149. Edwin Wolf 2nd, *Philadelphia: Portrait of an American City* (Philadelphia: Camino Books, 1990), 304.

150. Adrian, *History*, 132; Palmer, *Philadelphia Workers*, 78; Dudden, "City Embraces 'Normalcy,'" 608–9; John F. Bauman et al., eds. "Depression Report: A New Dealer Tours Eastern Pennsylvania," *Pennsylvania Magazine of History and Biography*, 104, no. 1 (January 1980): 97.

151. Dudden, "City Embraces 'Normalcy,'" 611; Bauman, "Public Housing," 236; Coode and Bauman, *People, Poverty*, 177.

152. Licht, *Getting Work*, 174, 195; Ryan, *AFSCME's Philadelphia Story*, 4.

153. Luconi, "Machine Politics," 40; Greenberg, "Philadelphia Democrats," 231; Coode and John F. Bauman, *People, Poverty*, 176.

154. Philip Jenkins, "'It Can't Happen Here': Fascism and Right-Wing Extremism in Pennsylvania, 1933–1942," in *Pennsylvania History: Essays and Documents*, ed. Jeffrey A. Davis and Paul D. Newman (Upper Saddle River, NJ: Prentice Hall, 2010), 295; Franklin, "Voice," 270; Wolfinger, *Philadelphia Divided*, 21.

155. Luconi, "Changing Meaning," 572–73.

156. Ryan, *AFSCME's Philadelphia Story*, 44.

157. Jenkins, "'It Can't Happen Here,'" 293; Cole, *Wobblies*, 21; Wolfinger, *Philadelphia Divided*, 79; Birte Pfleger, "German Immigration to Philadelphia from the Colonial Period Through the Twentieth Century," in *Global Philadelphia: Immigrant Communities Old and New*, ed. Ayumi Takenaka and Mary Johnson Osirim (Philadelphia: Temple University Press, 2010), 147; Philip Jenkins, *Hoods and Shirts: The Extreme Right in Pennsylvania, 1925–1950* (Chapel Hill: University of North Carolina Press, 1997), 10–11; Finkel, *Insight Philadelphia*, 162–63.

158. Lyons, *Philadelphia Communists*, 24–25; Wolfinger, *Philadelphia Divided*, 42; Jenkins, *Hoods and Shirts*, 4.

159. *Investigation of Un-American Propaganda Activities in the United States*, vol. 4: *Executive Hearings* (Washington, DC: Government Printing Office, 1941), 2543.

160. "Education Board Votes 'Red' Probe at Broome Request," *Philadelphia Inquirer*, May 7, 1936, 1.

161. *Investigation of Un-American Propaganda*, 4:2544.

162. Glen Jeansonne, *Women of the Far Right: The Mothers' Movement and World War II* (Chicago: University of Chicago Press, 1996), 123.

163. "People," *Time*, April 3, 1939, accessed December 14, 2022, https://content.time
.com/time/subscriber/article/0,33009,771631,00.html.

164. "Teacher Retires in Bigotry Row," *New York Times*, March 12, 1941, 23; *Investigation of Un-American Propaganda*, 4:2632; Jeansonne, *Women of the Far Right*, 123; Jenkins, *Hoods and Shirts*, 204.

165. Wolfinger, *Philadelphia Divided*, 45.

166. Bauman, "Public Housing," 227; Coode and Bauman, *People, Poverty*, 57–58.

167. Keels, *Forgotten Philadelphia*, 190–91; Jenkins, "'It Can't Happen Here,'" 47.

168. Joseph F. Guffey, *Seventy Years on the Red-Fire Wagon* (self-pub., 1952), 128.

169. Beers, *Pennsylvania Politics*, 37; Leichtman, "Machine," 114; Samuel J. Astorino, "The Contested Senate Election of William Scott Vare," *Pennsylvania History*, 28, no. 2 (April 1961): 189; Ryan, *AFSCME's Philadelphia Story*, 11.

170. Lukacs, *Philadelphia: Patricians and Philistines*, 225; Astorino, "Contested Senate Election," 190.

171. Guffey, *Seventy Years*, 75. See also Luconi, "Machine Politics," 37; Luconi, "Bringing Out," 253–54; Wolfinger, *Philadelphia Divided*, 30.

172. Beers, *Pennsylvania Politics*, 62; Wolfinger, *Philadelphia Divided*, 47.

173. J. David Stern, *Memoirs of a Maverick Publisher* (New York: Simon & Schuster, 1962), 205. See also John P. Rossi, "The Kelly–Wilson Mayoralty Election of 1935," *Pennsylvania Magazine of History and Biography*, 107, no. 2 (April 1983): 173; John L. Shover, "Ethnicity and Religion in Philadelphia Politics, 1924–40," *American Quarterly*, 25, no. 5 (December 1973): 506; Greenberg, "Philadelphia Democrats," 210; John L. Shover, "The Emergence of a Two-Party System in Republican Philadelphia, 1924–1936," *Journal of American History*, 60, no. 4 (March 1974): 985–96; Finkel, *Insight Philadelphia*, 33; Heineman, "Tale of Two Cities," 323.

174. Greenberg, "Philadelphia Democrats," 214; Ryan, *AFSCME's Philadelphia Story*, 34–35.

175. Dudden, "City Embraces 'Normalcy,'" 583–84; Rossi, "Kelly–Wilson," 172; Luconi, "Bringing Out," 277–79; Wolfinger, *Philadelphia Divided*, 55.

176. Wolfinger, *Philadelphia Divided*, 80; Mitch Kachun, "'A Beacon to Oppressed Peoples Everywhere': Major Richard R. Wright, Sr., National Freedom Day, and the Rhetoric of Freedom in the 1940s." *Pennsylvania Magazine of History & Biography*, vol. 128, no. 3 (July 2004), 288.

177. Adrian, *History*, 371.

178. Shover, "Emergence," 993.

179. Treadway, *Elections*, 34; Jenkins, "'It Can't Happen Here,'" 297.

180. Luconi, "Changing Meaning," 569; Shover, "Ethnicity," 506; Eric Ledell Smith, "'Asking for Justice and Fair Play': African American State Legislators and Civil Rights in Early Twentieth-Century Pennsylvania," *Pennsylvania History*, 62, no. 2 (Spring 1996): 193; Greenberg, "Philadelphia Democrats," 228; Bauman, "Downtown Versus Neighborhood," 12; Wadhwani, "Soothing the People's Panic," 27; Heineman, "Tale of Two Cities," 311; Stanley Keith Arnold, "The Great Depression and World War II," in *If There Is No Struggle There Is No Progress: Black Politics in Twentieth-Century Philadelphia*, ed. James Wolfinger (Philadelphia: Temple University Press, 2022), 77.

181. Luconi, "Bringing Out," 262; Shover, "Ethnicity," 513.

182. Stern, *Memoirs*, 207. See also Greenberg, "Philadelphia Democrats," 230.

183. Luconi, "Machine Politics," 42; Greenberg, "Philadelphia Democrats," 215; Stern, *Memoirs*, 228. See also Coode and Bauman, *People, Poverty*, 184–85; Wolfinger, *Philadelphia Divided*, 235.

184. Shover, "Emergence," 996; Coode and Bauman, *People, Poverty*, 186; Ryan, *AFSCME's Philadelphia Story*, 42.

185. Bauman, "Public Housing," 230–31; Bauman, "Black Slums," 312.

186. Ervin, *Homegrown Liberal*, 38. See also Abernathy, "Progressivism," 526; Licht, *Getting Work:*, 178; Palmer, *Philadelphia Workers*, 18; Elizabeth Fones-Wolf, "Industrial Unionism and Labor Movement Culture in Depression-Era Philadelphia," *Pennsylvania Magazine of History and Biography*, 109, no. 1 (January 1985): 3.

187. Pepper, *Philadelphia Lawyer*, 263.

188. Treadway, *Elections*, 102, 124–29.

189. Wolfinger, *Philadelphia Divided*, 98.

190. Gannon, "Pennsylvania," 234; Merl E. Reed, "Black Workers, Defense Industries, and Federal Agencies in Pennsylvania, 1941–1945," in *African Americans in Pennsylvania: Shifting Historical Perspectives*, ed. Joe William Trotter Jr. and Eric Ledell Smith (University Park: Pennsylvania State University Press, 1997), 367; Jeffrey A. Davis and Paul D. Newman, "Pennsylvania and the Second World War," in *Pennsylvania History: Essays and Documents*, ed. Jeffrey A. Davis and Paul D. Newman (Upper Saddle River, NJ: Prentice Hall, 2010), 303–4.

191. Maryann Lovelace, "Facing Change in Wartime Philadelphia: The Story of the Philadelphia USO," in *Pennsylvania History: Essays and Documents*, ed. Jeffrey A. Davis and Paul D. Newman (Upper Saddle River, NJ: Prentice Hall, 2010), 304–7; Wolfinger, *Philadelphia Divided*, 98.

192. Palmer, *Philadelphia Workers*, 99.

193. Wolfinger, *Philadelphia Divided*, 103.

194. Coode and Bauman, *People, Poverty*, 213–15.

195. Reed, "Black Workers," 368.

196. Wolfinger, *Philadelphia Divided*, 144.

197. Licht, *Getting Work*, 217–18; Wolfinger, *Philadelphia Divided*, 151.

Chapter 9

1. Mark McColloch, "Glory Days," in *Keystone of Democracy: A History of Pennsylvania Workers*, ed. Howard Harris and Perry K. Blatz (Harrisburg, PA: Pennsylvania Historical and Museum Commission, 1999), 213; Philip S. Klein and Ari Hoogenboom, *A History of Pennsylvania*, 2nd ed. (University Park: Pennsylvania State University Press, 1980), 499; Philip S. Jenkins, *The Cold War at Home: The Red Scare in Pennsylvania* (Chapel Hill: University of North Carolina Press, 1999), 198–99; Philip S. Jenkins, "The Postindustrial Age: 1950–2000," in *Pennsylvania: A History of the Commonwealth*, ed. Randall M. Miller and William Pencak (University Park: Pennsylvania State University Press, 2002), 318–20; Scott Gabriel Knowles, "Staying Too Long at the Fair: Philadelphia Planning and the Debacle of 1976," in *Imagining Philadelphia: Edmund Bacon and the Future of the City*, ed.

Scott Gabriel Knowles (Philadelphia: University of Pennsylvania Press, 2009), 78; Jordan Stanger-Ross, *Staying Italian: Urban Change and Ethnic Life in Postwar Toronto and Philadelphia* (Chicago: University of Chicago Press, 2009), 13; Stefano Luconi, *From Paesani to White Ethnics: The Italian Experience in Philadelphia* (Albany: State University of New York Press, 2001), 5; Matthew J. Countryman, *Up South: Civil Rights and Black Power in Philadelphia* (Philadelphia: University of Pennsylvania Press, 2006), 9; Diane Sicotte, *From Workshop to Waste Magnet: Environmental Inequality in the Philadelphia Region* (New Brunswick, NJ: Rutgers University Press, 2016), 117.

2. Jenkins, "Postindustrial Age," 325.

3. Alyssa Ribeiro, "'We Want Both': Pressuring Philadelphia Unions for Inclusion and Equity During the Long 1970s," *Labor History*, 60, no. 5 (June 2019): 560.

4. Jenkins, "Postindustrial Age," 332; Marcus Anthony Hunter, *Black Citymakers: How* The Philadelphia Negro *Changed Urban America* (New York: Oxford University Press, 2013), 118; James Wolfinger, *Philadelphia Divided: Race and Politics in the City of Brotherly Love* (Chapel Hill: University of North Carolina Press, 2007), 179; Stanger-Ross, *Staying Italian*, 12; Luconi, *From Paesani*, 126; Abigail Perkiss, *Making Good Neighbors: Civil Rights, Liberalism, and Integration in Postwar Philadelphia* (Ithaca, NY: Cornell University Press, 2014), 23; Timothy J. Lombardo, *Blue-Collar Conservatism: Frank Rizzo's Philadelphia and Populist Politics* (Philadelphia: University of Pennsylvania Press, 2018), 38.

5. Jack M. Treadway, *Elections in Pennsylvania: A Century of Partisan Conflict in the Keystone State* (University Park: Pennsylvania State University Press, 2005), 5; John Kromer, *Philadelphia Battlefields: Disruptive Campaigns and Upset Elections in a Changing City* (Philadelphia: Temple University Press, 2020), 59.

6. James Reichley, *The Art of Government: Reform and Organization Politics in Philadelphia* (New York: Fund for the Republic, 1959), 68–69. See also William J. McKenna, "The Negro Vote in Philadelphia Elections," in *Black Politics in Philadelphia*, ed. Miriam Ershkowitz and Joseph Zikmund (New York: Basic Books, 1973), 76; Stanger-Ross, *Staying Italian*, 17–18; Sicotte, *From Workshop*, 85; Lisa Levenstein, *A Movement Without Marches: African American Women and the Politics of Poverty in Postwar Philadelphia* (Chapel Hill: University of North Carolina Press, 2009), 11; Douglas S. Massey and Nancy A. Denton, *American Apartheid: Segregation and the Making of the Underclass* (Cambridge, MA: Harvard University Press, 1993), 71; Carolyn Adams et al., *Philadelphia: Neighborhoods, Division, and Conflict in a Postindustrial City* (Philadelphia: Temple University Press, 1991), 75; Eric C. Schneider, *The Ecology of Homicide: Race, Place, and Space in Postwar Philadelphia* (Philadelphia: University of Pennsylvania Press, 2020), xvi.

7. Erika Lee, "Immigration," in *Myth America: Historians Take on the Biggest Legends and Lies About Our Past*, ed. Kevin M. Kruse and Julian E. Zelizer (New York: Basic Books, 2022), 63; Stanger-Ross, *Staying Italian*, 3–4; *Immigrant Philadelphia: From Cobblestone Streets to Korean Soap-Operas* (Philadelphia: Welcome Center for New Pennsylvanians, 2004), 22–23; Luconi, *From Paesani*, 121.

8. Kathryn E. Wilson, *Ethnic Renewal in Philadelphia's Chinatown: Space, Place, and Struggle* (Philadelphia: Temple University Press, 2015), 43, 51.

9. *Immigrant Philadelphia*, 34–68.

10. Sicotte, *From Workshop*, 94; Carmen Teresa Whalen, *From Puerto Rico to Philadelphia: Puerto Rican Workers and Postwar Economics* (Philadelphia: Temple University Press, 2001), 2; Sabrina Vourvoulias, ed., *200 Years of Latino History in Philadelphia* (Philadelphia: Temple University Press, 2012), 21.

11. Melissa Cahnmann, "Over Thirty Years of Language-Education Policy and Planning: Potter Thomas Bilingual School in Philadelphia," *Bilingual Research Journal*, 22, no. 1 (Winter 1998): 67–70; John Lippincott, "Latin Is Dead! Long Live Latin!," *Humanities: National Endowment for the Humanities*, 2, no. 3 (June 1981): 11–12.

12. Wolfinger, *Philadelphia Divided*, 179; Sicotte, *From Workshop*, 101; Steven Conn, *Metropolitan Philadelphia: Living with the Presence of the Past* (Philadelphia: University of Pennsylvania Press, 2006), 134; Stephanie R. Ryberg, "Historic Preservation's Urban Renewal Roots: Preservation and Planning in Midcentury Philadelphia," *Journal of Urban History*, 39, no. 2 (April 2012): 198.

13. Guian McKee, "Edmund Bacon and the Complexity of the City," in *Imagining Philadelphia: Edmund Bacon and the Future of the City*, ed. Scott Gabriel Knowles (Philadelphia: University of Pennsylvania Press, 2009), 54–55.

14. "Urban Redevelopment Law," Pennsylvania General Assembly, Unconsolidated Statutes, accessed September 17, 2020, https://www.legis.state.pa.us/cfdocs/Legis/LI/uconsCheck.cfm?txtType=HTM&yr=1945&sessInd=0&smthLwInd=0&act=0385.

15. Joseph S. Clark Jr. and Dennis Clark, "Rally and Relapse," in *Philadelphia: A 300-Year History*, ed. Russell F. Weigley (New York: W. W. Norton, 1982), 670; Hunter, *Black Citymakers*, 123.

16. *Greater Philadelphia Movement: Annual Report of 1955 Activities* (Philadelphia: Greater Philadelphia Movement, 1956), 15.

17. Interview with Joshua Eilberg, January 29, 1996, Feinstein Center for American Jewish History at Temple University, 14, accessed January 25, 2021, https://libdigital.temple.edu/oralhistories/catalog/transcript:TOHFCJZ2016020016xp16002coll22x198; interview with Joseph Burke, March 15, 1979, Walter Massey Phillips Oral Histories, Temple University, 5–7, accessed January 25, 2021, https://libdigital.temple.edu/oralhistories/catalog/transcript: AOHWMPJZ2014120008xp16002coll22x59; Nochem S. Winnet, *Vignettes of a Lucky Life* (Philadelphia: Fox Rothschild O'Brien and Frankel, 1989), 148. See also Joseph D. Crumlish, *A City Finds Itself: The Philadelphia Home Rule Charter Movement* (Detroit: Wayne State University Press, 1959), 33. In his biography of Frank Rizzo, Sal Paolantonio goes so far as to call the GPM the "power behind the power." Sal Paolantonio, *Frank Rizzo: The Last Big Man in Big City America* (Philadelphia: Camino Books, 1993), 55. See also Hunter, *Black Citymakers*, 116; John Logan and Harvey Molotoch, *Urban Fortunes* (Berkeley: University of California Press, 2017), ix–x; Amy E. Menzer, "Exhibiting Philadelphia's Vital Center: Negotiating Environmental and Civic Reform in a Popular Postwar Planning Vision," in *A Greene Country Towne: Philadelphia's Ecology in the Cultural Imagination*, ed. Alan C. Braddock and Laura Turner Igoe (University Park: Pennsylvania State University Press, 2016), 156–57.

18. Reichley, *Art of Government*, 61; Nathaniel Burt, *The Perennial Philadelphians: The Anatomy of an American Aristocracy* (Boston: Little, Brown, 1963), 11.

19. "City Planning Progress," *American City*, 62, no. 2 (1947): 86. See also Dan Rottenberg, *The Outsider: Albert M. Greenfield and the Fall of the Protestant Establishment*

(Philadelphia: Temple University Press, 2014), 245; Gregory L. Heller, *Ed Bacon: Planning, Politics, and the Building of Modern Philadelphia* (Philadelphia: University of Pennsylvania Press, 2013), 48.

20. Kromer, *Philadelphia Battlefields*, 42; Gregory L. Heller, "Salesman of Ideas: The Life Experiences That Shaped Edmund Bacon," in *Imagining Philadelphia: Edmund Bacon and the Future of the City*, ed. Scott Gabriel Knowles (Philadelphia: University of Pennsylvania Press, 2009), 29; Heller, *Ed Bacon*, 5.

21. Interview with Ed Bacon, January 9, 1975, Walter Massey Phillips Oral Histories, Temple University, 10, accessed January 25, 2021, https://libdigital.temple.edu/oralhistories/catalog/transcript:AOHWMPJZ2014110011xp16002coll22x2.

22. "Republican Party Platform of 1948," ed. Gerhard Peters and John T. Woolley, American Presidency Project, accessed January 25, 2021, https://www.presidency.ucsb.edu/node/273392. See also R. Craig Sautter, *Philadelphia Presidential Conventions* (Highland Park, IL: December Press, 2000), 225.

23. "Democratic Party Platform of 1948," ed. Gerhard Peters and John T. Woolley, American Presidency Project, accessed January 25, 2021, https://www.presidency.ucsb.edu/node/273225. See also Sautter, *Philadelphia Presidential Conventions*, 253.

24. Heller, *Ed Bacon*, 3.

25. Lombardo, *Blue-Collar Conservatism*, 31; Steven Conn, *Americans Against the City: Anti-Urbanism in the Twentieth Century* (New York: Oxford University Press, 2014) 167.

26. Heller, *Ed Bacon*, 75–76; Menzer, "Exhibiting Philadelphia's Vital Center," 166; Lombardo, *Blue-Collar Conservatism*, 32; Conn, *Americans Against the City*, 152; Ryberg, "Historic Preservation's Urban Renewal Roots," 196.

27. Heller, *Ed Bacon*, 2–5; Jane Jacobs, *The Death and Life of Great American Cities* (New York: Vintage Books, 1992), 416.

28. Heller, "Salesman of Ideas," 47.

29. Adams et al., *Philadelphia*, 73.

30. Interview with Augustus Baxter with Diane Turner, Charles L. Blockson Afro-American Collection, Temple University, June 2, 2011, 8; Hunter, *Black Citymakers*, 118; Wilson, *Ethnic Renewal*, 43.

31. *To Secure These Rights: The Report of the President's Committee on Civil Rights*, accessed November 16, 2020, https://www.trumanlibrary.gov/library/to-secure-these-rights#VII. See also interview with Walter Gay, May 22, 1984, *Goin' North: Tales of the Great Migration*, Louie B. Nunn Center for Oral History, University of Kentucky Libraries, accessed January 25, 2021. https://goinnorth.org/items/show/1053

32. Peters and Woolley, eds., Democratic Party Platform. See also Wolfinger, *Philadelphia Divided*, 197.

33. "Progressive Party Platform," in *Congressional Record: Proceedings and Debates of the 80th Congress Second Session*, appendix: vol. 94, pt. 12: June 19, 1948, to December 31, 1948 (Washington, DC: Government Printing Office, 1948), A5091. See also Sautter, *Philadelphia Presidential Conventions*, 291.

34. Barbara A. Gannon, "The Wars That Ended No War: Pennsylvania Military History After World War II," in *Pennsylvania: A Military History*, ed. William A. Pencak, Christian B. Keller, and Barbara A. Gannon (Yardley, PA: Westholme, 2016), 238.

35. Interview with Joseph Burke, 1; Jenkins, *Cold War*, 12; Paul Lyons, *Philadelphia Communists, 1936–1956* (Philadelphia: Temple University Press, 1982), 138–39.

36. Jenkins, *Cold War*, 1–8; Lyons, *Philadelphia Communists*, 153.

37. Interview with David Cohen, January 11, 1996, Feinstein Center for American Jewish History, Temple University, accessed January 25, 2021, https://libdigital.temple.edu /oralhistories/catalog/transcript:TOHFCJZ2016020013xp16002coll22x217; McColloch, "Glory Days," 226.

38. Charlene Mires, *Independence Hall in American Memory* (Philadelphia: University of Pennsylvania Press, 2002), 207.

39. Pennsylvania Loyalty Act, Pennsylvania General Assembly, accessed January 6, 2021, https://www.legis.state.pa.us/WU01/LI/LI/US/PDF/1951/0/0463.PDF. See also Clark Byse, "A Report on the Pennsylvania Loyalty Act," *University of Pennsylvania Law Review*, 101, no. 4 (January 1953): 481; Jenkins, *Cold War*, 119.

40. Clark and Clark, "Rally and Relapse," 659. One, Goldie E. Watson, went on to become Model Cities director and deputy mayor. Allener M. Baker-Rogers and Fasha M. Traylor, *They Carried Us: The Social Impact of Philadelphia's Black Women Leaders* (Philadelphia: Arch Street Press, 2020), 9.

41. Sherman Labovitz, *Being Red in Philadelphia: A Memoir of the McCarthy Era* (Philadelphia: Camino Books, 1998), 2. See also Lyons, *Philadelphia Communists*, 159–60.

42. Interview with John B. Summers, February 15, 1984, *Goin' North: Tales of the Great Migration*, Louie B. Nunn Center for Oral History, University of Kentucky Libraries; Wolfinger, *Philadelphia Divided*, 204; Sicotte, *From Workshop*, 86; Paul Lyons, *The People of This Generation: The Rise and Fall of the New Left in Philadelphia* (Philadelphia: University of Pennsylvania Press, 2003), 19; Thomas J. Sugrue, *Sweet Land of Liberty: The Forgotten Struggle for Civil Rights in the North* (New York: Random House, 2008), 102–4.

43. Andrea Niepold, "Discovering Chestnut Hill: James Bond Slept Here—for More than 30 Years," *Chestnut Hill Local*, July 16, 2015.

44. Marc Stein, *City of Sisterly and Brotherly Loves: Lesbian and Gay Philadelphia, 1945–1972* (Philadelphia: Temple University Press, 2004), 25.

45. Stein, *City of Sisterly and Brotherly Loves*, 138–45.

46. Stein, *City of Sisterly and Brotherly Loves*, 109.

47. According to Jane Jacobs, "Several decades ago Washington Square became Philadelphia's pervert park, to the point where it was shunned by office lunchers and was an unimaginable vice and crime problem to park workers and police." Jacobs, *Death and Life*, 92. On police brutality and gay people, see Bob Levin, *Cheesesteak: The West Philadelphia Years* (Portland, OR: Spruce Hill Books, 2018), 42. See also Stein, *City of Sisterly and Brotherly Loves*, 84–85.

48. Interview with Joshua Eilberg, 4; interview with Boyd Barnard, April 10, 1979, Walter Massey Phillips Oral Histories, Temple University, 8, accessed January 25, 2021, https://libdigital.temple.edu/oralhistories/catalog/transcript:AOHWMPJZ2014110013xp 16002coll22x8. See also Paul B. Beers, *Pennsylvania Politics Today and Yesterday: The Tolerable Accommodation* (University Park: Pennsylvania State University Press, 1980), 193; Kromer, *Philadelphia Battlefields*, 36; Peter Binzen and Jonathan Binzen, *Richardson*

Dilworth: Last of the Bare-Knuckled Aristocrats (Philadelphia: Camino Books, 2014), 126–27; Burt, *Perennial Philadelphians*, 539.

49. Rottenberg, *Outsider*, 238; Hunter, *Black Citymakers*, 124.

50. Binzen and Binzen, *Richardson Dilworth*, 96.

51. Klein and Hoogenboom, *History of Pennsylvania*, 500; Rottenberg, *Outsider*, 226–27.

52. *Kefauver Committee Report on Organized Crime* (New York: Didier, 1951), 165. See also Binzen and Binzen, *Richardson Dilworth*, 98.

53. Dan Burt, *You Think It Strange: A Memoir* (New York: Overlook Press, 2013), 16; Beers, *Pennsylvania Politics*, 200.

54. Francis Biddle, *A Casual Past* (Garden City, NY: Doubleday, 1961), 346; Mary W. Bond, *Ninety Years 'At Home' in Philadelphia* (Bryn Mawr, PA: Dorrance, 1988), 65; Crumlish, *City Finds Itself*, 17; Kromer, *Philadelphia Battlefields*, 42.

55. Reichley, *Art of Government*, 6; Binzen and Binzen, *Richardson Dilworth*, 94–95.

56. Reichley, *Art of Government*, 41; Jenkins, *Cold War*, 63.

57. Treadway, *Elections in Pennsylvania*, 116–19; McKenna, "Negro Vote," 74.

58. Interview with Edward G. Bauer Jr., November 28, 1978, Walter Massey Phillips Oral Histories, Temple University, 2, accessed January 25, 2021, https://libdigital.temple .edu/oralhistories/catalog/transcript:AOHWMPJZ2014110014xp16002coll22x10; interview with Thacher Longstreth, December 5, 1976, Walter Massey Phillips Oral Histories, Temple University, 28, accessed January 25, 2021, https://libdigital.temple.edu/oralhistories /catalog/transcript:AOHWMPJZ2015010023xp16002coll22x171. By the 1960 presidential election and for the rest of the twentieth century, Pennsylvania had more registered Democrats than Republicans. See Treadway, *Elections in Pennsylvania*, 34; McColloch, "Glory Days," 245; Kromer, *Philadelphia Battlefields*, 50–51.

59. Crumlish, *City Finds Itself*, 2.

60. Marilyn Gittell and T. Edward Hollander, *Six Urban School Districts: A Comparative Study of Institutional Response* (New York: Frederick A. Praeger, 1968), 36; Lombardo, *Blue-Collar Conservatism*, 25.

61. Crumlish, *City Finds Itself*, 13.

62. First Class City Home Rule Act, Pennsylvania General Assembly, *accessed September 17, 2020*, https://www.legis.state.pa.us/WU01/LI/LI/US/PDF/1949/0/0155.pdf; Clark and Clark, "Rally and Relapse," 627.

63. Crumlish, *City Finds Itself*, 19; Reichley, *Art of Government*, 51; Lombardo, *Blue-Collar Conservatism*, 26.

64. Crumlish, *City Finds Itself*, 8; James McClelland and Lynn Miller, *City in a Park: A History of Philadelphia's Fairmount Park System* (Philadelphia: Temple University Press, 2016), 278.

65. Winnet, *Vignettes*, 150–52. See also Klein and Hoogenboom, *History of Pennsylvania*, 501; Beers, *Pennsylvania Politics*, 202. On the GPM's role, see Heller, *Ed Bacon*, 55.

66. Klein and Hoogenboom, *History of Pennsylvania*, 544.

67. Bill Shull, *Philadelphia Television* (Charleston, SC: Arcadia, 2015), 33.

68. Levin, *Cheesesteak*, 64.

69. Winnet, *Vignettes*, 239; *Greater Philadelphia Movement: Annual Report of 1955*, 4.

70. Burt, *You Think It Strange*, 71.

71. Interview with Augustus Baxter, 3; interview with Richard Watson with Diane Turner, Charles L. Blockson Afro-American Collection," Temple University, October 10, 2011, 5, accessed January 25,2021, https://digital.library.temple.edu/digital/collection /p16002coll1/id/27/; interview with Arthur Dingle, July 11, 1983, *Goin' North: Tales of the Great Migration*, Louie B. Nunn Center for Oral History, University of Kentucky Libraries, accessed January 25,2021, https://goinnorth.org/arthur-dingle-interview; Clark and Clark, "Rally and Relapse," 658; Klein and Hoogenboom, *History of Pennsylvania*, 528; "U.S. Gang Problem Trends and Seriousness, 1996–2009," *National Gang Center Bulletin*, no. 6 (May 2011); Cindy D. Ness, *Why Girls Fight: Female Youth Violence in the Inner City* (New York: New York University Press, 2010), 32; Jenkins, "Postindustrial Age," 340; Jacobs, *Death and Life*, 76–77.

72. Lombardo, *Blue-Collar Conservatism*, 35.

73. Interview with Joshua Eilberg, 17; John Daly and Allen Weinberg, *Genealogy of Philadelphia County Subdivisions*, 2nd ed. (Philadelphia: Philadelphia Department of Records, 1966), 88; Kromer, *Philadelphia Battlefields*, 49.

74. Wolfinger, *Philadelphia Divided*, 179; Levenstein, *Movement Without Marches*, 15.

75. Robert J. Mason, "Metropolitan Philadelphia: Sprawl, Shrinkage, and Sustainability," in *Nature's Entrepôt: Philadelphia's Urban Sphere and Its Environmental Thresholds*, ed. Brian C. Black and Michael J. Chiarappa (Pittsburgh: University of Pittsburgh Press, 2012), 196.

76. Heller, *Ed Bacon*, 153–57.

77. Conn, *Metropolitan Philadelphia*, 117–19; Mason, "Metropolitan Philadelphia," 194.

78. Heller, *Ed Bacon*, 73.

79. Joe Queenan, *Closing Time: A Memoir* (New York: Penguin Books, 2009), 29; Stein, *City of Sisterly and Brotherly Loves*, 35; Mires, *Independence Hall*, 225.

80. Ryberg, "Historic Preservation's Urban Renewal Roots," 195.

81. Ryberg, "Historic Preservation's Urban Renewal Roots," 194.

82. Edmund N. Bacon, "Philadelphia in the Year 2009," in *Imagining Philadelphia: Edmund Bacon and the Future of the City*, ed. Scott Gabriel Knowles (Philadelphia: University of Pennsylvania Press, 2009), 42; Heller, "Salesman of Ideas," 31.

83. Constance M. Greiff, *Independence: The Creation of a National Park* (Philadelphia: University of Pennsylvania Press, 1987), 40–41.

84. Greiff, *Independence*, 49–50.

85. Greiff, *Independence*, 55–56, 69.

86. Bacon was explicit about this, noting in 2004 that he hoped his designs would affect "the collective unconscious, and then the collective unconscious penetrated the brains of the people, and then as a three-dimensional experience they were influenced by it and acted in ways in accordance with how I hoped they would." Sasha Isenberg, "My Philadelphia Story: Edmund Bacon," *Philadelphia Magazine*, May 2004, 69.

87. Leonard Blumberg, Thomas E. Shipley Jr., and Irving W. Shandler, *Skid Row and Its Alternatives: Research and Recommendations from Philadelphia* (Philadelphia: Temple University Press, 1973), xiv, 3; Wilson, *Ethnic Renewal*, 73; Mires, *Independence Hall*, 220; Conn, *Americans Against the City*, 166. Jane Jacobs memorably described Philadelphia's

skid row as a "place where the homeless, the unemployed and the people of indigent leisure gather amid the adjacent flophouses, cheap hotels, missions, second-hand clothing stores, reading and writing hobbies, pawn shops, employment agencies, tattoo parlors, burlesque houses, and eateries." Jacobs, *Death and Life*, 92.

88. Heller, *Ed Bacon*, 117.

89. Isenberg, "My Philadelphia Story," 69.

90. Philadelphia City Planning Commission, *Land Use in Philadelphia, 1944–1954* (Philadelphia: City of Philadelphia, 1956), 11; Heller, *Ed Bacon*, 133; Rottenberg, *Outsider*, 238.

91. Heller, *Ed Bacon*, 118.

92. Interview with Ed Bacon, 10, 19. See also Rottenberg, *Outsider*, 238; Binzen and Binzen, *Richardson Dilworth*, 160–61; Heller, *Ed Bacon*, 125.

93. Heller, "Salesman of Ideas," 42; Heller, *Ed Bacon*, 123.

94. Rottenberg, *Outsider*, 244–45.

95. Jeffrey Lin, "Understanding Gentrification's Causes," *Economic Insights*, 2, no. 3 (2017): 10; Jim Saksa, "Four Reasons Why Philadelphia Is Gentrifying," WHYY, September 17, 2017, accessed December 13, 2022, https://whyy.org/articles/four-reasons-why-philadelphia-is-gentrifying/; Jake Blumgart and Jim Saksa, "From Slums to Sleek Towers: How Philly Became Cleaner, Safer, and More Unequal," WHYY, March 12, 2018, accessed December 13, 2022, https://whyy.org/segments/slums-sleek-towers-philly-became-cleaner-safer-unequal/.

96. Lin, "Understanding Gentrification's Causes," 9; Blumgart and Saksa, "From Slums to Sleek Towers."

97. Heller, *Ed Bacon*, 110.

98. James Reichley, "Philadelphia Does It: The Battle for Penn Center," *Harper's Magazine*, February 1, 1957, 49.

99. Penny Balkin Bach, *Public Art in Philadelphia* (Philadelphia: Temple University Press, 1992), 130–32.

100. Executive Order No. 1-91: City of Philadelphia Public Art Program Procedural Guidelines, February 28, 1991. accessed March 22, 2021, https://www.phila.gov/ExecutiveOrders/Executive%20Orders/1991_EO01-91.pdf.

101. Kromer, *Philadelphia Battlefields*, 122–33.

102. Clark and Clark, "Rally and Relapse," 689; Klein and Hoogenboom, *History of Pennsylvania*, 569–70.

103. Larry Santucci, "Documenting Racially Restrictive Covenants in 20th Century Philadelphia," *Cityscape*, 22, no. 3 (2020): 247.

104. "Zoning Variances and Exceptions: The Philadelphia Experience," *University of Pennsylvania Law Review*, 103, no 4 (January 1955): 526.

105. Jake Blumgart, "Zoning (Philadelphia)," *Encyclopedia of Philadelphia*, accessed September 26, 2022, https://philadelphiaencyclopedia.org/essays/zoning-philadelphia/.

106. This was far from unique to Philadelphia; see Jacobs, *Death and Life*, 358.

107. John Gunther, *Inside U.S.A.* (New York: Harper & Brothers, 1947), 605.

108. This was not unusual; some homes in South Philadelphia still did not have indoor plumbing. Ray Bilecki, *Blessings on Ellsworth Street: The Culture and History of*

Growing Up During the 1940s, '50s, and '60s (Falling Waters, WV: Academic Systems International, 2007), 39.

109. Heller, "Salesman of Ideas," 34; McKee, "Edmund Bacon," 59; Binzen and Binzen, *Richardson Dilworth*, 148; Heller, *Ed Bacon*, 69–71.

110. Wolfinger, *Philadelphia Divided*, 186–87; Burt, *Perennial Philadelphians*, 558. This was far from unique to Philadelphia; see Jacobs, *Death and Life*, 400.

111. See also Luconi, *From Paesani*, 141.

112. "Long-Contested Housing Project Opens Amid Calm in Philadelphia," *New York Times*, November 28, 1982, 65. See also Paolantonio, *Frank Rizzo*, 221–22.

113. Wolfinger, *Philadelphia Divided*, 200.

114. Hunter, *Black Citymakers*, 116–17; Amy Hillier, "Redlining in Philadelphia," in *Past Time, Past Place: GIS for History*, ed. Anne Kelly Knowles (Redlands, CA: ESRI Press, 2002), 86; Conn, *Americans Against the City*, 177.

115. For perspectives on white poverty in Philadelphia during this period, see Queenan, *Closing Time*, 3 and David Brenner, *Soft Pretzels with Mustard* (New York: Berkley Books, 1983).

116. Ira Katznelson, *When Affirmative Action Was White: An Untold History of Racial Inequality in Twentieth-Century America* (New York: W. W. Norton, 2005), x; Wolfinger, *Philadelphia Divided*, 197.

117. McKenna, "Negro Vote," 79; Miriam Ershkowitz and Joseph Zikmund, "Introduction," in *Black Politics in Philadelphia*, ed. Miriam Ershkowitz and Joseph Zikmund (New York: Basic Books, 1973), 58; Paolantonio, *Frank Rizzo*, 65; Reichley, *Art of Government*, 70; Perkiss, *Making Good Neighbors*, 21; Countryman, *Up South*, 1; Levenstein, *Movement Without Marches:*, 18.

118. Heller, "Salesman of Ideas," 46; Harry A. Bailey Jr., "Poverty, Politics, and Administration: The Philadelphia Experience," in *Black Politics in Philadelphia*, ed. Miriam Ershkowitz and Joseph Zikmund (New York: Basic Books, 1973), 171–72; Wolfinger, *Philadelphia Divided*, 207–8; Levenstein, *Movement Without Marches*, 4.

119. Richard Rothstein, *The Color of Law: A Forgotten History of How Our Government Segregated America* (New York: Liveright, 2017), viii.

120. Perkiss, *Making Good Neighbors*, 17.

121. Hillier, "Redlining," 8679–82; Heller, *Ed Bacon*, 59–60.

122. Sicotte, *From Workshop*, 86.

123. Countryman, *Up South*, 53–56. See also Matthew F. Delmont, *The Nicest Kids in Town: American Bandstand, Rock 'n' Roll, and the Struggle for Civil Rights in 1950s Philadelphia* (Berkeley: University of California Press, 2012), 15.

124. James Wolfinger puts the matter succinctly, concluding, "the suburbanization of work in the 1950s effectively robbed African Americans of their advances." Wolfinger, *Philadelphia Divided*, 3.

125. Lombardo, *Blue-Collar Conservatism*, 40.

126. Wolfinger, *Philadelphia Divided*, 180; Murray Friedman, "From Outsiders to Insiders? Philadelphia Jewish Life, 1940–1985," in *Philadelphia Jewish Life, 1940–2000*, ed. Murray Friedman (Philadelphia: Temple University Press, 2003), xxix.

127. William T. Coleman Jr., *Counsel for the Situation: Shaping the Law to Realize America's Promise* (Washington, DC: Brookings Institution Press, 2010), 186–88. See also

Conn, *Metropolitan Philadelphia*, 134; Lombardo, *Blue-Collar Conservatism*, 31; W. Benjamin Piggot, "The 'Problem' of the Black Middle Class: Morris Milgram's Concord Park and Residential Integration in Philadelphia's Postwar Suburbs," *Pennsylvania Magazine of History and Biography*, 132, no. 2 (April 2008): 174; Rothstein, *Color of Law*, 147; Sugrue, *Sweet Land of Liberty*, 202; Abigail Perkiss, "Postwar Philadelphia," in *If There Is No Struggle There Is No Progress: Black Politics in Twentieth-Century Philadelphia*, ed. James Wolfinger (Philadelphia: Temple University Press, 2022), 98–99.

128. Conn, *Metropolitan Philadelphia*, 139.

129. Murray Friedman and Carolyn Beck, "An Ambivalent Alliance: Blacks and Jews in Philadelphia, 1940–1985," in *Philadelphia Jewish Life, 1940–2000*, ed. Murray Friedman (Philadelphia: Temple University Press, 2003), 87–88.

130. Adams et al., *Philadelphia*, 77; Sugrue, *Sweet Land of Liberty*, 204; Conn, *Americans Against the City*, 97–98.

131. "Mount Airy Integration: Oral History Interviews About Life in the 1950s: Doris Polsky," *Germantown Crier*, 59, no. 1 (Spring 2009): 20. See also Wolfinger, *Philadelphia Divided*, 177–78; Stanger-Ross, *Staying Italian*, 10, 16–17; Perkiss, *Making Good Neighbors*, 25; Lombardo, *Blue-Collar Conservatism*, 44.

132. Interview with Edward W. Robinson and David P. Richardson, January 17, 1988, African American Migration to Philadelphia Oral Histories at Temple University, accessed January 25, 2021, https://libdigital.temple.edu/oralhistories/catalog/transcript: BOHWPMJZ2016020052xp16002coll22x260. Achieving and maintaining integration required some social engineering; see "Mount Airy Integration," 19. See also Perkiss, *Making Good Neighbors*, 2.

133. "Philadelphia's New Problem," *Time*, February 24, 1958, 18. See also Wolfinger, *Philadelphia Divided*, 188; Stanger-Ross, *Staying Italian*, 16; Lombardo, *Blue-Collar Conservatism*, 31; Sugrue, *Sweet Land of Liberty*, 205.

134. Conn, *Americans Against the City*, 9.

135. Interview with Joshua Eilberg, 19.

136. Interview with Walter Gay; Reichley, *Art of Government*, 51; Jonathan Hadley Strange, "Blacks and Philadelphia Politics, 1963–1966," in *Black Politics in Philadelphia*, ed. Miriam Ershkowitz and Joseph Zikmund (New York: Basic Books, 1973), 110.

137. Evelyn Brooks Higginbotham, *Righteous Discontent: The Women's Movement in the Black Baptist Church, 1880–1920* (Cambridge, MA: Harvard University Press, 1994), 192; Sugrue, *Sweet Land of Liberty*, 293.

138. Lombardo, *Blue-Collar Conservatism*, 78–79; Patricia Anne Masters, *The Philadelphia Mummers: Building Community Through Play* (Philadelphia: Temple University Press, 2007), 75–78.

139. Lyons, *People of This Generation*, 14; Hunter, *Black Citymakers*, 145; Sicotte, *From Workshop*, 86.

140. Michael Awkward, *Philadelphia Freedoms: Black American Trauma, Memory, and Culture After King* (Philadelphia: Temple University Press, 2013), 29; Levenstein, *Movement Without Marches*, 17.

141. Interview with Richard Watson, 29–30. Some Black people found Moore's stridency problematic; see interview with R. Sonny Driver with Diane Turner, Charles L. Blockson Afro-American Collection, Temple University, June 20, 2011, 28, accessed

January 25, 2021, https://digital.library.temple.edu/digital/collection/p16002coll1/id/24/rec/1.

142. Reichley, *Art of Government*, 13.

143. Interview with Walter Gay.

144. Interview with William R. Meek, May 22, 1979, Walter Massey Phillips Oral Histories, Temple University, 13, accessed January 25, 2021, https://libdigital.temple.edu/oralhistories/catalog/transcript:AOHWMPJZ2015010032xp16002coll22x180. See also Reichley, *Art of Government*, 79.

145. Paul Lermack, "Cecil Moore and the Philadelphia Branch of the National Association for the Advancement of Colored People: The Politics of Negro Pressure Group Organization," in *Black Politics in Philadelphia*, ed. Miriam Ershkowitz and Joseph Zikmund (New York: Basic Books, 1973), 146–54; Luconi, *From Paesani*, 129; Perkiss, *Making Good Neighbors*, 24–25; Countryman, *Up South*, 1–2; Sugrue, *Sweet Land of Liberty*, 292.

146. Lombardo, *Blue-Collar Conservatism*, 91; Gittell and Hollander, *Six Urban School Districts*, 38.

147. Coleman, *Counsel for the Situation*, 194–96.

148. Interview with Richard Watson, 20; interview with Kenneth Salaam with Diane Turner, Charle L. Blockson Afro-American Collection, Temple University, May 9, 2011, 30.

149. "Martin Luther King, Jr. at Girard College in Philadelphia, 1965," *BillyPenn*, January 15, 2022, accessed January 6, 2021, https://billypenn.com/2020/01/20/video-martin-luther-king-jr-in-philadelphia-1964/.

150. In his essay "White Backlash," historian Lawrence B. Glickman notes, "Commentators often misassign responsibility for backlashes . . . by implying that African American activists are the responsible party, assigning agency and causality not to the backlashers but to the movement for social equality." As originally written, this chapter fell into that paradigm, and I am pleased that I came across his essay with enough time to correct that construction in this text. Lawrence B. Glickman, "White Backlash," in *Myth America: Historians Take on the Biggest Legends and Lies About Our Past*, ed. Kevin M. Kruse and Julian E. Zelizer (New York: Basic Books, 2022), 213.

151. Quoted in Levenstein, *Movement Without Marches*, 189.

152. Wolfinger, *Philadelphia Divided*, 4; Jenkins, *Cold War*, 46–47; Delmont, *Nicest Kids*, 21; Levenstein, *Movement Without Marches*, 7; Rothstein, *Color of Law*, 33.

153. Interview with Edward G. Bauer Jr., 3. See also Binzen and Binzen, *Richardson Dilworth*, 171.

154. Kevin Phillips, *The Emerging Republican Majority* (Princeton, NJ: Princeton University Press, 2015), 15. See also Luconi, *From Paesani*, 129.

155. Elizabeth Hinton, "Police Violence," in *Myth America: Historians Take on the Biggest Legends and Lies About Our Past*, ed. Kevin M. Kruse and Julian E. Zelizer (New York: Basic Books, 2022), 240.

156. Elizabeth Hinton, *From the War on Poverty to the War on Crime: The Making of Mass Incarceration in America* (Cambridge, MA: Harvard University Press, 2016), 1–6; Hinton, "Police Violence," 201–42; Khalil Gibran Muhammad, *The Condemnation of Blackness: Race, Crime, and the Making of Modern Urban America* (Cambridge, MA: Harvard University Press, 2019), xv–xxiii.

157. Emily Langer, "Al Primo, Creator of 'Eyewitness' Local News, Dies at 87," *Washington Post*, October 5, 2022, accessed December 13, 2022, https://www.washingtonpost.com /obituaries/2022/10/05/al-primo-eyewitness-local-news-dead/; Layla A. Jones, "Lights. Camera. Crime," *Philadelphia Inquirer*, March 28, 2022, accessed December 13, 2022, https://www.inquirer.com/news/lights-camera-crime-20220328.html; Clem Harris, "The 1960s and Expanding Ideas of Black Rights," in *If There Is No Struggle There Is No Progress: Black Politics in Twentieth-Century Philadelphia*, ed. James Wolfinger (Philadelphia: Temple University Press, 2022), 114.

158. Jones, "Lights. Camera. Crime"; Lee Winfrey, "Anchorman Larry Kane: A Fast Talker with a Disappearing Act," *Philadelphia Inquirer*, August 8, 1974, 5C.

159. Daniel Romer, Kathleen Hall Jamieson, and Sean Aday, "Television News and the Cultivation of Fear of Crime," *Journal of Communication*, 53, no. 1 (March 2003): 89.

160. Interview with Kenneth Salaam with Diane Turner, Charles L. Blockson Afro-American Collection, Temple University, October 9, 2011, 16; W. M. Kephart, *Racial Factors and Urban Law Enforcement* (Philadelphia: University of Pennsylvania Press, 1957), 25, 114–19; James Forman Jr., *Locking Up Our Own: Crime and Punishment in Black America* (New York: Farrar, Straus & Giroux, 2017), 107–8; Wolfinger, *Philadelphia Divided*, 207; Stanger-Ross, *Staying Italian*, 24; Luconi, *From Paesani*, 127.

161. Heller, *Ed Bacon*, 191; Hunter, *Black Citymakers*, 143; Friedman and Beck, "Ambivalent Alliance," 90; Luconi, *From Paesani*, 130.

162. Jeffrey A. Davis and Paul D. Newman, eds., "Race Riots in Philadelphia and Pittsburgh, 1964 and 1968," in *Pennsylvania History: Essays and Documents* (Upper Saddle River, NJ: Prentice Hall, 2010), 344–45; McKee, "Edmund Bacon," 52–53; Paolantonio, *Frank Rizzo*, 75.

163. Interview with Sadie Tanner Mossell Alexander, October 12, 1977, Walter Massey Phillips Oral Histories, Temple University, 12, accessed January 25, 2021, https://libdigital .temple.edu/oralhistories/catalog/transcript:AOHWMPJZ2014120029xp16002coll22x1; interview with Karen Jordan with Diane Turner, Charles L. Blockson Afro-American Collection, Temple University, undated, 4, accessed January 25, 2021, https://digital.library .temple.edu/digital/collection/p16002coll1/id/26/rec/1; interview with Mel Dorn with Diane Turner, Charles L. Blockson Afro-American Collection, Temple University, May 22, 2011, 30, accessed January 25, 2021, https://digital.library.temple.edu/digital/collection /p16002coll1/id/30/rec/1; Coleman, *Counsel for the Situation*, 180; Lombardo, *Blue-Collar Conservatism*, 99–102.

164. William W. Cutler III, "Public Education: The School District of Philadelphia," *Encyclopedia of Greater Philadelphia*, accessed January 10, 2021, https://philadelphiaencyclopedia .org/archive/public-educationthe-school-district-of-philadelphia/. See also Lyons, *People of This Generation*, 14–15; Gittell and Hollander, *Six Urban School Districts*, 24–25; Henry S. Resnick, *Turning on the System: War in the Philadelphia Public Schools* (New York: Pantheon Books, 1970), 4.

165. Supplement to the Philadelphia Home Rule Charter: Approved by the Electors at a Special Election, May 18, 1965, Pennsylvania Legislative Reference Bureau, accessed January 2, 2021, http://www.palrb.us/pamphletlaws/19001999/1965/0/chart/charter.pdf; Gittell and Hollander, *Six Urban School Districts*, 44–50.

166. Wendell W. Young III, *The Memoirs of Wendell W. Young, III: A Life in Philadelphia Labor and Politics*, ed. Francis Ryan (Philadelphia: Temple University Press, 2019), 134. See also Klein and Hoogenboom, *History of Pennsylvania*, 543; McColloch, "Glory Days," 250.

167. Interview with Peter Binzen, November 27, 1979, Walter Massey Phillips Oral Histories, Temple University, 11, accessed January 25, 2021, https://libdigital.temple.edu /oralhistories/catalog/transcript:AOHWMPJZ2014110019xp16002coll22x9; Cutler, "Public Education"; Camika Royal, *Not Paved for Us: Black Educators and Public School Reform in Philadelphia* (Cambridge, MA: Harvard Education Press, 2022), 22–25.

168. Rizzo disputed having said this, but witnesses on the day reported hearing it. Moreover, Rizzo used racist language like this on other occasions; see Young, *Memoirs*, 154.

169. Interview with William R. Meek, 7; interview with Eugene Dawkins with Diane Turner, Charles L. Blockson Afro-American Collection, Temple University, June 24, 2011, 7, accessed January 25, 2021, https://digital.library.temple.edu/digital/collection/p16002coll1 /id/24/rec/1; Clark and Clark, "Rally and Relapse," 676; Paolantonio, *Frank Rizzo*, 91–94; Lyons, *People of This Generation*, 16; Resnick, *Turning on the System*, 11.

170. Interview with Edward W. Robinson and David P. Richardson, 33–34; interview with Bernyce Mills-DeVaughn with Diane Turner, Charles L. Blockson Afro-American Collection," Temple University, June 25, 2011, 5, accessed January 25, 2021, https://digital .library.temple.edu/digital/collection/p16002coll1/id/31/rec/1; Friedman and Beck, "Ambivalent Alliance," 91–92; Sugrue, *Sweet Land of Liberty*, 295; Alyssa Ribeiro, "'Asking Them and Protesting': Black and Puerto Rican Civic Leadership in Philadelphia Neighborhoods, 1960s–1970s," *Pennsylvania History: A Journal of Mid-Atlantic Studies*, 86, no. 3 (Summer 2019): 361; Baker-Rogers and Traylor, *They Carried Us*, 327.

171. Quoted in Friedman and Beck, "Ambivalent Alliance," 92. See also Awkward, *Philadelphia Freedoms*, 3; Countryman, *Up South*, 3.

172. Omari Dyson, "A Dialogue with Clarence 'Stretch' Peterson," *Spectrum: A Journal on Black Men*, 5, no. 1 (Fall 2016): 161; Baker-Rogers and Traylor, *They Carried Us*, 25.

173. Karen Bojar, *Feminist Organizing Across the Generations* (London: Routledge, 2021), 1.

174. Bojar, *Feminist Organizing*, 19.

175. Bojar, *Feminist Organizing*, 49–50.

176. Bojar, *Feminist Organizing*, 22.

177. Mires, *Independence Hall*, 256.

178. Thacher Longstreth noted that because he and Dilworth were WASPS, "both of us operated out of shared notions and manners and social obligations" despite being members of different parties. W. Thacher Longstreth with Dan Rottenberg, *Main Line WASP* (New York: W. W. Norton, 1990), 15. See also Rottenberg, *Outsider*, xii. See also Crumlish, *City Finds Itself*, 6; Reichley, *Art of Government*, 25, 81; Gunther, *Inside U.S.A.*, 603.

179. Interview with Cliff Brenner, March 26, 1997, Feinstein Center for American Jewish History, Temple University, 25, accessed January 25, 2021, https://libdigital.temple .edu/oralhistories/catalog/transcript:TOHFCJZ2016020011xp16002coll22x219; interview with Ed Bacon, 11; Lombardo, *Blue-Collar Conservatism*, 48.

180. David R. Roediger, *Working Toward Whiteness: How America's Immigrants Became White* (New York: Basic Books, 2018), 136.

181. Longstreth with Rottenberg, *Main Line WASP*, 250.

182. Quoted in Luconi, *From Paesani*, 135. See also interview with Sadie Tanner Mossell Alexander, 11; Young, *Memoirs*, 153; Kromer, *Philadelphia Battlefields*, 92.

183. Interview with William R. Meek, 2; interview with Peter Binzen, November 27, 1979, 21; Paolantonio, *Frank Rizzo*, 69, 97; Lombardo, *Blue-Collar Conservatism*, 2.

184. "Tough Cop for Mayor," *Time*, May 31, 1971. See also Longstreth with Rottenberg, *Main Line WASP*, 249–57; Paul M. Washington, *"Other Sheep I Have": The Autobiography of Father Paul M. Washington* (Philadelphia: Temple University Press, 1994), 155; Jerry Blavat, *You Only Rock Once* (Philadelphia: Running Press, 2011), 206; Dennis Clark, "From Periphery to Prominence: Jews in Philadelphia Politics, 1940–1985," in *Philadelphia Jewish Life, 1940–2000*, ed. Murray Friedman (Philadelphia: Temple University Press, 2003), 79; Luconi, *From Paesani*, 134–35.

185. Interview with Thacher Longstreth, 41. See also Interview with William Austin Meehan, March 23, 1977, Walter Massey Phillips Oral Histories, Temple University, 9–10, accessed January 25, 2021, https://digital.library.temple.edu/digital/collection/p16002coll12/id/1764/rec/; Luconi, *From Paesani*, 133.

186. Longstreth with Rottenberg, *Main Line WASP*, 233; Bond, *Ninety Years*, 148. Paul Lyons accurately calls Rizzo "a critical factor in Philadelphia politics by the late 1950s; by the middle and late 1960s, he was *the* dominant issue and story." Lyons, *People of This Generation*, 13.

187. Paolantonio, *Frank Rizzo*, 154–55.

188. Eisenhower to E. N. Eisenhower, 8 November 1954, *The Papers of Dwight David Eisenhower*, vol. 15, ed. Alfred D. Chandler Jr. (Baltimore: Johns Hopkins University Press, 2003), 1386.

189. James M. Cannon, "Federal Revenue-Sharing: Born 1972. Died 1986. R.I.P.," *New York Times*, October 10, 1986, sec. A, 39. See also Matthew J. Countryman, "'From Protest to Politics': Community Control and Black Independent Politics in Philadelphia, 1965–1984," *Journal of Urban History*, 32, no. 6 (September 2006): 846; Timothy Weaver, *Blazing the Neoliberal Trail: Urban Political Development in the United States and the United Kingdom* (Philadelphia: University of Pennsylvania Press, 2016), 163–64.

190. Weaver, *Blazing the Neoliberal Trail*, 182.

191. Paolantonio, *Frank Rizzo*, 138. This was not an isolated case; see interview with Richardson Dilworth Jr., February 6, 1979, Walter Massey Phillips Oral Histories, Temple University, 15, accessed January 25, 2021, https://libdigital.temple.edu/oralhistories/catalog/transcript:AOHWMPJZ2014120022xp16002coll22x83; W. Wilson Goode, *In Goode Faith* (Valley Forge, PA: Judson Press, 1992), 101.

192. Goode, *In Goode Faith*, 256; Schneider, *Ecology of Homicide*, 95. The police also intimidated white Philadelphians; see Queenan, *Closing Time*, 198.

193. Gregory Jaynes, "Philadelphia's Message to Rizzo: 'Enough,'" *New York Times*, November 9, 1978, A23. See also Luconi, *From Paesani*, 141–42, and Timothy J. Lombardo, "African American Politics in Frank Rizzo's Philadelphia," in *If There Is No Struggle There*

Is No Progress: Black Politics in Twentieth-Century Philadelphia, ed. James Wolfinger (Philadelphia: Temple University Press, 2022), 137.

194. Melvin G. Holli, "American Mayors: The Best and Worst Since 1960," *Social Science Quarterly*, 78, no. 1 (March 1997): 153.

195. Adams et al., *Philadelphia*, 70.

196. Sicotte, *From Workshop*, 97.

197. Gunther, *Inside U.S.A.*, 607. See also Sicotte, *From Workshop*, 117; Burt, *Perennial Philadelphians*, 553.

198. Knowles, "Staying Too Long," 89.

199. Bacon, "Philadelphia in the Year 2009," 10; Heller, *Ed Bacon:*, 185.

200. Knowles, "Staying Too Long," 106; Paolantonio, *Frank Rizzo:*, 154; Heller, *Ed Bacon*, 190; Mires, *Independence Hall*, 261.

201. Paolantonio, *Frank Rizzo*, 207–8; Heller, *Ed Bacon*, 190.

Chapter 10

1. Philip S. Jenkins, "The Postindustrial Age: 1950–2000," in *Pennsylvania: A History of the Commonwealth*, ed. Randall M. Miller and William Pencak (University Park: Pennsylvania State University Press, 2002), 353.

2. Timothy Weaver, *Blazing the Neoliberal Trail: Urban Political Development in the United States and the United Kingdom* (Philadelphia: University of Pennsylvania Press, 2016), 161.

3. John Kromer, *Philadelphia Battlefields: Disruptive Campaigns and Upset Elections in a Changing City* (Philadelphia: Temple University Press, 2020), 88.

4. "A City Transformed: The Racial and Ethnic Changes in Philadelphia over the Last Twenty 20 Years," *Philadelphia Research Initiative*, Pew Charitable Trusts (2011): 4, 9. See also Matthew Smalarz, "The 'White Island': Whiteness in the Making of Public and Private Space in Northeast Philadelphia, 1854–1990" (PhD diss., University of Pennsylvania, 2016), 340; Kromer, *Philadelphia Battlefields*, 59; "Congressional Interactive District Map," *Legislative Guide to Redistricting in Pennsylvania*, accessed February 21, 2021, https://www.redistricting .state.pa.us/maps/.

5. M. K. Asante, *Buck: A Memoir* (New York: Spiegel & Grau, 2014), 131. See also Elijah Anderson, "The Emerging Philadelphia African American Class Structure," *Annals of the American Academy of Political and Social Science*, 568 (March 2000): 64; Elijah Anderson, *Streetwise: Race, Class, and Change in an Urban Community* (Chicago: University of Chicago Press, 1992), 198; Elijah Anderson, *Code of the Street: Decency, Violence, and the Moral Life of the Inner City* (New York: W. W. Norton, 2000), 16–17; John R. Maneval, *An Ethnic History of South Philadelphia, 1870–1980* (Philadelphia: Balch Institute for Ethnic Studies, 1992), II104–II107.

6. Audrey Singer, Domenic Vitiello, Michael Katz, and David Park, "Recent Immigration to Philadelphia: Regional Change in a Re-Emerging Gateway," *Metropolitan Policy Program*, Brookings Institution (November 2008): 1, https://www.brookings .edu/research/recent-immigration-to-philadelphia-regional-change-in-a-re-emerging -gateway/.

7. "City Transformed," 1; "Philadelphia in Focus: A Profile from Census 2000," *Brookings Institution Center on Urban and Metropolitan Policy* (November 1, 2003): 4.

8. "City Transformed," 1; "Philadelphia in Focus," 4; Domenic Vitiello, Hilary Parsons Dick, Danielle DiVerde, and Veronica Willig, "Mexicans and Mexico," *Encyclopedia of Greater Philadelphia*, accessed October 5, 2022, https://philadelphiaencyclopedia.org/essays/mexicans-and-mexico/.

9. Jenkins, "Postindustrial Age," 340–41.

10. Nate Silver, "The Most Diverse Cities Are Often the Most Segregated," *FiveThirtyEight*, May 1, 2015, accessed March 13, 2021, https://fivethirtyeight.com/features/the-most-diverse-cities-are-often-the-most-segregated; Singer et al., "Recent Immigration," 14; "Philadelphia in Focus," 4.

11. Peter Binzen and Jonathan Binzen, *Richardson Dilworth: Last of the Bare-Knuckled Aristocrats* (Philadelphia: Camino Books, 2014), 131, 134; S. A. Paolantonio, *Frank Rizzo: The Last Big Man in Big City America* (Philadelphia: Camino Books, 1993), 65.

12. James Reichley, *The Art of Government: Reform and Organization Politics in Philadelphia* (New York: Fund for the Republic, 1959), 11; Binzen and Binzen, *Richardson Dilworth*, 167; Dennis Clark, "From Periphery to Prominence: Jews in Philadelphia Politics, 1940–1985," in *Philadelphia Jewish Life, 1940–2000*, ed. Murray Friedman (Philadelphia: Temple University Press, 2003), 76.

13. W. Wilson Goode, *In Goode Faith* (Valley Forge, PA: Judson Press, 1992), xiv; W. Wilson Goode, *Black Votes Mattered: A Philadelphia Story* (Pennsauken, NJ: BookBaby, 2018), 57; David Gambacorta and Barbara Laker, "The Rizzo Legacy," *Philadelphia Inquirer*, June 4, 2020, A13. See also Hizkia Assefa and Paul Wahrhaftig, *The MOVE Crisis in Philadelphia: Extremist Groups and Conflict Resolution* (Pittsburgh: University of Pittsburgh Press, 1990), 100.

14. Tina Rosenberg, "The Deadliest D.A.," *New York Times Magazine*, July 16, 1995, sec. 6, 22.

15. "A Life in the Balance: The Case of Mumia Abu-Jamal," Amnesty International, February 2000, 2, accessed March 18, 2021, https://www.amnesty.org/download/Documents/136000/amr510012000en.pdf.

16. Lynette Tolbert Hazelton, "Philadelphia Mayors Promised to Solve Philadelphia Poverty for Decades," *Philadelphia*, September 5, 2020, accessed March 20, 2021, https://www.phillymag.com/news/2020/09/05/philadelphia-poverty-history-mayors/; Roger D. Simon and Brian Alnutt, "Philadelphia, 1982–2007: Toward a Postindustrial City," *Pennsylvania Magazine of History and Biography*, 131, no. 4 (October 2007): 405.

17. Joe Davidson, "Philadelphia Liberal to Take Reins from Rizzo Monday," *Washington Post*, January 1, 1980, accessed March 20, 2021, https://www.washingtonpost.com/archive/politics/1980/01/01/philadelphia-liberal-to-take-reins-from-rizzo-monday/3134c131-e058-470f-815f-7860e28dd416/.

18. Goode, *In Goode Faith*, 152; "Philadelphia Mayor in Trouble over Minority Aid," *New York Times*, May 17, 1982, sec. B, 16. See also Marcus Anthony Hunter, *Black Citymakers: How* The Philadelphia Negro *Changed Urban America* (New York: Oxford University Press, 2013), 185.

19. Larry Kane, *Larry Kane's Philadelphia* (Philadelphia: Temple University Press, 2000), 96–100.

20. The *New York Times* noted, "Mr. Rizzo, who was host of a popular radio talk show last year, does not make overtly racist statements, but his campaigns act as lightning rods for racism in a city." Michael Decourcy Hinds, "Philadelphia Journal: Frank Rizzo Is Back, Making Waves (Again)," *New York Times*, February 1, 1991, sec. A, 12. See also Weaver, *Blazing the Neoliberal Trail*, 190; Smalarz, "'White Island,'" 293, and John F. Bauman, "W. Wilson Goode: The Black Mayor as Entrepreneur," *Journal of Negro History* 77, no. 3 (1992): 142.

21. Stefano Luconi, *From Paesani to White Ethnics: The Italian Experience in Philadelphia* (Albany: State University of New York Press, 2001), 142.

22. Goode, *In Goode Faith*, 148. See also Matthew J. Countryman, "'From Protest to Politics': Community Control and Black Independent Politics in Philadelphia, 1965–1984," *Journal of Urban History*, 32, no. 6 (September 2006): 846.

23. Keshler Thibet, "Breaking Barriers and the Evolution of Black Female Politicians in Philadelphia," *Hidden City Philadelphia*, November 9, 2020, accessed October 5, 2022, https://hiddencityphila.org/2020/11/breaking-barriers-and-the-evolution-of-Black-female-politicians-in-philadelphia/; Allener M. Baker-Rogers and Fasha M. Traylor, *They Carried Us: The Social Impact of Philadelphia's Black Women Leaders* (Philadelphia: Arch Street Press, 2020), 331–32.

24. Baker-Rogers and Traylor, *They Carried Us*, 329–30.

25. Goode, *In Goode Faith*, 141. See also Hunter, *Black Citymakers*, 168, 184; Countryman, "From Protest," 816; Weaver, *Blazing the Neoliberal Trail*, 164; Camika Royal, *Not Paved for Us: Black Educators and Public School Reform in Philadelphia* (Cambridge, MA: Harvard Education Press, 2022), 32.

26. Goode, *Black Votes Mattered*, 49; "Black History Today: Philadelphia Leaders and Their Legacies," *Philadelphia Public Record*, February 23, 2018, accessed March 17, 2021, http://www.phillyrecord.com/2018/02/Black-history-today-philadelphia-leaders-and-their-legacies/.

27. "City Transformed," 1; Judith Goode, "Polishing the Rustbelt: Immigrants Enter a Restructuring Philadelphia," in *Newcomers in the Workplace: Immigrants and the Restructuring of the U.S. Economy*, ed. Louise Lamphere, Alex Stepick, and Guillermo Grenier (Philadelphia: Temple University Press, 1994), 215; Victor Vázquez-Hernández, "From Pan-Latino Enclaves to a Community: Puerto Ricans in Philadelphia, 1910–2000," in *Puerto Rican Diaspora: Historical Perspectives*, ed. Carmen Whalen and Victor Vázquez-Hernández (Philadelphia: Temple University Press, 2005), 101.

28. Robert P. Inman, "How to Have a Fiscal Crisis: Lessons from Philadelphia," *American Economic Review*, 85, no. 2 (May 1995): 379; "J. F. White, Sr., Political Strategist, 75, Dies," *New York Times*, September 17, 1999, sec. A, 21; Sabrina Vourvoulias, ed., *200 Years of Latino History in Philadelphia* (Philadelphia: Temple University Press, 2012), 112; Holly Otterbein, "New Sanders Aide Apologizes for Race-Baiting '99 Website," *Politico*, March 22, 2019, accessed March 4, 2021, https://www.politico.com/story/2019/03/22/sanders-speechwriter-racially-inflammatory-website-1232953. See also Jenkins, "Postindustrial Age," 335.

29. Goode, *In Goode Faith*, 185–193; Goode, *Black Votes Mattered*, 70. See also Kromer, *Philadelphia Battlefields*, 135; Hunter, *Black Citymakers*, 187; Countryman, "From Protest," 848; Bauman, "W. Wilson Goode," 146; Weaver, *Blazing the Neoliberal Trail*, 190.

30. Weaver, *Blazing the Neoliberal Trail*, 192.

31. Goode, *Black Votes Mattered*, 82–83. See also William K. Stevens, "Philadelphia Mayor Warns Union He'll Use Private Garbage Collectors," *New York Times*, March 17, 1988, A28. See also Weaver, *Blazing the Neoliberal Trail*, 193; Bauman, "W. Wilson Goode," 153.

32. Bauman, "W. Wilson Goode," 143; Ayumi Takenaka and Mary Johnson Osirim, *Global Philadelphia: Immigrant Communities Old and New* (Philadelphia: Temple University Press, 2010), 6; Smalarz, "'White Island,'" 287–88; Carolyn T. Adams, "The Philadelphia Experience," *Annals of the American Academy of Political and Social Science*, 551 (May 1997): 227.

33. Robin Pogrebin, "Edmund Bacon, 95, Urban Planner of Philadelphia, Dies," *New York Times*, October 18, 2005, accessed March 21, 2021, https://www.nytimes.com/2005 /10/18/arts/design/edmund-bacon-95-urban-planner-of-philadelphia-dies.html#:~:text= Edmund%20N.,by%20his%20daughter%20Elinor%20Bacon.

34. Goode, *In Goode Faith*, 199–200.

35. Michael J. Lewis, *Philadelphia Builds: Essays on Architecture* (Philadelphia: Paul Dry Books, 2021), 215–20.

36. Natalie Kostelni, "Willard Rouse, 60, Dies; Transformed Phila.'s Skyline," *Philadelphia Business Journal*, May 28, 2003, accessed March 18, 2021, https://www.bizjournals.com /philadelphia/stories/2003/05/26/daily6.html; Victor Fiorello, "Disgraced Ex-City Councilman and Wife Sue 'Luxury' Drug Rehab," *Philadelphia*, January 4, 2013, accessed March 18, 2021, https://www.phillymag.com/news/2013/01/14/lee-diane-beloff-sue-luxury-drug -rehab/; Philip Leonetti with Scott Burnstein and Christopher Graziano, *Mafia Prince: Inside America's Most Violent Crime Family and the Bloody Fall of* La Cosa Nostra (Philadelphia: Running Press, 2014), 216.

37. Dylan Gottlieb, "Penn's Landing," *Encyclopedia of Greater Philadelphia*, n.d. accessed March 18, 2021, https://philadelphiaencyclopedia.org/archive/penns-landing/. See also Inga Saffron, *Becoming Philadelphia: How an Old American City Made Itself New Again* (New Brunswick, NJ: Rutgers University Press, 2020), 9, 30, 41.

38. Goode, *In Goode Faith*, 202–3; Inman, "How to Have a Fiscal Crisis," 381.

39. Goode, *Black Votes Mattered*, 71–72.

40. Roger Gastman and Caleb Neelon, *The History of American Graffiti* (New York: Harper Design, 2010), 20; Tyler John Mitman, "Rebels, Artists, and the Reimagined City: An Ethnographic Examination of Graffiti Culture in Philadelphia" (PhD diss., Drexel University, 2015), 8; Jeffrey Ian Ross, ed., *Routledge Handbook of Graffiti and Street Art* (New York: Routledge, 2016), 480.

41. Jane Golden, Robin Rice, and Monica Yant Kinney, *Philadelphia Murals and the Stories They Tell* (Philadelphia: Temple University Press, 2002), 8–20.

42. According to historian Julian E. Zelizer, by the end of President Ronald Reagan's second term, his administration had cut social safety net programs by between 6 and 10 percent. Julian E. Zelizer, "Reagan Revolution," in *Myth America: Historians Take on the*

Biggest Legends and Lies About Our Past, ed. Kevin M. Kruse and Julian E. Zelizer (New York: Basic Books, 2022), 291.

43. Eric C. Schneider, *The Ecology of Homicide: Race, Place, and Space in Postwar Philadelphia* (Philadelphia: University of Pennsylvania Press, 2020), 93; Debbie Beecher, *Private Property and Public Power: Eminent Domain in Philadelphia* (New York: Oxford University Press, 2014), 37.

44. George Bush, "Inaugural Address of George Bush," January 20, 1989, Avalon Project, accessed December 14, 2022, https://avalon.law.yale.edu/20th_century/bush.asp.

45. Goode, "Polishing the Rustbelt," 201; "Philadelphia in Focus," 4–5.

46. Weaver, *Blazing the Neoliberal Trail*, 172–83; Inman, "How to Have a Fiscal Crisis," 380.

47. "The Cost of Local Government in Philadelphia," Pew Charitable Trusts, March 2019, 1–4, 12; Goode, "Polishing the Rustbelt," 201; "Comparing State and Local Taxes in Large U.S. Cities," *New York City Independent Budget Office*, February 2007, accessed March 22, 2021, https://ibo.nyc.ny.us/iboreports/CSALTFINAL.pdf.

48. Simon and Alnutt, "Philadelphia," 396.

49. Adams, "Philadelphia Experience," 226.

50. Lynette Hazelton, "Fattah: Not Just Another Candidate," *Philadelphia Tribune*, February 23, 1982, 3. This was in line with the way Philadelphia was marketing itself at the time; see Bauman, "W. Wilson Goode," 142.

51. Inman, "How to Have a Fiscal Crisis," 379. See also Takenaka and Johnson Osirim, *Global Philadelphia*, 6; Weaver, *Blazing the Neoliberal Trail*, 202; Goode, "Polishing the Rustbelt," 200; Adams, "Philadelphia Experience," 228.

52. Dan Royles, "Taking It to the Streets: AIDS, Race, and Protest in Philadelphia," *Pennsylvania Legacies*, 16, no. 1 (Spring 2016): 27–29.

53. Dan Royles, "AIDS and AIDS Activism," *Encyclopedia of Greater Philadelphia*, n.d. accessed March 16, 2021, https://philadelphiaencyclopedia.org/archive/aids-and-aids -activism/; Frank Trippet and Margaret Kirk, "Congress Goes Home Again in Philadelphia," *Time*, July 27, 1987. 26.

54. Executive Order No. 4-92, City of Philadelphia, accessed March 13, 2021, https:// www.phila.gov/ExecutiveOrders/Executive%20Orders/4-92.pdf. For recent rates of infection, see "HIV in Philadelphia," Department of Public Health, City of Philadelphia, 2002, 9.

55. Royles, "AIDS and AIDS Activism."

56. Jenkins, "Postindustrial Age," 340–41.

57. Robert A. Silverman, "Marvin Eugene Wolfgang," *Proceedings of the American Philosophical Society*, 148, no. 4 (December 2004): 547; Elizabeth Hinton, *From the War on Poverty to the War on Crime: The Making of Mass Incarceration in America* (Cambridge, MA: Harvard University Press, 2016), 225.

58. John DiLulio, "The Coming of the Super Predators," *Weekly Standard*, November 27, 1995, accessed October 5, 2022, https://www.washingtonexaminer.com/weekly -standard/the-coming-of-the-super-predators.

59. Clyde Haberman, "When Youth Violence Spurred 'Superpredator' Fear," *New York Times*, April 6, 2014, accessed October 5, 2022, https://www.nytimes.com/2014/04 /07/us/politics/killing-on-bus-recalls-superpredator-threat-of-90s.html; Anne Gearan

and Abby Phillip, "Clinton Regrets 1996 Remark on 'Super-predators' after Encounter with Activist," *Washington Post*, February 25, 2016, accessed October 5, 2022, https://www.washingtonpost.com/news/post-politics/wp/2016/02/25/clinton-heckled-by-Black-lives-matter-activist/.

60. Dan Baum, "Legalize It All: How to Win the War on Drugs," *Harper's*, April 2016, accessed March 18, 2021, https://harpers.org/archive/2016/04/legalize-it-all/.

61. *Hearing Before the House of Representatives Select Committee on Narcotics Abuse and Control* (Washington, DC: Government Printing Office, 1980), 80.

62. Philip Jenkins, "The Speed Capital of the World: Organizing the Methamphetamine Industry in Philadelphia, 1970–1990," *Criminal Justice Policy Review*, 6, no. 1 (1992): 22, 31–32.

63. Robert P. Fairbanks, *How It Works: Recovering Citizens in Post-Welfare Philadelphia* (Chicago: University of Chicago Press, 2009), 5.

64. Frederick F. Wherry, *The Philadelphia Barrio: The Arts, Branding, and Neighborhood Transformation* (Chicago: University of Chicago Press, 2011), 58–59.

65. Corey Davis, "Philadelphia Ends 2019 with 356 Homicides, the Most Since 2007," 6ABC News, January 1, 2020, accessed March 18, 2021, https://6abc.com/murder-rate-philadelphia-homicide-homicides-in/5802150/#:~:text=PHILADELPHIA%20(WPVI)%20%2D%2D%20The%20city,that%20left%20a%20woman%20dead; John N. Mitchell, "Officials: Race Played Role in Policing of Crack," *Philadelphia Tribune*, February 16, 2018, accessed March 18, 2021, https://www.phillytrib.com/news/officials-race-played-role-in-policing-of-crack/article_d3997b4e-02a1-5209-8a3d-65f5e4b60c60.html; John L. Puckett and Rosalie Jackson, "An End of Drug Destruction: From Heroin to Crack Cocaine," *West Philadelphia Collaborative History*, accessed March 18, 2021, https://collaborativehistory.gse.upenn.edu/stories/era-drug-destruction-heroin-crack-cocaine.

66. Asante, *Buck*, 3; Schneider, *Ecology of Homicide*, xix, 18.

67. Larry Eichel and Meagan Pharis, "Philadelphia's Drug Overdose Death Rate Among Highest in Nation," Pew Charitable Trusts, February 15, 2018, accessed March 22, 2021, https://www.pewtrusts.org/en/research-and-analysis/articles/2018/02/15/philadelphias-drug-overdose-death-rate-among-highest-in-nation; Alfred Lubrano, "How Kensington Got to Be the Center of Philly's Opioid Crisis," *Philadelphia Inquirer*, January 23, 2018, accessed March 22, 2021, https://www.inquirer.com/philly/news/kensington-opioid-crisis-history-philly-heroin-20180123.html.

68. Laurel Wamsley, "American Life Expectancy Dropped by a Full Year in 1st Half of 2020," NPR, February 18, 2021, accessed March 22, 2021, https://www.npr.org/2021/02/18/968791431/american-life-expectancy-dropped-by-a-full-year-in-the-first-half-of-2020#:~:text=Life%20expectancy%20at%20birth%20for,0.9%20year%20decrease%20from%202019.

69. Rendell characterized himself as having taken "an aggressive, no-plea-bargaining approach to violent crime," a prosecutor who proudly and publicly criticized "judges who gave out lenient sentences to violent offenders, going so far as including 'worst sentences of the month' in our office newsletter." Ed Rendell, *A Nation of Wusses: How America's Leaders Lost the Guts to Make Us Great* (Hoboken, NJ: John Wiley & Sons, 2012), 21; Robert Huber, "Ed Rendell Still Has a Few Things to Say," *Philadelphia*, February 22,

2020, accessed March 22, 2021, https://www.phillymag.com/news/2020/02/22/ed-rendell
-interview-joe-biden-democratic-party/; Rosenberg, "Deadliest D.A.," 22. Reporter Larry
Kane noted that the culture of "tough on crime" was so pervasive that Mayor Frank Rizzo
called him a "pussy" after Kane pushed for a light sentence for a mentally disturbed man
who had threatened him. Kane, *Larry Kane's Philadelphia*, 54–55.

70. Michael Coard, "'Deadliest D.A.' Wants to Kill Justice in Philly Again," July 15, 2017,
Philadelphia Tribune, accessed March 22, 2021, https://www.phillytrib.com/commentary
/coard-deadliest-d-a-wants-to-kill-justice-in-philly-again/article_e3b28437-3671-5444
-a788-a732aad9566e.html; "America's Top Five Deadliest Prosecutors: How Overzeal-
ous Personalities Drive the Death Penalty," Fair Punishment Project, June 2016, accessed
March 22, 2021, https://files.deathpenaltyinfo.org/documents/FairPunishmentProject
-Top5Report_FINAL_2016_06.pdf; Steven Conn, *Americans Against the City: Anti-
Urbanism in the Twentieth Century* (New York: Oxford University Press, 2014), 9; Jenkins,
"Postindustrial Age," 340; Jacob Kang-Brown, Eital Schattner-Elmaleh, and Christian
Henrichson, "Incarceration Trends Pennsylvania," Vera Institute of Justice, n.d., accessed
March 6, 2021, https://www.vera.org/downloads/pdfdownloads/state-incarceration-trends
-pennsylvania.pdf.

71. Ed Pilkington, "A Siege. A Bomb. 48 Dogs. And the Black Commune that Would
Not Surrender," *Guardian*, July 31, 2018, accessed March 20, 2021, https://www.theguardian
.com/world/2018/jul/31/a-siege-a-bomb-48-dogs-and-the-Black-commune-that-would
-not-surrender.

72. Tajah Ebram, "'Can't Jail the Revolution': Policing, Protest, and the MOVE Organization in Philadelphia's Carceral Landscape," *Pennsylvania Magazine of History and Biography*, 143, no. 3 (October 2019): 333.

73. Goode, *In Goode Faith*, 164.

74. Kitty Caparella, "Cop's Death in Clash Was a Spark," *Philadelphia Inquirer*, May 10,
2010, accessed March 20, 2021, https://www.inquirer.com/philly/news/special_packages
/dailynews/20100506_Cops_death_in_78_clash_was_a_spark.html-2.

75. Goode, *In Goode Faith*, 256. The district attorney at the time, Ed Rendell, recalled
that his office was split on even trying the police officers involved, with some attorneys
believing that the unarmed Africa "deserved" the brutal beating. Rendell, *Nation of Wusses,*
24–25. See also Anderson, *Code of the Street*, 320–22.

76. Goode, *In Goode Faith*, 227.

77. Ed Pilkington, "The Day Police Bombed a City Street: Can Scars of 1985
MOVE Atrocity be Healed?," *Guardian*, May 10, 2020, accessed March 13, 2021, https://
www.theguardian.com/us-news/2020/may/10/move-1985-bombing-reconciliation
-philadelphia.

78. "'Did I Make a Mistake? Yes,'" *Time*, November 18, 1985, 47; Goode, *In Goode
Faith*, 233–34.

79. Bauman, "W. Wilson Goode," 152.

80. Paul M. Washington with David McI. Gracie, *"Other Sheep I Have": The Autobiography of Father Paul M. Washington* (Philadelphia: Temple University Press, 1994),
188–89.

81. Michelle Tranquili, "MOVE Through the Years," *Philadelphia Inquirer*, May 6, 2010, accessed March 24, 2021, https://www.inquirer.com/philly/news/special_packages /dailynews/MOVE_through_the_years.html.

82. Melvin G. Holli, "American Mayors: The Best and the Worst Since 1960," *Social Science Quarterly*, 78, no. 1 (March 1997): 153.

83. Thomas J. Gibbons Jr., Rich Heidorn Jr., and Sara Kennedy, "400 Protest at Home of Blacks in S.W. Philadelphia," *Philadelphia Inquirer*, November 21, 1985, A1.

84. Amy Linn, "Neighborhood Is a 'Ticking Time Bomb,'" *Philadelphia Inquirer*, November 24, 1985, A21; Tom Infield and Julia Cass, "Black Couple Decides to Leave Neighborhood," *Philadelphia Inquirer*, November 26, 1985, A1.

85. Steve Lopez and Thomas J. Gibbons Jr., "34 Charged for Defying S.W. Phila Protest Ban," *Philadelphia Inquirer*, December 1, 1985, A1.

86. Walter F. Naedele, "4 Charged in Arson in S.W. Phila," *Philadelphia Inquirer*, January 8, 1986. A1.

87. Smalarz, "'White Island,'" 291–92.

88. Philip Lentz, "Honeymoon over for Philadelphia Mayor," *Chicago Tribune*, December 8, 1985, accessed March 17, 2021, https://www.chicagotribune.com/news/ct -xpm-1985-12-08-8503240756-story.html.

89. Conn, *Americans Against the City*, 7, 274.

90. Luconi, *From Paesani*, 142.

91. Simon and Alnutt, "Philadelphia," 409.

92. "The Future of Fiscal Oversight in Philadelphia," Pew Charitable Trusts, January 7, 2020, 2, accessed March 20, 2021, https://pew.org/39JeUUA.

93. Weaver, *Blazing the Neoliberal Trail*, 194, 203.

94. "Future of Fiscal Oversight," 3.

95. Weaver, *Blazing the Neoliberal Trail*, 208. On the legislature's hostility, see "Philadelphia Stalls Bankruptcy," *New York Times*, September 22, 1990, sec. 1, 10.

96. One contemporary recalled of the campaign, "We laughed our way through it. We went into it knowing Joe was a pretty significant underdog." Robert Moran, "Joseph M. Egan; Ran for Mayor Against Rendell," *Philadelphia Inquirer*, April 26, 2009, accessed February 13, 2021, https://www.inquirer.com/philly/obituaries/20090426_Joseph_M__Egan _Jr___ran_against_Rendell_in_1991.html.

97. Chris Brennan and Holly Otterbein, "The Rizzo Statue? It's Staying Put Until After Kenney's 2019 Reelection Campaign," *Philadelphia Inquirer*, August 9, 2018, accessed March 6, 2021, https://www.inquirer.com/philly/news/politics/the-rizzo-statue-its-staying -put-until-after-kenneys-2019-reelection-campaign-clout-20180809.html.

98. Quoted in Jonathan Chait, "Are Public Unions All-Powerful?" *New Republic*, March 2, 2011, accessed March 21, 2021, https://newrepublic.com/article/84469/are -public-unions-all-powerful. See also Royal, *Not Paved for Us*, 9.

99. Rendell, *Nation of Wusses:*, 69; Kane, *Larry Kane's Philadelphia*, 155; Beecher, *Private Property*, 41.

100. The book's tagline—"They said it was a place that couldn't be saved. One man decided to save it"—aptly showcases Bissinger's framing, as does the author's assertion that

Rendell and the book's other subjects were each, in their own way, "heroic." Buzz Bissinger, *A Prayer for the City* (New York: Random House, 1997), xiv.

101. Hazelton, "Philadelphia Mayors"; Laura M. Holzman, *Contested Image: Defining Philadelphia for the Twenty-First Century* (Philadelphia: Temple University Press, 2019), 31.

102. Goode, *Black Votes Mattered*, 73; Simon and Alnutt, "Philadelphia," 430; Hunter, *Black Citymakers*, 186; Weaver, *Blazing the Neoliberal Trail*, 201–2.

103. Hazelton, "Philadelphia Mayors."

104. Holzman, *Contested Image*, 31–33; Stephen J. McGovern, "The Insurgence Nature of Black Politics in Contemporary Philadelphia," *in If There Is No Struggle There Is No Progress: Black Politics in Twentieth-Century Philadelphia*, ed. James Wolfinger (Philadelphia: Temple University Press, 2022), 191.

105. Weaver, *Blazing the Neoliberal Trail:*, 162; Inman, "How to Have a Fiscal Crisis," 380; "Philadelphia's Poor: Who They Are, Where They Live, and How That Has Changed," *Pew Charitable Trusts* (November 2017): 1.

106. Saffron, *Becoming Philadelphia*, 11–12.

107. Robert Puentes and David Warren, "One-Fifth of America: A Comprehensive Guide to America's First Suburbs," *Brookings Institution* Center on Urban and Metropolitan Policy (2006), 3.

108. Weaver, *Blazing the Neoliberal Trail*, 214.

109. Elizabeth Milroy, "'Pro Bono Politico': Ecology, History, and the Creation of Philadelphia's Fairmount Park System," in *Nature's Entrepôt: Philadelphia's Urban Sphere and Its Environmental Thresholds*, ed. Brian C. Black and Michael J. Chiarappa (Pittsburgh: University of Pittsburgh Press, 2012), 52; Weaver, *Blazing the Neoliberal Trail*, 205.

110. Weaver, *Blazing the Neoliberal Trail*, 231.

111. Aaron Moselle, "15 Years Later, Appraising the $300 Million Effort to Transform Philly Neighborhoods," WHYY, July 20, 2015, accessed March 16, 2021, https://whyy.org/articles/15-years-later-appraising-300-million-effort-to-transform-philly-neighborhoods/.

112. Alex Peay quoted in Jake Blumgart, "How Redlining Segregated Philadelphia," *Philadelphia in Flux: A Public Exploration of Philadelphia's Changing Communities* (Philadelphia: Next City, 2017), 5. See also Stephen J. McGovern, "Philadelphia's Neighborhood Transformation Initiative: A Case Study of Mayoral Leadership, Bold Planning, and Conflict," *Housing Policy Debate*, 17, no. 3 (January 2006): 531.

113. "White, Kemp, and 10 Others Charged in Philadelphia Corruption Case," FBI National Press Releases, June 29, 2004, accessed March 18, 2021, https://archives.fbi.gov/archives/news/pressrel/press-releases/white-kemp-and-10-others-charged-in-philadelphia-corruption-case; Craig R. McCoy and Mark Fazlollah, "Ten Years Ago, a Bugging at the Mayor's Office Shook Philadelphia," *Philadelphia Inquirer*, October 5, 2013, accessed March 18, 2021, https://www.inquirer.com/philly/news/20131006_Ten_years _ago__a_bugging_at_the_mayor_s_office_shook_Philadelphia.html.

114. Michael A. Nutter, *Mayor: The Best Job in Politics* (Philadelphia: University of Pennsylvania Press, 2018), 40. In 2000, Larry Kane noted, "crime is a major issue," despite declining crime rates. Kane, *Larry Kane's Philadelphia*, xv.

115. Nutter, *Mayor*, 32.

116. Yvonne Latty and Sammy Caiola, "Former Philly Mayor Michael Nutter Stands by Stop and Frisk, Despite Being Stopped by Police Multiple Times," WHYY, December 6, 2022, accessed December 14, 2022, https://whyy.org/articles/stop-and-frisk-philadelphia -mayor-michael-nutter-episode-4-political-will/.

117. Nutter, *Mayor*, 94.

118. "The Plan," Philadelphia2035, accessed March 24, 2021, https://www.phila2035 .org/plan.

119. Holzman, *Contested Image*, 32.

120. Holzman, *Contested Image*, 34.

121. Rebecca Yamin, *Digging in the City of Brotherly Love: Stories from Philadelphia Archeology* (New Haven, CT: Yale University Press, 2008), 46.

122. Edward Lawler Jr., "The President's House Revisited," *Pennsylvania Magazine of History and Biography*, 129, no. 4 (October 2005): 372.

123. Roger C. Aden, "Redefining the 'Cradle of Liberty': The President's House Controversy in Independence National Historic Park," *Rhetoric and Public Affairs*, 13, no. 2 (Summer 2010): 78.

124. Seth C. Bruggeman, "Review: 'The President's House: Freedom and Slavery in the Making of a New Nation,'" *Journal of American History*, 100, no. 1 (June 2013): 156, and Edward Lawler Jr. "The President's House in Philadelphia: The Rediscovery of a Lost Landmark," *Pennsylvania Magazine of History and Biography* 126, no. 1 (2002): 5–15.

125. Yamin, *Digging*, 46.

126. Avenging the Ancestors Coalition, accessed October 5, 2022, http://www .avengingtheancestors.com/.

127. Jill Ogline, "'Creating Dissonance for the Visitor': The Heart of the Liberty Bell Controversy," *Public Historian*, 26, no. 3 (Summer 2004): 51; Gary B. Nash, "For Whom Will the Liberty Bell Toll? From Controversy to Collaboration," *George Wright Forum*, 21, no. 1 (2004): 48.

128. Bruggeman, "Review: 'The President's House,'" 155.

Conclusion

1. Inga Saffron, *Becoming Philadelphia: How an Old American City Made Itself New Again* (New Brunswick, NJ: Rutgers University Press, 2020), 4.

2. "The Plan," Philadelphia2035, accessed March 24, 2021, https://www.phila2035.org /plan.

3. Jeffrey Lyons and Stephen M. Utych, "You're Not from Here! The Consequences of Urban and Rural Identities," *Political Behavior*, 2021, https://doi.org/10.1007/s11109 -021-09680-3; J. G. Gimpel et al., "The Urban–Rural Gulf in American Political Behavior," *Political Behavior*, 42, no. 4, (December 2020): 1344, https://doi.org/10.1007/s11109-020 -09601-w; S. Mettler and T. Brown, "The Growing Rural-Urban Political Divide and Democratic Vulnerability," *Annals of the American Academy of Political and Social Science*, 699, no. 1 (2022): 130–42, https://doi.org/10.1177/00027162211070061, 131.

4. Michaelle Bond and John Duchneskie, "Census Shows Changes in Income Across the City," *Philadelphia Inquirer*, December 8, 2022, 1; Aseem Shukla and Michaelle Bond, "In Diversifying Nation, City Remains Divided," *Philadelphia Inquirer*, October 24, 2021, 1.

5. Jeffrey Lin, "Understanding Gentrification's Causes," *Economic Insights*, 2, no. 3 (2017): 11; Seth Chizeck, "Gentrification and Changes in the Stock of Low-Cost Rental Housing in Philadelphia, 2000 to 2014," *Cascade Focus* (January 2017): 1–2.

INDEX

ACKNOWLEDGMENTS

This is my seventh book, and it has been a labor of love over the past seven years. Books like this always reflect the assistance (and forbearance) of people whose names do not appear on the cover. In particular, I want to thank my editor at the University of Pennsylvania Press, Robert Lockhart, whose sage advice, focused critiques, and commitment to the project are largely responsible for the best elements of this book. In addition, I would like to thank my copyeditor, Ron Silverman, whose attention to detail and knowledge of proper grammar have made my last three books publication worthy. My fact checker, Laura Daly, pointed out several errors in the manuscript; any that remain are entirely my fault. In addition, John Milner, Jared Cram, Amanda Saslow, Dolores Pfeuffer-Scherer, Ted Smith, and Timothy Lisko read early drafts and offered me needed support and suggestions, and I am grateful for their help. Tara Snyder Murphy has proofread almost all of my books and (amazingly) still responds to my text messages. I want to thank my amazing children, Alec, Zoe, and Lucy: though J. R. King is my favorite Philadelphia lawyer, these three are my favorite people, and I love you all. Finally, to my wife, Jennifer Murphy: "If I gotta be damned, you know I want to be damned/ Dancing through the night with you."